INTERNETWORKING

THE WAY TO A STRUCTURED NETWORK

JOIN US ON THE INTERNET VIA WWW, GOPHER, FTP OR EMAIL:

WWW: http://www.itcpmedia.com
GOPHER: gopher.thomson.com
FTP: ftp.thomson.com
EMAIL: findit@kiosk.thomson.com

WebExtra[SM]

WebExtra gives added value by providing updated and additional information about topics discussed in this book. Items included in the WebExtra for *Internetworking: The Way to a Structured Network* are:

- Headline news items that keep you up to date on developments about LAN Hardware, Ethernet and Token Ring, FDDI, TCP/IP, Virtual LANs, Frame Relay, ISDN, SONET, SNA, Internetworking Hardware and Software, Bridges, Routers and Gateways, and Remote Access of LANs.

The WebExtra feature outlined above is available free of charge (except for the charges associated with accessing the Internet and the World Wide Web). Just go to the Web site for International Thomson Computer Press. The URL is:

http://www.itcpmedia.com

A service of I(T)P®

INTERNETWORKING

THE WAY TO A STRUCTURED NETWORK

PETRA BOROWKA

International Thomson Computer Press

I(T)P® An International Thomson Publishing Company

London • Bonn • Boston • Johannesburg • Madrid • Melbourne • Mexico City • New York • Paris
Singapore • Tokyo • Toronto • Albany, NY • Belmont, CA • Cincinnati, OH • Detroit, MI

Copyright © 1996 DATACOM-Verlag
Internetworking: Konzepte, Komponenten, Protokolle, Einsatzszenarios

Copyright ©1997 International Thomson Publishing
Internetworking: The Way to a Structured Network

I(T)P® A division of International Thomson Publishing Inc.
        The ITP Logo is a trademark under license.

For more information, contact:

International Thomson Computer Press
Berkshire House
168–173 High Holborn
London WCIV 7AA
United Kingdom

International Thomson Computer Press
Königswinterer Strasse 418
53227 Bonn
Germany

Thomas Nelson Australia
102 Dodds Street
South Melbourne, 3205
Victoria
Australia

Nelson Canada
1120 Birchmount Road
Scarborough, Ontario
Canada M1K 5G4

International Thomson Publishing Southern Africa
Bldg. 19, Constantia Park
239 Old Pretoria Road, P.O. Box 2459
Halfway House, 1685 South Africa

International Thomson Computer Press
20 Park Plaza, 13th Floor
Boston, MA 02116
USA

International Thomson Publishing Asia
60 Albert Street #15-01
Albert Complex
Singapore 189969

International Thomson Publishing Japan
Hirakawacho Kyowa Building, 3F
2-2-1 Hirakawacho
Chiyoda-ku, 102 Tokyo
Japan

International Thomson Editores
Campos Eliseos 385, Piso 7
Col. Polanco
11560 Mexico D.F. Mexico

International Thomson Publishing France
Tours Maine Montparnasse
33 Avenue du Maine
75755 Paris Cedex 15 France

British Library Cataloguing-in-Publication Data
A catalogue record for this book is available from the British Library

Library of Congress Cataloging-in-Publication Data
A catalog record for this book is available from the Library of Congress

ISBN: 1-85032-137-X

Commissioning Editor: Liz Israel Oppedijk   Publisher/Vice President: Jim DeWolf, ITCP/Boston
Project Director: Chris Grisonich, ITCP/Boston   Manufacturing Manager: Sandra Sabathy Carr, ITCP/Boston
Marketing Manager: Kathleen Raftery, ITCP/Boston

Production: Jo-Ann Campbell • *mle design* • 562 Milford Point Road • Milford, CT 06460

Printed in the U.S.

Contents

Preface

It is no longer a matter for discussion nowadays that local and wide-area networks have gained significance in the computing of every medium-sized and large company. Growing outlays for networking in the DP department budget tell their own tale. If networks are not already implemented to differing degrees, then at least the planning and implementation of a computer network either locally or via remote data connection is on the agenda. According to IDC, the market for integrated IS networks will grow from a seller-oriented (i.e., mainly homogeneous) size of 350,000,000 users between 1986 and 1992 to a buyer-oriented (i.e., heterogeneous) size of 2,450,000,000 users in the years 1993 to 1999.

However, the physical network expansion and, to a growing degree, the number of stations which can be linked up in individual LANs are limited. As complexity and size increase, it becomes more and more vital to find structured ways and means to lift these restrictions.

Networking has long outgrown its infancy and relatively carefree beginnings, and in the last two or three years company networks are increasingly demanding the integration of developed network islands with a view to future functional and capacity expansion, as well as meaningful structuring and management functionality. The question asked in relation to network structuring is no longer "whether," but simply "how." The most diverse switching elements have been developed for solving this task; the market for bridges, routers, protocol converters and gateways has exploded before the users' eyes, to the extent that considerable effort is needed to gain an overview and find the optimal solution for the functions to be handled in the individual firm.

The initially heated debates about "Bridges—or Routers," or more recently "Routing and LAN Switching versus ATM," which led the various advocates to speak out strongly in favor of their own products and against those of the competition, are superfluous. Switching elements such as bridges, LAN switches and routers have their legitimacy and broad application areas parallel to ATM switches; no philosophy will drive the others out of the market for the time being. ATM, the death of bridges and routers? By no means. At any rate not so long as a single conventional LAN protocol is still in operation.

Sales of internetworking components alone (such as bridges, LAN switches, routers—globally 3.8 billion U.S. in 1995) represent a high demand in this market segment.

The majority of this equipment is again in the heterogeneous, i.e., Ethernet/FDDI/ATM, sphere; the boom in the Token Ring market segment has significantly abated in the last two years.

Many people have contributed with advice, tips, technical discussions and practical work to the conception and creation of this book. My sincere thanks to all of these.

I should especially like to thank (in alphabetical order)

Mr. H. Bazzanella, NCB
Prof. Dr. Ing. H. Beilner, University of Dortmund
Mr. Z. Bronstein, 3Com Israel
Mr. I. Dautzenberg, IBM Germany
Mr. J. Deibert, Munich
Mr. R. D. Härter, Inteco
Mr. K. Lipinsik, DATACOM Publishing Company, Bergheim
Mr. J. Obermann, Cisco Europe
Mr. E. H. Pröfener, DATACOM Publishing Company, Bergheim
Mr. J. Read, Digital Equipment Germany

Mr. G. H. Schimpf, IBM Germany
Mr. J. Schlosser, Cisco Germany
Mr. R. Seinsche, Novell Germany
Mr. H. Soldan, Aachen
Mr. J. Stöckner, Datakom
Dr. J. Suppan, ComConsult Kommunikationstechnik GmbH

Suggestions, supplements, corrections, reviews, comments and readers' letters are greatly appreciated. (Please direct letters to ITCP, Berkshire House, 168-173 High Holborn, London WCIV 7AA, U.K. or 20 Park Plaza, 13th Floor, Boston, MA 02116, U.S.A.)

All of Europe is networked by now. All of Europe? Not yet! There's a little village in Gaul... This is how a seminar began at the University of Dortmund on local networks and distributed systems. And this is why here and there in this book a few words are also dedicated to the ancient Gauls.

New developments, new images: In addition to the ancient Gauls, various examples were created in this new edition which have grown up around a toy manufacturer, United Barbie Dolls (UBD).

Petra Borowka
Aachen, Germany

1 The Development of Interconnected Networks

Although the computer industry is relatively young in comparison to other sectors (motor vehicles, textiles, chemicals, etc.), it has developed rapidly during that time. Starting from the individual computer, through the multi-console system, to the mainframe with several thousand terminals and finally to independent workstations with multiple communication links, requirements for an infrastructure to connect the various systems developed. A wide range of connections can be made today on the basis of such an infrastructure: connections between host systems and end systems, links between host systems of the same manufacturer, connections between host systems of different manufacturers, connections between PCs, connections between PCs, and host systems, etc.

Current developments are dominated by the slogan "Workgroup Computing," meaning the formation of any group of individuals into distributed workgroups for projects. Along with workgroup computing are requirements in terms of constant specialist activities (which are often performed on the basis of long-established host applications). This trend of changing task-related communications links on the one hand, and of the continuous use of particular established applications on the other hand, requires a flexible network structure, which allows both demarcation as well as cross-border communication.

Current operating situation

Technical know-how regarding LAN (WAN) interconnection technology is meanwhile the basis for many "commodity products." A wealth of "internetworking hardware" and "connectivity software" makes the market increasingly significant, with the trend being towards the tailored "internetworking box" corresponding to the specific working environment of a corporate network.

A series of technological and applications-related trends dominate and are altering the internetworking landscape:

- Proprietary architectures, such as DECnet or SNA as a corporate backbone, which dominated the scene in the seventies and even in the late eighties, find themselves increasingly having to step aside for multi-protocol backbones as the basis for heterogeneous multi-vendor networks.

- The market for front-end processors is in sharp decline (negative growth).

- The market for bridges, routers and hubs is booming with growth rates in double figures, despite the climate of general economic recession.

- Bridges, routers and hubs are developing from a symbiotic into a competitive relationship and from complementary into competing products.

- The originators of the large network, IBM and DEC, which have persisted in using their own protocol worlds (SNA and DECnet) as the basis for the corporate network, find themselves increasingly having to include "foreign protocols" such as IPX and AppleTalk in their network strategies, to say nothing of the long-avoided open TCP/IP environment (in the absence of broad OSI acceptance and availability).

- Growing user pressure for the integration of various environments have resulted in the launch recently of products such as boxes, box modules, dedicated or non-dedicated PCs with software, servers with software and similar items, which appeal to network operators with a high degree of incompatibility and which significantly complicate and/or make consistent planning for expansion with a multi-vendor model impossible.

- As the LAN turns increasingly into a LAN-WAN combination, the availability of high-capacity WAN connections and corresponding WAN services and the interconnection components that implement these, is increasingly becoming the key issue in further development opportunities. It is not possible to obtain solutions with sufficiently mature products at present in the USA, let alone in Europe. A further impediment to the expansion of LANs, in Germany in particular, are the exorbitant pricing policies of the telecommunications monopolies. If there is not a dramatic reduction in tariffs for lines with megabit capacities in Germany, even technical feasibility combined with mature products will not result in implementation of new technologies, given the current corporate policy of restrictive budget planning.

- The user's dream of simply calling up a range of applications by clicking the mouse on various windows/icons, where the user is unaffected by the physical location of the application or via which protocols and actual network paths it can be called up (and operate!), is turning into a nightmare for network operators: each additional protocol and every further component manufacturer makes the operation of such a network more complex, more unwieldy, more prone to errors (multiplication factor of the failure probability), and the demand for availability and services rises.

- Network management is becoming a matter of life and death for network operation, starting purely from clear documentation of the current position in terms of components and applications installed (in large networks sensibly based on an SQL database in most cases) through to central and distributed management consoles for the most important configuration and online monitoring tasks.

The brief summary of the development of Local Area Networks that follows is to provide an understanding of the different network structures and architectures and the resulting structuring requirements.

1.1 Centralized and decentralized Architectures

Communication links between various systems began in centralized architectures, in which a mainframe served a range of distributed workstations in the form of terminal connections. In the early days of data communication, the only type of connection between machines was a wire from one machine to another, so to speak. The first development from this was the multiplexer, which allowed at least several physical terminal connections with the host machine to be combined in a single cable.

Centralized architecture

Typically traditional mainframe architecture can be found in system environments of long-established computer manufacturers (e.g. Siemens and IBM). The hierarchy descends from the mainframe via various front-end processor stages finally through to the end device (terminal or terminal emulation), at which the user sits. Various communications processes (protocols) can be used on the various connection paths, as illustrated in figure 1.1. Digital and Hewlett-Packard also started to follow the route to data communication through centralized host-terminal structures but branched off relatively quickly in the direction of Local Area Networks and computer systems sharing equal communication rights.

The IBM SNA architecture is the only example given in this book of a centralized architecture, since it is the most widely used within hierarchical host environments (and presumably also with the longest life-span). The end devices (i.e., terminals), are connected via coaxial cable and also via a coaxial terminal protocol to a control unit, which talks to a communications computer (also a front-end processor/communications controller), which in turn talks to the host via a channel connection (with channel protocol, e.g. CTC, ESCON). Several communications computers can also be cascaded for more complex structures (normally, via SDLC), until finally reaching the host. This relatively expensive architecture can serve large numbers of terminals across extensive long-distance networks.

The requirement arose in the subsequent phase for the possibility of exchanging data between several computer systems (hosts) based on remote and distributed end station connection. Since "any to any" connections would have been required for a complete direct communications capability (n*(n-1)/2 links for n systems)—the connection was also intended to be via point-to-point "wires"—network structures were developed with which many systems could exchange data with one another via a common cable. The idea of decentralized architectures on the basis of a common infrastructure began to prevail.

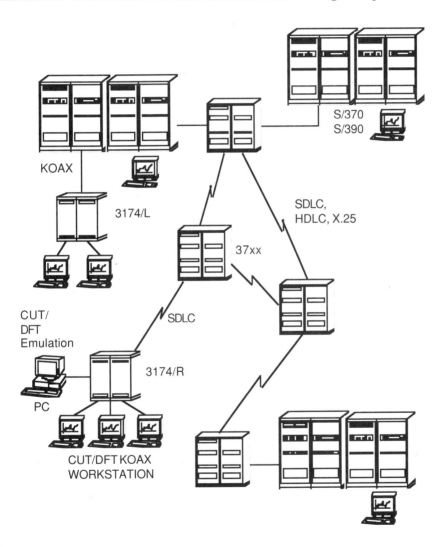

Figure 1.1: Centralized network structure

Decentralized topologies and their development

LANs (Local Area Networks), which were confined to individual buildings and individual sites at first, were developed as a solution to the problem of achieving decentralized architectures. As the Local Area Networks began to operate, various topologies arose with correspondingly different access methods, of which the most important are given below (see Figure 1.2):

- star topology,

- bus topology,

- tree topology,

- ring topology.

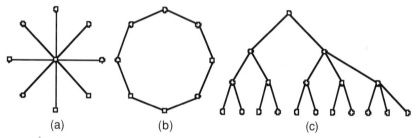

(a)   (b)   (c)

Figure 1.2: Possible network topologies (star, ring, tree)

In contrast to long-distance networks, the routing problems of meshed structures did not exist initially in simple bus, tree, and ring LANs; this did not occur until later with the combination of simple LANs.

The star topology is clearly the centralized approach), (i.e., various systems can communicate with one another but the connection path always passes via a central switching system) which obviously is an extremely critical component in the overall communications infrastructure. Added to this, is the considerable expense for cabling from outstations to the center.

In the case of the bus topology, all the end stations are connected to one central transmission cable, the bus, to the ends of which suitable terminating element modules are connected. An example is given in Figure 1.3. Different bus segments can be connected by what are known as repeaters. Bus structures are still used today in the low-cost Ethernet variant 10Base2.

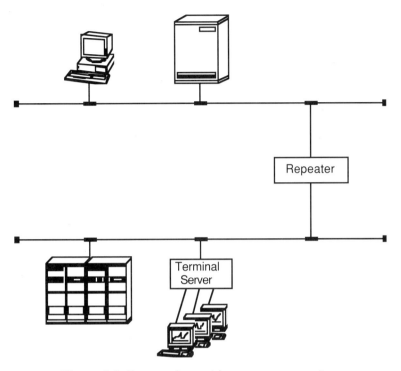

Figure 1.3: Bus topology with repeater connection

The tree structure consists of bus branches developed out of the bus structure for a more flexible network design, but it does not include any loops. There is a precise route between two connected end systems. A tree topology is achieved through the use of interconnection components with more than two ports (e.g., hub systems, see Figure 1.4).

A piece of information is propagated on both sides of the transmitting station throughout the entire network in both the bus and tree structure and can be received by the addressee destination station (if this is active). The packet is finally discarded by the end resistors (terminating element modules) of the bus.

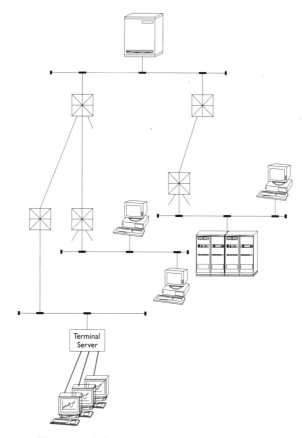

Figure 1.4: Tree topology with hub systems

In the ring structure, all network nodes are connected to a common transmission cable sealed to form a physical ring. This is generally "ring-star" cabling, in which the terminal systems are connected in a star configuration to a distributor and the individual distributors are connected to one another in the form of a ring. Overall, a single large ring results through laying double cables for the star connection (see Figure 1.5). Since a transmitted packet does not automatically disappear from the network as with the bus and tree topology, it must be explicitly removed from the ring, so as not to circle endlessly. This can be performed by the transmitter or receiver.

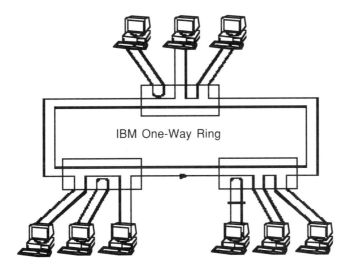

Figure 1.5: Ring topology with distributors

Medium Access Control

In order to achieve communication among many systems via a common cable (or equivalent connection paths, e.g., satellite channels), regulations were required regarding who can occupy the cable with data, for what reason, when, how, and for how long: Medium Access Control was born. It regulates the access of all systems to a common transmission channel according to the following principles:

- Fairness (everyone has the opportunity to be able to transmit at any time);

- Security (as far as possible only one party should be transmitting at any one time);

- Efficiency (as many parties as possible should be able to transmit as much as possible) and;

- Stability (when overloaded, the throughput should not collapse like a house of cards).

The access process can be divided into two fundamentally different categories:

- deterministic access processes.

- non-deterministic access processes.

Both categories are described in greater detail in Chapter 12.

1.2 The Importance of Standards: OSI Communication

To exchange data between two application processes on computer systems of the same or of different manufacturers requires more than the physical connection in the form of the cable. Rules of engagement for both sides and the structure of the exchanged data must be established. This occurs via protocols (analogy: the behavior protocol for an embassy reception; each participating diplomat knows to whom he may or may not say what, when and how). In order to achieve communication between various computer systems, it is possible to adapt one system to the conventions of another (i.e., to perform conversion routines between the two systems which transform the data so that it

can be interpreted and processed correctly in the other system). This has the disadvantage that a conversion unit is required for every combination of different systems (what is known as a gateway). For N systems, this generates the use of N*(N-1)/2 gateways, meaning a cost of O(N2), which is an expensive, inefficient and impractical solution.

The alternative to the gateway solution is the use of standardized communication protocols: each system adapts itself to a uniform standard and therefore requires only one conversion module. This reduces the cost for N systems to N conversion modules, which means linear growth of conversion modules in a growing range of systems and therefore represents a practical solution.

1.2.1 The OSI Reference Model

The reference model of the ISO (International Standards Organization) for open communication, known as the OSI reference model (Reference Model of Open Systems Interconnection/OSI), represents a general model for standardized communication between computer systems.

The most important principle of the reference model is the division of the communication process into various functions, which are performed by what are known as Layers. Seven Layers are defined overall; the OSI reference model therefore also became known as the 7 Layer model. The seven Layers are shown in Figure 1.6.

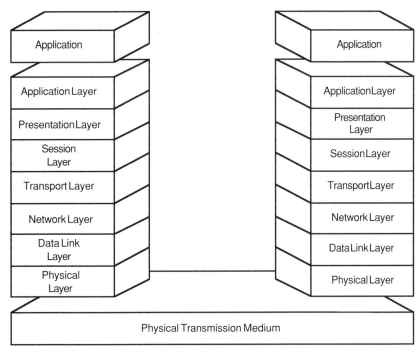

Figure 1.6: The OSI reference model

The communication process has a vertical and horizontal component: each Layer N communicates in one system with the Layer N in another system on the same level. This horizontal communication is termed peer-to-peer communication. The rules and formats for communication between two Layers N are established in a protocol (for the level N, N-layer protocol). For all Layers, apart from the lowest Layer 1, this is logical communication; only on Layer 1 is there actual physical transmission. A data unit which is exchanged between two peer Layers, is known as a PDU (Protocol Data Unit), therefore DPDU = Data Link Protocol Data Unit, NPDU = Network Protocol Data Unit, TPDU = Transport Protocol Data Unit, etc.

Vertical communication actions are defined in order to fetch the data units from the application to the cable and back from the cable to the application: each Layer performs particular services, which they provide to the next highest layer. In this way, each layer accesses the services of the next lowest Layer, which it uses to perform its own functions. Interfaces are defined between the two Layers in the framework of the standard protocols, to which particular services are offered via so-called Service Access Points (SAPs). The services of a Layer are allocated into hierarchies, one hierarchy of the layer N is an N hierarchy (see Figure 1.7).

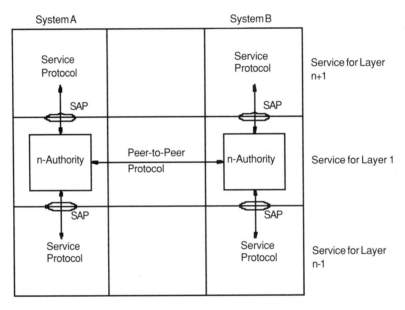

Figure 1.7: Principle of vertical and horizontal communication in the layer model

Each Layer embeds the payload data in protocol information so that it can be processed and conveyed by the peer Layer. The pieces of protocol data are called headers (at the start of the packet) and trailers (at the end of the packet); protocol data is termed the protocol overhead, in contrast to the payload data. Important elements in the protocol overhead include, for example, receiver and sender addresses on different layers, in particular in the case of communication via bridges and routers, addresses on Layers 2 and 3, or the entry of the protocol type to distinguish between different protocols. Payload data is therefore provided with protocol information six times in the process from the application to the transmission (protocol overhead arises every time), and the protocol information of a higher Layer is viewed as payload data by the lower Layer (i.e., handled transparently). On the lowest Layer, the information is converted into a bit stream including all protocol information and transmitted via the physical medium. The reverse process is followed on the receiver side: during packet processing, the protocol information of the peer Layer is interpreted in each Layer and removed after implementing the corresponding services. The remaining information is passed on to the next highest Layer, which repeats the packet processing procedure described above. If the information makes it to the application, all protocol information is removed, and only the payload data is passed on to the next Layer. (See Figure 1.8).

In the case of communication between two end stations, intermediate systems can also be employed as relay systems, which perform only a certain range of transmission functions but have not implemented all Layers. Such relay systems, e.g. bridges and routers, include those which transmit the functions up to Layer 2 or Layer 3.

1.2.2 Tasks of the Seven Layers

The Physical Layer

The lowest Layer of the OSI reference model describes the electrical and mechanical specifications which are required to send and receive unstructured bit streams, in particular transmission technology (baseband, bandwidth, etc.), transmission medium, data rates, electrical signal form and, under certain circumstances, plugs, and sockets.

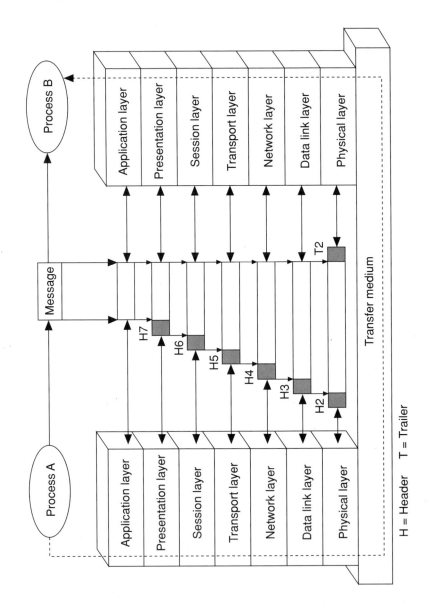

Figure 1.8: Data exchange between applications via Peer-to-Peer communication

The Data Link Layer

Layer 2 makes a secure and transparent data transmission available for Layer 3. In particular, this contains error detection and the processing of transmission errors, flow monitoring and Medium Access Control. Checksums are performed on all bits of a packet after the CRC process (Cyclic Redundancy Check) in order to detect any transmission errors. The packets in Layer 2, the frames, are transmitted sequentially. An acknowledgment mechanism is employed depending upon the protocol for flow control (mutual adaptation of transmission speeds) and acknowledgment of the packets received (ACK).

Layer 2 is divided into two sub-layers for local area networks: the Medium Access Control (MAC) and the Logical Link Control (LLC). The MAC layer regulates the important function of medium access.

Overview of Medium Access Control

A distinction must be drawn between centralized and decentralized Medium Access Control. In the case of centralized access control, the access privilege is allocated by means of a central dedicated device (e.g., packet switching, host polling). No such control centers exist in decentralized environments; the stations must "negotiate" with one another as to which acquires access next, a typical situation in LANs. The decentralized processes can be divided further into deterministic and non-deterministic access control.

In the case of the deterministic process, a protocol exists. This protocol determines how a station can access the transmission medium without competition, i.e., in agreement with all other stations. At the time the station holds access privilege, no other station behaving according to the protocol may claim this access. There is a sequential arrangement and the access time of an individual station is limited so that an upper time limit (deterministic time) for access privilege can be set for each station wishing to transmit. This feature is particularly important in real-time environments.

In the case of non-deterministic processes, access is competitive, not coordinated. If two stations try to access the medium at the same time, the transmitted packets collide (collision), and both packets are destroyed by the mutual signal collision and must be retransmitted. Since the access is not coordinated, no upper time limit for an individual station to receive guaranteed media access can be set. Examples of deterministic and non-deterministic processes are given in Figure 1.9.

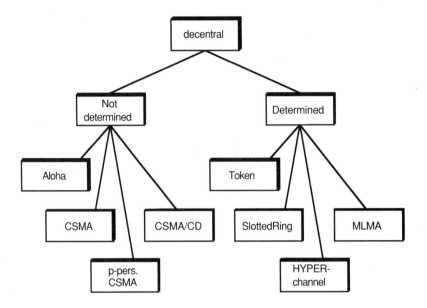

Figure 1.9: Decentralized media access methods

The Network Layer

The functions of the Network Layer include:

- routing

- multiplexing of Layer 2 connections

- sequencing of packets (division into suitable lengths)

- flow control

- acknowledgments

- error processing

- prioritized transmission

The Network Layer provides an end-to-end link between two end stations on the network. Routing is therefore the most important of the functions listed above. A distinction must be drawn here in particular between static processes with fixed routing determined by tables and dynamic processes with load-dependent routing and account taken of the currently active topology alternatives. These are discussed in greater detail in later chapters. Two important categories of network services are the connectionless service (datagram service) and the connection-oriented service. The conclusion of the Network Layer is often described as the interface between the "network protocols" (Layers 1–3) and the higher "application protocols." This Layer represents the transition from the network infrastructure to the host.

The Transport Layer

The Transport Layer provides an end-to-end connection between processes in two networked computer systems where the data transfer via the network for the processes is transparent. The Transport Layer is therefore the highest network-dependent and lowest application dependent Layer. The term end-to-end communication (between processes) is used here in contrast to end-to-end connection at the network level. Transport protocols are usually divided into 5 Classes (Class 0 to Class 4) with increasing functionality. Class 0 contains only the transmission of data on the basis of the service quality offered by Layer 3, Class 4 contains error recognition and error correction including multiplexing, sequencing, flow control and acknowledgments. This is the popular protocol class for LANs. Classes 1 to 3 contain various sub-groups of Class 4 (see [TANE89]).

The Session Layer

The Session Layer governs the control of communication between two applications processes. This includes the mutual issuing of transmission authorization, the definition of synchronization points and reset mechanisms. These services are combined into various functional units, the use or non-use of which must be negotiated by the stations making the connection.

The Presentation Layer

The range of functions of the Presentation Layer include essentially all coding and presentation tasks (i.e., character set and syntax and the use of a mutually accepted data structure for the transfer of information between two systems). The agreements for these presentation aspects are established via various transfer syntax descriptions with the aid of the ASN.1 description language.

The Application Layer

The Application Layer provides application-specific protocols. Their functions can roughly be divided into the provision of basic functions, which are used by all applications (Application Control Service Elements/ACSE) such as constructing and deconstructing connections and action control in distributed systems (Commitment, Concurrency and Recovery/CCR). The application-specific protocols regulate special functions such as file transfer (FTAM), the virtual terminal (VTS), mailing (Message Handling Systems/MHS, X.400) and similar matters.

"Industry standards" or de facto standards have been established in addition to the OSI standards. These are published protocols which can be adapted and implemented by each manufacturer as public domain. These can be found, in particular, in the TCP/IP environment (FTP, TELNET, NFS, etc.). More recent attempts at de facto standards have been made, in particular, in the framework of the OSF (Open Systems Foundation) in the field of network management (Distributed Management Environment/DME) and client/server computing (Distributed Computing Environment/DCE).

1.3   LANs of the First, Second and Third Generation

Various LANs were developed in the "first generation" based upon the different topologies and media access processes. The first generation include: ALOHA, CSMA, p-persistent CSMA, CSMA/CD, Token Ring, Slotted Ring, HYPERchannel, BRAM (Broadcast Recognition Access Method), MSAP (Mini Slotted Alternating Priorities), MLMA (Multi Level Multi Access). Fortunately, only two of the LANs are widely used. These are the two standardized LANs: CSMA/CD and Token Ring, which will be discussed in greater detail later.

1.3.1 The protocol survivors of the first generation: DIX and IBM

There are basically two protocol survivors of all the alternative LAN developments, i.e., protocols established on a wide basis, two survived. One is non-deterministic, and one is deterministic:

- IEEE 802.3 CSMA/CD, Ethernet 2.0 (DIX), CSMA/CD and;

- IEEE 802.5 Token Ring (IBM Token Ring).

CSMA/CD as an established non-deterministic process (Carrier Sense Multiple Access with Collision Detection) was originally developed by DIX: Digital, Intel, and Xerox at XEROX PARC (Palo Alto Research Center). It was called Ethernet, and is still used today in the version Ethernet 2.0 by a series of de facto standards. The IEEE 802.3 version of CSMA/CD differs from Ethernet in some ways, but it essentially corresponds overall; both variants can be operated in parallel on the same transmission cable and in part on the same adapter. Most system manufacturers, in particular Apple, Digital, Hewlett Packard, Sun Microsystems, Siemens/SNI, and others have implemented CSMA/CD as a LAN connection. Slowly and gradually IBM systems are also acquiring a CSMA/CD connection.

The deterministic IBM Token Ring, adapted as the IEEE 802.5 standard, can be found predominantly in computing environments with IBM hosts. The Token Ring was termed the "IBM LAN" for a long time but has achieved a broader base (and wider product range) since 1991, particularly in connection with the construction of PC networks, which required an IBM host connection.

The deterministic variant Token Bus (IEEE 802.4), devised primarily for the manufacturing sector in association with MAP (Manufacturing Automation Protocol), was not able to establish itself. There are currently discussions regarding the use of MAP on Ethernet (despite the theoretical lack of real-time capability).

1.3.2 The Second Generation: FDDI, LAN-WAN Connections

Current requirements are extending beyond simple local networks and heading towards site networks and Metropolitan Area Networks (MANs) with high capacity backbone structures. This new generation is leading the transition to high speed LANs in the range of 30 to 100 Mbit/s or even Gbit/s transmission capacity. Important developments to be mentioned here are FDDI (Fiber Distributed Data Interface), in the field of LANs and MANs, and ATM (Asynchronous Transfer Mode). FDDI seems to be restricted predominantly to the site and town sector because of its limitation to 100 km; ATM is standing out as a further development of the third LAN generation. ATM is a strategic high speed process in the public sector, since DQDB has not proved a success. Unfortunately the product situation in the ATM sector is still very unsatisfactory; FDDI has reached a broader level of acceptance.

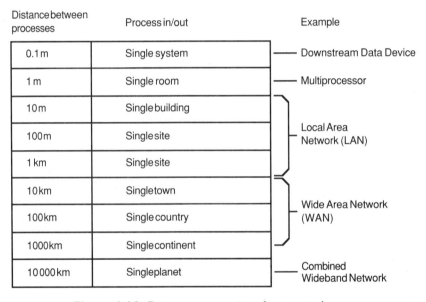

Figure 1.10: Distance categories of connected processors

The development of corporate networks has not stopped at MANs; it has extended to inter-site LAN-WAN connections over hundreds and thousands of kilometres of public networks. A market sector arose for the connection of outstations with corresponding branch office products. Frame Relay as a simple protocol for data transfer in the WAN sector has good prospects of establishing itself as an alternative to X.21 and X.25 (currently up to 2 Mbit/s) and will be available for use in the high speed sector in future (G.703 up to 34

Mbit/s). This is particularly important because ATM still cannot be used seriously in LAN-WAN combinations because of the high tariffs and immature products. ISDN is an alternative in the low capacity sector, which is currently experiencing very strong acceptance in the market.

In Figure 1.10, the distances between the two connected communicating processors is divided into distance categories to give an overview of examples of the increasing distances which have been and are being bridged in the context of data communication.

1.3.3 The Third Generation: Switched LANs and High Speed LANs

In the face of growing terminal numbers and of increasing network load per terminal, ways of expanding currently available technologies such as Ethernet, Token Ring and FDDI and developing variants of the standard LANs, which enable higher transmission capacities are being sought.

LAN Switching

In place of the "shared LAN" concept, joint LAN capacity is an alternative which provides a series of terminals in a LAN segment. Many connections are being combined with one another via a LAN switch in what is known as micro-segmenting, where each individual end station has full LAN capacity. For more details, please refer to Chapter 7.

Fast Ethernet

Two fast Ethernet variants are combined under Fast Ethernet: the first proposal was 100BaseVG by HP and AT&T at the end of 1992, the second proposal 100BaseX was from a consortium of Cabletron, 3Com, and Synoptics. After lengthy debate, the IEEE decided to develop two standards both of which are further developments of IEEE 802.3 and use 100 Mbit/s transmission capacity: IEEE 802.3u with 100BaseX and IEEE 802.12 with 100BaseVG, 100VG-AnyLAN.

The attraction of IEEE 802.3 100BaseX (100BaseT and 100BaseFX) is that the fundamental CSMA/CD technology is retained with tenfold nominal capacity in comparison to conventional Ethernet. The widely-established Ethernet know-how can continue to be used, not only by end-users but also by manufacturers, which has decisive benefits for product development. The possible distances for this are limited (max. 500 m with fiber optics, 100 m with Category 5 UTP or 10 m with Category 3 UTP between hub systems and a maximum of three cascaded hubs).

The attraction of 100BaseVG is the use of a cost-effective type of cable (voice grade, i.e., Category 3 UTP). Unfortunately, VG uses eight strands instead of just four in the case of 100BaseX, in order to reduce the electromagnetic radiation with Cat3 UTP to the required extent. Anyone without enough strands, must lay new cables. Using fiber optics, the maximum distance between two hubs is two kilometers. A second advantage lies in the fact that VG-AnyLAN also functions for Token Ring and provides bandwidth reservation for isochronous traffic (voice, video). The result is the specification of a new MAC process, which retains only the CSMA/CD frame format: demand priority with two priority values for high and low priority transmissions, high priority for voice and video, low priority for data transfer. The issuing of a new 802 number (802.12) leads to the assumption that this is a new LAN process.

Further FDDI developments

FDDI II and FDDI Follow On LAN (FFOL) are among the further FDDI developments of the ANSI X3T9.5 committee which might still be relevant in the future. FDDI II has already been in the specifications pipeline for some time, but has not yet learned to stand on its own. Both processes divide the bandwidth fully and reserve a smaller portion for synchronously clocked isochronous traffic (several channels have 64 kbit/s). The remaining bandwidth is placed as shared medium at the disposal of the asynchronous LAN traffic, which is prone to bursts. Two MAC modules are required for such an implementation, one for the time-critical isochronous traffic and one for the asynchronous traffic. Guaranteed delays can be anticipated of 125 µs for FDDI II and 5 µs for FFOL. FFOL standardization is currently still at a very early stage. Some claim that FFOL is practically ATM, since it is intended to be specified for copper and LWL, based on the Physical Layer on SDH, and FFOL uses ATM cells for asynchronous transport of data packets.

High Speed Token Ring

While Ethernet and FDDI are fighting for survival, Token Ring will not be left out. An IEEE 802.5 working group was established for this standard in July 1993. It is not yet clear whether Token Ring is intended to use the same signaling for High Speed Token Ring as for 100BaseVG, or as for FDDI or something totally separate.

Fiber Channel

ATM had hardly been introduced when a new competing standard surfaced on the horizon: Fiber Channel. Under the motto: "The copper age is over, long live fiber optics," the ANSI X3T9.3 committee began conceiving cost effective solutions with continuous fiber optic cabling. Fiber Channel is significantly more cost effective than ATM, since the high speeds (133/266/530 Mbit/s and 1 Gbit/s) can be achieved with conventional technology. Connection extensions are not supported under Fiber Channel however, and connections must be in a fixed configuration. This means less flexibility than with ATM, and the possible distances are less than with ATM, (25 m with 1 Gbit/s on coax, 100 m with 133 Mbit/s). The focus of Fiber Channel is more in the field of computer peripheral connections and LAN segments. In any case, some important commitments to the Fiber Channel, have been made by HP, IBM, and Sun.

Where next for the High Speed LAN?

There is the sixty four thousand dollar question for network managers and planners:

Your network is reaching its performance limit in terms of bandwidth. Some users have already begun to notice, and the coffee consumption has clearly increased. The more advanced users in your company are suggesting monitoring the coffee machine with multimedia—a service, which you must soon provide. ATM has not yet come down from its cloud. You need a solution NOW. Which of the following high speed technologies solve your current network performance and represent a practical migration path towards ATM?

- FDDI
- CDDI

- FDDI II

- FFOL

- Fiber Channel

- High Speed Token Ring

- Isochronous Ethernet

- Fast Ethernet (100Base VG)

- Fast Ethernet (100 Mbit/s CSMA/CD)

- ATM (ASAP)

- LAN Switching

- several of the above

- none of the above

- all of the above

Found a solution? Wrong! There is no solution, at least no universal solution for today's patchwork LAN collections in typical medium to large companies: for a home-baked PC network with a network word-processing system and file server, good old Ethernet is good enough every time; for a graphic cluster, you may already be thinking of possibly upgrading to 100BaseVG; you should be connecting up your R&D Suns and the Simulations Cray with Fiber Channel.

If you prudently chose "several of the above," you should show this book to your boss and ask for a rise: you have recognized the problem, several favorable alternatives strike you at the moment, and you later can sort out those which do not make it in the market.

Despite the current phase of technological uncertainty, several assessment criteria can be used for future network extensions. These include:

- actual bandwidth growth achieved per terminal

- compatibility with existing installations

- use of existing cabling, new cabling expense

- costs

- manageability, if necessary integrated management of "old" and new technology

- future-proofness

- extendibility

Actual increases in bandwidth

By skillful segmenting of the shared media (i.e. LANs), the performance of a network can be tweaked for a long time to come. The actual growth in bandwidth in increasing the LAN capacity depends upon the number of terminals used: exchanging Ethernet for FDDI or Fast Ethernet brings a factor of 10 into the equation; using 25 connected terminals, a LAN capacity of 100 Mbit/s does not mean more than 4 Mbit/s per terminal, provided that the communication is shared completely equally. In such a case, Ethernet Switching (10 Mbit/s per connected) therefore provides the greater increase in performance. If, in another case, 10 clients are talking to one superserver, there is an asymmetric communication distribution, and the server can claim a larger portion of the total bandwidth. In this case, the increase from 10 Mbit/s to 100 Mbit/s total capacity has certain advantages, since the server can use more than 10 Mbit/s of the bandwidth.

An increase in capacity in the ATM network is implemented totally differently: a dedicated connection with precisely defined capacity is newly created via a further point-to-point connection. While this new connection closes a "hole," an increase in capacity also results in the creation of other routes through a distribution of the load (the exact value of this, however, can be calculated only with a precise knowledge of the communication profile as regards the capacity utilization share of the various datastreams at the new connection). In particular, the simple extendibility by accepting a further point-to-point connection for a further "hole" in the network is not given in the well-known LAN processes. It is comparable in principle to LAN segmenting using bridges and routers.

In this respect, the protocol-determined overhead as a ratio of payload data to overhead must be examined closely (as a percentage: (100/#payload bytes) x

(#overhead bytes): ATM, praised as the top performer, can proudly offer 10.4 percent. Fiber Channel, on the other hand, has a 36 byte header with a 2112 byte payload, (only 1.7% overhead).

In the case of Fast Ethernet, the nominal capacity must be set against the achievable capacity utilization, since this process is afflicted by collisions in the same way as its predecessor. In the worst case (with file transfer applications), capacity utilization of a maximum of 70% to 80% can be achieved, which restricts the capacity to 80 Mbit/s from the outset. LANs with the token process, on the other hand, can achieve capacity utilization of over 90% (tests by Interlab achieved FDDI capacity utilization of up to 96%).

Capacity is only one side of the coin, however. The response time is often much more important to network operation, in particular, in the high load scenario. Here, the shared media processes appear to be inferior to the cell transfer processes because of the bursts occurring and long packet sizes. This restriction applies overwhelmingly for time-critical isochronous traffic and many different session pairs. In the case of server concepts (asymmetric communication), an HS LAN process can mean a more efficient solution because of lower overheads.

The simple bandwidth calculation using capacity is also not tenable with priority-controlled processes (ATM, FDDI II, HS Token Ring), since the low priority applications acquire a smaller share of capacity in the high load scenario (or even none at all). At the same time, prioritized applications do not always receive direct access, since they compete with other participants of the same priority.

The transition to new technologies always requires a connection with at least bridge functionality. The actual bandwidth and/or the more important measure of delay, is increased by the processing time in the interconnection component, which is dependent in turn upon the bus and buffer capacity. For datastreams crossing subnetworks, the throughput capacity of the interconnection components used and of the connection process represents an upper capacity limit.

Compatibility with existing installations

Speed alone does not make a network run—careful tests must be performed to determine whether, when changing to switch technology, the existing installations in the subnetwork area can continue to operate as before. Does the switch support the existing address structure of all the protocol environments in operation? Changing from bridge to switching technology often requires a laborious configuration of virtual LANs, which in turn requires significant input of working time to implement the migration. Since no standard has yet been approved for the LAN emulation, it is necessary to work with proprietary solutions—which in turn places in question the future compatibility with other products.

Scalability

In the same way as the compatibility with existing equipment must be taken into consideration, extendibility must also be considered. If a component cannot be extended in a modular manner, can new services be integrated? Is the capacity of the backplane sufficient for capacity extensions? Are there convenient introductory solutions? These and similar questions must be clarified for each network extension (i.e., when really making the transition to new technology).

Use of existing cable, new cabling expense

The additional installation of fiber optic cabling, particularly in the backbone field, is generally both technically and financially achievable. It is a different matter in the end station sector, since totally different connection volumes must be handled here and productive network operation is considerably impeded by changes at the workstation. In many cases, the forced change to fiber optics through to the workstation will therefore impede the migration (currently still with FFOL, FDDI II, Fiber Channel).

Costs

With regard to hardware and software investments, the costs for the various different new technologies differ greatly. An FDDI connection for fiber optics costs between $2,750 and $3,450 per PC, including concentrator port, a copper connection costs about $1,700. Some forecasts for 1996 are below $1,350 per connection. ATM is more expensive at over $4,750 per connection. On the other hand, 100Base VG comes in at around $475 per connection for an adapter as a dumping element.

Costs arise not only as a result of the investments to be made for hardware and software in the technology change. A considerable share of the cost lies in the necessary personnel capacity for conversion of the network operation and permanent care of the extended service offer. Consideration of the migration to a new technology must take careful account of the labor costs of the installation and operation. For example, if a company currently operates predominantly Ethernet, the change to Switched Ethernet or Fast Ethernet involves the least increase in know-how and conversion expense.

Manageability

The same basic principles apply for the expansion of a network using new technology as generally apply for a complex network: installing new components in an integrated management concept must be possible, and these should be manageable with the platforms in use. The topic is dealt with in detail in section 15.1.

Investment-protection

Since the market will accept only a limited number of different LAN processes, the crunch question must naturally be posed: Which will survive? Some of the models which the IEEE and ANSI are supporting so enthusiastically at present and likewise some of the (switching) models, for which there is no standardization, will certainly end up in the "oh yes, back then there was ..." basket. The number of major manufacturers who support a process cannot be ignored.

FDDI is the clear winner in this respect: more than 100 manufacturers can be considered as a solid base. Things are much tighter with ATM with around a dozen manufacturers and a series of planned products (the ATM forum has over 600 members). Fiber Channel, with less than 20 members in the Fiber Channel Association, is still in the early stages of development, but it already has well-known sponsors such as HP, IBM, and Sun.

Ethernet Switching is supported by a series of manufacturers but is not based on a standard, as is the case with FDDI and Token Ring Switching. There are still no products for the latter and only very few commitments.

Those which have fallen from favor with the manufacturers include an HS variant for Token Ring, isochronous Ethernet, and Full Duplex Ethernet, even if IBM wishes to support all these processes as a major manufacturer.

The OSI reference model and standard network architectures can be dealt with only in a very cursory manner in this book in order to lay the basis for further understanding. For further details please refer to Tane, 1989; MSKR, 1993; and Kyas, 1994a.

2 Network Structuring: A Systematic Introduction

To introduce the topic of network structuring, the most important LAN standards are compared with the limitations of an individual LAN (subnetwork), and the resulting typical reasons for structuring are discussed. The various classes of network interconnection components are briefly described for some general definitions.

2.1 The LAN Standards for Simple Networks

The most important protocols are described briefly in the framework of currently established LAN standards:

- CSMA/CD

- Token Ring

- FDDI

For further details, refer to [KAUSUP], [TANE89], and the relevant ISO standards.

2.1.1 CSMA/CD

Ethernet Version 1.0, the first CSMA/CD process (Carrier Sense Multiple Access with Collision Detection) to establish itself in the market was developed by Digital, Intel, and Xerox, also became known as the DIX standard. It was later modified to Ethernet 2.0. This is a protocol which currently is used in a series of LANs, particularly in the DEC environment. The IEEE standard 802.3 regarding the CSMA/CD process broadly corresponds to Ethernet 2.0 but there are several differences, which are briefly discussed below, to the extent required to understand how bridges and routers operate.

CSMA/CD is a non-deterministic access process with a transmission rate of 10 Mbit/s. The essential elements of the process can be deduced from the name: Multiple Access—all stations compete for access to the same transmission medium; Carrier Sense—each station listens to the channel before transmitting and transmits only when the channel is free; Collision Detection—each station also listens to the channel during transmission to detect any collision as early as possible and implement corresponding error correction. Despite Carrier Sensing, collisions may occur if two stations attempt to transmit simultaneously. The CSMA/CD process with competing media access is illustrated in Figure 2.1.

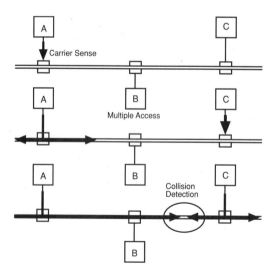

Figure 2.1: CSMA/CD access method

The maximum time in which a collision may occur is called the "collision window" and depends upon the maximum length of the transmission distance. In order to restrict the collision window, the segment length is limited to a maximum of 1500 m (including repeaters). If a transmission process proceeds during the collision interval without a collision, the channel is then "conquered," since the signal has been propagated over the entire medium and received by all stations wishing to transmit via their carrier sensing. The maximum time before a collision is detected is twice the collision interval, since the superimposed signal must, under certain circumstances, propagate once more to the transmitting station at the other end of the transmission medium. A message must therefore have a minimum transmission time of twice the collision window, (i.e., have a minimum length in bytes so that the collision can definitely be detected). This minimum length is 64 bytes (46 bytes data plus overhead). If the data portion is not long enough, the frame is enlarged to the required length with "padding." Following a collision, all participating stations suspend the transmitting procedure and implement the Binary Exponential Backoff-Algorithm (BEB) for error processing: they wait for a renewed transmission attempt for i*collision window, where the following values apply:

i   =   random number from the interval $0 < i < 2k$

k   = $\min(n, 10)$

n   =   number of transmission attempts performed

A transmission attempt is naturally undertaken only if the channel is free after the backoff interval according to Carrier Sense. After sixteen fruitless transmission attempts, transmission is interrupted with an error message (and under certain circumstances reinitiated by higher layers). The random size of the waiting interval avoids the fact that two stations which have generated a collision, generate a collision once more after the end of an identical waiting interval by attempting their next access at the same time.

A station wishing to transmit:

- listens to the channel for transmission activity, before it commences transmission,

- begins at the earliest 9.6 μs after transmission is completed on the channel (Inter Packet Gap),

- monitors the channel also during transmission (Collision Detection),

- interrupts transmission immediately after detecting a collision and begins to transmit an interference signal so that all other participants are also sure to note the collision,

- becomes inactive for the BEB period,

- attempts transmission once more after expiry of the backup interval.

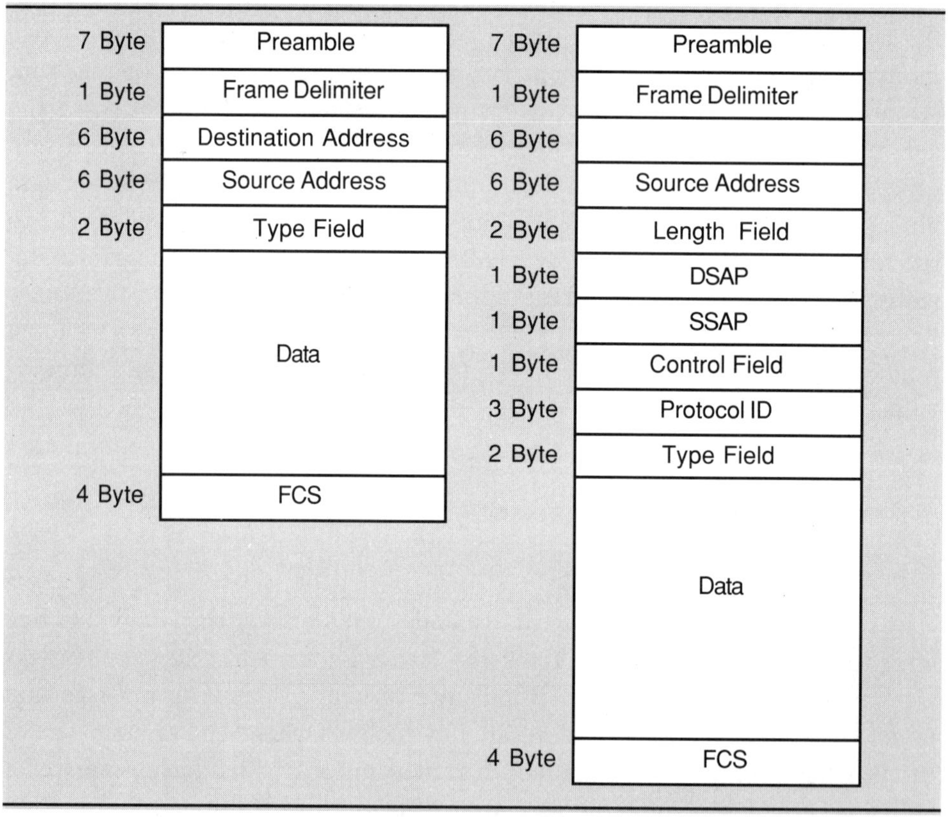

7 Byte	Preamble	7 Byte	Preamble
1 Byte	Frame Delimiter	1 Byte	Frame Delimiter
6 Byte	Destination Address	6 Byte	
6 Byte	Source Address	6 Byte	Source Address
2 Byte	Type Field	2 Byte	Length Field
		1 Byte	DSAP
		1 Byte	SSAP
	Data	1 Byte	Control Field
		3 Byte	Protocol ID
		2 Byte	Type Field
4 Byte	FCS		Data
		4 Byte	FCS

Figure 2.2: Ethernet and IEEE 802.3 frame format

The essential difference between Ethernet 2.0 and IEEE 802.3 lies in the frame format: after the destination and source address, a 2-byte long type field in the Ethernet frame follows, into which the type value of the higher protocol used is entered, after which follows the data portion. The different frame formats are shown in Figure 2.2. In the IEEE 802.3 frame, there is a length field instead of the type field, into which the frame length is entered. The DSAP and SSAP (Destination Service Access Point and Source Service Access Point) of the LLC layer following this, which is omitted in the Ethernet frame. These differences mean that stations which use Ethernet 2.0 cannot communicate with IEEE 802.3 stations. Both variants can be run in parallel on the same transmission medium, however, since the access process is performed in an identical manner. The different frame format has consequences for the use of filters, which is dealt with in greater detail in later chapters.

2.1.2 Token Ring

The Token Ring process (IBM Token Ring, 4 Mbit/s) was developed by IBM and used extensively in purely IBM environments in the early years. It was not until around 1990 that Token Ring began to be used on a broader level for LAN networking. The Token Ring variant expanded to 16 Mbit/s has established itself since 1991. The Token Ring process uses a token to control the transmission sequence. The token is a distinct bit sequence that circulates on the ring. The form of the token indicates whether the channel is free or occupied. A station wishing to transmit, which receives a free token, follows the sequence below:

- converts this into an occupied token and

- transmits its frame(s) (connected directly to the token) until either

- all frames have been transmitted, or

- the maximum time permitted for transmission has expired;

- removes a transmitted frame from the ring once more,

- converts the token into a free token after use and sends it to the subsequent station.

The receiver station copies the frame for further processing and places a corresponding bit flag at the end of the frame, in order to signal whether the frame was identified and correctly copied (Address Recognized Bit, Frame Copied Bit). If the subsequent station wishes to transmit, it occupies the token, if not, it continues on to the next station. The action sequence in transmitting a frame is illustrated in Figure 2.3.

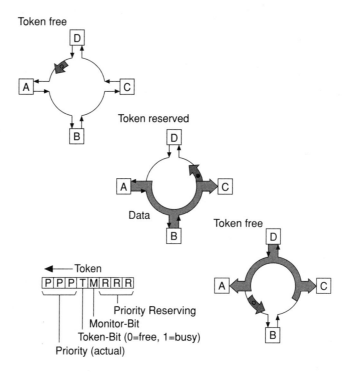

Figure 2.3 Token Ring Process

The Early Token Release Option can be used with 16 Mbit/s Token Ring in which a new free token is generated at the end of the transmitted message, only after the transmitted message has been removed from the ring completely. Further variants include Multiple Token processes, in which several tokens can circulate on the ring. This is sensible only with very high transmission capacities, otherwise the storage capacity of the ring (maximum number of bits, which can be on the ring at the same time) is too small, meaning that the use of several tokens is neither feasible, nor efficient. (The following is an example of loading capacity: for a ring of length, L = 5 km, data rate, D = 4 Mbit/s and a signal propagation speed of V = 200 000 km/s, according to the formula N=D*L/V 100 bit, barely 13 bytes fit onto the ring.)

The station connection in Token Ring is active, i.e., each frame passes through the connection point of each connected station. If a connection point fails, the cable path is interrupted (for the short-term).

Error correction mechanisms, which are implemented partly by a particular connected station, the so called monitor are provided in the Token Ring protocol for a series of error situations, which may confuse the process.

Link or end station failure caused by physical fault: to bridge (automatically or manually). Lost token caused by noise or signal interference: new token generated by monitor when timer expires. Token rotating through noise or station fault: If it happens for a second time, the token is removed from the ring and the management station generates free tokens. Double token caused by noise or station error: Examine the source address in the token following a message from the management platform; remove and reconfigure. Monitor failure through Hardware or Software error: Standby-monitor takes over after the operation of a timer.

Using the description of possible error situations, it becomes clear that the "monitor station" function provided according to the protocol which is performed by a specified (but in principle any) connected station, represents a central element in the Token Ring. It is activated and maintained by corresponding protocol mechanisms in each Token Ring.

The token principle is also used in the Token Bus process. In the absence of the physical ring to define the sequence, a logical sequential number (address) is allocated to the connected stations and each station passes on the token to its logical successor station.

2.1.3 FDDI

FDDI (Fiber Distributed Data Interface) is also a standard LAN with a token process (ANSI X3T9.5) based on a contraflow double ring (primary, secondary ring). The specified transmission capacity is approximately 100 Mbit/s, meaning that FDDI must be considered a high speed network according to current categorizations (ten years ago, Ethernet and Token Ring were still described as such). Fiber optics are generally used for transmission and copper cable also for very short distances (< 100m). The maximum network extension is 100 km; the maximum distance between stations is 2 km. FDDI is currently used frequently as a fast LAN Backbone and more rarely as a LAN for end system/ computer system connection.

The FDDI specification, as with all other standard LANs, includes the two lower Layers of the OSI reference model. In contrast to the LANs discussed so far, the specification of the Physical Layer is divided once more into PMD (Physical Layer Medium Dependent) and PHY (Physical Layer Protocol). PMD essentially defines requirements of the fiber optic transmission medium and optical components. PHY defines the medium-independent transmission processes, e.g. coding of the signals. A token process is used on the MAC Layer and the IEEE 802.2 standard on the LLC Layer. A separate standard module, SMT (Station Management), defines management mechanisms for FDDI. Such mechanisms include coordination of the ring structure when accelerating networks and network portions, status reports on ring and station status, and collection of statistical values. SMT is divided further into RMT (Ring Management) and the more important CMT (Connection Management), which takes care of the ring structure, reconfiguration in the event of correctable errors and statistical values. The individual standards and their relationship to one another are presented in Figure 2.4.

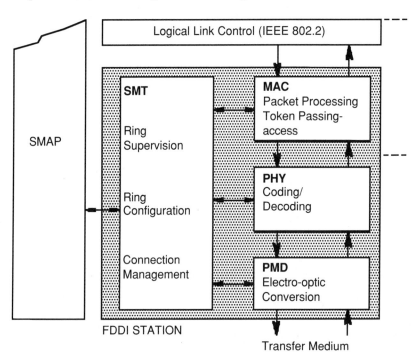

SMAP= Station Management Application Program

Figure 2.4: Set of FDDI standards

The token process used is a multiple token process: a transmitting station generates a new free token at the end of its message. A station wishing to transmit can place its message onto the ring immediately after receipt of the free token (see Figure 2.5). With the high transmission speed, under certain circumstances, so several messages can fit onto the ring, several tokens may be found on the ring at the same time (but with only one free token, however).

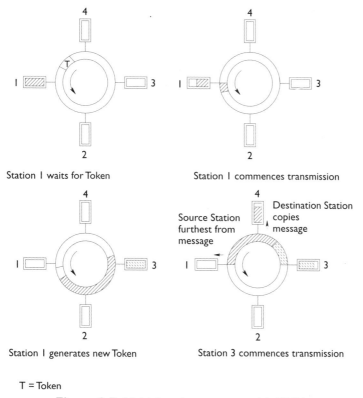

T = Token

Figure 2.5: Multiple token process with FDDI

FDDI connections can be divided into two classes: Class A and Class B stations. Class A stations are connected to both rings directly; Class B stations are connected to the double ring via distribution stations, concentrators, which can each connect several Class B stations (see Figure 2.6). Components can be classified according to the MAC and PHY module used:

- Single MAC Dual Attachment Station (SM-DAS, Class A)
- Dual MAC Dual Attachment Station (DM-DAS, Class A)
- Single MAC/Single Attachment Station (SAS, class B)
- Dual Attachment Concentrator (DAC, Class A)
- Single Attachment Concentrator (SAC, Class B)

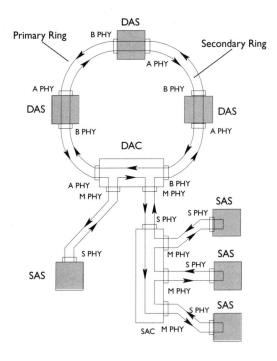

Figure 2.6: FDDI station types

These attachment possibilities give more complex FDDI networks a "Ring of Trees" topology as illustrated in Figure 2.7.

In the event of a line failure, Class A stations can switch to the other ring by means of an optical bypass, so that a backup connection is enabled and communication is not interrupted. Finally, some differences are given in tabular form in Figure 2.8 between the three standard LANs described.

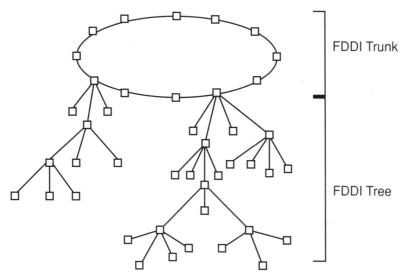

FDDI Trunk

FDDI Tree

Figure 2.7: Trunk and tree fields of the FDDI topology

	Ethernet	**Token Ring**	**FDDI**
Data Rate (Mbit/s)	10	16/4	100
Range	2.5km	800m	100km
Topology	Bus/Tree	Ring	Duplicate Ring/Star
Connection number	1024	260	1000
Error rate	10^{-9}	10^{-9}	2.5×10^{-9}
Net connection class	—	—	Class A; Class B
Reaction with cable errors	—	diversion through short circuit	diversion through short circuit
Physical Layer	not affected	not affected	affected: PMD, PHY
Frame length	1.5K	2K, 5K	9K
Management Standard	—	—	Station Management SMT (CMT, RMT)

Figure 2.8: Differences between Ethernet, Token Ring and FDDI

2.2   Limitations of an Individual Network

An individual network is clearly limited in its configuration and complexity (see also section 2.1). Limitation factors are

- physical expanse
- number of attached stations
- bandwidth/capacity utilization

Physical expanse

In the case of growing physical expanse (e.g., in connecting separate office buildings on a site), a LAN must be divided into segments based on the existing length restrictions (individual length restrictions were given in section 2.1 LAN Standards). This restriction is caused by the transmission technology. With Ethernet for example, the restriction of the maximum collision window (time in which the transmission channel is "conquered") determines the length restriction.

Number of attached stations

The maximum number of attached stations varies according to the standards for Local Area Networks, (Ethernet: 1024 stations, Token Ring: 256 stations). If the limit is exceeded, subnetworks must be formed, and in each of the subnetworks, a maximum number of stations can then be alloted. As is explained later, only in very rare cases should the maximum number of stations (i.e., a single subnetwork) be used.

Bandwidth/capacity utilization

The maximum transmittable load is restricted by the established transmission capacity. While this value is so high in FDDI that there is still plenty of capacity for most of today's networks, the load limit can be reached, in Ethernet and Token Ring LANs when using end stations with fast interfaces (Workstations, Power-PCs).

2.3 Typical Structuring Tasks

There are a number of good reasons to structure Local Area Networks even those with a far smaller layout than the maximum segment length or the maximum number of stations (e.g., already with 20 to 40 stations):

Load reduction

With a rising number of attached end stations with communication-intensive applications and powerful LAN interfaces, the network load can assume critical values long before reaching the maximum permitted number of stations. The result is exponentially decreasing response times and users who are constantly complaining. It may not be possible under certain circumstances to boot time-critical applications (e.g. LAT [line adapter]). As a last resort, but preferably long beforehand, suitable measures are required to reduce the load.

So as to prevent the total load of all areas propagating throughout the whole network (not every employee needs to participate in a company-wide test of proficiency in "Larry," "Tetris," "Block Out" or NSNIPES), subnetworks are formed in order to break down local loads. This structuring means that internal communication and the resulting internal load in individual subnetworks is limited to those subnetworks only.

Only inter-subnetwork communication continues to place a load on more than one subnetwork. As a network expands, the probability increases that structural subdivisions exist. These subdivisions communicate predominantly internally and rarely, in relation to this, between one another. Thus that the necessary structuring into subnetworks can be reasonably implemented on the basis of a universal, flexible cabling system.

Security

Security-critical data should not generally be distributed over areas beyond the absolutely essential portions of the network. Subnetworks which work with corresponding data must therefore be protected by suitable interconnection components, even with an otherwise low total load, and separated from other areas of the network.

Restricting errors

Division into subnetworks makes it possible to restrict defective packets (resulting from hardware defects) and to broadcast inundation and overloading of parts of the total network. If no structuring is undertaken, error situations in any end station, adapter cards, or cable sections affect the entire network. That is, all attached end stations would be affected.

Management

LAN management and error analysis become increasingly more complex as the network grows and more vital factors in ensuring smooth operation. Subdivision into subnetworks enables decentralized management and separate analysis of the subnetworks. A bridge or router port using management software can be disabled to facilitate an organized error search according to the "divide and rule" principle. With many interconnection components with corresponding intelligence, agent functions are implemented beyond this to create a management system for the entire network that can address all interconnection components.

Network portion management information can also be sensibly integrated (e.g., in networks with a LAN probe (RMON) in each subnetwork), to regularly transmit a status report to a management console in the support center. The result is that network management does not have to be performed solely within the subnetwork.

Redundancy

Large networks require sufficient backup structures for the active routes in normal operation, which can be activated and deactivated explicitly or automatically if necessary. Consequences of this are structuring into segments (with segmented backup connections) and the production of redundant connections between segments. When using corresponding interconnection components (bridges and routers), it is also possible to use redundant connections not only in backup cases but also for the distribution of the load and therefore achieve more efficient network operation through better exploitation of the total capacity.

LAN-WAN connections

The connection of geographically distant LANs (branches of a company in different cities) is becoming more widespread and leading to the construction of "extended" LANs. These LANs consist of subnetworks (e.g., a branch each) which are connected to one another by long-distance lines. Maximum lengths can be exceeded even within a site LAN at large company sites, meaning that it becomes necessary to divide into several subnetworks.

Site connection to high capacity backbone

Any-to-any communication on a company site, increasing multi-protocol operation across several buildings, central server concepts, and similar factors lead to significant load growth rates for site networks. A site combination derives from island networks with the need for the least possible operating personnel. The result of this is a growing need for backbone connections with high transmission capacities in the site field, which must be covered by suitable backbone concepts. Various backbone concepts are dealt with in greater detail in a later chapter.

At this point, the question of how far a particular or even worse, a "typical" user network is affected by the high capacity backbone problem might arise. The difficulty of describing the character features of a "typical company network" is: there is no "typical" network! To consider this in detail, i.e., taking into account all company-specific peripheral conditions, there are never even two identical networks: networks in operation at present vary in terms of size, physical scope, and heterogeneity. An attempt shall be made at this point, to categorize networks according to several instances of uses which clearly differ with regard to their requirement for high speed transmissions.

Case 1: PC network

In small companies, which have moved into data processing at a time when it was not necessary to connect up to a host system or even acquire such a system, LANs have often been installed with purely PC-based client server environments with Ethernet or Token Ring. Typical network-capable integrated data processing applications are used (word-processing, graphics, spreadsheets), consistent file and program storage via servers, and, where necessary, access to a network-capable database. For the network environment described here, the established network technology is totally adequate and ATM, FDDI or other visions of the future will not be an issue in the next few years. Should the need arise, LAN Switching will be the next step.

Case 2: "True Blue" IBM user

Quite frequently an almost exclusively IBM-dominated network environment is to be found in medium-sized and larger companies, particularly in the service sector: /370 or /390 host, front-end processors with, or even sometimes without Token Ring connection, likewise 3174 control units, Token Ring LANs with IBM PC bridges, many 3270 terminals and to an increasing extent, PS/2 systems with 3270 emulation and MS Windows, or occasionally OS/2, networked via IBM LAN/Server as the network operating system (NOS). Depending upon the state of development of the LAN and distribution of the company sites, a company may have its own LAN-WAN backbone, which is operated in parallel to the SNA backbone; full integration of the SNA backbone into the LAN-WAN composite occurs only in very rare cases. An increased bandwidth capacity can be expected here in the coming years, if:

- SNA and LAN applications are integrated in a joint multi-protocol backbone

- archives or databases are distributed by down-sizing onto PC or UNIX servers, if necessary, with optical, cascaded access media, which are attached directly to the network (CD-ROM disk arrays or servers with direct access with Gigabyte capacities)

Case 3: Average building/site network

Companies in a more technical field or manufacturing environments demonstrate a more heterogeneous environment in contrast to case 2. UNIX systems (Workstations, Minis), DEC environments or a series of other MDT systems (including also AS/400) are encountered here with PCs (mostly of these PCs are manufactured by one of three to four manufacturers, depending on the specialization of the department). These PCs are connected not only to a server but also to other hosts via TCP. Connection technology is predominantly via

Ethernet rather than Token Ring; the size of the network requires some care in planning a backbone, which will still be sufficiently powerful and extendible even several years from now. The need for high speed networks must be envisaged here for an increasing number of subnetworks for

- the backbone

- a growing number of terminals for server sites and centrally connected storage media and

- growing workstation clusters for simulation, development, and construction tasks in the front-end sector.

Case 4: Large multi-vendor network

Large multiuser networks which integrate administration, development, and production environments at large locations with several sites, can be characterized by the slogan: "Everything you could possibly imagine." An example here would be the case of a large German chemical company, in which 50 protocols are operated in department networks, sub-backbones, and backbones. Similar multi-vendor component collections occur in the field of operated systems, network hardware, and cabling. The PC must access not only its own server and the IBM host but also DEC and UNIX computers. Often there is no complete overview (no useable documentation to speak of) regarding systems, cable and network growth, at least not at one site under one person's control. Distributed responsibilities make planning, operation, and structured integration and expansion difficult. Token Ring and Ethernet are obvious features here, as are SDLC/coax connections in the SNA area, flanked by TDM and other point-to-point links for older systems, partly X.25 in-house networks and not least an FDDI backbone for connection to buildings with the heaviest communication load. The requirement for high speed transmission links is the combination of requirements under cases 2 and 3.

Case 5: Distributed sites

Medium-sized and even large organizations fall under this category in the strongly sales and service-oriented sector. These companies typically require international, nationwide, or more or less regional coverage (insurance companies, electricity generators, public authorities, monopoly operations, etc.). These enterprises typically have a hierarchical organization (central offices, sub-centers, outstations of various importance and even a further tier). The central offices usually fall into case 3 or 4 and the outstations are mostly categorized similarly to case 1 or 3 (small). The communications structure corresponds predominantly to that of the centralized corporate structure. "Case 5 networks" tend to arise in the case of organizational decentralization (greater processing and decision-making powers in sub-centers and outstations to increase proximity to the customer and production, with simultaneous central control and a central database), and give rise to a high speed WAN requirement over the medium term through increased online access.

2.4 Structuring and Interconnection Components

The following term "segment" has the same meaning as subnetwork. Although strictly speaking, a segment cannot have repeaters or hub systems, a subnetwork may have such components, however. Network interconnection components can be divided into various classes according to complexity and range of functions:

- repeaters
- bridges
- routers
- intelligent hubs
- gateways

These different interconnection components create functionally different network transitions between two or more subnetworks. A brief description is given below of the method of operation and configuration features of the interconnection components of various classes. The quality of the interconnection is described based on the OSI reference model (for further information see [CHHE87], [MMOS87]).

Repeaters

A repeater provides an interconnection between two network segments in accordance with Layer 1 of the OSI reference model (see also Figure 2.9). The main function of repeaters is to amplify the signal and therefore overcome the length restriction of an individual cable segment. It is therefore possible to extend the topology of the network.

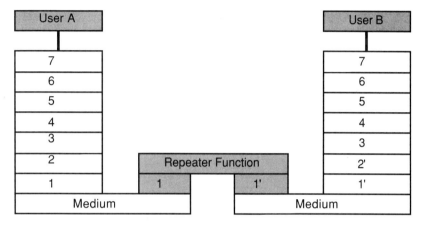

Figure 2.9: Repeater coupling according to the OSI reference model

This involves only signal processing; discarded signals, i.e., signals which can no longer be recognized by a repeater, are not transported. A distinction is made between what are known as "simple" and "buffered" repeaters. The former transport all received signals immediately, and the latter provide buffer storage for a message until it is received in full and only then transport it. They thereby provide the following functions:

- signal generation

- carrier sensing (listening to the transmission channel)

- preamble generation

- extension of fragments up to at least 96 bits (including preamble)

- collision detection

- JAM signal generation, if necessary

- self-test function

Errors on higher Layers, e.g., bit transmission errors, are not detected. Interconnection components with greater communications functionality must be used for that purpose. It is, in particular, not possible to separate the load using repeaters.

Repeaters are used mostly in Ethernet networks (the copper amplifier 8219 in Token Ring networks is no longer in demand). A repeater can either combine two LAN segments directly (if they are not more than 100 m distant from one another, since each transceiver cable cannot exceed 50 m) or connect two segments across a fiber-optics-based link segment (up to 1000 m) in what is known as a half repeater (as a pair).

Multiport repeaters have several LAN ports as their name would suggest, and can therefore connect several segments to one another. It must always be remembered here that there may be no more than 4 repeaters between any two end stations (according to IEEE 802.3; a maximum of 2 repeaters or 4 half repeaters according to Ethernet 2.0).

According to the IEEE 802.3 standard issued in 1988, what is known as auto-partition functionality is defined for repeaters: if a repeater or one of its connected segments is defective, it is separated from the rest of the network, so that the entire network does not come to a standstill because of collisions. The trend is for the use of repeaters to decline in favor of hub systems with fiber optic transitions to connect over larger distances. Figure 2.10 shows the maximum configuration using repeaters.

A bridge connects subnetworks according to Layer 2 of the OSI reference model (see also Figure 2.11). Most bridges connect subnetworks of the same type on the MAC layer, in the form of MAC layer bridges. The OSI definition does not restrict a bridge connection to LANs of the same type, however, and different MAC layers can also be connected (Ethernet–Token Ring, Token Ring–Token Bus, Ethernet/Token Ring–FDDI).

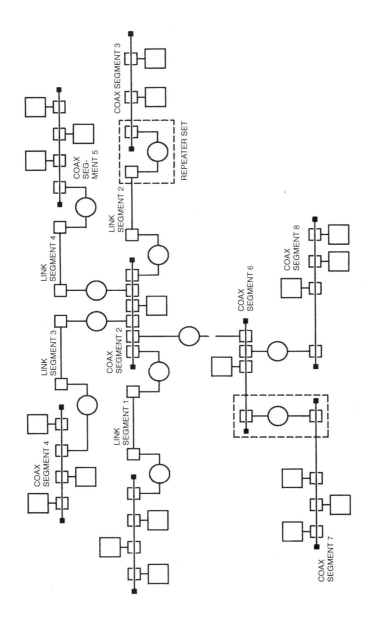

Figure 2.10: Network interconnection using repeaters and half repeaters

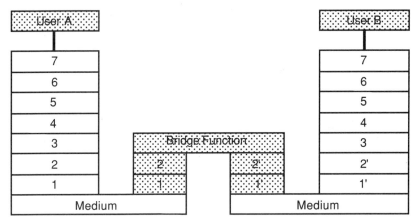

Figure 2.11: Bridge interconnection according to the OSI reference model

An interconnection of physically independent networks is achieved, which overcomes the LAN restrictions for maximum segment length and maximum number of stations. The functions of the MAC layer are also performed (i.e., the checksum and frame length are checked), for example. Defective frames (e.g., defects that are the result of transmission errors or collisions) are not transported, meaning that an error is confined to the subnetwork in question.

Local traffic is also separated from inter-subnetwork traffic, meaning that the load is divided and greater network capacity is achieved (see Figure 2.12). Data is transmitted on the basis of MAC addresses, which must be unambiguous throughout the whole network for bridge interconnection. In order to take the transport decision, all packets are interpreted (method: promiscuous mode). As a default, i.e., if the bridge cannot decide whether this is local or non-local traffic, packets are transported in order to ensure the communication capability between subnetworks. The result is that broadcasts and multicasts are transported and also any packets with unknown destination addresses.

Despite the separation of load, bridges represent a protocol-transparent subnetwork interconnection since they do not interpret the higher protocol layers. In practice, this means that without taking any decisions, a bridge transmits all protocols, which arrive on the connected MAC layers, e.g., AppleTalk, DECnet, IPX, LAT, NetBIOS, OSI, TCP/IP, XNS, etc. on an Ethernet basis.

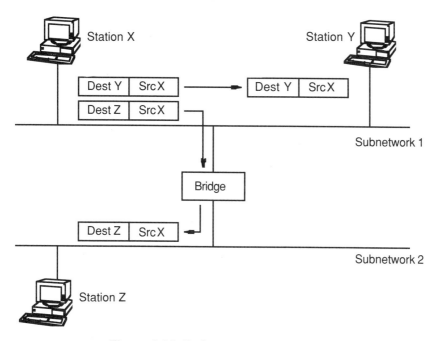

Figure 2.12: Packet transport via a bridge

Loop recognition and suppression mechanisms allow for redundant network structures which are not possible without bridges (or higher interconnection components) to be constructed using bridges (route redundancy, bridge redundancy). Such an algorithm does not always operate between bridges of various manufacturers, even as a standard implementation. In any case, a pilot test is required when using different manufacturers products on the same network.

Because of the provision of MAC functionality, bridges require a processing time in the range of microseconds to milliseconds for packet processing. For major inter-subnetwork traffic, a bridge constitutes a potential bottleneck. In this case, the subnetwork structure must be redesigned under certain circumstances.

According to the terminology, we talk of a repeater interconnection of segments and a bridge interconnection of subnetworks. A subnetwork can therefore contain several (repeater coupled) segments, but inversely, a segment cannot contain several subnetworks. This terminology is no longer strictly adhered to. Below, in the case of bridge or router interconnection, the term segment is used synonymously with subnetworks or network portions.

Routers

A router connects subnetworks according to Layer 3 of the OSI reference model (see also Figure 2.13). This involves, in particular, routing functionality as the central function of Layer 3. Since Layer 3 is different for all currently established industry standards, router interconnection is protocol dependent with regard to the higher layers, i.e., a router must "speak" all protocols which it is intended to process.

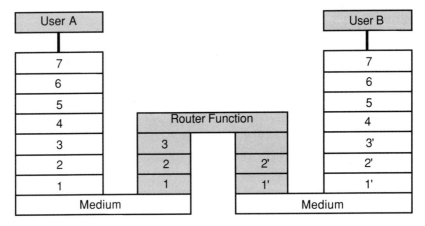

Figure 2.13: Router interconnection according to the OSI reference model

Different Layer 2 protocols can be exchanged very cleanly technically by means of an interconnection on Layer 3.

Based on the routing protocols implemented, a router interconnection provides a more complex and, in certain circumstances, a more efficient option in comparison to bridge interconnection. This is important for exploiting redundant network structures with regard to dynamic routing and alternative routes.

Hierarchical network structures can be achieved using network addresses (subdivision into logical subnetworks as a combination of a sum of individual network nodes).

In contrast to bridges, a router interprets only the packets which are addressed directly to it and does not transport any packets as a default. Only if the destination network is known, is the packet transported. Broadcasts are not transported but processed by the router using routing-capable protocols.

Because of the more complex routing functionality and the ending of default transport, routers are particularly suited to LAN interconnection across Wide Area Networks.

Intelligent hub systems, concentrators

Intelligent hubs, or concentrators, are derived from hub system technology. In addition to integrating various media via concentrator modules, several and different standard LANs can be operated in parallel (generally Ethernet, Token Ring, FDDI, and, in the future, ATM) in one intelligent hub system. Bridge or router, converter, RMON probe, terminal server modules, etc. can also be integrated in card form (OEM modules of bridge/router/terminal server manufacturers). The function description makes it clear that hub systems are acquiring increasing importance as structural components because of their high degree of functional integration. They have clear limits, however in comparison to bridges and routers, as shown in Chapter 14.

Gateways

A gateway connects various protocol environments according to OSI Layer 7 (see also Figure 2.14). The functionality serves primarily the explicit conversion of the various manufacturer protocols into one another (in many cases for communication between SNA and another manufacturer such as Digital, Hewlett-Packard, Apple, etc.) and not subnetwork structuring in the strict sense, even if in many cases, a gateway also forms the physical connection between the two worlds.

The gateway "understands" both protocols totally and is an addressable network node in both worlds. The full conversion entails:

- conversion of the addresses

- conversion of the formats

- code conversion

- buffering of the packets

- packet acknowledgment

- flow control/speed adjustment

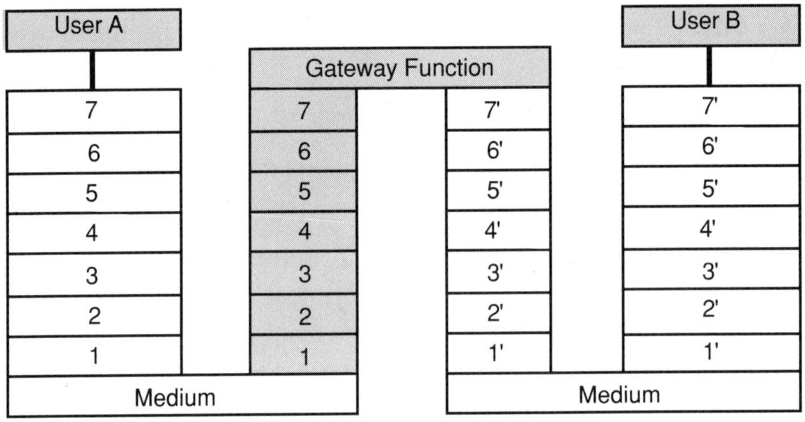

User A		Gateway Function		User B	
7		7	7'	7'	
6		6	6'	6'	
5		5	5'	5'	
4		4	4'	4'	
3		3	3'	3'	
2		2	2'	2'	
1		1	1'	1'	
Medium			Medium		

Figure 2.14: Gateway connection according to the OSI reference model

Because of the complete processing of all communication layers, a gateway often provides greater functional quality for the connected protocol worlds in terms of terminal emulation, graphics capabilities, program to program communication, file transfer, and a number of possible parallel sessions as jointly useable standard protocols. The gateway connection is generally restricted to two protocols, as shown in Figure 2.15. A disadvantage is the restriction to two different protocols, which requires n*(n-1)/2 gateways when using n protocols (an increase by a squared factor!), with corresponding support expenditure and an inability to review the logical network structure. This problem is illustrated in Figure 2.16.

Gateways, which are intended to provide high performance, require sufficient memory and process capacity because of the complex processing. Despite this, the processing time is clearly higher than in bridges and routers.

There are no standards regarding a Gateway connection between different protocols, and for this reason, the incompatibilities between different products are even greater than with bridges and routers.

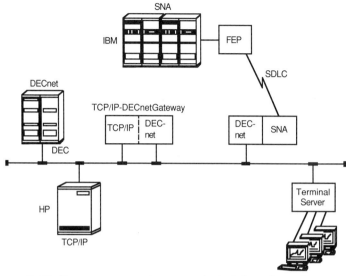

Figure 2.15: Gateway connection: more logical than physical structuring

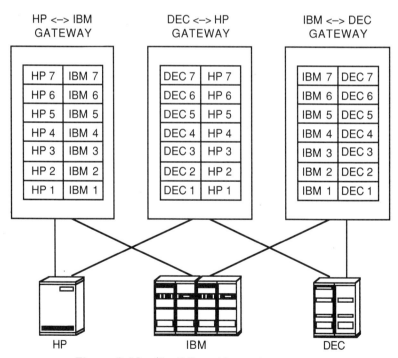

Figure 2.16: n*(n-1)/2 problem using gateways

2.5 Subnetwork Migration

According to the current state of the art, Local Area Networks are constructed using structured cabling concepts with uniform cabling and are simple to modify. The use of modular systems such as intelligent hubs and multiport bridges/routers allows a gradual extension of the network with a growing number of end stations, a growing level of service in the network, and therefore an increasing requirement for network structuring using interconnection components such as bridges and routers.

2.5.1 Strategies

The terms interconnection and coherence are defined in order to explain the various strategies for the construction of a network infrastructure:

Coherence Communications volume/network load within a physical subnetwork, "local" traffic

Interconnection Communications volume/network load between different physical subnetworks, which must be transported via interposed interconnection components, "cross-subnetwork traffic."

Building orientation

Conventional network planning has often favored a standard concept which is oriented to the geographical dimensions of the network. Interconnection between individual site areas is usually either primary area to secondary area, or secondary area to tertiary area. This means that the riser into a building is separated from the location backbone (primary-secondary interconnection) at the point of entry into the building by an interconnection component (bridge, router), and the individual floors in the building are separated from the riser using interconnection components (secondary-tertiary interconnection), as shown in Figure 2.17. This cabling strategy takes the security aspect into account, restricting hardware errors to the smallest possible area around the source of the error.

The concept is sensible for an efficient network operation with an increasing number of end stations and as a result of an increasing network load only if network portions are formed in which predominantly local, i.e., coherence datastreams, occur. This often applies to a building (end stations which work on a host in the building, PC networks, which are supplied from a server within in the building), and in rare cases to individual floors. Here, the contrary principle applies: if following new acquisitions or reorganization, all the staff in a project group (workgroup) or department actually acquire offices on the same floor, this means difficult times for network operators, and, according to the statistics, 25% to 40% of staff within a company move within one year!

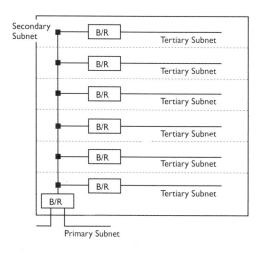

Figure 2.17: Geographically oriented network concept

The response to this is either a corresponding routing through the floors or communication via two interconnection components for all users who do not work on the same floor, on which the server/host is connected. With an increasing number of routings, a corresponding routing significantly impairs the ability to review network structure. Communication via two interconnection components implies large interconnection datastreams. "Looping cabling behind you" on floors with false floors does not prove to be an advantage for an ordered network operation, and after the third or fourth move this occasionally leads to the maximum permitted cable lengths being exceeded and therefore to non-deterministic errors in the network.

The negative consequences of such building-oriented network infrastructures are:

- Strong interconnection effects: since a large proportion of the network load passes via the interconnection components, the interconnection components are overloaded. This leads to poor performance behavior in the network.

- High maintenance expense for the interconnection components distributed over all floors (issuing of management addresses, configuration, software system updates,...).

- High costs: separate bridges on every floor result in high equipment costs.

- Poor flexibility: if it is intended to operate the network with an optimized load, there is little flexibility for moves and new installations.

- Insufficient cabling: if inter-floor subnetwork connection is attempted, despite the building-oriented separation, this leads to a significant lack of cabling.

If there is no separation for the above reasons, and a maximum repeater configuration is operated via hub systems, the negative effects become noticeable in larger segments, i.e., greater coherence in the network:

- capacity problems through excessive sum loads

- performance problems in peak situations (simultaneous booting of terminals and workstations in the morning leads to spontaneously rising coffee consumption amongst terminal users since the terminals cannot prevail against the long packets of the workstations and run into cyclical time-outs)

- addition phenomena of creeping fault situations: several small interference factors (jitters, cable quality, dirty bending radii, adapter capacity, ...) add up to clear deterioration in network throughput as the result of mutual impairment effects. This ultimately leads to network crashes in peak situations

- CPU loading of the user systems as the result of high broadcast volume

- reduced availability: all hardware faults of individual active and passive components, which lead to a network failure, affect the entire network

It is clear that neither a rigid floor separation nor the operation of maximum possible configurations allowed by cabling technology in heterogeneous network environments lead to an efficient structure and low operating costs. The objective of an efficient infrastructure must therefore be to find an optimum position between interconnection and coherence, i.e., maximum coherence with minimum interconnection.

Organizational orientation

Maximum coherence in network units of a reasonable size results from an organizationally oriented (i.e., logical), structure to the network within the building. Suitable components for this are either modular concentrator systems (intelligent hubs) or multiport interconnection components (bridges/routers/LAN switches). This should be clarified in the following examples.

The company UBD, United Barbie Dolls is intended as an example of organizationally-oriented network development of a typical industrial network operator in various development and expansion phases.

Phase 1

United Barbie Dolls is establishing itself in the European toy market under the logo UBD as the license holder for the series of dolls developed by Peter Frogger. These dolls are manufactured in the Far East, meaning that only a small sales branch is required in Germany. Several rooms are rented in an office building in a commercial district with favorable communications connections. Unfortunately, these are divided over three floors. The necessary data processing is operated via Novell on a PC network. The network infrastructure can be easily achieved via Ethernet hubs as stackable hubs or standalone introductory devices with a single Ethernet backplane and repeater function (fiber optics module) in the riser area. Network interconnection is neither necessary nor sensible given the small number of end stations and low network load. The configuration is given in Figure 2.18.

Phase 2

The UBD toys are selling so well that UBD expands the European center. Peter Frogger has become a partner in the company, moved into the European center and designed new models. The series has become a family of dolls with pets. The departments of auditing, bookkeeping, accounts; product planning, export, sales; and advertising now form separate workgroups and therefore acquire their own subnetworks. A central engineering room is established, in which the current three PC servers are set up. Fortunately additional offices can be rented on other floors, since the Swiss insurance company, Ladies First, is putting the building over to commercial use. This leads to an inter-floor distribution of departments, which for the sake of simplicity, we shall term A, B, and C. A hub is installed on two floors with an expanded backplane (multiple Ethernet) for extended network operation, a powerful backbone hub is installed in the central engineering room onto which the three physical subnetworks are looped across floors. The small amount of inter-departmental communication is performed via an internal backbone bus (segment 4) and bridge modules between the busses for departmental subnetworks and the backbone bus. The expanded configuration is shown in Figure 2.19.

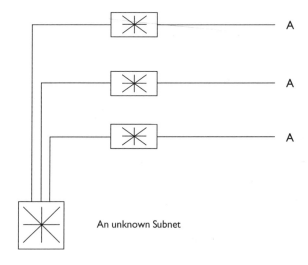

Figure 2.18: First sales branch of "UBD"

Phase 3

In order to be represented in the market with a broad product spectrum, a further development team was employed under Hein Langhaar who develops the appropriate houses, garages and farms for Peter Frogger's family of dolls. UBD now has permanent shelf space in the toy departments of many major department stores.

The company now has its own development and design department, which operates a workstation cluster, not with Novell, but with TCP/IP applications. Since these applications are working under high pressure, the workstations must be connected using FDDI.

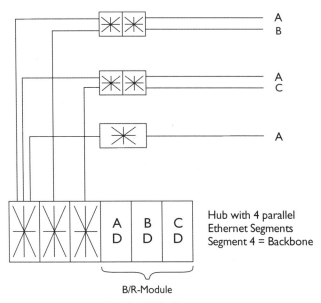

Figure 2.19: UBD European center

It was also possible to rent further rooms on the ground floor for the newly established warehouse and logistics department to supply the department store groups. UBD intends to acquire further segments of the market, possibly by purchasing a company with a suitable product range.

The UBD network is expanded as shown in Figure 2.20: the backplane of the central backbone hub and of the floor hub on the third floor is expanded with

FDDI using an upgrade kit. A more powerful hub is also installed on the first floor with a multiple Ethernet backplane. For reasons of performance, a separate bridge/router component is used to connect the subnetwork. The departmental distribution is now as follows:

- auditing, bookkeeping, accounts (A)

- development, design (B)

- product planning, export, sales (C)

- marketing, advertising (D)

- warehouse, logistics (E)

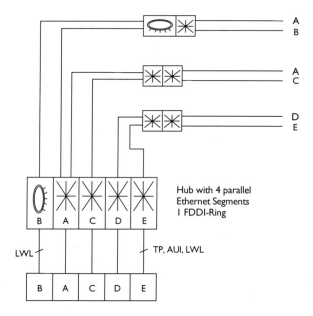

Figure 2.20: UBD following "Dixie Longhair Town" expansion

Phase 4

UBD expands and establishes the joint venture company Barbie-Stouberg Ltd. with the Stouberg Corp. of Patty Stouberg (puzzles, games, and building blocks for construction games) with direct marketing and catalogue sales.

The European center acquires part of the neighboring large car park area (commercial district) and builds a further building there for Barbie-Stouberg Ltd. The design and development departments are combined, the advertising department and ordering are expanded with a series of offices and one open office to cater to the catalog business, which is rapidly gaining a foothold. Patty Stouberg is married to Ken Olsson, the sales manager of a leading branch of IBM, and IBM hardware and software range can be entrusted with the significantly enlarged administration and customer transaction department. Barbie-Stouberg Ltd. and UBD acquire a joint computer center with a host system.

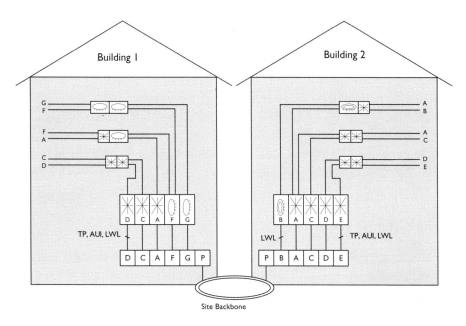

Figure 2.21: UBD and Barbie-Stouberg Ltd. corporate network

Fortunately, the development of the company was foreseen by the network planning group, and with the product lines used for hubs and bridges/routers, the corporate network can be extended with Token Ring subnetworks and FDDI, as shown in Figure 2.21. The connection of the building networks in the location area (P, primary area) is performed using an FDDI backbone. The departmental distribution is as follows:

- auditing, bookkeeping, accounts (A, Ethernet)

- development, design (B, FDDI)

- product planning, export (C, Ethernet)

- advertising (D, Ethernet)

- warehouse, logistics (E, Ethernet)

- sales, ordering (F, Token Ring)

- board, business management, associated departments (G, Token Ring)

2.5.2 Backbone concepts

Network portions in buildings on floors can be connected to one another by means of two fundamentally different backbone concepts:

- Distributed backbone

- Collapsed backbone

Both backbone principles are explained below with their various advantages and disadvantages.

Distributed Backbone

Distributed backbones are constructed using a fast backbone LAN (Ethernet or FDDI) and bridges/routers or bridge/router modules in hubs (see Chapter 14), which connect various buildings or floors. The principle of "divide and rule" applies here: divide the load and confine faults using segmentation. The bridges/routers in turn attach all the hubs (and therefore the end stations) of the individual segments to the BB (see also Figure 2.22). Bridges have the disadvantage here that different LANs (Ethernet, Token Ring, FDDI) cannot be connected for all protocols without sacrificing performance, which is unavoidable when using non-routeable protocols. FDDI bridges are often marked by a lack of WAN interfaces, which means that a site backbone can be connected to other sites only by using a separate device. The trend, at least for the site backbone, is towards the hybrid router, in order to exploit its advantages for WAN attachment and at least for routeable protocols. "Distributed" technology is used: communication is governed essentially through the routing (bridging) distributed to all backbone routers.

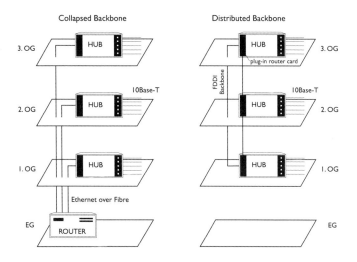

Figure 2.22: Collapsed and Distributed Backbone

The maximum aggregate throughput of distributed backbones (i.e., the sum of all inter-subnetwork datastreams) is derived from the capacity of the backbone LAN: 10 Mbit/s for Ethernet, 100 Mbit/s for FDDI. It must be noted here, however, that bridges often achieve a maximum throughput of only 50% for small packets in Ethernet (64 bytes).

The advantages of the distributed backbone are:

- The solution can be produced efficiently using hub modules.

- There is no Single Point of Failure (SPoF), in particular when using FDDI

- Depending upon the device, there can be more flexible configuration of bridge and router functions: in some devices, the router function cannot be configured for each interface but only for a device as a whole. The use of several devices offers more flexible configuration possibilities here.

- The local subnetwork traffic (where present) is cleanly separated, which means that faults are clearly confined to the subnetwork.

- The solution is possible for large distances.

- in LAN-WAN composite networks, a distributed network is the only possibility.

- The structure favors the formation of interfaces for distributed responsibilities (local network managers).

- By using several devices there is greater combined performance.

The following aspects must be considered disadvantages:

- Greater cascading: instead of one interconnection component, at least two interconnection components are always passed through for peer-to-peer communication in different subnetworks (occurs with TCP applications, for example).

- Distributed maintenance: more routes must be made for physical access, more downloads are necessary for software updates.

One area of application for this is the field of concepts with central servers (e.g., file management, mail servers, central databases) at larger sites with several buildings where users from all buildings must have access to the servers. These sites are then attached to the backbone allowing equal access privileges for all connected subnetworks. All traffic passes via interconnection components but a separation of end station segments from around 30 to 80 devices is recommended for security reasons. Communication via an interconnection component forms the most favorable compromise here (if central servers are positioned on floors, many users must access the server via two interconnection components).

A further use is the operation of terminal networks, which are served via central hosts in the computer center and/or departmental computers. Here also, users access the central computer from all buildings on a site.

Running workstation and terminal operations in a network via distributed departmental computers and central hosts can be more convenient, because of the resulting different load profile, by operating two parallel backbones (e.g., Ethernet) instead of a joint high speed backbone (FDDI. ATM). An unstructured network with mixed terminal operation is shown in Figure 2.23. All combined loads are sent to each terminal server, at the departmental computer and in particular at the host. The broadcast volume to be processed can be a significant drain on CPU performance. Figure 2.24 shows a remedy for this by creating a two site backbone for host access and the departmental computer composite.

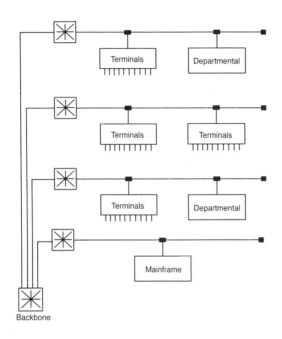

Figure 2.23: Terminal operation: critical situation

Collapsed Backbone

In the collapsed backbone (box backbone, router backbone or hub backbone), only one single central router or hub is used (or several routers/hubs at a central point), to which all buildings/floors are attached via hubs (see also Figure 2.22). Segmentation and correct transmission are achieved using the central router(s). The name originates from the fact that the previously distributed routers are now combined in one multiport device (not from the fact that the backbone collapsed and no longer exists; which does occur, however, if the central router ever fails).

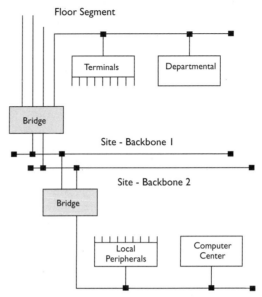

Figure 2.24: Terminal operation: redesign

The maximum aggregate throughput of a collapsed backbone (i.e., the possible sum of all inter-subnetwork datastreams) is given by the capacity of the router backplane. The backplane in this case should be in the region of several hundred Mbit/s and therefore clearly only high-end devices can be used for a collapsed backbone. The accumulation of Megabits is deceptive however: the throughput is also restricted by the CPU-controlled processing time in the router (100 μs up to milliseconds per packet). This limit is often far below the aggregate throughput of the backplane. Naturally, this does not apply if several smaller routers are used at a central network node instead of the central router: these must be connected to one another by a LAN. The solution actually constitutes a mixed concept along the lines of the distributed collapsed backbone (the collapse must extend to several routers before inter-subnetwork traffic is brought to a standstill) but stands out from migration from the distributed to the collapsed backbone.

The advantages of the collapsed backbone are as follows:

• Inter-floor subnetworks can be easily installed and modified/expanded.

- If the backbone is formed by a central hub, central service providers, such as data servers, program servers, mail servers, database servers, archive servers, or departmental computers can be attached conveniently via the hub.

- For routeable protocols, the use of a central multi-protocol router means a problem-free transition between all attached LANs without an interposed backbone LAN.

- Cascading for inter-subnetworking traffic is reduced for all protocols.

- The router, and therefore backbone, is centrally manageable and accessible, which, in cases of analysis in particular, allows all segments to be examined from one room. With a distributed backbone, this is possible only through distributed analyzer concepts (probes, RMON).

- Both central servers and departmental servers (which are attached to the departmental hub) can remain at the Computer Center.

- Hub-router pairs can generally be combined at will.

- Concentration in one device means savings on components. The infrastructure costs per end station and/or per hub or router port are lower.

The following aspects must be considered as disadvantages:

- The central interconnection component is a Single Point of Failure (SPoF). Even with a redundant design for the most important system components (power supply, CPU, cooling, management card), software errors in the system software can lead to a failure situation.

- The central backbone component must demonstrate very high performance and be equipped with hardware of a corresponding quality. A greater number of ports always constitutes a potential performance bottleneck.

One area of application for a collapsed backbone for example, is a building with workstation clusters (development, design) and terminal operation or PC networks. The high file transfer rates of the workstations are a hindrance to other protocol worlds, particularly when booting, which leads to the collapse of the boot process, and, in certain cases, to permanent rebooting. A corresponding configuration is shown in Figure 2.25. A collapsed backbone is a remedy here which separates the protocol worlds from one another and therefore achieves efficient tuning of the network throughput. The separation of workstations and terminal operation is shown in Figure 2.26.

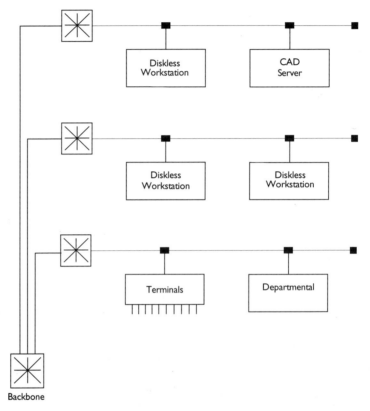

Figure 2.25: File transfer: critical situation

Bridge modules in departmental hubs are offered as a mixed concept and for further structuring after the introduction of a collapsed backbone. This is both for reasons of security and to optimize the load (if there is sufficient local traffic) and therefore take the burden off a central router.

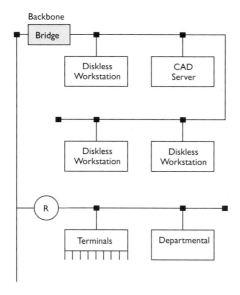

Figure 2.26: File transfer: redesign

3 Bridges

Bridges, in contrast to repeaters and concentrator modules in hubs, are the first devices in the hierarchy of network interconnection elements to which a certain degree of intelligence can be attributed with regard to the data transmission to be performed. This is expressed in three important intrinsic features of bridges.

Intrinsic features and definition

First: Bridges are capable of expanding the boundaries of a network with regard to the number of stations and the overall distance. If a network is structured by means of bridge interconnection into two subnetworks, each subnetwork can then receive the full number of stations and overall length corresponding to the defined standard (e.g., Ethernet, Token Ring, etc.) (see Figure 3.1).

Second: Bridges achieve a simple error limitation functionality. Layer 2 error packets are not forwarded. The result of this is that such error packets remain restricted to the subnetwork in which they arise and are not distributed to wreak havoc over the entire network (see Figure 3.2).

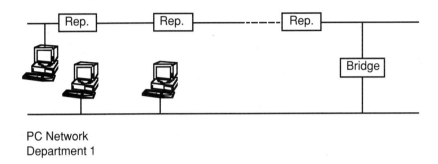

PC Network
Department 1

Figure 3.1 Removal of length restriction

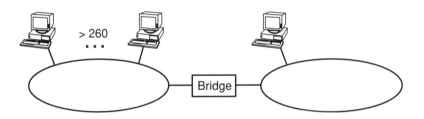

Figure 3.2 Removal of the restriction on the number of stations

Third: Bridges restrict the local traffic to the subnetwork in which it was generated; i.e., if a packet is sent to a station within the subnetwork of the sending station, the bridge does not forward this packet. This third feature is indeed the most important, since it can make a decisive contribution to load reduction in a large network (see Figure 3.3).

Beyond the definitive features given here, high quality products may implement further functions for more efficient control of the LAN traffic; these are dealt with in greater detail in the following chapters (filter functions, load distribution).

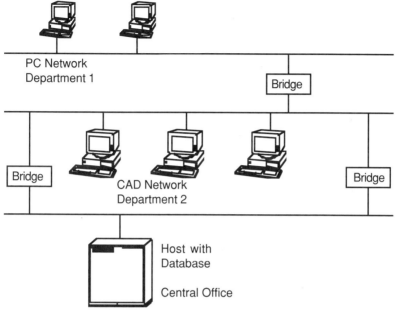

PC Network
Department 1

Bridge

Bridge

CAD Network
Department 2

Bridge

Host with
Database

Central Office

Figure 3.3 Separation of local traffic

Bridges combine subnetworks in accordance with their OSI definition according to protocol Layer 2a (MAC Layer) of the ISO OSI model. Independence is achieved from the physical transmission medium through such an interconnection and from the MAC layer, but the same LLC protocol (Layer 2b of the ISO model) or an empty LLC layer in the subnetworks is required, which are linked by the bridges. The standards IEEE 802.1D (Ethernet, FDDI) and DIS 10038 DAM 2 (Token Ring) define the bridge function.

The standard does not specify how many ports one bridge may have. Bridges with more than two ports may therefore operate totally in line with the standard, if they comply with the functionality detailed in the standard.

The way in which bridges operate is characterized by the protocol functions of Layer 2. The central information of Layer 2 here is the physical address, also termed the MAC address. The data stream is controlled by the bridges with the aid of the MAC addresses. Since MAC addresses are structured identically in all IEEE and ISO standards, bridges are also flexible interconnection elements between subnetworks of different types. A structure of subnetworks connected by bridges appears to an end station as a large unstructured network. The advantage of this method of structuring to the operator is considerable: he or she does not have to perform any bridge-specific configurations in the end stations (as is the case when using routers). Bridges are the LAN structuring elements with the lowest operating overhead as the result of their "plug and play" characteristics.

Definition: A bridge is an interconnection component which connects physical subnetworks with the same or different media access method on Layer 2 **according to the ISO OSI model.**

A key intrinsic feature of bridges is transparent network interconnection with regard to higher layer protocols. For the area of application, this means that all higher layer protocols which are on a particular MAC or LLC layer are passed on transparently, i.e., uninterpreted by the bridge. In this way, a single interconnection component ensures the connection of various higher layer protocol worlds (e.g., AppleTalk, DECnet, LAT, IPX, TCP/IP, OSI, XNS, etc.). The interconnection is performed without special configuration in the end systems of the attached subnetworks.

3.1 Types of Bridges

Even if the basic functionality (interconnection on Layer 2) is identical for all bridges, there are different implementations of this type of interconnection element, and each version has various peculiarities. The following section makes subdivisions into the various types of bridges.

3.1.1 Local Bridges

Local bridges actually embody the bridge per se, since they are the origin of the current family of bridging elements. In their simplest form, they have precisely two ports. Each of these ports combine two LANs, their two attached subnetworks. In most cases, these are LANs of the same type, e.g., Ethernet–Ethernet, Token Ring–Token Ring, but sometimes also different types such as Ethernet–Token Ring, Ethernet–FDDI, Token Ring–FDDI, or Ethernet–ATM, Token Ring–ATM.

Local bridges connect LAN segments as a subnetwork interconnection within a site network. The connection is made via the LAN input ports and output ports of the bridge, e.g., with input and output speeds of the LAN bandwidth. If these are LANs of the same type, the connection is made quite easily. If there are different MAC protocols on the input and output ports, there must be sufficient buffer space for intermediate storage of the packets from the "faster" LAN (e.g., 100 Mbit/s) to the "slower" LAN (e.g., 10 or 4 Mbit/s).

3.1.2 Remote bridges

Remote bridges connect subnetworks over long distances links, simple backbone links without any connected end systems. These bridges clearly operate as groups; they always occur at least as pairs, often in threes or fours. At both ends of a long distance link between two LAN subnetworks, a remote bridge is installed, which has led to the use of the term "half bridge."

A remote bridge may have one or more LAN ports and one or more remote ports. Most entry devices (low-level components) have precisely one LAN port (Ethernet or Token Ring), and, as required, one or two remote ports, e.g., X.21 (9.6 kbit/s to 2 Mbit/s) and ISDN (64 kbit/s). Multiport devices essentially concentrate more remote ports, e.g., up to 8 ports on one card, or in total up to 20 or 40 ports. Sometimes the aggregate bandwidth of a card, also known as the aggregate capacity, is limited to a maximum of 2 or 4 Mbit/s, however (i.e., all eight ports cannot be installed with 2 Mbit/s—this would exceed the processing and buffer capacity of the bridge at full utilization of all long distance links).

Remote bridges must compensate for very large capacity difference from LAN to WAN, depending on the capacity of the telecommunication lines. Buffer space (absorption of load peaks) and buffer organization play a significantly greater role in this case than in the case of local bridges for pure LAN-LAN interconnection. The implementation of a Spanning Tree algorithm (suppression of packet loops, which is described in the following chapters) is more complex. A mixed configuration with local and remote bridges is shown in Figure 3.4.

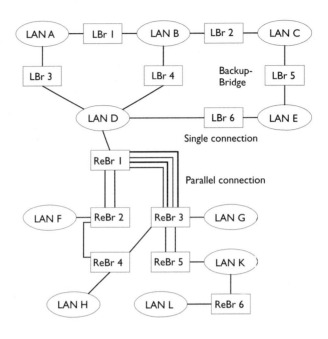

ReBr = Remote Bridge
LBr = Local Bridge

Figure 3.4 LAN configuration with bridges

3.1.3 Multiport Bridges

After two-port bridges dominated the market for a long time. The requirement came up for multiport bridges with more intensive structuring of the networks and the resulting trend for many subnetworks. Various manufacturers offer such multiport devices and in this way connect between four and twenty subnetworks. The use of multiport bridges or multiport LAN switches (see Chapter 7) may be considered absolutely essential in large networks for suitable subnetwork structuring.

The term multiport bridge was first established in association with remote bridges, but this term has since been used for local bridges. A multiport bridge is simply a bridge with more than two ports. It implements a star interconnection of several LANs and/or parallel connections between two LANs. Local multiport bridges offer the option of connecting more than two LANs via a device (which is usually a device from ACC, AEG, 3Com, or Retix). Many multiport devices are boxes with slots, into which LAN and WAN interfaces can be freely inserted.

Multiport bridges simplify the construction of a tree structure (multiple branching) in contrast to the strict bus topology (single branching). Furthermore, as the result of the concentration of several ports in a single bridge, the number of bridges required is reduced and the load distribution simplified to various connections. Multiport bridges are very well suited to subnetwork planning within buildings (secondary sector), since they can connect several subnetworks. Moreover, the cost share per LAN for bridges is reduced through the use of this type of bridge. The use of multiport bridges instead of two-port bridges is not free from increased complexity, however.

- Multiport bridges require a hardware concept with several CPUs. A multiport bridge with only one CPU represents a potential performance bottleneck in comparison to the throughput capacity of the other LAN components. When using a multiport bridge, its performance behavior with simultaneous loading of all ports or the possible loss of performance resulting from such a load failure must be observed.

- Multiport bridges and LAN switches intensify the load problem: All broadcasts and multicasts and all packets with unknown destination addresses are conveyed to all ports at which they were not received.

- Multiport bridges can significantly complicate the use of filters, since the filter setting in a multiport bridge between two different ports must be considered for all possible port to port connections. A well thought through filter program concept by the manufacturer is required.

- Multiport bridges and LAN switches can demonstrate interesting paths for FDDI migration, if they also allow integration of FDDI cards.

In the future, a market is certainly to be anticipated for multiport MAC layer devices. The trend must be monitored here of using routers with bridge capabilities as multiport devices. Although this is a very expensive solution, it contributes to a reduction in the variety of products in large networks under certain circumstances.

3.2 "Transparent" Interconnection: The Way Bridges Function

A bridge is extremely curious and examines all packets that it encounters. This method of operation is termed "promiscuous mode." The bridge must constantly make decisions: all packets which it passes must be inspected with regard to whether or not each packet should be forwarded.

The principle functioning elements of a bridge for the performance of its interconnection task are covered by the standard (IEEE 802.1D):

- to filter and transmit packets (frames)

- the information storage and maintenance required for filter and forwarding decisions (address tables and filter tables),

- management functions for the above-mentioned tasks.

Why, when, and how a bridge transmits which packet is considered next, starting with the description of the service which a bridge should provide on the MAC layer.

3.2.1 Connection of MAC Layers

The intrinsic features defined by the standard (IEEE 802.1D) of a network, which is structured by MAC Layer Bridges, are:

- MAC service quality as in a non-coupled LAN

- no direct addressing of the bridge by end systems: packets bear the MAC address of the partner station as the destination address, with which the communication is performed, not the MAC address of a bridge;

- connection-oriented service between bridges and end systems or between bridges is not supported (therefore no reception confirmation or packet repeats are sent);

- Unambiguity of all MAC addresses within the entire network, which is connected by bridges;

- topology and configuration of a LAN with bridge interconnections must not result in any restrictions for MAC addresses of the end systems;

- support of redundant network paths between end systems in order to enable further network operation in case of a failure situation;

- ease of prediction and configuration of the route which a packet takes from the transmitting station to the receiving station.

To summarize, a network with MAC bridges should actually seem to the end systems to be a single large network without bridges. Bridges must behave as transparently as possible and may at best be of benefit behind the scenes (load division, error restriction, redundancy possibilities, see Chapters 3 and 4).

The bridge performs the conversion from one MAC layer to another MAC layer on the basis of its internal intelligence, termed "internal sublayer service" under the standard.

Bridges frequently connect subnetworks that use the same protocol on the MAC layer, (e.g., Ethernet–Ethernet, Token Ring–Token Ring). They do not perform any protocol conversion but only the LAN extension and error restriction functions detailed above. The interconnection level is illustrated in Figure 3.5.

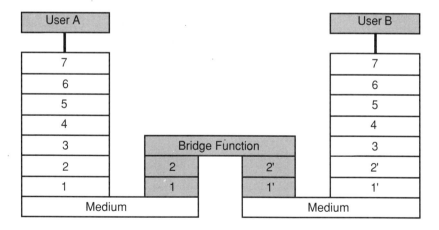

Figure 3.5 OSI Layer 2a connection: Bridges

An advantage of the network interconnection at a relatively low level, as is achieved by bridges, is the upward protocol transparency: the connection is therefore independent of the implementation of the layers above the MAC layer. DECnet, XNS, OSI, TCP/IP, NetBIOS, NetWare, VINES, AppleTalk, etc. can run on one and the same bridge. The bridge is totally indifferent as to whether a packet is an IP packet, an AppleTalk packet or an IPX packet. It forwards only one Ethernet Frame or a Token Ring Frame; it therefore "thinks" on a lower OSI layer.

If a network is intended to function as described above, in which the bridge interconnection is used, certain factors, called quality of service parameters, must be observed:

- availability

- packet loss

- packet sequence

- duplication of packets

- transit delay in the bridge

- lifetime of packets

- error rate

- maximum length of a packet

These are considered in greater detail below.

Availability

Availability is measured as (overall time-downtime)/downtime and should naturally come as close as possible to the 100% limit. The use of bridges may cause harm or benefits in this respect; generally, it should be assumed that the benefit predominates (otherwise an incorrect product or purchase decision was taken somewhere by someone). Availability consists, for example, in the fact that the readiness for operation of the network is retained in the event of partial failures (broken cable, defective repeater, failed wiring concentrator or optical fiber converter), by simply activating the alternative connection paths (which have been set up beforehand). The network reconfigures itself with the aid of the bridges. If no backup paths exist, all undamaged subnetworks still function internally and can communicate with all other subnetworks, which are likewise undamaged and reachable via bridges.

A reduction in availability occurs if the filter capacity of the bridge is exceeded. In this case, the bridge cannot process all arriving packets and therefore destroys the packets in its buffer memory which it cannot process quickly enough, and/or does not save the packets at all. As a result of this, communication for end systems is suspended temporarily; availability therefore falls. A distinction must be made here between pure filter capability and forwarding capacity: the filter capability relates to the number of packets which the bridge can receive under any circumstances; forwarding capacity, or throughput capacity, relates to the number of packets which it can forward. (An interesting side aspect is that the vendors/manufacturers generally state the throughput capacity of a bridge in frame/s and have used minimal frames in this measurement; they state the throughput in byte/s and have used maximal frames in this measurement, which naturally increases the data rate, since the bridge must interpret and process all control information much more rarely). The availability of the network should generally not be restricted by the filter capacity of the bridge, i.e., the filter capacity of the bridge should correspond to or exceed the maximum transmission capacity of minimum length frames (in Ethernet, including preamble, a minimum of 576 bit, for 9.6 μs IPG therefore a maximum of approximately fourteen 880 frames per second).

A second reduction factor not to be underestimated is failure, ie., the physical and intellectual breakdown of a bridge: if there is no redundant connection via other bridges the result is that communication by the attached subnetworks with the outside world is destroyed. Communication capabilities are possibly even destroyed within the subnetwork if the network adapters of the bridge "flip out" and produce, for example, permanent error packets. A redundant bridge connection serves no further purpose here.

Packet loss

There may be various reasons for the loss or discarding of packets in a bridge. First: The packet arrives damaged (too short, too long, transmission errors, etc.). In this case, it is a contribution to the general good that the bridge suppresses its forwarding. Second: The lifetime of the packet will be exceeded before the bridge can process it. Even in this case, the discarding of the packet is mostly a positive factor because the packet has already been circulating helplessly in the network far too long, without having found its destination station. Third: The buffer memory of the bridge is exhausted and cannot accept any further frames (packets). This is bad luck for the end stations. Fourth: The (correct) size of an arriving packet exceeds the maximum permitted size of the subnetwork MAC layer onto which the packet must be forwarded. Even in this case, the discarding of the packet is the correct action since the destination stations might not be able to receive it because of the excessive length; there is little sense in hacking off the tail which is too long. The transmitting station must therefore be organized by higher protocol layers to send sufficiently small packets. Fifth: The network reconfigures itself, because bridges or cable paths have been removed or added. Packet loss must be accepted here until a consistent configuration of the network is achieved once more.

Overall, the effect of the use of bridges is a minimum level of packet loss which is generally so well cushioned by the control mechanism of higher protocol layers that the end user does not notice anything.

Packet sequence

A bridge, if it behaves according to the standard, should not change the packets received in any way, but instead it should process the packets and forward them in the same sequence in which they were received. This applies in particular to bridges which have more than one port and can use redundant ports for the load distribution process (this is described in later chapters). This process may increase the transmission efficiency, but strictly speaking this process does not comply with the standard, since it may lead to changes in the packet sequence (if a packet overtakes a packet previously ahead of it on a different route). There are protocols which cannot cope with such a change in sequence and react with a communication shutdown (e.g., the LAT protocol).

Duplication of packets

A bridge should not duplicate data packets under any circumstances (in contrast to certain BPDU control packets, as will become clear in later chapters). This relates both to possible retransmission of packets and also the duplication of a packet in order to forward it over several ports on different routes. Both alternatives are not part of the functionality of a bridge, since they no longer represent transparent behavior.

Transit delay in the bridge

In order to transmit a packet to be forwarded from one port to the next and from there to the corresponding cable, the bridge generates different transit delays, depending on the quality of the internal architecture and the MAC protocol used.

The transit delay is the time which passes between the arrival of a MAC request at the receiving port and the completed transmission of the packet at its port of departure (MAC data indication). The minimum transit delay consists of the time required for the complete reception of the packet and its complete transmission. In this case, the processing speed of the bridge would be infinitely high for further internal control mechanisms (forwarding decision, check of additional filters, etc.). An additional implementation-specific period of time is required for the performance of these internal tasks until the final transmission of the packet is complete.

Packet Lifetime

In order not to allow a packet to circulate permanently in the network and to guarantee the function of higher protocol layers, a packet must not exceed a particular lifetime. The bridge has no access to the time stamp of the packet since it does not interpret this frame field. It therefore does not know how much of the lifetime has already expired. It may, however, limit the duration of the packet in the bridge itself between arrival and dispatch, i.e., it may discard the packet in the bridge after a maximum transit delay. How high this limit may be set, depends on the number of bridges used and the maximum lifetime.

Error rate

The error rate on the MAC layer is in general relatively low because of the checksum process used (10^{-13}). If the bridge converts two different MAC protocols into one another (e.g., Ethernet–Token Ring or Ethernet–FDDI), then it must recalculate the checksum. The result of this is that the probability of errors increases slightly, since errors may occur in the recalculation itself. When using the same MAC layer protocol, this effect does not occur.

Maximum Packet Length

Different packet lengths apply for different MAC protocols. An Ethernet frame may, for example, be 1,500 bytes long, a Token Ring frame 1500 bytes, 2k, 4k, or 16k. The bridge may forward only the smaller supported frame size for the connection of two LANs with different MAC levels; it may not transmit larger packets. On Token Ring with PC-Host communication via SNA and when using the IBM PC network operating system LAN Server, the 2k size is often use, caution is advised when using an IBM LAN bridge 8229 to connect with Ethernet: the bridge behaves according to the standard, i.e., it does not forward frames which are larger than 1,500 bytes. The parameters of the end systems must be set so that no frames are sent which are too large.

Throughput

The throughput of a network on the MAC layer may be increased significantly by the use of bridges, since bridges separate local traffic within a subnetwork from the rest of the network world. What is otherwise distributed over the entire network is limited to its actual target environment.

On the other hand, the network throughput may be reduced if the forwarding capacity of the bridge is not high enough for the arriving "non-local" traffic. However, this second aspect predominates in very few cases. If the network structure is wrong in some way as the result, of the planning and implementation of the use of the bridge, which is the case, for example, if the subnetworks interconnected by bridges have more cross-subnetwork traffic than local traffic. In this case, the use of a bridge is quite an example of misunderstood network technology.

In order to achieve the described connection of subnetworks on the MAC layer, Ethernet and FDDI bridges use processes which differ from Token Ring bridges. The operation of Ethernet/FDDI bridges is described first below, because they have the major market share.

4 | Transparent Bridging, Spanning Tree Bridges

4.1 What is Where? The Learning Mechanism

In order to perform its essential tasks, i.e., to forward or not to forward an arriving packet, an Ethernet/FDDI bridge must know which end stations are attached to which LAN and/or via which local or remote port of the bridge these stations are reachable. A MAC Layer bridge obtains this information independently by implementing a self-learning algorithm, the learning process of the above-mentioned internal intelligence module "Internal Sublayer Service" (see Figure 4.1).

This self-learning mechanism saves the manual configuration of address tables in bridges or end systems. When booted, the bridge automatically builds the address tables, the address database or filter database which enables it to decide independently whether to forward or discard a packet (see section 4.2). The forwarding module accesses the filter database and retrieves information from it regarding forwarding or discarding of a buffered frame. Some bridges hold one address table per port, and others use a joint address table and mark a registered address with the port ID of the port at which this address was seen.

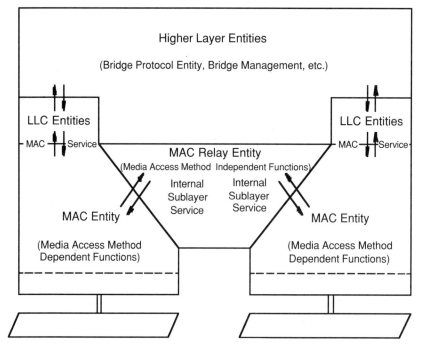

Figure 4.1 Connection of MAC layers in different subnetworks with MAC bridges

How large should the address table of a bridge be? Based on the CSMA/CD standard, a maximum of 1024 stations may be attached to each port of a bridge (maximum number of stations for a physical CSMA/CD subnetwork). Is 1024 enough? No, because a bridge operates transparently; it does not know whether a packet has already been forwarded by another bridge and the transmitting station is therefore remote to the bridge! Imagine a well-structured large network with internal building backbones, subbackbones for several buildings, site backbones, and perhaps even a WAN backbone. Now imagine the bridges between the subbackbone and the internal building subnetwork: this bridge must learn all the stations of all other buildings and sites on its "backbone port"! It therefore follows that:

The address table of a bridge must be large enough per port so that all attached stations of the entire network can be learned.

The bridge checks all the packets it receives at a port from other stations with regard to the packet source address—and it "receives" all packets which come past. If the address has not yet been entered in its address database, an entry is made which associates the source address with the port (LAN segment) on which the data packet (frame) has arrived. At the same time, a time stamp is recorded with the time of arrival. If the source address of a packet has already been entered, only the time stamp is updated (see Figure 4.2). Bridges often have one address table per port in order to be able to look up the address table more easily. The addresses are also sometimes stored in a common table, depending upon implementation by the manufacturer. Over time, the bridge gets to know all stations on all ports of those LAN segments to which it connects.

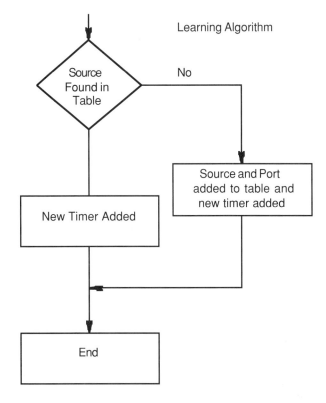

Figure 4.2 Learning Algorithm

Only individual source addresses are learned in this way, (Unicasts), i.e., no broadcasts or group addresses. This also makes sense, since the members of a group (and the addressees of a broadcast) may be distributed over several sub-networks and such an address cannot therefore be attributed to a clear source network. In contrast, the bridge would be extremely confused if it had to allo-cate the group address alternately to different LANs on which it appeared. Apart from this, a group address generally occurs only as a destination address and not as a source address in any case.

Self-learning bridges include products from the following companies, for example, Allied Telesyn, ACC, Conware, Digital Equipment, 3Com, RND, Network Systems, Retix, Shiva, which is by no means an exhaustive list. Starting a bridge is performed simply, since it is fully automated. The building of tables is performed within a few seconds or minutes (for large networks), i.e., from the time the first packet from an unknown station is received by the bridge.

If new stations are added to the network, they are integrated into the exist-ing address tables immediately (most stations, with the exception of such nasty end systems as hardware or protocol analyzers, register themselves when booting with what is known as an "I'm alive" packet). Stations which do not send such an initialization packet are not identified until there is desire for communication with some other end system, regardless of which higher pro-tocol they use (XNS, TCP/IP, SNA, Novell, etc.). A configuration with an address table and resulting load division is shown in Figure 4.3.

A performance limit is provided in theory for self-learning bridges by the limit of the address tables, but in practice the address table is generally large enough to accept all attached stations (e.g., for Ethernet a maximum of 1024 per segment). One performance criteria here is the implementation of the table lookup process which should be implemented as a hash process, in order to deliver a rapid inspection. If such a table should not record all addresses which the bridge learns, the standard implies that newly learned addresses can be entered at the expense of old addresses, which are then deleted.

Bridges which are able to restrict portions of the traffic to particular seg-ments and therefore have the effect of a load filter, are also known as filter bridges. This applies in particular if further "filters" can be set, in addition to the address tables.

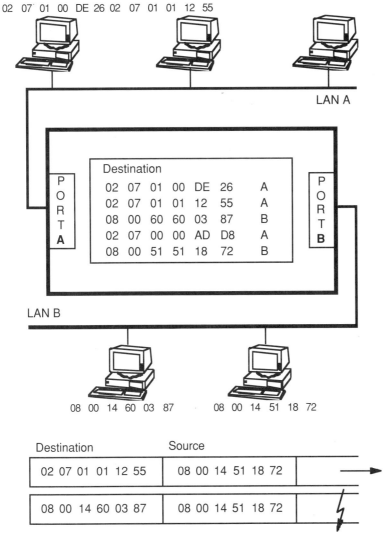

Figure 4.3 Bridge address table

4.2 The Forwarding Decision

The forwarding decision is made regarding further packet processing after passing through the learning process. The destination address is now inspected in addition to the source address. If the destination address if found in the table (i.e., a packet with this address as the source address has already been received in the past), there are two possibilities.

Firstly: the frame has arrived at the same port, which is associated with the destination address. At this time, the packet is recognized as local traffic and not forwarded, and processing is complete. Secondly: the source address has arrived at a port different from that which the destination address is associated. The packet is recognized as non-local traffic and forwarded to the associated port.

The most worst case scenario is if the destination address is not entered in the address database. The bridge must then forward the packet to all other active ports, with the exception of the receiving port. This measure ensures that packets reach their destination if the station in question has not yet surfaced as a source address (has not initiated any communication into a LAN connected to the bridge). Since the bridge does not know in this case to which port to send the packet, it uses all possible paths and a certain degree of overhead arises as a result. Forwarding to several ports occurs only in the case of multiport bridges, since only one forwarding possibility is given in the case of two-port bridges. Multiple transmission occurs only for a short period, however, since the bridge learns the source address with the first response packet and can associate this with the relevant port. The forwarding algorithm is outlined in Figure 4.4 as a flow chart.

Over time, the bridge learns all the stations of the relevant LAN segments to which it connects and is therefore in a position to filter local traffic completely and to make the load division between the segments.

It may occur in non-standard implementations that there is no common address database, but that each port holds its own address table. If the destination address is not found in the address table of the receiving port, the forwarding algorithm may terminate without investigating the other active ports; the packet is transmitted to all other active ports as non-local traffic. This saves processing time in the bridge but in the case of more than two ports, leads to a higher network load than would be necessary. This must be noted in particular for remote multiport bridges, since here the low transmission capacity always represents a bottleneck and any unnecessary overhead should be avoided. It is important that the forwarding algorithm takes account not only of the separating of local traffic (source port = destination port) but also uses the address tables, in order to route a frame with a known destination address explicitly to the port with which it is associated according to the table (Source <-> Port), and not to all other active ports. For standard compliance, explicit forwarding is mandatory, and a product should be checked for this under all circumstances before making a purchase decision.

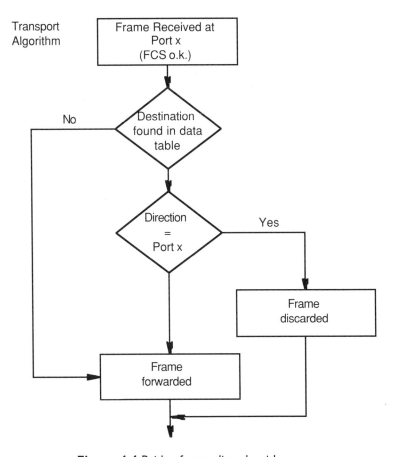

Figure 4.4 Bridge forwarding algorithm

For many bridges, the learning mechanism can be deactivated. The deactivation offers the advantage of a shorter packet processing time, since further addresses no longer have to be entered. At that point the bridge can no longer learn any newly attached station addresses, and the forwarding module operates only on the basis of the address database frozen at that time. Therefore the learning task should be deactivated only in an extremely stable configuration and the network operator must be aware of potential fault situations resulting from station addresses not included. It makes generally more sense to use a sufficiently powerful bridge which has the capacity to perform the necessary packet forwarding in parallel to the activated learning table.

As described until now, the following operating situation exists if the bridge has been up and running for some time.

- The bridge has learned the overall configuration of its attached segments (subnetworks) bit by bit and in this way carefully built up its address database.

- The bridge makes forwarding decisions in the sense of load division and explicit forwarding correctly to a particular port.

The question must now be posed: What happens in the event of a change of network topology?

4.3 Always Staying Up-to-date: Address Database and Aging Process

Topology changes in the form of moves may cause difficulties for a simple self-learning bridge: let us assume that a station "Asterix" is attached in the segment "Gallic Village." The stations "Obelix," "Majestix" and "Miraculix" are connected in the same way. Asterix, Obelix, and Miraculix can therefore discuss plans with one another within their Gallic village (i.e. they can communicate locally with one another.) The bridge has learned this function as required and does not forward packets with corresponding destination and source addresses out of the Gallic village, so as not to allow any village secrets to reach the ears of the Romans. "Asterix" then makes a trip to the "ROME" segment. As the reader will remember, Majestix ends up in some mess or fight and sends a message to Asterix for help. Unfortunately, the latter is cut off from communication with his Gallic village, since the bridge does not transmit any messages to "Asterix" from "Gallic Village"—it assumes that Asterix is still at home. This is bad luck for Majestix. It is also bad news for the bridge, if Asterix for his part sends a call for help from ROME for some unknown reason, since the discovery that a message with the source address "Asterix" is arriving at the port of the "ROME" segment, while the source address "Asterix" is associated with the "Gallic Village" segment in the address database, will cause considerable confusion in the bridge.

In the event of a move, the network manager would have to delete the address entry in order to enable a correct new entry. More convenient bridges can avoid these fault situations automatically through the so-called "aging mechanism" (the implementation of which is specified as mandatory by the standard for MAC bridges). The ageing process is shown in Figure 4.5.

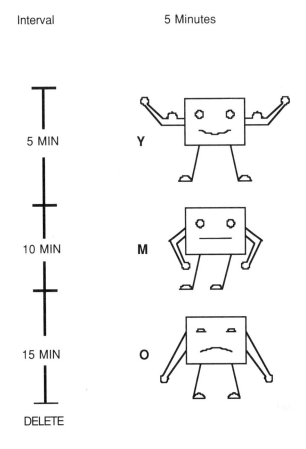

Figure 4.5 Aging Function Interval

4.3.1 Dynamic Address Database

The addresses of a bridge "learned" in the promiscuous mode with an active self-learning module (looking at all packets) are entered in what is known as a dynamic address database, from which they are then removed automatically after a certain period of time, since network topologies are deceptive: such is the experience of anyone who has operated a large network over a long period.

The aging function has the effect that each address entry is provided with a time stamp, sometimes in three stages (young, middle, old). After a fixed or configurable interval, the age is increased or the address deleted, if it has reached "old." The suggested default value for the lifetime of an entry according to the standard (for all three intervals Y, M, and O see Figure 4.5) is around 300 seconds (it may be set at 10 to 1,000,000 seconds according to the standard). In the event of a move, it must be assumed that the period of the move exceeds the "lifetime" and the address is deleted, if the station is connected in the new segment. A further possibility to manage the move situation is the implementation of a function of the type "search for the source address, which arrives at port X in the table of port Y; if it is there, delete it and enter it for port X." This is not mentioned in the standard however, and most bridges don't have that function implemented.

The aging function also makes sure that the address table of a bridge is always up-to-date (i.e., inactive stations no longer have to be taken into consideration). The number of address entries is minimal and as a consequence, the time is optimized for looking through the address table and packet processing can be performed more quickly.

Disadvantage of aging

In the case of longer inactivity pauses, parts of the address table must be rebuilt and packets forwarded unnecessarily. In order to avoid this with a stable network topology, the aging function is generally implemented such that it can be activated/deactivated as required; the aging timer can also be set so that an entered address "survives" inactivity periods.

The aging function is also indispensable in the event of a change to network topology through new bridges or failed bridge connections. It ensures that the addresses can be deleted and learned once more according to the new topology. In the case of reconfiguration on the basis of a modified bridge situation, the aging timer is essentially shortened temporarily in order to delete the obsolete configuration. This situation is dealt with in more detail in section 4.4.

4.3.2 Static Address Database, Operator Entries

In addition to the dynamic address database—a function which most bridges perform—a bridge should offer the possibility of making static (i.e., fixed) entries, which are not affected either by the aging function nor by a reboot action. These entries are edited manually by the network manager and updated or deleted as required. Such static entries may be not only for individual addresses (for stations fixed with nails on the ground), but also group and broadcast addresses. Static entries must specify precisely at which port a packet with a particular address may arrive (i.e., be received), and to which port/s the packet is forwarded. In addition, some internal addresses (i.e., group addresses) can be initialized as fixed in the static address table, addresses which the bridges use between one another using a special bridge protocol. These cannot be changed even by the network manager. The same applies also for the group addresses for standard protocols reserved according to the standard (01_80_C2_00_00_00 to 01_80_C2_00_00_0F), the group address for management actions 01_80_C2_00_00_10 or the functional address for Token Ring MAC frames 03_00_00_00_80_00.

If a bridge runs solely on the basis of its static table with the aging function deactivated and the learning process deactivated, this method of operation is termed Protected Mode, in contrast to Promiscuous Mode, since only the known entered addresses are forwarded and other stations no longer have the possibility of being included in communication across bridges. In cases of extreme security, this mode may be applied under certain circumstances, but the network operator must be permanently aware of the potential source of errors from the failure to forward to a non-entered address in the case of a topology extension.

Static Bridge

Similarly to the static address book, a static bridge is a bridge which has only static entries at its disposal and has not implemented any self-learning algorithm. Only packets are forwarded, whose addresses for source and destination are found in the address table.

A static bridge or simple bridge works with a limited strict address table, which was preconfigured in advance and does not modify itself in continuous operation. The entered addresses are MAC addresses (e.g., Ethernet addresses) and serve as a positive ~filter?~: packets are forwarded to the port which is entered in the bridge table for the destination address; a packet which arrives on the same line on which it should be forwarded according to the table, is discarded: this packet belongs to the local (i.e., internal) subnetwork traffic.

A static bridge achieves load division, by limiting local traffic to the local segment. It is inflexible with regard to topology changes in the network (extensions, moves, partial failure), and it must be reconfigured manually by the network manager. A packet whose destination address is not entered in the table is discarded.

The result is that the number of attachable stations is limited to the size of the address table (this may be smaller than the possible number of stations based on the LAN technology!) Such bridge technology is considered obsolete. The "static bridge" type is worth mentioning only for historical reasons; any worthwhile bridge product which operates on the MAC level has implemented at least a self-learning algorithm.

The operating situation for a network can be described as follows with the bridge functions detailed so far:

- The bridge has learned the overall configuration of its attached segments (subnetworks) bit by bit and in this way carefully built up its address database.

- The bridge takes forwarding decisions in the sense of load division and explicit forwarding correctly to a particular port.

- The bridge can react to topology changes via its aging mechanism and manage the corresponding reconfiguration of its address database.

4.4   Redundancy and Loop Suppression

A simple bridge configuration is not always sufficient, since in the event of errors, the network no longer operates correctly. Redundancy is therefore required. This requires additional intelligence in a bridge, however, as shown in the following example.

The bridge between ROME and the Gallic Village is known as "Una." The situation now changes as follows: a new subnetwork, the "KLEINBONUM" segment, has been created. A street is constructed from KLEINBONUM with bridge connection "Duo" to ROME. Likewise, a street is constructed with bridge connection "Tres" to the Gallic village, which creates a cyclical structure (Obelix: "They 're crazy, those Romans"). Since Caesar is currently staying with Cleopatra in Egypt, there is also a bridge "Quatro" between Rome and Egypt. (The configuration is shown in Figure 4.6.) Majestix sends a complaint to Caesar regarding damage to the landscape between KLEINBONUM and the Gallic Village. This packet travels as follows: the bridge Una forwards the packet as non-local traffic from the Gallic Village to ROME, bridge Quatro forwards it on to EGYPT. At the same time, the bridge Duo also recognizes that the packet is not local and forwards it on to KLEINBONUM. Bridge Tres then forwards it from there to the Gallic Village. Bridge Una then recognizes it as non-local traffic and passes it on to ROME, etc. If they had not been destroyed in the Gallic wars, they would still have been sending the complaint packet from Majestix around in a loop today. The same happens in practice with all broadcasts and multicasts.

The brief conclusion from this long operating experiment is that, self-learning bridges without an implemented loop prevention mechanism (Loop Detection, Spanning Tree Protocol) require a loop-free network topology, since they would continue to pass on circulating packets. No header with possible routing information is interpreted, and the overall topology is not known to an individual bridge. It takes a forwarding decision using the address table; as a consequence it cannot decide whether or not a loop has arisen. If redundant structures exist, the network manager must manually deactivate corresponding backup links or backup bridges and activate them in the event of failures.

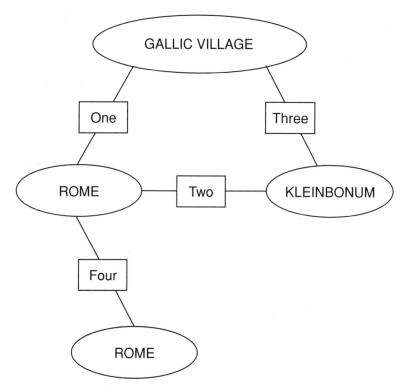

Figure 4.6 Redundant Configuration

4.4.1 Redundant Network Design

The disadvantage of such a configuration is obvious: in the event of faults, fault correction is very expensive, since reconfiguration must be performed manually, or it is simply impossible because the network does not contain any backup connections because of the necessary loop prevention. Regarding the current degree of complexity of operated networks and the dependency of the productive networks on high availability and fault tolerance, such a topology is no longer sustainable.

It is therefore necessary from design onwards to provide redundant structures in the form of backup paths and backup bridges to a sufficient extent and to implement these at the time of installation and startup. Despite this, permanent circulation of any packets in the network must be prevented, since it both exponentially increase the network load and potentially leads to protocol errors. The desired loop prevention within a network with the simultaneous existence of backup structures (parallel paths, redundant bridges) is achieved using a loop suppression mechanism, also termed a Spanning Tree Algorithm in a particular incarnation.

A Spanning Tree Algorithm is today of particular importance and necessary in practice for tree structures. It is particularly important for Ethernet bridges and ring structures with FDDI to make sure to prevent loops of a load once transmitted onto the network. Because this type of transmission does not change the communication process within the end stations in any way, the method is also called Transparent Bridging. For Token Ring configurations, a different process is generally used, the source route bridging process which is described later.

4.4.2 Spanning Tree Algorithm

What does a loop prevention mechanism do? In the network example described, it has the effect that the complaint from Majestix on the one hand is certain to reach Caesar in EGYPT but on the other hand does not wander constantly between ROME, KLEINBONUM, and the GALLIC VILLAGE and create confusion on the network.

How does loop prevention work? Primitive loop detection, as it was partly in the first implementations, basically operates as follows: A bridge transmits what is known as a HELLO packet; if a HELLO packet comes back to the bridge, the latter detects that a loop exists. A loop prevention algorithm is started, which results in the deactivation of corresponding bridges or particular bridge ports. The algorithm is open in principle, it must simply provide transition into an active configuration in which a unique path exists between any two bridges or network segments. State of the art bridges no longer randomly send packets to themselves however, rather they detect and deactivate the loops according to a standardized "Spanning Tree" algorithm (IEEE 802.1D), which will be described in greater detail.

According to network technology, implementation of a loop prevention algorithm makes it possible to reduce physically redundant meshed structures into a (loop free) tree structure. This is done by deactivating redundant links which form loops, in such a way as to "leave behind" a tree structure of active link paths. The randomly meshed network topology from a mathematical perspective is reduced to what is known as a "Spanning Tree." The mathematical essence of a Spanning Tree is such that all meshed nodes are connected by at least one, and only one, link. This implies the following characteristics:

- all network nodes are reachable from all other network nodes,

- there is one, and only one, defined path between any two network nodes,

- there are no loops between any two network nodes.

In practice, you can imagine it like this: If as a data packet you leave a segment in a Spanning Tree network, use only active bridge ports and do not change direction, you arrive at some point in a "cul de sac segment," from which you can go no further.

All superfluous links, ports, and even entire bridges are set to an inactive status in which they receive only control information but no longer forward any data packets. The deactivated, redundant links, ports or bridges are on hot standby, so, in the event of faults they are reactivated immediately and enable communication to be maintained.

There are two process algorithms: Spanning Tree according to the DEC implementation (DEC developed the first Spanning Tree implementation onto the market) and Spanning Tree according to IEEE 802.1 Part D. All networks today operate Spanning Tree according to IEEE 802.1, with a few exceptions, since Digital has also adopted this process in its bridges. The actual implementation of the HELLO protocol is not compatible among all manufacturers, however.

Spanning Tree Algorithm

In order to produce an STP algorithm, there are three essential preconditions:

- There is a well-defined group address, which is received by all bridges in a network (i.e., packets with this address as their destination are received). Packets with this destination address are processed by the bridge protocol module in a bridge.

- Each bridge has a unique identifier (a priority field and its own universal Ethernet address).

- Each port of a bridge must have a unique identifier within the bridge. This port ID may be set independently from other bridges.

The necessary identifiers are set in the bridge architecture and do not necessarily have to be allocated by the network manager.

In order to achieve a functioning configuration from these preconditions, three further configuration findings are required:

- a process to allocate relative priority to each bridge with regard to all other bridges in the network,

- a process to allocate relative priority to each port of an individual bridge with regard to all other ports of this bridge,

- a process to allocate path costs to each port according to its link capacity (LAN or WAN link).

The unique bridge ID is composed of a two byte relative priority part and the MAC address of the bridge. The priority value can be set by the manager. The lower numerical value here defines the higher priority. The setting of a bridge priority is of relatively great importance for the resulting network configuration which will be dealt with in the further description of the algorithm. In the case of bridges with equal priority, the numerically lower MAC address tier breaks. The port ID similarly consists of one priority byte and a byte for consecutive numbering of all bridge ports. The numerically lowest value once more achieves the greatest priority. The path costs must be set by the manager; however, there are defaults recommended as standard:

```
Path costs = 1000/link capacity in Mbit/s
```

The result from this for Ethernet, for example (10 Mbit/s) are path costs of 100 for 4 Mbit/s Token Ring, path costs of 25 for 16 Mbit/s Token Ring, path costs of 62.5 (if it is intended to use Spanning Tree in a Token Ring network; Source Routing is today used in most cases), and for FDDI, a path cost of 10. Remote links are clearly more important in terms of path costs, a link with 64 kbit/s costs 15,625, a link of with 256 kbit/s on the other hand costs 3906 and so on, the example is infinitely extendible. Naturally, a network manager can also disregard this recommendation and set the cost relationships freely in the framework of the value scale from 1 to 65,535 (2 byte integer).

A line with a capacity of 9.6 kbit/s would result in costs of 104,166, a value which cannot be described in the specified range. The standard obviously does not provide for such a slow wide area link. If it is installed, however, the network manager would have to set his or her own cost values in a corresponding relationship, for the other link capacities.

The active configuration, or topology, of a network in a stable condition is determined by the three important factors detailed above:

- unique bridge ID
- path costs
- unique port ID

according to the following algorithm.

Using the bridge ID, a Root Bridge is first established. This is the bridge with the highest priority, which results in any case from the priority value set and the unique bridge MAC address. According to this, every other bridge decides which of its ports lies "in the direction" of the root bridge. This is the port that offers the most cost-effective connection to the root, i.e., the port that offers a connection path to the root bridge that causes the lowest path costs. This port is known as the "Root Port." The path costs are calculated from the total of all individual path costs which arise on the route to the root bridge, maybe via several other bridges. If there are two or more paths via two or more different bridge ports, which both show the lowest path costs, the port with the higher port priority (numerically lower value) becomes the root port. If the ports unfortunately all have the same priority as the result of careless configuration, there is a solution: the port with the lower ID number wins (which is determined in the second byte). The determining of a root port can therefore be made in all cases and in an unambiguous manner.

Finally, similar to the "Root Port," a "Designated Bridge" is determined for each LAN (segment) and/or a "Designated Port" in this bridge which represents the most cost-effective connection to the root (bridge). If several bridges/ports meet the criteria to become a designated bridge/designated port, the decision is made using the set priority or bridge address and/or sequential port number, (the lowest address/port number "wins"). The designated bridge and the designated port are therefore just as unambiguously determinable as the root port. All traffic which is not local runs over the designated bridge.

The root bridge is the designated bridge for all attached LANs, i.e., in the case of the root, all ports which do not produce a parallel connection to one and the same LAN are active.

After completion of the Spanning Tree procedure, each bridge has only the following ports active (Forwarding State): the root port and all ports which connect LANs, for which the bridge is the designated bridge. All other ports are deactivated (Blocking State). They have a backup function, i.e., they can be activated immediately in the event of a fault.

Bridges which have implemented a loop prevention algorithm according to the Spanning Tree standard process use what is known as a Bridge Protocol to maintain the derived Spanning Tree topology. At fixed or a configurable intervals (HELLO time is typically 1–4 seconds), the bridges repeatedly exchange protocol information which has become known under the name "HELLO packets," according to the DEC process (formal OSI terminology: BPDU/Bridge Protocol Data Units).

There are two different types of BPDUs. Firstly: HELLO packets from the root bridge, which are forwarded via the designated bridges to all segments. If these packets are missing, a Spanning Tree recalculation is triggered by the remaining bridges after the expiration of a timer. Secondly: HELLO packets, which each bridge sends on all its ports. These packets are not forwarded, but interpreted by other bridges on the same LAN. If the packets from the designated bridge fail to appear on one LAN, the backup bridges on this LAN become active after a time-out, and the bridge with the next best cost to the root bridge becomes the new designated bridge. This has one major advantage: only if the root bridge fails a Spanning Tree recalculation happens. The failure of any other bridge is corrected "locally", i.e., the rest of the network continues to work without any interruption.

The BPDUs contain information regarding which bridge is the root, what distance (cost) exists to the root bridge, the bridge, and port ID of the transmitting bridge including time stamp when transmitting the BPDU. As the result of peer communication regarding the sending and answering of such BPDUs, the failure of network ports can be detected and a corresponding recovery started accordingly (activating any existing backup connections or bridges). The appearance of a loop is likewise prevented: if a new bridge is introduced, and its participation results in a loop, corresponding other bridges or ports are deactivated. The individual protocol actions may be examined in the relevant standard (IEEE 802.1D).

The configuration algorithm described can be clarified with an example (see Figure 4.7). In the example network, there are no bridge priorities issued for the sake of simplicity, the root bridge can be determined solely on the basis of its MAC address. This is bridge No. 1 between the GALLIC VILLAGE and ROME (address 08007C000165). The root bridge naturally has no root port.

For bridge No. 2, the most cost-effective path to the root bridge is via the GALLIC VILLAGE segment (cost = 100), its root port is therefore its port 1. For bridge No. 3, the most cost-effective path to the root bridge passes via the ROME segment (cost = 250), and its root port is likewise port 1. Similarly the path to the root for bridges No. 4 and No. 5 is via ROME, since the other connections are laden with higher costs. The root port of bridge No. 4 is port 1, and port 2 for bridge No. 5. The calculation for bridge No. 6 becomes interesting: the lowest costs arise in the root via the EGYPT and ROME segments with bridge Nos 5 and 4 (costs = 62 + 3 906 + 250), although one more bridge is involved than in the direct connection to ROME via bridge No. 3. Since this connection is much slower (lower capacity, costs = 15,624), the other connection is selected. The root port of bridge No. 6 is therefore its port 1. Root ports are termed RP in the configuration example shown.

Which bridge now serves which LAN and/or is the designated bridge for a particular segment? Root bridge No. 1 is simultaneously the designated bridge for the GALLIC VILLAGE and ROME segments attached to it, and as a consequence, all ports of No. 1 are active. The KLEINBONUM subnetwork is served by bridge No. 2, since costs arise to the root of only 100, instead of 250 in the case of bridge No. 3. Similar considerations make bridge No. 5 and not bridge No. 6 the designated bridge for the EGYPT segment. Ports with LAN connections which are not designated become inactive and go into backup mode (blocking state). The designated bridge for a particular segment is termed DB in Figure 4.8 and inactive ports B (blocking).

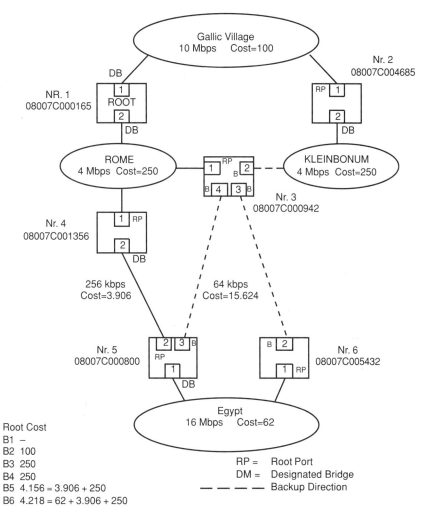

Figure 4.7 Topology of active paths after STP

After the bridges have now tuned their active and inactive ports to one another with more or less difficulty, the Romans attack. There is a battle between Caesar and Majestix, and bridge No. 1 is destroyed. There is a fault situation in the connecting network; and it is rather a nasty one at that, since of all the bridges, it was the root bridge which caught it. After the other bridges have not heard anything from bridge No. 1 for a long time (i.e., not received any more BPDUs), the Spanning Tree algorithm activates itself once more and the bridge with the lowest address is elected to root bridge. This is bridge No. 5. Since bridge No. 5 is at the other end of the network "world" so to speak, the entire network topology is shaken up: "Long live No. 5," the root.

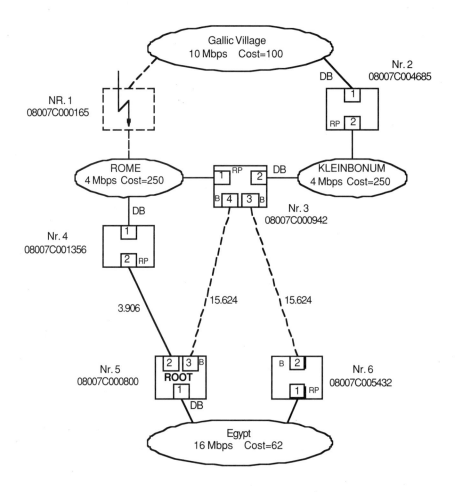

Figure 4.8 SPT reconfiguration after fault situation

After this, it is also the designated bridge for the EGYPT subnetwork. Bridge No. 1 is no longer taken into consideration, since it has failed. For bridge No. 2, the most cost-effective path to the root bridge is now via the KLEINBON-UM and ROME segments and bridge No. 4 (costs = 250 + 250 + 3906), although one more bridge is involved here than in the path via KLEINBONUM and bridge No. 3. Port 2 becomes the root port of bridge No. 2. The most cost-effective path to the root bridge for bridge No. 3 passes via the ROME segment and bridge No. 4 (cost = 250 + 3906), the root port continues to be its port 1, as before the fault situation. Bridge No. 4 has a direct serial link to the root via its port 2, and port 2 becomes the root port. Bridge No. 6 now has a much shorter path to the root than before, between itself and the root lies only the EGYPT subnetwork (costs = 62). The root port of bridge No. 6 is therefore its port 1. Root ports are termed RP in the configuration example shown.

Which bridge serves which LAN in the new configuration and/or is the designated bridge for a particular segment? Root bridge No. 5 is at the same time the designated bridge for the Egypt segment attached to it. The KLEINBONUM subnetwork is served by bridge No. 3 and GALLIC VILLAGE by bridge No. 2. The designated bridge for the ROME segment is bridge No. 4 and not bridge No. 3, since costs to the root of only 4,156 arise here, while the costs via bridge No. 3 would be 15,624. Ports with LAN connections which are not designated become inactive as in the first example, and go into backup mode (blocking state). The designated bridge for a particular segment is termed DB in Figure 4.8 and inactive ports B (blocking).

The example also makes clear how dubious it is to use several or even many bridges in a redundant structure, relying on the "self-configuration" of the topology using bridge hardware addresses. The connection structure which arises after the fault situation is very unfavorable, particularly since the connection structure represents a type of cascade leading through all subnetworks. This means that control packets must be forwarded from root bridge No. 5 to bridge No. 2 via two LANs and a serial connection. Bridge No. 3, on the other hand, has a central position in the topology and would be much more suitable as the root. By setting corresponding priorities (bridge No. 3 with higher priority than bridge No. 5), the desired configuration can be achieved (bridge No. 3 as the root). When planning a complex network, increased care is required when issuing priorities for bridges. This applies in several ways.

Normal Operation

Which is the most favorable tree structure to ensure that the shortest paths result between all attached subnetworks?

Network Extensions

How can potential network extensions be included so that the optimal network structure is not destroyed by newly-added bridges and their priority?

Fault Situations

How must priorities be issued, so that if certain central bridges fail, the new resulting topology contains the shortest possible connection paths?

For all cases, particularly for conceivable failures, a calculation must be made as to what topology results from a recalculation of the Spanning Tree and/or must the new topology be controlled previously by setting corresponding bridge and port priorities. Anyone failing to take such care should not be surprised at a later stage if a high network load suddenly occurs on a segment because of reconfiguration where it is totally unanticipated.

The reader should now ask a further question: What happens to the learned address tables after a reconfiguration, as described above? Bridge No. 3, for example, learned all addresses from the GALLIC VILLAGE in the first instance at its port 1 and as a consequence does not forward messages with such destination addresses. After the reconfiguration this is necessary, however, since the bridge is now the active connection to the GALLIC VILLAGE subnetwork. If aging is set at 15 minutes, the tables would not reflect the correct situation until 15 minutes later. That must not occur, and the standard therefore has a fast acting solution prepared for such an eventuality: if reconfiguration is performed, all bridges involved do not forward any packets until the new topology is definitely active and all dynamic address entries in this period are deleted. All addresses are relearned accordingly after a reconfiguration. A port in the "blocking" state naturally does not learn any addresses and therefore cannot make any further contribution to the general confusion.

Let us turn briefly to the protocol overhead: if necessary, a bridge forwards a self-prepared BPDU for a BPDU, which it receives from the root bridge. This is necessary at each port at which a LAN is attached, for which it is the designated bridge. Since there is only one designated bridge for non-local traffic, BPDUs are also forwarded into the LAN from outside only via a single port. Each LAN must therefore cope with at maximum as many BPDUs as overhead, as the root bridge transmits.

Networks at the Starting Stage

In small and less complex networks, which (e.g., for reasons of cost), are not designed as redundant, bridges do not require a Spanning Tree protocol in order to guarantee a correct LAN extension, since no loops exist. A Spanning Tree process here means only unnecessary protocol overhead: the active bridges send thousands of HELLO packets and responses for no reason (in the case of a HELLO interval of one second per bridge, this is almost 86,000 packets per day). For such loop-free configurations, it is advisable to use products in which the Spanning Tree process can be deactivated. A series of products on the market offer this option.

Bridges with implemented loop prevention of the Spanning Tree type include, for example, products from Allied Telesyn, Conware, Digital Equipment, 3Com, RND, Network Systems, Retix, and Shiva amongst others.

The Time Factor

In order to guarantee correct and sufficiently fast data transfer in a bridge-interconnected network, the standard offers some default values with regard to processing time and bridge performance:

- There should be no more than seven bridges connected in cascade between any two end systems (this also guarantees compatibility with Token Ring environments, as described in Chapter 5).

- The processing time (delay) should not exceed one second (recommended value). According to the standard, it may be a maximum of 4 seconds (absolute maximum).

- The hold time (minimum time between two transmitted HELLO packets) is exactly 1 second.

- The maximum error in the aging of a received HELLO packet is 2 seconds (maximum message age increment overestimate).

- The interval between two HELLO packets is 2 seconds according to the default; permitted values are between 1 and 10 seconds. The latter value is interesting for WAN configurations particularly, since the Spanning Tree overhead is reduced in this way by a factor of 5 in comparison to the default.

It is guaranteed in this way that minimum synchronization is achieved, even with differently implemented components by separate manufacturers. If bridges are operated in a network which support only the maximum values at the same time, bridges are operated that support the default values. This functions for at least three bridges in cascade (see IEEE 802.1D, appendix B4). This is calculated as follows:

Delay ≤ 2.0 s
Error ≤ 2.0 s
Hold Time $= 1.0$ s

It makes no sense to set the HELLO interval lower than the Hold Time. Likewise, it serves no purpose to set the HELLO time higher than two times the process period. The result of this is as follows:

$$1.0 \leq \text{HELLO} \leq 4.0$$

in order to operate a cascade of a maximum of three bridges in a synchronized manner.

Remote Bridges

If a network consists not of interconnected local (sub)networks only, but instead of a LAN-WAN combination with remote bridges, the topology calculation becomes increasingly more complex through the Spanning Tree.

- The strong capacity differences between LAN and WAN connections lead to a more complicated connection structure, paths over several LANs and a long-distance section with relatively high capacity (e.g., 2 Mbit/s) are preferred to a direct connection across a long-distance link with lower capacity, although more bridges are then involved for packet forwarding. The same applies to a connection path between two end systems across several long-distance links with high bandwidth, the total cost of which is lower than a direct long-distance connection with lower capacity (i.e., higher costs).

- WANs as a backbone are essentially less reliable than LANs, and WANs therefore have more redundant structures (alternative paths across several remote connections or direct parallel connection between two

LANs). All redundant links and bridges are involved in a reconfiguration. This increases the overhead and the SPT calculation time.

Obviously for a consistent network configuration, all bridges throughout the network, in particular at both end points of a remote link must use the same HELLO protocol and the same datalink WAN, i.e., the bridges must be produced by the same manufacturer in many cases, since bridges from different manufacturers "obviously" cannot talk to one another, although they should be able to do so after implementation of the standard. Compatibility with IEEE 802.1D and transparency sometimes exists however, two different bridges do not make one another mutually unserviceable—provided that the tree structure of the network is retained (one exception is bridges from NSC and Digital, since there is a cooperation agreement here and the bridge protocols are developed to be compatible with one another). If bridges from different manufacturers are to be in a network, the functional capability of the Spanning Tree algorithm must be tested beforehand in all cases (or the relevant test results obtained from the supplier).

The SPT algorithm was not provided originally to include WAN connections; it is therefore not optimally suited to a LAN-WAN mixed configuration. Since there is no other process available for bridges, however (not to mention standardization), LAN-WAN configurations with bridge connections represent the lesser of two evils.

There are local networks which can be connected redundantly without the SPT algorithm. They form, so to speak the "blue" counterpart to the Spanning Tree world, i.e., they occur almost exclusively in a "blue" environment (IBM, Token Ring). A process is used here for loop prevention, which is known as Source Routing and is described in the next chapter.

5 | Source Routing Bridges

Source Routing Bridges are specific to Token Ring networks (IEEE 802.5). Although in theory the source routing process would also be possible in FDDI and CSMA/CD networks, it is implemented only in Token Rings. Source routing bridges stand out somewhat from the rest of the bridge world since they make the forwarding decision with little independent intelligence, and in plain words they can be described as rather dumb. The IBM style Token Ring (with the source routing process) has clearly established itself in the LAN market in the last two years, as it has experienced a considerably increased product range from non-IBM producers. It is therefore questionable whether Token Ring variants without source routing (and with Spanning Tree) will prevail over source routing over the long term, or whether source routing will be retained by the hard-pressed user for the next ten years. At the same time there has been an ISO draft on this topic as a Token Ring Supplement (see [ISO 12]).

A fierce debate has taken place over the years regarding the advantages and disadvantages of source routing in comparison to Spanning Tree. This debate is similar to the one over Token Ring and Ethernet. Over time—and after both processes had proved themselves in practice—the controversies over Token Ring and Ethernet were cushioned by compromises (where the standard was represented primarily by IBM and IBM users). Feelings have quieted down to the extent that a standard has now been developed by both sides in the frame-work of the IEEE organization to connect Source Routing (SR) and Transparent Bridging (Spanning Tree/TB) in one bridge. Such a bridge can combine subnet-works which use SR with subnetworks which operate with TB. The operation of this bridge is termed Source Routing Transparent Bridging (SRT). It is described later in this book.

Source routing is not part of the Token Ring standard IEEE 802.5, but instead it is the specification of a forwarding algorithm for Token Ring net-works with bridge structures. It is the complementary process to the Spanning Tree algorithm that makes redundant structures possible. A supplement is under development in the framework of the IEEE standard: Source Routing Supplement to IEEE 801.1D (DIS 100038 DAM 2).

The essential difference between Source Routing and Spanning Tree lies in the storage of information which is required for the forwarding of a packet from the sender to the destination station. As the name already suggests, the route of a packet is specified by the source (i.e., its sender). The bridge does not hold the information on the route of the packet, but instead the transmitting station manages the routing table on all open (active) connections. Address table management is therefore transferred from the bridge to the end stations, and each station naturally takes care of the addresses of its own connection partners and not of those of the entire subnetwork (as is the case with bridge tables).

The term source routing is actually misleading, since the process does not represent a "routing protocol" in the OSI sense (on Layer 3). A more correct term which is also sometimes encountered in the literature is "Source Route Bridging," since extended bridge functionality is achieved in a similar way to Spanning Tree Bridging.

In the same way as with the Spanning Tree process, several prerequisites are necessary for implementation of source routing. The process requires:

- a routing information indicator in the frame
- a routing information field in the frame
- a search algorithm for route finding, also termed "Route Discovery Algorithm"

Routing Information Indicator

The Routing Information Indicator (RII) consists of a single bit in the MAC address of the source station. It is also termed the source routing bit and is the first bit of the source address (most significant bit/MSB); the RII determines whether the frame in fact contains routing information (i.e., a routing information field). RII = 0 means that the packet does not contain a routing information field. RII = 1 means first, that a routing information field is present, and second, that it can be interpreted. Figure 5.1 shows how the MAC address is made up.

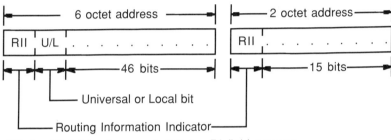

Figure 5.1 Source address field

Routing Information Field

The RI field consists of a 16-bit long routing control field (RC), which contains the control information and one or more route designators (RD fields), which define the route. The RC field contains in sequence, the routing type (RT), the length of the total RI field (LTH), what is known as a direction bit (D, direction), the maximum frame size supported (LF) and four further bits, which are reserved for other higher tasks. (See Figure 5.2.)

The RT type field is three bits long. The following values are defined:

- Type 0xx
- Type 100
- Type 110
- Type 111

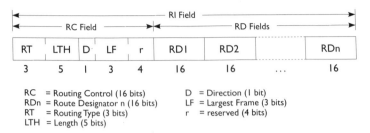

Figure 5.2 Routing Information Field RI

Type "0xx" means that the RD fields contain a specific route to the desired destination station (recorded MAC destination address). Such a frame is never an explorer frame but always a data frame. Type "100" means an "All Paths Explorer Frame," which is forwarded over all loop-free routes which are possible throughout the network. It is used in the route discovery process described later. Type 110 means a Spanning Tree explorer frame and is used if the bridges are organized at the same time between each other by means of a Spanning Tree despite the route discovery process. In this case, the packet is forwarded along the distinct Spanning Tree route. Type 111 means a Spanning Tree routed frame, which contains no dedicated route in the second part of the RI field (RD fields), since the path via the Spanning Tree is clearly defined.

The length field LTH consists of the next 5 bits and contains the length details of the RI field in bytes. In theory the maximum length is 31 bytes, but since only whole lengths are used, it is 30 bytes in practice, the 2-byte RC field and the 28-byte RD field (i.e., a maximum of 14 RD fields, or a maximum of 13 bridges). In IBM implementations only a maximum of 8 RD fields are permitted, which means a maximum of seven bridges between two terminal stations.

The direction bit D specifies the direction in which the RD fields must be interpreted. A 0 means an interpretation from left to right (sequence of the entries RD 1 ... RD N); the 1 means an interpretation from right to left (reverse sequence of entries RD N ... RD 1). This bit is not technical junk to confuse the user but is technically significant, which will be dealt with later.

The last three important bits of the RC field specify the maximum frame length supported (Largest Frame/LF, user data).

Possible sizes:

'000'=   516 byte, min. frame size under ISO 8802-2 LLC and ISO 8473
          (Connectionless mode),
'001'=   1500 byte, max. frame size under ISO 8803-3 (CSMA/CD)
'010'=   2052 byte, max. RU size for 3270 data stream, 80x24
'011'=   4472 byte, max. frame size under ISO 8802-5 for THT = 9 msec,
          max. frame size for FDDI
'100'=   8191 byte, max. frame size under ISO 8802-4 (Token Bus)
'101'=   11407 byte under ISO 8802-5 for Token Ring LANs
'110'=   17800 byte under ISO 8802-5 for Token Ring LANs
'111'=   65535 byte under ISO 8348 Network Service Definition

The routing control field is not interpreted by the bridge for each arriving packet, however. In order to decide whether a routing control field exists, the bridge checks the RII bit. Only if it has the value 1, is the routing information entered in the control field. If the MSB has the value 0, this is local traffic. The frame is then copied only if the destination address is the address of the bridge itself.

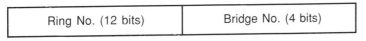

| Ring No. (12 bits) | Bridge No. (4 bits) |

Figure 5.3 Route Designator Field (RD)

For the RD fields (see Figure 5.3), the routing information consists of a series of segment identifiers and bridge numbers. These identifiers specify in sequence precisely those segments and bridges which the packet has passed through or is intended to pass through, in order to reach the destination address = destination station. An RD field consists of 12 bits for a ring number (subnetwork number RN) and 4 bits for a bridge number (BN).

Successive RD fields describe the exact route, e.g. "Ring 001/Bridge No. 1; Ring 004/Bridge No. 2; Ring 002/Bridge No. 5." The content of the RD fields is prepared with the aid of the address tables which the terminal station manages. An end system sets up (and manages) a table which contains the routes to desired partner stations. The routing control or transport decision is therefore transferred in a multi-ring configuration (see Figure 5.4) from the bridges to the end systems.

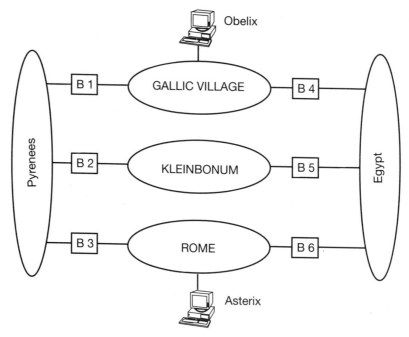

Figure 5.4 Multi-Ring Configuration

Each bridge has an identifier which is unique within the segments attached to the bridge (a "house number," "bridge number") and is initialized with the unique identifiers in the overall network (numbers) for the LAN segments that it connects. There are precisely two, if it is not a multiport bridge. Each sequence—segment number—bridge number that is used for the forwarding decision by the bridges must be unique (as explained later). The necessary unambiguity of the sequence "segment ID, bridge ID" determines an intrinsic restriction on the number of bridges used in the segment.

Since only 4 bits are available for the bridge ID, no more than 15 parallel bridges are used between two segments, ("0" is not allowed as a bridge ID), which is also totally sufficient. If a parallel Token Ring backbone is introduced to the site for reasons of redundancy, both backbone rings may be connected with more than 15 bridges between Ring 1 and Ring 2 (if you actually plan this, you have presumably made a design error).

First, we will describe the route discovery process below through one terminal station, which initiates a communication process with another end system, which gets to know the associated route via the subnetworks between the stations. After this, "normal traffic" is described in the communication process (for permanent routes).

The emphasis here is in the aspect of how source routing bridges behave or should behave within the flow of communication.

5.1 Route Discovery

Let us now imagine that the Roman world did not have a large Spanning Tree network but a large Token Ring network—to the joy of IBM. The sender of a message tries to obtain the necessary routing information with the aid of a test frame (TEST or XID = Exchange Identification Command as LLC-PDU). This is transmitted to the "Null-SAP" SAP X'00', since this SAP then also allows a station a response, even if there is no fixed link installed.

Definition

- Ring-In is the port of a bridge, on which it has received a particular packet (for which it must consider whether it should transport it).

- Ring-Out is the port of a bridge, on which it forwards a particular received packet (if it has arrived at the decision that it wishes to transport it).

Route Discovery is described with the aid of the example configuration in Figure 5.5.

The starting shot: Imagine that in the GALLIC VILLAGE, Obelix wants to invite Asterix on a wild boar hunt, so he first looks to see whether Asterix is staying in the village. He sends Asterix an LLC-PDU packet to SAP X'00', in which the RII is set at 0, because there is still no path information available and there is also no intention to collect any, if Asterix is in the village (i.e., attached to the same ring).

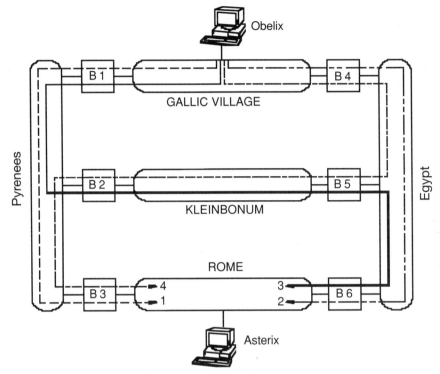

Figure 5.5 Route Discovery

If Asterix is at home, he will respond to the invitation packet and communication will be achieved solely via the MAC addresses entered (destination and source). Details of a route are not required, the RII bit remains set at 0 in all further packets. If Asterix is not at home however, Obelix must send a search dispatch, which results in the following actions. The search: Obelix starts the route discovery algorithm. He sets the RII bit to 1. After this, he sets the routing type in the first three bits of the RC field (also termed broadcast bits), which determines which of the two possible types of route discovery will be followed, i.e., which broadcasts will be sent:

- All Paths Exploration (type 100) or

- Spanning Tree Exploration (type 110), also termed single route broadcast or restricted broadcast.

Since the traditional type of source routing is all paths of exploration (also termed general source routing), it is described first. Each bridge that receives the packet in the GALLIC VILLAGE segment, interprets the RI field and then decides on forwarding (e.g., to the PYRENEES segment). The frame is forwarded, if

- the RI field has still not reached the maximum length (2 < RI < 18 or 30); and

- the last ring number (RN) is the same as the Ring-In of the bridge; and

- the number of the Ring-Out LAN of the bridge is not yet in the RI field (if it is there, the frame has already been in the said ring once and a loop would be produced); and

- the number of the Ring-In LAN and its own bridge number are not yet in the RI field (if they are there, the bridge has already forwarded the frame once); and

- the last RN-BN-RN sequence in the RI field is not Ring-Out, BN, Ring-In for the bridge in question (in such a case, there is a double ring number).

The bridge then enlarges the RI field: it enters the distinct sequence BN-RN (bridge number-ring number of Ring-Out) into the RC field. Therefore, it modifies the RI field:

- If the length of the RI field is less than 2, there was no RD field entered. The bridge adds the number of its Ring-In LAN behind the RC field, next it adds its own BN number, and then the number of its Ring-Out LAN. Finally, it adds four null bits for the next bridge number to be entered. It increases the value in the length field from 2 to 6.

- If the length of the RI field is greater than or equal to 6 and less than 18 or 32, its own BN is entered in the last available RD field and a further RD field is added with the Ring-Out of the bridge and 4 null bits for the next bridge. The value in the length field is increased by 2.

In addition to the routing information, the bridge also examines the maximum supported frame length entered. If it is larger than the maximum possible frame length of one of the LANs which are attached directly to the bridge, it replaces the entered value with the smaller value. As a result of this, the "minimum consensus" applies with regard to the frame length between two end stations, i.e., only frames which are large enough to be supported by all intervening LAN segments are forwarded. If the first largest frame size value was forwarded by all bridges unmodified, it may occur that between two end stations which both support large frame lengths, frames are transmitted which are not supported by the intervening LANs. As a consequence these frames are not forwarded via this LAN, but instead are discarded here. The result would be either a break in connection or an infinite loop, depending upon the quality of the higher software.

A frame which was forwarded to another ring segment, is of course, also removed from the bridge once more (i.e., deleted), if it has passed around the ring once.

As a result of the gradual construction of routing information, the originally transmitted frame is changed in each forwarding bridge. This means that the FCS (Frame Check Sequence) is always performed fresh and there is no end-to-end transparency of the FCS between end stations. In order to avoid loops, the bridge checks whether its Ring-Out has already been entered somewhere in an RD field to determine whether the packet was already forwarded onto this sub-network. If it has already been forwarded, it is discarded.

The number of intervening bridges between two stations is limited to 7 to ensure that route discovery frames are not processed endlessly on the network. Whether or not the 7 bridges are exceeded by a packet is determined by what is known as a hop count value, which is set to 7 at the start (or lower depending on the configuration) and reduced by one in each bridge. If the hop count stands at 0, the packet is no longer forwarded over any succeeding bridges.

If a broadcast packet reaches the destination station, it then takes the complete route from the routing control field and enters that route into the control field of the response packet. It is transmitted not as a broadcast, but as a normal packet and precisely according to the route via which it arrived. This is where the direction bit becomes useful: for the response packet, the route is not entered in the reverse sequence but instead the direction bit is simply changed from 0 to 1. The result is that the RD fields are interpreted in the reverse sequence and the packet therefore takes the reverse direction as its return route.

The upshot of all this is that the original transmitting station takes the routing information from the response packet which it needs for its routing table and the duration of the connection.

If redundant structures exist within the overall network (parallel bridges and redundant backbone links), the broadcast packet is forwarded by each bridge and is therefore reproduced. Several routing packets reach the destination station (with different recorded routes). The destination station acknowledges each packet with a response packet, into which it enters the route received. The original transmitting station may then select a suitable (i.e., cost effective) route, from the various response packets. In the current IBM implementations, this is the route of the first arriving response packet, since this route appears to be the shortest. The source routing standard also allows other criteria:

- The first response with less than x RD fields.

- The response with the shortest route within a particular time interval.

- The first response with a largest frame size (LF) greater than x.

- The response with the largest LF within a particular time interval.

- The first response with less than x RD fields and with an LF greater than y.

- The response with fewest RD fields within a particular time interval, which also fulfills the LF criteria.

- The response with the largest LF within a particular time interval, which has less than x RD fields.

If by chance, Asterix is staying in ROME, this process means work for him and the network. He must respond individually to all arriving route discovery frames. In the configuration shown, only three subnetworks are connected via backbones, which leads to the fact that four route discovery frames are received (see Figure 5.4):

Route 1= GALLIC VILLAGE - B1 - PYRENEES - B3 - ROME
Route 2= GALLIC VILLAGE - B4 - EGYPT - B6 - ROME
Route 3= GALLIC VILLAGE - B1 - PYRENEES - B2 - KLEINBONUM -
         B5 - EGYPT - B6 - ROME

Route 4= GALLIC VILLAGE - B4 - EGYPT - B5 - KLEINBONUM - B2 - PYRENEES - B3 - ROME

If ten subnetworks were connected in this way, Asterix would receive 18 route discovery packets.

How is the entire procedure structured with a single route broadcast? In this case the bridges are organized among one another according to the Spanning Tree process, i.e., they have corresponding ports deactivated, as these corresponding ports would result in loops. The route discovery frame is forwarded along the unique Spanning Tree path to the destination station. It therefore arrives just once at the destination station. Happy Asterix! He only has to answer one packet. He does this cunningly for his part with a response which has the routing type "all paths explorer." It is forwarded on its path to the transmitting station as a broadcast over all possible routes, and the participating bridges in turn enter the routing information according to the process described above and the minimum supported largest frame size.

This brings two advantages with it:

- The broadcasts are generated not by the inquiry process, but by the response flow and are therefore reduced by around half. The transmitting station receives precisely as many response packets as in the first process.

- If the destination station cannot be reached, no broadcasts result.

However attractive this process seems, an unexpected danger is hidden in its application: the Token Ring bridges must somehow be taught the Spanning Tree process. This occurs either through manual configuration or through the selection of a feature "automatic single route broadcast." Only the latter can be seriously recommended. If the Spanning Tree configuration is performed by hand, a manual reconfiguration must be performed in every error situation, and the prospect of the network manager going on holiday or becoming ill becomes a nightmare scenario for management and users.

If the option "manual single route broadcast" is selected when initializing a bridge, and there is no actual manual configuration, all ports of a bridge will find themselves in the active state by default, with the result that all ports forward all broadcasts of the "Spanning Tree explorer" type. The destination station then receives as many route discovery packets as in the all paths broadcast. The broadcast inundation is not yet at an end, however: all these nice, small packets are answered with an all paths explorer packet, which is then reproduced over all possible routes. In the example described with three subnetworks, which are connected via 6 bridges and two backbones, this leads to the generation of 4 x 15 frames, (i.e., 60 frames), in the response process. Therefore, stay away from a manual single route broadcast configuration. If, it must be used at all, then use it only in the automatic mode, in which the bridges determine their designated ports independently and reliably according to the Spanning Tree standard described in Chapter 4.

Multiport Bridges

The source routing process does not envisage that a packet is forwarded by a bridge two or more times. If a bridge connects three or more Token Ring segments, it must forward the arriving frame several times in the route discovery process, which at present contradicts the protocol specification. In the case of existing multiport products, this problem has been solved using manufacturer-specific technology. Some manufacturers have developed source routing internally as if the multiport device consisted of many two-port bridges, which are all attached with an "internal port" to an internal backbone ring. A ring number must be issued for this ring in accordance with the process. A multiport device path therefore requires two hops: from the bridge entry port to the internal backbone and from the internal backbone to the bridge exit port. Other manufacturers ignore the protocol specification and reproduce broadcasts, multicasts, and route discovery packets in the bridge (see also Figure 5.6).

In the case of multiport bridges, where two ports could also be attached to the same LAN segment, unambiguity requires that for these ports a bridge number must be defined for each, to guarantee the unambiguity of the "ring-in, bridge number, ring-out" sequence, since there is no port identification as in the Spanning Tree process.

Hardly any special Token Ring multiport bridges have been developed. Almost all multiport devices, which can be used as Token Ring bridges, can also be used as routers with appropriate software expansion.

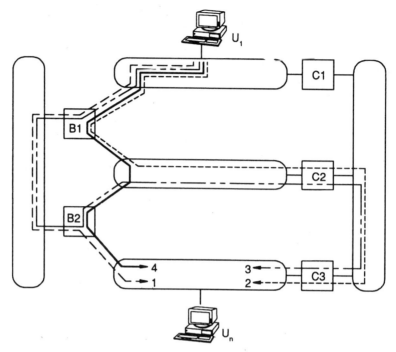

Figure 5.6 Possible Route Discovery with Multiport Bridges

Protocol Overhead

Depending upon the complexity of the overall network, a definite increase in the network load is created by the broadcast packets when searching for a route.

The United States Department of Defense (DoD) calculates that when using source routing with general broadcast (which should be as efficient as Spanning Tree), it would take 108 years for a once-initiated route discovery to settle down (i.e., all packets which were generated had disappeared again) in the admittedly large and intermeshed DoD network. The DoD therefore decided not to employ this "efficient" process.

The disadvantageous aspect which emerged in the source routing process is that the route discovery overhead increases significantly when there are many stations transmitting. This means increasing overhead with increasing user data, which is precisely when the network least needs the overhead. In contrast to this, Spanning Tree overhead depends only on the number of bridges used and therefore remains constant in the event of increasing user data as a result of greater transmission activity.

5.2 Source Routing after Determining the Route

Heaven comes to those who wait: the station wishing to communicate has incorporated the routing information into its address table and now can use it when sending. It sets the RII bit to 1 for each packet, and along with the destination address, enters the routing information into each packet in the routing control field of the packet header. "0xx" is set as the routing type to signify that this relates to an explicitly prescribed route and not a route discovery frame. The D bit is set to zero indicating that the route designator fields are to be interpreted from right to left.

A bridge which receives such a packet limits itself in the tiresome forwarding query to a simple string match process, according to which it decides whether the packet should be forwarded and to which segment. As described above, each bridge has a unique identifier within its segment (bridge number). Each bridge is also initialized in the overall network with the unique identifiers (ring numbers) of the LAN segments, to which it connects. There are precisely two of these. If the bridge lies on the route which the source station has allocated to the packet, the bridge finds its own bridge number in the routing control field. This bridge number is framed by the ring numbers of the two segments which it connects; this sequence "RN_A, BN, RN_B" is unique. The bridge forwards the frame when and only when

- the RII bit is set to 1; and

- it finds the sequence "RN_A, BN, RN_B;" and

- the sequence is in the order ring-in, BN, ring-out (i.e., it has received the packet at the port), to which the first ring number of the sequence is allocated.

Since the route was established previously by the transmitting station, the error cannot occur "packet arrives on the wrong side after a loop and is forwarded despite this." If a packet does arrive on the wrong side however, it has already been forwarded by the bridge and the bridge deletes it from the ring.

A frame is therefore copied (prepared for forwarding) only if

- the string match process results in a match with the source routing bit (RII = 1) and

- the string match process within the routing control field results in a match with the sequence "ring-in, BN, ring-out."

The destination station can take the routing information for the response packet from the packet header when receiving a packet and enter it in the header of the response packet with the D bit = 1. The return route is therefore determined as precisely the same as the original route in the opposite direction. The station can also take the routing information from its address table provided that it has a route entered there.

Local Communication

If two stations are communicating with one another in the same ring (for example, if Obelix and Asterix are both at home) the RII bit remains set at 0. The bridges attached to the GALLIC VILLAGE ring interpret the RII (the first item in the source address after the token) and then become immediately inactive again.

In this way, source routing avoids the situation where frames which do not have to be forwarded are copied.

This represents an essential difference from other bridge processes in which the bridge does not receive all frames unless it is in promiscuous mode and then decides whether the packet should be forwarded. The key element here is the transfer of the address tables from the bridges to the end stations.

For a long time Token Ring bridges could only be obtained as an IBM software product (IBM Token Ring bridge program) on a per PC basis, but the market has since become more diverse (Andrew, Galaxy, Netronix, RND). IBM is also moving away from the PC-based solution as the further development of the 8209 to the local Token Ring bridge makes clear.

5.3   Spanning Tree versus Source Routing

Although both processes have established themselves in practice, the advocates of each side fiercely contest the advantages of one and the disadvantages of the other. It is a fact however, that both processes will remain available to the user for the foreseeable future, since Digital Equipment and the rest of Ethernet bridge providers will not abandon Spanning Tree, and IBM, as the force behind source routing, will not employ Spanning Tree in the further development of its own products. In order to offer the reader an overview and the power to choose, the comparative features are detailed below:

Advantages of the Source Routing (SR) method

- Since several redundant bridges are used in parallel for data transmission, there is better load distribution and exploitation achieved of the redundant LAN transmission capacity.

- SR bridges do not have to manage any cumbersome address tables, and can therefore take forwarding decisions more quickly than Spanning Tree bridges; their throughput may be higher than that of Spanning Tree bridges. Source routing bridges must interpret the routing information field in the forwarding scenario, which somewhat offsets the processing time advantage once more.

- SR bridges do not have to manage any information regarding the overall topology of the network (such as for example, the root bridge in Spanning Tree) and all overhead of its own bridge protocol is dispensed with in the source routing case. SR bridges require only knowledge of their local environment (own bridge numbers and attached LAN numbers).

- As a result of the routing information which is included in all packets, corresponding network management information can be obtained more easily in the event of errors than in the case of Spanning Tree bridges. The routing tables constructed in an end station may also be evaluated for statistical analysis purposes (performance analysis).

Disadvantages of the Source Routing (SR) method

- The processing service which is required for the forwarding decision, no longer takes place in the bridges but instead in the end stations, where it no longer leads to negligible communication overhead (route discovery, table management per session). This takes capacity from the end station for the processing of its actual main tasks (applications programs). The communication work is performed by general purpose end systems instead of by interconnection elements (bridges) specially designed for this task.

- Error situations are noted only by the end stations. These are then responsible for the generation of new updated routing information. The probability of a time-out on higher protocol layers before the new route is established, is relatively high. The time taken for the total reconfiguration of the network depends on the speed and efficiency of the end stations.

- The unambiguous numbering of bridges, which are also clearly restricted in their numbers (16 per LAN, even less in the case of multiport bridges), is an impediment to and inefficient for the establishment of an open topology. The diagnosis of connection errors, which may occur as the result of duplicate ring numbers and bridge numbers (because of manual configuration), is relatively serious and time-consuming.

- There is no possibility of issuing priorities for preferential exploitation of some (faster) bridges for packet forwarding.

- There is no opportunity to occupy different paths with different costs, which has a negative effect, particularly when using remote bridges. The path via a remote bridge in the case of source routing is handled in principle on a totally equal basis as the path via a local bridge.

- At the start of each communication session, the necessary path information must be obtained once more, which requires renewed processing expense for repeat processing of facts which have actually been known for a long time. (This is necessary in order to include any errors which have occurred in the meantime.)

- In extremely intermeshed networks (i.e., in the case of extensive redundancy) the broadcast used for route discovery is increased exponentially. The corresponding number of "search packets" may burden the network in terms of capacity to such an extent that it can no longer be ignored. This proves particularly disadvantageous in the use of remote bridges where in some cases up to 50% of a remote link of correspondingly low capacity (e.g., 9600 bit/s) may be exploited by Token Ring broadcasts alone.

- The route discovery overhead increases significantly when the user data also increases (in the case of a rising number of transmission events).

Advantages of the Spanning Tree method (Transparent Bridging/TB)

- The forwarding of the frame is totally transparent to the end stations, and they only have to enter the destination address of the desired partner station in the header.

- The "forwarding work," which is required for the connection of bridge-interconnected networks, is achieved by the bridges, which may and should have hardware specially designed for this task (although some incorrigible producers still manufacture bridges based on PC architecture).

- In the case of source routing each end station must maintain the necessary address tables since the knowledge regarding the possible connection paths is stored at many locations in the network. Thus a single bridge holds the information required for the forwarding decision for all end systems on the attached LANs. Instead of the processing power of many individual machines being required for redundant information processing, processing power is necessary in only a single machine.

- An error situation because of bridge or cable failure, is noted by the participating bridges and may be corrected before the session reaches a time-out in the end station.

- In the simplest case, a TB bridge may be constructed according to the motto "plug and play." It can be run with the manufacturer's default settings. Neither unambiguous ring numbers nor unique bridge numbers need to be issued, which proves to considerably reduce complexity in particular when combining larger networks.

- The path that a frame normally takes between two end stations is determined precisely by a corresponding configuration of the Spanning Tree parameters. It alters itself at most in the event of errors. Such a definition may be very desirable for security reasons: a very simple example is that of a pharmaceuticals group whose data regarding circulation enhancement drugs should not wander around in the same network environment as the data for sleeping drugs. In the same way, there may be good reasons for the finance department not to want the data regarding management salary payments to travel over the LAN to where the union employee representation is connected. Further examples can be imagined.

- Different paths with different costs can be occupied depending upon the desired traffic density. The load flow can therefore be controlled explicitly by the LAN.

Disadvantages of the Spanning Tree method (Transparent Bridging/TB)

- In each case only a single path is held active between two terminal stations, all others are redundant connection possibilities on "hot standby," which means that they are activated only in the event of faults if a previously active route is no longer possible. This results in deficient utilization of the LAN capacity that is actually available.

- In more complex networks, such as those that combine subnetworks, careful configuration of bridge priorities is required even with TB bridges (active paths and ports determined depend on the priorities), as was made clear in the description of the Spanning Tree algorithm. This makes the apparent initial configuration advantage relative, since the issuing of priorities has a great influence on the distribution of network load and occupancy for individual bridges. This is not the case in the issuing of bridge and ring numbers for source routing, the result of which is that at least as much attention must be given to the issuing of priorities as to the issuing of numbers in source routing.

- The interim buffering of all packets which arrive at all ports of a bridge, until the forwarding decision is taken (i.e., at least until after interpretation of the destination and source addresses), requires high memory capacity, more complex buffer management, and greater CPU performance for a Spanning Tree bridge than for a source routing bridge.

Neither source routing nor Spanning Tree are restricted in theory to Ethernet or Token Ring. In reality, however, source routing is implemented only on Token Ring bridges and not for Ethernet bridges. Transparent bridging (Spanning Tree) was implemented for some Token Ring bridges (IBM competitors), since it offers applications in the PC world which can also be set up on Token Ring without source routing. As has already been stated, source routing that is not part of the 802.5 MAC standard which uses Token Ring as its medium, does not necessarily also have to support source routing. The whole range of PC networks must be mentioned here (NetWare, 3+ Open, VINES, LAN Manager) whose higher protocols are based purely on the Token Ring MAC specification and, where applicable, offer source routing as an additional option (this is also sometimes only on very recent releases). IBM LAN Server supports source routing as a default (via the OS/2 Communication Manager).

Why use Token Ring in the first place, if it is not intended to use the advantages of source routing? Such use may be totally justified in some cases:

- If there is already a Token Ring installation it can be used to attach IBM terminals to a host or for PC IBM connection. It can also be used to implement Ethernet for a PC network and manage the associated support complexity in terms of hardware it is assumed that two parallel networks would be both inefficient and senseless, since the PC networks can also be set up on Token Ring.

- Token Ring was, and is more popular with many users as a deterministic access protocol than the randomly controlled CSMA/CD protocol, even if practice has shown that both networks are thoroughly suitable for Joe Average users (under certain circumstances, there was also a good consultant at the plant who did the necessary convincing).

- If it is intended to attach PCs not only in a PC network but also make a host (server) connection, it would not be sensible to equip the PC with a Token Ring card for the host connection and an Ethernet card for the server connection. The gateway alternative (PC-gateway-host) is likewise often not desirable and so the PC is attached to the Token Ring as a workable compromise (it would be too much to hope for that the host was Ethernet-capable).

- The PC dealer who supports the user, is a pro-IBM Company and in this example has more Token Ring know-how than Ethernet experience. Since the user does not want to recruit a whole troop of network staff and has only one or two network managers, he will rely on such support in the future and decides on Token Ring.

5.4 The Synthesis: Source Routing Transparent

After years of committed argument over the advantages and disadvantages of Spanning Tree and source routing, in which both Digital and IBM were dedicated to supporting the front lines, it became clear that neither process can be dismissed by argument, and based on the numbers of installations made in the meantime by both sides, neither is going to disappear overnight. IBM installed the source routing process in all LAN components and LAN capable end systems (both from the PC via 3174 or 3172 control units and 3745 or 3746 frontends to the AS/400 or 9370 host and also in the newly appeared UNIX world with RISC/6000 machines) for both political and technical reasons, which is also implementable in theory for Ethernet bridges. Digital continued to persevere with the Spanning Tree process implemented for Ethernet, which in theory is also implementable for Token Ring bridges. A start was made on standardization with IEEE 802.5D/D15, 802.5M-90, 802.5M/D4 and 802.5M/E1, to create a connection possibility for both worlds with an SR-TB bridge definition or SRT definition.

SR-TB Interconnection

In principle, there are two possibilities for constructing mixed networks in which some end stations use source routing and others not:

- a single heterogeneous domain, in which source routing and transparent bridging stations are colorfully mixed among one another, termed a single heterogeneous domain under the standard.

- many homogeneous domains whose end systems all support only source routing or transparent bridging, also termed multiple homogeneous domain under the standard.

The following applies to a heterogeneous domain: SR bridges forward only source routing frames (RII = 1) and no Spanning Tree frames (RII = 0); inversely, transparent bridges forward only Spanning Tree frames (RII = 0) and no source routing frames (RII = 1). The various end stations can therefore coexist but not talk to one another. Different LANs can be connected to one another by SR bridges or TB bridges, which guide the relevant frames over the network independently of one another.

The SR end stations in such a heterogeneous world also have extended intelligence: if a route discovery process, which has been initiated by a station to communicate remains unsuccessful, it transmits a frame without routing information in the hope that perhaps Spanning Tree bridges will open up a path to the desired destination station. A TB end station does not bother about any source routing packets, if it ever discovers any.

Enough TB bridges must be installed so that all pairs of end stations which support Spanning Tree actually find a path to one another, which passes only via TB bridges. The same applies to SR bridges and pairs of SR end stations. This means, however, that two parallel bridge backbones must be installed to connect the various systems. Simply put, the cost would be doubled, and the support capacity and complexity would at least double. A company that can afford such a configuration should either increase its dividend or lower its prices and build a sensible network configuration instead.

For a homogenous domain or several of these, the bridge-interconnected network world is subdivided into individual domains, of which each uses either source routing or transparent bridging (Spanning Tree). The different domains cannot talk to one another; a deficiency which the SR-TB bridge (source routing-transparent bridging) remedies, as it connects both sides. It has an SR LAN attached to one port and a TB LAN attached to the other accordingly.

An SR-TB bridge works as if it were connecting two different networks (see also Figure 5.7). It translates one protocol (e.g., Spanning Tree) into the other (e.g., source routing) and stores the required information if necessary, in order to ensure the return path for the response packet to a forwarded frame. In the case of arriving route discovery frames (on the SR side), the route is stored through to the SR-TB bridge with the associated address pair (source address/SA, destination address/DA) and removed from the frame. After this, the route discovery is continued on the TB side with a Spanning Tree frame (type 110). If this frame is answered from the TB side, the bridge forwards the response to the SR side as follows: it adds its own bridge number to the stored route and the segment number of the Spanning Tree side and holds this route stored with the DA-SA address pair in its internal table.

If the reverse occurs and a Spanning Tree search frame arrives on the TB side, the address pair is saved, and a route discovery is started in the SR side direction. If this gets a response on the SR side, the bridge saves the route with the address pair in its internal table and forwards the response as a Spanning Tree response.

For communication over several domains, the route is always entered in the frame on the source routing side; in the case of transition to the transparent bridging site, it is deleted from the frame and saved in the bridge. This process can be cascaded for any sequence of SR and TB LANs, provided that the tables in the SR-TB bridges have constructed the necessary information and the necessary routes can be found in their SR table for the relevant DA/SA pairs. The Spanning Tree bridges have dynamic address tables for all stations per port, as described previously.

The draft standard described here cannot be considered to have a bright future in light of its complexity, and has not established itself in the marketplace.

All in One: SRT

In order to end the fighting, IBM changed from the role of adversary to peace envoy: in summer 1990, a proposal was submitted by IBM to the IEEE to connect both logical systems, source routing and Spanning Tree, in one single intelligence module as a bridge "brain" to end the strict division between source routing and transparent bridging. It was intended for a Token Ring bridge of this new era to be relatively indifferent as to whether a Spanning Tree frame or source routing frame arrived at a port, and this frame would be processed by the relevant parts of the "brain." This meant that IBM developed an intelligent solution (single heterogeneous domain) proposal for the "mixed pickles" configuration described above that does not require parallel TB and SR backbones, since an SRT bridge can do both. The model is contained in the standard proposal ANSI/IEEE Std. P802.1x/D1 MAC Bridges. Source Routing Supplement and 802.5M and PDTR 10734 [ISO 13].

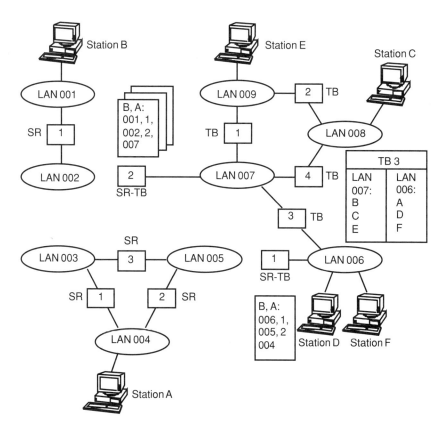

Figure 5.7 Connection of SR and TB networks

Such an SRT bridge has a joint Spanning Tree with all TB bridges. The internal logic is shown in Figure 5.8. If a Spanning Tree broadcast frame now arrives with a Spanning Tree group address (routing type 110) or a Spanning Tree data frame (routing type 111), it is forwarded to the Spanning Tree intelligence module of the bridge for processing. It is "routed" by the SRT bridge according to the Spanning Tree rules along the joint Spanning Tree. In other words, it is forwarded, only if the ring-out port of the bridge works according to the Spanning Tree configuration with "forwarding" status (i.e., is the designated port for the attached LAN). The same occurs with all frames that have no routing information since they originate from a TB sector (RII = 0). The transparency feature of Spanning Tree bridging (transparent bridging) is therefore retained for this frame when forwarded over the SRT bridge.

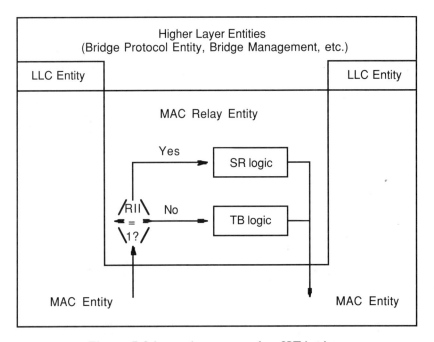

Figure 5.8 Internal structure of an SRT bridge

If a frame arrives with source routing information (RII = 1), it is passed by the SRT bridge to its own source routing intelligence module for processing, and the forwarding decision is taken according to the source routing process and implemented. This relates to all frames with a specific route entered to the destination station (routing type 0xx); the forwarding decision is performed for such frames according to the string match process described earlier. The bridge forwards the frame if it discovers its own combination ring-in—bridge No.Ñring-out in the routing information field. All-paths-explorer frames are also processed by a source routing bridge (broadcasts in the case of route discovery, routing type 100) (check loop and hop count, then possibly enter its own bridge number and ring-out and largest frame [LF] size, calculate fresh FCS).

The difference between such an SRT bridge and the SR-TB model is demonstrated in seven areas:

- The subdivision of the entire network into a Spanning Tree domain, a transparent bridging domain, and an SR-TB domain no longer applies, and the user does not have to think about efficient orientation, maintenance, and extension planning for this relatively complex domain design. This is not to mention the fact that under certain circumstances, the user must first learn what a domain concept entails. This frees time for other useful activities within the company network. The rules for connection of network portions with transparent bridging and source routing are far simpler in the case of SRT bridges (between any two stations, that use TB, only one path must be possible via any TB and SRT bridge and between any two stations that use source routing one path via any SR or SRT bridge).

- The complex storage mechanisms for routes within the SR-TB connection bridges no longer apply. This is a performance advantage for the SRT bridge. A bridge that combines the intelligence of both processes, which is also the case for the SRT bridge, always remains a potential bottleneck for the bridging technology within a large network. Attention must be paid here through suitable subnetwork structuring to ensure that not too much traffic passes over the bridge (which can be avoided in most cases through skillful subnetwork planning).

- SR bridges and TB bridges can be mixed in a joint LAN with the greatest possible topology freedom.

- SR and TB terminal stations can be mixed in a joint LAN with the greatest possible topology freedom.

- There is no change for the whole world of purely TB bridges and TB terminal devices.

- The difference between Spanning Tree explorer frames (type 110) and Spanning Tree routed frames (type 111) no longer applies and only the routing type 11x is necessary.

- The lower level of complexity of an SRT bridge in comparison to the SRTB bridge makes the manufacture of the SRT possible at a lower cost.

End stations that are connected to one another via several SRT bridges can create a communication session under different route discovery implementations: Spanning Tree routing or source routing. The intelligent end station can use both processes as required. Generally, the end station will first attempt the source routing type route discovery, and if that does not work, a Spanning Tree controlled attempt is subsequently performed. The user then takes responsibility for the fact that a station pair wishing to communicate can also speak the same language, ensuring that at least one process is supported by both sides. Since any network can be depicted here in the most appealing terms, the only recommendation can be to introduce a house standard in the company, either source routing or transparent bridging. Applications which do not support the chosen standard are therefore struck off from the set of services supported by the company's own computer team. SRT should be used only when it is totally unavoidable.

SRT standardization is interesting and necessary because, among other reasons, an SRT bridge may be the basis for the FDDI bridge interconnection between Token Ring and Ethernet. At present, there are almost no products which can sensibly make this connection. Access to directly-attached mainframes via FDDI by stations on Token Ring is therefore generally not possible.

The use of mixed processes is generally suitable only for transitional and migration solutions—in which case the presence of SRT bridges is required. Mixing the two technologies on a broad basis is not advisable, for reasons of support complexity and an increased probability of errors.

Five Rumors about SRT

Rumor 1

SRT bridges perform a translation in the sense that applications, which produce "transparent" packets, can communicate with source routing applications.

The standard does not offer any solution to the problem addressed here. A station with a "source routing" application cannot talk to a station that speaks "transparent bridging." Both languages are different, as has been described in detail.

Rumor 2

SRT bridges are compatible with existing SR bridges and SR end system software.

It is important to remember that the source routing part of an SRT frame using the SRT standard, is not compatible with current source routing for bridges or stations:

- A-bit and C-bit: some IBM end station software requires that these bits are set,

or

> it sends the packet again,
>
> it generates an error message, or
>
> it sends the packet afresh and generates an error message.

SR bridges set the A-and C-bit, if they forward a packet. The SRT standard submitted does not specify on the other hand, how the bridges maintain the A and C bits. An implementation may therefore comply with the standard draft, and despite this, not be able to collaborate with IBM adapters.

- The Spanning Tree protocol, which is used in the case of single root broadcast in IBM bridges, is unique to the manufacturer and not published. It is not compatible with the SRT standard.

Rumor 3

SRT bridges and existing transparent bridges may coexist in one and the same network.

Transparent bridges forward packets on the basis of the learned addresses and leave the source routing information here in the packet, since they do not change this. SRT bridges do not forward any packets that contain routing information. If SRT and transparent bridges are on the same network, loops may arise, because of which duplicate packets may be sent to the destination station instead of only one packet.

Rumor 4

A bridge, which supports source routing and transparent bridging, is an SRT bridge which complies with the standard.

The user must ask specifically whether or not the function is performed according to the standard.

Rumor 5

SRT is necessary for all environments with several subnetworks.

This is not the case if all subnetworks run source routing. If source routing is made the "house standard," it makes no sense to invest in restructuring the network with additional SRT bridges for reasons either of money or support capacity. Simply because it is possible, it does not mean that it has to be implemented everywhere. This also applies to the use of PC network operating systems other than the IBM LAN Server (which is capable of source routing), such as Novell or VINES. Since these systems also support IBM type source routing, there is absolutely no need to use SRT bridges if there is no intention to use the advantages of transparent bridging.

The starting position for a network is represented by the bridge functions described until now, as follows:

* The bridge has learned the entire configuration of its attached segments (subnetworks) bit by bit, and thereby carefully constructs its address database;

or

the bridge is a source routing bridge and does not need an address database.

- The bridge takes forwarding decisions correctly in the sense of load division and dedicates forwarding to a particular port. For this purpose, it consults either its port-related address table or, in the case of source routing, the string match process with regard to its own bridge number and numbers of attached segments.

- The bridge may react to topology changes via its aging mechanism and initiate a corresponding reconfiguration of its own address database;

or

the path information is restructured via the source routing process in the case of a new communication session, so that alternative routes can be sought in the event of topology changes.

- The desire for a reasonable redundancy design to the network infrastructure, both with regard to bridges and cable paths, can be fulfilled by means of the multiple installation of bridges and cable paths. The unambiguity of packet forwarding is assured in this case either according to the Spanning Tree or source routing process.

6 Further Functions: Filters, Load Distribution, Connection of Different MAC Levels

lmost as soon as the user implemented redundancy functionality in his or her network, he or she realizes there are two further requirements.

First: A bridge should control the packet flow in a more dedicated way, with respect to authorized and unauthorized communication. No sooner said than done; in the course of its development, a MAC bridge has acquired various functions to permit or deny inter-subnetwork data flow through the division of local traffic. This function is made available through filter mechanisms.

Second: The redundant links and bridges should not remain unused when implementing the Spanning Tree process (pre-requirement: the products purchased are of outstanding quality and therefore totally reliable and fault-free). Does it not make far more sense to exploit these alternative paths also in Spanning Tree networks in terms of their capacity for load distribution? No sooner said than done; the implementation of load distribution functionality in MAC bridges also eliminated this deficiency.

The following two chapters are dedicated to the two features referred to here—filters and load distribution.

6.1 Filter Mechanisms

The task of a filter is as follows: traffic, which passes across a bridge, is filtered via the "normal" local load division. Packets which actually belong to the inter-subnetwork traffic are not allowed through, and therefore ought to be forwarded.

What is a filter? A filter is a bit pattern that describes a particular part of a MAC frame, combined with the action which is performed with the recognition of this bit pattern in a frame. These patterns are:

- a dedicated destination address

- a dedicated source address

- a broadcast address

- a type field

- a mask

- logical combinations (and, or, not, and not, etc.) of several of the above-mentioned filters

All filters relate to MAC frames and/or the control and information fields which they contain. Access to the information flow for configuration purposes is therefore performed on a relatively low communication layer. Filters can be set both in Token Ring and Ethernet bridges. However, there are often more extensive functions available in Ethernet bridges.

A bridge in which filters are set, examines for the case that this relates to non-local traffic. After processing the "normal" forwarding decision all arriving frames are examined with regard to the bit pattern determined by the filter. If a frame coincides with the bit pattern of the filter at the point to be investigated, a match is made with the filter. If the frame does not agree at the investigated point with the filter, there is a mismatch. The bridge then performs the action with the frame which the filter program defines for match and mismatch cases. When programming, attention should be paid to the fact that actions for matches and mismatches must be programmed with logical reasoning, since the bridges permit unreasonable combinations in some cases, as is demonstrated in later examples.

A filter can be defined positively or negatively (see Figure 6.1 and 6.2). In the terminology of this book, this means that as its sign suggests, a positive filter has the effect that precisely those packets for which a match is made with the filter setting are forwarded. A negative filter has the opposite effect: packets with a filter match are not forwarded; packets with a filter mismatch are let through (if they are not local traffic).

POSITIVE

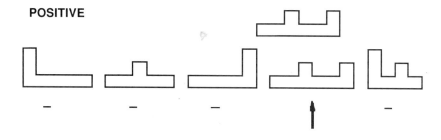

Figure 6.1 Positive Filter

NEGATIVE

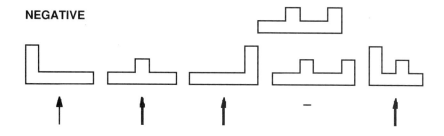

Figure 6.2 Negative Filter

Manufacturers and suppliers excel in interpretation of the terminology through maximum non-uniformity. In one book (and also in the implementation of the bridge) the concepts "positive" and "negative" are used according to their mathematical meaning; in another book, the philosophy is that a filter, as its name suggests, "filters out" and therefore a positive filter filters negatively and conversely, a negative filter filters positively, etc. In each case, the user must clarify the terminology of the manufacturer and the underlying philosophy (through extensive exercises with filters in a test installation) before launching into fully-fledged filter programming.

Address filters relate to explicitly-addressed source or destination stations, and/or their addresses. Theses filters can explicitly allow or deny communication with particular end stations via their addresses. Positive address filters perform explicit forwarding for the addresses entered, which is particularly relevant in the case of remote bridges and multiport bridges (which are explained in detail later) with regard to explicit port allocation for some addresses. Negative source or destination filters prevent access by particular stations to particular segments, which is to say, they suppress certain routes explicitly. In the example network (Figure 6.3) from the world of ancient Gaul and Rome, a negative source or destination address filter acts on the address of Majestix in bridge No. 1 and bridge No. 2 (connection of the GALLIC VILLAGE and ROME and/or KLEINBONUM), with the effect that Majestix cannot communicate with any of his tribal brothers and sisters outside the GALLIC VILLAGE. Any packet that Majestix tries to send out from his village detailing his source address (or at least the response to such a packet, which lists Majestix as its destination), is not forwarded by bridges No. 1 and 2. In this way, Majestix cannot start any argument with other villagers, much to the joy of Cervesia, but rather is restricted to communication with his own village residents (and they have plenty of experience with disputes). Negative source address filters therefore prevent access by particular end systems to resources outside their own subnetwork (other departmental servers, hosts, etc.).

Furthermore, the filter prevents, for example, Miraculix's address from being sounded out by any smart Romans and prevents the recipe for the legendary magic potion being divulged. Transferred to today's application scenario, such a filter is applied for stations with data in particular need of protection (laboratory data, staff data, etc.), which should not leave its own subnetwork under any circumstances and to which no one should be able to log on from outside.

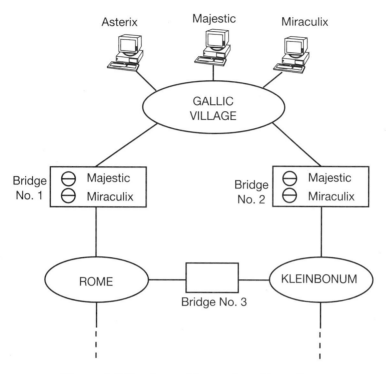

Figure 6.3 Topology with negative address filters

The other Gauls, who do not know the recipe, may communicate happily with the rest of the world; their packets are forwarded by the bridge in the tried and tested manner.

Positive source address filters (see Figure 6.4) take effect on port B in combination with the action "discard on mismatch," such that only certain end systems (through their unambiguous MAC addresses) have access to subnetwork A from outside. All others are forbidden access. It is assumed that bridge No. 1 was biased by entering the addresses of all Gauls living in ROME as positive filters. All Gauls can now communicate from ROME with the GALLIC VILLAGE and the Romans (whose addresses are not entered) fall victim to the action "discard on mismatch" and are once more screened out.

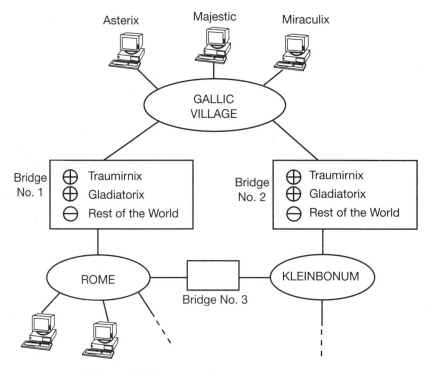

Figure 6.4 Topology with positive address filters

It becomes clear in this example that entering positive address filters and then selecting the action "forward on mismatch" makes no sense as the action for the mismatch. (A mismatch relates mostly to the default setting for a port, since when filters are not set, all packets are processed as if there was a mismatch.)

Broadcast filters relate to the frames directed to all participants in a particular protocol, whose identifier is the broadcast address in the destination address field in place of a dedicated address. A variation on the broadcast filter is a multicast filter, which relates to a group address as the destination address (e.g., the group address of the bridge protocol in the Spanning Tree process).

Sensibly, this filter is set only as negative (who wants to distribute massive broadcasts explicitly over the entire network?), in order to contain the herd-type incidence of broadcasts in subnetworks where they have nothing to find (since the broadcast-producing protocol is not used here). As a result of this, the burdensome characteristic of bridges of (1) not entering broadcasts in the address tables (since they are not addressed to anyone) and (2) generally forwarding by default (which is thoroughly sensible in many cases) are avoided.

Negative broadcast filters are very useful under certain circumstances: a bug which arises occasionally in IP implementations (of older varieties), is the non-agreement of what should be interpreted as a broadcast address. A frame which is sent in one subnetwork as a broadcast can be interpreted in the next as a "normal" packet; consequently, the IP systems there try to forward the packet. For this purpose, they generate new broadcasts which causes a wave of secondary broadcasts, which is often termed a broadcast storm. A further error with serious consequences results from error messages generated when misinterpreting broadcasts.

A message of the type "destination not attainable" is not sent to the sender, but rather to the same broadcast address that was misinterpreted. If two or more hosts exist on the network that have this error, the consequence is an endless to-ing and fro-ing of broadcasts, which are a burden on all systems (as is the nature of broadcasts). Over the long term these broadcasts damage to the network, also termed "Ethernet meltdown." For obvious reasons, such packets are sometimes termed Chernobyl packets. Broadcast filters are an effective counter agent here.

Type filters relate to the type of higher protocol used on Layer 3 (TCP/IP, DECnet, XNS, NetBIOS, IPX, etc.), which is entered in a specific part of the frame. This entry is found in the Ethernet frame after the source address (13th byte). In IEEE 802.3 CSMA/CD frames, it cannot be located here, since this field is used according to the standard for the length details. In this case, the SNAP protocol (SubNet Access Protocol, RFC 1042) can at least take remedial action for the TCP/IP world, assistance which provides the entry at a different permanently defined position in the frame (which can then be examined according to the type value). Figure 6.5 gives a comparison of the formats for Ethernet 2.0 and IEEE 802.3 with SNAP.

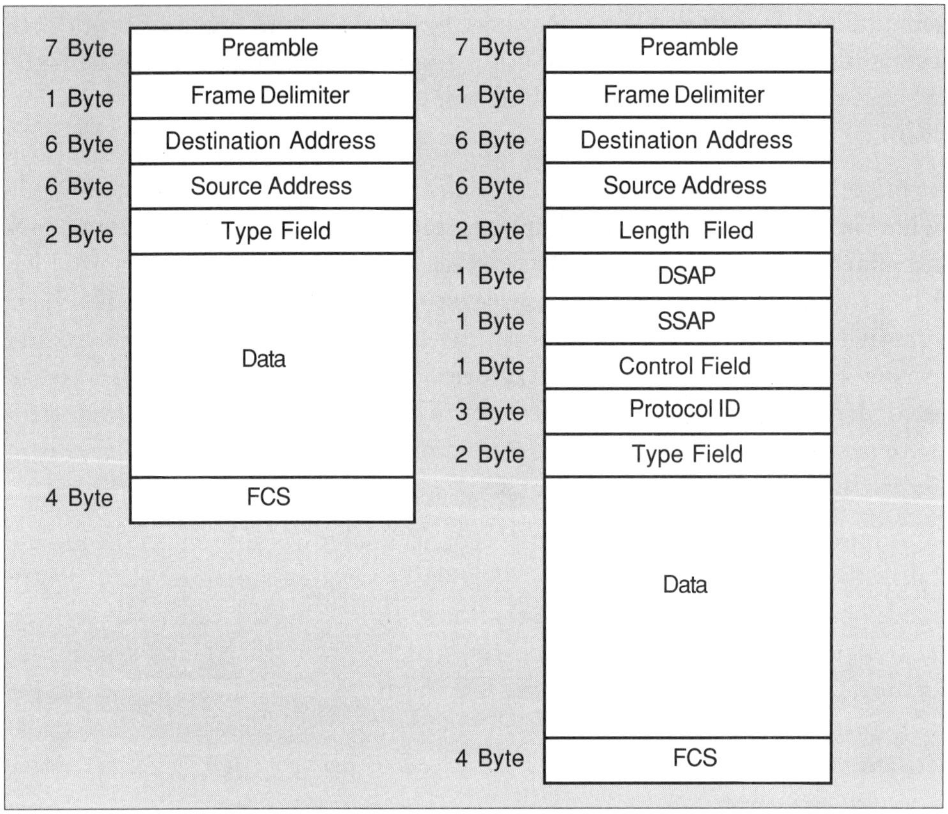

7 Byte	Preamble	7 Byte	Preamble
1 Byte	Frame Delimiter	1 Byte	Frame Delimiter
6 Byte	Destination Address	6 Byte	Destination Address
6 Byte	Source Address	6 Byte	Source Address
2 Byte	Type Field	2 Byte	Length Filed
		1 Byte	DSAP
		1 Byte	SSAP
	Data	1 Byte	Control Field
		3 Byte	Protocol ID
		2 Byte	Type Field
4 Byte	FCS		Data
		4 Byte	FCS

Figure 6.5 Frame format of the SNAP protocol

Protocol type filters exclude particular protocols from certain LAN segments (negative filter function) or allow precisely these protocols as an intersegment application (positive filter function). If the filters can be activated dynamically, particular protocols can acquire exclusive access from outside into the LAN (segment) in certain high load situations (e.g., booting). The use of a positive type filter (e.g., on the "Gaul" type in combination with "discard on mismatch"), can set the traffic within a subnetwork to a single protocol. The use of a negative type filter (e.g., on the "Roman" type) can exclude a single protocol definitively from the subnetwork. The latter is thoroughly conceivable in subnetworks, which consist partly of PC networks and partly of DECnet/LAT configurations. If none of the networked PCs has to talk to the DEC world, it makes sense to exclude all DECnet frames from the relevant subnetwork and conversely not allow any PC network traffic into DECnet subnetworks (which are already used sufficiently by broadcasts and DECnet protocol traffic). Some protocol identifiers are combined in Figure 6.6.

Type Field in hexadecimal	Type Field in decimal	Protocol
0600	1536	Xerox IDP
0800	2048	IP
0804	2052	Chaosnet
0805	2053	X.25 Level 3
0806	2054	ARP
6001	24577	DECnet
6002	24578	DECnet
6003	24579	DECnet
6004	24580	DEC LAT
6005	24581	DECnet
6006	24582	DECnet
8035	32821	Reverse ARP
809B	32923	AppleTalk
8137	?	NetWare

Figure 6.6 Type field values for higher protocols

Mask filters relate to any position in the frame, at which, for example, there is particular information on protocols of higher layers (Layers 4 to 7), particular protocol options are specified, the ID of the selected PC server is entered, etc. Mostly, the bit pattern specified for a mask filter may be a maximum of two bytes long. The start of the bit pattern in the frame is specified via a corresponding offset value. In some bridges, type filters may be programmed only via masks "on foot" so to speak, but in other products a "type filter" function is implemented. This type filter requires only details and knowledge of the type value without the necessary offset. Figure 6.7 gives an overview of filter types.

In some products (e.g., Conware, 3Com), several filters can be combined with one another via logical functions (AND, OR, NOT) and forwarding/not forwarding is performed in the case of a match with the more complex logical filter function presented here. Such filters can also be termed combination filters.

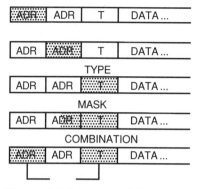

Figure 6.7 Summary of filter types

Of the features described (see Figure 6.8), by no means are all implemented in all bridges. In some bridges, no mask filters can be set; other bridges interpret only the filters set and have no feature of the type "action for mismatch." Only a few bridges can connect several filters through logical associations, etc. The user must investigate the products relevant to his or her requirements with regard to their filter capabilities (or lack of the latter).

- First Address e.g. 0800 1450 7C38

- Group Address e.g. Micom/Interlan 02 07 01

- Both source and destination address

- Protocol e.g., DECnet 6003

- Data of arbitrary length

- Subnetworks e.g., exclude Segment A

- Direction flow e.g., exclude Segment A

Figure 6.8 Various filter possibilities

Risks of using a filter

The additional functionality achieved by using filters brings with it advantages for the configuration of the network, but problems also arise, and filters must be used with care. Typically, the problems that arise are:

- performance loss, and

- increased risk of errors in the event of cable or bridge failure.

Performance loss

By exploiting all the available filter options, the flow of traffic between sub-networks may be subjected to a relatively complicated configuration. It is easy to imagine how this would occur, particularly when using many filters in an individual bridge with noticeable performance loss. Eventually, the bridge must check all filters set for each non-local packet. (Some bridges also decide after the first positive match. If, for example, a positive filter is set on a source address and a negative filter on the TCP/IP protocol, the packet is forwarded in the event of a match with the source address, even if it has the TCP/IP protocol as a higher protocol. In this case, the correct sequence of filter setting must also be observed in addition to filter logic.) The potential performance sacrifices in an interconnection element, which is in fact designed for rapid forwarding and high throughput, makes the extensive use of filter programs dubious—at least in every realistic case, the performance sacrifices must be weighed up against the additional configuration acquired.

Error Risk

A potential hazard source not to be underestimated is to be found in the use of filter programs in redundant networks. If a bridge with negative filters suddenly becomes the backup bridge for traffic as the result of Spanning Tree reconfiguration, what happens to traffic that does not normally have to be transported via this bridge? The user should play through the conceivable fault and failure situations of his or her network configuration before activating the planned filters in order to determine whether the traffic flow is also definitely guaranteed in the backup scenario. Filter programming, which takes redundant network design to absurd extremes by preventing communication via backup paths though negative filters, makes little sense.

Moreover, address-based filters become ineffective if the excluded or explicitly permitted stations change their address as the result of a defective or new adapter card. The filters set must then be reconfigured immediately or the desired functionality is lost.

Conclusion

The use of a few well-considered filters can only mean more efficient distribution of the traffic load in subnetworks and targeted control of traffic flow. The excessive use of the widest range of filters following the motto "if it's there, use it" conceals a high risk of faults (packets, which actually have to be forwarded, remain at some negative filter at some hard to identify bridge) and leads to a total lack of transparency for non-insiders regarding the actual active network configuration.

After investigating the advantages of skillful use of bridges, it remains clear that filter programming is, strictly speaking, nothing more than bit manipulation on the MAC layer, even if this is hidden behind attractive menus and seemingly easy use of filter settings (in user-friendly products). As already stated, this is not an argument against sensible and limited filter programming, only against its excesses.

6.2 Load Distribution

An even more extensive load regulation process can be seen in "Distributed Load Sharing" (DLS) (e.g., Conware, 3Com, Retix, RND). The process achieves load distribution via redundant bridges/links (if present), without destroying the Spanning Tree protocol (STP), however. Ports, which are in the blocking state under STP, are activated via DLS and used for the distribution of the current network load. A distinction can be drawn between two types:

- DLS within an individual bridge via several outgoing parallel bridge ports. These are mostly remote ports but can, in principle, also be local ports (see Figure 6.9).

- DLS between different bridges, where redundant paths are used simultaneously between bridges (see Figure 6.10).

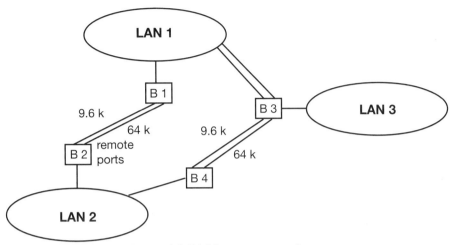

Figure 6.9 DLS between several ports

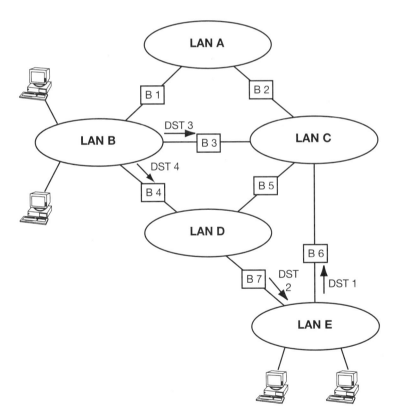

Figure 6.10 DLS between different bridges

In the same way as the implemented filter functions, the implemented DLS processes are not standardized. Bridges of different manufacturers, which are operated with DLS, are therefore not even theoretically compatible (a claim made by vendors of pure Spanning Tree bridges complying with the standard but which mostly cannot be proved in practice).

An important factor for the use of DLS is the observation of FIFO traffic. Some protocols (e.g., LAT) must be processed on the MAC layer in FIFO sequence. In other words, the packets must arrive at the destination station in precisely the same sequence as that in which they were sent by the sender. If this does not occur, a protocol error arises, with resulting failure. When using such protocols, only a DLS process can be used which takes account of the FIFO sequence (see Figure 6.10). If a non-FIFO DLS process was implemented by the manufacturer, only non-FIFO protocols (e.g., TCP/IP, IPX. XNS, etc.), which correct the confused sequence of the packets on the MAC Layer on higher protocol layers, can be processed with DLS, while FIFO protocols must be filtered at ports, which are not included in DLS.

In the case of DLS over several outgoing ports of a bridge (in contrast to DLS over several redundantly connected bridges), the process is presented as "single queue multiple server." A joint outward queue exists in the bridge, in which the packets, which are waiting to be forwarded, are processed in sequence (see Figure 6.11). They are distributed to various output ports, according to the free capacity of the ports. If, for example, port A is working, the frame is sent via port B and vice versa.

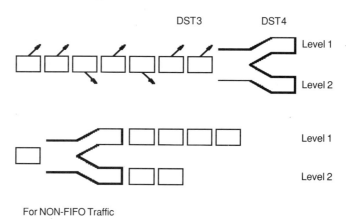

For NON-FIFO Traffic

Figure 6.11 Single Queue Multiple Server with DLS

Implementation of DLS functionality for remote bridges with a maximum of two remote ports is often used in a type of "triangular configuration." Three bridges, each with two remote ports, are connected in a triangular circuit, so that all packets can be forwarded directly or via an intervening bridge to the destination LAN. This DLS function is termed "triangulation" (see Figure 6.12).

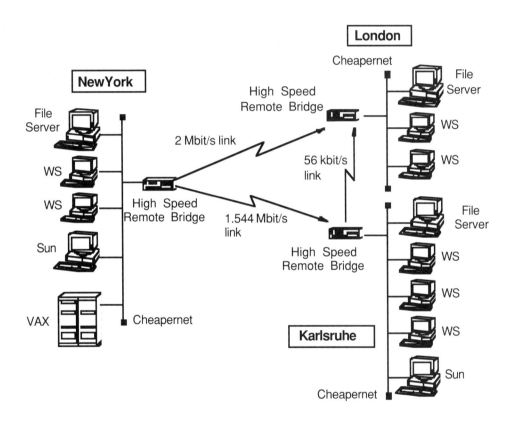

Figure 6.12 Triangulation DLS

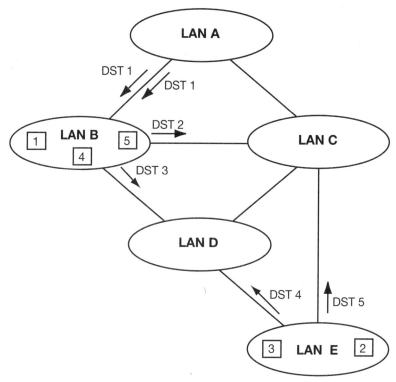

Figure 6.13 Load distribution when using bridges

The production of duplicates (parallel forwarding of the same frame via different links) is avoided by both DLS variants described. In the interplay with DLS, the SPT protocol is dominant. Therefore, if as the result of a link/bridge failure, a DLS path must migrate to the SPT path, the DLS protocol becomes inactive and the corresponding path is integrated into the Spanning Tree. The DLS processes described are used for local bridges only in the Ethernet or CSMA/CD sector, since Token Ring bridges perform a DLS strategy implicitly via the source routing process described (see Figure 6.13). In the field of remote bridges, DLS is offered both for Token Ring and for Ethernet bridges. Bridges which offer load distribution functionality, include, for example, products from NSC, RND, Retix, and Conware. The traffic flow in a redundant topology example is explained, in order to clarify the interplay between Spanning Tree and DLS (see Figure 6.14).

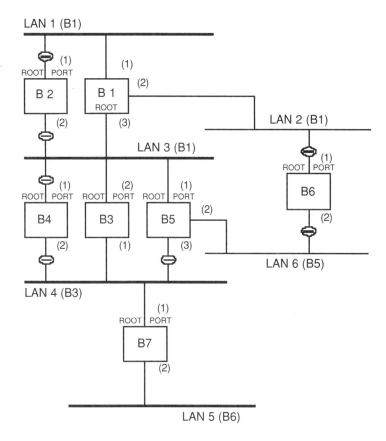

Figure 6.14 Topology example for Spanning Tree and DLS

The condition after the process of the STP algorithm is first described for the example in Figure 6.14. The "size" of an identifier and of the associated priority is given by its name, B1 is therefore less than B2 and has higher priority, P1 is similarly less than P2. For each LAN and each bridge, which bridge is the designated port and/or which port the root port is specified in brackets. B1 is the root, since it has the lowest ID and highest priority. It is the designated bridge for all attached LANs (1, 2, and 3), and consequently all ports of B1 are active. B3 is the designated bridge for LAN4, since it has the same costs as B4 and B5 with regard to LAN4 and has the lowest address. B2 has P1 as root port, since both ports have equivalent costs with regard to the distance from the root, but P1 has the lower port ID. The root bridge naturally has no root port. The bridges B2, B4, and B7 are in the blocking state after running the SPT algorithm, i.e., backup mode. They do not forward any information frames. By activating the DLS, those bridges also become active and take over some of the frames, which they forward in the direction of the destination station in place of the designated bridge (see Figure 6.15). B2 forwards some of the LAN1 to LAN3 traffic, B4 forwards some of the LAN3 to LAN4 traffic, B7 forwards some of the LAN1 to LAN6 traffic, etc.

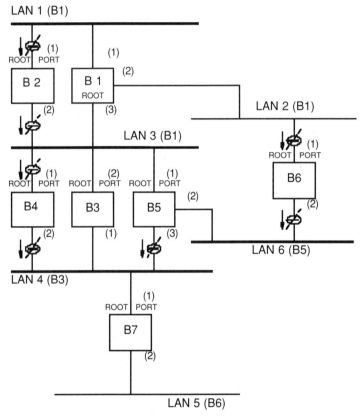

Figure 6.15 Topology example for Spanning Tree and DLS

If B3 failed, B4 would receive no further BPDUs from B3. After a timeout and Spanning Tree reconfiguration, B4 would delete B3 as designated bridge for

LAN4 in its topology database and assume the forwarding of packets to LAN4 totally. B4 now has the functionality of a designated bridge, which dominates the DLS functionality.

If B5 failed, B7 would receive no further BPDUs from B5. After a timeout and Spanning Tree reconfiguration, B7 would delete B5 as designated bridge for LAN6 in its topology database and assume the forwarding of packets to LAN6 totally. B7 now has the functionality of a designated bridge, which dominates the DLS functionality.

Filter functions and DLS cannot replace any explicit flow control or the use of more complex metrics (see Chapter 8), as are implemented in a router, but they clearly make a contribution to load control/regulation and therefore assume routing functions. This activity is often supported by extensive management statistics which give an insight into the current load situation and network topology. With this insight, a corresponding dynamic bridge configuration becomes possible on the part of management personnel.

The starting situation for a network can be depicted as follows, with the bridge functionality described up to this point:

- The bridge has learned the overall configuration of its attached segments (subnetworks) bit by bit and in this way has constructed its address database;

or

the bridge is a source routing bridge and does not require an address database.

- The bridge takes forwarding decisions correctly in the sense of load division and dedicated forwarding to a particular port. For this purpose, it consults either its port-related address table or, in the case of source routing, the string match process with regard to its own bridge number and numbers of attached segments.

- The bridge may react to topology changes via its aging mechanism and initiate a corresponding reconfiguration of its address database;

or

the path information is restructured via the source routing process at the time of each new communication session so that alternative routes can be sought in the event of topology changes.

- The desire for a reasonable redundancy design for the network infra-structure, both with regard to bridges and cable paths, can be fulfilled by means of the multiple installation of bridges and cable paths. The unambiguity of packet forwarding is assured in this case either according to the Spanning Tree or source routing process.

- Bridges can achieve particular access control to selected subnetworks via the implementation of more or less convenient filter functions. This applies both to Spanning Tree bridges and source routing bridges, where the filter functions in Spanning Tree bridges are generally more distinctive than with source routing bridges.

- The utilization of redundant bridges and link capacity is achieved though explicitly implemented load distribution processes or implicit alternative path selection in source routing.

Once the user has implemented this functionality in his or her network a further idea occurs to him or her: Why should a bridge not actually connect two different MAC layers in one network? The achievement of this task is described in the next chapter.

6.3   Interconnection of Different MAC Layers

If identical MAC layers are connected with a bridge, the subnetworks differentiate between one another only on Layer 1, that is differentiation is made with regard to the type of transmission used. The common MAC layer of both connected network portions forms an interface above which the different protocols used can be transmitted transparently. The behavior is different in bridges which connect different MAC layers. Here, different MAC layers must be converted into one another, which generates communication problems in several respects. Two important bridge types in which these problems must be handled are bridges for the connection of subnetworks via an FDDI backbone and bridges for the interconnection of different subnetworks such as Token Ring and Ethernet.

At present, there are still no standards or standard models, with the exception of SNAP (SubNetwork Access Protocol), to connect two different MAC layers in a bridge, either between Ethernet and Token Ring or between FDDI and Ethernet or Token Ring. The need for inter-MAC bridge interconnections has existed for a long time however, and has led to the development of corresponding products, which basically use two processes to connect two different MAC layers via bridges: encapsulation and translation. Both processes are at present implemented in products to perform tasks like, for example, forwarding data packets by means of bridges via an FDDI backbone. Upward protocol transparency, i.e., with regard to higher protocol layers, is achieved to a great extent in this type of interconnection. Both processes are described in the example of the FDDI interconnection.

6.3.1 Encapsulation

In this process, for the sake of simplicity, the frame (Ethernet packet or Token Ring packet) is left entirely as it is and encapsulated into an FDDI MAC frame as shown in Figure 6.16. The FDDI bridge manages a dynamic (self-learning) address table, into which all addresses of active stations of the attached sub-network for the non-FDDI port are entered. The MAC address of each active potential destination station (in some remote subnetwork) is entered for the backbone port and associated with the FDDI MAC address of the FDDI bridge, which connects the relevant destination subnetwork to the FDDI backbone. If this bridge is not known, the FDDI bridge, which connects the subnetwork of a source station wishing to send to the backbone, generates a "search frame" to all FDDI bridges in order to receive the desired bridge address as a response. The bridge, which finds the desired destination station as a "local" subnetwork station in its address table, answers the frame with its FDDI MAC address as the desired bridge address. The enclosed data packet can be sent from the "searching" FDDI bridge via encapsulation to the FDDI bridge, which responded. Since the address tables build themselves dynamically in self-learning mode in the same way as simple local Ethernet bridges, no configuration cost is required for commissioning.

Based on the encapsulation technique, this frame contains the MAC addresses twice (e.g., Ethernet for source and destination station, FDDI for the first and last bridges, which are passed over) and two checksums (FCS). The destination LAN must always run the same MAC protocol as the source LAN (Ethernet–FDDI–Ethernet or Token Ring–FDDI–Token Ring). Thus, FDDI can be used only as the backbone, and end systems (hosts or workstations) attached directly to FDDI cannot interpret the frame. There is no option of accessing a device attached to the backbone from a subnetwork.

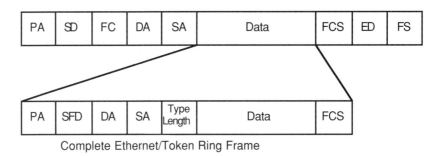

Complete Ethernet/Token Ring Frame

Figure 6.16 Encapsulation

The destination bridge is addressed directly on the FDDI network. The bridges do not work in promiscuous mode here, and there is no filter cost for this. In principle, a bridge that works with encapsulation can be considered as a "half bridge" in a similar way to a remote bridge: a bridge pair is required, in order to communicate between two same structure subnetworks via an FDDI backbone. The reader needs only to imagine replacing the slow remote link with a super fast FDDI network.

An encapsulation bridge does not actually achieve a genuine interconnection of different MAC layers, since no genuine translation of information takes place. It is only made possible to use a different carrier network as the "transit network" between subnetworks of the same type. In concrete terms, this means that a frame from an Ethernet subnetwork cannot be sent onto the FDDI backbone in order then to leave in the direction of a Token Ring subnetwork. This would often be desirable for a heterogeneous network configuration, however. When using products with encapsulation technology, the user is tied to one manufacturer, since products from different manufacturers are producer-specific, given the lack of standardization, and therefore not compatible with one another. The current maximum achievable compatibility is the parallel operation of different products in-the form of coexistence without making themselves mutually unable to function. The advantages and disadvantages of the process must be weighed before use.

Advantages

- The hardware cost is small, since the packets are in practice only pushed through and provided with the additional header and trailer of the new MAC process.

- High throughput is easily achievable, since no filtering has to be performed on the FDDI side: each packet that arrives on the backbone is addressed to the bridge, which downloads it once more from the backbone.

- The original FCS is retained, which minimizes the potential for errors in end-to-end transmission.

- Type field/length field are retained, regardless of whether this is an Ethernet frame or an IEEE 802.3 frame.

Disadvantages

- The model does not behave in accordance with OSI, since the frame format no longer corresponds to the MAC standard address because of the double MAC addresses.

- The technique is practical only for backbone networks, since the FDDI bridges with encapsulation can use the FDDI network only as a transit network.

- Only LANs of the same type (Ethernet-Ethernet or Token Ring-Token Ring) can be joined. A connection of subnetworks with different MAC layers is not possible, since the original frame (Ethernet or Token Ring) is not converted.

- Directly attached FDDI stations cannot be included in the communication, since they cannot interpret the encapsulated frames.

Encapsulation can be considered only as transitional technology in light of the limitations described. This technology was developed in the run-up to suitable standards as a result of the urgent demand for interconnection and will not be able to survive once a relevant standard is approved.

If the user decides to use such technology at present, he or she must clarify precisely whether it will be possible to convert to the emerging standards in the future, and if so, whether this will involve justifiable financial and support expenditure. Otherwise the user should accept depreciating the investments made over the medium term making new investments for suitable FDDI interconnection elements. For Ethernet–FDDI bridges, the encapsulation phase has already passed its peak, but Token Ring–FDDI bridges can still be seen as state of the art.

6.3.2 Translation

In the translation process, the LAN frame (e.g., Ethernet, FDDI or Token Ring) is converted into the frame of the other standard LAN (translation), and a genuine conversion takes place of the different MAC protocols into one another. An Ethernet protocol framework is replaced by an FDDI protocol framework, for example. The frame experiences various changes here: a new frame header and a new checksum (FCS) result. In the case of Ethernet frames, the type field is removed from the frame, since this is not provided for in the FDDI protocol. The lost protocol type information can be reinserted only in the destination LAN, if the bridge there can take the type from the protocol information of higher layers (e.g., using the SNAP protocol, RFC 1042). Translation with SNAP is shown in Figure 6.17.

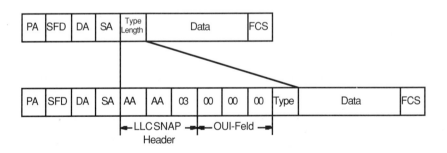

Figure 6.17 Translation with SNAP protocol

In translation technology, the LAN-FDDI bridges manage port-related dynamic address tables similarly to self-learning Ethernet bridges. The addressing is performed via details of the MAC destination address and the MAC source address of the communicating end stations in the frame. These addresses are taken over into the FDDI frame and forwarded as the LAN destination address and LAN source address via the FDDI network. An FDDI bridge must then search its address tables to see whether a destination address is attainable via Spanning Tree in one of its attached subnetworks. If it is, the FDDI bridge will forward the frame and thereby convert the FDDI format into that of the corresponding subnetwork (e.g., Ethernet). This corresponds to a totally normal forwarding decision in a totally normal Spanning Tree bridge-interconnected network. Likewise, the bridge behaves by default as a standard MAC bridge: if a destination address is not known, the bridge forwards the frame to the attached subnetwork/s. Direct addressing of the bridge (as in encapsulation) does not occur, except for BPDUs of the bridge protocol to maintain the Spanning Tree or in other management actions (control frames on the MAC level).

As a result of the complete conversion of the frame into an FDDI frame, stations, which are attached to the FDDI network directly, can also receive the frame and interpret it correctly. The advantages and disadvantages of the process are compared briefly below.

Since the FDDI bridge must operate in promiscuous mode in the translation process, where each frame is examined for forwarding or non-forwarding, considerable processor performance is required in the bridge for sufficiently fast processing. The bridge must examine destination addresses at 100 Mbit/s, and while doing so buffer the frame. It must also take the forwarding decision at the LAN speed and, where applicable, be able to forward packets onto an attached subnetwork. The throughput rate for the bridge must be set correspondingly high.

This "more open" technology in comparison to encapsulation is already significantly more advanced for the Ethernet-FDDI connection than for the Token Ring-FDDI connection: the FDDI bridges have still not learned source routing. If they had it, FDDI could pass cleanly as a particularly fast Token Ring. The statements of manufacturers and suppliers to support source routing in FDDI bridges, often are merely an encapsulation process, so that source routing is supported only "outside" the FDDI backbone for attached Token Ring subnetworks. That is relatively easy to implement.

Ethernet–FDDI products generally support a Spanning Tree algorithm according to IEEE 802.1D and occasionally DEC. Interoperability between bridges of different manufacturers is therefore more likely in theory than in the case of encapsulation (in practice, however, this has not yet been thoroughly tested), since an implementation is at least oriented to standards.

An aspect already indicated has proven to be problematic in the case of translation bridges. This is an aspect which is totally alien to encapsulation bridges, however, because of their different type of design. Differences between Ethernet 2.0, IEEE 802.3 and IEEE 802.5 must be translated into one another, since it is now thoroughly possible to send a packet from an Ethernet subnetwork and receive it on a Token Ring subnetwork. This proves to be critical, particularly in the case of highly interlocking structures. This is dealt with in greater detail in section 6.3.3.1.

Advantages

- The model behaves according to OSI, since the frame format observes compliance, particularly with regard to MAC standard addressing.

- Translation is practical for FDDI subnetworks and for backbone networks. Subnetworks in which standard MAC processes are used (e.g., IEEE 802.3, IEEE 802.5) can be connected to one another in any sequence.

- Connection of subnetworks with different MAC layers is possible (e.g., Ethernet and Token Ring), since the original frame (Ethernet or Token Ring) is first converted into FDDI format and then into the MAC format of the destination network. In this sense, FDDI can be understood to be the translation platform for the widest range of subnetworks into one another.

- Directly attached FDDI stations can be included into the communication, since they can interpret the FDDI frames produced by the bridge according to the standard.

Disadvantages

- The necessary processing overhead must first be made possible via a correspondingly high level of hardware capacity. This relates to processor performance, memory space, and also internal management of bridging components (bus, network adapters, CPU, memory, etc.).

- Products with comparable levels of hardware capacity achieve lower throughput with translation than with encapsulation because of the more complex processing (filtering on the FDDI side, frame conversion).

- The original FCS is changed by the conversion and newly calculated in each bridge, which increases the error potential in the case of end-to-end transmission.

- Differences between the various MAC formats must be taken into account in the conversion. This proves to be critical in particular in the case of type field/length field in Ethernet/IEEE 802.3 frames, since the FDDI format does not provide for any type field. Remedial action can be taken here only by the filing of the type information in higher protocols such as SNAP (RFC 1042).

6.3.3 Application Possibilities

The connection of subnetworks or network islands with different MAC access processes via relatively simple bridge interconnection as "plug and play" technology, is of interest in a series of application cases in which end stations with several higher protocols are intended to communicate with one another easily via different LANs. Three key areas of use for bridges between different MAC layers can be detailed at present:

- connection of Token Ring and CSMA/CD networks

- connection of Token Ring and CSMA/CD subnetworks via FDDI networks

- connection of Token Ring and CSMA/CD subnetworks via a broadband backbone

An obvious requirement is the connection of Token Ring and Ethernet, since presently these two processes clearly dominate the market of installed LANs. The translation process is generally supported here. The IBM LAN bridge 8229 (formerly IBM 8209) was for a long time the only product on the market that allowed a bridge connection between Ethernet and Token Ring (not least in order to establish Token Ring as a common backbone for Ethernet and Token Ring subnetworks). The other manufacturers dragged along two years later. Meanwhile there are a series of established manufacturers that support this function with their multifunctional interconnection elements (e.g., Bay Networks, 3Com, Cisco, IBM, Proteon, Retix).

The connection possibilities and problems when using a bridge connection between CSMA/CD according to Ethernet or IEEE 802.3 and Token Ring are discussed below.

6.3.3.1 Ethernet–Token Ring Connection

For the purposes of simplicity, a bridge is considered with an Ethernet or IEEE 802.3 segment and a Token Ring connection. Such a bridge achieves the network connection on OSI Layer 2. It converts Ethernet frames into Token Ring frames without accessing the higher protocol layers. These are forwarded transparently via the bridge, this generally involves SNA, NetBIOS, TCP/IP, or OSI. The Token Ring and IEEE 802.3 protocols operate on the LLC layer, but on Ethernet on the MAC layer with the LLC layer empty.

The resulting conversion is different for Ethernet and IEEE 802.3, with the easier case being IEEE 802.3 and Token Ring (IEEE 802.5). If information is sent from Token Ring to IEEE 802.3, the bridge removes the Token Ring header, stores the routing information in an internal database, and generates a CSMA/CD packet according to IEEE 802.3. The LLC protocol information is fed through unchanged from IEEE 802.3 and IEEE 802.5, the MAC headers from 802.3 (preamble) and 802.5 (Token and routing information field) are exchanged and the checksum recalculated. If a transmission is made from CSMA/CD to Token Ring, the bridge adds the source routing information from the internal database to the packet (see also Figure 6.19).

If information is sent from Token Ring to Ethernet, the bridge removes the Token Ring header, stores the routing information in an internal database, and generates a CSMA/CD packet Ethernet version 2.0. In order to be able to enter the information on the transmitted higher protocol into the Ethernet type field provided for this purpose, the Token Ring packet must have the SNAP format, in which the type information is entered from byte 20. If information is transmitted from Ethernet to Token Ring, the bridge adds the source routing information from the internal database and the type information via the SNAP protocol (Subnetwork Access Protocol, RFC 1042) into the packet (see also Figure 6.18).

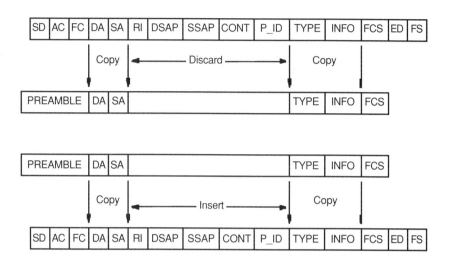

Figure 6.18 Ethernet - Token Ring conversion with SNAP

The question arises as to why the DSAP/SSAP field of the LLC layer is not simply interpreted for the type value, since this also contains a code for the higher protocol used. The problem in each case is that the DSAP/SSAP field is only one byte long, of which only 6 bits are available for type identifiers. Only 64 different type values can be coded, and this is totally inadequate. For a long time the international standards body has not given all known protocols a standardized value. There is not even a DSAP/SSAP value for such common protocols as ARP.

If a CSMA/CD station initiates a connection, the bridge can make an entry in its address table as to whether this station speaks Ethernet 2.0 or IEEE 802.3. Imagine the opposite situation: a Token Ring station starts a communication link to a CSMA/CD server, or the packet must be forwarded via a Token Ring backbone once more into Ethernet. From where is the bridge intended to know whether it should generate an Ethernet 2.0 or IEEE 802.3 packet? in this case, a default mode must be set for CSMA/CD: either IEEE 802.3 or Ethernet. This default is used for Token Ring packets, which must be forwarded to a destination station on the CSMA/CD side, whose address has not yet been learned. If the default is set to Ethernet for example, and a Token Ring packet arrives at the bridge with an unknown destination address which must be forwarded, it is converted into an Ethernet frame and not into an IEEE 802.3 frame. Depending on which end stations are used in the CSMA/CD sector, attention must be paid to the correct setting of the default, otherwise the end stations cannot receive the packet under certain circumstances: there are still adapter cards and software which cannot handle both packet types.

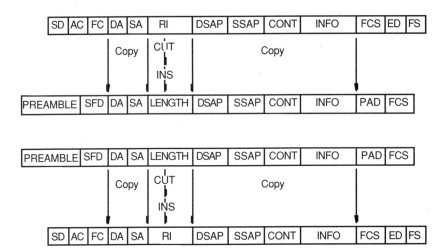

Figure 6.19 IEEE 803.2 – Token Ring conversion

Some manufacturers, can avoid this problem by generating all three packet types: Ethernet 2.0, IEEE 802.3, and IEEE 802.3 with SNAP. This increases the network load unnecessarily, until a particular MAC address of the correct packet type is learned. There are also manufacturers (e.g., Madgel/Lannet) that support " tunneling" (encapsulation) for backbone configuration, in which an additional parameter is sent between backbone bridges regarding whether the original packet was an Ethernet or IEEE packet.

When making a bridge interconnection via IBM 8229 or other products, attention must be paid to the fact that the Token Ring end systems do not send any frames which are longer than 1500 bytes. The default RU size for SNA communication in the OS/2 Communication Manager is 2048 bytes, for example. This is also used in client/server communication in the IBM LAN server (network operating system). If for example, a domain server is used that is on Ethernet with an additional server, that is on Token Ring, the two do not negotiate the packet size 1500 when making the connection. Therefore when the additional server sends packets that are too long, the bridge does not forward the packets, instead it destroys them. The result is a repeated attempt to make a connection (via NetBIOS), which finally ends in a timeout.

On the other hand, client stations on Token Ring are clever enough to adapt to the packet size of the domain server, even if they have been entered as RU size 2048. A simple parameter comparison does not lead to error recognition. In different end systems (server, client), the same parameter value leads to different communication results. In this case, the only assistance is the error search with the analyzer. It is therefore pointless to blame the 8229 bridge since it is behaving totally correctly: frames, which are too long may not be forwarded, since they cannot be received. Once more, the dirty implementation of communications software on the higher layers (in this case NetBIOS), causes the difficulties.

Problems may also occur in other cases, if "identical" protocols are achieved in a different way above the MAC layer. Some older IPX versions from the NetWare protocol stack use the broadcast permitted in Token Ring C0_00_FF_FF_FF_FF, as "Nearest Server Request," while IPX on Ethernet accepts only the broadcast FF_FF_FF_FF_FF_FF. A server on Ethernet therefore does not react to the Nearest Server Request, which was generated on Token Ring. The same phenomenon can also occur on AppleTalk.

Each NetWare/AppleTalk packet, which was generated for the Token Ring cannot therefore be interpreted correctly on Ethernet. This error situation cannot be blamed on the method of operation of the bridge. Instead it should be blamed on the unequal (not to say dirty) implementations for Ethernet and Token Ring. Other protocols also struggle with the problem of unequal protocol stacks for Ethernet and Token Ring (e.g., Microsoft's LAN Manager, DECnet, and AppleTalk).

One of the main problems here is the rotation of the MAC address bit: the Most Significant Bit (MSB) which is the highest value bit of a byte, is transmitted first whilst in Token Ring, the Least Significant Bit (LSB) is transmitted first in Ethernet. This means that between Ethernet and Token Ring, the MAC addresses must be rotated bit by bit, rotation which is implemented for example, via internal bridge conversion tables (which does nothing to hasten packet processing...). Unfortunately, the MAC addresses are sometimes also used in the higher protocol layers (i.e., "further back" in the frame), where no byte rotation takes place. A frame can arrive at the end station under certain circumstances, containing two inconsistent MAC addresses and be rejected as a protocol error. Some protocol examples given below should clarify the problem.

The ARP request of the IP protocol passes via a MAC broadcast to an IP address. The response packet contains the MAC address in the data section, which belongs to this IP address. The bridge therefore rotates the address also in the data section of the ARP packet when in doubt. With transparent operation, there is not much more to do, but at least it functions. In the case of IPX, the MAC address is contained in the network address once more. Here also, inconsistent values may arise as the result of rotation, values for which the bridging function then no longer supports. In the case of AppleTalk, the network addresses have variable lengths. It would not be clear, in which byte the addresses would then have to be rotated.

If the Token Ring is used only as a backbone, the error situations described above do not occur since the twofold conversion eliminates inconsistencies.

The error situations described give an insight into how little space the connection of Ethernet and Token Ring occupied in the minds of manufacturers before 1990. Otherwise, attention would have been paid to the uniform realization of higher protocol stacks. Developments later revealed the harsh reality.

Various application possibilities can be imagined for Ethernet–Token Ring bridges:

- Token Ring as a backbone to connect Ethernet networks for any higher protocols, particularly TCP/IP on computers of different manufacturers (see Figure 6.20). The communicating end systems are both attached to Ethernet.

- The connection of Ethernet and Token Ring subnetworks, where at present a sequence of Ethernet and Token Ring subnetworks in any order is still not possible (Ethernet–Token Ring–Ethernet is the maximum cascade, see also Figure 6.21).

- Communication between different IBM host and end systems on Ethernet and Token Ring via SNA and NetBIOS.

- Communication by end systems of different manufacturers on Ethernet and Token Ring via TCP/IP.

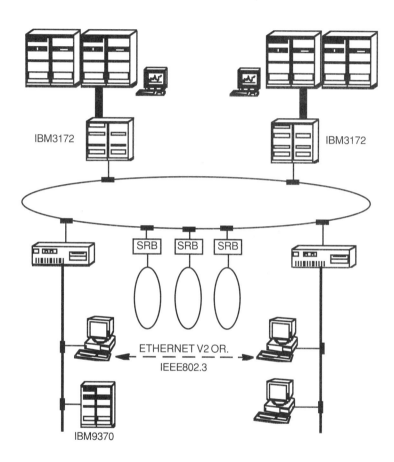

Figure 6.20 Backbone Configuration

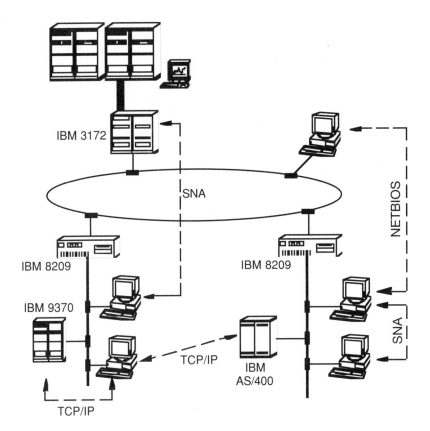

Figure 6.21 Ethernet–Token Ring interconnection

The connection of Token Ring subnetworks via an Ethernet backbone or via any sequence of Ethernet and Token Ring subnetworks does not function correctly at present. The hope remains that the function will be extended consistently in the future. An improvement is also anticipated here with the use of the future SRT standard.

Problems

As with previous examples, the following problem factors must currently be noted in the use of a bridge interconnection for an Ethernet–Token Ring connection:

- The exchange of headers and trailers in each packet to be forwarded costs processing time.

- When forwarding from Ethernet to Token Ring, the bridge must initiate the route discovery in order to be able to generate the RIF. This leads to a long processing time and response time when making connection between two stations.

- The default mode Ethernet 2.0 or IEEE 802.3 used must correspond to the operating mode of the stations in the CSMA/CD area.

- When using Ethernet 2.0, the SNAP protocol must be followed in Token Ring, since not all higher protocol type values are coded with DSAP/SSAP.

- For stations on Token Ring, the frame length must be restricted to 1500 bytes.

- Only protocols or implementations may be used, which use the same broadcast on the Ethernet and Token Ring side (generally FF_FF_FF_FF_FF_FF).

- Ethernet and Token Ring subnetworks cannot be cascaded in whatever sequence desired.

- Different implementations of higher protocols for Ethernet and Token Ring lead to a breakdown in communication, although the bridge operates correctly (duplicate and inconsistent MAC addresses following the bit by bit rotation on Layer 2 and Layer 3).

6.3.3.2 LAN-FDDI Interconnection

If Ethernet or Token Ring network islands are to be connected at the current point in time via a backbone or if a Token Ring or Ethernet fiber optic backbone is already present, the loading of which is approaching the capacity limit, the question must be posed regarding the use of or migration to FDDI. Instead of interconnecting Ethernet and Token Ring between one another via an Ethernet–Token Ring bridge, which represents a performance bottleneck under certain circumstances, the alternative is to offer using FDDI as a common intermediate network in the backbone sector. An interconnection via FDDI is becoming attractive, in particular with the future availability of an

SRT standard, since the latter will enable the requirement for a uniform interconnection of Ethernet and Token Ring networks.

At first sight, the interconnection of LANs via FDDI bridges appears attractively simple. The standardized IEEE address structures on Layer 2 (MAC addresses) do not point to any particular difficulties. On closer inspection however, some manufacturer-specific peculiarities can be found which lead to problems. In particular, irregular subnetwork structures can be observed here with a high level of switching in the different networks.

- Ethernet 2.0, the manufacturer-specific version of IEEE 802.3, demonstrates some differences to IEEE 802.3 CSMA/CD in the frame format: the LLC layer is missing, and the length field of 802.3 is a type field. In Token Ring, the MAC addresses are compared with Ethernet and IEEE 802.3 in reverse sequence and the mirror image is therefore transmitted (see also section 3.5.3.1). These differences make the Ethernet–IEEE 802.3–Token Ring conversion via FDDI more difficult.

- The combination of nested subnetworks with source routing and Spanning Tree bridges, redundant configuration design in Ethernet and Token Ring, and changing routes in the case of source routing leads to very complex processing mechanisms in the bridges, if a totally flexible interconnection is indeed achievable with currently available products.

- MAC addresses, often described as "locally administered," set using software (DECnet, Token Ring) regularly lead to problems when combining previously independent network parts. Manufacturers that do not use unambiguous hardware addresses must here answer the charges of a simple lack of foresight and a lack of technical specialist know-how.

- The broadcast problem is not avoided by FDDI bridges. For universal network interconnection, the broadcasts of the various higher protocols must be transmitted via FDDI into remote subnetworks (LAT, NetWare, TCP/IP, XNS, etc.). The result is a relatively high broadcast load on the backbone, which also cannot be restricted by setting filters in the case of unrestricted communication.

- In the case of the direct connection of high performance end systems to the FDDI backbone, attention must be paid to which protocols these stations can communicate; the attainability of directly attached IBM hosts must be investigated here in particular.

According to [KAUSUP92], the following interconnection features in particular must be checked before using a product and guaranteed by written confirmation from the supplier:

Interconnection feature 1

FDDI connects Ethernet subnetworks transparently and in a manufacturer-neutral manner.

Interconnection feature 2

FDDI connects IEEE 802.3 subnetworks transparently and in a manufacturer-neutral manner.

Interconnection feature 3

FDDI connects Ethernet and IEEE 802.3 subnetworks transparently and in a manufacturer-neutral manner.

Interconnection feature 4

FDDI connects Token Ring subnetworks transparently and in a manufacturer-neutral manner.

Interconnection feature 5

FDDI connects Token Ring and Ethernet subnetworks transparently and in a manufacturer-neutral manner.

Interconnection feature 6

FDDI connects Token Ring and IEEE 802.3 subnetworks transparently and in a manufacturer-neutral manner.

Interconnection feature 7

FDDI connects FDDI stations (SAS and DAS, in particular: IBM mainframes) with stations in CSMA/CD subnetworks transparently and in a manufacturer-neutral manner.

Interconnection feature 8

FDDI connects FDDI stations (SAS and DAS, in particular: IBM mainframes) with stations in Token Ring subnetworks transparently and in a manufacturer-neutral manner.

The currently available products for LAN-FDDI interconnection unfortunately fulfill only some of the required interconnection features. The user must exercise particular care when investigating and where applicable weigh up the different limitations posed by the various products well before making a decision.

Despite the difficulties, presently, a clear trend can be seen both on the part of users and manufacturers towards FDDI.

Increased subnetwork interconnection and greater transmission capacity in the end systems used (workstations, power-servers) make FDDI use achievable for a series of complex corporate networks.

6.3.3.3 Broadband Backbone

A further area of use of bridge interconnections despite different MAC layers is the use of a broadband backbone. Although at present in new cable installations, fiber optics is preferred as a medium for site cabling and backbone formation because of its simpler planning, more flexible use, and easier installation, there are still broadband installations present which represent a market for bridge interconnections via broadband.

If Ethernet is used both in the subnetworks and on the broadband, a bridge interconnection needs only to handle the different media (analogue broadband technology and digital baseband technology in the subnetworks). If it is intended to connect Token Ring subnetworks however, this protocol cannot be dragged over the broadband, since the Token Ring process cannot be used on broadband. There remains only the option described above of an Ethernet–Token Ring connection with Ethernet on the broadband backbone (IBM 8229 with broadband connection), or alternatively the option of a Token Bus–Token Ring connection with Token Bus as the backbone protocol. In the latter case, Token Ring–Token Bus bridges are available on the market (e.g., from Fubastar, Galaxy, TokenMaster). The problem, as already described, remains with regard to the IBM 8229 bridge, of different permitted frame sizes in Token Ring (2k up to approx. 5k) and Token Bus (8k).

Which protocol is used on the broadband backbone depends upon the other applications which run on the subnetworks. The bridge interconnection is exchanged accordingly. If, for example, Token Bus is already used in manufacturing environments for various applications and there are no Ethernet applications, the user will not be in a desperate hurry to run Ethernet over broadband; the user may need Ethernet only to connect Token Ring subnetworks with one another via the backbone. If the connection is possible via Token Bus, implementation of a further MAC protocol results merely in unnecessary complexity and cost. The sensible decision here is the use of a Token Ring–Token Bus bridge. Since Token Ring–Token Bus bridges generally operate as encapsulation bridges, end systems on the backbone cannot be addressed in this alternative and included in the communication. The Token Bus serves only as a transit network to connect Token Rings.

If it is necessary to attach both Token Ring subnetworks and Ethernet subnetworks to the backbone, the user has the dilemma of the following choice:

- The Ethernet protocol is generally used on the backbone, which brings with it the advantage of a lower range of protocols. This option narrows the selection of products for the Token Ring attachment considerably (at present almost entirely to the IBM 8229 LAN bridge). Since the IBM 8229 is not capable of operating as a purely Ethernet bridge, a second bridge product must be used in any case for the attachment of the Ethernet subnetworks. Since the IBM 8229 is a translation bridge, devices that are attached directly to the broadband can also be addressed.

- Ethernet and Token Bus are run on the backbone. Different bridges must be used to attach the various subnetworks. One advantage in the choice of products from a group of devices may be the uniform user interface and the therefore reduced support complexity. On the other hand, end systems, which are attached directly to the broadband cannot be addressed from Token Ring subnetworks because of the encapsulation technique.

It is sensible to make the product selection in the case of equivalent alternatives from one source, (i.e., from one manufacturer), who offers both an Ethernet broadband bridge and a Token Ring–Token Bus bridge in one product family. If possible, the product line should be modular to the extent that bridges are also possible for the direct connection of two subnetworks (Ethernet–Ethernet, Token Ring–Token Ring without an intermediate backbone) and other products therefore do not have to be used for this type of network interconnection.

The interconnection of subnetworks via a broadband backbone can be considered as a trend towards the use of existing equipment in the sense of an investment saving, rather than as the "use of obsolete stock." The corresponding bridge interconnections cannot be considered to be in the high end sector of bridging technology. Current developments are heading more in the direction of FDDI, which, in the same way as Token Ring, cannot be used on broadband. A broadband configuration is shown in Figure 6.22.

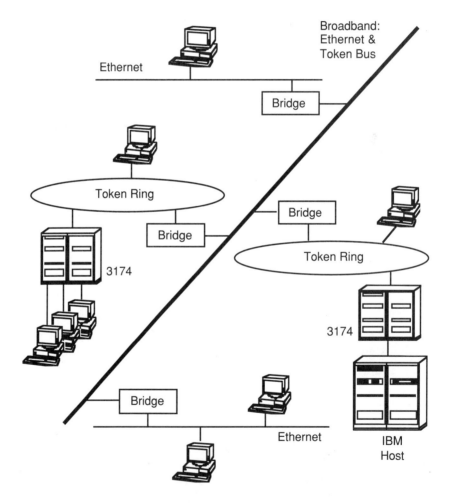

Figure 6.22 Subnetwork connection via broadband backbone)

7 | LAN Switches

Bridges are out, LAN switching is in and has become the new buzzword. This field of internetworking has developed into a market in which approximately 60 manufacturers compete. A description of LAN switches, their application possibilities, and an evaluation of this new technology is therefore an essential part of this book. LAN switches have the advantage of a clearly lower packet processing time in comparison to bridges and particularly in comparison to routers: 20 to 50 µs is required for LAN switching in contrast to 100 to 500 µs and more for multi-protocol routers.

There are LAN switches for Ethernet, Token Ring and FDDI. Since FDDI switches work quite similar to Ethernet switches and have made little impact on the market because costs for FDDI end systems remain relatively high, they shall not be considered within this book.

Why LAN Switches?

When considered from an objective, pure technical perspective, a LAN switch is often no more than a multiport bridge which has been extended in terms of ports and end system attachment possibilities and has lost interconnection functionality (filter, packet buffer load distribution, WAN attachment). This architecture belongs to a new generation of devices, since the backplane has greater capacity and ASICs are used for packet processing in place of CISC or RISC processors with firmware. The products currently available are equipped more sparingly with packet buffers in comparison to bridges, which can lead to a performance lack in cases of high load. Some devices continue to operate with RISC processors and firmware but are still sold as switches. Long live marketing.

Why LAN switches? Based on the hardware/software functionality and price, good old multiport bridges are thought of as interconnecting a limited number of segments each with many users (80 to 200) or entire LANs via WAN backbones. Depending upon the end system capacity and the hunger for bandwidth of established applications, Ethernet and Token Ring begin to falter with 10 or 20 attached power users (Pentium PC, RISC or Alpha Workstation). This has led to microsegmenting, in which no more than 10 to 24 users are attached to one segment. A logical further development of this idea is the dedicated LAN with a single attached end system which entails one server or individual workstations, which are combined in a cluster and operate on a peer-to-peer basis via a LAN switch.

LAN switches are products that are tailored precisely to this requirement: microsegmenting and the dedicated LAN. Three features are displayed accordingly:

- high port concentration (many micro-segments, many individual users)
- possibility to attach end systems directly to a port
- high bandwidth

WAN ports are not found on a LAN switch.

The following chapters deal with the method of operation of LAN switches and various architecture concepts. Possible LAN switch configurations, network scenarios, and limitations for LAN switches are illustrated.

7.1 Method of Operation

Despite sales claims by switch vendors and suppliers regarding astronomical throughput and minimal delay, there is nothing magical about the operation of LAN switches: LAN switches operate quite simply on MAC LAN standards.

They interpret MAC frames and make the forwarding decision by evaluating the MAC information. Each port has the full LAN capacity available to it, which is 10 or 100 Mbps for Ethernet, 4 or 16 Mbps for Token Ring. If a single end system is attached to a port, it has the full LAN capacity available to it on an exclusive basis, and communication with all other devices is **always** performed via the switch. If a segment is attached, the port capacity is shared among packets which must be forwarded to another port among all attached stations. Stations on this segment communicate with one another directly. Overall, as it was before, with the sum of the local and non-local load on a switch-attached LAN segment, you don't have more than the LAN capacity. This means that the network must always be structured so that no individual port of the LAN switch is overloaded with receiving or sending.

The interconnection logic of a LAN switch does not behave essentially different from a multiport bridge for standard, error-free, frames. For Ethernet and FDDI switches, this means packet forwarding via address tables, and for Token Ring switches, forwarding using the RIF information or similarly to Ethernet, the evaluation of address tables. A series of basic switch functions therefore correspond to the functions of bridges and are not explained again in detail. They can be found in Chapters 5 and 6.

7.1.1 Ethernet Switches

Ethernet LAN switches can be obtained as fixed configuration or modular boxes and moreover increasingly as plug-in modules in hub systems. The earliest manufacturer was Kalpana (now Cisco) at a time (approx. 1991) when the market knew very little about how to start using LAN switching. Fore Alantec is also long established in the LAN switching market.

The key functioning elements of an Ethernet switch are as follows:

- address tables
- port-specific packet forwarding
- default packet forwarding
- filter setting
- support of redundant link configuration

Address Tables

An Ethernet LAN switch constructs port-related MAC address tables on a self-learning basis, where a switch learns all systems attached to a port via their source address. Depending upon the hardware, the addresses are stored in one or more tables. The possible number of addresses may be limited per port, e.g., to 1 (Grand Junction), 64 (UB Networks), 1024 (Bay Networks), or per device [e.g., 16000 (3Com/Chipcom)]. Please note here that this restriction applies also to what is known as the backbone port of a LAN switch, which connects the LAN switch with the rest of its site network! Basically, the address restriction was often proposed in order to save memory space and address administration overhead to be able to produce the product cheaply. In former times, bridges also went through the same childhood illness.

If the address table is too small, all active addresses cannot be entered. All packets with destination addresses which are not entered in the table, are then forwarded like multicasts, to all ports. It is easy to see that considerable overhead can arise in the entire network in this way. There are also switches, that forward unknown unicast addresses only to the backbone, therefore take care! LAN switches with more product maturity lift the address restriction: the manufacturers have recognized that LAN switches are no longer used only in the low-level workgroup sector.

Port-Related Packet Forwarding

A switch which has all ports configured with standard CSMA/CD 10 Mbps is considered as entry point. If a packet arrives at a port, the destination address is interpreted. If the associated station is attached to the same port, the processing is terminated, and the buffered packet is discarded. If the station is attached to a different port, the packet is forwarded to that port or to the LAN attached at that point. It is not forwarded to all other ports. Because of the high processing capacity of the internal switch busses and ASICs, communication can be performed in parallel for many port pairs. Figure 7.1 shows an example of this: the switch has learned of one attached station at each of its ports 1, 2, 4, 6, 7, and 8. Ports 6 to 8 are server ports, ports 1, 2, and 4 are workstation ports for "Power Users." Port 5 attaches a segment with three workstations. Port 3 is still unoccupied. The following connections for example, can be served via the switch in parallel, i.e., independently, of one another: Hugo talks peer-to-peer with Otto, Eva talks with Kirk, Leo talks with Spocky. The port pairs are disjunct, and each peer communication can utilize 10 Mbps capacity. If communication takes place from two ports simultaneously with another port, the total throughput is once more restricted to simple LAN capacity: communication between Hugo, Otto, and Galaxy can never amount to more than 10 Mbps total capacity. The same also applies to parallel communication between Ari, Uri, Leo, and Kirk, or if Ari talks to Kirk and in parallel, Uri with Spocky.

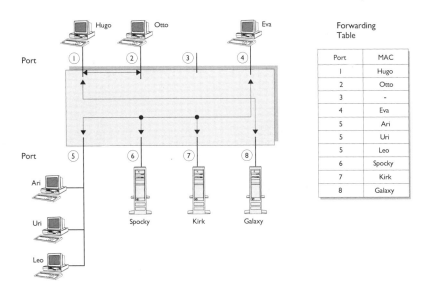

Figure 7.1: Parallel packet forwarding via a LAN switch

Default Packet Forwarding

Until now we have dealt with packet processing for simple unicasts. What does a LAN switch do with broadcasts and multicasts? Since it has not learned them as the source address of a station, it forwards these packets to all ports. In the case of networks with broadcast/multicast intensive protocols such as LAT, LAVC, HP-Cluster, NetBIOS, and SAP, the resulting load can very quickly lead to losses in performance, since the broadcast load takes up capacity at each port, which is then no longer available for the specific unicast traffic.

This must be taken into consideration particularly when using LAN switches with higher port concentration (e.g. 128): each broadcast/multicast that arises at one port is forwarded to all other 127 ports. Consider, in contrast, the following example:

A multiport bridge connects 10 segments, which each generate 100 minimal packets (512 bits) per second, i.e., approximately 50 kbps (0.5% of the Ethernet capacity), as broadcasts. This means a broadcast/multicast load on all ports of the following:

10 * 50 kbps = 500 kbps, i.e., 5% of the LAN capacity (10 Mbps)

95% of the LAN capacity is available for unicast data traffic. In the case of PC and workstation traffic with long packets, up to 80% of the capacity of Ethernet may be exploited and the remaining user data capacity is therefore

9.5 Mbps * 0.8 = 7.6 Mbps

for each LAN segment. If the calculation is reduced to 70% of the maximum attainable throughput based on the current small broadcast packets, there remains

9.5 Mbps * 0.7 = 6.7 Mbps

available for each LAN segment. A LAN switch with 100 ports, to which only half, i.e. 0.25% of broadcasts are attached, generates on all ports a broadcast/multicast load of

128 * 25 kbps = 3200 kbps, [or 32% of the LAN capacity (10 Mbps)]

Since these are small packets, the collision limit for Ethernet has almost already been reached in this example, and there is hardly any real capacity left for unicast traffic! In order to tackle this problem, LAN switch manufacturers have developed functions to divide the ports into what are known as virtual LANs. These are described in greater detail in Chapter 12.

Filter Definition

Filter definition in LAN switches functions very similarly to those of bridges and therefore filter setting does not need to be discussed in detail. In particular, it is used for the reduction of the default forwarding described earlier.

Filter setting obviously functions only in switches, which buffer a packet up to a length, in which the filter bytes can be checked: in order to implement a type filter effectively, a packet must be checked, i.e., buffered, up to byte 14 or with SNAP up to byte 22. For filters on higher protocols, the buffering must contain even more bytes. Complex filter setting is therefore possible only with Store & Forward Switches and leads to a longer processing time. Only filters on destination MAC addresses are also possible for Cut Through Switches (see section 7.2).

Redundancy Configurations

For larger network configurations, it is necessary when using several LAN switches in a backbone configuration to construct redundant connections, since a switch failure would be at least as fatal as a bridge failure. For corresponding redundant links, many Ethernet LAN switches support the IEEE 802.1D Spanning Tree algorithm. They can then also be operated redundantly in an internetwork together with normal bridges (take care of the Spanning Tree compatibility of different manufacturers and test thoroughly!).

7.1.2 Token Ring Switches

In contrast to the well established Ethernet switching technology, Token Ring network operators stood outside in the rain longer, as far as greater bandwidth via dedicated LANs was concerned. Token Ring LAN switches are now available on the market in a moderate product range. The first switches were the Elite/1 from SMC and the Speedswitch 100 from Centillion (now Bay Networks). Other manufacturers include Cisco/IBM/Madge (which have formed a development trio for Token Ring switches), 3Com, Nashoba (Cabletron partner), NetEdge, NetVantage, and Xylan (as OEM of NSC and IBM). The initial price per port for Token Ring switches was three times as high as for Ethernet switches. It was always rather more expensive to have "blue" taste.

Token Ring switches are available as fixed configuration boxes or modular chassis devices, similar to Ethernet switches with high speed backbone connections such as FDDI or ATM. Token Ring switch modules for hub systems were rarely available at the time of editing this book.

The key function elements of a Token Ring switch are:

- address tables

- token process

- source routing

- port-related packet forwarding

- default packet forwarding

- filter setting

- redundant link support

Address Tables

In contrast to Token Ring bridges, some Token Ring switches operate with address tables in the same way as Ethernet switches (e.g., Centillion/Bay Networks: 10,000 addresses per device). This process is also called "transparent" mode (similar to transparent bridging). Obviously, this mechanism was considered by a series of manufacturers as more efficient and cost-effective than source routing even for Token Ring environments. The switches use only the Token Ring media access process and the Token Ring frame format, both according to IEEE 802.5. The port-related and default packet forwarding function as they do in Ethernet switches. It should be noted, however, that Token Ring switches, which run purely in transparent mode, are incompatible with existing Token Ring installations. On the other hand, the maximum cascade of 7 hops no longer applies: the transition from one switch segment to another switch segment is no longer considered a hop. For segments which operate with source routing, the transition is transparent and not considered a hop.

Token Method

If the Token Ring switch operates according to the Token Ring standard IEEE 802.5, there must always be a wait at the output port for a free token, and consequently, buffer space must be provided. The more stations it is intended to attach in a specific operative network at one switch port, greater attention must be paid to sufficient buffer space in the product to be used, since the receipt of a free token takes longer if more stations are active on the ring.

In the case of dedicated attached end systems (end system per port), Full Duplex Token Ring (FDT) is a further topic for switch ports, however there is only an IEEE working group here, and (as of September 1996) there is no standard specification. Since 1996, an IEEE working group has started to work out an FDI specification under IEEE 802.5, IBM supports FDT for the LANstreamer, even if the standard is still not completely specified. A Full Duplex Token Ring process has parallel 16 Mbps transmission and reception capacities. For 4 Mbps, the process is not implemented, since the 16 Mbps standard already provides more capacity here. The Token Ring card in the attached end system must be FDT-compatible to the attached switch. FDT "bends" the token process, such that there is no more token in fact: a circulating token can only be occupied by only one single transmitting station, and not by two (transmitter-transmitter and receiver-transmitter)! Since only one station is attached to the switch port, there may not be any concurrent access to this port. The token therefore has actually become superfluous (fervent Ethernet advocates have been of this opinion for a long time).

Source Routing

Some Token Ring switches forward packets using the information in the RIF (Routing Information Field). The packet must be buffered intermediately at least until this field is received (18 to 30 bytes), as the result of which the latency period is increased. Each switch port must contain a clear ring number (segment number), and the restriction to seven hops, which means a maximum of seven cascaded switch ports, applies as in Token Ring bridges. IBM and Madge prefer the pure source routing solution.

In the case of source routing switches, there can be a considerable reduction in the explorer packets (route discovery) in the network if the switch stores route information in its cache memory. If the switch sees a routing information field in a packet which is waiting at any switch port, it notes this route and maps it to the MAC address. The MAC address is entered in the frame as the destination address. If the switch has to process a route discovery with this destination MAC address, it forwards the route discovery broadcast only in the direction of the learned route and not to all ports. This leads to a clear increase in efficiency particularly in the case of the high port concentration, which is typical for LAN switches. It also leads to poorer utilization of alternative paths, however, since these alternatives are no longer discovered by the route discovery transmitted explicitly to a port. RIF caching is currently supported only by Centillion/Bay Networks.

For doubters from the SNA world: Have you configured more than one front-end processor with the same MAC address for backup purposes and attached them to different rings? The Token Ring switch functions correctly here also, since it forwards packets with different entered routes to different ports if necessary.

Similar issues apply to NetBIOS broadcasts: NetBIOS name caching and therefore filtering on a higher protocol layer are supported by, for example, Centillion, Madge (and therefore also Cisco), and NetVantage.

Packet Forwarding, Filter Definition

The port-related and default packet forwarding functions as in Token Ring bridges. The same applies to filter definition. These points do not need to be discussed further.

Combination of Transparent Mode and Source Routing

In the case of the key question of forwarding via address tables, as in transparent bridging or via source routing, Token Ring switches behave as hybrids: several ports are combined to form a "virtual" Token Ring and given the same ring number. Within the "virtual rings," processing is performed via an address table, which connects the virtual rings to one another via source routing. (Centillion Speed Switch 100, Xylan Omniswitch, and the 3Com Lanplex 6000). An individual port can be run in transparent mode, in SRT mode, or in source routing mode. Care is required when configuring, however: a port that is configured in transparent mode no longer performs source routing correctly. In the case of network nodes and redundant circuits, which operate with source routing, which applies to SNA devices generally, problems can therefore arise.

Figure 7.2 shows a configuration example: an individual Token Ring segment may include a maximum of 260 stations according to the standard as before, and use its own token. In theory, a multiple of 260 stations can be attached to a virtual ring. Whether such a configuration still makes sense in terms of load and security is questionable, however.

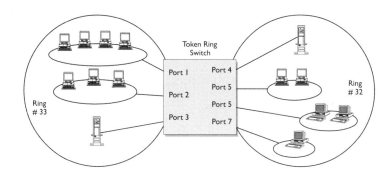

Figure 7.2: Mixed operation with source routing and transparent mode

As a rule of thumb, it can be established that transparent mode is the more suitable process for minigroups (workgroups) and source routing for backbone connections.

Redundant Designs

Token Ring switches, which are cascaded redundantly, operate with source routing. Switches which operate purely in transparent mode would have to support Spanning Tree instead. I am not aware of any Token Ring switch that exhibits such a function, however.

7.1.3 Layer 3 Switches: Routing Extensions

In relation to the formation of virtual LANs (see Chapter 12), LAN switches with extended routing functionality have become established in the market. They are termed Layer 3 switches in the example below. Anyone not yet acquainted with the basic principles of routing should skip this section and read Chapters 8 and 9 first.

For some manufacturers the first step in the direction of the Layer 3 switch is the implementation of IP fragmentation. Packets that are too long for an output port, are split in to smaller packets, a typical Layer 3 function. This function can be very useful for switches with an FDDI Uplink, and the result is that the maximum permitted packet length of 4500 bytes in the FDDI ring can be exploited, instead of 1546 bytes in CSMA/CD.

Layer 3 switches evaluate not only the MAC header for the forwarding of a packet, but also the information of the network layer, in particular, the network addresses. Using this method, a subnetwork can, on the one hand, be spread over several ports/LAN segments and, on the other hand, one port can be configured with dIfferent logical subnetwork addresses, as is shown in Figure 7.3. These are ideal prerequisites for complete movement flexibility without enforced configuration changes in end systems. If two stations belong to the same subnetwork, the forwarding is performed according to bridging technology/LAN switching, but if two stations belong to different subnetworks, broadcasts are suppressed and packets routed according to the switch tables. These are more comprehensive than conventional routers, however, since the same subnetwork no longer can be configured only at one port. Rather a subnetwork can be configured at many ports, even across more than one switch.

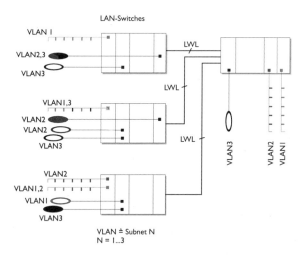

Figure 7.3: Formation of logical subnetworks with Layer 3 switches

A Layer 3 switch therefore evaluates not only the network part of the destination address but also the host part. After this, it checks the port to which this address is attached and forwards the packet accordingly, either to a normal LAN port or at a high speed backbone port to the next switch. Not all Layer 3 switches support several subnetworks per port, some support only one subnetwork per port (Newbridge), and as a result, the flexibility is clearly restricted. Whether a Layer 3 switch can still be termed a LAN switch in the strict sense can be argued without success long into the night.

The operation of Layer 3 switches is dealt with in greater detail in Chapter 12, since the necessary details of routing processes should be understood by the reader by Chapter 12.

7.2   Switch Types and Architecture Concepts

What is switching? The underlying principle stems from the ancient switching technology of analog telephony: Each input can be switched **simultaneously** to any output, the connection is "switched through" for a limited period. A switching matrix is used for switching through, also called "switching fabric" in modern internetworking technology. As in a telephone conversation, a sender—receiver address pair is connected together for the duration of the communication connection after determining the MAC addresses (telephone numbers), and when the communication is finished, they are separated once more. The principle of a switching matrix is demonstrated in Figure 7.4. In the case of older telephone switching systems, the switching matrix consisted of hundreds of clicking relays; in the case of modern LAN switches, the hardware has shrunk to a few ASICs. The fast processing technology means very short delay times for an individual packet in the switch. A matrix switch is not always physically present in the hardware. There are also concepts with a central memory and high capacity backplane which simulate the operation of a matrix switch.

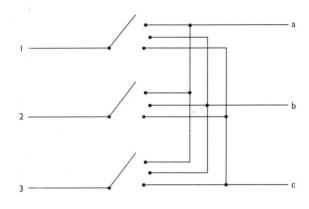

Source - Datacom

Figure 7.4: Switching matrix principle for LAN switching

The development of an ASIC for LAN switching required not inconsiderable expense: individual ASICs sometimes cost 150 person years to develop. The use of ASIC technology has several advantages, that lead to expectations of a return on investment:

- The packet processing is "cast in the hardware" and runs considerably faster. As a result of this, a new higher performance generation of components has arisen.

- An ASIC is specially developed and optimized for the relevant packet processing.

- There is significantly more functionality integrated into a single chip.

- By reducing discrete hardware components and therefore saving on connection logic, the hardware costs fall and at the same time, the MTBF time of the entire system increases.

LAN switches can be roughly divided into two categories: Cut Through switches, and Store & Forward switches. The switching matrix principle in the form of a hardware matrix is used in particular in hardware switches, which operate in Cut Through mode. In Store & Forward switches with a central CPU, a broadband backplane simulates the switching matrix.

Cut Through Switches (CT)

As the name suggests, Cut Through switches (CT) are designed for extremely fast throughput with short latency periods. They buffer an arriving packet until the MAC destination address is received, and after evaluating the destination address according to the address table, forward it as quickly as possible to the output port. Collision prevention, CRC error detection, and the use of other filter mechanisms are no longer possible. The processing time is reduced to a minimum, however. For optimal support of CT technology, two architectures have been developed: a hardware matrix switch (cross-bar) or a cell backplane. Both architectures use ASICs for implementing the switching logic.

Architectures with **matrix switching**, can be found, for example, at Cisco/Kalpana or Madge/Lannet. As soon as a matrix switch decodes the destination address and has allocated the relevant output port, it switches the input port through to the output port and forwards the remainder of the packet, as in a simple repeater function. If the output port is already occupied because another input port is switched through to the output port, the packet is parked in the input buffer of the receiver port as long as the switch has free buffer space. Generally, if no output buffers are available, the switching relay is performed from the input buffer. If there is no more buffer space available, the packet is discarded and must be repeated by the sending station. The principle of a matrix switch architecture is shown in Figure 7.5.

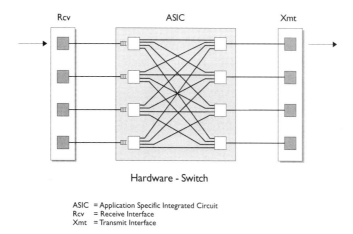

Hardware - Switch

ASIC = Application Specific Integrated Circuit
Rcv = Receive Interface
Xmt = Transmit Interface

Figure 7.5: Matrix switch

The matrix architecture is well suited to unicast traffic, but it can also lead to blockages. Consider the example in Figure 7.1. If workstation Hugo sends a data packet (e.g., 1024 bytes) to server Kirk, the output port 7 is blocked until the packet has been sent completely by Hugo. If workstation Leo sends an acknowledgement (minimum packet) to Kirk during this period, it remains in the input buffer of port 5, until port 7 is free again (clear to send). If only one input queue and no multiple input queue is implemented and the station Ari, which is also attached to port 5, sends a packet to Spocky in this period, the input buffer is possibly blocked in this way. This means that communication between port 5 and port 6 is blocked, although port 6 is not occupied!

The architecture has problems with broadcasts/multicasts: since only one connection is switched through between two ports and there is no central accessible packet buffer available, the forwarding of a broadcast to all ports by means of successive switching of the input port to all other ports is performed serially. In the case of an architecture with several ASICs, which are connected via parallel links, the switching can be performed in parallel, but the packet is still always explicitly copied and forwarded through the switch several times. The overhead becomes larger if the port concentration of the switch is higher. In the case of high broadcast/multicast overhead, performance losses may occur. If the switch has only very small buffers, this can lead to relevant, remarkable performance deterioration. Tests on switch architecture, which were performed in 1994 by IBM at the Zurich laboratory, showed that matrix switches with single input buffers could already reach their throughput limit with a 58% load.

Cell backplanes create the illusion of a matrix switch through a high capacity backplane which can process the input ports in the same time as a matrix circuit (see Figure 7.6). The backplane capacity is structured so that it is larger than the total capacity of all switch ports. It can then work in time division multiplex mode (TDM).

backplane capacity ≥ total port capacity + necessary TDM overhead

In this way, blocking of the input ports is avoided. Packet buffering is performed via output buffers. For cell backplane architectures, the term "self-routing" is sometimes used. There are architectures with fixed buffers per port or with a joint central buffer. The best results in the IBM investigation detailed above were achieved with separate output buffers per port. The individual switch modules or switch ports are attached to the cell bus. As soon as a packet arrives, it is segmented into cells, provided with a header which specifies the output port, forwarded via the bus to the output port or to the central packet buffer, reassembled here and buffered until the output port is free.

By dividing into small cells of a fixed size, packets that are waiting at different input ports can be processed almost in parallel (as different tasks by a CPU in the round robin process): each input port sends one cell in the TDM process to the bus. As a result, a long packet is no longer blocking the bus disproportionately, and all waiting packets are transmitted "practically" in parallel via successive cells. The cells of a complete LAN packet arrive at the output port in the same sequence in which they were transmitted via the bus and can be reassembled again in an ordered fashion to form the original LAN packet.

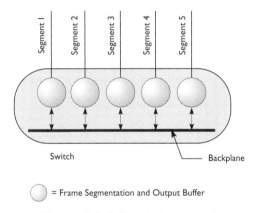

Figure 7.6 Cell backplane switch

The latency period in a CT switch is relatively constant given normal load, since the forwarding is performed independently of the packet length and amounts to around 10 to 30 µs. In the high load scenario, the processing time depends on the buffer design: if input buffers and/or output buffers that can accept many packets are available, the packet received last must wait until all previous packets have been processed. The latency period therefore does not always meet the minimum value of 10 to 30 µs even with CT switches.

Store & Forward Switches (SF)

Store & Forward switches (SF) buffer the packet received first (as also in a bridge) and can then apply fault detection and other packet processing procedure to the frames, for example filter functions, (see Figure 7.7). One reason that they work faster than many established multiport bridges is the use of backplanes with high capacity and ASIC technology for the implementation of switching logic. It is disputed whether SF switches are in fact "genuine" LAN switches or merely modified multiport bridges. The fact is that these products are marketed and sold as LAN switches.

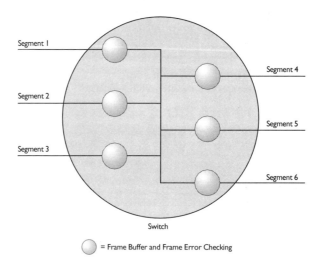

Figure 7.7: Store & Forward Switch

The considerable effect of packet buffering on the latency period was described for a Token Ring minimum packet in Chapter 7. The following calculation applies for Ethernet: in the case of a transmission capacity of 10 Mbps, 10 bits are sent/received in one µs (i.e., 1.25 bytes). The following results are achieved for the buffering of a minimum or maximum packet:

$$\frac{64 \text{ byte}}{1.25 \text{ byte} / \text{µs}} = 51.2 \text{ µs}$$

$$\frac{1500 \text{ byte}}{1.25 \text{ byte} / \text{µs}} = 1200 \text{ µs} = 1.2 \text{ msec}$$

Differences in manufacturer data also result here from the method of measurement: in the case of CT switches, the delay is generally measured between
the receipt and transmission of the first bit of a frame. In the case of SF switches, the delay must correctly be measured between the receipt of the last and
transmission of the first bit. If, however, measurements are made for receipt
and transmission of the first bit for a minimum packet, the resulting latency
period may never be less than 51.2 µs! The same also applies to bridges and
routers. Measurements are actually often taken here for receipt and transmission of the first bit. Considering the receipt and dispatch time of 2.4 µs overall for a long frame, the delay time of even 120 µs (with high load) is no longer
significant in a single SF LAN switch. Under certain circumstances, there is a
receipt delay of 1.2 µs in a super-fast LAN–ATM converter. This also buffers
the packet entirely before sending it on to the ATM backbone or to an attached
LAN segment.

If it is intended to switch between different MAC processes (Ethernet,
Token Ring, FDDI, ATM) or different speeds, only SF technology can be used,
Cut Through cannot perform a packet conversion (translation) and cannot
adapt different transmission rates from one process to another. If there is
reception at 10 Mbps and transmission at 100 Mbps, transmission gaps would
occur in CT mode since the packet is not received as fast as it has to be transmitted. In the case of a conversion from 100 to 10 Mbps, CT could be used.
This would have the result that the 100 Mbps port in the transmission direction is operating differently from the reception direction and is not recommended in practice.

Similar to the contrast of source routing to transparent mode, CT switches
have established themselves in the sector of microsegmenting (workgroups)
and SF switches in the backbone sector.

The Compromise: Mixed Forms

Some indecisive manufacturers have developed mixed processes under the slogan "partial buffering." Here, a packet is buffered for example, up to and
including the type field, in order to be able to apply corresponding filter functions to the MAC destination and source address or the protocol type (digital
gigaswitch). Alternatively, the first 64 bytes are buffered, evaluated, and
checked in order to suppress any errors in minimum packets, particularly
to suppress all collisions.

Token Ring Peculiarities

Token Ring switches sometimes continue to use an architecture with a central CPU and are strongly reminiscent in this case of Token Ring multiport bridges (IBM, Madge, and 3Com use one CPU per port). The question: "Central CPU or ASIC?" was already discussed exhaustively by Ethernet switch manufacturers and should not be resurrected here. Existing switch architectures with a CPU can be traced back to the fact that the temptation was too great to use the existing Token Ring chipsets and launch the product quickly on the market.

Token Ring switches have problems with the Cut Through mode: normally, there must always be a transmission buffer on the switch output, since it is necessary to wait here for the next free token and the packet must be repeated if necessary, if the AC bits are not set. A packet to be sent must be buffered at least until the free token is received and transmitted as an occupied token at the start of the packet. Given that (a) no station is sending that is at least 16 bit periods (at 4 Mbps, 4 µs) plus one bit period per attached station, and (b) there are many stations attached to the ring and sending, the waiting time increases into the millisecond range. This problem can be reduced if the LAN switch is given preference over normal stations by utilizing the option of higher Token Ring priority, (an option that currently is little used by manufacturers). This option is provided for in the 802.5 standard. Centillion (Bay Networks), 3Com, IBM, and Madge are working in this direction.

The token technology can then be suppressed only if an individual device is attached to this port. In that case, the process no longer operates in accordance with the IEEE 802.5 standard, as was discussed in Chapter 7.

If there is a switch from 4 to 16 Mbps, the packet must be buffered completely in any case, otherwise it could be transmitted on the faster output only with pauses, i.e., gaps. If there is a switch from 16 to 4 Mbps, input and output buffering must likewise be possible, since it is not possible to send as quickly as to receive.

For the reasons given, the majority of Token Ring switches are SF switches. The latency period problem in Token Ring is more serious than in Ethernet, however, since the maximum packet length is 4000 or 16000 bytes (Ethernet: 1512 byte). Buffering of a frame of 4000 bytes requires 2 msec at 16 Mbps capacity.

Madge and IBM are pursuing an ASIC based CT approach. 3Com is now shipping both a SF and a ASIC solution. Interestingly, IBM and Cisco/Madge are working on a CT technique with additional error checking (slightly delayed). It is termed Adaptive Cut Through: while the packet passes through the switch "on the fly," the complete Token Ring MAC check is performed. In this way, error packets can be discovered (not stopped!). If too many error packets occur, the corresponding port is switched to SF mode (mostly the complete module with all ports).

7.3 Switch Configuration

To summarize, LAN switches enable all essential types of attachment, which can be found in hub systems for end systems and segments. In comparison to bridges, there are essentially more ports concentrated in LAN switches. Magnitudes here are between 30 and 200 ports. The numbers indicate the purpose for which LAN switches are designed: to attach end systems or **small** segments (microsegmenting).

End System Attachment

The individual end systems can be attached for Ethernet via twisted pair with RJ-45 plugs or via DB-9 plugs to a LAN switch. For larger distances, some manufacturers support fibre optic ports with 10BaseFL. Such an attachment makes sense, for example, if the central infrastructure concentration point is not at the NOC for several cross-building subnetworks but the servers should all be located at the NOC for security reasons and for easier support. The first 100BaseTX ports have been available since mid 1995, e.g., for central high performance servers.

In the case of Token Ring switches, there are the known twisted pair possibilities available (RJ-45 or DB-9), and for fibre optic attachment of end systems, support of the IEEE 802.5J standard should be regarded. In the case of dedicated attachment of an individual terminal station to one port, the Token Ring can be run in full duplex mode FDT (Full Duplex Token Ring, proprietary, still no standard!).

Segment Attachment

Ethernet LAN switches support the attachment of segments via AUI, BNC, 10BaseFL, and in some cases, via 10BaseFB. In the case of the 10BaseFL attachment, the repeater rule must be observed (maximum 4 repeaters). Unfortunately, 10BaseFB is offered only by a few switch manufacturers and mostly only by hub manufacturers whose hub systems support 10BaseFB (e.g., Chipcom/Galactica, (3Com), Madge/Lannet). Direct attachment of a segment to the switch port saves installing a central hub system to connect the switch ports and segments or end systems. In the case of multiport bridges, such a hub is also required, since a bridge itself must be attached to a segment like an end system. Figure 7.8 shows the bridge connection in comparison to the LAN switch connection. A segment can also be attached via twisted pair if the RJ-45 connection of the LAN switch is made to a hub rather than to an end system. Token Ring segments are attached via twisted pair or fiber optic. The fibre optic attachment of segments is always proprietary and at best "IBM 8230 compatible," there is no IEEE 802.5 supplement for this.

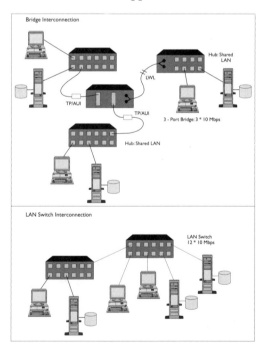

Figure 7.8: Interconnection via a multiport bridge in comparison to the LAN switch

An example shows different attachment possibilities for an Ethernet LAN switch in Figure 7.9 two local individual stations and a local server are attached via twisted pair and RJ-45 plugs. A distant server is attached via 10BaseFL. A distant hub system is connected via 10BaseFB and a local segment via BNC.

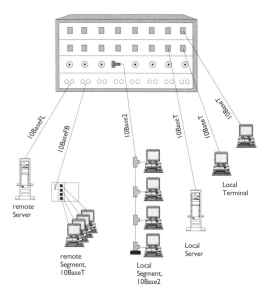

Figure 7.9: End System attachment when using LAN switches

Cascading, Uplinks

In order to connect LAN switches to each other, also called **cascading**, some manufacturers use the FDDI standard (e.g., Fore/Alantec, Chipcom, Cisco, 3Com), some ATM (e.g., Cisco, Digital, 3Com, NetEdge, Bay Networks/Centillion), some use 100BaseX (e.g., Bay Networks, Cisco), some use FDE (no standard!) and some use totally proprietary media access (Bay Networks, Cisco/Kalpana, Madge/Lannet, SMC, Retix). Even standard Ethernet can be found.

Connection via standard media access has the advantage that devices from different manufacturers can be connected together in a LAN switch configuration. This functions for FDDI with translation technology and for ATM, if the LAN emulation standard is implemented in the same version. In the case of proprietary cascading or encapsulation technology, the connection of different manufacturer types is not possible. On the other hand, the connection offers higher capacity, where applicable (Retix: 175 Mbps, Kalpana/Cisco: 280 Mbps). Some switch cascades are shown in Figure 7.10.

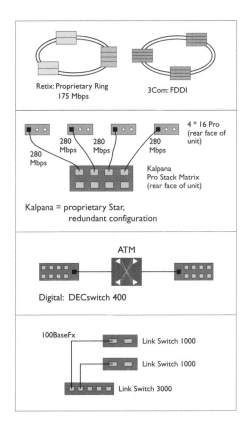

Figure 7.10 Switch cascades

The attachment of LAN switches to high speed backbones such as FDDI or ATM is often termed an **uplink**. FDDI uplinks provide a translation or encapsulation bridge function. ATM uplinks attach the conventional LAN world to an ATM switch or ATM backbone with several ATM switches. In this case, the LAN switch must achieve LAN-ATM conversion, and hopefully, LAN emulation (see Chapter 11). ATM uplinks can be found in the following products:

Ethercell/Bay Networks, Speed Switch/Centillion/Bay Networks, Catalyst/ Cisco, DEC-switch 100/Digital, Linkswitch 2000/3Com, ATM Connect/ NetEdge, to name a few.

At this point, it must be noted once more that when using different LAN accesses and speeds, Store & Forward technology must always be used. This causes a high latency period, particularly for long packets. Caution must always be exercised when dealing with "wire speed throughput data" from the manufacturers with regard to backbone attachments.

7.4   Areas of Application: Possibilities and Restrictions

This chapter handles aspects of practical network operation when using LAN switches. It describes various possibilities for using LAN switches efficiently in data networks, in order to tune the network. At the same time, it shows some of the problems and risks, which must be avoided when using LAN switches wherever possible.

7.4.1 Bandwidth Gain and Total Capacity

Bandwidth gain through the use of LAN switches can be achieved via various configurations.

Scenario 1

The advertising department of UBD (United Barbie Dolls) is so successful that it develops into a profit center. The departmental manager, Bangermann-Uss, proceeds to establish a further subsidiary UBM (United Business Marketing Ltd). This company provides its advertising and PR knowledge also to other enterprises in the leisure industry, particularly in the sport and DIY market. These of course are not competitors of UBD or Stouberg Ltd.

The newly-established UBM moves into a newly constructed building on the acquired site, where the loss of parking space is minimized. The text processors and graphics staff use Apple machines (AppleTalk) for DTP which are networked via Ethernet. The other staff use WfW (Windows for Workgroups) and MS-Mail. There is no central data storage, instead there is distributed access to local files in the workplace computers. Since projects are often handled by a single text processor or graphics person, the network load is so low that no further structuring seems to be required. Thirty of the 50 staff are networked to one another via stackable hubs. The host connection is made for all staff via a 3270 emulation on Ethernet, which is converted to Token Ring via a gateway PC in building 1.

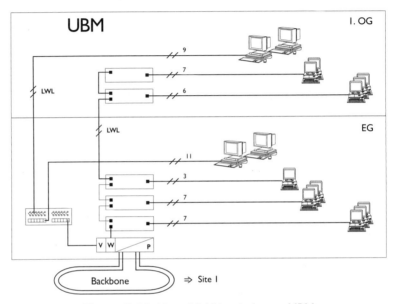

Figure 7.11: Use of LAN switches at UBM

UBM is dealing with the production of video sequences on DIY application possibilities for certain tools. The videos are intended to be produced together with written explanations and instructions on CD. Twenty workstations are operating on this in a cluster. They are attached to an Ethernet segment in the first configuration and therefore have 10 Mbps transmission/reception capacity available. Each workstation has local data, which is made accessible via NFS to everyone else. In this way, peer-to-peer traffic arises with equally distributed transmission/reception profiles. The capacity of shared Ethernet is no longer sufficient. If each workstation is attached to a separate LAN switch port, 20/2 * 10 Mbps transmission/reception capacity can be achieved, i.e., a total capacity of 100 Mbps. The workstations on the 1st floor receive an LWL attachment with 10BaseFL (to reach the distance requirement) and the workstations on the ground floor receive a TP attachment. The multiport bridge between the advertising center and the backbone is supplemented with an Ethernet interface for access to the resources of the general network and attached to the LAN switch. The configuration for the two story "advertising center" is shown in Figure 7.11.

Incidentally, the claim that a LAN switch can put through 200 Mbps on 20 ports which are configured with 10 Mbps standard CSMA/CD, is simply technical nonsense (each input packet is at the same time an output packet on a different switch port), or the manufacturer has calculated each packet twice, once when arriving at the switch and once when leaving the switch.

Scenario 2

After the advertising department has moved out, the UBD export department finally has space to expand, constructs a "foreign branch" business area, and moves its staff from building 2 into building 1. It uses a further server; product planning with 30 staff members receives its own server and moves entirely to building 2, but must still have access to export data. The two servers, which are attached to a separate CSMA/CD backbone each serve 60 users in one building subnetwork. Together, they have a capacity of 10 Mbps availability and also serve all workplace systems of the export staff. Performance bottlenecks arise.

Each server is now attached to its own LAN switch port and the users are split onto two LAN segments, each of which is attached to its own switch port. Each server therefore has 10 Mbps transmission/reception capacity available and the users of each LAN segment also have 10 Mbps transmission/reception capacity. The total transmission/reception capacity has therefore been increased by a factor of 2. The broadcast load must be subtracted from this, which is present at all ports, so that a factor of approx. 1.9 results. The attachment is achieved, for reasons of cost, via a LAN switch module in the existing hub system (see Figure 7.12).

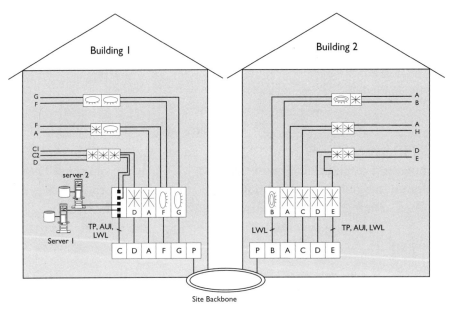

Figure 7.12: Export expansion at UBD

The departments are now divided into subnetworks as follows:

- control, bookkeeping, accounts (A, Ethernet)

- development, design (B, FDDI)

- export (C1, C2, Ethernet)

- product planning (H, Ethernet)

- advertising (D, Ethernet)

- warehousing, logistics (E, Ethernet)

- sales, orders (F, Token Ring)

- board, business management, associated staff (G, Token Ring)

Scenario 3

An individual server serves 120 users which are attached to two different physical subnetworks. If the server receives a 100 Mbps adapter and is attached to a LAN switch port which is configured at 100 Mbps, it can process 20 Mbps without a problem, which may occur as the total capacity of the two attached LAN segments. Cut Through technology is no longer possible between server and clients, however. Since CSMA/CD at 100 Mbps was approved by the IEEE as a standard under IEEE 802.3u, there is a sufficiently broad product range of compatible adapters and switch ports available (in any case, the compatibility of adapters and switches for 100 Mbps must be tested thoroughly beforehand!). The same tuning effect can be achieved with established 10 Mbps adapters, if the server is given several adapters. In this case, Cut Through technology can be used on all ports (see Figure 7.13).

The use of Full Duplex Ethernet Adapters (FDE) does not contribute much, since servers mostly transmit considerably more than they receive or vice-versa. They are therefore in a poor position to exploit the duplex functionality.

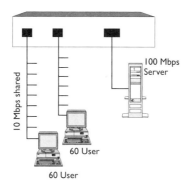

Figure 7.13: Scenario 3

Scenario 4

Four workgroups with a total of 100 PCs are attached to four different subnetworks and are each served by one server per subnetwork. This configuration provides a total capacity of 40 Mbps minus the occasional inter-subnetwork server access. The subnetworks are connected by a multiport bridge for <u>occasional</u> access by a PC client to another server. If the multiport bridge is replaced by a LAN switch, on which each server receives a dedicated port and each workgroup is attached to the LAN switch as a segment, no greater total throughput will be achieved. No client can access his or her server directly (via the same LAN segment with minimum response time!). You will also require, double the number of switch ports in comparison to the multiport bridge. The LAN switch contributes only minimal advantages, such as a lower latency period than the multiport bridge.

If the scenario is modified so that all servers are accessed by all users as central servers (e.g., a program server, a file server, a database server, a mail server), improvements in load distribution are possible via the LAN switch.

Do not allow yourself to be talked into replacing your multiport bridge with a LAN switch for the configuration described in scenario 4. A significant throughput increase results only if each centrally-used server receives greater access capacity (e.g., 100 Mbps), and the clients are divided into more than four segments.

7.4.2 Switch Categories

LAN switches can be divided into different categories. Each category generally demonstrates different functional features with regard to

- maximum number of ports
- range of supported LANs
- total performance
- architecture
- buffer space
- filter functionality

Workgroup Switches

Workgroup switches have a lower number of ports (12 to 14 ports), and all ports support the same LAN type (either Ethernet or Token Ring). The switches have little buffer memory or filter function, they are not modular, and they may operate well with Cut Through technology, since forwarded error packets remain restricted to a subnetwork and are not forwarded onto the backbone. Workgroup switches are available as standalone boxes or hub inserts (e.g., the LattisSwitch 28000 from Bay Networks, the Etherswitch from Cisco/Kalpana, the LANplex 2016, Linkswitch 1200 from 3Com, the Fastswitch from Grand Junction, the NV7500 from NetVantage, the Powerpipe from NetWorth, and the LANbooster from Ornet).

Department Switches

Department switches can be extended in a modular manner with a moderate maximum number of ports (30 to 60 ports) for department servers, "Power Users" and/or many attached microsegments of a LAN type (either Ethernet or Token Ring). They require high buffer memory and high capacity ports for attachment to the site backbone and for larger central servers, e.g., 100BaseX (IEEE 802.3u.) or FDDI. Basic filter functions should be present. The switch operates in Store & Forward mode on the high capacity ports used. Modules, whose ports all have the same capacity, can operate within the module with cut through. Examples include the Powerhub from Fore/Alantec, the Galactica from Chipcom, the DECswitch 400 from Digital, the 4-Slot LANplex 6000 from 3Com, the SwitchStack from Retix, and the Elite/1 from SMC.

Campus Switches (Enterprize Switches)

Campus switches can be extended in a modular manner with a high maximum number of ports (50 to 100 ports), sufficient buffer memory at the transition to high capacity ports for backbone or servers, support for the established access processes in one (CSMA/CD, Token Ring, FDDI, ATM), and support of good filter possibilities. The switch must be operated in Store & Forward mode for the high performance ports and filters. Examples include the LANplex 6000 and the Catalyst 5000.

7.4.3 Overload Situations

Overload situations can lead to considerably greater losses of performance when using LAN switches than when using multiport bridges. If a block results at a time of high load, the buffers overflow faster than in conventional bridges, since they are of a smaller size. This leads to increased packet repeats, and in the case of continued high load, to the collapse of the network. If a switch has more ports, there is a greater probability that several datastreams will arrive in parallel at one of these ports and lead to an overload. The switch manufacturers, however, interestingly give no recommendations as to how many network nodes of a particular type (PC, server, workstation) can be attached to a switch port.

When using individual 100BaseX ports for servers, an overload may arise at the 10 Mbps Ethernet ports: if the server transmits at 100 Mbps, the 10 Mbps ports must be capable of buffering bursts, which the server sends to a microsegment (see Figure 7.14). LAN switch ports are intended to be monitored carefully for spontaneous or regular overload situations. Some manufacturers (Madge/Lannet, NetWorth, Ornet, and Cabletron) have implemented flow control mechanisms in the switch, to avoid an overload.

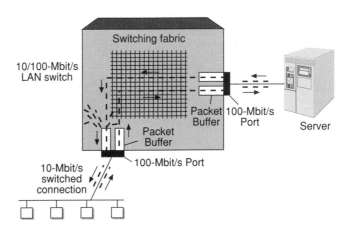

Figure 7.14: Planning errors when using switches

Let us consider the broadcast/multicast problem which is often overlooked when using switches: a multicast, which arrives at a port, is forwarded not only to 20 ports, but under certain circumstances to 40 or 90 ports. This occupies the switch intensively for a while with copy actions. The unicast traffic is reduced to many small segments through microsegmenting. The broadcast/multicast traffic from all microsegments remains in the overall network which is interconnected via LAN switches. In the case of a large number of microsegments (e.g., 90 segments), this leads to a relatively high broadcast/

multicast proportion per microsegment, and in this way considerably reduces the useful capacity for unicast traffic.

In the case of excessive broadcast/multicast overhead, a two-tier structure is recommended in place of a pure LAN switch configuration: LAN switches on a departmental level or workgroup level and router interconnection on the backbone (see Chapter 8). Another alternative is the formation of VLANs (see Chapter 12).

Here are a few rules for avoiding overload situations:

- *Ask resellers and manufacturers for the maximum achievable capacity utilization per port for their switch, if all ports are loaded in parallel.*

- *For "light" users in who require only terminal access to a UNIX host and occasionally mail access: do not attach more than 70 PCs to one switch port.*

- *For power users (graphics, spreadsheets, frequent transfers of large texts, use of OLE host access, access to networked databases, E-mail): do not attach more than 20 PCs or 8 UNIX workstations to one switch port.*

- *For UNIX high performance workstations (simulation, CAD, image data processing): no more than 2 to 3 users per port.*

7.4.4 Management Aspects

In all the examples referred to, it should be recorded, monitored and evaluated whether and how often switch ports reach an overload situation at peak times. If overload situations occur repeatedly, the configuration must be adjusted (modified segmenting, more ports, set ports from 10 to 100 Mbps, etc.).

A question is posed here, which may appear stupid to the naive user at first: How is a switch port monitored? The spontaneous answer is, by monitoring, obviously.

Parallel monitoring of 90 attached microsegments on a campus switch may create some problems, even if a port is free on each microsegment in order to attach an analyzer or probe, for an analyzer can monitor only one switch port (i.e., segment) at a time. Analysis data would have therefore to be transmitted to a central management system 90 times—no small load on the network to which the NMS is attached! You should therefore plan for a separate LAN for your management traffic.

How is a monitor attached if the port is operated as a dedicated port? The port is occupied with the server connection, and the network manager is left holding the analyzer and searching in vain for an attachment option. In this case, there are various options, but to return to the monitoring data:

Y-cable: Instead of a simple attachment cable, a Y cable is attached to the switch port, which connects the attached network nodes, the analyzer and the switch. The method comes from from WAN analysis, the attachment of a Y cable often can be performed so quickly that no session timeouts occur. The disadvantage is that the analysis is restricted to one port.

Minihub, two port repeater: A minihub or two-port repeater can be inserted just as easily as a Y cable. The connection cable between the hub and switch port must be alternated however. Monitoring is restricted to one port.

Monitor ports: Some switches (Fore/Alantec, Cisco, 3Com, Grand Junction, SMC) support a monitor port on which the data traffic can be reflected from any switch port or port pair. In this case, monitoring can be switched using software from one port to another. Despite this, it is more like a nightmare than sensible management to be monitoring 90 ports by constantly switching to and fro. Further developed functionality means several ports can be monitored simultaneously. The danger exists that the monitor port becomes a bottleneck, if it has the same capacity as the monitored ports: the monitor port of the Cisco/Kalpana EPS2015 can monitor all 15 ports. This can reach approx. 100 Mbit/s of communication throughput at times of high load. This would be a hopelessly excessive requirement for the monitor port. Cisco/Kalpana and other manufacturers that support multiple port monitoring recommend that the number of monitored ports is not configured too high, even if it is possible to display all ports of a LAN switch on the monitor port using the management software.

SNMP agent: Some switch manufacturers implement an SNMP agent for the entire switch, the basic values (# packets, # byte, # MAC error packets, collisions, etc.) are collected for all ports together, and these are passed to a management system. The disadvantage of this solution lies in the communication load between the switch and the central management system, and in the low statement quality for the collected data if only the standard MIB II is used. If it is intended to collect more data, a proprietary expanded private MIB is used.

RMON agent: RMON functionality means that considerably more monitoring data can be evaluated per port than with SNMP MIB II. RMON agents are still relatively expensive, however. In addition, the implementation of an RMON agent in the switch must combine and prepare the data before it is sent to the management system, otherwise the same load problem arises between the switch and management system as in conventional probes (see above). If RMON data is preprocessed in the switch, however, a relatively high CPU loading arises, which may lead to losses in performance.

A sensible compromise seems to be what is known as "light monitoring:" normally only the basic data is monitored and collected and in the event of errors, detailed statistics are collected from the defective ports.

A further problem, even when using RMON, lies in the fact that only per port data and no data between communication pairs (conversation data) can be collected. Load relevant network tuning, e.g., positioning servers, cannot be performed: if the statistics say that the server has sent 1000 packets, information to whom it sent the latter on to is also important. If, for example, 100 packets were sent to local clients but 900 packets were sent via two backbones to the other end of the site network, the server should be positioned at the other end of the site network or attached to a central backbone.

7.4.5 Distinction between Alternatives: FDDI, Multiport Bridges

FDDI versus LAN Switching

LAN switches are often considered as an alternative to FDDI backbones because of the price advantage, if it is a matter of constructing client/server networks. The following table is intended to help clarify the various consequences of a LAN switch configuration and of an FDDI configuration.

FDDI	LAN Switches
100 Mbit/s shared capacity	10 Mbit/s per port, 100 Mbit/s for individual ports
Capacity division is not necessarily set as equal for all servers	Capacity—port capacity
Throughput restricted by the throughput capacity of the FDDI—Ethernet bridges or routers used	Throughput restricted by the capacity of the LAN switch
Existing FDDI installations can be used	
Standard—inherent redundancy	SPT—redundancy, proprietary redundancy or **no** redundancy
Large expanse	Expanse limited to maximum cascade
High capacity, if only one or two servers used	High capacity, if more than one adapter can be used per server, which is not supported by all protocols
Subnetworks can be interconnected via routing or bridge functions (Ethernet—FDDI router, translation bridging)	Subnetworks (i.e., VLANs) can be interconnected only via separate routers (i.e.,) greater cascading, danger of bottlenecks
Unpredictable response times because of shared medium	Response times more deterministic if only one device is attached per port
Error detection performed according to specified FDDI standard	No error detection performed in Cut Through LAN switches
Different manufacturers products can be cascaded in one network via the FDDI standard	Cascading is possible only with products from the same manufacturer
Expensive FDDI adapters required	Cost-effective Ethernet adapters possible
Higher costs	Lower costs

Multiport Bridges versus LAN Switches

It is becoming increasingly difficult to draw distinctions between a fast multiport bridge and a LAN switch, particularly if the LAN switch operates in SF mode. Despite this, we shall now attempt such a summary.

LAN Switch	Bridge
Processing time: 20 – 50 µs	Processing time: 90 – 120 µs
Lower buffer capacity per port	Higher buffer capacity per port
Critical as collapsed backbone, only with low network load	Collapsed backbone is possible in small to medium-sized networks
Lower filter functionality	High filter functionality
Segment attachment and end system attachment	Only segment attachment
Higher number of maximum possible ports per device	Lower number of maximum ports per device
Lower price per port	Higher price per port
No error restriction in Cut Through	Full error limitation on MAC layer
Floor sector, workstation clusters: substitute for FDDI	./.
./.	Remote connection via WAN
Virtual LANs, i.e., formation of separate broadcast domains, connection between the VLANs only via routers	./.

7.4.6 Conclusion

Both in the definition of what a LAN switch is and in the recommendations for the use of LAN switches, there are a series of outstanding matters which require further technical development. LAN switches can contribute to network tuning in a series of use scenarios (see section 7.4). The advantages and risks/disadvantages of using LAN switches are summarized below:

Advantages

+ *LAN switches enable a scalable expansion of the network through modular extendibility to up to 100 ports.*

+ *The costs per port are clearly lower than for multiport bridges and in particular multiport routers.*

+ *Any type of mixed configurations can be formed with microsegments and dedicated LANs.*

+ *The latency period is low.*

+ *The configuration expense is considerably lower than for routers.*

+ *LAN switches are well suited to hub plug-in modules.*

+ *Increased movement flexibility can be achieved through the configuration of virtual LANs (see Chapter 12).*

Disadvantages

• *There is no standard for LAN switching.*

• *Cut Through switches do not perform any error correction and cannot therefore be used as backbone switches.*

• *Overload situations must be carefully avoided, since they may lead to the collapse of the network.*

• *There is often no possibility of monitoring all ports adequately via management software and of obtaining statistics and error analysis.*

• *If monitoring is possible, the management cost increases considerably as the result of microsegmenting.*

• *Many manufacturers connect LAN switches via proprietary protocols instead of via ATM or FDDI. The products of different manufacturers cannot therefore be cascaded in one network.*

• *Not all LAN switches support Spanning Tree according to IEEE 802.1D, some manufacturers use their own redundancy algorithm (Bay Networks LattisSwitch 28000). There are therefore no redundant configurations possible with different products in a larger network combination.*

The Question of Price

Since the hardware cost of CT switches is often more expensive than for SF switches, the price per port for these devices is higher than that for SF switches. On the other hand, better performance values can be achieved in good architectures. If the price per megabit/s throughput is calculated, rather than the price per port, the results for individual switch manufacturers alter dramatically.

If operating expenditure is also included in the calculation (switches with lower management functionality generate higher operating costs than switches with good management functionality), the price ratio moves once more in the direction of higher device quality, i.e., higher investment costs.

8 Routers

As regards their historical development, routers predate bridges: WANs were first configured using switching computers which possessed router functionality. Routers or computer systems with implemented routing functionality were also later used in more complex LANs (TCP/IP, DECnet). The routers used at that time (six to ten years ago) were capable only of routing one LAN protocol each. A separate router had to be used for each network protocol (TCP/IP, DECnet, XNS, X.25, etc.). Routers were sometimes termed gateways at this time. (This continues today in some product descriptions and protocol names, e.g., Exterior Gateway Protocol/EGP, Interior Gateway Protocol/IGP.)

With the increasing number of parallel protocols in one LAN and the arrival of MAC layer bridges, these devices lost their appeal. They had lower throughput, were more expensive, and had less flexibility in their application than bridges.

Routers have enjoyed a renaissance in the last two years. This is due to several factors:

- The new generation of routers have a considerably greater throughput rate in comparison to the devices originally used. Because of improved architectures, the throughput rates are comparable to bridges.

- With increasing size and the growing together of the most diverse end systems and network islands, a new category of heterogeneous "networked networks" arose. They are still too complex to configure with ease using bridges.

- The development of multi-protocol routes (see below) made it possible to handle several protocols in one device. This was not possible with the previous generation of routers.

- Router manufacturers extended the capability of their products with additional bridge functionality.

Key Features and Definition

Over the course of time, routers acquired different names: Interface Message Processor (IMP), Intermediate System, Network Relay, through to Gateway. According to the definition, routers provide a connection between two or more subnetworks on the Network Layer (ISO Layer 3) and provide the functions through to the Network Layer (Physical, MAC, LLC, Network). The central function of the Network Layer is to select the route from the transmitting through to the receiving station, which is the establishment, maintenance, and orderly shutdown of an end to end connection of two end systems. Routers therefore continue one step beyond where bridges stop and implement at least Layer 3 of a higher protocol above the LLC layer (IEEE 802.2). Well-known protocols include, for example:

- IP (Internet Protocol), Layer 3 of the TCP/IP family

- IPX (Internetwork Packet eXchange), Layer 3 of NetWare

- NS (Network Services), Layer 3 of DECnet IV

- IDP (Internet Datagram Protocol), Layer 3 of XNS (Xerox Network Systems)

- DDP (Datagram Delivery Protocol), Layer 3 of AppleTalk

- OSI CNLS (Connectionless Network Layer Service, ISO 8473)

- Layer 3 of VINES (IP derivative)

- X.25 as ITU-TS standard for WAN connections

The important aspect here is that Layer 3 is always the same in a router interconnection from the source system through to the destination system; it "runs through." Routing does not mean connecting IP with IPX or IPX with CNLS! Routing means producing a connecting route on the basis of the protocol information from the same Layer 3 passing through (see Figure 8.1).

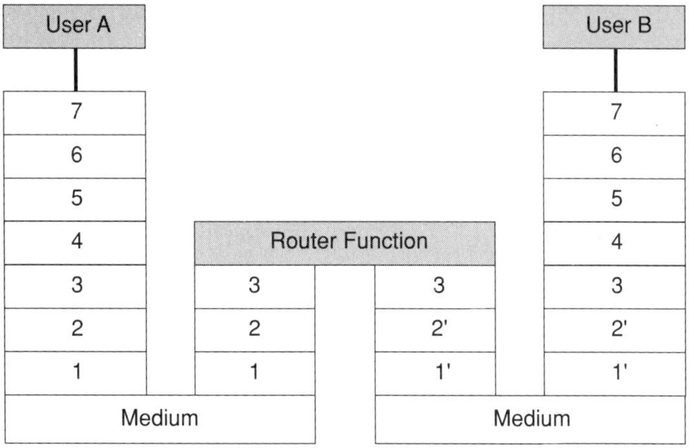

Figure 8.1 OSI Layer 3 - Router connection

Regarding the key features in relation to the extension of restrictions of a simple subnetwork, routers achieve the same as bridges and more:

First: routers are capable of extending the limits of a network with regard to station numbers and physical distance. If a network is split into two subnetworks using a router, each subnetwork can acquire the full number of stations and physical distance in accordance with the defined standard, provided that narrower limits are not set for the number of stations in the framework of the routing protocol used.

Second: routers achieve error limitation on Layers 2 and 3. Both error packets on the Data Link Layer as well as packets with a correct Data Link Layer, but incorrect network layers are not forwarded. The result is that such error packets remain restricted to the subnetwork from which they originated and are not distributed to wreak havoc over the entire network. Routers sometimes generate additional error messages with the reason for the failure to forward. Bridges do not do this, they simply discard the error packet.

Third: routers create a restriction on local traffic to the subnetwork in which it arises, i.e., if a packet is sent to a station in the subnetwork of the sender, the router does not concern itself with this packet.

Fourth: through implementation of Layer 3, routers perform complex route selection functions to optimize the route which a packet takes from the transmitting station to the destination station. This is the most important distinguishing difference from bridges.

Fifth: by using network addresses, routers achieve a logical subdivision of a network into subnetworks. Under certain rare circumstances routers also perform this function within a physical segment. This makes the introduction of address, and therefore subnetwork hierarchies possible in contrast to the flat MAC address world.

Definition: A router is an interconnection element which connects subnetworks on Layer 3 (Network Layer) according to the ISO OSI reference model.

Central key features of routers are the subdivision of a network into logical subnetworks, the performance of complex routing functions to optimize the route a packet takes from the source to the destination station, and for this purpose, the interpretation of network protocols and non-transparency with regard to higher protocols. A router must be able to "speak" all network protocols that are used in a subnetwork if it is intended to connect the subnetwork with other subnetworks that use these protocols.

Each protocol is served by a different router, or, more commonly today, by a different protocol stack in a router. By using network protocols, the router is "transparent" with regard to the lower layers (up to Layer 2). The layers are relatively easy and cleanly interchangeable in technical terms. In this sense, a router behaves as a complement to bridges, which operate transparently for higher protocols but have their difficulties in interconnecting different MAC Layers.

8.1 Router Types

Even if the basic functionality is the same for all routers (interconnection on the Network Layer), there are different versions of these interconnection elements with different particular features. The various types are differentiated below.

8.1.1 Single Protocol Router

The single protocol router is today a low-end product, even if a variety of such devices are in operation (see Figure 8.2). This type of device does not feature highly in purchases of new routers, and it can be said with some justification that the single protocol router has become marginalized. It connects LAN subnetworks on the basis of a single higher protocol and hence its name. The connection may be a LAN-LAN connection or a LAN-WAN connection, mostly via X.25, but sometimes via X.21. An example of a single protocol router is a DECrouter, which connects two or more subnetworks by means of DECnet routing and X.25. The classic example of a single protocol router is an X.25 network node, since routing clearly has its origins more in the WAN sector than in the LAN sector.

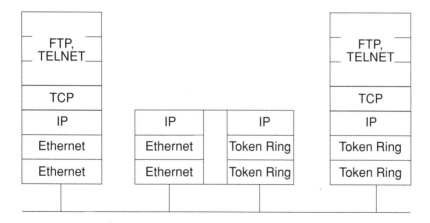

Figure 8.2 Single Protocol Router

8.1.2 Multi-protocol Routers

Multi-protocol routers (MP router: Multiple Protocol Router) have been developed more intensively in recent years. As a result of this development, the use of routers has generated renewed interest given the complexity of today's networks as an alternative to the use of bridges. MP routers are capable of handling several protocols in parallel, in contrast to single protocol routers. Different logical networks are connected to one another (DECnet-DECnet, IPX-IPX, IP-IP, etc.) via different protocol stacks (implementation of several Layer 3 protocols, see Figure 8.3), implemented in one device. In this way, multiple backbones are eliminated (a logical backbone with a single protocol router type for each protocol) and a single type of device is sufficient on the backbone to interconnect all protocol worlds. When receiving a packet, the router establishes which protocol the packet contains via the network address and other information, and processes it further with the corresponding protocol routine for this protocol. The connection of different protocol worlds is also performed in multi-protocol routers in the sense of a LAN-WAN-LAN interconnection (e.g. DECnet - X.25 - DECnet, IP - X.25 - IP) and not between different LAN protocol worlds (DECnet - IP). A gateway is required for this.

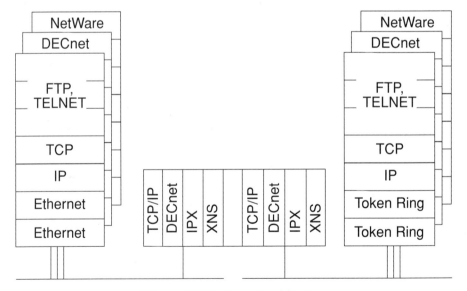

Figure 8.3 Multi-protocol Router

8.1.3 Hybrid Routers, Routers with a Bridging Function

The ultimate multipurpose machine in terms of bridges and routers can be found in the bridge/router as an extended multiple protocol router. All packets that cannot be routed (because the relevant protocol is not implemented in the router or simply cannot be routed) are forwarded in the bridge manner, or not at all. In this way, the device operates in promiscuous mode once more by receiving all packets for further processing (see Figure 8.4).

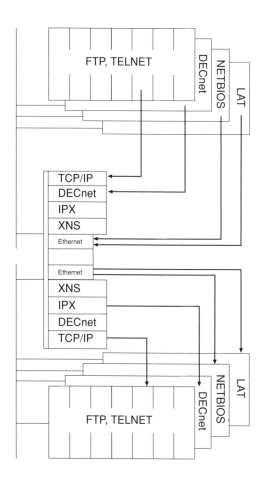

Figure 8.4 Hybrid Routers, Routers with a bridging function

After the control information has been interpreted, a decision is made as to whether the packet is routed or bridged, or discarded from the buffer. Generally, identical LANs are connected according to bridge functionality (Ethernet–Ethernet, Token Ring–Token Ring). One advantage is the "new" protocol independence achieved in the development cycle: all applications can now run "transparently" once more over a bridge/router. This functionality is also clearly reflected in the price, however (bridge: US $6750 to $3375, multi-protocol router US $13,500 up to several $67,500).

Examples of this new development include the multi-protocol routers with additional bridge functionality from ACC, Cisco, 3Com, NSC, Retix, Proteon, Schneider & Koch, and Bay Networks.

8.2 Interconnection on the Network Layer: Router Functioning

An interconnection is possible on the Network Layer if two requirements are present. First: the Network Layer is present as its own layer and accessible from outside via its own addresses. Second: Network addresses are used which can be split into a network part and a host part (end system ID, network node ID).

Only in this way is it possible to form a hierarchy according to logical subnetworks and end systems within these subnetworks. A protocol or protocol stack, that meets these requirements is termed a routable protocol in general technical parlance (e.g., TCP/IP, NetWare/IPX, AppleTalk/DDP, DECnet/ NS, OSI/CONS, XNS/IDP, etc.).

Now to interconnection: a router is not as curious as a bridge and is concerned only with the packets which are addressed directly to it. If a packet arrives at a port, the packet is accepted for processing of the protocol information of its Network Layer. Issues of why, when, and how which packet is forwarded—and if yes, to where—is dealt with below, starting with the description of the service which a router is intended to provide on the Network Layer.

8.2.1 Connection of Terminal Devices: Interface Between Network and User

The general task of routers is to produce an end to end connection between two end systems requiring communication on the Network Layer. By possessing communication capability up to and including Layer 3 of the OSI reference model, routers provide the interface to connect to the lower network layers, the network infrastructure so to speak (see Figure 8.5). Routers make the interface between the subnetwork-dependent (network infrastructure) protocols and the host-dependent (applications) protocols.

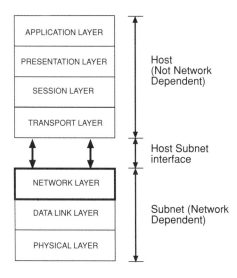

Figure 8.5 Link between network and applications protocols

In order to connect end systems on different subnetworks on the Network Layer, routers must have a series of basic components.

- A process for identifying the stations in relation to the router and vice versa (e.g., ARP).

- An algorithm for "non-local" packets, in order to select the next router to receive the packet (e.g., RIP); the algorithm is termed "routing," after the central function of a router, which is the self-explanatory name for the device.

- A header for information such as the destination address of the end station, lifetime (time stamp), fragmenting, and reassembly (e.g., IP header).

The basic functions here are in line with [ISO02]:

- The formation and maintenance of a routing information database (more simply known as a "routing table") with information on routes and their costs and additional forwarding conditions such as filters.

- Information collection for the maintenance of the routing information database (evaluating messages from neighboring and more distant systems to receive and send updates, to evaluate management information, to measure delays, to interpret routing protocol information).

- Passing on information for the databases of other systems.

- Calculation and maintenance of the necessary routes. This includes in particular, the decision of whether a packet should be forwarded, and if yes, to where.

Terminology

According to ISO OSI terminology, a router is termed an "intermediate system" (IS). An overall network is divided into subnetworks. The service which the router/intermediate system provides is the corresponding subnetwork service for the end systems. A subnetwork or routing domain is a collection of end systems which speak a common language, i.e., use the same Layer 3 protocol. A hop is the passage of a packet through a router/intermediate system on the way from the sending station to the receiving station. A distance of two hops means that two routers are passed through en route from the source to the destination. The OSI terminology draws a distinction between intermediate systems and relay systems. The former can be any routers or hosts with routing intelligence and the latter are purely "connecting elements", i.e., only routers). The ISO has had this perspective on a cascade of possible intermediate systems since 1988 (see [ISO07]). Previously, definitions were made only for neighboring systems.

Distinctions must be drawn between three protocol elements for communication on Layer 3: the routable Layer 3 protocol (e.g., IP). which specifies the packet format and the addressing and the communication between end systems; the ES-IS protocol (e.g., ARP, OSI ES-IS), which regulates communication between end systems and routers, particularly for the connection establishment phase; and the router-router protocol or routing protocol, which runs between routers and enables the dynamic construction of routing tables.

These three elements are not divided into separate protocol modules in every protocol. For example, in NetWare, there are only two modules, IPX (routable protocol and ES-IS protocol) and RIP or NLSP as routing protocol. This distinction often is not made clearly for implemented protocols, since in English both are termed "routing protocols." ES-IS protocols can also be termed "routable protocols" and IS-IS protocols "router protocols" in order to clarify the difference. Known router-router protocols include, for example:

- RIP (Routing Information Protocol) and OSPF (Open Shortest Path First) for TCP/IP,

- RIP and NLSP (NetWare Link Services Protocol) for NetWare/IPX

- RIP for XNS/IDP,

- DRP (Digital Routing Protocol) for DECnet/NS,

- IS-IS (Intermediate System - Intermediate System) for OSI/CLNS,

- RTMP (Routing Table Maintenance Protocol) for AppleTalk/DDP.

The interplay between routed protocol (data transport), forwarding decision, routing table (routing information base), and routing update is shown in Figure 8.6.

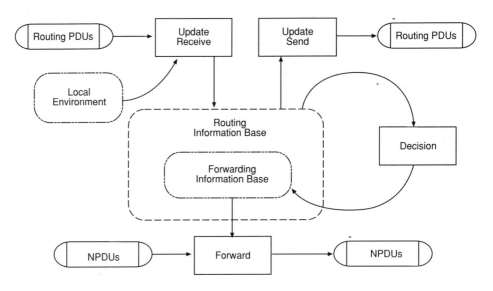

Figure 8.6 Representation scheme of routing functions

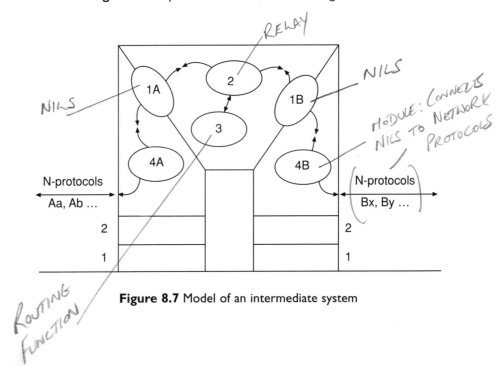

Figure 8.7 Model of an intermediate system

The inner workings of a router can be described according to [ISO01] with the model shown in Figure 8.7. There is a Network Internal Layer Service (NILS) which acts as the interface between the network service (NS) according to the protocol and the relaying and routing functions. The elements 1A and 1B represent the NILS in the Intermediate system. The heart of a router is formed by elements 2 and 3, the relaying and routing function. Element 2 connects the two NILS entities, the routing function provides the algorithm in order to make the connection. Elements 4A and 4b are modules which connect the NILSs with the network protocols supported on both sides. A connection between end stations may naturally be possible via several ISs connected between one another (Interconnected Intermediate Systems), as shown in Figure 8.8.

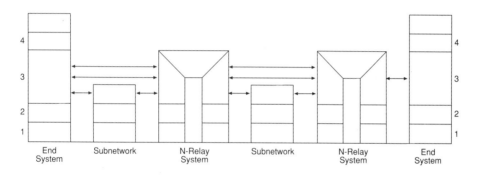

Figure 8.8 Connection via interconnected intermediate systems

The NILS has a range of tasks. A series of service primitives and parameters of the NILS which belong to the network service must be managed.

NC Establishment

A connection on the Network Layer must be established by an IS, with the purpose of transferring user data back and forth between users on both sides of the IS, although one or more subnetworks and ISs are involved.

QOS Selection

Network protocols can sometimes support "Quality of Service" parameters which determine a particular level of quality in establishing the connection for the duration of the connection (OSPF V2, IS-IS, ...). Such parameters include, for example:

- throughput (sender-receiver direction),
- throughput (receiver-sender direction),
- processing time in the IS,
- access protection (authentication required, determining of a fixed route),
- priority.

Data Transfer

Arriving packets (NPDUs) must be forwarded in sequence and transparently for the end user (the ultimate purpose of the entire exercise).

Flow Control

The data rate at which transmission and reception occurs, can be controlled between neighboring ISs (if flow control is supported, e.g., X.25).

Segmentation

Support of segmentation means the option of dividing arriving packets into several packets so that they can be combined together correctly again at the end. Relevant identifiers must be used for this purpose as control information (IP, IPX, OSI).

Expedited Transfer

This is an option for preferential forwarding, i.e., prioritization of particular message types (control information, error messages, etc.).

Confirmation of Receipt

NSDUs received can be confirmed as an option (OSI CONS, e.g., X.25).

Connection Reset

In the case of mutual reception confirmation, the transfer can be repeated at a defined point following an error situation (lost or defective packets), without having to send all packets again.

Connection Shutdown

The shutdown of a connection can be "normal" or due to defects—when errors occur which require shutdown. In the case of a defect connection shutdown or non-forwarding (discarding) of a packet, a control message can be generated with the reason.

Connection-Oriented Mode

A logical fixed connection exists between the ISs. This is established at the start of communication and terminated once more at the end or "dissolved."

Connectionless Mode

No logical connection exists, and no connection establishment and shutdown occurs.

In addition to the elements of the Network Layer, additional elements are handled within the IS and therefore do not occur in end systems.

Addresses

There are calling and called addresses (from ISs), source and destination addresses (from end systems), error addresses, and others. All these addresses are network addresses of the relevant protocol used.

Lifetime

The lifetime parameter specifies the life of a packet. It is reduced accordingly in each IS which is passed through. If the lifetime has expired or would have been exceeded by the next IS, the packet is discarded.

Router Recording

During the transfer, information on the route that the packet is currently taking is entered as control information.

Connection Control

The connection control is achieved by means of the option of ISs exchanging information regarding what is actually happening on the network and with an IS. It is not until the information exchange that collaboration between the different ISs can be achieved in the sense of a successful end to end connection of end systems.

Error Acknowledgement

An IS can send diagnosis reports with regard to connection reset and defect connection shutdown. For example:

- permanent connection shutdown
- temporary connection shutdown
- destination not attainable
- destination address not known
- QoS is temporarily not available to the required quality
- QoS is permanently not available to the required quality
- overload
- source routing error (e.g., IP)
- source routing, unknown address (e.g., IP)
- source routing, specified path unacceptable (e.g., IP)
- source routing is not supported (e.g., IP)
- route recording is not supported
- lifetime expired
- access protection error

This is provided for only in ISs, which operate in a connection-oriented manner.

Accounting Information

Accounting information between ISs is information that relates to the "costs" of a connection (number of ISs to be found between two end systems, duration of the connection, capacity of the lines used, etc.).

8.2.2 Connection on Network Layer: Upward Protocol Dependency

In order to clarify protocol dependency, an example is given from the post routing analogy (see Figure 8.9). The Chinese scientist Wi Tu Sen in Peking sends a research report to his colleague Mu Tu Schaun in Wuhan. He writes the report in Chinese and gives it to his secretary. The secretary places Wi Tu Sen's report in an envelope with the precise address (name, university, street = network address of the end station) of Mu Tu Schaun. After this, the envelope sits in a postal sack in the post room of the university of post office (network). From here, it is forwarded by whatever means (bus, train, carrier pigeon) to its correct destination, Wuhan.

The post bag from Peking finally arrives in the cellar of Wuhan university. It is opened, and a letter to Professor Mu Tu Schaun appears. This is forwarded to a secretary who removes it from the envelope and places the report for Mr. Mu Tu Schaun on his desk. The enthusiastic response from Mr. Mu Tu Schaun to Professor Wi Tu Sen follows the same pattern in the reverse direction.

The routers in the example given, come into action when the post bag is lying in the cellar. It is therefore important that they know the language used, the address convention, and the route from Peking to Wuhan and/or the individual stages and can guarantee the relevant transport.

This may be handled in different countries of the world (different protocol worlds) quite differently. The router therefore must be capable of speaking the "network language." Unfortunately, no two protocol worlds speak a common network language, since together with Layer 3, the higher layers are included at the same time (a Chinese letter does not have an American address) for all currently implemented protocol worlds (AppleTalk, DECnet, NetWare, TCP/IP, XNS, etc.).

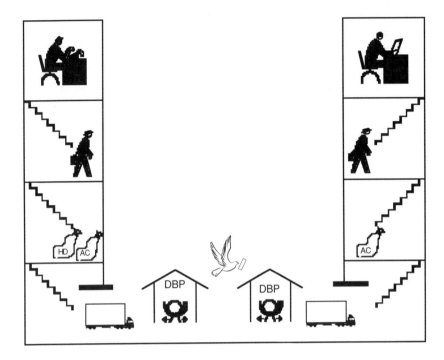

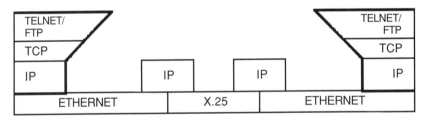

Figure 8.9 Postal route analogy to routing

Given the situation described the following situation results, if the router is used:

- A router enables a connection between end systems, where the end systems do not bother about the route which lies between them.

- The router uses a special protocol from the Network Layer in each case to make the connection route.

If the connection on the Network Layer is made between end systems, the desire arises to make this connection via different networks. It should be possible between any LAN and WAN networks. The question arises as to what happens if the networks support different packet sizes and the end systems do not agree on the smallest size. In this case, bridges must discard packets that are too long.

8.2.3 Downwards Transparency: Connection of Different MAC Layers

The choice of Layer 3 as the connection layer makes matters dependent upon the higher protocols used but independent of the protocols used on Layer 2, on the other hand. Thus, they can be used transparently. Where the MAC Layer bridge which provides "upward" transparency on the basis of identical MAC Layers, the router offers "downward" transparency. Routers behave in a complementary manner to bridges in this sense. In particular, they can produce Ethernet–Token Ring, Ethernet–FDDI and Token Ring–FDDI connections via the same Layer 3 protocol.

Reference is made here once more to the post-routing analogy: Wi Tu Sen, his secretary, and the post bag are totally indifferent in principle as to whether the letter is forwarded by bus, train, aircraft, or carrier pigeon; the main objective is that it arrives safely at its destination (such trivial aspects as performance are put aside for once). In this example, bus and train represent Ethernet and Token Ring. For instance, the aircraft may be FDDI, and the carrier pigeon is a at 64 kbit/s line.

In the event that the MAC Layers which are being connected use different packet sizes, routers are often used because the packets are split when changing from one LAN to another and therefore modified—segmented and reassembled—a function which a bridge does not generally perform, since it does not modify packets.

Routers now cover the following functions:

- A router enables a connection between end systems, where the end systems are not concerned over the route which lies between them.

- The router uses a special protocol from the Network Layer in each case to make the connecting route.

- It connects different LANs and WANs, even if these support different packet sizes.

8.3 The Central Functions

How can many LANs and WANs be cascaded between two end systems without the connection suffering? The central tasks (i.e., the central functions) which a router undertakes are considered in greater detail for that purpose. The route selection for a packet to be forwarded and the end to end connection on the Network Layer are examples of these central tasks. The essential elements for this are given in Section 8.2.1:

- A process for identifying the stations in relation to the router and vice versa (network address, MAC address, protocol ID).

- An algorithm for "non-local" packets in order to select the next router, which is intended to receive the packet (the algorithm is termed "routing," after the central function of a router, as is easily recognized from the current usual name for the device).

- A header for information such as the destination address of the end station, lifetime (time stamp), fragmenting, and reassembly (all control information from the network protocol).

8.3.1 Arriving Safely: Packet Forwarding between End Systems

In order to produce an end to end connection between end systems wishing to communicate (i.e., to forward of packets from the sender to the receiver), two end stations (sending station and receiving station) must be unambiguously identifiable from their network addresses. The routers lying between these end stations can forward the packet from the transmitting station via the first router to the second, from there to the third and so on, according to their routing tables, until finally, the "last" router on the route through the various subnetworks forwards it to the receiver station. The routing tables (in each router) contain the information for the relevant router regarding in which direction a packet with the specified destination network should be forwarded.

Since a station is generally allocated to a particular router, no dynamic load distribution via different routers (similar to DLS or source routing in bridges) can be achieved within a logical subnetwork on the Network Layer which contains several physical subnetworks. This application scenario rarely occurs, however. In the case of different connecting routes between different subnetworks, load distribution is possible. Routers achieve adjustment to the current load situation by, for example, exchanging and periodically updating control information on all subnetworks. (This functionality is not provided by all routing algorithms, however, see section 8.3.3). The overhead here rises in proportion to the number of subnetworks. If each router passes on its own table via all known subnetworks to all other routers, the overhead rises quadratically with the number of subnetworks. This results in corresponding costs, in particular for WAN connections. This is the case in some implementations.

In some protocols, regular control packets are required between routers and stations so that the router is always informed with regard to active stations (DECnet IV). This generates considerable overhead. If routers exchange information on all attached stations (DECnet), the overhead is increased further and rises in proportion to the number of attached stations. In contrast, the overhead when using bridges for the calculation of the Spanning Tree, does not increase with the number of stations. Instead it increases in proportion to the number of bridges.) In order also to be able to control the establishment of routes manually, despite automatic adjustment possibilities, a network manager must be capable of activating, updating, and deleting as many routes generated in the router in continuous operation as possible. This is extremely necessary, in particular in the event of errors (isolation and remedying).

Routers manage access to the network on a subnetwork level. Here also, there are filter options, where the filters are set to network addresses. Stations from outside which are not entered in the routing table do not achieve access, and arriving packets are discarded. Conversely, this applies in the same way to stations which are attached in the subnetwork and wish to communicate outwardly. A bridge can achieve this function under certain circumstances through complex filters. What it cannot do in contrast to the router, is to make access restrictions within a physical segment if corresponding network addresses are assigned with filters in the router such that they are forwarded only to other specific network addresses of the segment. This achieves a logical subdivision of the segment, e.g., according to user groups. Therefore, a (physical) load division within the same segment cannot be achieved, since the transmitted message is transmitted physically over the entire segment and only logically (i.e., on the Network Layer), and cannot be interpreted by the "blocked" stations. The load occurring is even greater in this case. Inter-group data traffic is sent twice: from the transmitting station to the router and from the router to the receiving station. A similar procedure must also be established in network operating systems if a physical segment is subdivided by several servers into logical segments. For a user, only one server for example, can be addressed, although the data packets are physically present at all servers.

8.3.1.1 Addressing

In contrast to bridges, routers are addressed explicitly in LANs. They do not have to filter all arriving packets in promiscuous mode, they only process broadcasts and the messages addressed directly to them (the degree of inquisitiveness of a router is consequently lower than that of a bridge). In order to clarify this with an example such as the one in Figure 8.10, we turn to our friends the ancient Gauls once more.

If Asterix and Obelix live in different quarters of the village, it may be that Miraculix and Majestix control what happens in the village. If Obelix wants to invite Asterix on a wild boar hunt, he must engage Miraculix and Majestix as intermediate carriers. He prepares a message with the following content: "Let's go and hunt some wild boar." The network source Obelix sends the data to the network destination Asterix. On the MAC layer, however, Obelix addresses the first intermediate station, i.e., Miraculix: MAC source is Obelix, MAC destination is Miraculix. Miraculix checks the genuineness of Obelix's invitation and submits it in an amended form, that is, with modified addresses and a modified checksum (CRC). For this purpose, Miraculix knows that the next intermediate station is Majestix. He enters in the packet (MAC source Miraculix to MAC destination Majestix) "Let's go and hunt some wild boar." the information on the Network Layer remains unchanged. The network destination is Asterix, and network source is Obelix. Majestix receives the packet from Miraculix, checks for his part whether Obelix may invite Asterix, and forwards the packet with MAC source = Majestix, MAC destination = Asterix. The network addresses are not modified. After this multitude of successful communications operations, Asterix can finally consider whether he would like to go hunting with Obelix.

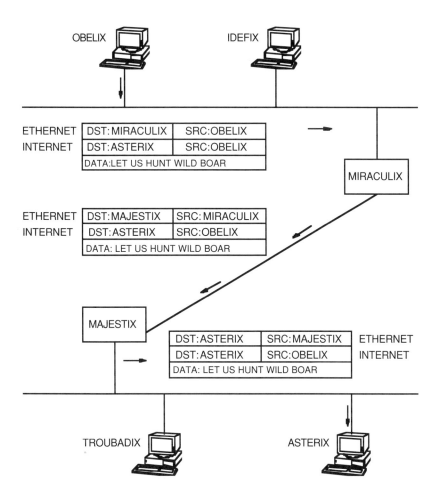

OBELIX   IDEFIX

ETHERNET	DST: MIRACULIX	SRC: OBELIX
INTERNET	DST: ASTERIX	SRC: OBELIX
DATA: LET US HUNT WILD BOAR		

MIRACULIX

ETHERNET	DST: MAJESTIX	SRC: MIRACULIX
INTERNET	DST: ASTERIX	SRC: OBELIX
DATA: LET US HUNT WILD BOAR		

MAJESTIX

DST: ASTERIX	SRC: MAJESTIX	ETHERNET
DST: ASTERIX	SRC: OBELIX	INTERNET
DATA: LET US HUNT WILD BOAR		

TROUBADIX   ASTERIX

Figure 8.10: Addressing on Layer 2 and Layer 3 when using routers

Despite the specific packet acceptance (via direct addressing), processing in the router takes longer than in a bridge, with a few exceptions, since all control information from Layer 3 e.g., lifetime, address conversion, header checksum, etc. must be interpreted and renewed. In some implementations, a default router is always selected within a subnetwork, which addresses a router (if necessary) that can forward the packet to the desired subnetwork. The process is helpful but makes the default router a potential bottleneck: if it fails, the subnetwork is totally cut off from external communication even if other routers which could enable a connection are active in the segment.

The address conversion has the effect that MAC addresses have to be unambiguous only within a subnetwork and no longer cross subnetworks, which considerably increases the number of attachable stations. It is also not advisable when using routers to use the same MAC addresses if it can be avoided, since this always creates the potential for inconsistencies during moves and topology changes. Hierarchical schemes can be used for addressing (while bridges operate with a flat address space). In this way, the size of the address table is reduced: there are only as many entries as there are subnetworks present. (In the case of bridges, the table size corresponds to the number of stations.) For non-local traffic, the router holds only the "rough information" on the next highest hierarchy layer for the forwarding of the packet. With each hierarchy layer, the number of possible stations increases exponentially, and the processing time, on the other hand, grows logarithmically, i.e., far slower than the number of stations.

Packet Modification

There is always a snag. As the result of converting the address and packet changes generally, the checksum (CRC, FCS) must be recalculated. This means that a strict end-to-end control is no longer possible in the sense of a fully transparent transmission of the packet. Hierarchical addressing often can lead to frequent address changes in the event of configuration changes to the network (in the event of a move), and therefore to corresponding reconfiguration expense and, in the event of errors, to connectivity losses. For all table savings, the processing time for the router is often longer than for bridges, even if performance falls only logarithmically, since the protocols must be interpreted and processed up to Layer 3, particularly, if the router is handling several protocols in parallel. This applies even if many stations are attached (i.e., despite complex bridge tables). The advantages of using the router in contrast to bridges lie not in the shorter processing time, but in the utilization of logical configuration mechanisms, more complex routing functions and saving on network load by reducing broadcast traffic.

8.3.1.2 Packet Processing in the Router

The processing of a data packet in the router, given the example of a router with assumed average architecture is demonstrated below. The example is a router with four LAN interfaces, two Ethernet, and two Token Ring LANs, each on a LAN interface board. The LAN boards are controlled by a CPU board or by their own CPUs on the relevant board (see Chapter 14), which regulates the coordinated processing of the arriving forwarding request (for receiving "upward" and for sending "downward"). In light of possible failures, the configuration of the router is backed up in non-volatile memory (mostly diskette, more rarely onboard RAM). At this point, attention is drawn once more to the fact that it is sensible to have the configuration stored a second time. This is achieved by simply backing up the diskette, and in the event of errors, it saves the work which manual reconfiguration entails. Additional memory for the buffering of packets arriving and those in processing, is also provided. The CPU interacts with the attached LAN interfaces in the master/slave process. An individual LAN board processes the packets arriving and those to be sent each via a FIFO queue in the hope that the CPU is quick enough to prevent any FINO (First In Never Out).

In addition to the input and output queues of each LAN interface, the router generally has a queue for each possible routing protocol that it can process. A packet is not recopied from queue to queue during protocol processing. Instead it is stored once in the buffer memory and processed via pointer references which are passed on from queue to queue (input interface queue to protocol queue to output interface queue). The constant recopying when passing through the various queues would only consume unnecessary processing time.

Which path does a TCP/IP packet now take from one of the attached Ethernet LANs to one of the attached Token Rings? (See Figure 8.11)

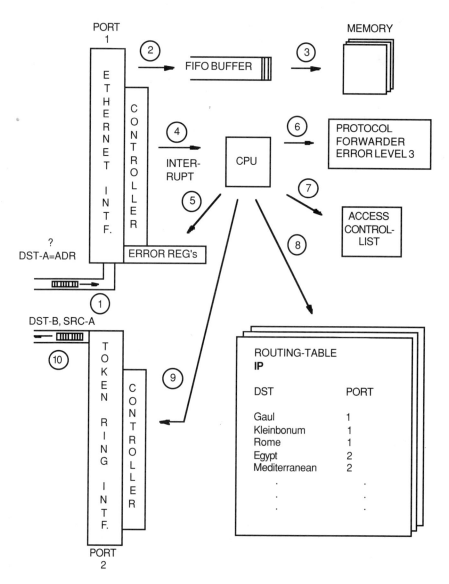

PORT
1

MEMORY

② → FIFO BUFFER

③ →

ETHERNET INTF.

CONTROLLER

④ →

INTER-
RUPT

CPU

⑥ →

PROTOCOL
FORWARDER
ERROR LEVEL 3

⑤

⑦ →

ACCESS
CONTROL-
LIST

?
DST-A=ADR

ERROR REG's

⑧

①

DST-B, SRC-A

⑩

TOKEN RING INTF.

CONTROLLER

⑨

ROUTING-TABLE
IP

DST   PORT

Gaul   1
Kleinbonum   1
Rome   1
Egypt   2
Mediterranean   2

PORT
2

Figure 8.11 Packet processing in the router

Let us assume that the TCP/IP protocol suite is activated in a router: an Ethernet interface discovers a packet which has its own MAC address as its destination address (1). It places the packet in its on-board FIFO buffer (2).

After this, the controller transfers it into the router main memory and sets a corresponding pointer, which it passes on to the input queue of the Ethernet interface in question (3). The CPU receives an interrupt which reports the arrival of the packet (4). A first service routine checks all Ethernet protocol details: FCS errors, length errors, type errors, etc. (5). This routine is responsible for all Ethernet interfaces. There is only one version of the Ethernet protocol software active in the router. It is assumed that the packet is error free on the MAC (i.e., Ethernet, Layer) and has a protocol type that the router can interpret on Layer 3 (i.e., TCP/IP). The pointer is then set to the network header, and the control information from the Ethernet layers is then removed from the packet.

The IP protocol software receives a request, and the packet is then standing in the "IP queue." First, the IP task checks whether the version number of the protocol is correct (6). Only one common version is possible in one network. After this, the header length is checked in order to determine whether the control information has at least the minimum length; if not, the packet is binned. In order to guarantee that the packet has not suffered any forwarding damage, the header checksum is examined (unlike the MAC FCS, which is already removed). At the next stage, the actual packet length is compared with the entered length (length field of the frame). If it is too short, the route leads to the bin. If not, the formal error checks are ended at this point. With corresponding router intelligence and configuration, there is a logbook entry with source and destination address (network addresses) that an IP packet was correctly received here. If the network administrator takes the trouble to search for the log file, he or she will discover this packet in the log file.

If the packet has overcome all hurdles thus far, the question is posed as to whether and to where it should be forwarded. Even on the IP Layer, there are access filters in a control table (Access Control List) which explicitly allow or prevent the forwarding of particular IP addresses; if there is a negative filter match, the packet is still binned at this point although its form is correct (7). Otherwise, the routing table is consulted: if there is no route for the destination network present, the sender receives a message of the type "your destination network is not attainable." If there is an entered route, the protocol is processed further: the maximum packet size is checked, fragmentation performed if necessary, the time stamp entered (time-to-live, in order to avoid endless circulation), the check sum newly calculated, etc. (8).

Once all IP protocol actions have been completed, the packet is forwarded to the send queue of the LAN interface board which corresponds to the destination route. In the example selected, this is a Token Ring interface (9). All control information from the MAC layer which was removed in the processing of the packet is reproduced, in particular the MAC address of the router as source address and the MAC address of the next router or destination station (if no more routers lie in between) as destination address.

The starting position for a network can be represented as follows, with the router functionality described above:

- A router enables a connection between end systems, where the end systems do not bother about the route that lies between them.

- The router uses a special protocol from the Network Layer in each case to make the connection route.

- It connects different LANs and WANs, even if these support different packet sizes.

- By using unambiguous network addresses, MAC addresses only have to be unambiguous within the subnetworks.

- By using several routers, LANs and WANs can be cascaded for the connection between end stations. The route selection is regulated here by routing tables in the routers.

The user can now be certain that the packet will reach the receiver station from the transmitter station without being damaged in any way. This is not enough for him or her: the forwarding of the packet should be configured as well as possible. How should a routing algorithm be, to optimize forwarding?

8.3.2 The Essence of a Routing Algorithm

A routing algorithm establishes a process according to which the routing tables are constructed in the routers concerned. The algorithm also establishes unambiguous decision criteria (known as a metric), according to which the optimum route is determined between two destination networks. This route is entered in the table. Some algorithms also allow the entry of more than one route, either for backup purposes or for load distribution (e.g., OSPF). The essence of a routing algorithm is determined by two elements: the type of connection—connectionless or connection-oriented—and the requirements on the algorithm for route selection.

8.3.2.1 Virtual Circuit versus Datagram

End systems in a computer network have the illusion that they could "hold a conversation" with any other end system via any type of communication channel. Each end station actually communicates, with a switching computer (router), which in turn communicates with a router, and the series continues infinitely until the communication path finally reaches the destination host. The illusion that one end station can "talk" to another is maintained by the described communication network of routers and end systems. A point to point connection of this type offered by the network can exist in two different versions:

- Virtual Circuit (connection-oriented service)

- Datagram Service (connectionless service)

The first is often selected for WAN connections and the latter for less error-laden LAN connections (e.g., X.25). In the case of the Virtual Circuit (VC), the Network Layer offers the Transport Layer a perfect communication channel: freedom from errors and correct sequence for the transmitted messages. There is an explicit connection establishment, followed by a data transfer phase and an explicit shutdown. Once established, the connection is maintained during the entire communication period (error-free requirement).

An example of this is the public telephone network: the caller must first establish the connection (dial), then send messages (talk), and finally end the connection (hang up the receiver more or less firmly). During the conversation, both participants have the illusion of a direct connection, although the signal is actually running via a series of network points (in the LAN-WAN combination, routers). In particular, the information is forwarded in precisely the same sequence as that in which it is sent (words do not normally arrive in a garbled order on the telephone network).

In the Datagram Service, the network forwards each individual packet and tries to forward it as an isolated unit to its destination. Packets may arrive in a different sequence from that in which they are sent or even not at all. The Datagram Service does not contain any explicit connection establishment and shutdown.

The postal analogy to the Datagram is the letter system. Each letter is forwarded independently as an isolated unit, letters sent after one another do not have to arrive in the same sequence, and lost letters are not re-sent automatically. The differences between the Datagram and connection-oriented service are summarized in Figure 8.12.

	Virtual Connection	Datagram
Destination Address	Required close to the building	Needed in every packet
Error Handling	in Subnet Service	in higher layers (End Stations)
Flow Control End-to-End End Station	Through the Subnet	Through higher layers
Packet Sequence Source-Destination	Arrival in Sequential Order	Arrival in Non-sequential Order
Explicit Building Connections	Yes	No

Figure 8.12 Differences between Datagram and Virtual Circuit

Connections

At the outset, the Datagram Service seems to be the less convenient of the two alternatives. It may prove advantageous, however:

- A communication process does not require any packet sequence.

- There are applications for which automatic transmission repetition in the event of errors is not desirable: in the case of a (digitized) telephone connection, it is better that a participant hears a discarded packet (noisy word) than that he or she waits two seconds for a timeout and repeat transmission.

- If the end station performs a costly error treatment internally in any case (e.g., transport protocol Class 4), error treatment on the Network Layer is redundant and results in inefficiency. For example, Banks would not appreciate it if $1.00 became $4,097.002. Its applications generally demand far more costly error correction than the Network Layer achieves. These are then achieved on higher layers.

- Datagram Services have considerably lower overhead than Virtual Circuits and therefore enable a higher user data throughput. In the case of applications whose average communication time is very short, the costs increase for connection establishment and shutdown for the sending of the actual message.

- Because the packet forwarding is operated in a connectionless mode, i.e., without a fixed set route, dynamic diversion of the packct is possible in the event of errors. This is "dynamic rerouting." This is perhaps the greatest advantage of a Datagram Service.

Factors against Virtual Circuits include the following:

- Some network applications require sequential, error-free communication. If this function is achieved on the Network Layer, the higher layers, and therefore the application layers, the terminal stations are freed from this burden.

- The realization of these functions is performed in the router which is designed specially for the task, instead of in each end system (this discussion has also already occurred in the topic source routing—transparent routing). The operating system of the end station is freed from such annoying actions as error correction, sequence regulation, and flow control for the network connection.

In the event of errors, Virtual Circuits must first be reset and then established once more. Once selected, the connection path is fixed for the entire session (typically, for example, for highly secure virtual SNA connections, APPN in the LAN sector). Datagrams can affect balanced traffic flow, since the communication path between end stations can also be changed during the period of the connection.

8.3.2.2 Requirements of a Routing Algorithm

Regardless of the type of connection (LAN-LAN or LAN-WAN), some features are desirable or required for routing algorithms (see [TANE89]).

- Independence—from the network topology in order to guarantee later extendibility of the network.

- Correctness—each deliverable message should finally reach its destination. "Deliverable" here means that both the addressed destination station and a connection in the network to that destination are currently available and attainable.

- Simplicity—this hardly needs to be discussed; the simpler the algorithm, the easier it is to implement and the higher the performance.

- Robustness—once installed, the network should be capable as an entity, despite locally limited hardware and software defects of working without network-wide failure. The network must also be able to cope with topology changes and extensions and modified flow control without total failure.

- Stability—routing processes which do not have fixed route selection must make changes in the route selection according to set criteria. After implementing such changes, the network must return to a stable state, which is to say, a state of continuous change (oscillating of the routes) must not arise.

- Fairness—each end station should acquire network access on as equal a basis as possible.

- Optimization—the required end to end transparency of a packet should be minimized and the user data throughput maximized.

Unfortunately, some of these demands hinder one another. "Fairness and optimization" sounds as plausible as "Christmas and Santa" and no one would contradict this combined requirement. The objectives are actually in conflict, however, as the example in Figure 8.13 shows: it is assumed that the traffic between A and A', B and B', C and C' is sufficiently high, so X and X' are the first to be excluded from communication for reasons of throughput optimization. X and X' will hardly consider this perspective to be fair and not be very understanding.

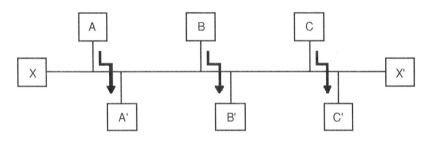

Figure 8.13 Conflict between fairness and optimization

Response time behaviors and total throughput may also form a trade-off: if the capacity is utilized very heavily (particularly in the WAN sector), long waiting times arise in the processing queues. This drastically increases the response time. As a compromise solution, many routing processes have tried to minimize the number of routers lying between the end stations in order to minimize the processing time in these interconnection elements and so to improve the throughput retrospectively. If this occurs without taking account of the intermediate performance capacity, there is no optimal throughput achieved (see Chapter 9)—a finding which new protocols such as OSPF or IS-IS take into account.

After presenting the requirements for a routing mechanism, a network with routers has the following functionality:

• A router enables a connection between end systems, where the end systems do not bother about the route which lies between them.

- The router uses a special protocol from the Network Layer in each case to make the connection route.

- It connects different LANs and WANs, even if these support different packet sizes.

- By using unambiguous network addresses, MAC addresses only have to be unambiguous within the subnetworks.

- By using several routers, LANs and WANs can be cascaded for the connection between end stations. The route selection is regulated here by routing tables in the routers.

- The underlying routing algorithm has the effect of optimizing packet forwarding through the network.

The user can now be sure that the packet will arrive at the destination and do so in the optimal manner. Our user is still not satisfied however, for optimum network operation there must also be utilization of redundant configurations. What is a router's approach to redundancy?

8.3.3 Different Route Selection Processes

Routing processes can be differentiated in principle into two strategies:

- static or non-adaptive routing
- dynamic or adaptive routing

Static Routing

Static routing, as the name suggests, is based on a fixed setting for the route between any two end systems. This setting is made when installing the network, and it is generally stored as a fixed table in the router. The end systems are each allocated to a router, and by this device they are attainable and can reach other destinations. The precise configuration of the network, number, and position of the routers, links used, and their transmission capacity must be known when determining the routes. The following are taken into account as configuration parameters:

- number and position of the end systems and routers,

- existing links and their capacity (high capacity links are more often used as routes than those with lower capacity),

- assumptions over the load to be expected (the computer games department of a mail-order firm tends to debug the network-capable versions on their own house network and therefore produces a considerably higher load than a sports clothing department),

- priorities among network participants.

In the event of modifications, a static route must be reconfigured manually (errors, extension, moves, etc.), at which point the disadvantage of the process becomes clearly evident. Static routes are therefore recommended only in two cases:

- in extremely stable configurations, in which there are almost never any topology changes or errors (and where have you ever heard of such a configuration),

- in cases of extreme security restrictions, where the route which a packet takes over the network must be 100% predetermined.

Dynamic Routing

An essential advantage of routers is the opportunity to establish routes dynamically, i.e., in continuous network operation as the network is extended or modify routes according to the load situation. These processes are also termed adaptive routing, since the route selection is adapted to the current network situation. The optimum route selection is determined according to an initial parameter setting only via the routing protocol, and therefore it is transparent to the user. Such dynamic routing protocols provide a central function of the network and take additional factors into consideration in comparison to static routing:

- Link and node failure; redundancy concepts may come in useful here with alternative routes.

- Knowledge of alternative routes to avoid certain sections of the network, e.g., during high load situations.

- Line overload.

- Overload of the processing queue (of the interface) in the router.

A dynamic process is impressive due to its flexibility, but a disadvantage comes as standard. In order to achieve the flexibility, the routers involved must talk to one another constantly regarding what is "in" on the network in order to control information on the current available configuration and exchange topology. This means additional overhead, which can be translated directly into additional network load, particularly for remote links, but also in LANs in the event of corresponding intensity (DECnet).

As has already been mentioned at other points, incompatibility also exists in most cases between different products, since manufacturers have implemented different dynamic processes or the implementation of the same principle is achieved in a different manner. Why should the world of routers be any "holier" than that of bridge products? Even in the case of implemented standards, inter-manufacturer communication using different router products is possible in far from all cases (see Networld and Interop).

All routing processes try to optimize the route between two end stations in some form, i.e., to make it as cost effective as possible. What cost effective means here depends on the decision criteria selected:

- number of hops from the source to the destination,

- cost of the line (in DM, $, SFR, £, etc.),

- capacity of the lines used,

- error rate for the lines used.

The above-mentioned decision bases are known as metrics.

An important criteria for dynamic routing processes is good convergence behavior (corresponding to the "stability" quality feature in Chapter 8), i.e., the speed with which a stable state is achieved once more after a change. The convergence is usually described as a function of the number of routers installed in a network, since it is particularly interesting how the convergence time grows with rising numbers of routers. If the convergence time increases, e.g., in proportion to n23, where n is the number of installed routers, the protocol cannot be used in large internetworks.

Two fundamentally different dynamic processes are currently implemented in routers:

- **Distance Vector Algorithm (DVA)**, also known by the name of the developer of such a process, Bellman-Ford algorithm (e.g., RIP),

- **Link State Algorithm (LSA)**, also known as Shortest Path First (SPF) or Dijkstra algorithm (e.g., OSPF, IS-IS, DECnetV/OSI).

Both processes are implemented as software modules in the router and generate information packets (update packets) dynamically for other routers. Based on the information received from other routers, the routing software generates its own routing table dynamically. This determines the path to all destination networks. The table is essentially a list of attainable networks (from the perspective of the router in question), with a reference as to which router port a packet should be forwarded and which has a particular destination network entered in the network part of the network address. From time to time, the table is newly calculated and then used in its new form until the next update. DVA and LSA differ fundamentally in the way in which the tables are calculated.

For a Distance Vector Algorithm, the best route is the shortest route. The distance forms the basis as a metric and is generally measured according to the number of hops (the route with the least hops via intermediate routers is the shortest for a packet). Other metrics include: estimated transmission time/delay (e.g., in addition to the hops for NetWare RIP) or bandwidth (e.g., for DECnet IV, converted into cost values as in Spanning Tree). All routers are basically considered to be equivalent here and not differentiated with regard to their position in the overall network. The underlying router topology has a completely flat structure. The Bellman-Ford algorithm uses a distributed calculation, where each router sends its complete table to all other routers when a change is noted and/or at intervals. This means that for n routers and k networks, n*k tables, where the table size also grows with the number of networks. The convergence time therefore grows in proportion to $n \cdot k$. Since $k \geq n$ always applies, this means an overhead of $O(n^2)$.

A router compares all the tables it receives and from this calculates the optimum routes for itself. If the new table has changed in relation to the old table, the updated table is sent to the neighboring routers at the time of the next update. The processing occurs under the slogan "first compute, then distribute." Particularly for networks with high levels of route redundancy, update packets for table updates circulate for a relatively long period over the network before convergence is established: update packets result in table changes in certain routers, which in turn cause update packets, which in turn produce table changes, etc. The Bellman-Ford algorithm also has advantages, however:

- simplicity

- easy implementation

- low memory consumption

These are typical characteristics and advantages of most initial processes.

In the case of the Link State Algorithm, a complete topology basis underlies the table calculation: the LSA database contains both information on distances to other routers and additional information on the hierarchical structure, in which routers are connected to one another. Typically, a distinction is made between "backbone routers" (hierarchy level 1) and "area routers" (hierarchy level 2) and there are at least two hierarchy levels present. In the case of table changes, only modifications are forwarded, and these are forwarded only to the neighbors within their own hierarchy level, not to all systems. Different metrics are possible for the calculation, thus the calculation not limited only the number of hops between two end systems.

The SPF algorithm tends less to produce loops in topology changes and converges, finding the consistently optimum route after changes in network operation more quickly. It also generates less overhead: routers do not send their complete table, they only send the information as to which are their direct neighbors. From this "distributed database" each router calculates the new routes. In the framework of the TCP/IP protocols, the SPF variant OSPF (Open SPF) has established itself as an alternative to RIP (Routing Information

Protocol), a variant which has been operated by an IETF group since 1988. DECnet will produce an SPF implementation for dynamic routing in Phase V and a corresponding SPF draft was submitted by DEC to the ANSI committee X3S3.3. LSA protocols have the following advantages over DVA protocols:

- lower overhead

- faster convergence

- wider range of metrics

- more suitable for large networks

Human communication is taken as an analogy, in order to make a final comparison of both processes, DVA and LSA. DVA protocols spread news like "rumors." A hears that B heard that C knows that D has a distance to E of 3 hops. As in life, each router changes the information by adding information from its own table. LSA protocols spread news like "propaganda," identical information is drummed into all participating systems again and again, until the last system has understood. The greater precision and faster convergence of an LSA protocol in relation to a DVA protocol can be seen from this comparison.

The question as to the router-router protocols used is an important criteria when investigating a router. Some products can process standard protocols between end systems and routers but use their own routing protocol on the router-router WAN connections (e.g., IGRP from CISCO). This is generally incompatible with other manufacturers. Personal router-router protocols are used, for example, by (TransPath) and RND (REB, RTB).

The starting position for a network can be represented as follows with the router functionality described above:

- A router enables a connection between end systems where the end systems do not bother about the route that lies between them.

- The router uses a special protocol from the Network Layer in each case to make the connection route.

- The router connects different LANs and WANs, even if these support different packet sizes.

- By using unambiguous network addresses, MAC addresses have to be unambiguous only within the subnetworks.

- By using several routers, LANs and WANs can be cascaded for the connection between end stations. The route selection is regulated here by routing tables in the routers.

- The underlying routing algorithm has the effect of optimizing packet forwarding through the network.

- By using dynamic routing processes, redundancy concepts can be taken into consideration.

- Explicitly established routes are also possible (backup considerations, overhead savings).

What happens in a network where links and/or routers are overloaded?

8.3.4 Overload Behavior

The problem of overload requires attention in relation to routing, particularly for WAN connections. Congestion or overload develops if the network (or links) or individual router interfaces can no longer process the arriving load and the router after some time "runs out of steam," i.e., has no more spare buffer space for intermediate storage of the packets. Actually, this is not really mind acrobatics, but too many network planners and managers try to tackle overload through additional capacity (and therefore additional budget). Ahead of capacity extension, tackling the overload through corresponding network management should first be attempted. In principle, the entire exercise of connecting LANs via slow WANs suffers from the overload problem. In order to handle these ugly phenomena, there are two strategies in principle:

- congestion avoidance (do not let the problem occur in the first place),

- error correction (eliminate the problem, which you should have better predicted).

In the strategy of congestion avoidance, routers discuss with one another a priori what is possible in terms of load. Thus the relevant buffer space is reserved before transmission and is therefore available when the packet actually arrives. In the case of error correction, an attempt is made to gradually break down the overload which has occurred by arranging with corresponding control information for the load source (the transmitting router or end station) to produce less load, until the congestion situation is remedied (e.g., choke packets in SNA). Explicit control packets and/or packet confirmations are required for all these processes (which a bridge cannot and may not issue).

8.3.5 Broadcast reduction

One reason for using routers instead of bridges is to suppress inter-subnetwork broadcasts. Mass broadcasts, known as broadcast storms, may arise as the result of protocol errors (see Chapter 6) but are forwarded only on the MAC layer. This type of error situation is caused by protocols, which work with broadcasts within the subnetwork even in normal operation (meaning a subnetwork on the Network Layer), e.g., ARP from the TCP/IP family, DECnet, Novell, etc.

A broadcast overhead of 20% of the network load is a more realistic value in some network configurations, which generates a correspondingly high "basic load" on a remote connection—for links with low capacity under certain circumstances 80%, so that no serious bandwidth remains for the user data throughput (0.5% Ethernet utilization means 75% utilization of a 64 kbit/s remote line; a 9.6 kbit/s line has therefore collapsed). In the case of protocols which work with broadcasts (generally for establishing connections), the broadcast load increases in a linear pattern with the number of attached stations. If subnetworks are interconnected via bridges (without setting filters), the load increases in a linear pattern with the stations attached in all subnetworks, since the bridges forward all broadcasts.

In the case of structuring on the Network Layer by means of routers, broadcasts are not distributed over all subnetworks, since the router interprets the network address and forwards or answers the broadcast in a targeted manner. Broadcasts therefore occur only between end systems and routers (in fast LANs, which can handle that) and not between two routers (e.g., in slow WANs). On the other hand, the most bridges can do is broadcast via filters. At the same time, the filters lead to the fact that no connection is possible to end systems in the subnetworks, and thus no broadcasts penetrate the subnetworks.

Broadcast suppression is naturally possible only for protocols which are routable. For LAT (Local Area Transport) and NetBIOS, this is not the case.

The disadvantage which is incurred by this configuration of the Network Layer is more costly configuration and, where applicable, the greater processing time in the router, depending on which device is used and how many protocols are operated in parallel.

8.4 Extended Functionality: Filter Definition

Even for routed connections, filter mechanisms can be set. The filter mechanisms relate at least to Layer 3 addresses and can be combined similarly to bridges—positively, negatively, and by means of mathematical logic functions. The filter lists are often termed access lists. Some router products support wild cards within address filters, so that entire logic subnetworks or address sectors can be filtered. Some filters apply to higher protocols such as, for example, SAP filters in NetWare or subnetwork, FTP filters in TCP/IP.

Similarly to bridge interconnection, performance losses must be taken into consideration when using filter setting extensively, losses in the region of 5% to 20% of throughput. Well planned and limited filter settings, in particular for WAN connections, make sense, but no more than this, since at some point on Layer 3 of the OSI reference model, the filter settings become confused with increasing numbers.

The starting position for a network can be represented as follows with the router functionality described until now:

- A router enables a connection between end systems, where the end systems do not bother about the route which lies between them.

- The router uses a special protocol from the Network Layer in each case to make the connection route.

- The router connects different LANs and WANs, even if these support different packet sizes.

- By using unambiguous network addresses, MAC addresses need only to be unambiguous within the subnetworks.

- By using several routers, LANs and WANs can be cascaded for the connection between terminal stations. The route selection is regulated here by routing tables in the routers.

- The underlying routing algorithm has the effect of optimizing packet forwarding through the network.

- By using dynamic routing processes, redundancy concepts can be taken into consideration.

- Explicitly established routes are also possible (backup considerations, overhead savings).

- Routers can produce mechanisms to control overload situations (depending on the protocol).

- Routers make a significant contribution to reducing inter-subnetwork broadcasts.

The functions listed are not enough for the operator of a complex network. Since he/she operates different protocol worlds in the network and wants to connect these via one and the same type of device, the search is for an interconnection element that can handle the various worlds in parallel. Which worlds does this relate to?

Routing Protocols: OSI- and De facto- Standards

The following section describes in more detail some important routing protocols which have become established as proprietary or standard protocols. These usually consist of a network protocol (routable protocol), which provides a network-layer service (usually datagrams), and a routing protocol, which creates tables and optimizes the routes. The routing protocol or the router-router protocol is used to create routing tables and specifies the exchange of check information between the routers required to create and update the tables. The network protocol determines the packet format and address structure for data packets and check packets and the actions between end systems and routers. The network protocol and the routing protocol are, therefore, always matched to each other.

9.1 TCP/IP Family

TCP/IP originated from the ARPANET (Advanced Research Projects Agency), which is a military network used by the DoD (Department of Defense). As the TCP/IP family is one of the oldest and most frequently used peer-to-peer protocols implemented on the majority of computer platforms (there are in fact no manufacturers who do not offer at least the minimum version of this protocol), this protocol will be described in more detail than the others. TCP/IP routing is used with a series of protocols serving the end system router and router-router communications: IP (Internet Protocol, RFC 791), RIP (Routing Information Protocol, RFC 1058), HELLO, ICMP (Internet Control Message Protocol, RFC 792), ARP (Address Resolution Protocol, RFC 826, 829) and EGP (Exterior Gateway Protocol, RFC 890, 827, 901, 911).

To explain the basic principles of routing for the Internet, we shall start with a brief look at the Internet architecture and philosophy. The internet architecture is designed as a stack of three blocks: first, a datagram service at network layer; second, a reliable transport service with suitable error correction mechanisms and packet acknowledgments; and third, the application services (application layers): file transfer, virtual terminal, and mail. The protocol stack is shown in Figure 9.1.

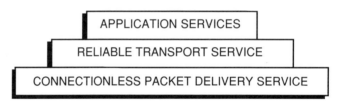

Figure 9.1 Architecture of the TCP/IP services

As the transport layer provides a highly reliable service, such reliability was deliberately omitted at the network layer; this layer uses a relatively simple datagram service. Fragmentation and reassembly (division and reconstruction of packets) are supported. Reassembly however, is not performed in every router; it is only performed at the destination station. A fragmented packet is like a broken flower vase: unless all the fragments are recovered, the vase cannot be restored to a usable (i.e., watertight) condition. Likewise, if fragments are lost on the route between the originator and the recipient, reassembly cannot be performed properly. The incoming fragments are destroyed and the entire packet has to be repeated. The minimum packet size supported by an internet implementation is 576 bytes.

9.1.1 IP Packet Format

Figure 9.2 shows the format of an Internet datagram. At the start of the pack-'
et, the VERS field contains the version number used for the IP protocol. This
ensures that the originator, recipient, and the router between them all use the
same version. Each device only accepts the version of the protocol which it has
itself implemented. In the event of a migration therefore, only stations and
routers with identical versions of the protocol are able to talk to each other. As
a rule, the migration must be performed as quickly as possible throughout the
entire IP network. The length field LEN shows the length of the header (the
unit of length is a 32-bit word); the most common length, if no options are
used, is 20 bytes, i.e., a length of 5. The total length of the IP packet in bytes,
i.e., header and data part is entered in the TOTAL LENGTH field.

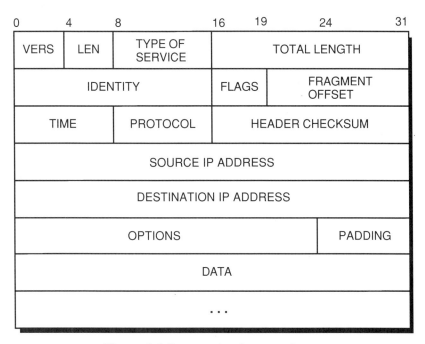

Figure 9.2 Format of an Internet datagram

The TYPE OF SERVICE field (TOS) places special conditions on the quality
of the service for the further transmission of the packet. It is 1 byte long with
the PRECEDENCE fields (3 Bit) and the D-bit, T-bit and R-bit (see also Figure

9.3). The last two bits are not assigned. Precedence may be assigned a priority value for priority transmission of between 0 (normal) and 7 (check information). A D-bit requires a connection with low delay, a T-bit requires high throughput, and an R-bit high connection reliability. Many implementations do not support the Type of Service field (i.e., they cannot interpret it).

Figure 9.3 Type of Service field

The next three fields contain information on fragmentation: FLAGS uses its three bits to control the fragmentation. The first bit is not assigned, the second bit is the "do not fragment" bit, since, when set to 1, no fragmentation may be performed. The packet is either transported in its entirety or not at all. The third bit is called the more fragments bit, because a 1 means that more fragments are following. Since the length field in the IP packet specifies the length of the fragment and not the length of the entire datagram, the destination station cannot use the length information to determine whether all the fragments have arrived. This makes the more fragments bit vitally important. The IDENT is a unique ID number identifying the datagram. A destination station can use this ID to gather together all the fragments of a specific datagram, since each fragment bears this unique number. The FRAGMENT OFFSET field shows the offset in length units of 8 bytes relative to the original datagram. The first fragment has an offset of 0. The destination station can use the offset information and the data lengths received to determine whether it is has received all the fragments. If one single fragment is missing from the sequence, the entire datagram will have to be sent and received again (see above).

The TIME field shows the lifetime of the packet in seconds. This information is important for preventing the packets from wandering round endlessly in an internet with many branches. Every router reduces the lifetime in accordance with the processing time expended in the router and the transit time assumed to have been taken for the packet to reach the router. This time is very difficult to calculate; to simplify the calculation, a standard time is specified for each transit.

Like an Ethernet-type field, the PROTO field specifies a specific protocol for the higher layers. HEADER CHECKSUM is an ·intrinsic checksum for the packet's check information (i.e., the header). Since this field is itself located in the header, a rule must be adopted for the calculation here: for calculating the header checksum, the content of the checksum field is assumed to be 0.

After the checksum, we finally see the destination and source addresses (network addresses, not MAC addresses), followed by the options. These are mainly used for test purposes and in error recovery protocols, not in normal data traffic. The OPTION field does not therefore, appear in all datagrams. Examples of important options include the record route option, in which the route actually taken by a packet is entered during transport (in the form of the addresses of the participating routers) and the source route option, in which the transmitting station specifies a fixed route on which the packet may be transported. Like the record route option, the time stamp option ensures that a time stamp is entered in every operational router. This enables the individual transport and processing times required to be understood more precisely.

9.1.2 IP Address Concept

An Internet address has a fixed length of 32 bits, the equivalent of 4 bytes. The individual bytes are shown as decimal digits and separated by point notation. It is easy to convert the decimal notation into the binary address:

Decimal notation: 10.20.30.40

Binary value: 00001010 00010100 00011110 00101000

It is divided into a network part (address of the network) and a host part (address of the end station in the network). All institutions and companies wishing to communicate with the international Internet in any way will be assigned the addresses for the network part centrally by the Network Information Center (NIC). The assignment of station addresses is left up to the organizations themselves. The international NIC in the USA has developed international address ranges which are managed and assigned by continental (ENIC, European NIC in Amsterdam) and national institutions (DeNIC in Karlsruhe).

Different numbers of bits may be selected for the network and the host. The idea behind this is the clever observation that not all networks have the same configuration: on the one hand, some networks have numerous subnetworks with only a few end stations each and, on the other hand, some are the exact opposite, networks with very few subnetworks, each of which has a large number of end stations. According to the traditional splitting into three, there is also a hybrid between the two. This is expressed formally by splitting the network addresses into three Classes, as shown in Figure 9.4:

- Class A has a 1-byte network part (network ID) and a 3-byte host part (station ID). More than 216 end stations (in words 65.636) per subnetwork and a maximum of 27 networks are possible in this gigantic dimension. However, it must be possible for all networks of this kind to be used worldwide, i.e., these network addresses are assigned centrally and have now all been assigned. Class A addresses are identified by a 0 in the first position leaving only 7 positions for the actual ID and hence 27 subnetworks.

- Class B has a 2-byte network part (network ID) and a 2-byte host part (station ID). A maximum of 214 end stations per subnetwork and a maximum of 216 subnetworks of this type are possible. The number of subnetworks is derived from the 14-position network address, as the first two bits are always assigned 10. Like the Class A addresses, the majority of the international Class B addresses are already assigned.

- Class C has a 3-byte network part (Network-ID) and a 1-byte host part (station ID). The network address starts with 110 which means a maximum of 221 subnetworks are possible, each of which may have up to 28 end stations.

Although the categorization into different network classes indeed allows for a differentiated approach, it does however, also have a few weak points:

- when the address Class changes (e.g., from C to B, if the networks are growing), all the devices have to be reconfigured and consistently.

- As IP implementations cannot usually handle two address Classes in parallel, it is not possible to perform the conversion for all devices step by step, which is in itself laborious enough; instead it has to be done in a global-galactic action (Friday night to Sunday night).

- The leap from 28 to 214 stations is relatively large, so an intermediate value, i.e., categorization into 4 Classes, is desirable under some circumstances. It is more flexible to have variable categorization into a network part and a station part, which may be governed by parameters.

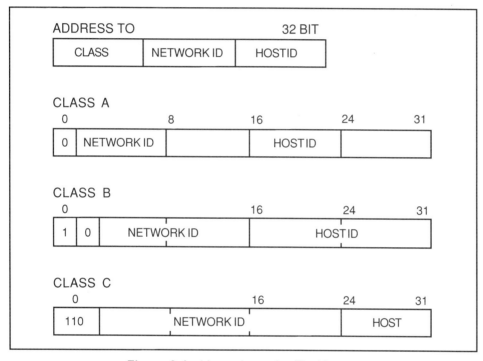

Figure 9.4 address classes for IP addresses

If different companies wish to pool their internets, careful coordination and planning of the current and future addresses is necessary to ensure that there is a favorable address structure but no duplicate addressees in the event of the participating companies not having international addresses. Even within each individual company, the implementation of TCP/IP networks should be planned and implemented from a long-term perspective (i.e., in relation to the final configuration stage), to avoid the change in address Classes with the implications described or error situations resulting from duplicate addresses as far as possible. This type of error may easily occur if, "for the sake of simplicity," equipment configurations are copied from new devices of the same type during installation and the person responsible forgets to change the IP address after copying.

The shortage of international Class B addresses has resulted in the development of two alternatives in recent years:

- the aggregation of Class C addresses by coherent Class C address blocks

- the use of gateways and a specified private address space that is not used by the Internet.

The aggregation of Class C addresses functions as follows: a user receives a coherent block of Class C addresses, which may be combined by an overlapping, i.e., shorter, subnetwork mask. This aggregation is known as CIDR (Classless Inter-Domain Routing) (RFC 1338, RFC 1519). The following shows an example with 16 Class C addresses, starting with the address 234.5.48.0:

Decimal Notation	Bit coding
234.5.48.0	11101010 00000101 00110000 00000000
234.5.49.0	11101010 00000101 00110001 00000000
234.5.50.0	11101010 00000101 00110010 00000000
234.5.51.0	11101010 00000101 00110011 00000000
234.5.52.0	11101010 00000101 00110100 00000000
234.5.53.0	11101010 00000101 00110101 00000000
234.5.54.0	11101010 00000101 00110110 00000000
234.5.55.0	11101010 00000101 00110111 00000000
234.5.56.0	11101010 00000101 00111000 00000000
234.5.57.0	11101010 00000101 00111001 00000000
234.5.58.0	11101010 00000101 00111010 00000000
234.5.59.0	11101010 00000101 00111011 00000000
234.5.60.0	11101010 00000101 00111100 00000000
234.5.61.0	11101010 00000101 00111101 00000000
234.5.62.0	11101010 00000101 00111110 00000000
234.5.63.0	11101010 00000101 00111111 00000000

All possible addresses for the last 4 bits in byte 3 "belong" to the user and may not be assigned to any other network. This address range may be aggregated with the following subnetwork mask.

Decimal Notation	Bit coding
Mask 255.255.240.0	11111111 11111111 11110000 00000000
Address 234.5.48.0	11101010 00000101 00110000 00000000

The subnetwork mask is 4 bits shorter than the Class C mask. One of the main advantages of this procedure is the fact that the entire address range may be managed in the Internet for all companies by a single entry in the participating router tables: the first address together with the abbreviation subnetwork mask, also known as the IP prefix. This abbreviated masking must be supported by the end system and the routers used. On the other hand, there are implementations which automatically set the subnetwork address to 255.255.255.0 for addresses with a value higher than 191.254.254.0. No CIDR may be used in this case.

When gateways are used, in accordance with RFC 1597, all internal company devices receive addresses from the following ranges:

- 10.0.0.0-10.255.255.255 (1 Class A)

- 172.16.0.0-172.31.255.255 (16 Class B)

- 192.168.0.0-192.168.255.255 (255 Class C)

These addresses are not assigned on an international level by the NIC and may be used "privately." If a company still wishes to allow some devices to talk with the Internet, international addresses will be requested for the devices which are to communicate with the Internet. A gateway will be set up to map the internal addresses for the devices in question to the international addresses. Within the company, all end systems communicate with the private addresses. A device logs on to the internet using its private address through the gateway which converts the private address into the international address before the packet is transmitted further to the Internet on the access router.

9.1.3 Routing Algorithm: RIP

An identical network address is used (network part of the network address) within one logical IP subnetwork, and packets may be sent directly to the station address (station part of the network address). Routers are not required as switching systems. Routing in its real sense will only be required if communication is required between stations in different subnetworks. In this case, the transmitting station must explicitly or implicitly address a router which will take over the responsibility for onward routing. In Internet terminology, routers are also called gateways, therefore, the word "gateway" is frequently found in the relevant TCP/IP literature. This manual uses the term "router" to designate a switching element at IP level.

In order to route packets correctly, each router has a table of reachable destination networks. This table only contains the reachable networks, not the end stations. If every router were to be constantly informed of which stations were active in which network parts, the overhead would be simply enormous. The network address is completely adequate for a routing decision, since the router only needs to know which stations are active in the subnetworks to which it is directly connected. The router interprets the network address and then decides whether to route the packet to an end station or to the next router (addressed =).

Imagine that the roads in ancient Gaul were connected not by bridges, but by routers. In the Internet network (see Figure 9.5), the connecting routers are shown with the applicable interface addresses. Although the network address for the station part always has the value 0, it must be possible to address the router interface as a station address, and so it has a full address (network part and station part). In the example of the network in the diagram, routers have the routing table shown in Figure 9.6. This should always contain the address of the destination network and the router interface address which has to be addressed for onward routing. Logically, this address is always the address of an "adjacent" router. The selected route is always the one with the fewest hops. If there are two routes of the same length, the one that was learned first remains in the table: changes are only effected in the event of improvements or discontinuation of communications (deterioration).

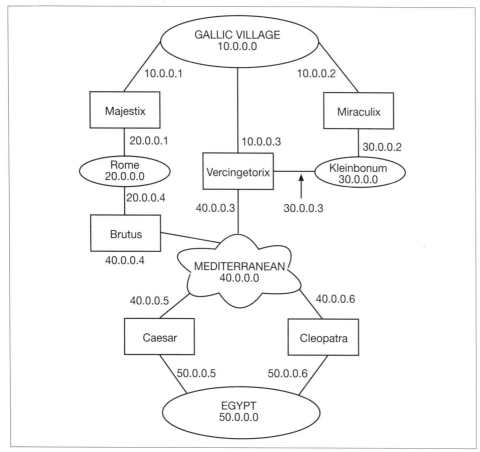

Figure 9.5 Example: Internet network

To keep the routing table small in complex networks, there is an option of setting default routers. All packets with network addresses which are not directly reachable are routed on to a defined default router which has more precisely specified tables. This alternative is useful for example, for connecting different sites (within one site, the routing is performed using network addresses and between sites a default router is used). This gives the possible routes a clearer structure, but redundancy is lost.

In static routes, the tables are applied manually; in dynamic routes they are learned "anyhow" by the routers. The calculation and updating of the tables in every router is facilitated by a router-router protocol, e.g., the Routing

Information Protocol (RIP). This was developed on the basis of the XNS RIP, and has become very firmly established as the BSD UNIX 4.x standard module, not because of its quality, but because of its ease of distribution. Many Internet networks have taken it over without worrying too much about its technical advantages or disadvantages. All routers send their own routing tables as a broadcast to other routers at intervals. The distance to other networks is proportionate from the point of view of their own routing tables. The routers use the tables they receive as the basis for calculating the shortest transmission distances to each destination network and take the adjacent router which provides the details of the distance as the destination router for onward routing. Figure 9.7 shows the update information sent by the routers Cleopatra and Majestix, i.e., reachable destination networks including learned distances.

Vercingetorix		Caesar	
For the Network	To Pass On	For the Network	To Pass On
10.0.0.0	ENDSTATION	10.0.0.0	40.0.0.3
20.0.0.0	40.0.0.4	20.0.0.0	40.0.0.4
30.0.0.0	ENDSTATION	30.0.0.0	40.0.0.3
40.0.0.0	ENDSTATION	40.0.0.0	ENDSTATION
50.0.0.0	10.0.0.1	50.0.0.0	ENDSTATION

Figure 9.6 Routing table for the routers Vercingetorix and Caesar

Sender: Cleopatra		Sender: Majestix	
Network	Distance	Network	Distance
10.0.0.0	1 Hop	10.0.0.0	0 Hops
20.0.0.0	1 Hop	20.0.0.0	0 Hops
30.0.0.0	1 Hop	30.0.0.0	1 Hop
40.0.0.0	0 Hops	40.0.0.0	1 Hop
50.0.0.0	0 Hops	50.0.0.0	2 Hops

Figure 9.7 Routing update information

The maximum distance may be 14 hops, so a value of 15 stands for "not reachable." This value seems fairly low, but the reason will become clear as follows: this procedure is very optimistic. It has the characteristic feature of disseminating "good news" (i.e., broadcasting new, shorter routes) very quickly and suppressing "bad news" for as long as possible. A simpler network configuration would be chosen for this: all routers are connected to each other in series (Figure 9.8).

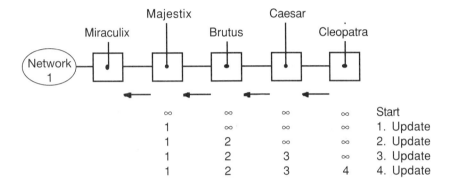

Figure 9.8 Learning new routes

Majestix, Brutus, Caesar, and Cleopatra have been active for a long time; Miraculix the druid is cutting mistletoe, and therefore, he is not ready. When he has finished doing that, he will participate in communications again. After four update intervals and transmission of the relevant information, all the others know that there is a route to network 1: on the first update Majestic, learns that there is a route to network 1 via Miraculix with 1 hop. On the second update, Brutus learns that Majestix has a route to network 1 with 1 hop, consequently Brutus has a route with 2 hops, as he has one hop to Majestix. On the third update, Caesar learns that there is a route to network 1 via Brutus with 3 hops and, on the fourth update, Cleopatra learns the same route with 4 hops (see Figure 9.8).

At this moment, Miraculix decides that he would rather be cutting mistletoe. Network 1 immediately becomes actually unreachable. Figure 9.9 shows the number of updates required for this to be recognized. For the sake of simplicity, the routers are designated A, B, C, D, and E. On the first update, C hears from B that he has a route to A with one hop, since B is in fact sending his "old" table. Brilliant, thinks C, that means I have a route to A with two hops since I take one hop to B. At the same time, C sends his own table to B. B has not received a direct message from A and is, therefore, no longer able to enter the route 1 hop to A. He receives the table from C and thinks: Brilliant! C has a route to A with 2 hops. That means I have a route to A with 3 hops, since I take one hop to C. B is not aware that C's information was based on the assumption of a route via B (which no longer actually exists). As a result, the routers mutually base their decisions on the "new" route and the value deteriorates by 2 hops.

It is only after fourteen updates (see Figure 9.9) that everyone is aware that network 1 is not longer reachable. This makes a restriction of the maximum distance to 14 hops very reasonable. In current implementations as in NetWare RIP, an improvement is achieved by the use of the Split Horizon procedure in which a router does not send updates on reachable networks on the port on which it received them (see also section 9.5).

9.1.4 Further Protocols

HELLO

The HELLO protocol functions in a very similar way to RIP, but it uses another metric. While RIP uses the number of hops needed as a metric, the HELLO protocol uses the transmission time (delay) for a communications route. This gives a clear advantage over RIP: two alternative links from A to B, both via two intermediate routers, are treated as completely equivalent in RIP. This is not the case if one of the links travels on lines with 9.6 kbps while the other travels on lines with 64 kbps. Consideration of the transmission time is an important criterion for route optimization.

Consideration of the "time" factor requires all routes to be synchronized with each other since every router has to know how things stand with the other routers. This, once again, requires check information which produces overhead on the network.

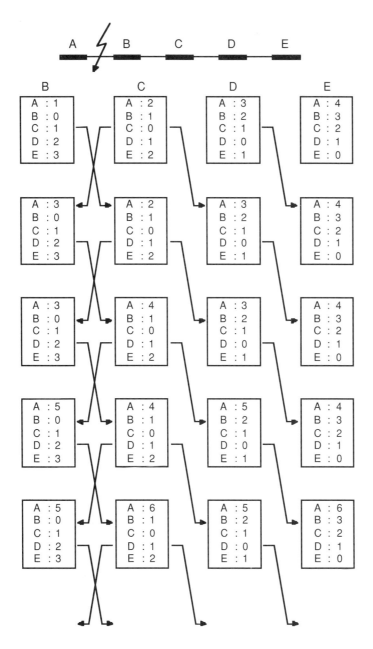

Figure 9.9 Learning unreachable networks

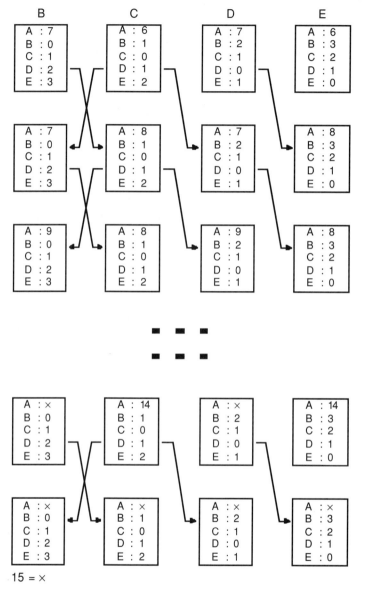

Figure 9.9 Learning unreachable networks (cont.)

In addition to the route information, every packet is given a time stamp when processed in a router. When it arrives at the next router, it calculates the delay in the connection made by subtracting the value of the time stamp from the estimated value for the current clock time of the adjacent router (the router from which it received the packet). Obviously, the router can only make assumptions of varying degrees of accuracy concerning the adjacent router's clock time and these assumptions should be checked from time to time. For this purpose, adjacent routers occasionally poll each other to find out each other's current clock time.

For reasons of stability, changing a route because of a shorter delay may only take place if a specific difference value is exceeded. Small differences upward and downward occur frequently as a result of synchronization differences and, if each one were to result in a change of route, the network would be caught up in a permanent game of "route roulette"—every network operator's worst nightmare.

ICMP (Internet Control Message Protocol)

RIP and HELLO protocols only provide the conditions for connections between end stations, not mechanisms for monitoring success with regard to the actual arrival of a packet at the destination station. The ICMP (Internet Control Message Protocol) therefore, fills this gap: it is used for error treatment and to monitor communications. It enables routers to notify errors and the causes of errors to other routers or end systems. It is mainly designed for error treatment between routers and end stations, but may also be used between routers.

ICMP is not a higher layer protocol, but, like IP, it is located at Layer 3 of the ISO model. It may be designated an ES-ES or ES-IS protocol (between end systems and routers). ICMP messages are transmitted like data packets as IP packets, based on the Internet service (datagram), there is therefore, no check on the actual arrival of an ICMP message. At this point, we should ask what would happen if an error message itself produces an error? To avoid producing an error message for an error message on a error message, it has been agreed that nothing at all will happen.

Instead of being followed by a data part with an ICMP packet, the IP header is always followed by a check or diagnostic part relative to the error situation determined. All ICMP packets have a TYPE field to identify the type of error (8 bit), a CODE field with extra information describing the type of error (8 bit) and a CHECKSUM field (16 bit), in which a checksum for the ICMP packet is entered (similar to the IP checksum). The ICMP packet also contains the first 64 data bits of the IP datagrams responsible for the error. This is more than the datagram header for the following reason: the recipient of an ICMP packet should also receive information on higher protocols and the application which are included in the 64 bits. This enables it to analyze the cause of the error more accurately. Most higher layer protocols are designed and implemented so that the central information may be found in the first 64 bits. Figure 9.10 shows some examples of ICMP packets. The source route option mentioned refers to an IP option, not to Token Ring source routing.

ARP (Address Resolution Protocol)

Formerly, it was frequently said that communication takes place via network addresses and that packets are sent "anyhow" to the correct addresses. How does a router or an end system learn which network address belongs to which MAC address? By means of an ES-IS protocol governing the communication between the router and the end station for a peer-to-peer link establishment phase. This task is administered by the Address Resolution Protocol. Where implemented, this protocol applies mapping tables to undertake the assignment of network addresses to MAC addresses. ARP is a typical ES-IS protocol (see section 8.2.1).

Since an Ethernet address is 48 bits long, it cannot be accommodated in a 32-bit Internet address. This means that no direct mapping (i.e., the derivation of the network address from the MAC address) is possible (as in other protocols, e.g., XNS, IPX). The necessary mapping table as shown in Figure 9.11, is applied on the basis of a dynamic inquiry algorithm: if end system A knows Internet address Ib and is searching for the associated MAC address Mb, it sends out a broadcast to end system B with Internet address Ib. The broadcast requests system B to respond with its MAC address Mb. This inquiry is received by all Internet systems, but only system B with Internet address Ib responds (hopefully, because protocol errors for this function may result in broadcast storms, for example).

TYPE	CODE
0	8

Echo   Request

0	0

Echo   Reply

3	0

Destination   Network
Inaccessible   Inaccessible

3	1

Destination   End Station
Inaccessible   Inaccessible

3	2

Destination   Protocol
Inaccessible   unavailable

3	3

Destination   Port Inaccessble
Inaccessible

3	4

Destination   Fragmentation
Inaccessible   Necessary, but "don't
                              fragment" rule

3	5

Destination   Source Route Option,
Inaccessible   Route Not Possible

Figure 9.10 ICMP examples

INTERNET	ETHERNET
89.0.0.2	08-00-14-65-02-03
89.0.0.3	08-00-C0-B8-41-25

Figure 9.11 ARP Table

If a router is located between the end systems, it responds to the broadcast with its own MAC address and then routes the incoming packets on the link onward in accordance with its routing table. This means that broadcasts overlapping subnetworks are suppressed by the router.

Now what would happen if the adapter card in a PC were replaced and hence the MAC address learned from other systems via ARP changed? Similar to what happens during the aging process in bridges, the ARP table is periodically refreshed (e.g., at half-hourly intervals). If a change is made in the meantime, errors may occur. In cases of doubt, the table has to be "deleted" and recompiled by restarting the TCP/IP protocols. The errors produced in this way remain within limits, since it is not to be expected that network adapters will have to be replaced all the time. The advantage of automatic address mapping (compared to manual entries) outweighs the disadvantage of occasional inconsistency.

Obviously the ARP only functions between end systems if both sides support the protocol. Unfortunately, it is not supported by all TCP/IP implementations.

EGP (Exterior Gateway Protocol)

RIP and HELLO introduced two protocols which can perform routing within complex networks. In Internet terminology, these kind of protocols are known as IGP (Interior Gateway Protocols). The EGP is intended to connect several complex networks which form a rather self-contained world and only occasionally (compared to internal communication) wish to talk with other networks. In TCP/IP terminology, this kind of network is called an autonomous system. It combines with other autonomous systems to form a "network of networks." In each autonomous system in the combined network, at least one "boundary router" is installed as an exterior gateway to connect the autonomous system with the other autonomous systems. The associated routing protocol is known as an Inter-autonomous System Routing Protocol (formerly also known as an Exterior Gateway Protocol).

The use of a higher ranking routing hierarchy has the advantage that not all internal routers have to exchange routing information with the other autonomous systems (overhead reduction). The disadvantage is that all communication with other autonomous systems takes place via this one (or a few) routers, which is not always the optimum route and means the boundary router is a potential bottleneck. Since cross-system communication is a low requirement, this last aspect is of subordinate significance. The failure of this kind of router should be seen as critical since it means no external communication is possible any more.

The EGP is mainly based on three mechanisms:

- First: Adjacent acquisition is supported. Thus, there is a mechanism by which one boundary router becomes acquainted with boundary routers in "adjacent" autonomous systems (router-router multicast between exterior gateways) and agrees with them to exchange routing information on the basis of the EGP. The term "adjacent" does not mean that they are physically adjacent, only that they have agreed to exchange information.

- Second: Adjacent EGP systems test at intervals to see whether the adjacent system is still alive (i.e., responds to inquiries). This prevents an infinite sequence of packets being sent over an autonomous system which in reality is no longer reachable. (As only datagrams are sent in the Internet, there is no packet-related check to see whether they actually arrive at their destinations.)

- Third: Adjacent EGP systems exchange information at intervals on which networks they are able to reach and they use this to update their routing tables according to the currently active topology.

Figure 9.12 shows a configuration with autonomous systems. See [COME88] for a more detailed description of EGP. In future, EGP will be replaced by the newer BGP (see also section 9.2.6).

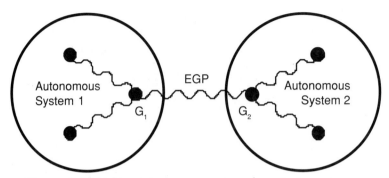

Figure 9.12 Linking autonomous systems by exterior gateways

9.2 Open Shortest Path First (OSPF)

OSPF is a routing protocol introduced in 1991 which will replace RIP in the short to medium term. The current version 2 is specified in RFC 1247. The weaknesses of RIP are discussed in section 9.1. The improvements offered by OSPF are as follows:

- hierarchical structure
- use of a Link State Algorithm
- bridging of distances larger than 14 intermediate systems
- more flexible metric

In principle, OSPF uses the same concepts as the OSI IS-IS described in the following section. Unlike the IS-IS, OSPF is designed for the address features and network structure of the TCP/IP or Internet world, while IS-IS requires OSI addresses.

9.2.1 Overview

OSPF is designed as an IGP, that is, it governs the routing within an autonomous system. It routes IP datagrams on the basis of the IP address and the TOS in the IP Header. No encapsulation into further check information takes place. OSPF is a dynamic routing protocol, i.e., routers have to exchange check information on the current network topology. It has the following design objectives:

- support for hierarchical network structures

- awareness of changes to the topology rapidly

- cycle freedom after convergence

- small overhead

To explain it further, let us start off by defining a series of terms used in OSPF:

- **Router**: Internetworking component which links networks at Layer 3 (called a gateway in earlier RFC standards).

- **Autonomous System, AS**: Group of routers which exchange routing information using a common routing protocol (IGP).

- **Area ID**: A 32-bit number assigned to an area. It has the same meaning throughout the network and may be the IP network number for the area. The backbone always contains the area ID 0.

- **Router ID**: A 32-bit-Number which every router under OSPF contains. The router ID must have the same meaning within the AS. It does not have to be, but may be, the router's network address.

- **Network, Net**: IP network or IP subnetwork. A physical subnetwork may contain several network numbers. It will then be treated as several separate networks.

- **Network Mask, Subnetwork mask**: A 32-bit number masking the address range of an individual network/subnetwork. A typical subnetwork mask for Class C networks is 0xFFFFFF00, in decimal notation 255.255.255.0.

- **Multi-Access Network**: A non-broadcast network to which several systems may be connected (e.g., X.25).

- **Interface, IF**: A link between a router and one of the networks to which it is connected.

- **Adjacent Routers**: Routers with interfaces to a common network. In multi-access networks and broadcast networks, adjacent routers are identified dynamically using the HELLO protocol.

- **Adjacency**: A communications relationship between adjacent routers for the mutual exchange of routing information, in particular their topological databases.

- **Link State Advertisement (LSA)**: The packet that contains information on a router or a network. LSAs are flooded. Collection of all Link State Advertisements forms the basis for calculating topological database. A router must await an inter-packet gap of at least 5 seconds between the transmission of LSA packets.

- **HELLO Protocol**: A protocol for establishing and maintaining adjacency. In multi-access networks and broadcast networks, the HELLO protocol is used to find adjacent systems dynamically.

- **Designated Router (DR)**: Every multi-access network and broadcast network has a designated router which performs special protocol actions. The designated router is selected using the HELLO protocol. It may be addressed using Multicast 224.0.0.6.

Establishing and Addressing Subnetworks

One of the most significant properties of OSPF is the option of grouping networks within an Autonomous System (AS). Like IS-IS, OSPF uses a hierarchical concept: a network group is an area and the higher-ranking hierarchy is the entire autonomous system. All areas are linked by a common backbone, together with this forming a partition of the Autonomous System. The topology of an area is screened from the rest of the Autonomous System (AS): the AS views the area as a separate subnetwork. This screening achieves a significant reduction in overhead. Routing within an area is solely based on the information on this area. Even the rest of the AS is screened from the area. As a rule, an area consists of several Class C IP networks or Class A/B subnetworks. OSPF addresses are not restricted to these address Classes: an area is defined by a list of network addresses and subnetwork masks, which could look as follows:

Network number	Address mask	Subnetwork size (#hosts)
128.185.16.0	0xFFFFF000	4094
128.185.1.0	0xFFFFFF00	254
128.185.0.8	0xFFFFFFF8	8

This means that a Class A, B, or C address may be structured by the subnetwork mask into larger or smaller subnetworks as required.

Topological Database and SPF Tree

Every router has a topological database, known as the Link State Database, for every area to which it is connected. The Link State Database is used to file all important topological information on the area. This database is the same for all routers in an area, but differs for routers in different areas (if a subdivision into areas has been performed, see below). Every router makes its personal details (current status, active interfaces, adjacent systems currently reachable), which contribute to the overall topology, known to the other routers within its area by means of broadcasts.

Every router uses the topological database to form its own "shortest path tree" in relation to the topology in which it regards itself as the root, and the paths in the tree are the shortest distance (as seen by the router in question) to each reachable destination. This method is known as the Shortest Path First (SPF) method since the shortest path is in each case (as seen by the router in question) selected as the route. If there are alternative routes of the same distance, the load is distributed equally. The tree structure produced is obviously different for each router. A router forms different trees for different metrics (costs or TOS: delay, throughput, reliability). The default cost metric is one in which every output interface is assigned costs (integral value). The other metrics are tailored to the specified types in the TOS field (type of service fields) in the IP frame.

The exchange of protocol information in OSPF is protected by authentication mechanisms, i.e., only authorized routers may participate in OSPF routing. Every area may use its own authorization.

Coexistence with other protocols

Routing information which originates from EGP or BGP information is routed onward transparently by an Autonomous System using OSPF.

RIP routes may be made known in the OSPF AS as external routes (AS external routes) by boundary routers between an RIP AS and an OSPF AS. The RIP routes are then static routes and are addressed via the boundary routers.

The following will first give a description of the elements used in OSPF and then use this as a basis for describing how the network topology is designed. The dissemination of topological information and error treatment is explained using examples.

9.2.2 Elements Used and Routing Philosophy

OSPF supports the following networks and links:

*   *Broadcast networks (LANs)*, in which more than one router may be stationed, but in which all routers may be reached with a single physical (broadcast) message. Adjacent routers are learned using the HELLO protocol.

*   *Point-to-point connections between a single router pair*, e.g.,. a 64 kbps serial line. Direct connections from end systems to routers (e.g., SLIP Serial Line Interface Protocol) are also treated as point-to-point connections.

*   *Non-broadcast multi-access networks* in which more than one router may be stationed but in which there is no broadcast mechanism to reach all routers with one message (usually public networks, e.g., X.25 networks, in the future ATM as well).

*   *Virtual links*, which, in the event of an error, maintain a perfect backbone connection if there is no physical link (see below).

OSPF topology is split into several layers:

*   network
*   area (group of networks)
*   backbone (linking areas)
*   Autonomous System (AS = all the areas connected by the backbone).

The hierarchical organization of an Autonomous System is one of the most important aspects of OSPF. A group of logically and physically connected networks may be combined to form an area. Areas may not overlap and are generally connected to each other by the backbone. The actual backbone is a (higher-ranking) area and is always assigned the area ID 0. Every area loads its own version of the SPF algorithm internally and so creates its own internal topological database. This means routers from different areas have different topological databases. A router that is connected to several areas in an area border router and has a topological database for each area. It must belong to the backbone area.

Two routers which are connected to the same area, have identical topological information for the area. The backbone includes all networks which are not assigned to an area, the routers in these networks, and all routers which are connected to several areas; the backbone must always be physically and/or logically coherent. If there is no physical link, a logical backbone connection must be configured as a virtual link, as is explained later. For the purposes of the protocol, a virtual link is treated as a point-to-point link. The actual backbone forms a "backbone area" with all the properties of an area: its own topological database, the contents of which are screened from other areas (just as the actual backbone does not "know" anything about other areas), and intra-area routing.

Different router types are assigned to the different levels:

- *Intra-area Router*: all networks connected to the router (router interfaces) lie within one area or all interfaces lie within the backbone.

- *Designated Router*: In LANs, the HELLO protocol selects a router to represent all the others as a designated router which exchanges topological information with the other networks.

- *Area Border Router*: all routers which are connected to an area and the backbone or to several areas are area border routers, i.e., they belong to at least two different worlds (e.g., two areas or one area and the backbone).

- *AS Boundary Router*: routers which maintain the link to one or several other AS and are able to provide their own AS with relevant routing information.

OSPF uses the following fixed parameters (architectural constants):

- The area ID for the backbone is 0

- The update period for LSA information is 30 minutes

- A router must wait for an interval (interpacket gap) of at least 5 seconds between the transmission of two LSA packets

- The maximum permissible age of LSA information in the database is 1 hour

- The checksum for a stored LSA must be checked every 5 minutes

- A flooded LSA has a maximum lifetime of 15 minutes

- The value for inaccessibility is 216 for router links (2 byte cost value) and 224 for summary links (3 byte cost value)

Routing Philosophy

There are two routing levels in an Autonomous System:

- Intra-area routing within an area

- Inter-area routing over at least one area border, i.e., using the backbone

Intra-area routing requires only the internal area topological information. In addition, only routers within this area participate in the onward routing process. This protects the routing process within an area from error conditions outside the area. Inter-area routing information is only used if it is really required, i.e., if a packet has to routed over area borders. In this case, area border routers, i.e., backbone routers, also participate in the routing process. If the routing takes place on a virtual link, it is performed in accordance with the regulations of the participating areas, even though it is in actual fact "backbone routing."

The exchange and notification of topological information is performed by means of what is known as "advertising." Every router advertises its own knowledge so it may be used. The associated messages are called advertisements.

9.2.3 Example of OSPF

An example of an Autonomous System is shown in Figure 9.13. In this example, no areas have been created. Circles and rounded rectangles denote multi-access networks (LAN, X.25); rectangles denote routers. Links between routers represent point-to-point links. Router interfaces in these links do not require the assignment of any Internet addresses. If, despite this, an Internet address is assigned, the interface is modeled as a stub link connection (dead end). The only point-to-point network in the example configuration with an interface assignment is the link between router 6 and router 10.

The rectangle designated H1 denotes a host which is connected to router 12 by means of a serial interface (SLIP). Router 12 disseminates information on a host route. The treatment of host routes falls outside the scope of this book, and it will not be dealt with in any great detail (for detailed information see [RFC1131]).

As output interfaces, all interfaces are assigned costs which may be configured. The lower the costs are set, the more attractive the use of this interface becomes and the more frequently it will be used for onward routing, as other alternatives are "dearer." No costs are specified for the route from the network to the router interface: the costs of an interface as an output interface include the entire route as far as the next router. Links from the network to the router, therefore, have the cost value 0.

Router 1 has, for example, two interfaces to two LANs, network 3 is connected to four routers, router 3 has two interfaces to LANs, an interface to a point-to-point link with router 6 etc. Router 5 is linked to three networks outside the AS, networks 12, 13, and 14. Router 6 only has interfaces to other routers, not to networks. Router 12, for example, has interfaces to two LANs and one host; network 6 is connected to three routers for which the route into the network has given rise to cost value 1 and the route out of the network to the router has the cost value 0.

Since no areas are configured, all the routers have the same database on the network topology. The routing tables for different routers are based on the calculated SPF-tree, in which every router sees itself as the root, since they are all different. In the next step, the routing table for router 6 will be reconstructed using the tree which it has compiled. The tree is shown in Figure 9.14.

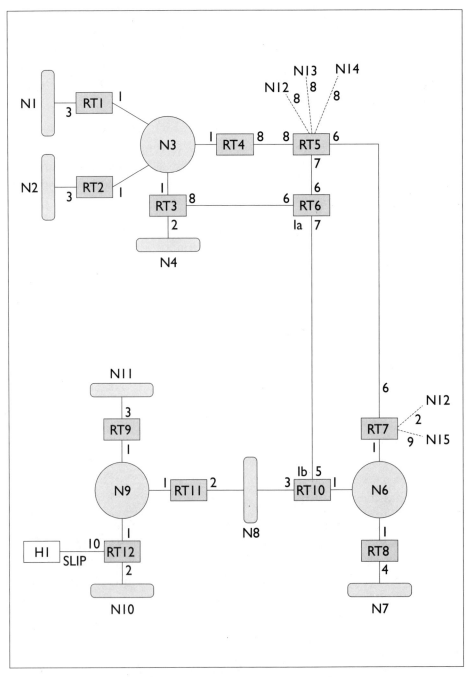

Figure 9.13 Example of an Autonomous System

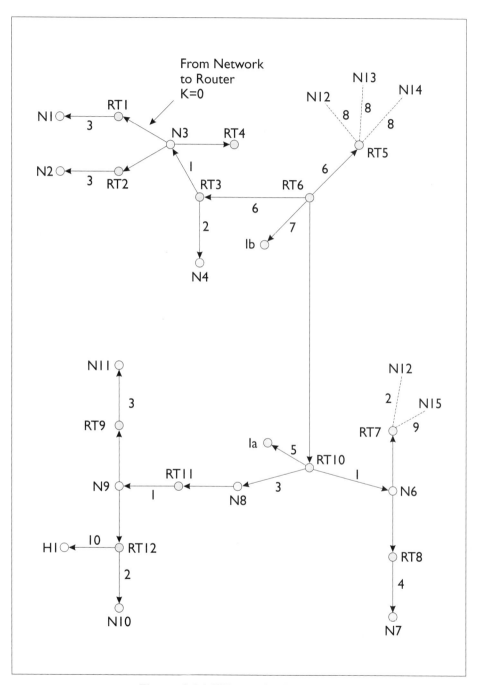

Figure 9.14 SPF- tree for Router 6

The SPF-tree designed by the router specifies the distances to all the reachable networks. However, to transfer a packet, it is always the next node (router) on the route which is addressed. The shortest distance to the next router is found from the SPF-tree. The distance from router 6 to network 9 has, for example, a cost value of 11, which is obtained from the total of 7+3+1 on the path via router 10 and router 11. The cost value for links inside and outside the AS are shown in Figure 9.15.

Destination	Next Hop	Distance
N1	RT3	10
N2	RT3	10
N3	RT3	7
N4	RT3	8
Ib	*	7
Ia	RT10	12
N6	RT10	8
N7	RT10	12
N8	RT10	10
N9	RT10	11
N10	RT10	13
N11	RT10	14
H1	RT10	21
RT5	RT5	6
RT7	RT10	8
N12	RT10	10
N13	RT5	14
N14	RT5	14
N15	RT10	17

Figure 9.15 Cost table for router 6

The example of a network with the original flat topology is now structured into areas. The new configuration is shown in Figure 9.16. There are three areas; area 1 contains router 1, router 2, router 3, router 4, and networks 1 to 4. Area 2 consists of networks 6 to 8 with routers 7, 8, 10, and 11. Area 3 encompasses routers 9, 11, and 12, host H1, and networks 9 to 11. Networks

9, 10, 11, and host H1 are combined again so that, from outside, they are declared to be a common "destination." (This feature is included for purposes of completeness, but no further details can be given in this manual. For further details see [RFC1131]).

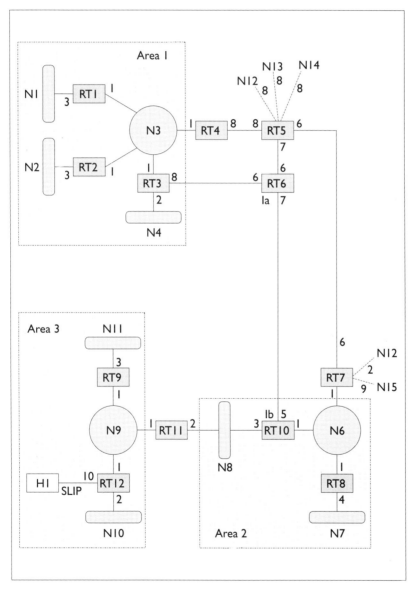

Figure 9.16 Example of an OSPF area configuration

Routers 1, 2, 5, 6, 8, 9, and 12 are internal routers. Routers 3, 4, 7, 10, and 11 are border routers. Router 6 is a pure backbone router, and therefore counts as an internal router (the backbone area). Routers 5 and 7 are AS boundary routers. Router 11 is a backbone router as it belongs to two different areas, but it is not connected to the rest of the backbone. Remedy? A virtual link is configured between router 10 and router 11.

Topology Calculation

This configuration is now used to compile the topological databases in the individual routers. Figure 9.17 shows the database for area 1. It is identical for routers 1, 2, 3, and 4 and shows how the world appears to internal routers 1 and 2. As area border routers, routers 3 and 4 have the tasks of making known the networks in area 1 which are reachable via the backbone, but without the associated topological information, just a corresponding cost value. For the area 1 database, these links take the form of stub links (dead-ends). In addition, border routers 3 and 4 should also notify the AS boundary routers together with the networks reachable through them. This information is entered into the databases as separate topologies.

In addition, border routers 3 and 4 must notify the backbone of the reachable area 1 networks. Once again, this is only based on cost value (distance), not topological information.

The notification is shown in the table in Figure 9.18. Router 3 disseminates cost value 4 to networks 1 and 2, distance 1 to network 3, and distance 2 to network 4. Router 4 sends advertisements with cost value 4 to networks 1 and 2, with distance 1 to network 3, and with distance 3 to network 4. This makes it clear that backbone routers for packets which have to go into network 4 will always address router 3 (as long as it is active).

The topology of the backbone is calculated in a backbone database. This calculation is performed by all border routers (routers 3, 4, 7, 10, and 11). The information on reachable area networks is contained in the backbone topology as stub links (see also Figure 9.19). Every border router hears from the backbone all advertisements put out by the other border routers with regard to reachable networks. It uses these messages to calculate the distances to the networks outside its own area and enters the distances in the database.

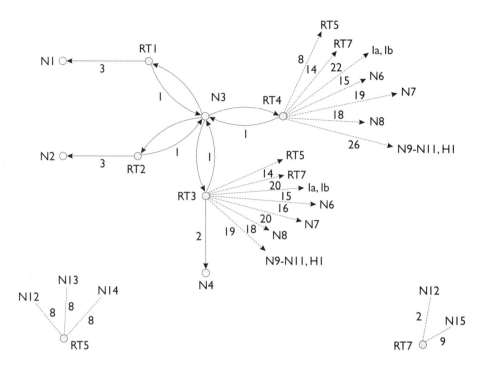

Figure 9.17 Topological database for area

Network	RT3 adv.	RT4 adv.
N1	4	4
N2	4	4
N3	1	1
N4	2	3

Figure 9.18 Notification of networks reachable to the backbone by routers 3 and 4

Using the example of routers 3 and 4, this looks as follows: first of all, they calculate their own SPF-tree for the backbone and so obtain the distances (cost values) to all the other backbone routers. Then they calculate the distances to networks in the backbone and to AS boundary routers. The calculated values are shown in the table in Figure 9.20.

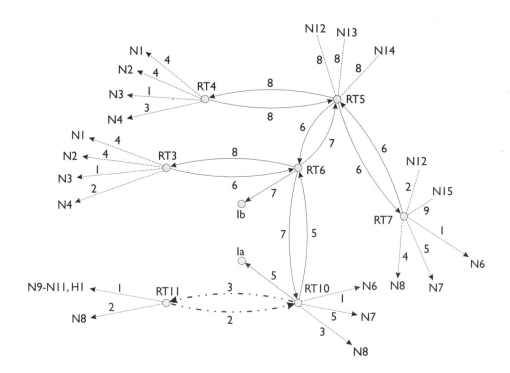

Figure 9.19 Backbone topological database

Area Border Router	Dist from RT4	Dist from RT3
to RT3	*	21
to RT4	22	*
to RT7	20	14
to RT10	15	22
to RT11	18	25
to Ia	20	27
to Ib	15	22
to RT5	14	8
to RT7	20	14

Figure 9.20 Backbone distances as seen by routers 3 and 4

In the third step, they incorporate the information (advertisements) from the other border routers and learn the distances which other routers are disseminating for "their" networks. Routers 3 and 4 again notify their own area of these networks and distances. The advertisements from routers 3 and 4 for their own area (area 1) are shown in the table in Figure 9.21.

Destination	RT3 Adv.	RT4 Adv.
Ia,Ib	15	22
N6	16	15
N7	20	19
N8	18	18
N9-N11,H1	19	26
RT5	14	8
RT7	20	14

Figure 9.21 Advertisements from routers 3 and 4 for area I

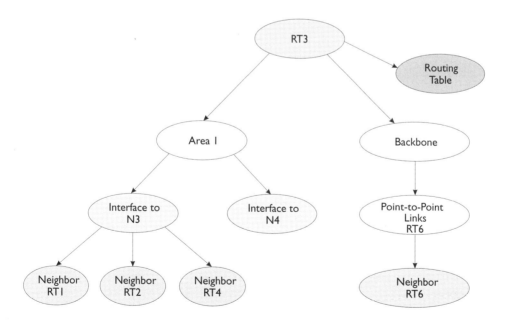

Figure 9.22 Data structure for router 3

To round things off, an example of router 3 is used to show the final data structure established by a router (see Figure 9.22). Router 3 belongs to area 1 and to the backbone. In area 1, it has interfaces to networks 3 and 4. It learns routers 1, 2, and 4 as its adjacent area 1 routers. It has an interface to the backbone which talks to router 6 via a point-to-point connection. Router 6 is also the only adjacent backbone for router 3.

9.2.4 Creation of OSPF table and routing

Before an OSPF-router data packet may be routed onwards, it must undergo a series of actions to construct its topological database and resulting routing table.

Acquisition of Adjacent Routers, Database Creation, Updates

A router's first activity after booting is to initialize its data structure and perform the usual self-tests (interfaces, lower-ranking LANs, etc.). During this time, it does not transport any data. Then it uses the HELLO protocol to acquire information on adjacent routers by acquainting itself with the adjacent routers. (The default setting for a HELLO packet is 10 seconds in the LAN and 30 seconds in the WAN). HELLO packets go to the IP multicast address AllSPF routers (224.0.0.5) and are interpreted by all OSPF routers.

If, with the aid of the HELLO protocol, two routers have agreed that they are adjacent, they exchange their topological information (database synchronization). To ensure that the exchange takes place in the proper way, the adjacent routers agree on which of them is to start first: the exchange takes place according to a master-slave arrangement. The router with the higher router ID is the master. The complete database is only exchanged between adjacent routers (otherwise it would be overdoing the gossip). This involves a router notifying its status at intervals ("my interface is out of action," "now it's working again"). This ensures that, in the event of a total failure, adjacent routers learn fairly rapidly that one of them is no longer alive. The surviving router then sends the sad tidings (for this there is a parameter known as router dead interval: a multiple of the HELLO intervals, e.g., 4*HelloInt).

After the initial exchange of databases, the databases then have to be maintained. To do this, Link State Advertisements (LSA) are exchanged between adjacent routers. LSA packets are transmitted periodically (at 30 minute intervals) or governed by events (active interface out of action, new interface activated). Event-controlled LSAs in particular cause the convergence behavior to be much better than it is with RIP. Obsolete link state information is deleted and re-requested by an aging timer.

Designated Router

As LANs are broadcast networks, all connected routers hear everything the others say about themselves. With 10 routers (e.g., on a site backbone), every router would have adjacency with everyone else which would result in permanent Link State Advertisements (LSAs). This is obviously absurd, as it is sufficient for a router to receive all the information and then transmit the LSA packets to the multicast address AllSPF routers (224.0.0.5), and all the others should "hear" this. This is covered by the concept of the Designated Router (DR). This establishes adjacency with all the other routers and exchanges the necessary database information with them.

The Designated router is selected using the HELLO protocol. Every router has a priority value (8-bit, interpreted as an integer), which it enters in the HELLO packet. The router with the highest priority is the DR. In the event of equal priority, the router with the highest router ID is the winner. It is evident that the Designated Router holds a critical position. If it fails, the information system collapses. Therefore, a Backup Designated Router (BR) is selected which works in hot standby and also maintains adjacency to all other routers but does not transmit any LSA packets. The selection principle is the same as for the DR. If the DR fails, the BR notices this after the expiry of a timer and is immediately activated as a new DR. At the same time, a new BR is selected. The DR and BR are addressed via the multicast 224.0.0.6.

Intra-Area Routing

The collection of all Link State Advertisements forms the basis for the topological database, its updating, and the design of the SPF-tree. The SPF-tree is used as a basis for the creation of the intra-arca routing table (which, for each destination network, specifies the next router on the shortest route). For all destinations it contains the following:

- destination type (network, border router, AS boundary router)

- area ID

- cost value

- next router (next hop)

No further information is required to implement the routing functions within an area: if a router receives a packet for onward routing within the area, it finds the next router and the associated output port. It address the packet to the router's MAC address and routes it onwards.

Inter-Area Routing

To be able to route over several areas, area border routers require additional information which they assimilate as an extract from the topology of all the rest of the AS in their data structure. This takes place in 3 steps; it should be noted that border routers are backbone routers and hence contain detailed information on the backbone area:

- *Step 1*: every border area router notifies in the form of address and cost value or distance all networks which are reachable via its area(s). The relevant advertisements are known as Summary Link Advertisements and are received by all backbone routers. Then every backbone router, and hence also every border router, has the summary information for all other areas.

- *Step 2*: A border router may use the summary information and the complete information on the backbone received previously to calculate the distances to all networks not within the areas to which it is directly connected.

- *Step 3*: The router notifies the calculated total costs to other networks in the area to which it is directly connected. All the border routers in an area do this. In this way, the internal routers in an area learn which border router is the best one for a specific destination (i.e., the one with the shortest distance).

External Routes

Yet another ingredient is added for external routes. The networks which may be reached by these routes are notified equally to all internal and backbone routers in the form of AS boundary routers and networks. They are flooded over the entire network and are contained in every topological data base.

Before giving an example explaining the various advertisements, let us group them into categories once more:

- *Router Links Advertisement*
  From: all routers
  Contents: own status, interfaces
  To: own area

- *Summary Link Advertisement*
  From : area border router
  Contents: networks outside own area
  To: all connected areas

- *AS External Link Advertisement*
  From: AS boundary router
  Contents: networks outside the AS
  To: all routers within the AS

- *Network Links Advertisement*
  From: designated router in a LAN
  Contents: a network's routers
  To: own area
  (will not be examined further)

When routing in accordance with OSPF, a router has to perform the following actions: it transmits

- Router Links Advertisements into each area to which it is connected

- Summary Link Advertisements for every destination outside the area (inter-area destination)

- AS External Link Advertisements to everything, if it is an AS boundary router

It should be noted that the backbone itself counts as an area. Let us now return to router 4: which advertisements does it send within OSPF to which networks? The committed OSPF fan can work it out before reading further.

Router 4 is an area border router or, to be more precise, a member of area 1 and a member of the backbone area. Router 4 sends five advertisements to the backbone:

- own interfaces (router links)
- network 1 (summary link)
- network 2 (summary link)
- network 3 (summary link)
- network 4 (summary link)

Router 4 sends eight advertisements to area 1.

- own interfaces (router links)
- router 5 (summary link relating to AS boundary router)
- router 7 (summary link relating to AS boundary router)
- 1a, 1b (summary link)
- network 6 (summary link)
- network 7 (summary link)
- network 8 (summary link)
- networks 9 to 11, host 1 (summary link relating to combined group)

As an AS boundary router, router 5 sends three advertisements which are routed on to all networks:

- network 12 (AS External Link Advertisement)
- network 13 (AS External Link Advertisement)
- network 14 (AS External Link Advertisement)

Error Response

What follows is an explanation of the actions which take place in OSPF in a normal case. Unfortunately the network world is not as healthy as the user might wish. Sooner or later (usually sooner rather than later), failures will occur, even in an OSPF network. What happens to the topological information in the event of an error? The error response is described below with the aid of a few examples. Figure 9.23 shows an Autonomous System with two areas. Router C and D are backbone routers. The link between routers A and B has just failed. The numbers at the junctions indicate costs and the numbers within the routers are interface numbers.

Router B learned at some stage that it has a neighbor A. When A ceases to respond, the timer RoutDeadInt times out at B. B recognizes that A is completely or temporarily "dead" and

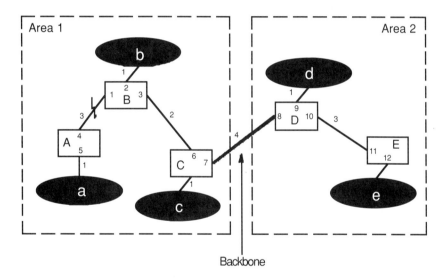

Figure 9.23 Error in OSPF

- B changes the status information on A from "UP" to "DOWN."

- B sends a router link advertisement within area 1 (event-driven advertisement) of the type "link 2, to network b, metric 1; link 3, to router C, metric 2."

- C replaces the old entry "network a, metric 6 with a new entry "network a, metric_."

- C sends a Summary Link Advertisement to the backbone "network a, metric _."

- D replaces the old entry "network a, metric 10" by the new "network a, metric _."

- D sends a Summary Link Advertisement to area 2 "network a, metric _."

- E replaces the old entry "network a, metric 10" with the new entry "network a, metric _."

Consequently: 3 updates are sufficient!

Compared with RIP, this achieves a considerable saving in time and information exchange. Manufacturers supporting OSPF include, for example, ACC, Bay Networks, Cisco, Digital, 3Com, IBM, Proteon, and Retix.

9.2.5 Comparison: OSPF and RIP

The following table contains a point-by-point comparison of RIP and OSPF:

	OSPF	RIP
Hierarchy formation	yes	no
Algorithm	link state	distance vector
Storage space	higher	lower
CPU performance	higher	lower
HELLO interval	10 sec. LAN 30 Sec. X.25	*****
Link state refresh	every 30 minutes	*****
Update packet	individual information (LSA)	complete table
Update confirmation	yes	no
Table update	*****	every 30/60 seconds
Metric	"costs"	hops
Convergence	better	worse
Overheads	lower	higher
Authorization	yes	no

9.2.6 BGP (Border Gateway Protocol)

BGP (Border Gateway Protocol) is a more recent protocol between Autonomous Systems, which is replacing EGP. It is now being used in version 4 according to RFC 1771. It is suitable for working with OSPF as an internal routing protocol. In particular, it supports route aggregation with CIDR. BGP is already used in the international Internet, and all routers which support this protocol are gradually being converted to BGP.

A BGP router talks to other BGP systems via a reliable transport protocol: TCP (not just IP). In an active state, it attempts to find other active adjacent BGP systems and establish a connection with them via TCP Port 179. Adjacent BGPs have physical links with each other without any other inter-posed BGPs. According to the conventional "hop-by-hop paradigm" a BGP-router notifies the routes which it itself is using. As in OSPF, every BGP router uses the sum total of the route information from other BGP routers, particu-larly adjacent BGP routers to create a database for routes overlapping ASs, which contains the routes to all reachable ASs.

If two adjacent BGP routers have identified each other and established a TCP link with each other, first they exchange their complete databases with each other. After this, only event-driven updates will be used if the network situation changes. Default updating at regular intervals is not specified. However, BGP routers do send regular KeepAlive packets via their TCP links so that their partners know they are still alive.

A BGP system creates three different databases, which are known as RIBs (Routing Information Bases):

- RIBs-In contain the routes which were learned from update packets

- Loc-RIBs contain the internal AS routes which are used by the BGP system itself

- RIBs-Out store the routes which the BGP system notifies to other BG partners (by advertisement). Only this route information is entered in update packets (advertisements)

RFC 1771 does not specify that this information really has to be stored in three copies. The different tables may also be compiled from one database using suitable pointer concepts.

Since there are no regular updates, a BGP system has to store the complete routing tables for all its partner systems (BGP systems with which there are TCP links), for the duration of the link. If a route is no longer reachable, a BGP system has three different ways of notifying this to its partners:

- The IP prefix (network address, subnetwork mask) is entered in an update packet in a special field—WITHDRAWN ROUTES. The recipients know that the router in question is no longer reachable.

- If there is an alternative route, this is notified in the NLRI (Network Layer Reachability Information) field in the same update in which the original route was disabled under WITHDRAWN ROUTES.

- The TCP link between BGP routers may be dismantled. This forces the participating routers to deactivate all routes which the two participating routers had notified to each other. This last possibility represents a type of emergency exit for serious error situations or inconsistencies.

The basic routing algorithm is a distance vector procedure: the update packets contain complete routes to reachable Autonomous Systems in each case as seen by the transmitted BGP router.

9.3 OSI

ISO-OSI IS-IS (Intermediate System to Intermediate System Protocol) in accordance with ISO Standard 10589 of 1992 is the routing protocol forming part of OSI routing. Communications between routers and end systems is regulated by the ES-IS protocol (End System to Intermediate System) in accordance with ISO Standard 9542, which was adopted in 1988 and expanded in 1994 by multicast definitions for connectionless services. IS-IS works according to similar concepts as OSPF (hierarchy and link state algorithm), but it is designed for OSI addresses and generally kept more global than OSPF. One of the favorite concepts within the framework of OSI is a domain concept, since, with domain concepts, things may be beautifully modeled globally, flexibly, and hierarchically. For example, the OSI network management also uses a domain concept.

A domain is usually "anything" partitioned from the rest of the work—a service company, a car production plant, a hospital, a building, a computer world, a town, an occupational group, etc. One important feature of a domain is that it may be further subdivided into sub-domains and sub-sub-domains etc. As part of OSI routing, it is planned to have two hierarchical levels, a domain (company network) split into sub-domains. The layers are called Level 1 (sub-domain) and Level 2 (domain). The IS-IS standard ([ISO06]) refers to the routing within a domain, which is called Intra-Domain Routing (Level 2). An IDRP, Inter-Domain Routing Protocol (IDRP) has been defined since 1994 in ISO Standard 10747 (/ISO08/) (the "metalayer" for Level 2 routing). The network service on which the routing protocols are based is connectionless (ISO 8473 CLNP, Connectionless Network Protocol). The connections between IDRP, IS-IS, ES-IS and CLNP are shown in Figure 9.24.

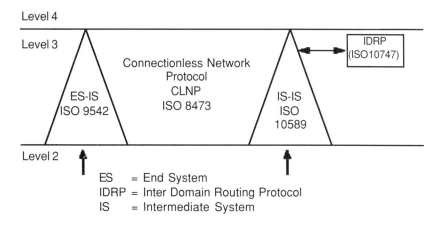

Figure 9.24 OSI routing protocols

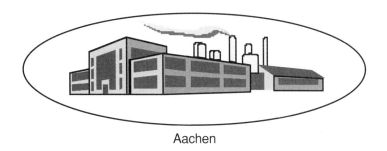

Aachen

Figure 9.25 City highway

As in many instances of OSI standardization, CLNP, ES-IS, IS-IS, and IDRP are based on a global model. To explain this, let us look at a model from our everyday environment, the international highway model. Picture a country which has four federal states. Each of the federal states has several cities. A six-lane highway ring has been constructed around each city as the city highway (Figure 9.25-9.28), obviously with several access and exit roads.

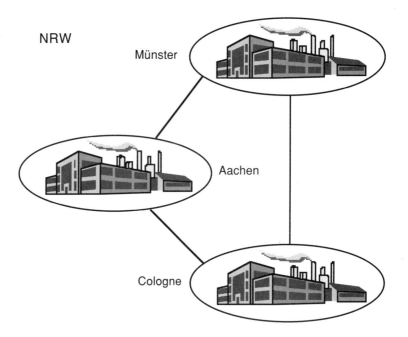

Figure 9.26 State highway

Within a state, the highway rings are linked to each other by state highways. Different states have different types and different numbers of state highways (e.g., Highway 61 goes to Tunica, Mississippi, while I95, 495, 90, and many others go to Boston, Massachusetts), but they do have one thing in common: there is always at least one link between any two cities. The state highways are linked to each other by national highways (just as the city highways are linked by state highways), which facilitate transit from one state to another (e.g., indicated by a sign stating "You are now entering the State of Pennsylvania"). In Europe, after the introduction of the EC internal market, international highways were created to connect the different countries so that there is always at least one possible route between any two countries. The same traffic regulations (passing on the left, slow driving on the right, no passing on the right) apply on all these international highways which link the national highways, which link the state highways which link the city highways.

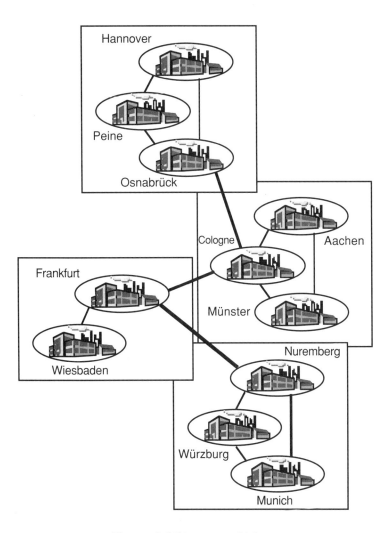

Figure 9.27 Interstate highway

This world corresponds exactly to an OSI network environment (Figure 9.28), except, unlike real life, all the "road" users in a network environment obey these rules of the "road." The buildings in the cities correspond to end systems (a to f). They start or end a communication process. The cars correspond to data packets moving through the world independently of each other. The city highways correspond to LANs. The transition from city highway to state highway takes place via a Level 1 router (A to C). A federal state corresponds to a Level 1 area, a country to a Level 2 backbone area or a domain in OSI terminology. The transition from state highway to national highway takes place via a Level 2 router (L2-1 to L2-4). Thus far, the IS-IS routing is sufficient. As with the EC internal market, full internationality has not yet been achieved. This is where the IDRP is supposed to facilitate the link between different domains; with a current interpretation of the term "domain" being a manufacturer's world! (SNA, DECnet, TCP/IP, etc.)

The routing algorithm for IS-IS is based on Digital Phase V (DECnet/OSI). The previous OSI routing was performed as static routing. IS-IS, on the other hand, is a dynamic procedure. The links examined are the same as with OSPF:

- LAN
- point-to-point
- multi-access (X.25, frame relay, ...)

The algorithm is suitable for both small and large networks (up to 10,000 routers and up to 100,000 end nodes). It is a dynamic Link State Algorithm. As with OSPF, there is a common connected backbone (Level 2) which connects Level 1 areas (which are already familiar to the reader as OSPF areas) and which itself forms a Level 2 area. If the physical backbone cohesion is incomplete, a virtual link is formed via Level 1 areas. Level 1 and Level 2 areas screen their topological information from each other.

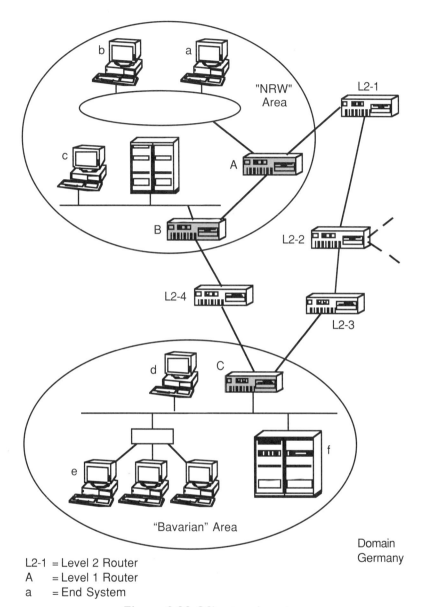

L2-1 = Level 2 Router
A   = Level 1 Router
a   = End System

Figure 9.28 OSI-network environment

IS-IS supports four different metrics, but only the default metric is mandatory, the others are optional:

- line capacity (default)

- processing time (transit delay, optional)

- costs (DM, $, SFR, £ etc. optional)

- the link's error rate (optional)

An Intermediate System may support any combination of these metrics. For every metric,. it calculates its own SPF tree and creates its own routing table. This means that if an IS is simultaneously a Layer 1 router and a Layer 2 router (OSPF border router) and supports all four metrics, it has eight databases and eight parallel Dijkstra algorithm processes for the Link State Routing—to the delight of the CPU industry. The use of different metrics makes complete sense because of the different possible networks (Ethernet, Token Ring, FDDI, X.25, Satellite), since, in one case, the most important criterion could be loading and in another it could be cost. As with OSPF, there are authorization mechanisms at every level.

Error Treatment by Backbone Links

If the link is interrupted within a Layer 1 area (the area is divided into two partitions), but links to all networks would still be possible via other areas, this link may be used as a virtual link between the partitioned areas. One precondition for this is that there must be at least two routers in the discarded Layer 1 area which are simultaneously Layer 1 and Layer 2 routers, and each of them must be located in a different partition. This is the only way a virtual link may be established using the backbone (see Figure 9.29).

An exchange of topological information at Layer 2 is used to identify whether an area has actually been partitioned. IS-IS protocol is used to define a "partition designated Level 2 IS" for each partition from Layer 2/Layer 1 routes, i.e., a Layer 2 system designated for a partition. The two designated routers in the two partitions establish a virtual link with each other by means of the backbone and the provisional link for the separated area parts joined together. The end points of the virtual link contain NSAP addresses. If a packet is to be sent over the virtual link, it is unchanged (with network source and destination address), and it is packed in another IP protocol frame, known as the CLNP Wrapper. The original address is retained. The additional external address uses the end point NSAPs in the virtual link.

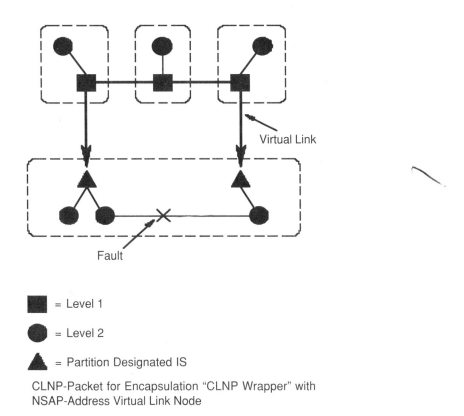

= Level 1

= Level 2

= Partition Designated IS

CLNP-Packet for Encapsulation "CLNP Wrapper" with
NSAP-Address Virtual Link Node

Figure 9.29 Error correction in a partitioned area

Addresses and Address Flexibility

An OSI address is known as an NSAP (Network Service Access Point) and is
defined in ISO 8348. Just as with IP, there is an internationally unambiguous
address, which an OSI user may, but is not required to use. The space for the
international address is known as the Global Network Addressing Domain and
is divided into Network Addressing Domains. Each domain is managed by one
institution (authority), which assigns the addresses. The Network Addressing
Domains form a partition of the global address space. This ensures that there
are no overlapping addresses. All institutions which are authorized to assign
addresses are entered into the address in the form of an international identification (AFI in the IDP), so that it is immediately possible to identify who was
responsible for assigning an OSI network address.

An OSI network address (NSAP) consists of two basic components, the initial domain part IDP and the domain specific part, DSP (see also Figure 9.30).

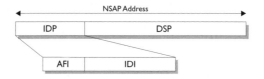

Figure 9.30: NSAP address structure

- IDP specifies the Network Addressing Domain mentioned above as the global address space. It consists of an AFI (Authority and Format Identifier) and an IDI (Initial Domain Identifier).

AFI consists of two decimal numbers (00..99) and specifies

- the format of the IDI

- the institution which assigned the IDI values

- the significance of leading zeros in the IDI (whether there are any or not)

- the syntax of the DSP

IDI specifies

- the network domain for which these addresses were assigned

- the institution which assigned the DSP addresses for this network domain

Two OSI network addresses may be completely different, depending on who assigned them and who uses them. Obviously, this is the result of a failure to agree (e.g., on the part of telephone users and data technicians) how a flexible address should appear. The coding has never been defined. However, binary byte coding (4-bit encoding of a decimal number) is explicitly permitted and proposed. With byte coding, the NSAP address has a maximum length of 20 bytes, the AFI only occupies the first 2 bytes.

The specified IDI formats with the AFI value and the associated IDP and maximum DSP length are shown in Figure 9.31. A comparison with the well-known address of the LAN emulation configuration servers in Chapter 11 shows that this uses ISO 6523 ICD format (AFI 47). The diagram also shows that an address-assigning "institution" (authority) is not actually a physical institution, but rather a standardization area.

IDI Format	AFI Value	IDP Decimal Length	IDP Byte Length	MAX DSP Byte Length
Local	49	2	1	19
ISO DCC	39	5	3	17
ISO 6523-ICD	47	6	3	17
X.121	37,53	16	8	12
E.163	43,57	14	7	13
E.164	45,59	17	9	11
F.69	41,55	10	5	15

Figure 9.31: AFI values, IDP- and DSP-lengths

For the domain specific part, there are a wide variety of format definitions, particularly of

- ECMA 117

- ANSI

- NIST

- EWOS Addressing Guide

- GOSIP Profiles

- Manufacturers (e.g., Digital for DNA)

As an example, the ANSI and GOSIP proposals for AFI 39 or 47 are developed further (see also Figure 9.32). For AFI 39 or 47, the maximum length of the DSP is 17 bytes. ANSI suggests the following fields for this:

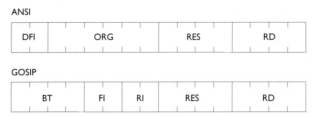

Figure 9.32: ANSI and GOSIP DSP formats

- DFI, DSP format identifier, 2 hexadecimal numbers/1 byte

- ORG is the international organizational unit identifier OUI, 6 hexadecimal numbers/3 bytes

- RES as reservation for future expansions 2 bytes: 0x'0000'

- RD for the routing domain, 4 hexadecimal numbers/2 bytes

GOSIP has a similar breakdown

- BT, area part with 4 hexadecimal numbers/2 bytes

- FI, format identifier, 2 hexadecimal numbers/1 byte, for GOSIP = 0x'01'

- RI, regional identifier, 2 hexadecimal numbers/1 byte

- RES as reservation for future expansions, 2 bytes: 0x'0000'

- RD for the routing domain, 4 hexadecimal numbers/2 bytes

This means that in each case 8 bytes of the maximum 17 bytes are specified. What happens with the rest of them? Once again we turn to the OSI NSAP specification:

- 8-byte network address which is divided differently into network ID and host ID according to the DSP

- 1-byte selector for different processes or transport protocols in the end system (similar to ports or sockets)

In Germany, NSAP addresses according to ISO DCC are assigned by the Deutsche Gesellschaft für Warenkennzeichnung GmbH (German Association for Merchandise Marketing) in Berlin. Host 343 in network 49 at Darmstadt University could then have the following address in DECnet V, OSI:

0x'39276F31000116000001030031AA00040057C521'

AFI	39
IDI	276F, 3 numbers international country code, padded with F to a whole number of bytes
DE_BT	3100, German area part (DFN)
FI	01, GOSIP FI
RI	16, RI for Hessen
RES	0x'0000'
RD	0103, routing domain Darmstadt University
area	0031, hexadecimal value for decimal 49
Node ID	AA00040057C5, C557 = hexadecimal value for area 49, node 343
SEL	21, OSI transport protocol

The question is posed for the entire address area as to how IS-IS implements multicasts: to all routers, to all Level 1 routers, to all Level 2 routers or to something else. The solution is not pretty, but it is practical: MAC multicasts are transmitted:

Multicast Destination	MAC-address	Description
AllL1ISs	01-80-C2-00-00-14	All Level 1 routers
AllL2ISs	01-80-C2-00-00-15	All Level 2 routers
AllIntermediateSystems	09-00-2b-00-00-05	All routers
AllEndSystems	09-00-2b-00-00-04	All end systems (hosts)

In the Token Ring networks, where devices impede these addresses (because otherwise they get tangled up with other functional addresses), the following multicasts should be used:

Multicast Destination	MAC-address	Description
AllL1ISs	03-00-00-00-01-00	All Level 1 routers
AllL2ISs	03-00-00-00-01-00	All Level 2 routers
AllIntermediateSystems	03-00-00-00-01-00	All routers
AllEndSystems	03-00-00-00-02-00	All end systems (hosts)

The use of different multicast addresses results in higher processing expenses in the router as it has to set the multicast LAN-specifically and cannot be used as a general constant.

One great advantage of IS-IS is the basic idea of area addresses as the basis for the architecture. In particular, it is possible to give one area more than one address, known as alias addresses. This greatly alleviates the necessary reconfigurations:

- An area address has to be changed for some reason or other (e.g., a new address convention). In this case, it may be assigned the old address and the new address in parallel. As long as both addresses are valid, it may be reached with both addresses. The network operator no longer has to convert all addresses in a single error-prone operation.

- Two areas are to be combined. All ISs in both areas then receive both the older addresses for a transitional period. The new common address will be gradually configured in the ISs.

- An area is divided into two areas. One of the new areas gradually receives one new address, the other area receives a second new address. When the new addresses have been assigned to both sides, the previously common address is phased out.

OSPF does not provide these options.

9.4 DECnet

Since the Digital Equipment Corporation was one of the first manufacturers to use LAN network technology, their DECnet in-house peer-to-peer communications protocol has been around for a relatively long time. (Version 1 became available in 1976.) DECnet was originally developed as a result of in-house requirements to link its own computers for internal use (at that time it was still using PDP11). The basic architecture is DNA, Digital Networks Architecture. The version currently implemented is version 4, DECnet Phase IV, in 1987 Phase V was announced and has since been specified, at least in a test in the Digital network, and finally released. Phase V includes both downward compatibility with Phase IV and the option of using OSI addresses and OSI routing.

DECnet mainly runs on all Digital systems and has gateways to other worlds. Digital is only expanding the TCP/IP functions very hesitantly.

While in DECnet Phase I, only similar computers were able to talk with each other, in Phase II communication was expanded to different computers (made by Digital), such as PDP11s and VAXs. File transfer, remote program execution, and access to remote peripheral equipment were possible, but only between devices which had a point-to-point link. Phase III introduced logical links over which any two nodes in the network could communicate, even if they did not have a point-to-point link. If there are two or more computers with the same operating system, a terminal with a physical connection to computer A could log on from here to computer B or C and the user could work as if on his own computer.

This phase was the first time routing functions which routed messages onwards using the most cost-efficient link were provided. DECnet Phase III used dynamic routing based on a Distance Vector Algorithm (DVA). This also implemented a congestion control: in the event of congestion, control functions operate causing the transmitting nodes to reduce the packet rate. However, this only takes place if the load is so high that packet losses may occur despite the congestion control.

Since Phase III, full function nodes, also known as end nodes, have been available. All nodes are able to exchange messages, but only the full function nodes are able to route (the similarly with IBM's brand new APPN with network nodes and end nodes should be noted here). The costs of a link were assigned manually as line costs, and it was possible for one link to have different costs depending upon which nodes it used. In the event of an error, the routing nodes would calculate alternative routes. In addition, Phase III also introduced management programs for monitoring and parameter tuning.

9.4.1 Phase IV

Phase IV was announced in 1982. Layer 2 supports a series of different protocols, an essential new feature in this version. The number of nodes supported was expanded to 64,000, and these may be distributed between a maximum of 64 logical subnetworks (each with a maximum of 1023 nodes, which matches the Ethernet capacity). Gateway products were introduced to provide connections to other protocol worlds (X.25 gateway, SNA gateways). At Data Link Level, the following protocols are supported:

- Ethernet V. 2.0

- FDDI

- X.25 (which goes higher than Layer 2, but is used by both IBM and DEC for LAN-WAN or SNA-WAN links at Layer 2)

- DDCMP (Digital Data Communications Message Protocol), a byte-oriented protocol which may be operated synchronously or asynchronously

- HDLC

- CI-bus (Computer-room Interconnect, 70 Mbit/s controller in VAX clusters)

Routing Protocol and Routing Function

The protocol which implements the routing layer is called the DECnet Routing Protocol (DRP). It is a distance vector procedure. The routing layer in DNA consists of two function modules:

- The control sub-layer handles the routing, congestion control, and service life of the packets.

- The initialization sub-layer provides for the establishment and physical supervision of links.

According to the DECnet Phase IV routing specification, the routing function consists of the following two databases and four processes:

- routing database

- forwarding database

- decision process

- update process

- forwarding process

- receive process

These elements will be explained in more detail later on.

Metric

The metric used calculates the route with the most favorable "costs," with every link between two DECnet nodes being assigned a configurable cost value. The costs are set for each output interface, as with the Spanning Tree procedure, but, unlike the Spanning Tree, there are no default values. Input interfaces do not result in any costs. The cost value K should be configured with

```
1 <=K <= 25
```

as an integral number. The cost calculation between two end nodes or the segments to which they are connected is performed by adding up the individual costs for all output interfaces from the router up to the end node segment. The total costs are limited within each area and between two areas by configurable parameters:

- Maxc = maximum total costs to reach node from route R within its area A

- AMaxc = maximum total costs to reach an area X from router R in area A

The upper limit for Maxc and AMaxc is 1022, the value 1023 is treated as not reachable.

If routes cost the same, there is an option of using "path splitting." The load is distributed over the equivalent routes in a round-robin procedure. In the example shown (Figure 9.33), the route via routers R2, R1, and R4 is taken from PC2 to VAXs 1 and 2 as they have the lowest costs (they are configured in this way because router R3 is an older model and is used as a backup router). The WAN link between routers R5 and R6 is an ISDN link and should therefore only be used for backup purposes. With the specified cost values, PC4 selects a route via R6, R7 and R5 to the VAXs.

Costs (PC2, R1, R2, R4, Vax1) = 5+3+3 = 11
Costs (PC2, R3, Vax) = 12
Costs (PC4, R6, R7, R5, R4, Vax) = 6+13+3+3 = 25
Costs (PC4, R6, R5, R4, Vax) = 22+3+3 = 28

Usually, LAN routes are always assigned lower costs than WAN routes; generally the costs are configured in approximately inverse proportion to the interface's transmission capacity, for example: Ethernet = 10, FDDI = 1, X.21 with 2 Mbps = 15, 64 kbps = 25. If you select this metric you will have problems with 622 Mbps ATM: the values can no longer be adequately coded as an integral value since it has to be selected as <1.

In addition to the path costs, the number of hops is calculated (the output router counts as hop 1). The maximum number of hops in a link has to be configured:

- Maxh = maximum # of hops from a router R to a node within its area A

- Maxh = maximum # of hops from a router R to an area X

For Maxh and AMaxh, the specification suggests that in each case twice the value of the longest possible route (measured in hops) be configured. Maxh and AMaxh may not exceed a value of 30, as the value 31 = Infh means "non-reachable:"

```
Infh = 31
```

If the maximum number of hops in a possible route is exceeded, the route in question is not taken, even if it is the most cost-efficient route (such a case is, however, unlikely in sensibly structured networks) or if it is more cost-efficient than other routes with fewer hops. In the example shown, the most cost-efficient router is not the one with the fewest hops.

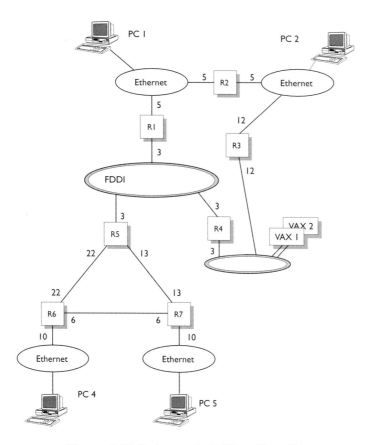

Figure 9.33 Path costs in DECnet Phase IV

Subnetwork Formation

Logical subnetworks are called areas and the connected systems end nodes. Unlike other protocol worlds, a DECnet area is not necessarily restricted to a physical LAN, but represents a logical grouping: an area may consist of several LANs which are connected by Level 1 routers. Subdivision according to intra-area routing and inter-area routing facilitates a hierarchical network structure, which is only loosely connected to the physical structure. Within the same LANs, it is not necessary for all nodes to belong to the same area; they may also be assigned to different areas.

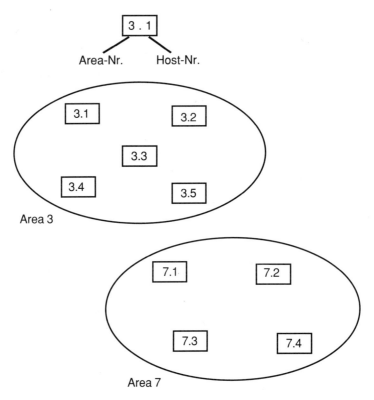

Figure 9.34 DECnet Phase IV addresses

This idea may have been hit upon by someone who, for reasons of security, only wished to allow communication between stations in the same physical subnetwork via Level 2 routing or who had no desire to reconfigure a station's DECnet address after it has moved to another. For reasons of performance, this is not recommended: the packet occurs twice on the physical LAN, since it is routed between the areas, and this will produce unnecessary routing overhead (update packets). Routing takes place in a two class system as Level 1 and Level 2 routing (as will be explained in more detail later). Several Level 1 and Level 2 routers may be stationed in one area. A router recognizes from a packet's address whether it should be routed on Level 1 or Level 2: the address has a network part in which the address of the area is entered and a host part in which the address of the end systems or router is entered. If the area numbers differ from the destination address and source address, Level 2 routing is required but, if they are the same, Level 1 routing is performed. As with IP, the area and host address are combined by integral values and the dot notation "Area.Host" to produce the complete DECnet address, as shown in Figure 9.34.

Addressing

This brings us to the subject of addressing. Every DECnet node is assigned precisely to an area. There are three types of node:

- end node

- Level 1 router

- Level 2 router

Unlike other routable protocols, a router in DECnet receives a single DECnet address and not one address per interface. Area identification and host identification have to be configured for every end node and every router. There are two bytes available for this.

Area ID = 6 bit (network part)
End Node ID = 10 bit (host part)

The value 0 is invalid. This results in the restriction to 63 logical subnetworks, each of which may be connected to 1023 hosts. Unlike in protocols such as IP or OSI however, this address does not just appear in a Layer 3 header, it is also coded in the MAC address. DECnet changes an adapter's hardware address by a software command, in a similar way to that used with "locally administrated addresses" in Token Ring environments. How can 16 bits be used for a 48-bit MAC address? The software places a DECnet identifier: AA_00_04_00 in the first 4 bytes. This identifier is also known to DECnet operators as the HIORD parameter. The DECnet identifier identifies a system as a DECnet node, or to put it another way: every system wishing to use DECnet IV services must use the identifier AA_00_04_00 in the first 4 bytes of the MAC address. This is followed by the 2-byte DECnet address, but it is inverted (we don't want to make things too easy for network users). The address is changed the moment the user goes up the DECnet protocol stack. This is explained using the example of station 08.15:

	Area ID = 8	End node ID = 15
	101000	000000011011
Bit code	1010 0000	0000 1111
Hexadecimal code	20	0F
Twisted	0F_20	
MAC address	AA_00_04_00_**0F_20**	

The hardware address for Digital Adapter (Digital OUI) is 08_00_2b.

The mapping between the network address and MAC address does not require an ARP request, as for IP, but takes place implicitly: every DECnet node may use the MAC address (destination and source) to calculate the DECnet address (destination and source) immediately. Therefore, there is no establishment of any caches, as with IP and ARP.

Incidentally, if TCP/IP is run in parallel with DECnet, consider what will happen to the ARP caches as soon as DECnet is started and the MAC addresses for the connected systems are suddenly changed. This may result in many duplicate IP address errors! Here's a tip: configure the system so that DECnet is loaded first and then the other protocol stacks are loaded.

In exactly the same way as with IP addresses, problems may occur with DECnet addresses due to manual configuration: if two networks are combined according to Murphy's law, duplicate addresses will always be presented first. This will obviously greatly interfere with communications. In addition to the network addresses, terminals may also be assigned logical names. The name <-> address assignment is usually administered by the network administrator in a central table, of which every network node has a copy.

Routing and Forwarding Database

The routing database for a Level 1 router contains parameters such as:

- all adjacent routers
- all interfaces associated with them
- output costs

- HELLO timer

- router priority in order to become a designated router

- current designated router

- Connectivity matrix: # of hops from router R to each destination

- Cost matrix: total costs from router R to each destination

- The router's area (home area)

For Level 2 routers, the routing database contains:

- The number of hops to every reachable area via every adjacent router

- Total costs to every reachable area via each adjacent router

- Minimum # of hops to every reachable area

- Minimum total costs to every reachable area

The forwarding database holds the following for Level 1 routers

- Reachable destination nodes ("0" represents the "next" Level 2 router)

- Output interface and next router for each reachable destination node and for Level 2 routers

- Reachable areas

- Output interface and next router for each reachable area

Decision Process

The decision process uses the routing databases as the basis for deciding whether a destination station is reachable, and if it is, which minimum total costs and which path length (# of hops). Then it checks whether the minimum total costs equal ≤ Maxh or ≤ AMaxh and whether the path length is ≤ Maxh or ≤ AMaxh. At the same time, the decision process supervises the course of various HELLO timers and the status of all interfaces and adjacent routers, which is quite important for calculating the forwarding database.

The decision process always becomes active when a status change is made or an update packet is received. It evaluates the information received and uses it to calculate the most currently efficient routes to all reachable destination stations. In this connection, we should refer again to the most important parameters, which need to be carefully coordinated with each other to enable the decision process to run correctly and efficiently:

- maximum number of areas which may support a Level 2 router
- maximum number of nodes per area
- interface output costs
- maximum path costs
- maximum path length

Finally, the decision process controls the service life of packets: every packet has a "visit field" which is set to 0 during the packet generation and is increased by 1 with every hop. If the field has exceeded a maximum value of Maxv with

Maxh ≤ Maxv ≤ 2*Maxh

the packet is discarded.

Update Process

The update process generates information packets for other routers (and end stations, as will be explained later), in which reachable destination stations and/or areas are notified. In particular, these stations contain the total costs and path length of the transmitting router to the destination. Update packets are not routed onward, but only evaluated. There are in the main six different update packets:

- *Routing Message*: This update packet is transmitted to all router interfaces (LAN and WAN) and serves as an update for all adjacent routers. The HELLO packet has the multicast address Ab_00_00_03_00_00 (all routers). Level 1 routers transmit update packets to all adjacent routers within their area, with information on the reachable end nodes. Layer 2 routers transmit update packets to all adjacent Layer 2 routers, with information on reachable areas. Update packets are sent event-driven (link up, link down, new networks, ...) and periodically (if the network is running without events).

- *Ethernet Router HELLO*: A router informs all DECnet nodes (end nodes) on a LAN from time to time that it is still alive. The HELLO packet has the multicast address Ab_00_00_04_00_00 (all end nodes).

- *Ethernet End Node HELLO*: A DECnet node informs all routers on a LAN from time to time that it is still alive. The HELLO packet has the multicast address Ab_00_00_03_00_00 (all routers).

- *Initialization Message*: This packet is transmitted while ascending a WAN link (non-broadcast: DDCMP, X.25) to the adjacent router.

- *Verification Message*: checks the initialized WAN link.

- *HELLO and Test Message*: checks the status (up, down) of an adjacent WAN-routers.

The update intervals for the routing-tables and HELLO intervals (transmission of HELLO packets to make themselves known to other hosts/routers) are configurable. This enables longer intervals to be used on slow WAN lines than on fast LANs.

A Level 1 routing message has the format shown in Figure 9.35:

Flags: A byte with the bit values
                    bit 0:   1 (control packet)
                    bit 1-3: packet type = 3
                    bit 4-6: reserved
                    bit 7:   pad Indicator = 0 (no padding)

Source Node: 2 bytes with the DECnet address for routers (6-bit area, 10-bit Host)

Res: 1 byte, reserved

Segment: variable length, divided into 2 byte COUNT, 2 byte STARTID and COUNT*2 byte RTGINFO, with count showing the number of nodes named, start-ID the first nodes (the 6 area bits to zero, then 10-bit host address), routing info the rest of the nodes together with 2-byte path information, which is as follows for all the nodes specified:
                    bit 0-9: costs

bit 10-14: # of hops

bit 15: 0

Checksum: 2-byte checksum (1st complement) throughout all segments to detect transmission errors and to ensure that Phase IV routing messages are not erroneously interpreted as Phase III messages.

Byte		Byte	
(0)	FLAGS	(1)	SRC NODE
		(3)	RES
(4)	SEGMENT:COUNT		
(6)	STARTID		
( )	RTG INFO		
( )	SEGMENT		
( )	...		...
( )	CHECKSUM		

Figure 9.35: Format of a Level 1 routing message

A Level 2 routing message has the format shown in Figure 9.36:

Flags: A byte with the bit values
bit 0: 1 (control packet)
bit 1-3: packet type = 4
bit 4-6: reserved
bit 7: pad Indicator = 0 (no padding)

Source Node: 2 bytes with the DECnet address of the router (6-bit area, 10-bit host)

Res: 1 byte, reserved

Segment: variable length divided into 2-byte COUNT, 2-byte STARTarea and COUNT*2 byte RTGINFO, with count showing the number of areas named, Area-ID the first area (the 10 host bits to zero, then 6 bit area address), routing info the rest of the areas together with 2 byte path information, which is as follows for all specified nodes:

bit 0-9: costs
bit 10-14: # of hops
bit 15: 0

Checksum: 2-byte checksum (1st complement) throughout all segments to detect transmission errors and ensure that Phase IV routing messages are not erroneously interpreted as Phase III messages.

Byte		Byte	
(0)	FLAGS	(1)	SRC NODE
		(3)	RES
(4)	SEGMENT:COUNT		
(6)	STARTAREA		
( )	ROUTG INFO		
( )	SEGMENT		
( )	...		...
( )	CHECKSUM		

Figure 9.36: Format of a Level 2 routing message

An Ethernet router HELLO has the in format shown in Figure 9.37:

Flags: A byte with the bit values
bit0:   1(ControlPacket)
bit 1-3: packet type = 5
bit 4-6: reserved
bit 7:   pad Indicator = 0 (no padding)

Version: 3 bytes with version number, ECO number, user ECO number or the DECnet Software

ID: 6 bytes, DECnet MAC address of the transmitting router, with the first 4 bytes AA_00_04_00, then the DECnet address

Info: 1 byte with the bit values:
bit 0,1: 2 = Level 2 router (10)
           1 = Level 1 router (01)
bit 2:   1 = verification required (only Ethernet)
bit 3:   1 = reject flag
bit 4:   1 = verification failed

bit 5: 1 = no multicast traffic
0 = multicasts are accepted
bit 6: blocking flag (for Ethernet = 0)
bit 7: reserved

Block size: 2 bytes for a maximum data link layer packet length

Priority: 1 byte priority value to determine the designated router

Area: 1 byte home area of the router

Timer: 2 byte HELLO timer (seconds)

MPD: 1 byte reserved (set to 0)

E-List: 1-244 bytes to define logical networks on a physical Ethernet (the starts of virtual LANs...). The E-List contains a 7-byte long name and then a list of routers, including status (up, down) and priority connected to this logical network.

An Ethernet end node HELLO has the format shown in Figure 9.38:

Flags: A byte with the bit values
bit 0: 1 (Control Packet)
bit 1-3: packet type = 6
bit 4-6: reserved
bit 7: pad indicator = 0 (no padding)

Byte		Byte	
(0)	FLAGS	(1)	VER
(4)	ID		
(10)	INFO	(11)	BLKSIZE
		(13)	PRIORITY
(14)	AREA	(15)	TIMER
(16)	MPD	(17)	E-LIST
	...		...

Figure 9.37: Format of a Ethernet router HELLO

Version: 3 bytes with version number, ECO number, user ECO number for the DECnet Software

ID: 6 byte, DECnet MAC address of the transmitting routers, with the first 4 bytes AA_00_04_00, then the DECnet-address

Byte	Byte
(0) Flags	(1) VER
(4) ID	
(10) INFO	(11) BLKSIZE
	(13) AREA
(14) SEED	
(22) NEIGHBOR	
(28) TIMER	
(30) MPD	(31) DATA
...	...

Figure 9.38: Format of a Ethernet end node HELLO

Info: 1 byte with the bit values:
bit 0,1: 3 = end node (11)
bit 2: 1 = verification required (only Ethernet)
bit 3: 1 = reject flag
bit 4: 1 = verification failed
bit 5: 1 = no multicast traffic
0 = multicasts are accepted
bit 6: blocking flag (for Ethernet = 0)
bit 7: reserved

Block size: 2 bytes for the maximum data link layer packet length

Priority: 1 byte priority value, to determine the designated router

Area: 1 byte home area of the router

Seed:　　　　8 bytes for verification entries, set to 0

Neighbor:　　6-byte DECnet MAC address of the adjacent system (with point-to-point links), of the designated routers in Ethernet

Timer:　　　2-byte HELLO Timer (seconds)

MPD:　　　　1 byte reserved (set to 0)

Data:　　　　1-128 data bytes for test purposes, each byte is set to octal 252 (decimal 160, bit value 10100000)

Forwarding Process

The forwarding process performs what is generally understood as routing: it handles the actual forwarding. This also includes a check as to whether the format is correct. If not, the packet is discarded, and an entry is made in the error statistics. If there is no free buffer space, the packet goes into the bin.

If the packet is correct, the output interface is determined according to the routing table and forwarded by Layer 1 routing or Layer 2 routing according to the destination address. If the source and destination are connected to the same LAN, the Intra-Ethernet bit is set, as will be explained later. A DECnet configuration with several areas and the resulting routing table for router 8.1 is shown in Figure 9.39 and Figure 9.40.

DECnet has a certain amount of access safety: first of all, end nodes cannot even talk to each other. In fact, they do not know to which LAN their partners are connected, since an area, as already described, may consist of several LANs connected by routers. End stations with no routing functions, and hence no routing table (end nodes), use a Level 1 router as a "designated" router, which is active during the establishment of a link between two end nodes within the same area. The designated router in DECnet is entirely different from the designated router in OSPF: it helps an end system to find out which destination partners are attached to the same LAN and hence may be addressed directly. The designated router on a LAN is the router with the highest priority. If two routers have the same priority, the one with the highest numerical DECnet address wins. The actions of end devices and routers are explained using example in Figure 9.41.

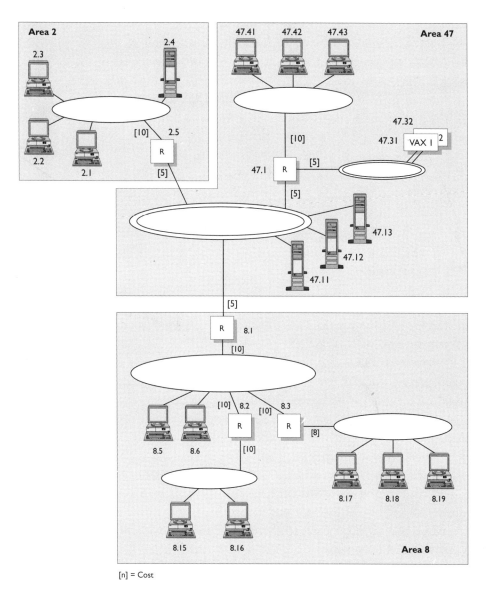

[n] = Cost

Figure 9.39: DECnet configuration with several areas

Level 1 Routing Table				
Destination	Cost	Hops	Next Hop	Interface
8.2	10	1	0.0	1
8.3	10	1	0.0	1
8.5	10	1	0.0	1
8.6	10	1	0.0	1
8.15	20	2	8.2	1
8.16	20	2	8.2	1
8.17	18	2	8.3	1
8.18	18	2	8.3	1
8.19	18	2	8.3	1
Level 2 Routing Table				
Destination	Cost	Hops	Next Hop	Interface
2	15	2	2.5	2
8	0	0	0.0	1
47	5	1	47.1	2

Figure 9.40: Routing table for the Level 1 and Level 2 routers 8.1

Area 2 consists of three PCs (2.1, 2.2, 2.3), a server (2.4), and a router (2.5). On start-up and then periodically, each end node sends an end node HELLO to the "all routers" address AB_00_00_03_00_00. The designated router receives all end node HELLOs and checks whether they have the same area ID as it does. If they do not, it ignores them. This ensures that it actually only learns the end nodes in its own area. In the example shown, the designated router learns that the four nodes, 2.1, 2.2, 2.3, and 2.4, are at its LAN interface. It enters the addresses learned in a cache, from which they are deleted again if, within a configurable timer (CACHETIMEOUT, default 1 minute), no packet with the relevant DECnet address is seen again. Since the designated router for its part is sending interval-control router HELLOs to the "all end nodes address AB_00_04_00_00," all end nodes learn which router is their current designated router. Turn back to the example and imagine that PC 2.1 wishes to talk with its server 2.4.

(1) Since it does not know whether 2.4 is attached to its LAN, it sends the first data packet to the MAC address for the designated router (2.5) and sets bit 5 in the FLAG field and the intra-Ethernet bit to 0. The DECnet ID for server 2.4 is the destination ID in the DECnet header for the data packet.

(2) The designated router looks in its cache and sees that server 2.4 is connected to the same LAN as PC 2.1. Thereupon, it sends the data packet to server 2.4 and sets the intra-Ethernet bit flag to 1.

(3) Server 2.4 enters the address 2.1 in its end node cache (for directly reachable destination stations) and sends a response packet (intra-Ethernet = 1) to PC 2.1.

(4) PC 2.1 now sends all packets directly to server 2.4. Both now know that they can communicate with each other directly (without interposed routers).

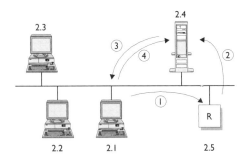

Figure 9.41: Link establishment within an area

If an area consists of several LANs which are linked by Level 1 routers, the forwarding of the packet within the area is performed by the Level 1 routers. To see an example of this, look at area 8 in Figure 9.42.

If node 8.15 wishes to speak with server 8.6, the designated router (8.2) recognizes that the destination address is on another LAN, forwards the packet to server 8.6, and sets the intra-Ethernet bit to 0. Server 8.6 sends the response to the router's MAC address which forwards it to 8.15. Now, both end nodes know that they cannot speak to each other directly, but only through their designated routers. If node 8.15 wishes to communicate with node 8.18, router 8.2 looks in its routing table for the next router on the most favorable route (8.3) and forwards the packet to it. Router 8.3 sends the packet to the destination station 8.18. In all packets, the intra-Ethernet bit is set to 0. Therefore, a routed packet always goes from the end system first to the designated router. There are three possibilities:

- The end system is linked to a LAN with which it has an interface: forward to the destination system

- The end system is linked to a LAN within the area to which it has an interface: forward to the next Layer 1 router via the most favorable route

- The end system is in another area: forward to the "next" Layer 2 router (router ID = 0)

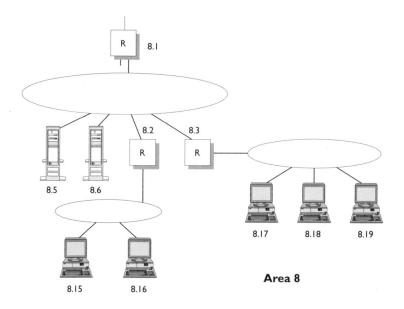

Figure 9.42: Area with several LANs connected by routers

Layer 1 routers do not have any inter-area route information stored in their tables, they only know the "next" Layer 2 router. They forward inter-area packets to this. Therefore, every area must have at least one at physical link to a Layer 2 router if they wish to speak with other areas.

Layer 2 Routing

Layer 2 routers forward packets between different areas, but not within one area. Layer 2 routers use update packets to exchange information with the Layer 1 routers in their area and also with other Layer 2 routers. In this way, a

Layer 1 router knows to which Layer 2 router it may have to forward a packet with another area number as the destination. A Layer 2 router knows which is the most favorable route to a specific area and to which Layer 2 router it should forward packets next on the same route. A packet whose sender and receiver are located in different areas, therefore takes at least the following route:

Sender, area S -> Layer 1 router, area S -> Layer 2 router, area S -> Layer 2 router, area R -> Layer 1 router, area R -> receiver, area R

A router may be a Layer 1 and Layer 2 router simultaneously. The minimum route, then, is as follows:

Sender, area S -> Layer 1/2 router, area S -> Layer 1/2 router, area R -> receiver, area R

A DECnet configuration with several areas is shown in Figure 9.9. To attain full connectivity, at least routers 2.5, 47.1 and 8.1 must be Layer 2 routers. A link between 08.15 and 47.11 takes the following route:

Sender 08.15 -> Layer 1 router 8.2 -> Layer 2 router 8.1 -> Layer 1/2 router 47.1 -> receiver 47.11

Bridge Link

Bridge links are transparent for DECnet. Several physical subnetworks connected by bridges count as a LAN. A bridge is never a Layer 1 or Layer 2 router.

Receive Process

In DECnet it is important to know that not only dedicated routers but also hosts take over routing functions as "full function nodes." This kind of "host-router" can, therefore, also receive quite normal data packets directed to it as a host. The receive process examines any packet received and forwards it to the next process according to its content:

- Routing message: to decision process

- HELLO: to a node listener process in the initialization sub-layer; this uses the HELLO timer to check the status of known nodes for activity packet to internal destination address: to end communications layer

- packet with outside

- destination address: to forwarding process

Access Protection

Access protection by means of passwords is only provided for point-to-point links However, access to specific node addresses via a router may be explicitly permitted or prohibited by means of filter lists (access lists) (as with IP).

9.4.2 DECnet/OSI Phase V

The situation in DECnet/OSI and multi-vendor environments could be described as follows: "When the lion roars, everyone expects all the other animals to turn and run." But, while Digital, the "Queen of Distributed Computing" is still announcing the era of multi-vendor networks with OSI, others have quietly implemented this concept; the router manufacturers have introduced parallel control of the protocol worlds. The standards supported by DECnet/OSI are listed in Figure 9.43.

Expanded DECnet functions in Phase V are:

- At Layer 2, ISO 8802.3 (IEEE 802.3) CSMA/CD and IEEE 802.5 are also supported in addition to Ethernet 2.0 (!).

- The assignment of addresses and logical names for end systems is automated by means of an auto-configuration mechanism. The manual configuration of mapping tables is, therefore, no longer necessary.

- Mapping tables no longer need to be held in each node, but in name servers.

- An additional service is to provide network-wide time synchronization (which is, for example, important for metrics that work on a delay basis).

- The former DVA has been replaced by IS-IS routing (the activities for the development of the IS-IS draft for OSI was heavily based on Digital, after all DECnet had hierarchical routing as early as Phase IV). The OSI standard (IDRP) to be agreed in the future will be used for inter-domain routing.

- In the event of overload, control functions operate early enough to ensure that there is no packet loss any more (as in Phase III and Phase IV), and the transmission rate is reduced at the correct time.

- In Phase IV, not all alternative routes are identified by the management with path splitting, but network management in DECnet/OSI provides information on all routes, even with path splitting.

- For X.25 links, dynamic links (DED, dynamic established data) are supported.

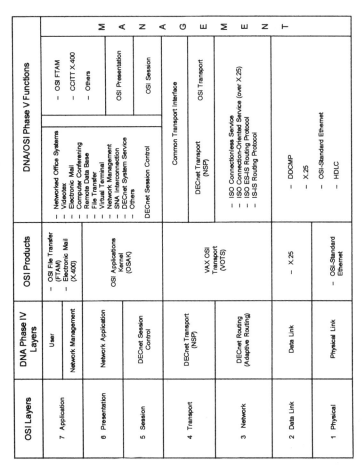

Figure 9.43 DNA Phase IV and DNA/OSI Phase V

The following table lists the differences between Phases IV and V.

Comparison of Phases IV and V		
	Phase IV	**Phase V**
Transport Layer	DEC's Network Services Protocol NSP	NSP; OSI TP0, TP2, TP4; TCP/IP
Node number	64.000	2160 nodes, virtually unlimited
X.25 support	only static links	static and dynamic links
Logical names	six positions	255 position in accordance with OSI
Format	in-house	OSI
Mapping tables	per node	Name server
Routing	Distance Vector	Link State Algorithm
Congestion behavior	Congestion control	Congestion control and congestion avoidable
CSMA/CD support	Ethernet V2.0	Ethernet V2.0, IEEE 802.3

9.5 NetWare

The NetWare protocols were developed as an XNS derivative. As XNS was produced before OSI, separation into seven functional layers was not strictly followed. In addition, NetWare does not use a peer-to-peer model like OSI, it uses a client/server model.

There are two different types of network nodes, clients and servers. Clients only talk to servers, never directly to each other. Clients are the workstation systems which use network applications (file management, text system, spreadsheet, printing ...), servers make these applications available as services. Different communication processes are implemented by different protocol stacks (NCP, SAP, RIP).

At the MAC layer (Ethernet, Token Ring, FDDI), IPX is used; above this are the higher protocols: NCP (NetWare Core Protocol), SAP (Service Advertising Protocol), and RIP (Routing-Information Protocol), as shown in Figure 9.44. NetWare routing can be implemented via pure network components, "NetWare router," and also via existing file servers (Novell calls them "internal routers," formerly "internal bridges"). The file server/router is also often called a gateway server.

Router manufacturers, supply pure routing functions without a file server function (NetWare-compatible routing). There are also servers/gateway servers which act as NetWare routers and routers which act as NetWare routers.

Addressing and IPX Packet Format

The NetWare datagram protocol at Layer 3 is IPX (Internetwork Packet Exchange) and was developed from the Layer 3 protocol by XNS (Internet Datagram Protocol/IDP). Like every correctly routable protocol, it defines network and end system addresses (host addresses), incorporating the "hardware address," i.e., the MAC address. As in XNS, an address consists of a 4-byte network part, the 6-byte system ID (hardware MAC address), and 2-byte socket number, which addresses a specific process in the end system. IPX addresses are, therefore, much longer than, for example, IP addresses (12 bytes compared to 4 bytes), but still shorter than OSI addresses. There are no different Classes of network addresses as in IP. The network part, i.e., the network address, must be unambiguous throughout the network. The use of the MAC addresses as a host address is not optimum, as network addresses should be completely independent of Layer 2. In addition, the repetition of the MAC address in the network part of the packet results in unwanted redundancy. The use of the MAC address does spare the tormented user from having to configure the host address in the system.

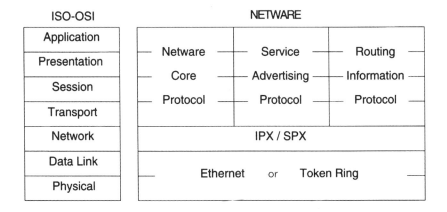

Figure 9.44 NetWare protocol structure

Important socket numbers are, for example:

- File server
  0451hex   NCP

- Routing
  0452hex   SAP
  053hex RIP

- Clients
  0455hex   NetBIOS
  0456hex   Diagnosis
  4000hex-6000hex   Client systems

Like IP, the IPX packet also contains a checksum, a length entry, a type entry and a control of the service life (transport control), see Figure 9.45.

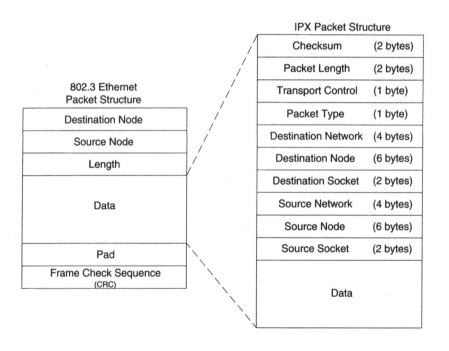

Figure 9.45 IPX format

The checksum is not used; it is always set to FFFF, since an error check takes place automatically at the MAC layer. The length entry refers to the IPX header (30 bytes) plus a data part. The maximum packet length is matched to the LAN; it is simply adopted: for IEEE 802.3 1500 bytes, for IEEE 802.5 4096 or 16 KB, for FDDI 4500 bytes. Transport control contains the number of hops behind the packet: during packet generation, the value 0 is entered. This is increased by 1 with each forwarding (by routers or file servers). If the value reaches 16, the packet is no longer forwarded. Defined packet types are:

0	Unknown
1	RIP
4	SAP
5	SPX
17	NCP
20	NetBIOS packet

9.5.1 Routing with RIP and SAP

The routing algorithm was borrowed from XNS and modernized (i.e., made more efficient) in several aspects, but there are about 10 years between them.

Link Establishment

Now, how does a client wishing to communicate reach its server? There is no special ES-IS protocol like ARP, with IP, so the necessary actions are performed by RIP, SAP, and NCP. The procedure which handles link establishment is probably familiar to most readers: it is found on many PCs in the form of IPX.COM. However, users will search in vain for a parameter in the NetWare client where they will be able to configure the network address. At the start of the communication, a client only knows that its host address is the MAC address. Consequently, its first action must be to find out its own network address. This may be done using one of the two traditional possibilities in life: waiting or acting.

Waiting: If the client can wait, after a minute at most, it sees an RIP update packet from a service or router on the local segment. As the RIP packet is a broadcast, the client interprets it and hence finds the IPX source address

(4-byte network, 6-byte router-MAC, 2-byte socket). It notes the 4-byte network ID as its own network. This is correct because the transmitting router/server is connected to the same LAN as the client.

Acting: The impatient client sends a get local target packet (request). This request is actually intended to ask for the shortest route to a specific destination network. With get local target, however, the destination and source network number is 0x'0000', because the network sought is not known. It is an RIP packet and receives a response from all routers on the same LAN with a give local target packet (response). The client interprets the IPX source address and so obtains its network number.

The client now knows which network it is connected to and next searches for a server: it sends an SAP packet with a get nearest server request. This request receives a response from locally connected servers and routers with give nearest server (response). The response contains the server name, the server address and the number of hops to the server.

The client now checks the server's network ID. If the server and workstation are in the same (sub)network, the network part of the source and destination address correspond, and no routing should take place. The client knows that it can speak with its server by means of direct addressing. A packet then looks as shown in Figure 9.46. If the server has a different network address from that of the client, IPX.COM must locate the shortest route to the server or the next router on this route. It sends a get local target with the server's network number as the destination entry. All routers which know this network respond and state the number of hops which they require on this route. The client selects the router which announces the fewest number of hops. It finds the router's MAC address in the IPX source address in the response packet.

Finally, it is now possible to put the link establishment into operation: the client sends an NCP request "create connection," to which it is hoped the server will make a response. In the response, the client receives a session number.

By the way: if there are no routers in the network, the client cannot find a server. However, it can still always try to establish communication with the network number 0x'0000', at least to local peers.

The principle actions in the establishment of a client/server link are summarized in Figure 9.47.

Figure 9.46 Transmitting within a subnetwork

Packet	Source	Destination	Protocol
Get Nearest Server	Client	Broadcast	SAP
Give Nearest Server	Router	Client	SAP
Get Local Target	Client	Broadcast	RIP
Give Local Target	Router	Client	RIP
Create Connection	Client	Server	NCP
Connection #x Assigned	Server	Client	NCP

Figure 9.47: Link establishment between client and server)

To offer their services to the client, all servers report themselves regularly once a minute with an SAP broadcast. Routers collect this information, store it in SAP tables, and forward it in their own update packets. Over time, every router learns where each server is and how many hops are required to reach it. The periodic SAP updates from routers are useful for ensuring that all routers keep as consistent as possible an information base regarding which servers are "up and running" and which are not. A typical SAP table contains the following parameters:

- server address

- server name

- service type (managed by Novell)

- # of hops from router to server

- interface (port) used to reach the server

- aging value

The aging value shows the actual "age" of an entry (e.g., in minutes). When the aging timer has expired (e.g., 4 minutes), the entry is deleted if the information has not been verified (i.e., received again).

When a NetWare router starts up, it asks for the available servers. It does this by sending out a "general" request in which the service type field is set to FFFF. Each local router responds to this with a "general" response containing all its SAP entries. Since only a maximum of eight servers may be coded in a response, a response may consist of several packets. The format of an SAP packet is shown in Figure 9.48. The operation code may assume four values for the different requests and responses:

1 = request (generally: opcode = FFFF; specifically: opcode < FFFF)

2 = response

3 = get nearest server request (generally: opcode = FFFF; specifically: opcode < FFFF)

4 = get nearest server response

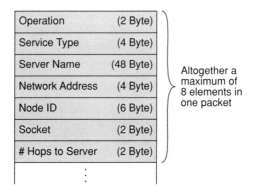

Figure 9.48: Format of an SAP packet

The SAP actions when a router starts up are shown in Figure 9.49.

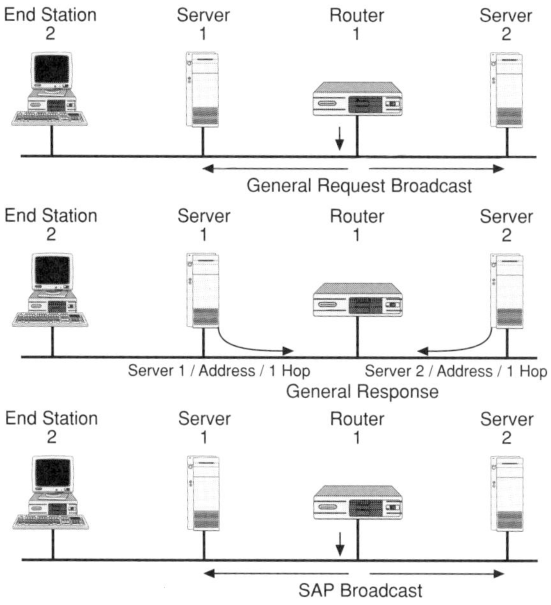

Figure 9.49: Actions to build up the SAP table

Routing Information Protocol (RIP) and metric

An XNS RIP derivative is used as the routing protocol. The XNS RIP has been improved with regard to the metric and routing algorithm. NetWare-RIP packets are transported on the basis of IPX packets, i.e., they use IPX Format (see also Figure 9.50). An OPERATION field indicates whether the packet is a request or a response (see below). This is followed by one or more information fields about reachable networks. A maximum of 50 networks may be entered in one RIP packet. The number of hops and the number of ticks needed to reach the network from each server are specified as a metric. A tick is a measure of delay (about 1/18 of a second, more precisely 18.21 ticks/sec). This is a decisive improvement over XNS because it enables the transport time to be taken into consideration. A routing decision is taken first on the basis of ticks and second on the basis of hops. (He who does not tick properly has to hop.)

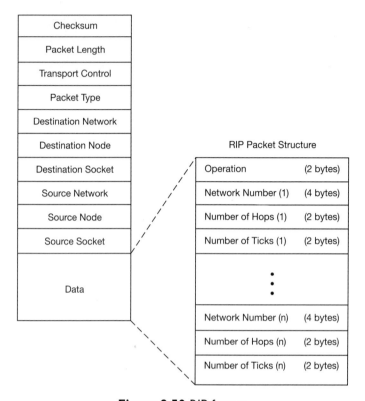

Figure 9.50 RIP format

An RIP request packet is used to ask for the shortest route to a specific network and contains only the network address. It does not contain route information (this should already have been requested). The fields for hops and ticks have the value 0. A response packet is sent as a response to a request packet and as a periodic broadcast. RIP governs the exchange of several pieces of information.

- A workstation looks for the shortest route to a specific server (in the form of a route request to a specific network).

- A server wants information on the availability of other servers (route request who is where?) to keep its internal tables up to date

- A server responds to requests from workstations or servers.

- Each server transmits broadcasts at intervals showing that it is still alive and what its routing tables look like (every 60 seconds).

- A server transmits broadcasts when it has noted a topological change (adjacent router dead, new adjacent router).

Network Number	Hops to LAN Segment	Ticks LAN Segment	NIC	Immediate Address of Forwarding Router	Net Status	Aging Timer [min]
00000001	1	2	A			0
00000002	1	2	B			0
FEED0038	1	20	C		R	0
FEED0035	2	3	B	00001B029927		1
000000FF	2	3	A	00001B0349B2		2
FEED0036	3	4	A	00001B0349B2		2

R = Reliable
LAN ≈ 1 Tick
T1 ≈ 7 Ticks

Figure 9.51 NetWare RIP routing table (source: Schneider & Koch)

Each router creates a routing table and updates it. Into this are entered details of all the reachable NetWare networks, the hops (transit router) and ticks required, the output port for a specific destination network (network interface card/NIC), the MAC address of the next router-servers, a status field (for "reliable" links) and an aging field (see Figure 9.51).

A LAN-link is generally assigned 1 tick, remote lines are polled to measure the current delay time in ticks. A non-overloaded T1 Link requires, for example, 6-7 ticks for packet transport. The aging entry is important to enable the reachability or non-reachability of a network to be determined quickly: since, like XNS RIP, NetWare RIP does not disseminate "bad news" very quickly, a network from which nothing has been heard for three updates is declared to be dead (aged out). It there were any active servers there, they would have had to have sent three broadcasts in this time; since none was received, the network is evidently not active.

Old NetWare versions (< 2.15c) keep all alternative routes in the routing tables in case there is an error. More recent versions only hold alternative routes with equally few ticks. This reduces the size of the routing table, but unfortunately it degrades it at the same time (possibility of no alternative route in the event of an error) and hence improves performance.

The routing algorithm uses the best information algorithm, which avoids some of the drawbacks of the RIP:

- *First*: although a router sends broadcasts to all connected segments, a broadcast does not contain any information received from the subnetwork to which the broadcast is transmitted.

- *Second*: a broadcast does not contain any information on the subnetwork to which it is transmitted.

Both measures are used to prevent gossip spreading (A has heard that B knows from C that D has a route to X, etc.). When a router becomes active, it first writes the network numbers for the subnetworks in its table to which it is directly connected (it makes sense to set these addresses at the start, and so ensures quick access to them, because this is where the majority of traffic for them occurs).

Then it sends several "start broadcasts" (see Figure 9.52): an RIP broadcast to the subnetworks to which it is connected to inform the routers there which subnetworks it is now able to serve directly; an RIP request to find out which other subnetworks and routers exist.

All routers respond to the request using the best information algorithm. Then, like all the others, at 60-second intervals it sends normal update broadcasts and broadcasts following the occurrence of topological changes. No interval broadcasts are sent on X.25 links to save on overhead. Only amendment broadcasts and start-up broadcasts are sent here.

As with NetWare routing, with RIP, the information on reachable file servers is disseminated with SAP and filed and updated in appropriate "server information tables" (every 60 seconds). The use of different protocols for routing information, file server reachability, and an additional third protocol for client/server action (NCP) is not as clean as in other routing architectures—it is evident here that NetWare routing is much more a network operating system process than a correct Layer 3 function; this is also expressed in the name "internal router" used by Novell for its routing (see chapter 6). It is worthy of note that in the protocol structure diagram, RIP, SAP, and NCP cover the same Layers (3-7), and they are therefore in fact protocol stack modules with different tasks.

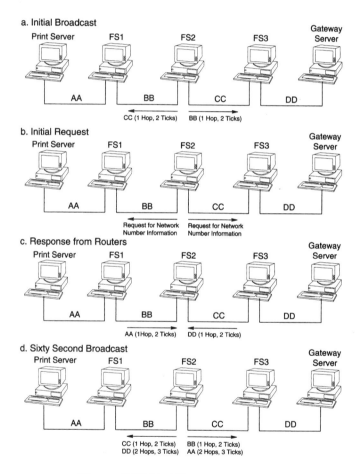

Figure 9.52 NetWare router start-up

NetBIOS

Some older Novell implementations use NetBIOS as a protocol. A NetWare router, therefore, has to grapple with NetBIOS packets and be capable of forwarding them. As with Token Ring source routing (the protocol cannot deny its origin), the NetBIOS packet contains the sequence of networks through which is passes. If a router receives a NetBIOS broadcast, it handles it as follows:

- It checks the value of the transport control field. It must not be greater than 7 since NetBIOS permits a maximum of 8 hops. If the value is ≥ 8, the packet is discarded.

- If transport control value is not greater than 7, the router examines the network numbers entered. If it finds the number of the network on which the packet was received, there is a loop and the packet is discarded. Otherwise, the router adds the network number for the network on which the packet arrived to the network numbers entered and increases the transport control value by 1.

- The router sends the expanded NetBIOS broadcast to all connected networks whose network numbers are not in the header.

9.5.2 Routing with NLSP

NLSP (NetWare Link Services Protocol) is derived from the OSI IS-IS and has been adapted to IPX networks. Just like OSPF, OSI, and DECnetV, NLSP uses a Link State Algorithm, many details of which are based on the IS-IS Standard ISO 10589. In routers there is a HELLO protocol; in LANs there are designated routers. Routers establish adjacencies, create Link State Databases, send Link State Packets (LSP), and calculate routes according to cost values.

However, there is small, but decisive catch with NLSP: it currently only implements Layer 1 routing in version 1.0. Hierarchical routing (intra-area, inter-area) is not yet possible, NLSP networks have to be configured for a large area.
A few new socket numbers were defined for NLSP:

Protocol	Socket	Packet type	
IPX ping	0x9086	0x00	
	IPXWAN2	0x9004	0x04
	NLSP	0x9001	0x00

The IPX ping protocol was included as an IPX expansion to test the reachability of specific destination networks in an uncomplicated way. The ping response is short and painless and has no wearisome information about hops and ticks and the like.

Addressing

The future form of hierarchy is already here. It is a mixture of OSI and OSPF: the area is coded by masking in the 4-byte network number:

Area ID   **4711A000**
Mask   **FFFFF000**

The relationship between the area ID and network number of the individual networks within an area is evident: each network within the area must correspond to the area ID in the masked bits, otherwise it does not belong there. An area may be assigned a maximum of 3 IDs (similar to IS-IS alias addresses).

NLSP uses Multicast addresses, but they are optional. As with IS-IS, one MAC Multicast is used and there is no Multicast at Layer 3. If a router does not support any Multicast addresses, broadcasts are transmitted (at MAC layer!!).

NetWare 3 and NetWare 4 servers or routers also have an internal network address, which must be unique throughout the network. The router ID (node ID) is always set to 1 (0x'00000001'). With IPX WAN, the router ID is the internal number extended by 0x'0000', i.e., 0x'<nnnnnnnn>0000'.

NLSP applies its own arrangements for Multicasts: there is a MAC Multicast "to all NLSP routers." However, this is different on all LANs:

LAN	Multicast
IEEE 802.3	09-00-1B-FF-FF-FF
IEEE 802.5	C0-00-10-00-00-00
FDDI	09-00-1B-FF-FF-FF

The use of different Multicast addresses results in more processing costs in the router, as it has to set the Multicast LAN-dependent and cannot use it as a general constant.

Designated Routers and LAN HELLO Packets

The priority of a router may be configured for each interface (default PRIO=44). If the priorities are the same, the router with the numerically highest MAC address is the winner. If, for operational or administrative reasons, a router must not become a designated router, the priority value 0 should be configured. This means it cannot become a designated router. For the designated routers, NLSP also takes into consideration LANs, in which routers occasionally crash and re-start or in which MAC addresses are changed as a result of interchanged adapter cards. If a router has become a designated router, its priority is increased by 20. This avoids another tie-break in the event of a failure as described above. The value 20 is a default and may (but does not have to) be implemented so that it can be configured.

HELLO packets help Layer 1 routers on the same LAN to find each other and to select the designated router. They contain a field LAN ID where the router ID for the transmitted router is entered. A router with several interfaces on the LAN reports to all these interfaces with the same node ID, since the router ID is made up of the internal network number and the node ID 0x'000001'. This means that HELLO packets from two different router interfaces can no longer be differentiated at IPX level. To facilitate this, all LAN interfaces are automatically assigned an ID by the router software (LocalLAN CircuitID, 1 byte). The two values together enable a unique assignment to be made once again.

The following applies to the generation of HELLO packets: a router, which takes a router other than itself to be the designated router, enters its LAN ID in its own HELLO packet.

Metric, Updates and Route Calculation

NLSP uses a cost metric. A network manager may configure the costs for every interface itself, or it can refer to default values for several established LAN and WAN interfaces. These are calculated roughly in relation to the throughput on a link and are shown in Figure 9.53. The second metric (delay value) is generally assigned 100 μsec for LANs; for WANs it is measured as described for IPXWAN.

Throughput*		Default Cost	Typical Media
At least	Strictly less than		
0 K	16 K	61	
16 K	32 K	55	
32 K	48 K	55	
48 K	64 K	45	
64 K	128 K	45	ISDN (U.S.)
128 K	256 K	40	ISDN (European)
256 K	512 K	35	
512 K	1 M	30	
1 M	2 M	27	T1 (1.5 M), Corvus Omninet (1 M)
2 M	4 M	26	Ef (2M), ARCnet (2.5 M)
4 M	8 M	25	Token Ring (4 M), Corvus Omninet (4M)
8 M	10 M	23	
10 M	16 M	20	Ethernet
16 M	32 M	19	Token Ring (16 M)
32 M	64 M	15	
64 M	128 M	14	FDDI (100 M), CDDI (100 M)
128 M	256 M	9	
256 M	512 M	9	
512 M	1 G	6	
1 G	2 G	6	
2 G	4 G	6	
4 G	8 G	3	
8 G	16 G	3	
16 G	32 G	3	

*K = 10^3 bits/second   M = 10^6 bits/second   G = 10^9 bits/second

Figure 9.53: Default cost values

Several values for the "best" route are used for route calculation in the sequence shown below:

(a) lowest end-to-end path costs

(b) highest net throughput end-to-end (i.e., restricted by the link with the lowest throughput on the route)

(c) lowest end-to-end delay

(d) highest end-to-end supported MTU value

(e) next hop with the lowest system ID

(f) interface (circuit) with the lowest LocalCircuitID on the local router

(g) remote neighbor with the lowest LAN MAC address

This means a best route is found deterministically, at any rate. This makes it easier, in the event of an error, to determine which route was previously unambiguously active. If routes cost the same, a procedure similar to OSPF and IS-IS load distribution may be activated. For this purpose, there is an MSD parameter, which restricts the maximum number of routes used in parallel. This is also useful in the event of fault location. If the NLSP metric has found m equal cost routes, the number R of routes used in parallel with load distribution is:

```
R = min(m, MSD)
```

During route calculation, it is essential to consider the routers and not the paths used: look at the example in Figure 9.54. Router D is a new arrival. Router A evaluates the routes to router D via router B and router C as only two, not three, different routes and sends the load from A to D equally distributed via router B and router C. As far as the two routes from A to B are concerned, once again load distribution is used. However, this was specified earlier for all packets from A to B, regardless of whether they were sent to router D or to router B or via router B in completely different network parts.

It is possible for an overloaded router to introduce a breathing space. It places an overload bit in its Link State Packet (LSP). This causes no more transit packets to be received, but only packets whose destination addresses are connected to the router's local LANs. The same applies to multihoming servers (with several LAN interfaces), which must not be misused as routers. They also set a bit, but then only calculate their own topological data base and are treated by the rest of the routers as an overloaded colleague.

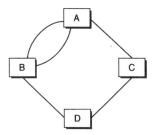

Figure 9.54: Evaluation of the node number, not the link number for load distribution

To keep the topological databases up to date, the routers send interval-driven LSPs, which contain individual pieces of information and a sequence number (PSNP Partial Sequence Number Packet). LSPs are sent on WANs as Unicast and confirmed by their sequence number. On LANs, LSPs are transmitted as Multicast (AllNLSP routers) and are no longer confirmed individually. In the event that a router should not receive an LSP, the designated router sends a CSNP (Complete Sequence Number Packet) group packet from time to time. This packet contains all the LSPs in its database with their LSP IDs and the associated sequence numbers. CSNP information is confirmed. If LSP information is missing from a router, it may request this after evaluating the CSNP packet.

In addition to this, in the following cases a router generates event-driven LSP and CSNP packets:

- An adjacency or a link fails or is started

- The costs for an interface change

- The router ID or its name change

- The designated router changes

- The network number changes

- SAP services or external RIP routes change

- The overload status changes (comes into being or finishes)

A whole series of timers apply to the whole operation of sending LSPs. Here are some of the most important of these:

- After the expiry of the **MaxAge** timer, LSPs are treated as obsolete, deleted and requested anew. The default is 7500 sec.

- The maximum interval within which LSPs must be resent periodically is configured by means of the **maximum LSP generation interval**. The default is 7200 sec (2 hours).

- To enable a few more data packets to be transported in the meantime, the minimum time interval between two LSPs is limited. The default for the **minimum LSP transmission interval** is 2 sec. It may be set differently for LANs and WANs.

- CSNP packets are transmitted in the interval between the **minimum complete SNP interval**, default 30 sec, and **maximum complete SNP interval**, default 5 sec.

- The maximum size of an LSP (**lsp buffer size**) is set by default to 512 bytes (including the IPX header, excluding the data link header).

- If a router in overload status wishes to return to normal status, it waits until the **waiting time** timer has expired. The default is 60 sec.

A special feature of NLSP is an enforced jitter assigned to the configured timer intervals: the actual interval between two transmitted packets is randomly distributed between 75% and 100% of the timer value. This is to prevent HELLOs and LSPs being synchronized and hence producing overhead peak loads.

Compatibility: RIP, SAP, NetBIOS

As before, a NetWare client learns from RIP to which network it is directly connected and which router knows the best route to a specific destination network. It is mandatory for the corresponding RIP request/response procedure to be supported by every NLSP router. The same applies to SAP packets which are sent by a server to announce its services.

The transmission and reception of RIP and SAP broadcasts may optionally be supported: there are three variants available for this:

- "On"—RIP and SAP broadcasts are generated. Received RIP and SAP broadcasts are evaluated and "absorbed," i.e., not forwarded.

- "Off"—RIP and SAP broadcasts are not generated and not absorbed.

- "Auto"—If an RIP/SAP router is detected on a link or LAN, RIP, and SAP broadcasts are generated. Received RIP and SAP broadcasts are evaluated and "absorbed," i.e., not forwarded. If no RIP/SAP router is identified, RIP/SAP is not generated and not absorbed.

It is advisable for the default mode to be "Auto," as this causes RIP to be masked in the places where there are no longer any RIP routers. This should gradually become the case in the entire network when the migration to NLSP is complete.

The following applies to NLSP routers: an RIP route is not selected if there is an NLSP route. If an RIP broadcast is generated, any NLSP part passing along this route will not be taken into consideration. At each interface, RIP routes may be explicitly approved or blocked by setting a filter. RIP routes which are entered in LSPs are not filtered. SAP is treated in a similar way.

RIP routes may be announced in NLSP as Xroutes (external routes). An Xroute contains the "distance" from an IPX network to the announcing router, coded as follows:

- network number

- number of hops

- RIP delay as number of ticks

SAP information which is announced in NLSP contains the following information:

- service name (47-byte text string)

- service type

- IPX network address for the network in which the service is offered locally

- number of hops required to reach the service offering the service

As with RIP routing, NetBIOS broadcasts are provided with packet type 20 and forwarded as described in Chapter 9.

IPX-WAN v2

Together with NLSP, a new WAN protocol was defined, IPX-WAN version 2 (IW2). It supports important new functions such as address-free WAN links (unnumbered links) and the direct connection of workstation systems (clients).

IPX-WAN v2 may be used in different WAN protocols, which may be supplemented in the future:

- PPP according to RFC 1331 and RFC 1552

- X.25 SVC and PVC

- Frame Relay

- IP Relay

With **PPP**, the link establishment is according to RFC 1552. IW2 only starts when the PPP link has attained "open" status. The Novell implementation does not support any of the IPXCP options. If other implementations support IPXCP options and if selected options later come into conflict with IW2, the IW2 options have priority. The data exchange uses normal PPP encapsulation according to RFC 1331 (for further details see /RFC1331/, /RFC1552/).

For **X.25** and SVCs, the protocol identifier 0x'800000008137' is entered in the call request packet. It is the identifier for a dedicated IPX SVC. IPX is encapsulated directly in X.25 without an intermediate header. With PVCs there is no call request, and the router leaves a functioning link as soon as the data link connection is established. If the router detects an interruption to the data link, it evaluates this immediately as a link abort and attempts to re-establish the link.

Frame Relay supports PVCs. The IW2 router periodically exchanges KeepAlive packets with the next switch, using the Frame Relay specification of either ANSI or Digital/Northern Telecom/Stratacom. Once again 0x'800000008137' is used as the network layer protocol ID (NLPID).

If there is a requirement to use dynamic rerouting in the WAN, but not parallel protocols, IW2 may be operative via **IP-Relay**. An IW2 link is then configured with two fixed end points with IP addresses like a PVC, although the actual WAN links used may be intermeshed. The route taken is regulated by

IP routing (RIP, OSPF). It is not TCP but UDP that is used here (UDP port 213). A maximum packet length of 1472-byte UDP packets (excluding UDP and IP Header) must be supported.

Overall five routing procedures are possible with IPX-WAN v2:

- NetWare RIP as previously

- Un-numbered NetWare RIP: point-to-point WAN links do not receive any network address

- On-demand static routing

- NLSP (which also uses un-numbered links)

- Client-router link: individual workstation systems are connected to the network by WANs

Link Establishment in IW2

As with every proper link state protocol, the database of adjacent routers may only be replaced in the master-slave procedure. The router with the higher internal router ID is the master. After this, timer packets are sent every 20 seconds, containing the supported parameters, such as routing types (see below), assignment of a network number and a network identifier, IPX header compression and assignment of node ID for clients.

If **RIP** is selected, the next and final IW2 step is an information request/response according to RFC 1362 (replaced by /RFC 1634/). After this, the link can now only be used for RIP and SAP; it can no longer be used for NLSP.

Unnumbered RIP is advisable for dedicated links to save configuration and maintenance of network addresses. Since the delay and number of hops are measured independently of the network number, the metric is retained even for un-numbered links.

On-demand static routing is for suitable for X.25 links or switched links. On-demand static routing is a way of killing two birds with one stone:

- Because of the static route definitions, no dynamic information has to be transmitted, neither RIP, nor SAP, nor NLSP. Incoming RIP and SAP packets must, however, be given a response.

- Since no routing information has to be exchanged, the participating routers do not need to establish any transparency, and no routing overhead is incurred. A link is only established if data are actually present. In the event of inactivity, the link is automatically cleared after a period of time.

With **NLSP**, the establishment sequence for a link is slightly longer (see also Figure 9.55). To apply the NLSP metric, throughput tests (throughput requests) are sent first and then response time tests (delay requests) to obtain the necessary input for route calculation. Finally, establishment is completed with an information request/response. If no response has been received after 16 requests (retransmission timer = 20 sec), the link is cleared.

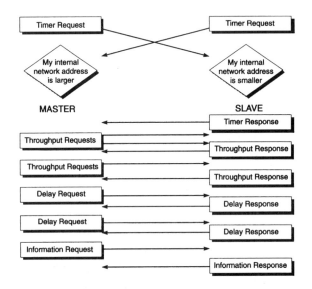

Figure 9.55: IW2 link establishment for NLSP

The throughput is measured as follows: the master twice sends a fixed packet size R, default = 512 bytes, and repeats this twice. This produces

```
R byte
—->
—->
            —-> t1
            —-> t2
thr1 = / (t2 - t1)
R byte
—->
—->
            —-> t3
            —-> t4
thr2 = / (t4 - t3)
THR = (thr1 + thr2) / 2
```

The delay value is calculated from the echo time with two values: transmission time through the medium and processing time in the router. The transmission time may be calculated reciprocally from the throughput. This produces the following equation which is to be resolved according to the variable delay:

```
Echo_time / 2 = delay + (1 / throughput)
```

The echo time is measured as follows:

```
576 byte
t1 —-> —->+
t2 <—- <—-+
echo1 = (t2 - t1) / 2          (μ-seconds)
576 byte
t3 —-> —->+
t4 <—- <—-+
echo1 = (t4 - t3) / 2          (μ-seconds)
delay = (echo1 + echo2) /2 - (1.000.000*8*576 / throughput)
(throughput in Mbps)
```

The calculated values are entered in the subsequent link state packets as NLSP delay and NLSP throughput. The specification permits the calculated values to be overwritten by a management command. However, with differently configured routes at the two ends of a WAN link, these may lead to different values and consequently to asymmetrical routers. In the event of an error, this will complicate the fault location.

A **client-router** link offers the possibility of connecting individual systems directly to a NetWare LAN via a WAN. In principle, client-router link establishment with IW2 takes place similarly to router-router link establishment. However, some additions are needed to cope with the asymmetric link structure. Furthermore, the client now has to learn address information from the router and support the re-establishment of crashed links (e.g., dialed connections) without interfering with its higher protocol layers, otherwise the service link is aborted.

Clients receive a network number and a network-wide unique node ID (pseudo MAC address, as the client does not have a LAN interface). However, they are spared the transmission and reception of RIP and SAP broadcasts. A client may, however, relocate specific RIP and SAP requests (request for *one* destination network or *one* service).

During link establishment, a client is always the slave. It sets its network number and node ID to 0. The router dynamically assigns it a network number and node ID. Two possibilities for this are left to the manufacturer-specific implementation: each client receives a unique network number and is treated like a single user network, or every client receives the same network number and a unique node ID. In the latter case, all the clients form a common network, and the router must forward all the broadcasts generated by clients to all the other clients.

The node ID should have the value 0x'02' in the first (most significant) byte, so that the address is not interpreted as a Multicast in any IEEE LANs (this is guaranteed by the fact that the two least significant bits of 0x'02' are always zero). The remaining address space occupies 5 bytes. Since, with this address size, a wrap-around is very unlikely, the specification suggests that the assigned node ID be increased by the value "1" with each new link establishment. This enables a client to retain its numbers in the event of an error and means it only needs to change them in the event of a complete new start.

During the re-establishment of a link (reset), the client only needs to inform the router of its previously assigned network number and node ID. This is only applicable if the client makes itself master for the parameter exchange. For this purpose, it sets its node ID in the timer request to 0x'FFFFFF', becomes a master, and the router does not have to devise any new network or node ID.

Differences Between NLSP and IS-IS, NLSP and OSPF

This section summarizes the main differences between NLSP, IS-IS, and OSPF. The differences start with the terminology. It is always a new challenge to become familiar with the different designations which mean the same thing, or possibly not the same thing.

Terminology

OSPF	IS-IS	NLSP
Router	Intermediate System	Router
Host	End System	End node
Autonomous system	Domain	Domain
Internetwork	Network	Internetwork
Area	Area	Area
Subnet	Subnetwork	Network
Packet	Protocol Data Unit	Packet

Addresses, Packet Format

OSPF uses IP addresses, IS-IS OSI addresses, and NLSP IPX addresses. The concept of alias names, i.e., of assigning several area-IDs for the same area, is limited to a maximum of 3 area IDs with NLSP, but not with IS-IS. There are no alias names in OSPF. OSPF uses IP headers; IS-IS uses CLNP headers and NLSP IPX headers.

OSPF specifies Multicasts as IP-addresses; IS-IS and NLSP specify different Multicasts as MAC addresses. NLSP allows broadcasts to be used if a router does not support any Multicast.

Data Link Layer

IS-IS specifies that a router automatically detects when a router at the other end of a WAN link starts. Here, NLSP implements an automatic status device which is also designed for inadmissible links which do not automatically send an "up" signal.

Routing

OSPF and IS-IS recognize Layer 1 and Layer 2 routing; NLSP only recognizes Layer 1 routing. OSPF and IS-IS each support several parallel metrics; NLSP only supports one, the cost metric. In IS-IS, LSPs are only transmitted if there are also some adjacent routers. In NLSP, a router babbles away to itself if it is completely alone. The priority of a router is not changed in the event of an overload in IS-IS; in NLSP it is reduced.

In IS-IS, Layer 1 LSPs contain links to other routers and to end systems. In NLSP, they contain links to other routers, to external routes, and to services. In addition, there is a management information field with the router names and the IPX network number. When the LSP sequence number arrives at a wraparound, the IS-IS router becomes inactive for a short time; the NLSP router only deletes the LSP and may optionally continue to operate. The maximum lifetime of an LSP is 120 minutes in NLSP, 20 minutes in IS-IS, and 60 minutes in OSPF.

Designated Router

The priority of a designated router is increased by 20 with NLSP and not increased in IS-IS and OSPF. In multi-access networks like X.25, SVCs are treated as separate point-to-point links. There are no designated routers as in OSPF.

Communication With End Systems

In OSPF, the end systems use ARP, in IS-IS the ES-IS protocol, in NLSP RIP and SAP.

Error Situations

During the partitioning of the area due to hardware errors (e.g., a bridge failure), rerouting is not possible in all cases. In IS-IS, this is provided by means of the defined CLNP wrapper.

Management

Network management is implemented in OSPF via SNMP on IP, in NLSP on IPX, and in IS-IS the network management runs on CMIP. Various MIB groups for NLSP MIB have already been defined:

- System

- Circuit (interface information)

- Forwarding (database info)

- Services (by means of SAP known services)

- Neighbors (neighbors and adjacencies)

- LSP (Link State database)

- Translation (mappings, e.g., between addresses and logical names)

- Graph (network topology)

- Traps

9.6 Routable and Routing Protocols

Finally, Figure 9.56 gives an overview of the routable protocols and associated routing protocols.

Routable Protocol	Routing	Stack
IP	RIP, OSPF, BGP, EGP	TCP/IP
CLNS, CONS	IS-IS	OSI
IPX	NetWare RIP, NLSP	NetWare
NSP	DRP	DECnet
IDP	XNS RIP	XNS
DDP	RTMP, AURP	AppleTalk

Figure 9.56: Routable protocols and routing protocols

10 | Multi-Protocol Operation: Network Structuring in Different Manufacturer Worlds

After examining different established routing protocols, let us now see how they are used in structured networks. The following describes how router usage and/or network structuring is handled in different protocol worlds.

10.1 DECnet, TCP/IP

Routers have been used for a long time in the conventional, primarily CSMA/DC-based DECnet and TCP/IP LAN protocol worlds. However, they really started to be used in earnest after the transition from LAN to WAN networks. For example, the first router products from Digital were pure LAN-WAN interconnection components. Depending upon the equipment configuration, a DECrouter pair connects two LANs by means of an X.21 or X.25 link.

In many cases, it is planned primarily to use bridges for a LAN-LAN link, not least because, in addition to DECnet, the non-routable LAT and LAVC are often operated in parallel as routable protocols in Digital environments. Coupled LAN subnetworks are generally viewed as one area, an extended LAN. Another similar method is the use of broadcast technology for link establishment, both under TCP/IP and under DECnet. About five to ten years ago, the capacity of a LAN in relation to the number of end stations connected and the throughput rate of terminals was still assessed so highly that the broadcast load generated was treated as negligible. The idea of restricting LAN traffic to within an extended site LAN in order to achieve a load reduction was not fashionable when DECnet and TCP/IP were becoming established. Only with the increasing numbers of end stations and the extension of the present-day LANs on the one hand, and the drastically increased end stations throughput rates on the other, have internal LAN structures with multi-protocol routers and with a view to broadcast reduction became a topical subject. On the other hand, load reduction for relatively expensive remote links over public networks has been an important aspect of network planning and operation from the very beginning.

TCP/IP and DECnet networks are also characterized by the use of host computers with routing functions. Previously, this was implemented to a greater degree than it is now since, with a lower network load, the routing tasks may be performed by the host CPU without too much expense. The current trend, however, is increasingly to perform routing on dedicated routers as interconnection components, because

- the hosts are to be relieved of loading

- routing as a typical network function is performed more efficiently by routers specially designed for the purpose

- dedicated routers are easier to incorporate in network management and support concepts than are hosts with application programs

It is only in UNIX workstations that the RIP daemon is often used so that configuration of the router to be addressed (known as a gateway) does not have to be performed manually for all destination systems in other networks. The workstation learns all the destination networks from RIP dynamically and independently. If the router is operated with OSPF, workstations cannot be incorporated in the dynamic self-learning process, unless the routers have activated the RIPs to which the workstations are connected in parallel to all interfaces.

10.2 PC Networks

The use of routers in small to medium PC networks is encountered more rarely than in extended DECnet- or TCP/IP-configurations. As pure PC networks, these networks are sometimes too small for the use of routers with the resulting build costs to be worthwhile. Inside a LAN, the traffic with moderate use of PC network applications is not high enough to require the use of routers.

Under the basic conditions mentioned above, subnetworks in pure PC networks may alternatively be configured via PC servers, which perform "internal routing" based on their network operating system. Often servers are also used to connect remote stations to a central station within a common network concept by performing the routing functions between the central station and a remote station.

In an integrated environment of PC and host networks or in PC networks with several hundred users, on the other hand, the use of routers is more interesting again (see section 10.5), particularly for the uncoupling of PC networks on a site-wide or company-wide multi-protocol backbone.

10.3 Non-Routable Protocols

Protocols which are not routable, i.e., which do not address any network, and which have implemented routing functions as described in the reference model, are nowadays seen as the "black sheep" of the LAN world. These protocols do not have any separate network addresses, which prevents their incorporation in a routing procedure. They include protocols such as Digital's LAT (Local Area Transport), LAVC (Local Area Vax Cluster), Digital's MOP (Maintenance Operations Protocol), and IBM's NetBIOS. These protocols were originally designed only for use in purely local environments, but nowadays, with the integration of departmental networks, site networks, and company networks they also have to be operated in highly structured environments. At the present time there is no other option than bridge coupling, although for remote connections, compression tools may be used to save costs.

One possibility for incorporating protocols without network functions into a routing concept is encapsulation, for example, in TCP/IP. Although, as already described in other chapters, this does have some drawbacks, encapsulation is nevertheless increasingly being used for non-routable "obsolete protocols," particularly in the SNA area (see section 10.4).

10.4 SNA Integration in Multi-protocol Backbones

For many years, SNA was established as a closed shop. Despite the frequently heard warning "never touch a running system," there is an increasing requirement to view the networked IBM system world in the overall context of a heterogeneous company network. The following describes the current possibilities for integrating SNA into multi-protocol networks. A small comparison: SNA is only two years older than Ethernet; IBM established SNA in the market in 1978, the first version, Ethernet V1.0, also known as DIX-Net (Digital, Intel, Xerox) was presented in 1980.

Under the concept of "SNA internetworking," a series of functions were developed for internetworking components to enable SNA to be fully integrated into the LAN-WAN combination. However, the dream of many network operators to put an end to the parallel backbone for SNA and LAN (i.e., to throw front-end equipment worth millions onto the second-hand market and replace it with "cheap" routers for everything) has so far only been implemented to a limited extent.

The current statistics keep the euphoria of the LAN "freaks" in the Internet community within bounds. Some of the installed SNA equipment is still fitted with SDLC or even BSC and other access modules which are alien to LANs. COAX cards are still being used for host connections in some PCs. Devices networked by Coax or Twinax like the 5394, 3174, 3274, and SNA-compatible third party minis are still found in some numbers (and some of them are a long way from being written off). The existence of these devices cannot be argued away overnight. Large-scale users are still operating networks in which 50% of the users work with a simple 3270 data terminal and in which the degree of networking between the PCs used is less than 30%. However, the reverse case is also found: pure PC and workstation environments at the workplace and full networking between workstation systems.

With increasing networking in companies, the trend is towards a halt in growth followed by a cutback in terminal usage. The networked PC with its advantages in IDP and the possibilities for a wide variety of host connections (not only to IBM systems) is increasingly becoming established.

To sum up, following core developments in the IBM environment, the following should be borne in mind:

- Multifunctionality at the workplace, including in Token Ring

- Possibilities for operating SNA by means of Ethernet

- 16 Mbit/s Token Ring with decreasing significance

- FDDI and ATM as high-speed backbone networks

- Transition from homogeneous network to heterogeneous network with multi-protocol applications

- Continuation of the SNA line by IBM

- Integrated applications with LU6.2

- APPN as dynamically routable carrier protocol and peer-to-peer basis for LU 6.2

- Expansion of the AIX Strategy

SNA and Multi-protocol Backbone

Parallel to and influenced by this development, the conventional hierarchical SNA structure is undergoing a drastic change: the coupling of LAN islands and their use as a backbone for a computer network has deprived the SNA pyramids of their traditional form: strictly hierarchical, host-based WANs changed into an unorthodox WAN network of equal ranking LANs in which gateways establish the host connection (see also Figure 10.1).

Token Ring LANs and the rest of the world grew together. The operation of parallel LAN and WAN backbones is, however, vague, expensive and labor-intensive. The logical progression is to replace it by a concentration of different LANs with a high-capacity backbone, e.g. FDDI or ATM. The functional progression of bridge-coupled Token Ring backbones will be the use of LAN switches and routers with additional bridge functions to enable the advantages of routing in multi-protocol environments to be exploited.

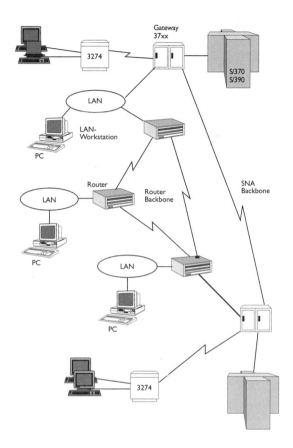

Figure 10.1: Parallel backbones

Now, exactly what is this "rest of the world" with which SNA is to be integrated? The most common protocols are TCP/IP, SNMP, NetWare, AppleTalk, NetBIOS, DECnet IV, DECnet V, LAT, OSI, VINES, and, in a few rare cases, XNS. The applications used on these protocols vary greatly and generate a wide variety of load profiles:

- File access and program access in client/server structures which have to operate using inter-networks, i.e., in the multi-site LAN-WAN network (TCP, IPX)

- Distributed databases which may be accessed by all users (in all buildings, departments, floors) (TCP)

- Graphics tools and a wide variety of IDP applications such word processing systems, electronic diaries, spreadsheets, and PC-Mail, at one workstation (minimally Windows, or X-Emulation; TCP, IPX, AppleTalk, DECnet)

- Host access: VT emulation and 3270 emulation expanded by File Transfer and local printing (SNA, DECnet, HP NS)

- Distributed development leading to faster development cycles, and consequently to faster application cycles (DECnet, TCP)

- Product planning (TCP, DECnet, IPX)

- Inventory control, logistics control (DECnet, LAT, TCP)

- CAD, CAE, CAQ

- A wide variety of product control systems (proprietary protocols)

- Multimedia applications which are flooding the market and which have the unpleasant feature of a rapidly growing bandwidth requirement (native ATM)

- Remote access for mobile employees to all the applications listed, for sales support, consulting, etc.

- … the list may be continued ad infinitum.

Several approaches for the local and wide area integration of SNA and the "rest of the world" with a bridge/switch/router backbone are described below:

- Token Ring with SRB bridge technology

- Ethernet with TB bridge technology

- SDLC-LLC conversion

- TCP encapsulation

- SDLC passthrough

- Remote polling

- Data Link Switching (DLSw)

- Proprietary routing in the WAN area

- APPN

- Protocol prioritization

- MPTN/AnyNet

- SNA Router, SNA encapsulation

- ATM backbone

- Router with channel interface

- TCP with TN3270

10.4.1 Token Ring with SRB Bridge Technology

The first stage for the integration of SNA in multi-protocol networks is often the installation of a Token Ring: the front-end processor or control unit (3745, 3174, 3172) is provided with a TIC and the heterogeneous world in the form of PCs, PC-Servers, UNIX workstations (usually RISC 6000), and X-Terminals. Some MDT-computers (Tandem, SNI) also may be linked by the Token Ring network. A link may also be established to the Ethernet world by means of routing with routable protocols (IP, IPX, AppleTalk, OSI,) and Ethernet Token Ring bridging with non-routable protocols (NetBIOS, DLC, also LAT to a limited extent).

From the viewpoint of the heterogeneous world, the pure SNA area is not routable and is operated by bridge coupling in the LAN. (Routers for LU2 and PU2 are defined statically in VTAM; they cannot be accessed by 3rd party routers, the SNA router is the FEP.) With advanced technology (multi-protocol bridge/routers), it is possible to implement collapsed backbone concepts in the LAN for Ethernet and Token Ring with routing and bridge technology, optionally configurable for each port, which facilitate SNA and multi-protocol operation by means of a common coupling element.

The advantages of Token Ring and bridge technology are:

- Lower configuration costs

- Routes no longer have to be defined statically in SNA; they are found automatically with source route bridging.

- Protocol transparency, including the NetBIOS protocol (which is now considered to be obsolete (once again non-routable) and which was very widely implemented in the first PC networks and LAN applications in the SNA environment) may be operated successfully with Token Ring and bridge technology.

- Standardized procedure (nowadays extension of ISO 100038, the Adaptation of IEEE 802.1D, including SRB)

The disadvantages of bridge technology are:

- Limited cascading: a maximum of seven bridges may be connected in series with source route bridging (RIF limited to 16 bytes and restriction of the Route Discovery Overhead). In the site area, with sensible structuring this is more than adequate, but there is a noticeable restriction when using several WAN levels (central station, subsidiary central station, site, remote station). A new version of the IBM bridge program has increased the cascading to more than 30, but the market has not adopted the expansion: universal bridge technology is no longer used in large networks.

- No rerouting in the event of errors: if the session is aborted, a new session has to be established with a new route discovery. This applies to the LAN and WAN area.

- Forwarding of broadcasts and multicasts.

- Considerable overhead from LLC acknowledgments, particularly from time-outs, if bridge technology is used in the WAN network. Too great a delay in LLC ACKs due to the WAN cascading of Token Ring bridges may result in the session being aborted.

- Route Discovery Overhead, which may even be significant in WAN networks with Single Route Broadcasting (IEEE simplifications of the original All Route Broadcast): a narrow hop count limitation, e.g., to 3 hops, is no longer possible, as this would mean that remote stations could not be reached from the central location. Consequently, the Route

Discovery, which in the LAN originates in the center, is forwarded to the entire WAN network. This may only be prevented by complicated filter settings.

- The absence of Token Ring acceptance and hence of a MAC link in the Token Ring network of established protocol worlds such as DECnet, LAT, HP-NS, MAP, SINEC AP, etc.

To avoid the restriction of 7 hops, some manufacturers have implemented what is known as "enhanced SRB" where the entire WAN backbone, throughout all site hierarchies, is configured as a hop and is given a virtual ring number (see Figure 10.2).

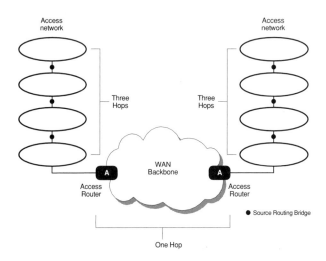

Figure 10.2: Extended source route bridging

Token Ring Switches

The first Token Ring LAN switches became available in 1995 (Bay/Centillion, Cisco/Madge, NetEdge, SMC, Xylan, and in the future 3Com, IBM, Nashoba (Cabletron OEM), NetVantage. As in the Ethernet area, the use of Token Ring LAN switches makes a scaleable increase in capacity easier to achieve, and bridge technology is taking on a new significance. Token Ring switches often work with a combination of TB and SRB. This eliminates the restriction to 7 hops.

10.4.2 Ethernet with TB Bridge Technology

Now that IBM has recognized Ethernet as an equivalent procedure, even traditional SNA components such as 3174 and FEP have an Ethernet interface. At least it is now possible with one 3174 to use SNA with DLC on Ethernet and to replace the Token Ring bridges and source routing with Ethernet and transparent bridging with Spanning Tree. This variant is even more interesting if Ethernet LAN switches are used in place of the bridges to increase the available bandwidth. In the PCs, emulation must be used as PU 2 instead of Token Ring on Ethernet, which is simple with established emulations. If, however the PC-PUs are combined by gateway technology, Token Ring is still required for host access. The SNA variant via Ethernet has not really established itself in the market. On the other hand, the SNA variant via TCP or IPX on Ethernet has undergone continuous growth.

10.4.3 SDLC-LLC Conversion

SDLC-LLC conversion is a technology developed in the last few years for SNA integration. The main advantage of this technology is that it uses existing LAN-WAN structure for the SNA traffic. SDLC-LLC converters or routers that perform the SDLC-LLC conversion are connected to the SDLC output line from a 3x74 control unit (or a front-end processor) and transform the relevant data flow from SDLC format to Token Ring LLC format (and vice versa). This means that there is no need to equip the control units with Token Ring interfaces and, with a LAN-WAN network with Token Ring (Ethernet), it permits the use of Front-End Processors at remote sites. This may result in considerable cost savings. The booming market for SDLC converters clearly reflects this trend.

At the host site, there must be either a Front-End Processor (3745/3746), a control unit (3174), or even a LAN interconnect controller 3172 with Token Ring or Ethernet interface and gateway feature or an LLC-SDLC converter (made by the same manufacturers as the SDLC-LLC converter) which retransforms the data flow back into SDLC format and transfers each SDLC link individually to the FEP (see Figure 10.3).

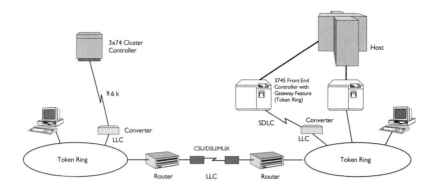

Figure 10.3: SDLC-LLC conversion

The use of LAN WAN backbones enables dedicated SNA wide area links to be saved (reduction of service complexity, reduction of operating costs). As the conversion in the LAN-WAN area is purely based upon source routing technology, in the event of an error, no dynamic rerouting can take place—the session must be re-established by route discovery. The restriction to 7 hops applies in the same way as before.

Of the possibilities described, coupling at Data Link Level (for example, SDLC and Token Ring) is the option with which the least complications may be expected. In theory, from an SNA point of view, the Data Link Layer is interchangeable at will, i.e., the higher SNA layers may be used with Token Ring, SDLC, or X.25, as desired. In practice, however, some slight side effects result when the layers are changed. These side effects make the procedure more annoying than the word "interchangeability" suggests:

- SDLC and Token Ring are distinct protocols, and each has its own different framing.

- SDLC is designed for point-to-point links. In practice, less than 20 terminals per link are handled.

- SDLC has no protocol mechanisms to support bridge links. In particular, it does not know the source routing functions.

- Since the concentration of several SDLC links multiplexes are implemented in higher SNA layers (NCP), the concentration of several SNA links via Token Rings and bridges/routers gives rise to problems.

SDLC-LLC conversion (also called SDLLC) also functions for Ethernet. This means that it is no longer necessary to establish a mini-Token Ring network purely for SDLC-LLC conversion at remote terminals where an FEP is to be used. The existing Ethernet may be used by the SNA traffic as a transit network. From IBM's point of view, this is a risky solution.

10.4.4 TCP Encapsulation

Encapsulation with TCP/IP is a technology for making non-routable protocols in the WAN area dynamically reroutable and, particularly during the use of Token Ring LANs, to eliminate the restriction to seven hops (seven bridges/routers). In the SNA environment, TCP encapsulation takes place for SDLC (also known as SDLC encapsulation) and LLC (also known as tunneling). In the WAN backbone, SNA encapsulation using TCP/IP and the corresponding TCP/IP routing is currently considered to be the state-of-the-art technology.

The advantage of this solution is the use of a common backbone. The disadvantage the relatively expensive non-OSI protocol technology for encapsulation, in which a complete frame with all the check information is embedded in a further quasi-enveloping protocol. This means twice the protocol overhead during transmission and encapsulation or decapsulation.

LLC Tunneling

With LLC tunneling, routers forward SNA traffic from different non-centralized Token Ring subnetworks via a WAN backbone (Figure 10.4) or a central Token Ring backbone. This, in turn, still has an interface (37xx, 3174, in future RS/6000?) to a conventional, more or less expanded SNA backbone.

Since by no means all terminals and hosts are networked by LANs and there is still a large number of installations with SDLC, complete integration of the SNA world by means of routers is only possible if these protocols are directly supported by the router (i.e., an additional protocol is added to the router's protocol stack). IBM equipment which does not have Token Ring capability, is supported in the form of SDLC Token Ring conversion.

SDLC Encapsulation

During SDLC encapsulation, routers are connected to the SDLC output line from a 3x74 control unit (or a Front-End Processor) (synchronous router interface) and forward the SNA traffic over the existing WAN network by means of IP routing to the host location. All remote integrated links are connected at the host location by corresponding SDLC router interfaces to one or more Front-End Processor(s). For host management (NetView), the WAN line serves as an error-free SDLC line (with suitable redundancy, the routers will perform dynamic rerouting) since NetView has no access to the router and TCP-based forwarding. The Front-End Processors and control units upstream and downstream of the router link are still manageable with NetView (see Figure 10.5).

The simplicity of this connection technology is fascinating. Metaphorically, it's like retaining the engine and gearbox in an old car and respraying the chassis, that is to say, embedding the SDLC packet in a TCP/IP frame and transporting it over the WAN router backbone. What arrives on one side is delivered to the other side. From one flag to the next, every SDLC packet is nicely packed and then unpacked again. The router network does not spend time interpreting the SDLC elements, let alone changing them. The only thing that is new compared to the encapsulation described above is the use of one or more ports with an SDLC capability in the router, so that SNA packets that arrive not via a Token Ring but via a traditional SDLC link may also be processed. Every SDLC link which is connected to an SDLC port in the router is connected logically by the router backbone to just one SDLC output port in a remote router (exception: Cisco supports point-to-multipoint links).

In SNA terminology, this may be expressed as follows: the SDLC line from a 37xx is connected to the SDLC port on an upstream router. The remote SNA units (3174, 3274, terminal) are connected to the SDLC port of a downstream router. After the activation of the sync passthrough, a fixed point-to-point link is switched between the two routers. The route using the router backbone is usually fixed. The combination of several physical downstream ports to form a port on the upstream router is not possible, nor is it possible to implement the concentration of several downstream ports by virtualization (representation of several physical downstream ports as several virtual links on an upstream port).

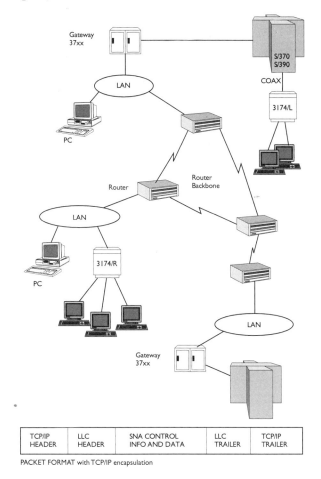

TCP/IP HEADER	LLC HEADER	SNA CONTROL INFO AND DATA	LLC TRAILER	TCP/IP TRAILER

PACKET FORMAT with TCP/IP encapsulation

Figure 10.4: SNA link via LLC tunneling

The advantages of the procedure are:

- use of the router backbone for SNA transmission

- existing know-how in the field of SDLC transmission

- no compatibility problems with higher SNA levels

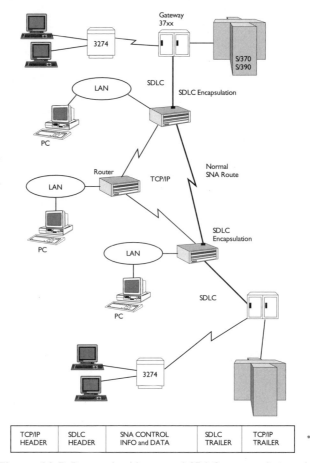

TCP/IP HEADER	SDLC HEADER	SNA CONTROL INFO and DATA	SDLC TRAILER	TCP/IP TRAILER

Figure 10.5: Router backbone and SDLC encapsulation

- avoidance of a new NCP generation when introducing this technology

- transparency for SNA management with NetView: the interposed routers do not hinder the management of the remote SNA components functionally.

The disadvantages of the procedure are:

- increased data and processor load due to encapsulation

- "invisibility" of the routers in NetView with the consequence of apparently extremely error-free SDLC links from the point of view of NetView, as the packet repetitions between routers are not identifiable in NetView

- usually no use of data compression, as the compression time in the router cancels out the time advantage in the transmission

- possibly higher response times for the SNA area, as the LAN traffic also passes over the router backbone

- changing response times (which produces dissatisfaction in the SNA user) as the LAN traffic has severe loading peaks

- need to provide the corresponding "over capacity" for the remote line to enable load peaks to be cushioned adequately, compared to the 9.6 kbps in SNA, by at least a factor of 4; associated higher line costs

- poorer response times in the LAN area, if the sync passthrough channels are assigned a higher priority to achieve constant SNA response time behavior

- transmission of all the polling traffic over the backbone (sometimes up to 50% of the overall traffic in a 24 hour period)

Table 10.1: Comparison of SDLC-conversion and encapsulation

Criteria	SDLC-LLC	SDLC (encapsulation)
Flexible bridge or router selection at both ends of the link	+	I
Flexible propagation in LAN and WAN	+	- (only WAN)
SDLC and LLC termination and hence tuning for both	+	+/- (not with all routers)
Point-to-multipoint links	+	+/- (with only few routers)
WAN-link speed	+	- limited to 19.2 k or new NCP-Gen required; FEP upgrade to 56k
WAN link management	+ (NetView)	- (only SNMP)

(continued)

Table 10.1: *(continued)*

Criteria	SDLC-LLC	SDLC (encapsulation)
No new NCP-Gen required	- (SDLC - Token Ring conversion)	+
No card/product change on the expansion of the router network	+	- possibly new converter cards with larger router model
Dynamic rerouting	-	+

In order to combine the advantages of both alternatives, it is possible to install mixed configurations: SDLC-LLC conversion is performed at the remote location, but it is forwarded in the WAN using bridge technology, TCP encapsulation not bridge technology. In the central station, reconversion is no longer performed according to SDLC; connection to the host is provided with LLC. In this case, it is necessary to perform regeneration in the FEP. All previous SDLC links must now be reconfigured into LLC links (see Table 10.1).

10.4.5 SDLC Passthrough

SDLC passthrough is an alternative encapsulation technology: the SDLC-packet is not packed in TCP, but in a MAC packet in the WAN. Spanning Tree bridge technology is used and hence automatic error tolerance achieved. Compared to TCP encapsulation, overhead is saved (the TCP/IP header consists of about 40 bytes). As with bridge technology generally, SDLC passthrough is also suitable for small to medium-sized internets with low levels of cascading.

Caution: The name SDLC passthrough is not used uniformly: some manufacturers call their SNA integration SDLC passthrough, but they have actually used TCP encapsulation.

10.4.6 Remote Polling

Remote polling, also known as poll-spoofing, is the next stage in the evolution of routers with an SNA capability: this avoids WAN capacity being wasted due to annoying idle polling; as the name indicates, the polling technology is led up the "garden path" or, to put it more simply, it is tricked. The trick is as follows: additional intelligence is implemented in the routers' SDLC ports. A primary module in the downstream router sends polls to the terminals and emulates an SDLC primary link station like the 37xx. A secondary module in the upstream router responds to the polls from the real 37xx. "At the top," a dummy (in the router) responds to the genuine poll, and "at the bottom," a dummy (in the router) sends pseudo-genuine polls, which causes the polling on the backbone to be masked out, i.e. tricked. Data is only transmitted over the backbone if SDLC information frames are involved (see Figure 10.6).

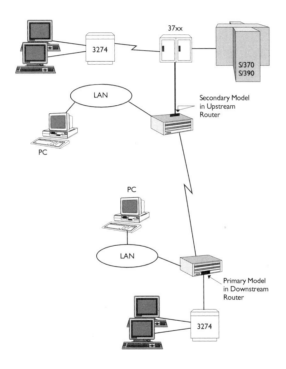

Figure 10.6: SNA link via router and remote polling

If a terminal really wishes to send data, the primary module (downstream router) gives the secondary module (upstream router) the hot tip that an actual data exchange is now taking place. This procedure is implemented in a router-router handshake protocol. The upstream router activates its port, sends a DATA READY signal to the 37xx and waits for the response. This should be SNRM (set normal response mode), and the data exchange can start. Acknowledgments may also be sent in this three-part way: the primary module confirms receipt of the packets to the terminals, the secondary module captures the confirmations from the 37xx for the received packets, the router modules use special protocol mechanisms between each other to ensure there is no packet loss. (Obviously the router-router protocol is proprietary and not standardized, which results in and entails incompatibility between different manufacturers.) If the secondary module has not received any messages about active terminals from the primary module, the secondary dummy behaves towards the 37xx as if the terminal were switched off.

The advantages of this procedure are:

- use of the router backbone for SNA transmission

- existing know-how in the field of SDLC transmission

- no compatibility problems with higher SNA levels

- avoidance of new NCP generation with the introduction of this technology

- transparency for SNA management with NetView: the interposed routes do not hinder the management of the remote SNA components functionally

- reduction of the traffic on remote links

- reduced probability of time-outs at Data Link Level due to delayed transmission on the backbone

- concentration of several physical downstream links (terminal–primary module) into one upstream link from the secondary module to the 37xx by virtualization; one terminal on each of several remote devices acts like several terminals on one remote line

The disadvantages of the procedure are:

- increased data load due to encapsulation

- "invisibility" of the router in NetView with the consequence of apparently extremely error-free SDLC links from the point of view of NetView, as the packet repetitions between routers cannot be identified in NetView

- possibly longer response times for the SNA area, as the LAN traffic also passes over the router backbone

- changing response times (ideal for producing dissatisfaction among SNA users) since the LAN traffic has severe load peaks

- no significant reduction in the necessary "over capacity" compared to sync passthrough, since the LAN traffic still affects the response times

- poorer response times in the LAN area if the poll-spoofing channels are assigned a higher priority to achieve a constant SNA response time behavior

10.4.7 Data Link Switching (DLSw)

Data Link Switching (DLSw) is a specification disclosed by RFC 1434 and RFC 1795, which is encapsulated in TCP like SNA and NetBIOS traffic in TCP and hence is dynamically reroutable in LAN and WAN backbones. The procedure is described in more detail in section 10.5 and will not be dealt with further here.

10.4.8 Proprietary Routing in WANs

Some manufacturers (for example, Andrew, CrossComm, RND) run proprietary routing for optimized SNA and NetBIOS transport in the WAN area. The link to the LAN functions like bridge technology. RND calls it SPF (shortest path first), CrossComm calls it the PIR procedure (Protocol Independent Routing). PIR uses either SDLC passthrough or SDLC-LLC conversion. SNA packets are provided with a type of network addressing and hence made routable. SNA traffic is prioritized in relation to LAN traffic. If a router is no longer reachable, CrossComm rerouting is faster than with DLSw, since no explicit link is established between routers as with DLSw (circuit establishment). However, here PIR was compared with RIP routing, not with OSPF routing.

Users who wish to use this kind of solution tailored to SNA should be aware of the fact that this increases dependence upon a specific manufacturer/supplier.

10.4.9 APPN

The first APPN specifications (Advanced Peer-to-Peer Networking) appeared in the mid-1980s under the names PU 2.1 and LEN (Low Entry Networking). APPN was conceived as a peer-to-peer expansion of the 3270 master-slave terminal traffic in SNA and incorporates about Layers 1 to 4 1/2 of the ISO-OSI reference model. Together with the peer-to-peer application protocol LU 6.2 or APPC (Advanced Program-to-Program Communication), it represents the adaptation of SNA architecture to client/server environments with intelligent clients instead of dumb terminals.

One advantage of APPN is the fact that it uses existing SNA formats as the SNA protocol. This means no encapsulation technology is necessary for SNA LU6.2, as with DLSw (LU 2 and LU 0/1/3 are also packed by the DLUR/DLUS functions—in LU 6.2).

APPN has a lively history behind it. Initial power games on the part of IBM had the objective of keeping the APPN network node function proprietary and only disclosing the end node specification. Later (1993), in response to consumer pressure, the NN code was expensively licensed (The Empire Strikes Back), which succeeded in ensuring that several internetworking manufacturers scratched their heads behind closed doors and, under the leadership of Cisco, came up with the counter-initiative APPI (Battlestar Galactica). APPI was intended to be an implementation of the end node function and to make APPN routable in TCP/IP by encapsulation. When Cisco announced its intention of acquiring an APPN license and implementing NN functions, the waters calmed down rapidly in 1994 and the APPI initiative was out. Native APPN or DLSw are now in.

Unlike other routable protocols, APPN routers (NN, network nodes) do not have a hop-by-hop routing table, but keep lists of reachable network nodes with complete routes in directory services. These are transmitted during session establishment of the transport layer for the initiating node (see Figure 10.7) and entered into every packet for the duration of the session (analogous to source routing). In the most recent version available (from VTAM v4.3), the protocol is dynamically routable with HPR; i.e., in the event of an error, no new session establishment is necessary, instead a new route is automatically sought by the transport layer RTP (Rapid Transport Protocol) after a time-out. The basic routing procedure, ANR (Automatic Network Routing, see Figure 10.8), is a mixture of source routing for packet forwarding and an OSPF-like link state procedure for route calculation.

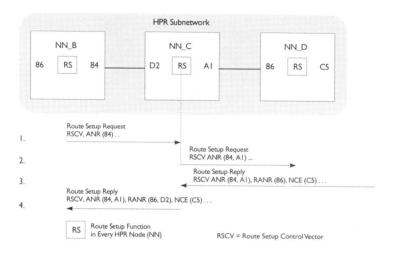

Figure 10.7: HPR session establishment: route definition

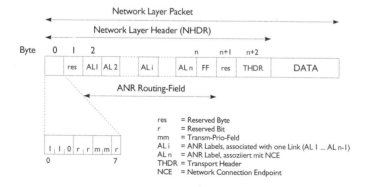

Figure 10.8: ANR format

APPN has some advantages for IBM environments:

- It greatly simplifies the configuration of SNA links;

- Together with the recently available HPR, it permits dynamic rerouting without session loss in the event of an error;

- It further develops the SNA sub-area concept;

- It contains SNA priority control and is a transport protocol which has been optimized for SNA traffic;

- The integration of the APPN NN functions as an independent protocol stack in routers enables SNA to be operated in integrated company backbones with multivendor products.

Network node functions, i.e., "SNA routing," may be implemented in the following equipment: IBM 3174, 3745/46, RISC/6000, OS/2, AS/400, 6611 MP routers, third-party routers. This means that SNA integration is possible as a "completely normal additional protocol" on a LAN basis (see also Figure 10.9): in parallel with protocol A to X: IP routing, IPX routing, DECnet routing, AppleTalk routing, VINES routing, etc., APPN is also loaded into the routers as protocol S (like SNA) and activated with the required memory configuration.

10.4.10 Protocol Prioritization

A core problem during multi-protocol operation with SNA involves achieving constant response times for SNA users, who have been spoiled in this regard. This is not really possible with FIFO processing with load profiles including megafiles and short terminal packets during periods of high loading. Many bridge/router manufacturers have therefore developed functions which assign different priorities to different protocols, and hence facilitate the priority processing of SNA traffic before other protocols.

The first job of a prioritization function is to arrange the incoming packets in several different queues. This requires filter functions to be configurable for different protocol types. Usually the LSAP value is used for this. Two rough classes of prioritization may be identified:

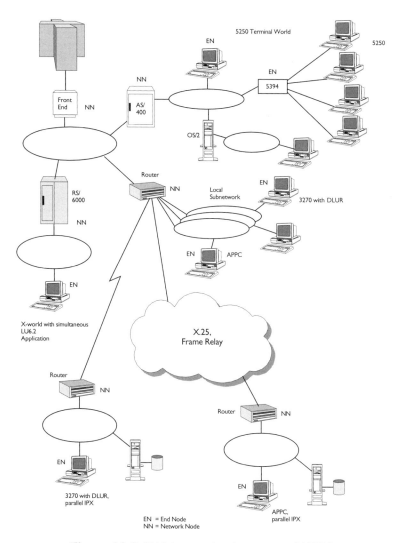

Figure 10.9: SNA integration by means of APPN

Absolute prioritization: Depending upon the priority class, a separate queue is established for processing. The queues (protocol types) are allocated a priority value: "high," "medium" or "low." Higher priority queues are processed until they are completely empty. Only then will lower priority queues be processed (3Com, CrossComm, previously also Cisco and Bay Networks). The algorithm scans the queues in priority order, but leaps back to a higher priority queue if a packet arrives there before the lower priority queue has been attended to. With high loads in a queue with high or medium priority, this procedure may result in the protocols with a low priority "starving" and time-outs will cause the session to abort. An example: a "high" priority is assigned to SNA traffic, "medium" to NetBIOS, because of the critical LLC timer, and "low" to the rest of the protocols : TCP, IPX, DECnetIV. If, in a high load situation, the WAN link is loaded with SNA packets, NetBIOS time-outs and session aborts take place, as the NetBIOS queue is not processed as long as there are SNA packets in the SNA queue.

Relative prioritization (bandwidth reservation): A separate queue is established for each priority class. This queue is assigned a greater or lesser share of the overall processing capacity (for example, SNA 60%, IPX 25%, TCP 15%). The algorithm scans the queues in accordance with the ratio of percentages assigned, i.e., in the example the SNA queue 12 times, the IPX queue 5 times and the TCP queue 3 times. If a queue does not contain any packets, its bandwidth may optionally be made available for other protocols (FIFO). Packets in different queues are processed according to the ratio of their assigned capacities (12 SNA packets, 5 IPX packets, 3 TCP packets, if all packets are approximately the same length).

However, once again there is a catch. Some LAN protocols, such as for example, TCP, adapt themselves to the available bandwidths: if the available bandwidth is low, TCP may automatically reduce the window size and hence indirectly the required bandwidth. In the routers, this results in this bandwidth being assigned to other protocols. Whereupon TCP reduces its window size again... and so on. At some stage, this mechanism causes the TCP to cut off its own life blood. Router manufacturers argue that this is a matter of tuning the application to correct this TCP behavior by changing parameters. This is not good news for network operators. They would prefer a prioritization algorithm from the router manufacturers which is able to process TCP without problems.

As standardization of priority mechanisms is not recognizable with multi-protocol operation, the implementations of manufacturers are different and incompatible with each other. In addition, the actual mathematical prioritization function is expensive to develop because the algorithm is only described incompletely in books.

The incompletely-developed technology for protocol prioritization in a heterogeneous LAN does hold some risks for user:

- The preference for SNA traffic increases the response times of other protocols, under some circumstance to time-out. This may occur if there is no relative prioritization, only absolute prioritization.

- During the prioritization of SNA and NetBIOS in combination with other protocols (TCP, IPX), NetBIOS still causes problems.

- If SNA and NetBIOS are transmitted with DLSw, not all manufacturers differentiate between the protocols since they receive the same LSAP and hence may no longer be assigned separate priorities. The result of this may be that NetBIOS appropriates more bandwidth and the response times are poor for SNA applications.

- The use of prioritization virtually commits the user to one manufacturer: the one who has the service capacity to deal with the effects and the tuning of two superimposed prioritization functions, even if the communication is still "functioning" because receiving routers do not interpret the prioritization, but only process incoming packets. The modeling of cascaded prioritization using different algorithms via, for example, interposed routers $(1 < n \leq 5)$, is clearly a rewarding subject for scientific work.

10.4.11 MPTN/AnyNet

Another approach to integration is MPTN (multi-protocol Transport Network) which IBM has being tried to implement since the announcement of Network Blueprints (September 1992). This involves the permanent association of an application with a specific transport protocol (TCP, IPX, APPN). For this purpose, a type of adaptation module (which is de facto a gateway at Layer 4) is inserted between the network and higher layers to fill the gap left behind by the missing link: it provides interworking with one of several networks/transport protocols available (see also Figure 10.10). For example, an application which was originally SNA may then be translated by TCP sockets and, vice versa, a UNIX application transported on SNA (nicknamed "SNAckets"). The adaptation module corresponds "upwards" to a CTS interface (Common

Transport Semantics), as defined by IBM, with which (newly written or ported) applications may be used independently of the underlying protocols .

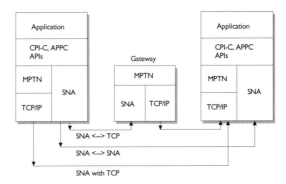

Figure 10.10: MPTN architecture

Admittedly, MPTN has advantages for IBM environments:

- in the future, the user will no longer be entirely dependent upon the SNA/APPN stack

- MPTN enables other protocols to be used with APPN and hence APPN may be made into a standard backbone protocol (similar to Cisco IGRP).

The last argument is particularly important to users to whom the 80/20 factor applies: at least 80% of incoming communication is SNA traffic, a maximum of 20% of the incoming communication is accounted for by all other protocols. In this case, the use of APPN has definite advantages.

Under close examination, two factors may be identified behind the MPTN approach, on the one hand the marketing attempt to obtain SNA structures for "alien protocols" as well, at least as a transport system, and, on the other hand, the rather overblown step of finally implementing TCP sockets, which most manufacturers have been doing for years now.

The question arises as to why new applications should be used on APPN (SNA), for example, if all routers support TCP/IP, but APPN is only implemented natively in individual products, and then only with a low degree of product development? To be quite frank: the MPTN product line is called AnyNet, but TCP/IP is already AnyNet.

For environments of a heterogeneous nature, besides simplified access to traditional SNA applications (and hence once again IBM equipment is affected), no other advantages may be foreseen, which places a question mark over company-wide MPTN implementation at the present time. The extent to which the MPTN approach will be able to establish itself in the market remains to be seen. The arguments to the contrary are:

- the need to adapt a gigantic applications base, which currently run on native protocol links;

- performance losses due to the adaptation module;

- increasing porting of many applications, first to native TCP, second to native IPX.

The following alternatives are establishing themselves more strongly than MPTN: SNA in the form of a 3270 emulation or APPC application is used in PCs on TCP or IPX and hence is routable in the WAN. The routing protocols used are known (TCP RIP, NetWare RIP). If the more modern OSPF or NLSP procedures are used, it requires the establishment of new know-how, but this will be necessary anyway when the existing PC network operation is converted to the new routing.

10.4.12 SNA Router, SNA Encapsulation

Smart developers have simply turned around the idea of replacing traditional SNA backbones by the up-and-coming LAN-WAN backbones. For example, a router made by packs the LAN traffic in SNA packets (LU 6.2) and forwards them over an existing SNA backbone by means of SDLC or X.25 to the destination LAN. This obviates the need to establish separate links to the LAN-WAN network. The protocols supported are NetBIOS, IPX, and TCP/IP, AppleTalk. Even IBM has recently introduced this kind of SNA router, the NWays multi-protocol concentrator (MpC) 2217. The IBM 2217 also supports APPN or MPTN.

This solution is suitable for networks in which the majority ($\geq 80\%$) of communication continues to be traditional SNA traffic, which also have to integrate a small amount of inter-site LAN traffic ($\leq 20\%$). Under these conditions, the following factors are seen as advantageous:

- optimized response times for SNA traffic;

- investment protection for installed SNA equipment;

- the use of existing WAN skills in the SNA area, instead of the establishment of new know-how for the operation of a LAN-WAN-BB.

However, this approach also has its disadvantages, particularly in view of
the fact that LANs have a tendency towards extreme growth and are constantly hungry for WAN capacity:

- Due to the equipment in existing front-ends, the line capacity is often
  less than 64 kbps (9.6 kbps or 19.2 kbps are commonly found), so that
  the manageable LAN traffic capacity is severely limited.

- With increasing capacity requirements, it will be necessary to upgrade
  front-end processors or control units, which, although a good excuse for
  enhancing the computer center, may cast doubt upon the flexible
  expandability of the solution in view of the known LAN growth rates.

10.4.13 ATM backbone

Another alternative to FDDI, Ethernet LAN switching, or Token Ring LAN
switching for SNA integration is the ATM backbone. The following approaches are possible:

- Token Ring integration using a hub system with a Token Ring backplane in which a LAN–ATM converter and an ATM uplink module are
  installed (site integration).

- The use of a Token Ring–ATM bridge, for example, IBM's 8281 (site
  integration).

- Connecting the front-end processor to a Frame Relay/ATM–Switch or
  by SDLC conversion to a router with an ATM uplink (WAN integration).

The achievable function is ATM LAN emulation or pure SNA–SNA with
ATM as the transit network (with FEP–ATM switch link).

10.4.14 Router with Channel Interface

As already described, the SNA support in the router may be restricted to the bottom two to four layers of the OSI model (SDLC, LLC, APPN) or it may reach up to the stars and extend into the SNA Layers 3–7 or it may be feasible to implement a complete SNA PU type 2 or PU type 4 intelligence. NSC and Cisco are going down this road and offering a channel interface in their routers (assuming that this thing can be called a router) (Cisco at present only for TCP, but in the future also for SNA).

A bus-and-tag or ESCON connection is an alternative for replacing cumbersome front-end processors. In terms of cost, they are more expensive than upgrading to a 3174 or 3172 device, but the router may be used for more than just SNA operations.

10.4.15 TCP with TN3270

We should not forget to mention a very simple approach which may be applied with all SNA integration, transformation, and encapsulation in internetworking backbones: instead of making routers more expensive by adding channel interfaces, SDLC interfaces, conversions software, and prioritization algorithms, application integration is used: the TCP stack on the host.

The TN3270 expansion of the Telnet protocol and FTP or NFS may be used to establish solid communication quality—on pure TCP/IP (for example, in a newsroom). The software price is extremely attractive. TN3270 is not a well-kept secret, but it has tended to be kept on the edge of the picture. However, it is now making a comeback on the crest of the current TCP wave as a cost-effective software solution:

- It offers the possibility for mobile users to dial in remotely using the same protocol in server and host(-server).

- There are no SNA address tables or static routes; network changes are easier to perform, even without APPN.

In this case, efforts at integration require nothing more than equipping the host and all end stations with TCP software and IP addresses. TCP becomes the company's backbone protocol. The equipment required for internetwork-

ing (LAN switches, router) is usually already present. As yet there is no official TN3270 standard, but the IETF has taken the matter in hand. Some new
RFCs have been developed are:

RFC 1647   B. Kelly, "TN3270 Enhancements," 07/15/1994 (Proposed
            Standard)

RFC 1646   C. Graves, T. Butts, M. Angel, "TN3270 Extensions for
            LUname and Printer Selection," 07/14/1994 (Informal)

RFC 1576   J. Penner, "TN3270 Current Practices," 01/20/1994 (Informal)

The achievable communication function is solid, but not brilliant:

- The PF keys on the 3270 terminal are shown as cryptic keys:

- TN3270 was originally described to enable VT terminals to have access
  to IBM hosts. Therefore, every symbol is transmitted separately:

- Expanded functions such as EAB, colors, or graphics are not supported
  as well as they are in traditional emulations.

10.4.16 Conclusion

The decision as to whether and how to employ SNA integration in a multi-protocol backbone is not simple and cannot be based simply on gut feeling or the
product price list.

What Could IBM Do?

Since this concerns the integration and survival of IBM's own architecture, we
have to ask what IBM could do to make life easier for the users. Here are some
suggestions:

- Make APPN available as a public domain code.

- Provide toolkits with applications interfaces with which IPX applications, AppleTalk applications, etc. can be used on APPN.

- Implement RFC 1795 in Front-End Processors and control units.

- Within the framework of MPTN: use 3270 applications on TCP, use
  APPC and 3270 on IPX.

- Install gateway functions in 3174 and 3172 products corresponding to third-party gateways such as NetWare for SAA, NT SNA Server, gateways from Attachmate, Wall Data, etc.

Recommendation

The following are some tips which could simplify the exit, transfer, and entry into ISI ("integrated SNA internetworks"):

- Route routable protocols;

- Avoid proprietary procedures and instead use open, standardized procedures (DLSw with RFC 1434 in the future RFC 1795;)

- Calculate the bandwidth requirements for the resulting SNA/multi-protocol mixture very carefully;

- Weigh up the advantages and disadvantages of SDLC-LLC conversion and the advantages and disadvantages of conversion with separate converters or with routers for the particular network, giving consideration to

  - management integration

  - service costs

  - diversity of the protocols used

  - costs for the provision of a Token Ring connection for SNA equipment

- Conduct a pilot phase with defined tests.

- *Pay attention to the increased redundancy requirements resulting from an integrated company backbone.*

10.5 Standard for SNA and NetBIOS: DLSw

TCP, which has been spurned for a long time by SNA gurus, is establishing itself as a standard for SNA integration in WAN and sometimes LAN backbones. Data Link Switching (DLSw) is a specification disclosed as an RFC as to how SNA and NetBIOS traffic are encapsulated in TCP and are dynamically reroutable in the WAN area.

The first proprietary implementations of TCP encapsulation for SNA were followed by a special IBM implementation for their multi-protocol router IBM 6611. To enable other manufacturers to use compatible implementations, the specification was published as RFC 1434 (current status: Informal). Data Link Switching was born. Although the document has the status of "Informal," DLSw was, according to RFC 1434, implemented by several established manufacturers. The successor RFC 1795 is still too new for wide dissemination, not to mention the compatibility of different manufacturers. One of the first implementations was introduced to the market by Cisco, which played a decisive role in the development of RFC 1795.

TCP encapsulation with DLSw is used as an alternative to the SDLC-LLC conversion for SNA traffic, and for SNA LLC (DLC) and NetBIOS. One objective of the DLSw specification was to make SNA routable without having to change the data link software in the end stations. DLSw terminated the LLC-Session on LAN-WAN transition by means of bilateral local polls and acknowledgments, as with SDLC poll-spoofing (see also SNA in Heterogeneous Networks: Integration Possibilities).

Data Link Switching supports SNA PU type 2, type 4, type 2.1 and optionally NetBIOS on 802.2 networks (standard LANs). SNA PU type 2 primary or secondary and PU 2.1 are also supported by SDLC. In DLSw, they are treated as LAN systems: every PU is assigned a data link address (MAC address, LSAP).

The Background

IEEE 802.2 LLC type 2 was developed on the assumption that the response time in the network is very low and deterministic (predictable). These are typical assumptions for LAN applications. Accordingly, the LLC procedure uses a fixed timer to identify packet loss. If the protocol for WAN operation is bent over bridge links, the assumptions are no longer true: the response time becomes too high and it is *no* longer deterministic, but extremely variable when there are overloads on the WAN link. The LLC timer runs out, and a packet repetition is triggered. However, if the original frame has not been lost, but only delayed, under some circumstances, extreme confusion breaks out in the LLC type 2 procedure, resulting in protocol errors and, in the worst case, to the link being aborted.

The following is a more detailed examination of the two RFCs for DLSw. Although RFC 1434 has officially been replaced by RFC 1795, the older RFC is also described, since all current implementations are based on this RFC.

10.5.1 RFC 1434

DLSw describes the encapsulation of SNA and NetBIOS in TCP as a backbone protocol. The routers which perform the encapsulation are known as Data Link Switches. No independent routing mechanism is defined, but it acts as a substitute for LLC or DLC a pure Layer-2 link which is switched between the Data Link Switches. The routing uses the known IP procedures (RIP, OSPF, etc.) The DLSw procedure addresses the following LLC weak points:

- DLC time-outs

- DLC acknowledgments via WAN

- flow control and congestion control

- broadcast control for link establishment

- restriction of the hop count limit with source route bridging to 7 hops

- the absence of dynamic rerouting in the event of an error

How does a Data Link Switch (DLS) work? To put it simply: towards the LAN, a DLS acts as though it were the communication partner and, towards the WAN, together with its DLS partner at the other end of the LAN-WAN-LAN network, it reliably ensures that link establishment, data exchange and automatic rerouting take place in the event of an error. A protocol was defined which facilitates the necessary links, the SSP (Switch-to-Switch Protocol). A single Data Link Switch with several interfaces may switch links internally between these interfaces. Obviously, it does not use a TCP for this; that would be a nonsensical internal overhead. Figure 10.11 shows the principle of intra-switch and inter-switch DLSw links.

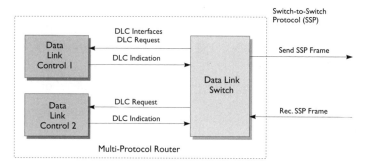

Figure 10.11: Inter-switch and intra-switch DLSw links

Hop count limit

The main difference between DLSw and SRB is that DLSw terminates the LLC link locally and also terminates the hop count limit. SRB does not do this (see also Figure 10.12). The LLC link is replaced in the WAN by a TCP link. This enables several LLC links to be multiplexed on a TCP link between DLSs (Data Link Switches).

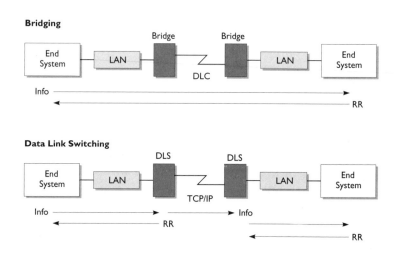

Figure 10.12: Comparison of DLS coupling with SRB coupling

DLC Time-outs, DLC Acknowledgments

The masking out of the LLC links in the WAN results in the local "remnants" of the LLC link on the two sides working completely independently of each other. The central task of the participating DLS pair is to keep the two isolated LLC parts synchronized and to supply packets properly. For this reason, the WAN uses the high link quality provided by the TCP service (link-orientated, error-tolerant, flow control), not only IP.

LLC acknowledgments (RR) are not forwarded into the WAN, but spoofed: The remote DLS sends RRs in its connected LAN and hence creates the illusion that the remote partner station would receive its communication partner's RRs (see Figure 10.12). The same applies to SDLC: polling and poll response are treated locally (poll spoofing).

Broadcast Control for Link Establishment

As soon as a Data Link Switch has learned where a specific destination system is to be found, it forwards broadcasts which contain a link establishment request for this destination system, not to all ports, but only to the specific switch behind which the destination system is connected (MAC address caching).

NetBIOS, SNA

During the establishment of NetBIOS sessions, DLSs use the NetBIOS names to forward packets to a specific address. NetBIOS packets use the LSAP 0x'F0'. During the establishment of an SNA session, TEST or XID packets are forwarded. They use the SAPs 0x'04', 0x'08', and 0x'0C'. This enables SNA packets and NetBIOS packets to be differentiated. A Data Link Switch makes a note of reachable NetBIOS systems by entering the names in a table (NetBIOS name caching). SNA stations are learned locally, using route discovery and remotely from responses from other switches. SDLC end stations are treated as LAN stations: they receive a MAC/SAP address in the switch that is mapped to the PU.

Data Link Switches

Before a single data packet can be exchanged between communication part-ners, the interposed routers or Data Link Switches must have established a TCP link from router to router. To this end, a DLS keeps a list of all other DLSs known to it. Every switch entry is marked with the status information - active/inactive. The following TCP parameters are used:

- Socket family   AF-INET   (Internet Protocol)

- Socket type   SOCK_STREAM   (Stream Socket)

- Read port number   2065

- Write port number   2067

For the end systems connected to the LANs, the switches are presented as source routing bridges. Therefore, a switch receives internally a virtual ring number: the ring number of the LAN. The communication via a switch pair for an end system appears as though it is communicating with the adjacent ring. Switches that are connected to the same LAN must receive this same vir-tual ring number on the relevant interfaces. This also applies if several source routing bridges are installed between the switches, i.e., the LAN consists of several Token Ring segments. As with source route bridging, the virtual ring number prevents a data package from being forwarded in parallel by two or more switches connected to the same LAN.

Link Establishment and Link Addressing

If there is a TCP link between two switches, they use the Switch-to-Switch Protocol (SSP) to establish an end-to-end connections, i.e., LAN to LAN "cir-cuits." The overhead for SSP is not low: control packets (with circuit estab-lishment and link establishment) have a 72-byte header and data packets have a 16-byte header. If the circuit exists, it is possible to talk end-to-end in LLC type 1. After the establishment of the circuit, an end-to-end link of LLC Type 2 may be set up between communication partners.

A link is defined as a logical association between two end stations. The link is assigned a 14-byte data link ID consisting of a 7-byte destination address and a 7-byte source address (6-byte MAC address, 1-byte LSAP). The circuit between the participating switches receives a 64-bit number for each individual participating DLS (4-byte DLC port ID, 4-byte data link correlator). Every DLS may be assigned an arbitrary, freely-available circuit number independently of the other DLSs for new links. (Similar to: X.25 VCs.) The circuit ID must be unique within a DLS. Together with the DLS IDs of the participating start and destination switches, there is a unique identifier for an end-to-end circuit. Every DLS keeps a table with the circuit ID pairs for the local and remote end points of a circuit. The switch that initiates the establishment of a circuit is called the origin switch, and its remote partner is called the target switch. Figure 10.13a shows the addresses used during the establishment of an end-to-end link.

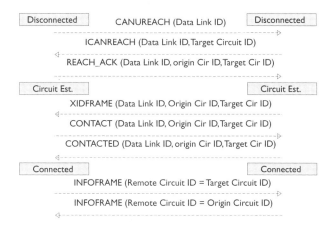

Figure 10.13a: Address during link establishment by DLSw

If the SSP link exists, the short header which only contains the circuit ID is used for info packets. With NetBIOS control packets, the entire NetBIOS DLC header is transferred into the data part of the frame: MAC header, RIF (padded to 18 bytes), LLC header. This affects the following NetBIOS packet types: Name Query, Name Response, Add Name Query, Add Name Response, and Dataframe. The remote DLS which receives these packets ignores the routing information entered (RIF).

The following describes the protocol sequence for an SNA link establishment: Peter Frogger from United Barbie Dolls wishes to speak with Patty

Stouberg. Peter sends a TEST command which is seen by the DLS (see Figure 10.13b). Then he sends a CANUREACH (can you reach) to the target DLS. If the origin DLS does not know the target DLS, it sets up a "canoe race:" it sends the CANUREACH to all DLSs. All DLSs search their local tables for the destination address or start a local route discovery, including the actual target DLS. It responds with ICANREACH (I can reach). If several DLSs are connected to the destination system's LAN, they all respond: the canoe race returns. As in source routing, the origin DLS snatches the first response and sends a REACK_ACK to the selected target DLS as confirmation. Link condition "circuit established" has now been achieved. End stations can exchange LLC type 1 packets over the circuit (for example, XID, TEST).

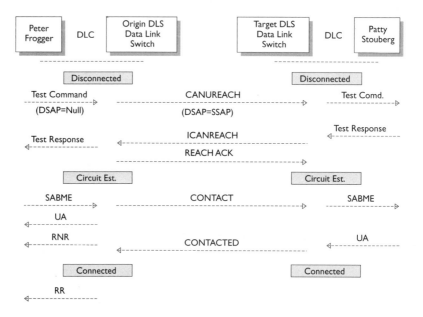

Figure 10.13b: DLSw link establishment

This is not enough. A "connection" is required to enable LLC type 2 traffic to be transmitted as well. To do this, Peter sends a SABME command. The origin DLS reacts to this by sending a CONTACT to the target DLS and simultaneously supplying Peter with a UA response. To prevent Peter chattering away in vain before the link is finally established, an RNR is sent afterwards.

But to return to the target DLS: after receiving the CONTACT, it sends a SABME to Patty, who responds with UA. This converts the target DLS into a CONTACTED at the origin DLS. The latter is not idle, and reacts by sending an RR to Peter. Both DLSs now have the status "CONNECTED." The LLC type 2 link between Peter and Patty is "up and running."

In the event of errors, a restart may take place during which the DLSs return to "circuit established" status to re-establish the link until "CONNECTED" status is achieved. Obviously, the link may also be cleared in a civilized manner. Figure 10.14 shows the automatic status device for each individual circuit. A DLS starts one automatic status device for each circuit. There are three stable status's: DISCONNECTED, CIRCUIT_ESTABLISHED, and CONNECTED. All others are transitional status'. Readers who get into a state when reading status transitions should simply ignore the figure.

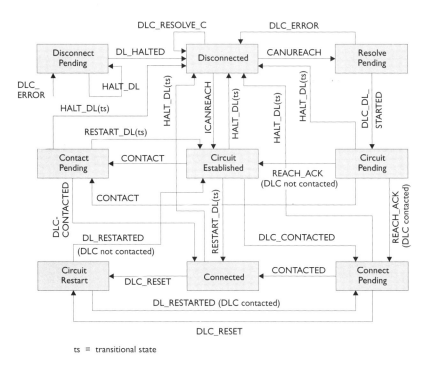

ts = transitional state

Figure 10.14: Automatic status machine for an RFC 1434 DLS circuit

10.5.2 RFC 1795

IBM's RFC 1434 resulted in a multi-manufacturer initiative to develop a more comprehensive standard together with the APPN implementors workshop. An initial document has been available in the form of RFC 1795 since April 1995. RFC 1795 replaces RFC 1434. It fills some gaps in the specifications in RFC 1434 and contains several expansions, particularly:

- Frame format

- Message types

- Link establishment

- Establishment of cache for MAC addresses and NetBIOS names

- Adoption of largest frame size

- Priorities for circuits

- Session numbering for NetBIOS

- Exchange of supported parameters on DLS-DLS link establishment (pacing, window sizes, NetBIOS Name Caching, MAC address lists, SAP lists)

- Flow control

Unfortunately, no explicit backwards compatibility was defined since greater innovations were introduced. Accordingly, RFC 1795 only deals very half-heartedly in several places with the older specification formats being described which are found in RFC 1434 and are no longer used in RFC 1795.

Future developments, for example, encapsulation in APPN instead of TCP, are feasible (announcement of 3Com, Cisco). The following discusses RFC 1795 and its main expansions.

Frame Format

The header lengths for check packets (72 bytes) and info packets (16 bytes) have not changed as RFC 1434 kept a series of bytes free "for future use." The formats for check packets according to RFC 1434 and RFC 1795 are shown in

Figures 10.15a and 10.15b. The changes in RFC 1795 are marked. Info packets use the first 16 bytes of check packets, so this format will not be described separately. The designation "remote" refers to the switch which is "remote" from the point of view of the transmitter. "Origin" designates the switch or the end station, that initiated the link; "target" designates the switch or the end station, that accepted the link or should accept the link. It should be noted that "target" and "remote" correspond only if the transmission is in the direction of the target switch!

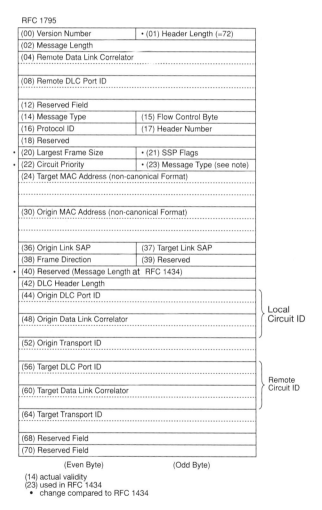

Figure 10.15a: Frame formats in RFC 1434 and RFC 1795

The Version number (offset 0) is 0x'31', the ASCII symbol for "1" (decimal code 49). The experienced reader will have already worked out for himself that this code stands for version 1. The header length (offset 1) is 0x'48' for check packets (72 bytes) and 0x'01' for info packets (16 bytes). The packet length (offset 2) shows the length of the data part which is transmitted after the header.

The code for the packet type has moved from byte 23 in RFC 1434 to byte 14. One byte was provided for flow control (offset 15). The protocol ID (offset 16) is "66", i.e. 0x'42'. The header number (offset 17) was set at 0x'01'. Other bytes encode the maximum packet length (offset 20), flags for the switch-to-switch protocol (offset 21), and link priority (offset 22). In Version 1.0, only one flag is defined: Bit7=1 means the packet is an explorer packet (CANUREACH_ex, ICANREACH_ex). Byte 23 was not assigned for reasons of possible compatibility with RFC 1434, as the "old" packet type is entered there.

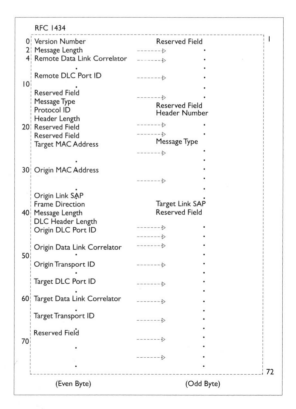

Figure 10.15b - Frame Format in RFC 1434

The route display (offset 38) has the value 0x'01' for packets from origin to target and the value 0x'02' for packets from target to origin. This field is used to determine how the "remote" parameters (data link correlator, port ID) should be set and to check that they have been set correctly: if "1" is set, the remote parameters correspond to the target parameters, if "2" is set they correspond to the origin parameters.

The DLC header length (offset 42) is 0 bytes for SNA 0 (0x'00') and 35 bytes for NetBIOS data packets, i.e., 0x'23'. It contains AC, FC, DA, SA, RIF, DSAP, SSAP, and the LLC check field. The RIF is padded to 18 bytes so that it is always the same length. Notice that the number is 18 instead of 16 bytes (maximum length according to IEEE 802.5). Since the DLSw cloud receives a virtual segment number, it may be necessary to enter one more route designator. In this case, the RIF increases from 16 to 18 bytes. Therefore, as before, the LAN side may use the maximum number of 7 hops.

Now let's look at addressing: as already described, a link is defined as a logical association between two end stations. From byte 24, the MAC target and source address for the participating end stations are entered. They are transmitted in the Token Ring format (non-canonical), i.e., with the MSB first. This is followed by the link SAPs (offset 36, 37), for example, 0x'F0' for NetBIOS or 0x'04', 0x'08', 0x'0C' for SNA. The link connection is assigned in a 14 byte-long data link ID which consists of the destination and source link address, each 7 bytes long, (6 bytes MAC address, 1 byte LSAP). This has the advantage that the end stations have no need to know which switch is actually taking over the data transport, making DLSw fully transparent for the end systems. In the SSP packets for a specific circuit, the origin DLSw acts as if the MAC address for the initiating end station were its own MAC address. Similarly, the target DLSw acts as if the MAC address for the destination station were its own MAC address.

A circuit is identified end-to-end by an ID pair: the circuit between the participating switches receives a 64-bit number for each individual participating DLS (4-byte DLC port ID, offset 44 and 56, 4-byte Data Link Correlator, offset 48 and 60). Every DLS may therefore be assigned any circuit number which it has available for new links independently of the DLSs (similar to: X.25 VCs). The circuit ID only has to be unique within a DLS. Together with the data link IDs for the participating start and destination stations. This produces a unique identification for an end-to-end circuit. Every DLS keeps a table with the circuit ID pairs for the local and remote end points of a circuit. The switch which initiates a circuit establishment is called the origin switch; its partner at the other end of the line the target switch.

The transport IDs identify the special TCP/IP port for a data link switch.

The Data Link Correlator, port ID, and transport ID have only switch-internal (local) significance. RFC 1795 explicitly specifies that they may not be identified. The values must be accepted unchanged into response packets by the partner switch ("as is echo").

SSP packets which cannot be assigned to a circuit are irrevocably rejected (with HALT_DL_NOACK, a link abort without waiting for an acknowledgment). This avoids error situations in which one switch has a defined circuit and another does not.

Message Types

The defined packet types are shown in Figure 10.16. Expansions in RFC 1795 compared to RFC 1434 are marked.

Order	Description	Type	Flags
· CANUREACH_ex	Can U Reach Station_explorer	0x03	SSPex
· CANUREACH_cs	Can U Reach Station_circuit start	0x03	
· ICANREACH_ex	I Can Reach Station_explorer	0x04	SSPex
. ICANREACH_cs	I Can Reach Station_circuit start	0x04	
REACH_ACK	Reach Acknowledgement	0x05	
DGRFRAME	Datagram Frame	0x06	
XIDFRAME	XID Frame	0x07	
CONTACT	Contact Remote Station	0x08	
CONTACTED	Remote Station Contacted	0x09	
RESTART_DL	Restart Data Link	0x10	
DL_RESTARTED	Data Link Restarted	0x11	
ENTER_BUSY	Enter Busy	0x0C	
· EXIT_BUSY	Exit Busy	0x0D	
· INFOFRAME	Information (I) Frame	0x0A	
HALT_DL	Halt Data Link	0x0E	
DL_HALTED	Data Link Halted	0x0F	
NETBIOS_NQ_ex	NETBIOS Name Query-explorer	0x12	SSPex
. NETBIOS_NQ_cs	NETBIOS Name Query-circuit setup	0x12	
. NETBIOS _NR_ex	NETBIOS Name Recognized-explorer	0x13	SSPex
. NETBIOS_NR_CS	NETBIOS Name Recog-circuit setup	0x13	
DATAFRAME	Data Frame	0x14	
· HALT_DL_NOACK	Halt Data Link with no Ack	0x19	
NETBIOS_ANQ	NETBIOS Add Name Query	0x1A	
· NETBIOS_ANR	NETBIOS Add Name Response	0x1B	
KEEPALIVE	Transport Keepalive Message	0x1D	
CAP_EXCHANGE	Capabilities Exchange	0x20	
· IFCM	Independent Flow Control Message	0x21	
· TEST_CIRCUIT_REQ	Test Circiut Request	0x7A	
. TEST_CIRCUIT_RSP	Test Circuit Response	0x7B	

· Change in comparison to RFC 1434

Figure 10.16: Packet types for DLSw according to RFC 1795

The simple CANUREACH and ICANREACH were replaced by the flag extensions _ex and _cs. The _ex types serve as pure explorer packets without any need for a circuit to be established between two switches. This reduces the overhead.

DGRMFRAME and DATAFRAME are both used for data transfer. The DATAFRAME contains data link IDs (MAC/SAP) as addresses. The DGRM-FRAME uses circuit IDs as addressing and may only be used if the link establishment (circuit establishment) is complete. The DATAFRAME is taken if the SSP link does not yet exist and the circuit IDs have not yet been exchanged.

The ENTER_BUSY and EXIT_BUSY types were added by several manufacturers after the publication of RFC 1434 to provide flow control. They are no longer used in RFC 1795 and have been replaced by pacing, as described later.

NETBIOS_NQ_cs and NETBIOS_NR_cs are not normally sent. They are there for compatibility with RFC 1434 switches. NB*_ex is now used instead of NETBIOS_NQ_cs and NETBIOS_NR_cs.

HALT_DL_NOACK requires an immediate link abort without waiting for acknowledgment from the distant station. It is used in error situations in which the partner switch is no longer able to respond in some circumstances.

KEEPALIVE may send a DLS to check its TCP link. This must be ignored by the distant station. KEEPALIVE makes sense, for example, if DLSs are connected to each other by other TCP routers. If the router link is destroyed, in some circumstances, the KEEPALIVE results in an ICMP message and the DLS recognizes an error situation, although the data link is actually idle.

Link Establishment

To save overhead, a switch may attempt to find a MAC/SAP destination without the preliminary lengthy establishment of a link with the partner switch. Only when the address is found (ICANREACH_ex arrived), will CANUREACH_cs be used to start a link establishment. A DLS which has the required destination it its cache may (optionally) respond directly to CANUREACH_ex without establishing an LLC link to the desired destination station beforehand (by TEST-Frame to the zero SAP). However, it may also activate the local LLC link to the destination station immediately (by sending

TEST). Figure 10.17 shows the process of link establishment. The actions listed under the switch symbol run internally in the switch between DLC and DLSw: for example, a TEST received by the LAN side results in an internal switch resolve request DLC_RESOLVE_C, which is forwarded to the DLSw network as CANUREACH_ex. An internal DLC_DL_STARTED in the target switch results in a ICANREACH_cs etc.

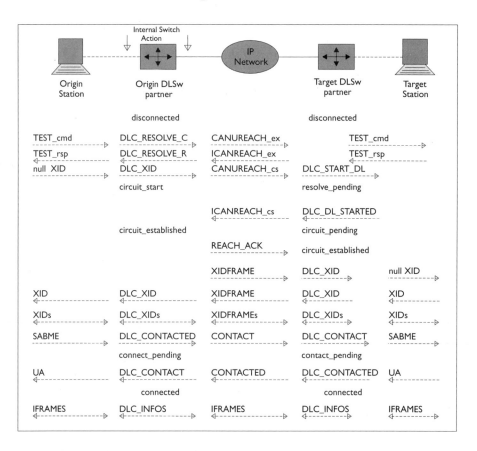

Figure 10.17: Link establishment by DLSw according to RFC 1795

Establishment of a Cache for MAC Addresses and NetBIOS Names

A switch that sees *_ex packets (for example, on the LAN backbone or in a intermeshed WAN backbone) may evaluate the information and use it to establish a cache for MAC addresses and NetBIOS names. This enables it, on request, to start a link establishment to these addresses directly without first having to send a CANUREACH_ex to all active switches. The link establishment may fail if the cache information is not up-to-date, i.e., if the desired address may no longer be reached via the switch in the cache. If abbreviated link establishment does not take place, a normal request has to be made.

The evaluation of a cache is always optional, and the RFC does not specify any timer values for information update (aging).

Adoption of the Largest Frame Size

The "largest frame size" byte in the SSP header is used to enable the maximum packet size to fly through the DLSw cloud and to transmit it between the two participating end stations along the DLSw link. Otherwise the transmitting station might use a longer packet length than the LAN for the destination station permits or vice versa. In both cases, this would lead to a link abort, unless the SSP were to define fragmentation. The inventors of DLSw saved themselves a lot of bother by ensuring that the maximum packet size is encoded according to IEEE 802.1D, Annex C, and is only used during link establishment (CANUREACHxx, ICANREACHxx, NETBIOS-NQ-ex, NETBIOS_NR_ex). This field should be ignored in all other packets.

Priorities for Circuits

Different DLSw links (circuits) may be assigned different priorities (CP, circuit Priority). The RFC does not say anything about which priority algorithm should be used (relative or absolute priority, which protocol receives which priority, etc.). The algorithm is left up to the implementation.

The priority is defined on link establishment, and after this, it cannot be changed until the link is cleared. The priority value is found in bit 0 to bit 2 of the priority byte. It encodes the following values:

000	Unsupported
001	Low priority
010	Medium priority
011	High priority
100	Top priority
101-111	Reserved (for future use)

How does the selection function? Figure 10.18 shows an example of this. First of all, the originator sets a CANUREACH_cs, for example, switch_A, the CP bits. This shows which priority is being given to the link, for example, '011'. The partner switch, for example, switch_B, sets the bits in the ICAN-REACH_cs response as the user would like to have the priority, for example, '010'. If the wishes are different, switch_A selects one of the values, and enters it in the REACH_ACK, for example, 010. This makes the value 010 valid, and it has to be accepted by switch_B. Switch_A does not have to take the lower value. Therefore, it could have selected '011'.

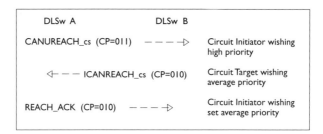

Figure 10.18: Selecting the priority

If a DLS does not support priority control, the value for "Unsupported" is entered.

Special Features of NetBIOS

During link establishment and for general check information, NetBIOS uses different routing types for source routing. These different packets must be treated appropriately by Data Link Switches. UI frames (unnumbered information) for directory services and/or datagrams often have a GA multicast (group MAC address) as the destination address. Since a group of end stations may be distributed between several LANs, the routing type in the routing control field is set to STE (Spanning Tree Explorer). They are listed here for the benefit of NetBIOS protocol specialists:

- NB_Add_Name_Query
- NB_Name_in_Conflict

- NB_Add_Group_Name_Query

- NB_Datagram

- NB_Datagram_Broadcast

- NB_Status_Query

- NB_Terminate_Trace

If a switch receives an NB_Add_Name_Query, it sends a NETBIOS_ANQ to all other active switches (which it knows from its cache table). A switch which receives a NETBIOS_ANQ, it sends it to all "normal", non-DLSw LAN segments, which are active according to Spanning Tree, as NB_Add_Name_Query (routing type STE).

The other GA-Frames are simply forwarded unchanged as DATAFRAME (i.e., without circuit establishment) to all other switches.

The NetBIOS packets

- NB_Add_Name_Response

- NB_Status_Response

- NB_Name_Recognized

have a specific MAC address (Unicast) as destination address, the routing type is, however, ARE (all routes explorer). If a switch_A receives an NB_Add_Name_Response, its sends a NETBIOS_ANR to the switch_B which connected the destination address locally (if switch_A's cache makes this information known). Switch_B forms a NB_Add_Name_Response (routing type ARE) from this and forwards it to the connected LAN segments.

The NB_status_Response has a MAC Unicast as the destination address and the routing type SRF (source routed frame), i.e., a normally entered route in the RIF. It is forwarded unchanged as DATAFRAME to all DLSs.

If a switch receives a NB_Name_Recognized, this was preceded by an inquiry regarding these names (NB_Name_Query), which was forwarded in the DLSw cloud as NETBIOS_NQ_ex and reconverted into NB_Name_Query in the connected LANs. The response NB_Name_Recognized is converted into a NETBIOS_NR_ex and forwarded to the switch which sent the NETBIOS_

NQ_ex. It forwards the whole thing as NB_Name_Recognized into the LAN to which the source station which started the original name query is connected.

During the explorer exchanges, a so-called "crossover" situation may occur: source_A sends a name query to destination_B. The associated switch_A makes this into a NETBIOS_NQ_ex (B) which is received by switch_B. At the same time, source_B has generated a name query to destination_A, the responsible switch_B has made this into a NETBIOS_NQ_ex (A) and sent it to switch_A. Switch_A may now create a match for source_A and destination_B and no longer has to wait for a NETBIOS_NR_ex response. However, the evaluation of crossover information is optional. The crossover situation may also occur if a switch has received a NETBIOS_NQ_ex, forwarded it as a name query to the connected LANs, and received a counter-query before the official response (NB_Name_Recognized) from the destination station.

Session Numbering for NetBIOS

During the name query (NB_Name_Query) and query response (NB_Name_Recognized), session numbers are exchanged between the end stations. To enable the exchange to function with DLSw as well, it is necessary to ensure that every NETBIOS_NQ_ex frame is converted by a switch into a name query with exactly the same, current session number. The session number may not therefore, be taken from the cache (only older session numbers for old queries may be stored here). If a switch receives two queries from the LAN for the same NetBIOS names with different session numbers, the query has to be processed separately for each session number. This also applies in the event of a crossover.

Exchanging the Supported Parameters during DLS-DLS Link Establishment

According to RFC 1795, DLSw have several functions which require the agreement of the participating switches, since they are only supported optionally or there are different value areas which have to be exchanged and sometimes selected. This includes, for example:

- Manufacturer's ID (3 byte, from IEEE assigned OUI)

- Version number of the DLSw standard (currently Version 1 Release 0)

- Version number of the manufacturer's software

- Number of TCP links supported

- Starting window size for pacing

- Filter lists for

  * MAC-addresses

  * NetBIOS names

  * LLC SAPs

The exchange of supported parameters (capabilities exchange) is always the first action on a newly established SSP link between two switches. It takes place by means of special SSP check packets which contain the packet type 0x'20' (capability exchange). The packet has the following format in the data part:

```
byte 0-1 2-3 4 to n
      +---+---+-----------------+
      | LL | ID | Control Vectors   |
      |    |    | x-times(L|T|Data) |
      +---+---+-----------------+
```

LL specifies the overall length (LL+ID+control vectors), ID has the value 0x'1520' for requests and 0x'1521' for responses. The parameters are encoded in so-called LT (length and type) control vectors which are familiar to all readers who have ever had to use GDS structured subfields in SNA. The first byte specifies the length L of a control vector (max. 255, since only one byte is available for the encoding), the second byte specifies the type T, and this is followed by a maximum of p bytes of parameter data where $p \leq 253$ (as the length L+T+p is). The defined vector types (IDs) are listed in Figure 10.19 for purposes of completeness.

The SAP list specifies the SAPs supported by the switch, for example, 0x'04', 0x'06', etc., 0x'EC' for SNA and 0x'F0' for NetBIOS. The exchange is important to avoid unnecessary overhead: if a switch does not support NetBIOS (the support of NetBIOS is optional), it does not need to receive the corresponding explorer frames. All SAPs used by SNA should, according to RFC 1795, always be fully supported.

Vector Description	Hex Value
Vendor ID Control Vector	0x81
DLSw Version Control Vector	0x82
Initial Pacing Window Control Vector	0x83
Version String Control Vector	0x84
Mac Address Exclusivity Control Vector	0x85
Supported SAP List Control Vector	0x86
TCP Connections Control Vector	0x87
NetBIOS Name Exclusivity Control Vector	0x88
MAC Address List Control Vector	0x89
NetBIOS Context Control Vector	0x8A
Vendor Context Control Vector	0x8B
Reserved for future use	0x8C - 0xCF
Vendor Specific	0xD0 - 0xFD

Figure 10.19: Defined control vectors in DLSw Version 1.0

A switch that receives a MAC or NetBIOS list (code 0x'89', 0x'8A'), may only use it as a filter list if the associated exclusivity vector (code 0x'85', 0x'88') defines it as a filter list with the value 0x'01'. Then only the specified addresses are reachable via the switch that sent the list. If the exclusivity vector has the value 0x'00', the specified addresses are, by definition, reachable via the switch, but there may be other addresses that are reachable.

If all the specified parameters are supported, the response is positive. Invalid capability packets or those with parameters which the address does not support receive a negative response. Here, the offset for the non-supported parameter and an error code (reason) are specified (see Figure 10.20). The initiating switch should react by aborting the TCP link. RFC 1434 implementations are recognized by the fact that they do not respond at all to capability exchange packets as they do not know them. For such a case, RFC 1975 does not specify that the TCP link must be aborted—it does not specify anything—and passes the buck to the implementation.

Flow Control, Pacing

Believing that merely having made a start is laudable, the standard describes a data flow control between the participating switches. Unfortunately, it does not describe how the flow control implemented may be converted to the DLC flow control for the LANs connected to the switches. The authors themselves describe their statements on the subject as "philosophical overview."

However, their intention is good: to push overload situations within the DLSw cloud back to the DLSw access points and so place the blame on the LANs which caused them. This means that respectable LANs, which do not produce any overloads, are guaranteed a sensible throughput through the DLSw network.

0x0001	invalid GDS length for a DLSw Capabilities Exchange Request (The value of Offset is ignored.)
0x0002	invalid GDS id for a DLSw Capabilities Exchange Request (The value of Offset is ignored.)
0x0003	Vendor Id control vector is missing. (The value of Offset is ignored.)
0x0004	DLSw Version control vector is missing. (The value of Offset is ignored.)
0x0005	Initial Pacing Window control vector is missing. (The value of Offset is ignored.)
0x0006	Length of control vectors doesn't correlate to the Length of the GDS variable.
0x0007	invalid control vector id
0x0008	length of control vector invalid
0x0009	invalid control vector data value
0x000A	duplicate control vector (for non-repeating control vectors)
0x000B	out-of-sequence control vector (for repeating control vector)
0x000C	DLSw Supported SAP List control vector is missing.

Figure 10.20: Error codes on negative response to capability exchange

Flow control takes place independently in both directions in every link (circuit). As with all orderly flow control between two switches, each gives the other the transmit authorization for a number of packets. This includes the packet types DGRMFRAME and INFOFRAME. Check packets are not included. The following describes the interaction between sender and receiver which takes place independently in both directions (every switch is simultaneously a sender and a receiver).

The sender has the parameters

- GrantedUnits number of packets which are (may be) transmitted

- CurrentWindow current window size which may be changed by the receiver

- InitialWindowSize initial window size which is the same for all circuits in the same TCP.

The receiver has the parameters

- *GrantedUnits*   number of packets which have to be received

- *CurrentWindow*   see above

- *InitialWindow*Size see above

- *FCACKOwed*   The sender must send an ACK (acknowledgment) before another transmit authorization is given.

The flow control byte is in the SSP header as described for offset 15. This means that it is also contained in INFOFRAMES with a short header, which permits piggybacking. The format is shown in Figure 10.21. FCI is the flag for a flow control action (flow control indication, FCIND), and FCA is used for an ACK (FCACK). FCO encodes the action (flow control operator) and has the following values:

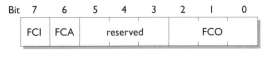

FCI   : Flow Control Indicator
FCA   : FLow Control ACK
FCO   : FLow COntrol Operator Bits

Figure 10.21: Format of the flow control byte

000	Repeat Window Operator (Rpt)
001	Increment Window Operator (Inc)
010	Decrement Window Operator (Dec)

011	Reset Window Operator (Rst)
100	Half Window Operator (Hlv)
101 to 111	reserved

Repeat means a transmit authorization of a further W packets, with W being the current window size, for example W=3. Increment increases the window size by 1 (W=3+1) and gives a transmit authorization for a further W packets. Decrement reduces the window size by 1 (W=3-1) and gives a transmit authorization for further W packets. Reset closes the transmit window. Half decreases the window size by half if it was previously larger than 1 (W=int(3/2)) and gives a transmit authorization for a further W packets. The maximum window size is restricted to 0x'FFFF'. The data flow control achieved in this way is based on the pacing in SNA.

If a switch has free buffer space, it applies the increment operator. If the buffer space is tight, it uses the decrement operator, or in a more serious case, the Half-Operator. The reset is for use in emergency only; it closes the transmit window as soon as it is received, even if not all the packets granted previously have been transmitted.

Every packet with flow control information (FCIND) must be confirmed (after sending an FCIND, the receiver set FCACOwed = TRUE) before the number of packets is increased again. The confirmation (FCACK) must repeat the values set in FCIND exactly. If FCACKOwed=TRUE is set, no new FCIND is transmitted. Therefore, there is never more than one FCIND open, i.e., unconfirmed, with one exception: in an emergency (buffer overflow), the reset operator is permitted even if the previous FCIND has not yet been confirmed. This makes sense because the reset closes the transmit window immediately, even if more packets have been granted. The sender must then confirm the reset in a pure check packet without data (IFCACK, independent FCACK), even if it has not yet confirmed the previously received FCIND.

An example: United Barbie Dolls (UBD) is expanding, and more proximity to the customers is required. Three regional sites are established for sales. Obviously these require host access via SNA and are given a mini Token Ring. To achieve dynamic rerouting in the WAN, the remote stations are connected with the UBD central station via Data Link Switching, as shown in Figure 10.22. The flow control between switch Arnie and switch Bernie, transmission direction Arnie -> Bernie, may take place as shown in Figure 10.23:

The InitialWindowSize is 2, the value for GrantedUnits is always 0 at the start of a link. The parameter are set as follows:

ARNIE (sender)
- GrantedUnits: 0

- CurrentWindow: 2

- InitialWindowSize: 2

BERNIE (receiver)
- GrantedUnits: 0

- CurrentWindow   2

- InitialWindowSize   2

- FCACKOwed   false

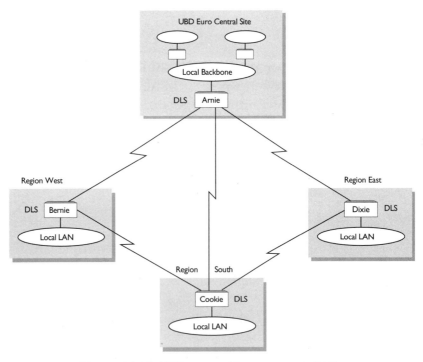

Figure 10.22: UBD regional locations with DLSw

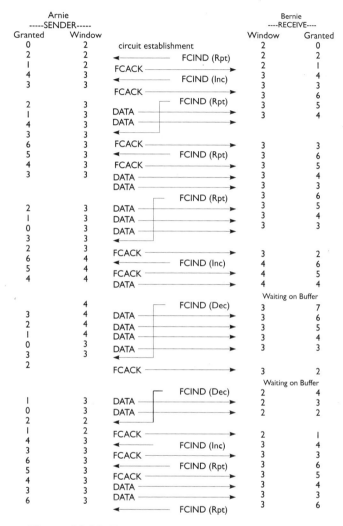

Figure 10.23: Flow control between Arnie and Bernie

The transmit authorization is given explicitly with the first flow control Information. Bernie sets the operator repeat, i.e., he increases the number of packets which Arnie is allowed to send (in the following simply called "packet number") by 2 units. Arnie sends a FCACK with the next data packet, which reduces the packet number to 2-1=1. Bernie still has some free buffer space and increases the window size to 2+1=3 and the packet number by 3. Arnie confirms with the next packet and then sends two data packets until the next FCIND arrives. Bernie has a stable buffer situation and sets the repeat operator which again grants 3 packets, Arnie can increase his granted units to 4. This takes place three times. Bernie has additional buffer space. He sets the increment operator, increases the window size to 3+1=4, and the packet number by 4. He has now taken on too much, a process with a higher priority uses buffer space. Luckily, the confirmation from Arnie arrives immediately, and Bernie can send a new FCIND in which he sets the decrement operator and reduces the window to 4-1=3, granting only 3 more packets. Before the next confirmation (FCACK), Bernie only has to cope with four data packets. In the meanwhile the buffer situation has gotten worse. Therefore, he sets the decrement operator again, etc.

An infinite number of different processes could occur, depending on the load situation and the implementation of the buffer management.

Conclusion

Despite a few bumpy bits in the specification, DLSw has emerged as the open standard approach for operating SNA and NetBIOS in integrated LAN and WAN networks using TCP/IP. It is supported by manufacturers such as Bay Networks, Cisco (not 1434), 3Com, IBM, and Proteon. Contrary to earlier announcements, the implementation of RFC 1434 was sometimes put before the implementation of APPN which is evidence of its increasing acceptance in the market. The introduction of a series of optional parameters in expansion of RFC 1795 may, however, lead to different implementations. Compatibility will then only be achieved by means of a common function subset which is supported by all participating router/Data Link Switches.

10.6 Integration and Parallelism

The use of several protocols within a company network in parallel network operation is an increasing requirement in developing networks. Differently configured subnetworks with different manufacturer and protocol worlds are to be connected by means backbone configurations. Deciding to use configurations with routers gives rise to the question as to whether a single common protocol or several protocols in parallel should be run on the backbone.

Integrated Approaches

To integrate IS-IS and TCP/IP OSPF, Digital developed RFC 1195 in 1990 (see [RFC1195]). At any rate, the protocol is intended to integrate the worlds (which is why it is called Dual IS-IS or Integrated IS-IS). The IS-IS frame is expanded by some information to enable IP communication to be performed. The integration achieved is however, at the cost of option possibilities in OSPF. Although OSPF increases the performance and functions of TCP/IP networks significantly compared to RIP, it does not offer OSI compatibility and functions. In particular, it does not support OSI addresses. While OSPF supports eight different metrics, integrated IS-IS only supports four; while OSPF does not restrict the number of possible hops, IS-IS supports a maximum of 1,024 hops (although at present it would be very unusual for this distance to be exceeded).

The aim of integrated IS-IS is quite obvious: the migration of TCP/IP towards OSI (the assumption behind this is that many customers will go over to OSI because DECnet Phase V means OSI). Unfortunately, at present OSI is only supported by Digital, Bay Networks, and 3Com work with integrated IS-IS.

To enjoy the advantages of integration means accepting some disadvantages:

- IS-IS and Integrated IS-IS have not yet been tested in wide areas of application outside Digital's own company network. Most router manufacturers support OSPF.

- Network managers have problems in defining a common metric for different networks like IP and DECnet, such as would be necessary in Dual IS-IS. The enforced use of a common metric results in higher costs, due to both increased line costs and to impaired performance due to less efficient implementation of the routing.

- It is very difficult to combine the historically developed, extremely different address structures of different protocol areas in a common structuring concept with the same address layout for all.

- On transition to OSI, it is necessary to ensure that all the routers used really also use the OSI protocol—otherwise "black holes" appear throughout the network, i.e., parts of the network which are suddenly no longer reachable.

- The decision between TCP/IP and OSI is not actually the choice the genuinely "better" alternative; at present it is a choice between two equally good, but different worlds.

Supporters of integrated IS-IS still hope that the approach with increased distribution will become established in the end.

Integrated IS-IS is not the only integrated approach for multi-protocol operation: Cisco has long been pursuing the aim of serving different protocol worlds with the same routing procedures with its proprietary IGRP (whose roots, incidentally, are in the good old XNS-RIP) and the new version of EIGRP (Enhanced IGRP). However, IGRP was never disclosed and, as a proprietary solution, it is not implemented by other internetworking manufacturers. With their MPTN architecture and AnyNet products, IBM is also trying to establish an integrated approach for SNA, TCP and in the future IPX in the market.

The discussion about integrated routing will be revived for ATM backbones (see also Chapter 11). The ATM Forum is working on an integrated routing procedure which at least combines the most established protocols (IP, IPX, and, possibly, OSI) with a uniform link state routing procedure. The draft versions are called IPNNI (Integrated Private Network-to-Network Interface) and MPOA (multi-protocol Over ATM), which was introduced into the ATM Forum by Cisco. Specific specifications are planned for the middle to end of 1996.

Parallel Protocols

While integrated IS-IS represents the standard approach, IS-IS and OSPF represent different "open" protocol worlds. Daily network practice involves several other routing protocols such as DRP, TCP/IP-RIP, NetWare-RIP, NLSP, or AppleTalk's RTMP. These protocols serve completely independent different manufacturer environments and all use different metrics and tuning parameters. However, they are able to coexist on a common network infrastructure (Ethernet, Token Ring, X.25, FDDI) if multi-protocol routers are used. They behave like "ships in the night." Different frames "are routed past each other without noticing each others presence"—just like ships in the night. This analogy is the source of the name given to parallel protocol usage: SIN (Ships In the Night). SIN enables network operators to set optimum tuning for all the different protocols, different protocols may be forwarded over different links or even use common links (as required by integrated IS-IS).

Like integrated IS-IS, retaining the diversity has its disadvantages:

- It requires the use of expensive multi-protocol routers. Servicing numerous protocols simultaneously is very complicated.

- A high CPU performance and memory is required of the routers.

- The overhead is high: for every participating protocol, separate routing tables are established, separate updates sent, separate timers are set, etc.

- SIN will cause a further delay in the distribution of OSI, i.e., the establishment of a final, generally valid communications platform.

- Looked at seriously, the SIN approach is a relapse to the gateway age, since a multi-protocol router is nothing less than a logical parallel relay for a wide variety of protocols.

The parallel operation of a wide variety of protocols together with the discernible bandwidth hunger of newer applications requires a higher bandwidth for each end system and backbone transmission capacities in the range of hundreds of Mbps or even Gigabit/s. There are also other problems which cannot be solved simply by increasing the speed:

- restrictive timers in traditional LAN protocols like NetBIOS, LAT etc., which were never meant to be used with multi-protocol networks (Campus, WAN);

- conversion problems when changing from Ethernet/Token Ring to FDDI or ATM (in migration stages);

- continuous changes in network addresses for routable protocols when moving;

- faulty router software, particularly with multi-protocol operation and after the appearance of new releases with several expanded functions;

- MP operation in the terminal: incompatibility of cards which load all protocols using drivers placed directly on the hardware with cards which use NDIS and also with cards with use ODI;

- multifunctional APS: how will the 640k restriction in DOS/Windows be handled with the 10th application? Which application will crash when the fifth protocol is loaded, even though it does not even use it?

- defective functions of the available management tools (no standard surfaces, insufficient integration of different components, insufficient automation of routing activities, inadequate help during fault location).

Conclusion

The more sensible approach is integrated IS-IS. The years of delay in OSI on the one hand and consistently strong expansion of TCP/IP installations on the other hand mean that, particularly with the availability of diverse multi-protocol router products, the SIN approach currently has clear superiority and practical advantages. However, large-scale network operators have frequently found that although the integration of the 13th protocol in the multi-protocol backbone is an extremely interesting challenge from a technical point of view, at the same time normal operation and fault location becomes extremely complex with an increasing number of protocols.

Here is a practical recommendation: try to tune the network to such a degree that it operates no more than three to four routed protocols or two to three routed protocols and parallel bridging in the backbone! Although this is a hard restriction for long-established large multivendor networks, it is the only way to provide an efficient network operation and sensible, structured growth in the medium term at a justifiable cost.

With all the router functions described so far, an initial network situation may be described as follows:

- A router provides a link between end systems with the end system not caring which route lies between them.

- The router uses a special protocol for the network layer to implement the route.

- The router connects different LANs and WANs, even if they support different packet sizes.

- The use of several routers enables LANs and WANs to be cascaded for the link between end stations. The choice of router is regulated by routing-tables in the routers.

- The basic routing algorithm optimizes the transportation of the packets through the network.

- The use of dynamic routing procedures enables redundancy concepts to be taken into account.

- Explicitly defined routes (safety considerations, overhead saving) are also possible.

- Routers may (depending on the protocol) implement mechanisms to regulate overload situations.

- Routers make a significant contribution to the reduction of broadcasts to multiple subnetworks.

- Multi-protocol routers are able to handle several important protocol worlds in parallel and hence to form an integrated network backbone. There are possibilities for using several protocol worlds with one standard routing procedure to reduce the overhead.

11 ATM, LAN Emulation and Multi-Protocol Operation

ATM is a new technology on the horizon of product development: the increasing communication load on cross subnetwork and multi-site traffic has resulted in an increasing requirement for high-capacity WAN transmission procedures. In addition, the idea of uniform transmission for data, video and voice in local and wide area network traffic is attractive and may even give rise to the euphoric statement "the cell will be the byte of the nineties," in anticipation of cell processing in the end system. It was in this regard that two and a half years ago ATM (asynchronous transfer mode) hit the headlines as a competitor to FDDI and other high-speed systems with a wide-area capability.

Like many technical innovations, ATM has two roots: Technology development and market pressure. The developers and planners of ATM have made it a matter of faith finally to integrate data, voice, and video for transmission and to cope with the constantly growing capacity requirements for the next decade. Increasingly more powerful end systems (the PC is slowly going out of fashion, the new trend will be for PWs–personal workstations) and the widespread use of client/server configurations, not only for file storage, but also as distributed databases or video servers, go beyond the limits of conventional

Ethernet networks using X.21/X.25. As always, new application requirements are resulting from:

- extremely large quantities of data (high throughput requirement)

- real-time applications (requirement guaranteed low delays with greatly varying bandwidth use, for example, video)

An example in connection with multimedia: If a 10-second long video clip is to be incorporated into a text document, this will require approximately 2 MB in compressed form—this is probably more than the length of the text; not to mention the matter of the load produced by a server which holds 10 minute-long video clips. To remain with the example of video; video conferences require low delay times in the transmission (even if throughput is not a problem when subscribers take long pauses for thought,) otherwise image and voice distortions occur.

From this we may deduce three central requirements for ATM technology:

- *Semantic neutrality (transparency):* it must be possible to transport both LAN protocols for data transfer and video and voice data

- *Time neutrality (isochronous behavior):* guaranteed maximum delay times should be maintained

- *Requirement neutrality (scalability):* both peak loads (bursts) and network extensions (increased number of inputs and outputs) and expanded services (different priorities) must gradually become possible.

11.1 Classification of ATM Components

Since ATM was originally planned for wide area corporate networks but was very quickly adapted by the "LAN developers," ATM networks may be divided into different classes according to functionality and range. These network classes are implemented by different ATM switch components:

- access components (DSU)

- adapter cards

- routers, hubs

- campus switches

- WAN switches

DSUs (Kentrox, Digital Link Corp., etc.) and **adapter cards** (Fore Systems, Interphase, National Semiconductor Corp., N.E.T., Network Peripherals Inc., Bay Networks, Transwitch Corp., etc.) are ATM access components with ATM adapter cards generating a native ATM data stream and DSUs transforming an incoming LAN or PBX data stream into an ATM data stream (ATM cells). Both classes of components work as real products, frequently in conjunction with just one switch product.

Classification is more problematic with **Routers** and **Hubs** (Cisco, Chipcom/3Com, Digital Equipment, 3Com, Madge/Lannet, LanOptics, NSC, ODS, Retrix, Bay Networks, etc.), which either generate an ATM data stream or format the outgoing LAN packets so that a DSU can interpret them and convert them into ATM cells. In the case of a hub, it is then necessary to differentiate as to whether there is a pure ATM module in the hub or a (possibly OEM) router module in the hub, or an ATM converter which connects incoming LAN traffic on a ATM backbone, but does not facilitate any direct link between the LANs (see also Figure 11.1).

Campus switches and **LAN switches** (Bay Networks, Cisco, Digital Equipment, 3Com, Fore Systems, NetEdge, N.E.T., NSC, Newbridge Networks Inc., ODS, etc.) are the key components for a local area ATM network. They are pure backbone switches without end system interfaces and switches which connect ATM end systems (i.e., workstation systems and servers with ATM adapters) to the ATM backbone. In the latter case, the name/expression LATM (LAN ATM) is also used by analogy with Ethernet-LAN or Token Ring–LAN. This switch class is designed with the capacity to transport LAN traffic and protocols. The number of available ports differs greatly from 2 to 90 according to the product.

Unlike Campus switches, **WAN switches** integrate ATM and the "established" WAN services like X.21/X.25, analog voice transmission, ISDN etc., and so permit a gradual migration of already installed links towards ATM. They are used to a greater degree than Campus switches for isochronous services (video, voice) and are, therefore, subject to tighter time restrictions which affects the processing time and buffer management in the switch. Moreover, the suppliers of WAN services are often contractually bound beyond the restrictions of purely technical feasibility to observe specific response times. This requires a correspondingly complex switch design.

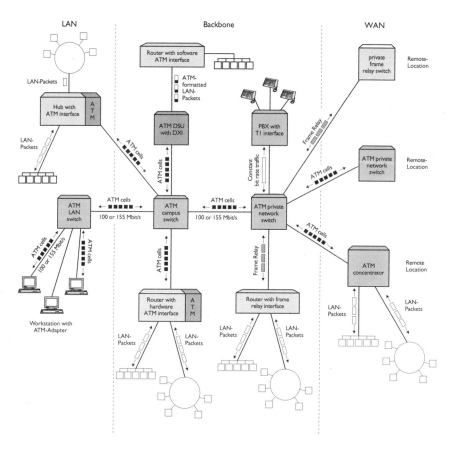

Figure 11.1 ATM components

As hub systems, bridges, and routers are predominantly used as access devices to ATM backbone networks or as Campus switches (hub systems with switch modules) in local areas, further examination of the subject will concentrate on the LAN aspects of ATM technology.

ATM as the final stage of a dedicated LAN

Although, at the end of the eighties, segments with approximately 300 nodes were connected by two-port bridges or two-port routers (in single protocol operation), the number fell rapidly in the new decade through approximately 100 nodes and multi-port coupling of hybrid routers, 50 nodes with hubs and bridge/router slide-in modules to 30 nodes to multi-segment switching modules in one hub (see also Figure 11.2). The current redesign of a large-scale automobile manufacturer is based on only 5 to 10 nodes per Ethernet or Token Ring segment. Taken to its logical conclusion, this development finally results in a dedicated LAN, i.e., full LAN bandwidth for each end station access, which then requires a backbone with hyper-LAN capacity (from 155 Mbps upwards) to connect the end systems—i.e., ATM.

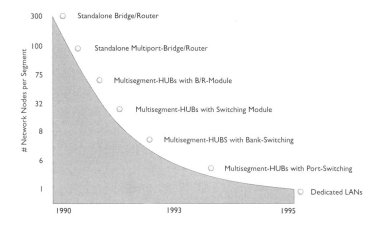

Figure 11.2: Development of segment size and use of internetworking devices

The department layer in an ATM scenario looks virtually the same as before, but the hub or router has an ATM interface, which links the departmental network with the backbone. Additional ATM interfaces may be used to link particularly fast workstations. In this development stage, normal workstations are connected in mini-groups or individually by Ethernet switching modules (micro-segmentation, dedicated LAN). The actual backbone consists either of a single ATM switch (collapsed BB in which the central router is replaced by a switch) or of several intermeshed connected ATM switches (distributed BB) according to the size of the network and the operator's ability to invest (see Figure 11.3). The common backbone protocol is ATM (AAL 5), like X.25 nowadays in WAN networks, but with a much lower overhead. However, this does not mean that conventional routing completely disappears, it is only moved to the ATM access points and possibly a central router/route server. From department layer, the conventional LAN packet is packed in an ATM packet and routed in accordance with ATM protocol specifications.

The scenario shows that ATM is clearly attempting to establish itself as a competitor to FDDI, which has only enjoyed limited success.

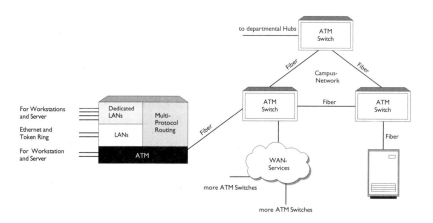

Figure 11.3: ATM scenario

Therefore, the first signs of a migration to ATM are already evident: at department layer only the HUB interface changes, otherwise Ethernet and Token Ring are connected as before. To assess the relationship: typically, hubs account for 75 to 80 percent of the amount to be invested and routers and switches for 20 to 25 percent. Nowadays, hubs are first fitted with an ATM interface, before giving way to new components which have internally been completely converted to ATM (ATM Box). However, with the current WAN tariffs, this development will be restricted to private Campus networks for the foreseeable future.

11.2 Architecture of ATM Switches

Put simply, ATM switches consist of a series of input lines, a series of output lines and an interconnecting network in between. The input lines are controlled by input controllers (IC), the output lines by output controllers (OC). The internal switch interconnecting network is made up of interconnected switching elements (See also Figure 11.4). To improve performance and avoid collisions, different types of parallel architectures are used, so-called "switching fabrics," synchronous switch mechanisms.

The operation, administration, and maintenance (OAM) of the parallel switching elements controls a control processor. Switching fabrics may be designed by their main architectural components:

- topology

- buffer layout

- treatment of concurrent access (collision prevention)

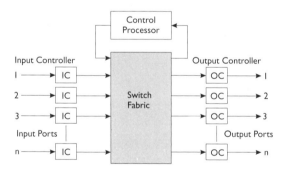

Figure 11.4: Structure of a switching fabric

Switching fabrics may be roughly divided into two categories

- blocking

- non-blocking

A non-blocking architecture has an internal design which ensures that inside the **switch, cells** do not compete with each other or generate a collision (sufficient bandwidth or parallel routes). With a blocking architecture, internal jams may occur. Of course, the internal architecture is not able to prevent external blockages, i.e., jams at one or more switch inputs.

Internal parallelism may be implemented either by increasing the internal processing capacity, i.e., time division (gigabit bus or gigabit ring) or by multiple routes, i.e., space division. In the case of several switching stages, space division is also called a multistage interconnection network (MIN). To reduce costs, it is a design goal if possible to use similar switching elements to establish the internal-switch networks. Typical switching elements have for example, two inputs and outputs (2x2 elements). The number of inputs/ outputs may be increased either by further elements connected in parallel or by increasing the switching stages. Figure 11.5 shows an overview of the procedures.

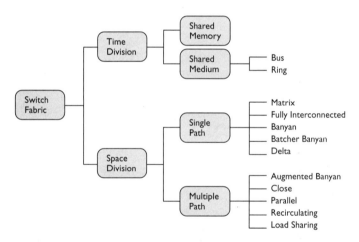

Figure 11.5: Classes of switching architectures

Another two-class differentiation is based on the forwarding principle used:

• self-routing switching

• table-driven switching

Self-routing switching elements interpret routing tags for forwarding—these are added as an additional header at the switch input to the data cell. At each switching stage, one tag is removed following interpretation and at the output of the switch, the data cell is reduced back to its original content. Table-driven switches apply a routing table for each switching element used to select the route. The establishment and management of these distributed routing tables is relatively complex, which is why preference is given to self-routing architectures, although this requires the internal processing capacity to be increased by the additional header length of each cell. The individual procedures cannot be dealt with in detail in this book, you are referred to further literature on this subject, for example, Kyas, 1993; Pryk, 1993.

The aggregated bandwidth (capacity of all ports) of an ATM switch is in the range of 2 to 20 Gbps. For example, a switch with 10 ports with a capacity of 155 Mbps aggregates to 1.55 Gbps. As with hubs, the architectures are very different, but they all use hardware-based cell switching (ASIC-chip or chip group). Differences may be identified in the bus links: some switches use a single (backplane) bus, to which all slide-in cards have access. The link between the cards and the ATM network is provided by an ATM switching module (switching fabric) which is connected to the other cards by the bus and serves as the link between the ATM network and the HUB-cards. Another approach implements ATM transmission on every slide-in card with every card having an internal point-to-point link to the ATM switching module. This alternative does not require any hyper-mega-backplane bus, as every card has its own link to the switching module. At the present time, however, it is still unclear, which switch manufacturers and which architectures will survive.

11.3 ATM Protocols and Transmission Characteristics

ATM provides link-orientated services insofar as a route between the sender and the receiver is defined during the link establishment and assigned identifiers which are used for the data transfer. The transmission of acknowledgments which, according to OSI also belongs to the line-orientated service, is not found with ATM. In analogy with the ISO-OSI reference model, the procedure may be divided into three separately specified functional layers: the physical layer, the ATM layer, and the adaptation layer. The individual layers and sublayers are shown in Figure 11.6.

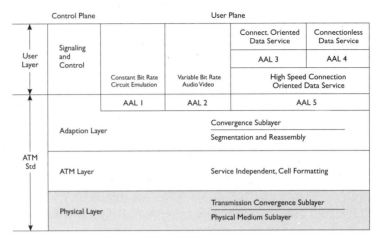

Figure 11.6: ATM protocol stack

Adaptation Layer

The ATM adaptation layer may be divided into two sublayers: a convergence sublayer CS and a segmentaton layer SAR (Segmentation And Reassembly).

To handle different types of data, adaptation protocols must be used which may possibly specify different priorities and assign the individual types of data to different logic channels. This is done by the convergence sublayer. The adaptation protocols (AAL, ATM adaptation layer) are implemented at the entry point or exit point of ATM networks (for example, in the router), not within the ATM networks. The functions provided depend upon the higher (to be adapted) layers. The CS layer (Convergence Sublayer) implements the basic CPCS functions (Common Part Convergence Sublayer) and a service-specific SSCS function (Service Specific Convergence Sublayer) implements the assignment of ATM packets, time/bit rate supervision, etc.

The SAR layer (Segmentation And Reassembly) divides the data units (PDUs) in the higher layer, for example, IP/IPX/MAC packets in LAN traffic, into the corresponding ATM payload parts (48 bytes) and, at the end of ATM network, puts them back together as the original packet.

It should be noted that the protocol overhead for AAL layers is transported not in cell's header, but in the payload part, which means an additional negative impact, albeit low, of the user data/overhead rate.

Overall, at present 5 types of AAL are defined:

- **AAL1** as a connection link switching service with a constant bit rate, CBR, (for example, T1 or S-ISDN primary multiplex connection through ATM)

- **AAL2** as a precisely time-synchronous (clocked) service with a variable bit rate (audio, video) VBR

- **AAL3/4** for connection-oriented or connectionless asynchronous services with variable bit rates, for example in data communication (SMDS, frame relay, UDP, TCP/IP, X.25)

- **AAL5** is a simplification of type 3/4 and intended for pure data packet exchange (LAN traffic). This type has the simplest structure, which is why it is also known as SEAL (Simple and Efficient Adaptation Layer) and in all probability will be one of the first implementation.

Since the AAL5 is of particular interest in connection with internetworking technology, the following will deal with the relevant protocol mechanisms in more detail. Multi-protocol operation based on AAL5 is dealt with in RFCs 1483 and 1577—there are two methods of using ATM as a transport medium for LAN traffic (see also section 11.5):

- multiplexing several LAN protocols using common ATM VC

- generating a separate VC for every LAN protocol transported

ATM Layer

The ATM layer as a second layer (to be fitted in between OSI Layer 1 and 2a) takes over the 48-byte payload (segmented MAC frames) from the AAL for further processing. It inserts the cell header and so forms all the ATM cells with the required fixed block size of 53 bytes. In addition, the ATM layer provides the routing and the transport through the ATM switch. The ATM layer in the last ATM switch on the route through the ATM network or the ATM LAN converter at the exit point to the LAN removes the header again and forwards the payload to the overlying adaptation layer. Virtual circuits and a multiplex function are supported for packet switching. Multicasts may be transported over separate VCs (see also ATM LAN emulation). As is evident from the name asynchronous transfer mode, different types of data (video, data, voice) may be transported on different logic channels (virtual circuit) in parallel (see also Figure 11.7).

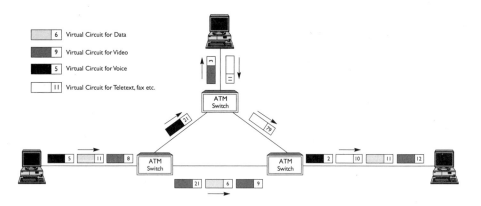

Figure 11.7: Transmission of different types of data on different VCs

The ATM layer acts independently of the physical layer used and implements a series of logical transmission functions for cell processing:

- generation and removal of the ATM header

- multiplexing and demultiplexing cells in different links which are recognized by different VCI/VPI values

- changing the cell ID i.e., VCI and/or VPI if necessary when changing from one link to another in a switch (routing)

- provision of the required quality of service (QoS) for the user of a VCC (virtual channel connection) or VPC (virtual path connection)

- management actions based on header information (overload indicator, flow control, etc.)

- flow control for the UNI using the GFC bits in the header, if they are present

The format of an ATM cell is shown in Figure 11.10 (see section 11.3.1).

The advantages of cell technology may be seen from two examples:

- segmentation, i.e., compiling the data block by analogy with framing in LANs

- processing time in the switch

An encoder producing a constant 64 kbps takes 6 milliseconds to encode a segment of 48 bytes (without overhead). If the segment size were 480 bytes, the segmentation would take 60 milliseconds. Together with the necessary latency in the switches between source and destination network, the delay time is unacceptable (a digital voice transmission rarely lasts longer than 15–20 ms).

It is assumed for the processing time in a switch that 20 logic channels are active in an ATM switch with E3 connection (34 Mbps). Assuming that the switch works with the round-robin procedure, the latency in the switch may be 0 to 19 times the processing time for an individual segment. At 34 Mbps, this is approximately 0 to 240 microseconds. With a segment size of 530 bytes or a variable segment size with max. 530 bytes the maximum latency is 0 to 2.4 ms.

In both examples, the use of small fixed data block sizes has advantages in respect of response times and capacity calculation.

A central requirement for the ATM layer is the forwarding of segments. Which rule applies in the event of two segments arriving simultaneously, which both have to be forwarded on the same logic channel? The simplest solution here would be to delete one of the two, but this would mean packet repetitions and hence increased loads. Therefore, the possibility of intermediate buffering must be provided in the switch which should also retain the sequence of the segments for the same logic channel, since not all higher protocol accept changes of the transmission sequence. The buffer size and strategy are characteristic features of a switch. If the switch is using non-blocking architecture, the buffer problem only occurs at the switch input and/or output, as described above.

Physical Layer

As with FDDI, the physical layer is divided into two sublayers, the PM layer and the TC layer (physical medium, transmission convergence).

The PM layer implements pure bit encoding and is media-dependent. In order to avoid re-inventing the wheel, quite deliberately, no special bit encoding layer (PM) was defined for ATM, instead existing standards were used. These include SONET (STS-3, 155 Mbps, FO, ITU-T), PDH, pure cell transmission (155Mbps, multimode-FO, 8B/10B encoding, without higher-ranking frames), DS3 (45 Mbps, FO) in the United States and E3 (34 Mbps, FO) in Europe, Japan, and Australia. The use of the FDDI physical medium-dependent layer (100 Mbps TAXI, 4B/5B encoding) is also specified. Nevertheless, IBM did attempt to re-invent the wheel and suggested a capacity of 25 Mbps specifically for ATM (based on 25 Mhz and 4B/5B encoding, a 32 Mhz clock rate is easy to achieve, which in turn may be transformed into 16 Mbaud or 16 Mbps in the Token Ring, etc.). The suggestion was accepted at the beginning of 1995 for category 3 copper cables. Figure 11.8 gives an overview of the PM specifications.

Definition of the Physical Layer of ATM					
Private UNI Physical Layer				Public UNI Physical Layer	
Frame Format	Bitrate/ Link capacity	Medium	Frame Format	Bitrate/ Link capacity	Medium
Cell Stream	25.6 Mbps/32 Mbaud	UTP3	DS1	1.544 Mbps	Twisted Pair
STS-1	51.84 Mbps	UTP3	DS3	44.736 Mbps	Coax
FDDI (TAXI)	100 Mbps/125 Mbaud	MMF			
STS-3c, STM-1	155.52 Mbps	UTP5			
STS-3c, STM-1	155.52 Mbps	SMF, MMF, COAX	STS-3c, STM-2	155.52 Mbps	SMF
Cell Stream	155.52 Mbps/ 194.4 Mbaud	MMF, STP	E1*	2.048 Mbps	Twisted Pair, Coax
			E3*	34.368 Mbps	Coax
STS-3c, STM-1*	155.2 Mbps	UTP3	J2	6.312 Mbps	Coax
STS-12, STM-4*	622.08 Mbps	SMF, MMF	n x T1*	n x 1.544 Mbps	Twisted Pair
* in Development	DS Digital Service		STM Synchrounous Transport Mode		
	MMF Multimode Fiber		STS Synchrones Transport System		
	SMF Single Mode Fiber		UTP Unshielded Twisted Pair		

Figure 11.8: Physical layers in ATM

The TC layer is independent of the transmission medium, and therefore may also use some of the PM specifications mentioned above. It implements cell generation including the header checksum HEC, cell transmission, synchronization between adjacent ATM nodes and, therefore, possibly the insertion of empty cells (cell rate decoupling) and an error check of a received cell.

Regardless of the signaling used, the physical layer always uses asynchronous time division multiplexing (ATDM) for the transmission of individual cells. ATDM combines the advantages of purely asynchronous (statistical) and purely time-controlled (time division) multiplexing: the time-controlled fixed clock rate in cell transport achieves a fair sequence regulation, the possibility of asynchronous transmission enables free slots to be used for bursts. This makes both guaranteed reaction times and greater efficiency than with TDM possible.

The suggestion was accepted at the beginning of 1995 for category 3 copper cables. Figure 11.8] gives an overview of the PM specifications.

The TC layer is independent of the transmission medium and therefore may also use some of the PM specifications mentioned above. It implements cell generation including the header checksum HEC, cell transmission, synchronization between adjacent ATM nodes and possibly the insertion of empty cells (cell rate decoupling), and a check on the correctness of a received cell.

Regardless of the signaling used, the physical layer always uses Asynchronous Time Division Multiplexing (ATDM) for the transmission of individual cells. ATDM combines the advantages of purely asynchronous (statistical) and purely time-controlled (time division) multiplexing: the time-controlled fixed clock rate in "cell transport" achieves a fair sequence regulation, the possibility of asynchronous transmission enables "free" slots to be used for bursts. This makes both guaranteed reaction times and greater efficiency than with TDM possible.

11.3.1 Cell Relay

The byte has been the dominant size for wide area transmission over the last 20 years, and now the "cell" could become the byte of the nineties. The characteristic element of ATM transmission is small data blocks of a fixed size. This type of packeting as a transmission procedure is also called cell relay. The use of cell relay, i.e., fixed data block size for transmission (also defined in IEEE 802.6 and ITU-T I.361) is a significant difference from frame relay and X.25.

A correct cell data block is exactly 53 bytes long, a 48-byte data part (**Segment, Payload**) and 5 bytes of control information (corresponding to a good 10% protocol overhead), a 4-byte header for segmentation and reassembly

(SAR), and a 1-byte access control field (ACF). **A fixed length is defined for every frame**. It makes no difference whether images, voice or data are transmitted. The length of 53 bytes according to IEEE 802.6 is, so to speak, a compromise between voice and data: a compromise between the American (64 bytes) and the European suggestion (32 bytes). The latter is based on the predominance of voice transmission with favorable very short data blocks, the former on the predominance of data transmission with longer data blocks, which has become much more established in America for wide-area networks than it is in Europe/Germany (particularly in Germany, the completely overdimensioned cost structure of the postal services monopoly impedes the use of fast WANs).

The MAC frame transmitted, *including the MAC headers and trailers* is broken down into segments, each with 5 bytes of protocol information (overhead) and 48 bytes of MAC data (payload). If the length of the MAC frame is not an exact multiple of the segment length (which is usually the case), the last segment is filled out by padding. If a 2-byte trailer, which is in some cases inserted in an overhead within the 48-byte payload, is also taken into account, together with padding, this gives an overhead of approximately 16 to 17%. Segmentation and frame format are shown in Figures 11.9 and 11.10.

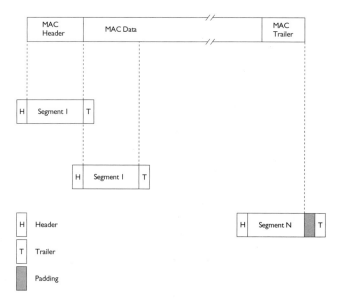

Figure 11.9: Segmentation of a MAC frame

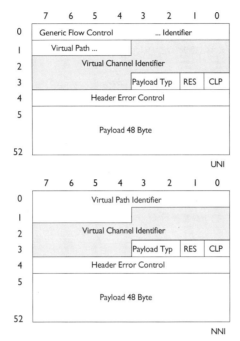

Figure 11.10: ATM cell format

The bytes in a cell are transmitted in ascending sequence (i.e., the first byte first), while the bits in the bytes are transmitted in descending sequence, i.e., the most significant bit (MSB) first. In the UNI specification, the header receives 4 bits for flow control (GFC).

Virtual Path Identifier (VPI, 8-bit) and Virtual Channel Identifier (VCI, 16-bit) include the routing information for correct forwarding within the ATM network.

The packet type (PTI, payload type identifier) is two bits long, followed by a reserved bit (R) and the "discard indicator" for cell loss priority (CLP). As with the DE bit in frame relay, the setting of this indicator may influence the potential packet loss: cells with a set CLP bit are the first to be removed from the buffer in the event of a buffer overflow.

The 8-bit long header checksum HEC may be used either to correct individual errors or to recognize double errors. All TC specifications use the same solution: usually, the receiver works in individual error correction mode. If an error is identified, it is rectified and the receiving logic switches to double error recognition mode. If a multiple error is identified, the cell received is rejected and the logic again switches to double error recognition mode. In error detection mode all packets with an error (in the header, because this is the only part the algorithm checks) are rejected. On the first error-free header, the receiving logic switches back to error correction mode. The CRC polynomial used is x8+x2+x+1.

The *segment trailer* (2 bytes) is entered within the 48-byte. It consists of the number of bytes actually transmitted from the original MAC frame (P_LENGTH, 6 bit), followed by the segment checksum (P_CRC, 10 bit) which is formed throughout the entire segment.

The use of cell relay avoids the mixing of short and long frames due to interactive applications and file transfer, which has always been an ideal recipe for producing completely unforseeable load profiles and consequently inadequate planning and provision of transmission capacity

Cell relay almost compels a hierarchical architecture with two layers: a software side as the higher layer, which establishes and clears the logic links, implements dynamic resource management and performs routing and cost calculations (all in the *millisecond* range), and cell relay hardware as the lower layer, which performs cell processing, i.e., segmentation into "cells," switching, and multiplexing (this is in the *microsecond* range). With a network configuration with routers and switches, it is advisable to move the software part to the routers and implement the cell relay hardware in the switches.

Conclusion

ATM/cell relay has both advantages and disadvantages.

The following aspects are advantageous

- ideally suitable for implementation in hardware and hence cost-effective to implement

- standard procedure for LAN and WAN, data, voice, and video (theoretically)

- queuing delay easy to calculate

- processing time easy to calculate

- necessary buffer size much easier to calculate than with variable frame lengths

- physical independence of LEC side and hence optional distribution of a LAN throughout the network

- use of the same access line to ATM backbone by several ELANs

- capacity increase in comparison with shared LANs due to point-to-point links. Restriction: broadcast/multicast capacity of the "weakest" LEC, i.e., 10 Mbps for Ethernet LECs

The following aspects are disadvantageous

- relatively higher overhead (10%–15%)

- increase in overhead from the headers in the ATM layer, which are inserted in the payload (1 byte for AAL type 1, 4 bytes for AAL type 4); only AAL type 5 remains without ATM layer overhead

- no overload control and error correction

- the smaller the frame size, the higher the switching rates (packet-throughput) required for comparable throughput

- cell relay is only worthwhile from speeds of at least 45 Mbps for data transmission

11.3.2 ATM and SONET/SDH

At Layer 1, ATM may be used on SONET or SDH (USA, Europe). The use of a Synchronous Digital Hierarchy (SDH) instead of PDH has a great advantage: the multiplex procedure used is transparent. The transparency of the proce-dure means that an individual 64 kbps channel may be decoupled directly out of the highest hierarchy layer or coupled into the highest layer. The reference size (stage 1) of the Synchronous Digital Hierarchy is 155.52 Mbps. The ATM cells are packed into a 2430-byte long SDH frame which is transported by means of STM1 signal generation (synchronous transport module at the first synchronous layer). The transport lasts 125µs, which in turn corresponds to the time difference between two PCM scanning values. Every SDH frame consists of 9 lines of 270 bytes each (see also Figure 11.11). Every line has a 9-byte header, the so-called section overhead (SOH) which gives a user data bandwidth of 150.34 Mbps. Every byte in the SDH signals corresponds to a transmission bandwidth of 64 kbps.

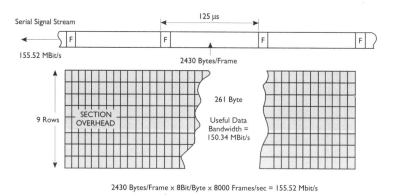

Figure 11.11: Format of the STM1 frame

The useful data packets are forwarded in so-called containers which contain STM1 frames, from one ATM node to the next. The SOH is used for the synchronization and monitoring of transmission links and contains, for example, transmission channels, i.e., bytes for network management or voice channels for maintenance services (1 byte = 1 channel with 64 kbps). At the end of a transport section, the SOH is again separated from the useful data. This means that the SOH is not adequate for the correct forwarding of a STM1 frame throughout the entire SDH network and another piece of overhead is added, the path overhead (POH). This makes the container into a so-called virtual container, containing information for the alarm monitoring and controlling the signal quality, and it is only removed at the exit point (path termination) of the ATM network. The POH is found in every STM1-line behind the 9-byte SOH. This further reduces the user data rate from 150.34 Mbps to 149.76 Mbps. Since the STM1 frame does not contain user data which is a perfect multiple of 53 bytes, there are ATM cell data flow cells which are divided into two STM1 frames.

Higher hierarchical layers with STM4 and STM16 are defined with 622.08 Mbps and 2.48832 Gbps respectively. Therefore, it is simple to derive the underlying law for the formation of the SDH as

```
STM n = n * STM1
```

Anyone who has rummaged through the data sheets for ATM products (or who intends to do so) has probably been irritated by the jungle of physical transmission interfaces. Therefore, the following examines the different specifications for PDH and SDH speed hierarchies in Europe and the USA in more detail.

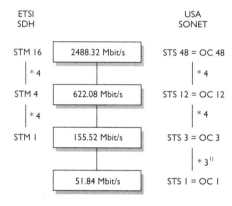

Figure 11.12: Hierarchy layers in SDH and SONET

The SDH concept was developed in the Bell Laboratories at the end of the 1908s to cope with the requirement for higher and variable transmission capacities. It was given the name SONET (Synchronous Optical NETwork). The currently valid ITU-T standard specifies two versions of SDH: ETSI-SDH (Europe) and ANSI-SONET (USA). The main difference between the two specifications is the basic transmission speeds referred to: SONET is based on 36.8 Mbps and 48.38 Mbps for better integration of the established PDH hierarchy (DS3 = 44.73 Mbps), SDH, on the other hand, is based on 149.76 Mbps. In addition, SONET has also been given a "siding" of 51.84 Mbps as STS1 (synchronous transport signal module) or also OC1 (optical carrier type 1) because of its suitability for DS3 signals. This speed was not however, adopted by ITU-T. STM1 has three times the capacity of STS1 and is therefore called STS3 or OC3 in SONET. STM4 and STM16 correspond to STS12/OC12 and STS48/OC48 (see also Figures 11.12 and 11.13).

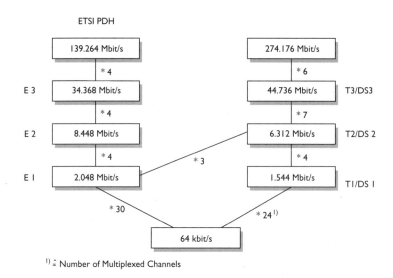

Figure 11.13 Hierarchy layers in PDH

11.4 The ATM Service LAN Emulation (ATM LE)

Summarized in one sentence, ATM LAN emulation (ATM LE) provides the following service: the ATM network acts as if it were one or more LANs, it emulates a LAN. In fact, a LAN connected to the genuine LANs by bridges (bridge functions). This is not so simple to achieve because, while LAN protocols work connectionless, ATM is connection-oriented and, while standardized LANs use shared media access, ATM works with point-to-point connections. All higher protocols may be used on ATM with the specified bridge function, both routable and non-routable (AppleTalk, APPN, DECnet, DLC, IP, IPX, LAT, LAVC, NetBIOS, OSI, etc.). With the routable protocols, an emulated LAN can only depict one single logical subnetwork.

The following question now arises: what is all this effort in aid of? The short-term advantage is considerable: when LAN emulation is used, all normal

LAN end stations which are supposed to talk to each other over an ATM backbone may be operated as before without further change and do not have to be fitted with an ATM interface or ATM software. Since the coupling achieved is a bridge coupling, ATM LE does however retain all the problems involved with a bridge-coupled network.

Version 1.0 of the specification for ATM LAN emulation was ratified in February 1995 by the ATM Forum. Immediately afterwards, the technical committee started work on Version 2.0, which is to define server-server protocols for LAN emulation, since this is the only way that different multivendor LAN emulation servers may be connected together compatibly in a network. As yet there is no scheduled date for the adoption of version 2.0 of the LAN emulation.

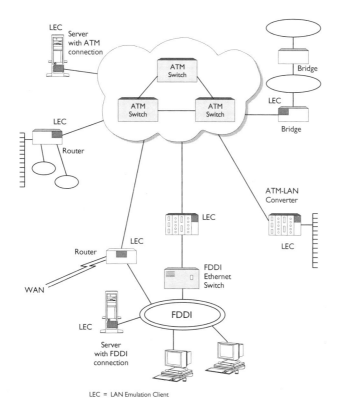

LEC = LAN Emulation Client

Figure 11.14: Internetworking scenario with ATM LE

The following describes the basic elements and functions of ATM LE and the use of internetworking components in ATM LE. A possible ATM scenario with different internetworking components is shown in Figure 11.14. The server on the FDDI ring may only be connected by the FDDI Ethernet switch since ATM LE does not directly support FDDI. Similarly, the router's WAN interfaces can only forward Ethernet or Token Ring frames by LE through the ATM network.

11.4.1 Conceptual Overview: Architecture and Components

The LAN emulation service enables LAN devices to communicate with each other using an ATM network or with end systems which are directly connected to ATM. For the purposes of LE, end systems are PCs, workstations, and servers, and also hub systems, bridges, and routers. In principal, as a B-ISDN service in accordance with ITU-T recommendation I.211; LAN emulation could emulate the MAC layer, Network Layer, or Transport Layer. The current Forum Version 1.0 specifies a pure MAC service. An emulated LAN (ELAN) has the following characteristics:

- connectionless service

- supports standard LANs, Ethernetv2.0/IEEE 802.3 and IEEE 802.5 (FDDI is ignored)

- broadcast/multicast-support

- supports NDIS (Microsoft, Intel, 3Com), ODI (Novell), and DLPI (UNIX International) as adapter-independent LLC interfaces for the higher layers.

- independence of physical end system site.

If FDDI packets are to be served by a LAN ATM converter via ATM LE, they first must be transformed into Ethernet or Token Ring packets. One solution to this is the additional implementation of FDDI Ethernet translation in the LE client. FDDI Token Ring translation is also theoretically possible, but actual implementation is improbable because of its greater complexity.

Overview

Picture a network with an ATM backbone connecting different LAN subnetworks together, and the main tasks of LAN emulation are clear:

- Coupling elements must be installed at the transitional points between LAN and ATM to convert the LAN packets into ATM. They are designated LAN ATM converters. This kind of converting intelligence may be implemented in hub slide-in modules, in bridges and LAN switches or in routers, with bridge functions.

- The reachable stations must be notified at the connection points between LANs and ATM network. This is performed by assigning the station addresses (by MAC addresses or route descriptors in the Token Ring) to the ATM access points, i.e., to the ATM addresses of the corresponding coupling elements. There is a piece of software called LAN Emulation Client (LEC), which notifies the locally reachable addresses.

- The LAN destination address/ATM address assignment is achieved by the establishment of suitable tables in a central server (LAN emulation server, LES) and using address resolution. If one LAN station wishes to communicate with another over the ATM backbone, at some time the packet lands in the LAN ATM converter with LEC function since the LAN is known to be a shared medium. If the ATM address, connecting to the destination LAN, is not known to the LEC, like TCP, it sends a so-called LE_ARP request regarding the desired destination address to which the LES responds with the associated ATM address. The destination LAN or the desired destination station may be reached via this "ATM exit point." If the LES does not know the address, there are further search mechanisms which will be described later.

- If the LAN destination/ATM destination address assignment is successful, data transfer from the source LAN passes throughout the converter (LEC), ATM backbone, converter (LEC) into the destination LAN. The communication sequence is shown in Figure 11.15.

- There is a requirement for a mechanism to forward broadcasts/multicasts so that they reach all stations belonging to the emulated LAN. This is the responsibility of another server, the BUS. Its mode of operation is described in more detail later.

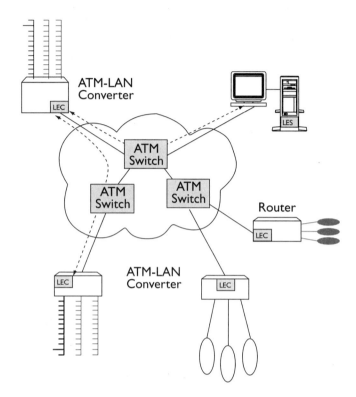

Figure 11.15: Communication sequence with ATM LAN emulation

Since an ELAN may be given an identifier or a name, the implementation of different ELANs in one network is possible and one end system could be connected to different ELANs. However, the ATM document only specifies the mode of operation of an individual ELAN and not how ELANs may communicate with each other or how ELANs may be implemented in parallel in end systems. According to the standard specification, these ELANs have no links between them. They may only be connected by external routers or bridges. The latter makes less sense: instead of coupling two ELANs by bridges, make the whole thing into a common ELAN with internal bridge function, unless the external bridge connection is provided with filters, with the caution advised in the section entitled "Bridge Functions."

Architecture

The LE architecture describes the logical relationship between individual ATM modules (see also Figure 11.16). A LAN emulation entity is built in between the ATM layers and the LAN protocols at Layer 2 (LLC). The LE entity <–> LLC interface to the higher protocol layers is used for transmitting/receiving data. Lower down, the LE entity is set to AAL type 5. The service-specific convergence sublayer is empty (zero SSCS).

All LAN packets are packed in ATM packets of AAL type 5. With the encapsulation technology used, it is evident that a Token Ring packet cannot arrive in an Ethernet LAN. Only LANs of the same type are connected. If an Ethernet wishes to talk with a Token Ring via an ATM backbone, an additional translation bridge function is necessary, which makes a correct Token Ring frame out of the unpacked ATM/Ethernet frame.

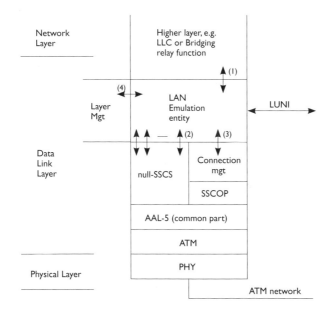

Figure 11.16: Architectural model of LAN emulation

The LE entity interface to the connection management contains, for example, functions for the establishment and clearance of ATM links (VCs, Virtual Circuits). SVC and/or PVC are supported.

Peer systems, usually LE client and LE server(s), communicate with each other using the LAN emulation User to Network Interface (LUNI). The LE entity sends information to the Layer 2 management at the same time. The protocol layers and conversions which are required between LAN devices and ATM devices with ATM LE are shown in Figure 11.17.

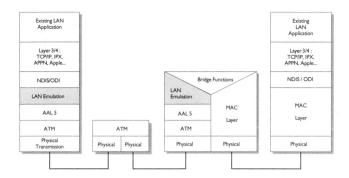

Figure 11.17 Protocol conversions with ATM LAN emulation

Physical Transmission

The LE client function may be implemented in an end system or in coupling devices (hub systems with ATM Uplink and ATM LAN converter, bridges, routers with bridge functions). The LE service functions may be implemented in an ATM coupling device or an ATM end system. The specification also permits LE client and LE service to be implemented simultaneously in a physical system to save hardware costs.

Components

Like all modern communications software, an ELAN functions using client-server mechanisms. The LAN type is either IEEE 802.3 / Ethernet V2.0 or IEEE 802.5 (Token Ring). An ELAN has the following components:

- LAN Emulation Client (LEC)

- LAN Emulation Configuration Server (LECS)

- LAN Emulation Server (LES)

- Broadcast and Unknown Server (BUS)

An **LE-client** is responsible for the data transfer and in the first instance for address resolution for all the LAN systems which it connects. Every LE client belongs to an ATM end system and serves a series of users via their unique MAC addresses. Every ELAN has at least one, usually several, LE clients.

An ELAN implements precisely one LE service which is provided by three different servers: the LE Configuration Server (LECS), the LE Server (LES), and the Broadcast and Unknown Server (BUS). The LE service may be implemented in an ATM end system or an ATM switch, on one physical system or distributed between several. The synchronization when the LE service is distributed between several machines' is not described in the ATM LE document and depends upon the implementation.

The **LAN Emulation Server (LES)** is responsible for recording all addresses (MAC addresses and route descriptors for Token Ring environments) notified to it by LECs and, if required, acts as the second instance for looking after the address resolution. It does this either by responding directly to requests (LE_ARPs) or by forwarding them to the LE clients, which are able to respond to them.

The **Broadcast and Unknown Server** (BUS) processes all broadcast/multicast traffic transmitted to it by LECs, i.e., it forwards this traffic to all concerned LECs. The BUS's multicast function should be consistent with ITU-T Recommendation X.6. The BUS also forwards a link's initial unicast traffic as long as the address resolution has not yet been performed successfully. The ATM Forum's specification supports just one bus over the LUNI interface per ELAN. If a manufacturer implements distributed or redundant BUS functions, the specification permits this, but the implementation must ensure that the distributed and/or redundant BUS behaves towards the LE clients in all functions in the same way as an individual component (single BUS server). If SVCs are used, the BUS must itself participate in the address resolution process by responding to LE_ARPs on the broadcast address (FF_FF_FF_FF_FF_FF) with its ATM address.

The **LAN Emulation Configuration Server** (LECS) is used to connect individual LE clients to different ELANs. The connection is made by LECS notifying an LE client of the ATM address of the LAN Emulation Server serving the ELAN to which the LEC wishes to be connected. Allocation may take place according to two criteria:

- physical location (ATM address of LE client)
- represented LAN destination (MAC address or route descriptor)

Connections

The LE client and LE Server communicate by means of LUNI using virtual channels (VCC, Virtual Channel Connections). There are VCCs for control connections and data connections. They are used to establish and clear the connection and other management actions, the latter for the orderly exchange of data packets. Control connections may occur as bi-directional (control direct VCC) or unidirectional (control distribute VCC) point-to-point connections and unidirectional point-to-multipoint connections. Unidirectional connections are only established from the server to the client. Data links are bi-directional and are established between LE clients and between the LE client and the BUS. To maintain the correct sequence of LAN data packets, the flush message protocol is defined as an optional expansion. A more detailed description may be found in the ATM LE specification V1.0.

Flush messages are the only ATM control data flow which may appear on a data connection. Any other overhead is sent on control connections. For broadcasts/multicasts, every LE client establishes a bi-directional link to the BUS (multicast send VCC). In return, the BUS establishes a unidirectional point-to-point or point-to-multipoint link to the LE client (multicast forward VCC). Both VCCs may be used by the BUS to sent/distribute broadcasts/multicasts, but a packet may not be sent in parallel on both links.

11.4.2 Functional elements of LAN emulation

The communication between LE peer entities via LUNI usually takes place in four steps from:

1. initialization
2. registration

3. address resolution

4. data transfer

The different functional elements are described in more detail in the following.

11.4.2.1 Initialization

When starting up, the LE client has a defined initial state. In this state, it only recognizes fixed preconfigured parameters such as:

- LEC ATM address(es)

- LAN type

- ELAN name

- max. frame size

- own local MAC address

- route descriptors

- LE client identifier with the value X'0000' (LECID)

- list of the desired multicast addresses

- segment number of the emulated LAN

- multicast send rate for peak and average

and a series of timers and retransmission counters.

It is configured with the help of the configuration servers (LECS) so that it may be connected to one of the emulated LANs. The initialization is complete when a successful JOIN has been performed and a permanent link to the BUS is established. The individual states gone through before initialization is complete are shown in Figure 11.18.

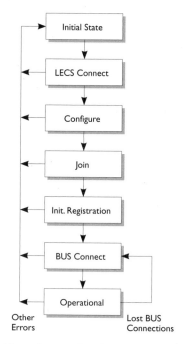

Figure 11.18: Flow diagram for the initialization of an LE client

LECS Connect and Configure

In the LECS connect phase, the LE client establishes a control connection to the configuration server (configuration direct VCC). In the configuration phase, fixed preconfigured parameters may be used in the simplest case (auto-configuration) to "find" the LE service. In more luxurious implementations, the LE client specifies the LE configuration protocol which may be used to deal with different parameters and which dynamically finds the LE service (LECS, LES, BUS). In particular, the LECS informs the LEC of the ATM address of the LES responsible.

The different measures used to find the configuration server are defined in an exact sequence:

1. *Find the LECS address using ILMI.* First of all, the management is addressed (Interim Local Management Interface). The LE client must transmit an ILMI Get or GetNext to obtain the ATM address of the

LECS. If the attempt to establish a UNI link to the address obtained fails, the LE client may transmit a Get/GetNext in order to obtain another LECS address (which is important for reasons of redundancy, because even a LECS fails sometimes).

2. If the ILMI remains silent about LECS addresses (does not provide any address as a response) or if the LE client is unable to establish any control connection (configuration direct VCC) to the ATM address obtained, the concept of "well-known address" comes into being. The LE client now tries to establish a link to the address X'470079000000000000000000-00A03E000001-00' (20 bytes, OSI-format). 00_A0_3E is the ATM Forum's OUI (Organizational Unique Identifier), 000001 was additionally defined by the ATM Forum.

3. If this attempt fails, there is a final alternative: the "well-known PVC." The LE client attempts to establish the configuration direct VCC link via PVC with VPI=0, VCI=17 (in decimal values).

JOIN

In the JOIN phase, the LE client establishes a control connection to the LES (control direct VCC between client ATM address and LES ATM address). The server may for its part establish a VCC to the client before terminating the JOIN phase which may also be used to transport control data for other LECs. The LE client has to accept this link, but only as long as the JOIN has not been completed. The conformity of the type of ELAN desired by the client and the type provided by the LES (IEEE 802.3, IEEE 802.5), and the corresponding maximum frame size is checked because a JOIN request must contain the LAN type, max. frame size, and ELAN name as parameters. In the event of a successful JOIN, the LE client receives the positive JOIN response and a network-wide unique identifier (LECID). During the JOIN phase, the client may record an individual MAC address or a route descriptor for a LES. This makes sense with hub systems, for example, which have only connected fiber optic routes and a single end system, for example, a server. Another example is a server with an ATM interface but which is implemented internally as an LEC and uses a MAC address. This enables the subsequent registration phase to be skipped.

Initial Registration

After a successful JOIN, an LE client may record all its local MAC addresses and/or route descriptors with the responsible LAN Emulation Server to check their uniqueness within the ELAN before entering the final operational status.

BUS Connect

In order to establish a link to the BUS, the LE client sends an LE_ARP to the broadcast address FF_FF_FF_FF_FF_FF. In response, the BUS establishes a multicast forward VCC to the LEC. If the BUS link is terminated, the LE client must attempt to re-establish it. If this is repeatedly unsuccessful, it has to return to the initial state and perform a new initialization. By the way, the BUS connect phase is the only step in which initialization may be repeated. In all other phases, interrupt or abort means: back to the start (see also Figure 11.18).

11.4.2.2 Registration

The most important task of the LES is to respond to LE_ARP requests as inquiries for specific MAC addresses (unicasts) or route descriptors (Token Ring) with the ATM address of the LE client which has a connection to the desired destination locally. This gives rise to the question: How does the LES receive the information on all these destination addresses? The response is provided by the registration protocol. It is sent via control connection between LE clients and the LE server and defines a procedure for LE clients to inform the LES of reachable MAC addresses or route descriptors. An LE client must either register all local addresses/descriptors with the LES or announce itself during the initialization in the JOIN phase as "proxy." The LES forwards LE-_ARPs to which it is unable to give a response to all LE clients which are connected as proxies to the ELAN.

A proxy is usually a Spanning Tree bridge or LAN switch with an ATM uplink and one or several LAN segments. It may not register the addresses which it learned at its LAN segments, but, as a proxy, it has to deal with the associated LE_ARP requests itself. This means that a Spanning Tree bridge does not register any local unicast MAC address. Addresses handled by the proxy function are also known as remote addresses. LE_ARP responses contain a "remote address" flag, which in this case is set to "1."

"Normal" (non-proxy) clients are, for example, hub systems with several isolated LAN segments and an LAN ATM converter module with no LAN bridge function, i.e., which only couples segments by ATM. A hub system with a LAN bridge slide-in module has both local and remote addresses as defined in the ATM LE specification. It announces itself as a proxy in the JOIN phase (for the bridge segments) and then records the local addresses for the segments which are not connected by bridge modules.

As addresses may also change, an LEC may delete a registered address with a suitable UNREGISTER control frame. However, access protection is implemented for various LE clients: An LE server may never accept an UNREGISTER from the LE client "Otto" to an address which was recorded by the LE client "Hugo." If an LE client only has one unicast address, it does not need to activate the registration protocol, if it has already registered the address during initialization (see section 11.4.2.1). Broadcast/multicast addresses or functional addresses (Token Ring) may never be recorded: all broadcast/multicast frames would immediately be sent to this LE client and would only be distributed in the LANs connected to it. The rest of the ATM network would stay empty.

Every successful registration is confirmed by the LES. In order to limit the whole registration overhead, a REGISTER request may only be repeated once a second.

Token Ring

In Token Rings, a destination station may be reached not only using its MAC address, but also using the route information in the frame. Therefore, two statements apply to a Token Ring ELAN:

- An ATM network which emulates a Token Ring receives a proper segment number like every normal Token Ring LAN.

- In the emulated Token Ring LAN, the reachable segments must be made known in corresponding lists of route descriptors.

The route descriptors are recorded in the LES. As described in the section on "Token Ring bridges," a route descriptor (RD) consists of 2 bytes,

```
X'LLLB' with
LLL=segment number, unique throughout the network (LAN_ID)
B=bridge number
```

A Token Ring bridge records all its locally directly connected Token Ring segments as reachable destination addresses in the form of route descriptors. An example of a configuration and the resulting table in the LES is shown in Figure 11.19. For purposes of simplicity, instead of the correct 20-byte OSI format, 4 hexadecimal digits were used for the ATM addresses for the source routing LE clients.

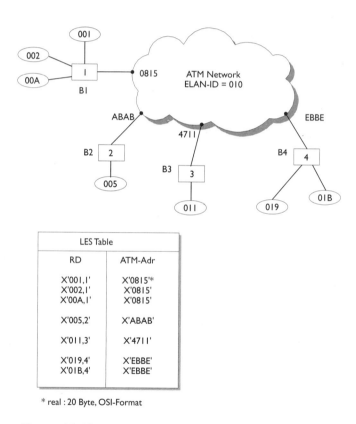

LES Table	
RD	ATM-Adr
X'001,1'	X'0815'*
X'002,1'	X'0815'
X'00A,1'	X'0815'
X'005,2'	X'ABAB'
X'011,3'	X'4711'
X'019,4'	X'EBBE'
X'01B,4'	X'EBBE'

* real : 20 Byte, OSI-Format

Figure 11.19: Registration of route descriptors in ATM LE

An LEC which is simultaneously a Token Ring bridge must be able to find from the RIF of the Token Ring frame whether it should transport it or. It does this in two steps:

- It identifies whether the route runs at least from the source LAN through the ELAN to a destination LAN via two source routing LE clients. The RIF then contains at least the hops LANs-ELAN-LANd (RIF=LLLsBs_LLLeBe_LLLd). It has a length of at least 6 bytes.

- It identifies whether the RIF contains a route descriptor as the "Next_RD" corresponding to its own bridge number and the number of a connected segment.

If the RIF is 6 or more bytes long, the LE client looks for the next route descriptor "Next_RD" in relation to the segment number of the ELAN (it is unique throughout the network). In Figure 11.20, RD_n is the route descriptor and the segment number of the ELAN is SEG_ID_n. A Token Ring source routing LE client finds the "Next_RD" in the following steps:

- It finds RDn with SEG_ID_n which provides a match with the segment number for the ELAN.

- It searches for "Next_RD" in relation to the D-bit:
  - if D=0, "Next_RD" is the segment number SEG_ID_{n+1} from RD_{n+1} and the bridge number BR_n from RD_n
  - if D=1, "Next_RD" is the segment number SEG_ID_{n-1} and the bridge number BR_{n-1} from RD_{n-1}

Obviously, it may also happen that there is no "Next_RD" at all. In this case, the ELAN is the last hop and the destination station is connected directly to the ELAN segment (for example, server with ATM interface). An LEC determines this as follows:

- D=0 and RD_n is the last RD in the RIF
- D=1 and RD_n is the first RD in the RIF

Like Token Ring source routing bridges, it does not forward the frame, but ignores it.

Even an LEC which is not a source routing bridge is able to interpret the RIF in accordance with the ATM LE specification (optional): in this case, the LEC should assume that, when D=0 then RD_n is the first RD in the RIF and, when D=1 then RD_n is the last RD in the RIF.

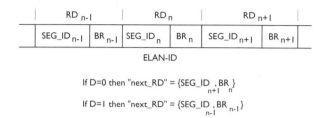

If D=0 then "next_RD" = {SEG_ID_{n+1} , BR_n}

If D=1 then "next_RD" = {SEG_ID_{n-1} , BR_{n-1}}

Figure 11.20: Finding the "Next_RD" in the routing information field

11.4.2.3 Address Resolution

To ensure that the data traffic is forwarded sensibly through the ATM network, a LAN destination (MAC address or route descriptor) must be mapped to the ATM address of the LE client providing the ATM connection to the destination LAN. The associated procedure is called address resolution. It enables the LE clients to establish data links between the transmitting station in the source LAN and the receiving station in the destination LAN using the ATM network (data direct VCC). The address resolution protocol uses the control connection between the LES and LE clients.

An LE client may never participate in address resolution before the JOIN has been successfully completed. This could lead to data loss and inconsistent network topology and is therefore strictly prohibited in the specification.

As an inquiry for an unknown MAC address, the LEC sends an LE_ARP request via its control connection to the LES. If the LES finds the relevant ATM destination address in its tables, its sends an LE_ARP response to the client with the desired ATM address. Otherwise, it forwards the LE_ARP request to all LE clients which are proxy clients. The algorithm for forwarding is not defined in the LE specification, but depends upon the implementation. If a response is received from a proxy, the LE server forwards it to the LEC which sent the original request. Alternatively, after evaluating the LE_ARP response, the LES may itself generate an LE_ARP response to the client. If an LEC receives an LE_ARP request for a MAC address for which it is responsible, it must respond to even this if it had registered the address in the LES. For example, it could be that the LES lost the address due to a memory overflow or false records, or it did not receive it as a result of a transmission error, or some similar mishap.

An LE client keeps a cache for all the LAN destination stations learned in which the active addresses (MAC addresses, route descriptors) are stored together with the associated ATM destination address (destination LEC). It must store at least all addresses for LE_ARPs which it has transmitted, but it may, in addition, store all addresses which it sees in LE_ARP responses (when forwarding). What does an LEC do if its cache is full but it still has outstanding LE_ARP? If a response is received for an open LE_ARP request, the LE client must free memory space for this. The specification does not say how this is to be done (possibilities: cache-expansion or deletion of the oldest entry).

After the expiration of an aging timer (between 10 and 300 sec, default=300) a learned address is deleted if it has not been seen in the interim, that is, if it has not been verified. "Seen" means a data packet, an LE_ARP response, or an LE_NARP request with this address has arrived. NARP requests are sent if a proxy thinks it is responsible for this new address after the conclusion of a topology change (Spanning Tree reconfiguration). Spanning Tree bridges should ignore LE_NARP requests, as they learn addresses more efficiently using the IEEE 802.1D learning mechanism. When the timer has expired, the address entry must not be used again. However, the LEC may generate an LE_ARP request on the expiration of the timer to test on its own initiative whether the questioned address is still active.

If the LE client is a Spanning Tree bridge, topology changes (failures, expansions) cause the Spanning Tree timer (IEEE 802.1D) to become active to delete the dynamically learned addresses. It has a higher priority than the normal aging timer.

For multicast addresses and broadcasts other than X'FF_FF_FF_FF_FF_FF' (for example, X'C0_00_FF_FF_FF_FF' in the Token Ring), no LE_ARP request may be transmitted. This would be the same as wanting to enter a multicast in the address table of a Spanning Tree bridge. It does not make any sense because multicasts/broadcasts are transmitted by a proper LE client to the BUS and then forwarded.

11.4.2.4 Data Transfer

If all control connections exist and registration and address resolution have been completed, the LEC may finally function meaningfully and forward the first data packet over the ATM network, as intended by the inventors of ATM LAN emulation. It recognizes from the first bit of the MAC address whether the frame is a unicast or broadcast/multicast. The LEC transmits it on the data connection to the destination LEC or the BUS as appropriate.

Unicasts

For unicast traffic, a bi-directional point-to-point data connection is established between the two participating LE clients (data direct VCC). As long as this link does not yet exist, an LEC may send the data over the multicast send VCC to the BUS, which then forwards it to at least all proxy clients, or even to all clients if the destination address is not registered. This produces a significant extra load in the ATM network. Therefore, the transmission rate to the BUS is limited for unicast traffic (number of frames = 1..10, default=1; transmission interval = 1..60 sec, default=1).

AN LEC implementation which does not send unicast traffic over the BUS runs the risk of failing to reach a MAC address which is connected via cascaded Spanning Tree bridges: under some circumstances, the bridges functioning as proxy agents do not know the address and in particular, do not know where the destination is. They will only flood the packet to all the connected LAN parts if they receive it from the BUS.

Broadcast/Multicasts

Broadcast/multicast-traffic is always over the BUS. Usually, an LE client uses a point-to-point link to transmit to the bus (multicast send VCC) which forwards the packets over unidirectional point-to-multipoint links to all clients (multicast forward VCC). The BUS may also use multicast send VCC, but not both to one LE client in parallel, to prevent duplications. Normally, an LE client may determine from its LECID in the packet header whether a frame which is transmitting the BUS originates from the LE client itself. In this case the LE client will ignore the frame. Spanning Tree bridges are unlucky: they are not able to filter a packets uniquely as it does not contain their address, but the address of the station connected to the LAN segment. Even with self-generated multicasts, for example, BPDU frames, the packet may be generated at bridge interface A (MAC_A) and forwarded by the BUS to all other interfaces (MAC_B, MAC_C, etc.). These do not recognize it as a self-generated packet and forward it to all the other bridge ports. The specification has obviously left some gaps here.

Packet Sequence

ATM LE only guarantees the packet sequence for pure unicast traffic, if—and only if—the flush message protocol is used which controls the packet sequence by additional control packets. For mixed data flows, for example,

1. MAC_Otto -> MAC_Hugo

2. MAC_Otto -> multicast

3. MAC_Otto -> MAC_Hugo

there is no guaranteed sequence, so the multicast frame could arrive later than the second packet sent by Otto to Hugo. A description of the flush message protocols is outside the scope of this book.

11.4.2.5 Link Management

Like every proper point-to-point connection, ATM LE connections are also controlled. This involves link establishment, the definition of VPI/VCI number, confirmation of establishment, ready indication for data reception, ready request when wishing to transmit, and link shut-down at the end of the session, upon the LEC's loss of the BUS connection, or after different time-outs. More detailed information may be found in the specifications UNIv3.0, UNIv3.1 and ATM LE Version 1.0.

11.5 ATM and Multi-Protocol Operation

The principles for multi-protocol operation based on AAL5 are defined in RFC 1483. RFC 1577 contains more detailed descriptions for IP and ARP. The ATM Forum has also suggested specifications for integrated routing over ATM:

Integrated Private Network-to-Network Interface (IPNNI) using PNNI and Multi-Protocol Over ATM (MPOA) which was introduced later in the work of the ATM Forum, primarily by Cisco.

11.5.1 RFC 1483

This defines two methods for using ATM as a transport medium for LAN traffic:

- **LLC encapsulation**, i.e., several LAN protocols are operated over a common ATM VC

- **VC multiplexing**, i.e., a separate VC is generated for every LAN protocol transported

In both cases, the LLC-PDU is completely transmitted in the ATM payload of the CPCS frame (Common Part Convergence Sublayer) of the AAL5. The specification assumes that the SCSS for AAL5 is "empty", i.e., is not used. However, if there is an SSCS, data units (PDUs) are transported using the higher-level multiplex method. One example of this is Frame Relay using ATM, as defined in RFC 1490. This uses a Network Layer Protocol ID (NLPID) to identify the protocol.

VC multiplexing should be chosen when it does not matter how many VCs are assigned, and if they may be dynamically generated without great expense. LLC encapsulation is the better alternative if VCs have to be reduced for reasons of cost, because the tariffs depend upon the number of VCs assigned, if the network is only provided with PVCs and the configuration of a VC for each protocol routed is too cumbersome.

The format of CPCS-PDU is shown in Figure 11.21. The CPCS-PDU is a maximum of $2^{16} - 1$ bytes long and, where appropriate, padded to make it divisible by 48. The UU field is used for the exchange of user information (user-to-user) and has no function with multi-protocol ATM encapsulation. Therefore, it may contain any values.

The CPI field (Common Part Indicator) extends the trailer for CPCS-PDU by one byte to 64 bits (8 bytes). If the field is only used for this alignment function, the value is 00 (hexadecimal). The length field shows the length of CPCS-PDU (max. 65535). The value 00 (hexadecimal) signifies a link abort. The CRC is calculated throughout CPCS-PDU, excluding the CRC field itself.

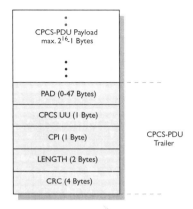

Figure 11.21: Format of AAL5 CPCS-PDU

LLC Encapsulation

With LLC encapsulation, the higher protocol transported must be entered in the PDU to enable different protocols on the same VC to be differentiated and demultiplexed. This information is entered in the LLC header. The following describes this for LLC type 1 (connectionless); it is just as possible for type 2 (connection-oriented), only the frame formats are different.

For routed protocols, the PDU has an IEEE 802.2 header and possibly also an IEEE 802.1a SNAP header (SubNetwork Attachment Point). The actual LLC header is 3 bytes long, DSAP, SSAP, and Ctrl. With LLC encapsulation the control field (Ctrl) always has the value 03 (hexadecimal) for a non-number data-PDU. The DSAP/SSAP for ISO protocols is FE (hexadecimal). The LLC header is followed by the identifier for the Network Layer (NLPID). Hence a connectionless ISO-PDU (CLNP) produces the CPCS-format shown in Figure 11.22 with the LLC value FE-FE-03 and the NLPID value 80.

The NLPID value 00 (hexadecimal) which indicates inactive Network Layer is not permitted with ATM encapsulation. Important NLPID values include

0x00   empty network layer (not in ATM)
0x80   SNAP
0x81   ISO CLNP
0x82   ISO ES-IS
0x83   ISO IS-IS
0xCC   Internet IP

Although IP was defined by the value CC (hexadecimal), *this value may not be used according to RFC 1483* but IP must be encoded by SNAP. The SNAP header is encoded by the LLC value AA-AA-03 and is found directly behind the LLC header. The SNAP header consists of 3 bytes OUI (Organizationally Unique Identifier referring to the organization which manages the following 2 bytes) and 2 bytes protocol type identifier (PID). The OUI 00-00-00 (hexadecimal) signifies an Ethernet protocol type. The format for non-ISO PDUs then looks as shown in Figure 11.22 and, specially for TCP/IP, the type field has the familiar value 0800 (hexadecimal).

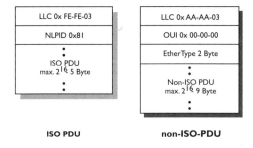

Figure 11.22: CPCS format of an ISO PDU and non-ISO PDU

LLC encapsulation for **bridged protocols** uses the OUI 00-80-C2 and encodes the bridged medium in the PID field. The encoding also shows whether the original FCS is still retained or not (if the MAC overhead changes, another CRC checksum is produced). Important codes include:

	FCS retained	FCS changed
802.3/Ethernet	0x00-01	0x00-07
802.4	0x00-02	0x00-08
802.5	0x00-03	0x00-09
FDDI	0x00-04	0x00-0A
802.6 (DQDB)	0x00-05	0x00-0B
Fragments		0x00-0D
BPDUs (IEEE 802.1D)		0x00-0E

Since the user data must always start at an offset in the frame which is divisible by 4 bytes (4-bytes alignment), if necessary, padding is inserted behind the PID field. The formats for bridged Ethernet, bridged FDDI and Spanning Tree protocol according to IEEE 802.1d are shown in Figure 11.23.

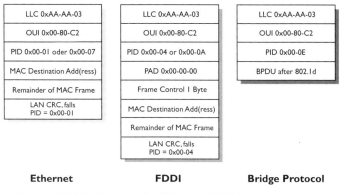

Figure 11.23: Formats for Ethernet, FDDI, bridge protocol with bridged LLC encapsulation

VC Multiplexing

With VC multiplexing, the protocol is identified implicitly by the special VC, which is configured between the two ATM stations for each protocol. This means that no further information is required in the AAL5 CPCS-PDU, which has the benefit of reducing the overhead. The encoding in VCs may be performed using a manually edited static configuration or dynamically during the connection establishment. Details for dynamic allocation will be dealt with in later RFCs.

VC multiplexing for routed protocols is performed entirely without overhead in the AAL5 CPCS-PDU—for bridged protocols the format is adopted from the PID field for the LLC encapsulation, as shown in Figure 11.24. Since the PID field is missing, the absence or presence of a LAN CRC is only made implicitly identifiable by differently configured VCs. PDUs with and without LAN CRC are also handled as different protocols, even if the bridged medium is the same.

For bridge function in ATM networks, an interface must be able to properly forward both multicasts and individual unicasts for dedicated MAC addresses. According to RFC 1483, multicasts may be either copied to every VC or forwarded over a separately defined VC. Here, compatibility needs to be taken into account if different equipment is used. For unicasts, an interface should normally have mappings between all potential destination partners on a MAC basis. As this may be unwieldy to varying degrees, however, VCs are established between physical LANs and the ATM interface looks into the CPCS-PDUs and, if they have been generated in accordance with the RFC, it can recognize the MAC source addresses entered in incoming PDUs and assign them to the relevant VC. *Hence, like remote bridges, ATM interfaces are able dynamically to learn MAC addresses and assign them to the associated ATM links (VCs).*

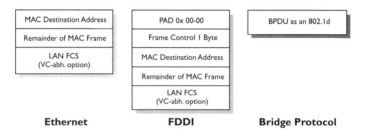

Ethernet FDDI Bridge Protocol

Figure 11.24: Formats for Ethernet-FDDI, bridge protocol with bridged VC multiplexing

11.5.2 RFC 1577

RFC 1577 describes LAN environments in which a LAN as a physical subnetwork is replaced by ATM; ATM only replaces the "wire" between the communication partners, nothing else. Instead of Ethernet, Token Ring, or FDDI, the IP packets are transmitted by ATM. RFC 1577 is based on the so-called "classical paradigm" for IP.

IP Model

The ATM network connects stations that are attached to the same logical subnetwork (SN), known as the Local IP Subnet (LIS). As before, different logical subnetworks are connected by routers and classical IP routing (RIP, OSPF, BGP, etc.). RFC 1577 does not include *any* bridge function or *any LAN* emulation. The link establishment and the establishment of the necessary cache tables is performed using ARP and inverse ARP, with ATM addresses being used instead of LAN addresses. Access control and access protection is performed, as in LANs, by routers, filter setting (Layer-3-Filter) in routers, and firewalls (use of gateways), as long as ATM does not offer any better safety and management functions than the current specifications. RFC 1577 describes the conversion of the ARP (according to RFC 826) and inverse ARP protocols defined for LAN (according to RFC 1293).

ATM Specifications

The following is specified for ATM use: RFC 1577 is an explicit extension of RFC's 826 and 1293 with an ATM capability, which means that stations which have correctly implemented RFC 1577 behave consistently with RFC's 826 and 1293. The ATM service used is AAL5, not AAL3/4. Public ATM networks and/or private ATM networks are connected by routers via PVCs. According to RFC 1577, both relevant address structures (private: OSI NSAP, public: E.164) and mixed environments *must* be supported for this. The signaling takes place according to Q.2931. According to RFC 1483, the IP/ARP packets are packed in LLC/SNAP.

All VCs use the same maximum packet size (MTU, Max. Transmission Unit). According to RFC 1577, this is 9180 bytes plus 8 bytes LLC/SNAP header, i.e., 9188 bytes. A smaller MTU size may only be used if this MTU size is configured for *all* stations on the relevant logical SN. A VC always only connects two stations in the same SN as a point-to-point link. The end-to-end routing procedure (RIP, OSPF, etc.) is not changed by RFC 1577.

Subnetwork Configuration

What does an IP subnetwork based on ATM look like? Just the same as a LAN-based subnetwork—only ATM addresses are used instead of MAC addresses: the hosts and routers in an ATM network form an enclosed logical subnetwork (SN). The hosts connected to an SN communicate with each other by direct IP addressing/ATM addressing. Different SNs operate completely independently of each other. The intra-SN communication runs on classic IP routing with the router being an ATM access point. Of course, a router with several interfaces may be connected to several SNs.

All stations (network nodes) in a SN have an identical network identifier (network part of the IP address) and an identical subnetwork mask. Every network node must support address resolution which uses ATMARP packets and

InATMARP packets (inverse ATMARP) to map IP addresses to ATM addresses. The underlying ATM topology is fully intermeshed, i.e., every network node has a VC to every other station in the same SN.

To function correctly, an IP station according to RFC 1577 must support the following parameters:

- *ATM address* (like the Ethernet address designated as a hardware address, although it is not really hardware-dependent, because OSI does not have any manufacturer recognition).

- *ATM request address*; this is the ATM address of the ATMARP server for a specific SN. This receives the ATMARP requests to which it responds with the ATM address for a desired IP destination station. The role of the ATMARP server is explained in more detail later.

A router serving several SNs must keep the specified parameters *for each* logical subnetwork and of course perform mapping between the parameters and the SN identifier. RFC 1577 recommends that a router for several SNs should have one physical ATM interface with several ATM addresses (one address per SN). This is the same principle as that of LAN technology: a router-LAN interface is assigned several IP addresses. This principle was simply transferred to ATM. However the difference is as follows: the router does not have to be configured with several OSI end system addresses (ESI, end system identifier); the SN differentiation is in the last byte, the selector (SEL) for ATM OSI address. This enables each NSAP to support up to 256 SNs.

Address Resolution

Two procedures are used to map IP addresses with ATM addresses: ATMARP and InATMARP. ATMARP corresponds to ARP according to RFC 826, InATMARP corresponds to inverse ARP according to RFC1293.

When **PVCs** are used, they must support LLC/SNAP encapsulation, otherwise it will not work. Now what does an IP/ATM station have to do to communicate with PVCs? It attempts to find out the IP address of the partner station by sending an InATMARP request ("Tell me the IP address for your ATM address"). The IP station evaluates the InATMARP responses from the partner stations on all PVCs and builds up the familiar ARP table in the cache.

However, it uses ATM addresses linked to IP addresses instead of MAC addresses.

When **SVCs** are used, the procedure is more complicated: since ATM is known to have a non-broadcast and non-multicast function (put simply: it is not a shared medium), similar to the ATM LAN emulation, an ATMARP service is established for the address resolution. In every logical subnetwork, there is one ATMARP service which is provided by one ATMARP server for each SN.

The initiative originates with the client (the IP station). It establishes a link to the server via the server's preconfigured ATM address (ATM request address for the station parameters named above). Then the server sends an InATMARP request to the client and receives its IP address in response. It proceeds in this way with every client and gradually compiles its ATMARP table in the ATMARP cache. If, subsequently, a client sends an ATMARP request to the server ("Tell me the ATM address for the IP address named in the request"), the server uses the table to respond to the request. If the server does not know the ATM address, it sends an ARP_NAK as a smoke signal saying that although the request has arrived, unfortunately no response can be given. Is this an unnecessary overhead? No, because the client can use the ARP_NAK to decide whether this is only a gap in the information or whether the server has crashed (in the latter case there would not be any response at all).

The defined single server model does not specify any redundancies (distributed or reflected server). This is left up to the implementation. It must function like a single client/server interface despite any redundancy.

Summary: If server and clients establish their ATMARP caches properly, the communication will work despite ATM.

11.6 ATM's State of Development

At present, ATM is mainly characterized by the fact that everyone is talking about it, but few actually have it, at least not with all its functions because ATM is not only the division of LAN frames into small blocks of fixed length (cells), it also includes numerous other specifications, some of which have not yet been completed and implemented, even if the ATM Forum (pooling of interests of the ATM manufacturers and large user companies) is working hard to supply the rather tardy ITU-T and ANSI committees with the relevant documents and, in the meantime, has even (contrary to early statements) started to look at compatibility tests.

Standardization

The standardization of all necessary functions is making slow, but steady, progress. Nevertheless, stable specifications are still lacking for many functions, some interfaces, and internationally agreed standards. The interfaces required for ATM are shown in Figure 11.25.

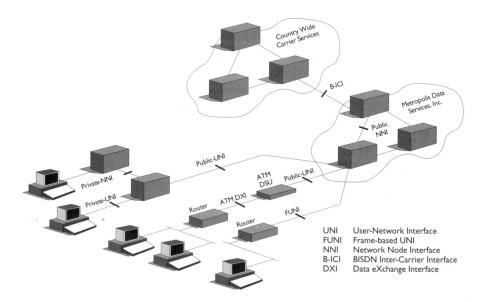

Figure 11.25: ATM interfaces

User to Network interface (UNI)

One of the most important interfaces for data communication is the UNI in version V3.0 and the upgraded version V3.1, which also supports SVCs. It is the interface between the user and the network. UNI V3.1 uses a Q.2931 derivative for signaling, which includes point-to-multipoint-links. The UNI is based on an end station, which is connected to an ATM switch. If the switch belongs to a public network, it is called a public UNI, if the switch belongs to a private network, it is called a private UNI. Unfortunately public and private UNIs are not entirely consistent. Although it is true that the UNIv3.1 specification deals with both of them, it does not specify which details belong to the public domain and which to the private domain. Even the physical layer is different public and private UNIs, as shown in section 11.3.

Signaling

A standard procedure for signaling is required to control virtual links dynamically. Without signaling, there can be no standardized use of SVCs. The ITU-T has defined Q.2931 (formerly Q.93B) for this purpose. The ATM Forum has defined its own signaling for UNIv3.0 which is not compatible with Q.2931. Although Univ3.1 is much closer to Q.2931, it is not fully compatible with it. Unfortunately, the adaptation of UNIv3.1 to Q.2931 has resulted in UNIv3.0 and UNIv3.1 also being incompatible with each other.

Addressing

The private UNI uses OSI addresses (20 bytes, GOSIP format), the public UNI telephone addressing according to E.164).

Quality of Service, Management

UNIv3.1 is an attempt to implement a QoS by a "terminal" (end system) having to specify the exact characteristics of the expected load before link establishment. Cells which exceed these characteristics are discarded with high priority in the event of bottlenecks. This kind of overload control is required only in the public domain and not in the private domain.

The management interface is different for private and public switches. The quick and dirty solution developed for the private UNI was the SNMP-like ILMI (Interim Local Management Interface). Public network operators have been flirting with OSI CMIP for a long time. Both ILMI and public switch management should become pure SNMP in the future. However, as the functions of ILMI are continuously being upgraded, we can assume that it still has a long time to live, as is so often the case with "handy interim solutions."

Flow Control

In the meantime, a requirement has arisen for a new type of ATM service in addition to CBR and VBR: Available Bit Rate (ABR) for non-time critical applications: the guaranteed transmission bandwidth is minimum, but if bandwidth is free, it is completely used for existing data. The provision of this service requires efficient flow control at cell level. Generally, with ABR a very low cell loss would be achieved. However, the store and forward approach known from X.25 was rejected by switch manufacturers (because they would have had to redesign all their switches as a result of changed buffer requirements and expanded software requirements for the input-output port synchronization!)

As an alternative, an end-to-end approach was selected: cells passing through an overloaded switch are marked with bitflags. The destination station which receives a marked cell, sees the bit, and provides the source station with a control cell which indicates to it that the transmission rate should be reduced. This solution is similar to the pacing principle found with SNA: the transmission rate is controlled end-to-end by control mechanisms between peer communication partners. The ATM Forum made a majority decision to use this approach in September 1994.

Access Components: DXI and FUNI

DXI (Data Exchange Interface) and FUNI (Frame-based UNI) are interfaces between ATM access components and private switches. Typically, routers and special ATM DSUs are used as access components which perform segmentation/reassembling. DXI has been available since August 1993. The DSUs used convert the router's data flow to the public UNI. If FUNI is used instead of DXI, normal DSUs may be used. This saves on equipment costs. The SAR function is then moved to the carrier network, and the router works like an end station which is connected directly to the public ATM network. Unfortunately the current carrier plans are not encouraging: the planned access rates are 56 kbps and 1.5 Mbps; these rates are so low that the cell overhead becomes unattractive.

The DXI between the router and the switch (similar to SMDS) may be implemented as HSSI with 45 Mbps with management data being exchanged over LMI (Local Management Interface) with SNMP. In mode 1, the DXI supports 1024 VCs, AAL type 5 and uses a 16-bit CRC and a maximum frame length of 8 kB; mode 2 supports 16 million VCs and AAL types 3 to 5, a 32-Bit CRC and a 64 kB frame length.

Private Network-to-Network Interface PNNI

This interface is to facilitate compatibility between multivendor switches by defining the interface functions between two switches. This includes traditional routing elements, such as topology information and route calculation (for VCs), or the current utilization of specific network resources (links, router interfaces, etc.). The routing procedure used is a Link State Algorithm. There are separate interfaces for public and private networks. The private interface P-NNI specification P-NNI phase I was modified in July 1996.

Multi-Protocol Operation using ATM

In the interim, the ITU-T has standardized AAL3/4 and AAL5. The main difference between AAL3/4 and AAL5 is as follows: AAL3/4 permits interleaving, i.e., cells in packets of different lengths are to be transmitted on the same virtual link interleaved with each other (similar to paddling: one rudder stroke to the right, one to the left). At one time, AAL5 only supports one single long packet on a virtual link. The consequence is evident: AAL3/4 has a significantly higher overhead. For public network operators, interleaving is an attractive function as it is a way of offering more favorable tariffs, but the manufacturers' attempts at interoperability are mainly directed towards AAL5. This conflict of interests is probably won by AAL5.

For the operation of different LAN protocols on an ATM network, RFC 1483 gives a basic description of how LAN packets may be encapsulated in AAL5 packets. RFC 1577 adds a few more details for IP and ARP. Other approaches include IPNNI (Integrated PNNI) and the later MPOA, which is mainly pushed by Cisco (multi-protocol over ATM).

The ATM Forum is working on the important missing supplements, for example,

- multicast proposal for ATM signaling

- B-ICI (Broadband InterCarrier Interface) for wideband between different carriers (for example, the transfer of a frame relay service to an ATM service, i.e., FR-ATM conversion)

- NNI (network-to-network interface) for the public network interoperability of different switch manufacturers

- PNNI (Private NNI) an interface between switches for local (private) local area ATM networks, phase 2

- IPPNI (Integrated PNNI)

- LAN emulation V2.0 with expanded function for compatibility, communication between ELANs, and communication between different LE servers

- multi-protocol operation over ATM for the established LAN protocols

- QoS definitions

- Standards for management including flow control and interoperability

- Standard addressing schemes for LANs and WANs with computer manufacturers fighting with telephone companies for telephone addresses (ITU-T E.164) or OSI-compatible addressing: here, geographical uniqueness comes into conflict with adaptation to geographically overlapping organizational hierarchies. At present, OSI addresses predominate in practice (NSAP addresses using GOSIP format), since ATM will be predominantly used in the private domain.

Unsolved Problems

The reluctance on the part of many, including large-scale users in employing ATM as a proprietary solution, is understandable and justified as long as the problems which remain open have not been resolved by stable specifications and their implementation:

- Flow control and overload control are missing, which is particularly disadvantageous in the WAN area. In the LAN area, this does not cause problems since with coverage in the kilometer range, only a few cells are transmitted simultaneously on the cable, and bottlenecks are identified relatively quickly. As the distance increases, this changes: at 5.500 km approximately 5.500 cells occur in parallel on a transmission route, and it takes double the route for a flow control message to be pushed through end-to-end. During this time, a number of data blocks are repeated due to time-outs, which increases the overload.

- Error correction only takes place at the ATM adaptation layer, i.e., end-to-end and not between switches.

- The actual mix of voice and data, i.e., low constant bandwidth with future mega-bursts has not yet been verified with practical expertise.

- Since only SONET/SDH has a fixed cycle for cell transmission, synchronization bits must be introduced for E1/T1, E3/T3, and other asynchronous types of LAN transmission, and this further increases the overhead.

- The signaling procedure is not standard, since Q.2931 and UNIv3.1 are not identical.

- There is no internationally agreed-upon standard for LAN emulation over ATM. The ATM Forum's specification V1.0 only defines the absolute basic functions and leaves a number of interpretation gaps open.

- With ATM LAN emulation, an LE client must keep tables with the addresses of all potential communication partners—which once again achieves the status of a completely flat communication hierarchy from which we were so happy to be resolved by routers; quite apart from the use of memory (with the any-to-any philosophy underlying ATM).

- ATM LE "only" implements a bridge coupling, therefore all the problems of purely bridge-coupled networks are retained with ATM LE.

- Routing over ATM has not yet been specified. There are only entirely proprietary solutions.

Conclusion

It still remains to be proven whether the increase in efficiency is in practice so high that it is able to cope with the (self-)imposed requirements. If ATM is actually available for high speeds in a few years, it is possible that completely different approaches will be available—ATM is definitely not the last word. In addition, the market acceptance of existing technologies such as FDDI, 100 Mbps Ethernet, or 1Gbps Ethernet in the future may act against the introduction of ATM if the prices are low enough.

The advantages of ATM are evidently the better scaling, the service-integration and the standardization of the transmission procedure for LAN and WAN communication. If you are planning to invest in an ATM network, the following check list may provide a few useful pointers.

Check List for ATM

- Do the hub systems support an ATM uplink which is compatible with the ATM switches used?

- Does the hub manufacturer offer his or her own switch modules for his or her hub system? Are OEM modules offered?

- Are the planned terminal adapters fully compatible with the switch? Do they support LAN emulation?

- Do the routers used support DXI or UNIv3.0 or UNIv3.1?

- Will LAN emulation be supported in compatibility with the current ATM Forum specification?

- Do the LAN ATM converters used also support FDDI (translation function)?

- Is SNMP used as a management protocol for all planned ATM components?

- Are there management applications for all planned ATM components which may be integrated under a common management platform? Are the components integrated in a graphical overall representation of the network?

- Which redundancy functions support the planned ATM uplinks and ATM switches? (Hot Swap, redundant links, redundant power supply, etc.)

12 Virtual LANs

The current state-of-the-art technology may be used to structure medium to large networks within a building using bridges/routers, while connections between buildings and LAN-WAN links are implemented using routers. Even if the subnetwork structures are optimized to match organizational relationships (see Chapter 2), some geographical orientation is required. The floor orientation may be broken down by multi-segment hub systems and multiport bridges or bridge modules in hub systems so that the organization orientation is reachable, inside a building at least. However, if distributed routers are used for backbone connection, logical (routed) subnetworks have to be physically connected and hence remain restricted to one building.

The Need for Virtual LANs

Conventional technology results in considerable expenses in daily network operation: moving from one building to another always requires the configuration of new network addresses in the end systems or suitable boot servers, which is a significant expense in view of the statistical frequency of moving of 45% a year. Another annoying fact is that the implementation of multi-protocol technology in multiport devices requires the implementation of logical subnetworks from different protocol worlds with more or less physical mapping to keep the structure reasonably transparent. Instead of this, it is desirable to separate physical and logical network structures—as implied by the name "logical subnetwork" (i.e., Layer 3 subnetwork). This is particularly applicable to the operation of different protocol worlds on a common network infrastructure.

Leaving aside the router software bugs which have now become an everyday occurrence, the throughput performance of routers still leaves a lot to be desired in the event of high-load and multi-protocol operation. Particular workstation clusters, in which every device can connect with the network at 20 to 40 Mbps (e.g. Alpha machines) or time-critical applications like real-time video or alarm handling in production environments using control technology, cause problems even for high-performance routers.

New approaches increase flexibility by the formation of virtual LANs. The competition for market shares in the VLAN market has plunged virtually all internetworking manufacturers into the chaotic process of VLAN invention: Agile (led by the founder of Wellfleet Seiffert), Bay Networks, Bytex/NSC, Cabletron, Chipcom, Cisco, 3Com, Fore, IBM, Madge/Lannet, Newbridge, Retix, UB Networks (to a limited extent only at present), to list just a few of the established names. The only identifiable conformity between the competitors is the fact that routers are still used, but only between, not within, the VLANs. The death of routers, which has been predicted by several market observers, seems to be some years in the future.

What is a VLAN?

Port switching hubs could be described as the precursors of VLANs (port switching is also known as per-port assignment); they are able to connect any ports in the same or different concentrator cards of *the same* LAN type (Ethernet, Token Ring, FDDI) by software mapping on the same internal LAN backplane bus to a physical LAN (Layer 1 connection). If further advances are made with the necessary microsegmentation, the approximately five to fifteen backplane segments will no longer suffice and alternative possibilities will be needed. One development in this field is Bytex hubs with which, like matrix switches, any ports on any cards may be grouped together to form a physical

LAN segment for Ethernet or for Token Ring, without restriction as to the maximum number of backplane buses.

As a VLAN standard is still "pie in the sky," as expected, different manufacturers have developed very different mixed concepts which make logical and consistent classification difficult. Nevertheless, Figure 12.1 tries to do this. Different approaches are used to form virtual LANs. Some use migration over LAN switches, which work without an ATM connection in the first phase and in the future will be able to work with an ATM connection. LAN switches may work at Layer 2 or Layer 3. In different VLAN concepts, the latter are also known as Layer 3 switches or multilayer switches or ridges or edge devices, etc.

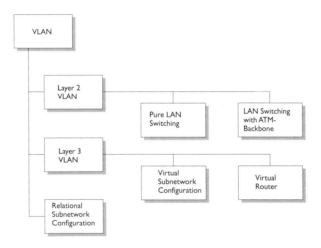

Figure 12.1 Classification of VLANs

Particularly in connection with ATM as the backbone technology, it is important to find out what a manufacturer understands by a virtual LAN. Some manufacturers (e.g., IBM) only understand this to mean the ATM backbone, because it is not actually a LAN, it only acts as if it were a LAN by means of LANE. Other manufacturers (e.g., Cisco, Bay Networks) support VLAN functions in the sense of additional organization-oriented network partitioning in their LAN switches combined with proprietary ATM LANE variants to connect the VLANs over an ATM backbone. ATM LANE according to forum document v1.0 has nothing to do with the division of the entire LAN into organization-oriented broadcast domains.

The formation of virtual LANs (VLANs) is achieved therefore, by means of LAN switching and/or virtual routing (Layer 2 and/or Layer 3 coupling); it is performed at Layer 2 and/or Layer 3 and, depending upon the (manufacturer's) definition, may be achieved by packet switching (frame switching, LAN switching) and sometimes also ATM cell switching (LAN emulation LANE, LE).

ATM LANE was described in Chapter 11 and pure LAN switching in Chapter 7. For the purposes of this book:

- the establishment of a pure ATM-backbone with standard LANE
- the use of pure LAN switching without additional functions to divide the network into broadcast domains

are not a virtual LAN.

For an unambiguous definition of the terminology for this book, in the following the term LAN switch will be used for Layer 2 switches which transport LAN packets in their full length (not as ATM cells); Frame switches which also or only use network layer information (i.e., the network address) will be called Layer 3 switches.

In addition, the following definitions apply:

VLAN: The formation of a broadcast domain, freely defined according to specific criteria on the basis of physical LAN segments, i.e., MAC link with or without additional evaluation of the Layer 3 information.

12.1 Layer 2 VLANs

VLANs which are formed purely by evaluating MAC information are used in the following approaches:

- LAN switches
- Native Secure Data Exchange, IEEE 802.10
- ATM with LAN emulation

LAN switches

VLAN functions may be found both with CT and with SF switches (see Figure 12.2). With pure CT switches however, VLAN functions are restricted to grouping MAC addresses or ports, as the frame contents cannot be expanded any further. Generally therefore, the switch manufacturer has to choose between the trade-off of short delay times and sophisticated VLAN functions. Some undecided manufacturers have developed mixed procedures using the "partial buffering concept." In these for example, the addresses and the type field (digital gigaswitch) or the first 64 bytes are buffered, evaluated and checked. This enables further filter functions to be set.

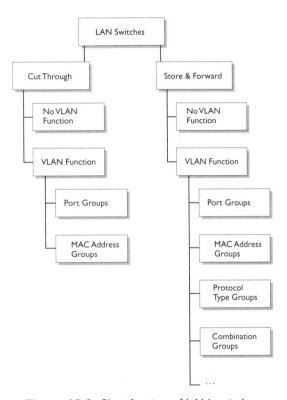

Figure 12.2: Classification of LAN switches

A Layer-2-VLAN groups the users on the basis of pure MAC links, usually address tables (Ethernet, Token Ring, FDDI) and, where appropriate, source routing in the Token Ring to a "LAN" i.e., a broadcast domain as shown in Figure 12.3. A VLAN receives an ID, usually a number (whole number). A differentiation should be made here between products which perform port-level allocation (Cisco Catalyst 5000, Catalyst 3000, Digital, Retix) and products which permit grouping of MAC addresses (Cabletron, 3Com, Xylan/NSC) or other filter conditions. The latter means greater flexibility, particularly if, after a move, the workstation system is automatically allocated to the same VLAN again. Within the defined VLANs, the packet transport is controlled by address tables. The VLANs do not usually have any communication with each other, unless this is provided by external links (exception: Bay Networks Speed Switch for Token Ring). This should be taken into consideration as appropriate when assigning the logical subnetwork addresses, i.e., the same subnetwork address must be provided and defined for bridge coupling and, for router coupling, the subnetwork addresses should be different. For example, different servers may be combined with their respective clients in different VLANs connected by routers. For centralized server concepts with separate server functions and access by all users to all servers, however, this kind of concept is not feasible.

Caution is advised for the bridge coupling of VLANs with non-routable protocols: the bridge coupling forwards all broadcasts/multicasts into all the connected VLANs. Nevertheless, there are some feasible applications for bridge coupling: if a LAN switch is not able to connect VLANs across several switches, LAT stations, which are connected to different switches, would have to be linked by bridges. In most cases however, it will make more sense to configure one VLAN instead of two bridge-connected VLANs.

Protocol-related VLANs are easier to establish if the grouping is not performed using MAC addresses but according to any other filter conditions applied to the MAC frame, e.g., the type identification for the higher protocol (type field, LSAP or SNAP). This is supported by Bay Networks/Centillion, Digital, 3Com or Xylan, for example. However, the same applies to VLAN formation according to filter conditions which are set to MAC frames as to bridge technology: correct filter setting requires extensive protocol know-how, and too many filters make the resulting structure unclear and hence no longer efficient to operate and maintain.

To form protocol-related VLANS in a heterogeneous network for the purposes of load optimization (Novell network, AppleTalk network, TCP network), a "VLAN switch" must allow one MAC address or one port to be assigned to several VLANs, namely for all systems which use more than one protocol stack (e.g., with Switch-Stack/Retix, LANplex, 3Com, Omniswitch/ Xylan alias Enterprise LAN switch/NSC). A practical expansion is the cascading of LAN switches and the formation of VLANs using several LAN switches (This does not work with Digital Gigaswitch, UB Networks DragonSwitch, for example.) A typical application scenario for this is the installation of services in the computer room, whereby end systems distributed all over the place are connected to random ports on other switches. The switches are suitably connected with high capacity, i.e., 100 Mbit, Ethernet, e.g., (proprietary) or FDDI (3Com, Cabletron) or completely proprietary (Retix with 175 Mbps, Bay Networks with 200 Mbps FDE Cisco/Kalpana with 280 Mbps) and, in future, where appropriate, ATM. Attention should be paid here to the size of address table, since, on its connection port to the next switch, a switch must be able to learn the addresses of all other connected stations. Products which are restricted to one (Cisco/Grand Junction) or 64 addresses per port, cannot be used for larger distributed VLANs; neither can products which only permit limited cascading.

An important aspect of the implementation of VLANs is the establishment of redundant links. This only works if the switch supports a separate Spanning Tree algorithm for each VLAN (e.g., Cisco), which is not the case with all manufacturers. If the switch has only one Spanning Tree, it is not possible to switch parallel links for two cross-switch VLANs and hence to distribute the load: one of the VLAN links is deactivated and hence the data traffic is suspended.

The following applies to the connection of different VLANs: routable protocols may be connected by external routers, non-routable protocols may be connected by external bridges. In this case, the routers/bridges are normally each connected by one interface to each VLAN.

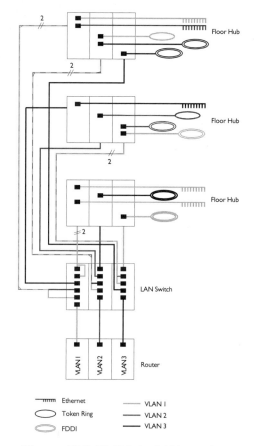

Figure 12.3: VLANs by LAN switching

Separating the Logical and Physical Structure: Consequences

If the logical and physical structure are separated from each other, LAN switches must be able to identify stations in the same VLAN across all switches and forward packets correctly within a VLAN. How does a LAN switch A, which at one port, has stations Hugo and Peter from VLAN_1, know that station Otto at switch B also belongs to VLAN_1? It definitely does not know this from the vibration of its chassis and does not hear it from the special transmission noise made by Otto's packets. A procedure must be implemented on a multiswitch basis which makes every separate VLAN completely reachable across all switches.

The transmission of the information as to which packet belongs to which Layer 2 (or Layer 3) VLAN (see below) may take place according to at least four different procedures:

- exchange of addresses/address tables

- time division multiplexing

- proprietary tagging (packet expansion with VLAN ID entry)

- group formation and tagging in accordance with standard specification IEEE 802.10

Exchange of addresses: If an end station boots on the LAN, the switch to which it is connected learns its address. After this, it sends a message (signaling message) with this new address and the associated VLAN number to the other switches. For synchronization between each other (e.g., because addresses are always being deleted from a table as a result of aging, etc.), at intervals, e.g., once a minute, switches transmit their complete address table, which is very reminiscent of Level 1 routing with DECnet IV. Obviously this results in overhead in the network. Address table exchange is used by Bay Networks (LattisSwitch 28000) and Madge/Lannet, for example.

Time Division Multiplexing: different VLANs are connected with each other by a high-speed backbone, and transmission takes place in time slots (e.g., for 10 Mbps capacity with an 175 Mbps-backbone in 17.5 µs a total of 1 msec transmission time). Every VLAN is assigned one or several time slots (e.g., Switchstak from Retix). This solution is only applicable to a small number of VLANs and hence is fairly limited. The advantage is the avoidance of overhead messages as to which address is connected to which switch. The disadvantage is that unused time slots cannot be used by other VLANs. The consequence: the backbone must be carefully monitored to check constantly whether the time slots were efficiently assigned during configuration of the VLANs or whether the VLAN on which the users usually sleep has received four time slots, while jams constantly occur in another VLAN because of a shortage of capacity.

Tagging: a switch which forwards a MAC packet to another switch adds a marker (tag) with the VLAN number at the start of the packet. Again, with this alternative, synchronization messages are not required, since every packet receives the VLAN identifier, i.e., a switch can decide on its reception whether to forward the packet and, if so, to which ports. The disadvantage is seen if a packet of maximum length has to be transported: the additional tagging bytes cause the maximum length to be exceeded and there is a code violation. Analyzers will record the packets as faulty packets. Standard components (e.g., bridges) will not forward the packets. Packets which are too long may give rise to non-specific protocol errors. Such a case would require the implementation of proprietary fragmentation. However, manufacturers argue that only the LAN switches are connected to the backbone, and they are able to interpret these over-length packets correctly. However, this only permits a very restricted usage of the backbone (i.e., only to connect the LAN switches).

The IEEE 802.10 procedure described in the following also uses tagging. Here, the standard gives a suggestion of how over-length packets should be fragmented.

IEEE 802.10 (SDE)

A standard-based VLAN variant may be implemented using the SDE protocol (Secure Data Exchange), IEEE 801.10. This is being attempted by Digital (Gigaswitch), Cisco/Grand Junction, Cisco, Racal and Bay Networks (Native Mode LAN, NML), for example.

According to IEEE 802.10, additional encapsulation is used to the add the information on group membership to a specific VLAN. The additional protocol bytes are divided into the clear header, protected header, padding trailer for additional encoding entries or the like, and integrity check value (ICV) to identify transmission errors. All these fields are optional. At present, only the clear header is used for VLANs. It consists of 3 bytes for SDE identification (twice the reserved LSAP for SDE and the LLC field "unnumbered control" with the value 11000000), the secure association identifier (SAID), and an optional field for processing information (MDF, Management-Defined field). The station ID field (protected header) receives the MAC address of the transmitting station starting with the first bytes. This makes transmitter authentication possible (remember that with routed packets the original MAC source address is exchanged during processing in the router). The format is in Figure 12.4.

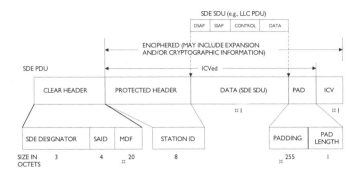

Figure 12.4: Format of a SDE-PDU

The SAID consists of 4 bytes which encode a single station or group identification, i.e. VLAN ID. In a group identification, the first bit of the first byte is set to 1, for individual identifiers it has the value 0. Current SDE implementations implement a subset of the IEEE 802.10, i.e., the insertion of group identifications called VLAN-IDs. Particularly in distributed backbone environments, this permits the formation of virtual LANs without the end stations having to be able to speak SDE: every switch/bridge/router port is assigned the corresponding VLAN IDs for the end stations which are connected to this port (Bay Networks calls this a closed user group ID, CUGID, for example). Between the backbone and a specific physical subnetwork, only those packets which have a CUGID configured for this port by access list (e.g., 100, 200, 300) are transported. On the destination subnetwork, the SDE packet is converted back into a normal LCC packet by the relevant coupling element.

Suitable negative filters may be used to completely separate VLANs from the backbone. Combining several VLAN IDs (e.g. an ID range from 101 to 120) to form a VLAN (range 100) enables the access control to be expanded to port level in hub systems. The administration of this kind of network is very complex however, since when a user moves, the new SAIDs have to be installed in a subnetwork, in some circumstances, at bridge level and hub level, or have to be deleted at the place being left. Without this cannot be used productively in large networks. The use of LAN switches for SDE is very dubious, as these devices have to rely on very high-speed packet processing due a shortage of buffer space and therefore are only rudimentarily equipped with filter functions.

The advantage is that the procedure functions for all standard LANs without proprietary gymnastics, hence different network components are compatible. This is not the case with switched virtual LANs with proprietary concepts. But even with 802.10, the problem is with the options: Bay Networks call the VLAN ID CUGID (closed user group ID) and uses the MDF field to insert the VLAN ID, while Cisco uses the SAID field. That is the end of all commonality, despite the standard. The Bay Networks format is shown in Figure 12.4a.

With collapsed backbones, one or more group IDs are configured at every port of the collapsed backbone switch/router. However, the additional SDE bytes now have to be inserted by the terminal.

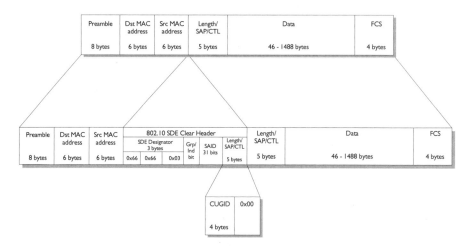

Figure 12.4a: Format of 802.10 SDE-PDU used by Bay Networks

To summarize: the advantages of VLAN formation by means of LAN switches are the greater total capacity available (compared with traditional Ethernet/Token Ring), the shorter processing time (only with LAN switches), and the flexibility to form multi-building LANs in accordance with the organizational and structural requirements and independently of higher protocols. A less attractive feature is the cabling costs: under some circumstances, one cable connection per workgroup to the switch. In addition, each VLAN connection requires a router port, which means a significant port concentration in the routers on the formation of collapsed backbones (to save processing time). Disadvantages of VLANs based on MAC include the absence of broadcast separation and access safety within a VLAN. Both are still only possible over routed links.

VLANs with ATM and LAN Emulation

ATM manufacturers see the upgrade of workgroup LAN switches with a so-called ATM uplink and replacement of the LAN switches in the backbone by an ATM switch as a further development of the virtuality of switched LANs. In this case, a procedure is required to connect pre-configured VLANs safely with each other over the ATM backbone. The preferred approach in this case is at present called LAN emulation (LANE, LE), in which the ATM backbone as an ELAN (Emulated LAN) acts as if it were an intelligently functioning LAN in ideal ATM conditions. ATM LE was described in Section 11.

If the virtual ELAN is made even more virtual, i.e., extended to several VLANS configured in a LAN switch, one ELAN will be required for every VLAN. The ATM standard for LE currently limits the number of emulated LANs to 1024, as one ELAN ID consists of 10 bits. This restriction is also found with manufacturers who are mainly trying to achieve VLAN formation in conjunction with ATM (e.g., Cisco). In addition, the ATM LANE document only describes how an individual ELAN functions, not how several ELANs are implemented. If different VLANs are to be mapped on as many ELANs, *each VLAN* will require the complete ATM LANE mimic: A LES, a BUS, a LECS etc. Nor does the ATM LANE document describe how different LESs may exchange information, whether and how different LESs may be implemented in network components, how ELANs are connected etc.

Just like switched VLANs, VLANs based on ATM LE must be configured by software configuration using a management console. However, they have the advantage of reduced cabling costs: just one cable with many virtual ATM channels runs from the floor hub to the central hub equipped with an ATM switch, instead of the separate cable connection for each VLAN used before (see Figure 12.5). According to the LE specification, the establishment of the link after a move is performed automatically throughout the entire VLAN network (the address information is deleted out of the LEC's address memories at intervals due to aging). However, manual reconfiguration is required if a user is to be integrated into another VLAN. Cabletron, Cisco, 3Com, Fore Systems, Hilan, IBM, and Bay Networks for example, work with LAN emulation.

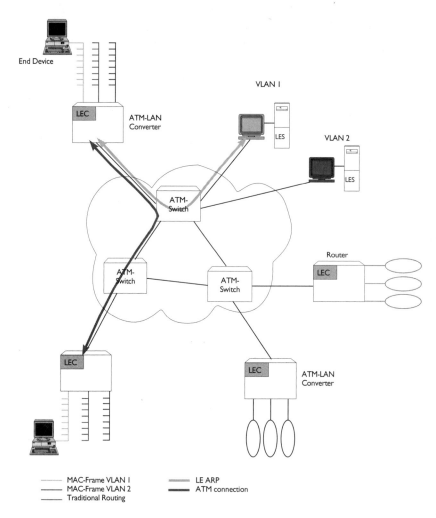

Figure 12.5: VLANs with ATM and LAN emulation

The connection between VLANs is achieved in the same way as with LAN switching over routers which have their own LEC implementation and can also be connected by one single ATM port instead of a separate port for each subnetwork. Obviously, this restricts the overall capacity of the routing throughput to the capacity of the ATM links. However, it is still able to support 622 Mbps. Nevertheless, the router still has the problem that it has to be able to push through approximately 400,000 packets on an interface to make full use of the link capacity. If the router does not have an ATM capability, the link may be established as before over a multiport LEC with several individual links to the router. They then only have LAN capacity (10, 16, 100 Mbps).

The problem here is that the current LE draft only provides for one VLAN (= one ELAN) per LEC. This means dependence between the physical and logical structure again, if several LECs are not to be used in one coupling element.

To summarize: the advantages of VLAN formation using ATM LE are the reduced cabling costs compared to LAN switching, the use of ATM scalability in the backbone area, and the automated integration of stations after a move within a logical subnetwork (IP, IPX, DECnet). Disadvantages include the fact that the coupling is still restricted to MAC level, which means the connection between VLANS is provided by traditional routing and hence is a potential bottleneck. Also, VLANs do not permit any physically distributed formation of the same logical subnetwork. Another disadvantage is the implementation which currently is completely proprietary, since, although Version 1.0 of the LE specification has been agreed by the ATM Forum, it still does not contain any sensible definition for VLAN emulation.

12.2 Layer-3-VLANs

VLANs based on Layer 3 information (logical subnetworks) may be established with Layer 3 switches or "virtual routing:" for the separation of the logical and physical network structure, this requires a further virtualization stage, virtual routing. Moves and changes may be performed separately from the physical network structure. Finally, the logical subnetworks at ISO-OSI Layer 3 have become real logical networks: a move means no compulsory change of address; an assignment to another work group no longer necessitates any physical recabling (connection to the relevant network). The main approaches to the implementation of virtual routing concepts may be divided into two directions: virtual subnetwork formation and virtual routers.

Layer 3 Switches

To forward a packet, Layer 3 switches evaluate not only the MAC header, but also the information in the Network Layer, particularly the network addresses. This method may be used on the one hand, to stretch a subnetwork over several ports/LAN segments and, on the other hand, to assign several logical subnetwork addresses to a port, as shown in Figure 12.6. These are ideal for complete flexibility in moving without enforced configuration changes in end systems.

If two stations belong to the same subnetwork, forwarding is performed using bridge technology/LAN switching; if two stations belong to different subnetworks, broadcasts are suppressed and packets routed in accordance with the switch tables. However, these are more extensive than in conventional routers, as a subnetwork may now be configured not just on one port, but on many ports with all the switches. A Layer 3 switch evaluates not only the network part of the destination address but also the host part. Then it checks to which port the address is connected and forwards the packet as appropriate, either to a normal LAN port or to a high-speed backbone port to the next switch.

Usually, during the formation of Layer 3 VLANs, a VLAN will be consistent with a Layer 3 subnetwork address. Between the different VLANs, there will then be only a routed link, either by externally connected routers (see Figure 12.6) or over internal routing functions (see Figure 12.7). However, not all Layer 3 switches support several subnetworks per port, some support only one subnetwork per port (Newbridge), which significantly reduces flexibility. With multi-protocol stations, the Layer 3 switch must allow one station to belong to several VLANs (e.g., IP VLAN_1, IPX VLAN_3, Apple VLAN_10).

Layer 3 switching poses the following question: where does the switch obtain its routing table, that is, the information by means of which it reaches other destination networks? At present there are in principle two approaches for this, a central approach and a decentral approach.

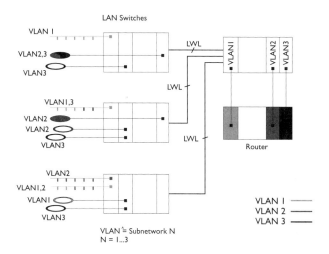

Figure 12.6: Virtualization with Layer 3 switches and use of external routers

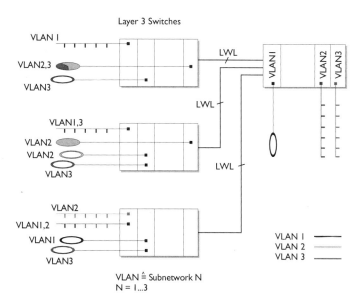

Figure 12.7: Virtualization of logical subnetworks with Layer 3
switches and internal routing

Virtual Subnetwork Configuration

The decentral concept is also called "virtual subnetworks." Every Layer 3 switch also functions as a router and sends updates about the networks and possible end systems connected to it. It is therefore a type of Layer 3 switch/router. The information on connected end systems is in any case proprietary as it is not defined in the standardized routing protocols (exception: DECnet IV, Layer 1). Every Layer 3 switch/router evaluates the update information received from all the others and uses this to create its routing switching tables.

Routing updates on routing protocols like RIP and OSPF are no longer sufficient for virtual subnetworks, as these may extend over several backbones with several ports and switches. The packet forwarding then poses the question: what does a Layer 3 switch/router do with a packet if it does not know its destination network? It no longer forwards packets which are addressed to a specific logical subnetwork on precisely one route because the subnetwork is physically distributed. Like the self-learning bridges, it can send this packet to all connected ports and wait to see which port generates the response packet. It has then "learned" the Layer 3 address as a source address at this port and in the future only forwards packets to this target address to this port. Another variant would be a "subnetwork ARP," to which all Layer 3 switches which know this subnetwork respond, i.e., which have stations connected in this subnetwork.

Like Layer 2 subnetworks, concepts based on ATM backbones use a (proprietary) expanded LANE to find out the ATM target address of the corresponding router or LAN-ATM converters before the router. With this expanded LANE, LE ARPs are not only transmitted for MAC addresses, but also for Layer 3 addresses being sought. Virtual subnetworks may be implemented over the ATM backbone and access routers at the transition between the subnetwork and the ATM backbone (see Figure 12.8). These routers could also be called "edge routers" or access routers and have an "ATM uplink", i.e., a UNIv3.x interface to the ATM backbone. In addition, they not only perform routing, but they are also able to combine several interfaces by LAN switching to form a subnetwork, even different LAN-interfaces such as Ethernet, Token Ring and FDDI.

Building up virtual subnetworks with ATM moves the routing from the collapsed backbone to the end system concentration points, i.e., the central building and, where appropriate, floor wiring closets. If there is a requirement to route between two connected end stations, the routing software becomes active, if there is only a bridging requirement, LAN switching comes into action. As an expansion in comparison with LAN emulation, not only are MAC addresses mapped to ATM addresses, but, by means of a "multilayer ARP," also network addresses. A router which needs to address a destination network sends an ARP on the ATM multicast channel, and the router on the ATM backbone that connects this destination network responds to the ARP request with its ATM address. Then, for example, over Q.2931, a link is established between the access routers which perform the LAN-ATM conversion of the packets.

The first approaches at standardizing virtual subnetworks may be found in RFCs 1483 and 1577. NetEdge, Digital, and Bay Networks follow the concept of virtual subnetworks. Parallel CPUs may be used to advantage with the access routers (familiar from the Bay Networks architecture) with one CPU running the table administration and dynamic routing protocols (OSPF, DRP, IS-IS), the interface CPUs performing the packet forwarding by bridge functions, LAN switching functions or routing functions and other CPUs controlling the ATM link establishment. In addition, the access routers can implement the LAN-WAN connection very well, which is still relatively far below ATM speeds.

Three problems remain with virtual subnetworks: first of all, in its current version (IPv4), IP has no Multimac functions, i.e., several interfaces of a router cannot be assigned the same network address in conformity with the standard. Second, the formation of distributed subnetworks is not desirable, as two or more routers would respond to the ARP request, and all packets would be sent on several routers or the routers would have to use additional information, such as an evaluation of the ARP caches (for the end systems connected to their own interfaces), to establish unambiguity. Since the ARP cache does not always contain all the addresses of the connected end stations, in a negative case the ARP would have to be forwarded to a router's corresponding virtual subnetwork interfaces, which means a significant additional overhead. However, logical subnetwork coupling by routing may take place between the interfaces of an "edge router."

All Layer 3 switches have a third problem with wretched, non-routable protocols such as NetBIOS, LAT, LAVC, SNA DLC. These cannot be operated with purely Layer 3 switching.

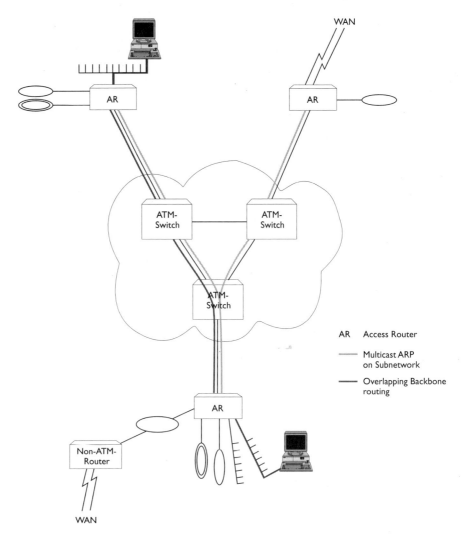

Figure 12.8: Virtual subnetworks

Reconfiguration on moves is always necessary if a device from a new sub-network is to be connected to a Layer 3 switch, or if all the stations in a configured subnetwork have moved and this subnetwork has to be deleted at the switch interface. At least it is no longer necessary to reconfigure host addresses if a user wishes to remain in his or her VLAN.

Virtual Router

Further progress has been made with the division of tasks in the central approach, "virtual routers." Cabletron, Cisco, Newbridge and MPOA are following this concept. The routing functions are distributed among several devices: a central component and Layer 2/3 switches (called multilayer switches by Cisco) as subordinate components. The central device (central routers, core routers, route servers) with a high-capacity connection to the ATM backbone runs the dynamic routing protocols (table update, transmission of update information) and acts as a route server which performs the route calculation and forwards the new route information to all Layer 3 switches at intervals or event-driven. To enable it do this correctly, the core routers/route servers are supplied with information on the connected subnetworks and/or end systems by all the Layer 3 switches. To implement this interplay, it is necessary to develop a *distributed routing protocol*. Cisco is investing a lot in this task. At least this company does have experience in the development of proprietary routing protocols (e.g., IGRP, EIGRP).

The Layer 2/3 switches perform the packet forwarding, i.e., they bridge, switch and route the packets according to the requirement. This approach is also used in the Cisco Fusion architecture. Cabletron is also following this approach, of course using a SPECTRUM application as the route server.

The concept of the virtual router lets the entire ATM network with core routers and multilayer switches at the ATM LAN transition points become a virtual router (as shown in Figure 12.9). Compared to conventional routers, multilayer switches correspond to the LAN-interfaces, the ATM backbone to the backplane, and the core routers to the central router CPU. The implementation of these kinds of architecture has always been proprietary—therefore why should it not be extended to a proprietary ATM network? The idea of the functional separation of packet forwarding and route administration is certainly plausible since it may greatly reduce the packet processing time for routed connections. However, as the route server no longer has one port for every subnetwork, but addresses the subnetworks over virtual channels (VCI/VPI), the connection of multilayer switches must be preconfigured manually or take place using so-called "well-known" addresses (addresses to be defined in a standard which does not yet exist).

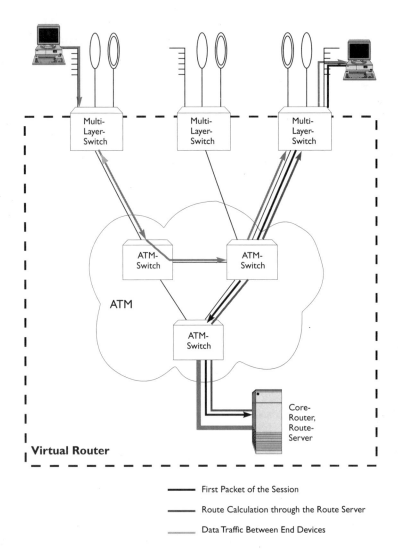

Figure 12.9: Virtual router

A Layer 2/3 switch must be able to serve end systems in the same logical subnetworks (SN) at different ports and find them using the route server. It must also be able to serve several SNs at one port (at least the backbone port). Consequently, it must make table entries for each end systems connected *and* each routed protocol—a memory-intensive solution. If a multilayer switch cannot find a desired destination in its cache, it starts an inquiry at the central router (ARP) from which it receives the desired target address. Anyone who remembers the good old SNA structures could also compare the route server with a host processor, and the multilayer switches with front-end processors. At least the route server represents, if not duplicated, a single point of failure.

The implementation of distributed logical subnetworks still has some snags even using virtual routers. At every Layer 2/3 switch, every subnetwork from which it has connected stations has to be configured. If a user moves onto a floor that belongs to a new subnetwork, this has to be re-installed at the multilayer switch. If the last user of another subnetwork moves out, this subnetwork has to be deactivated. Connecting a complete SN to a multilayer switch and only operating the connection of different SNs over the ATM backbone is much simpler. However, this also involves increased reconfiguration costs for the end systems when moving.

To summarize: the advantages of Layer 3 subnetwork formation are the achievement of the desired flexibility of movement with a simultaneous reduction in broadcasts (fewer broadcasts than with traditional bridging, more than with traditional routing) and access control through logical subnetwork formation instead of the (manual) grouping of MAC addresses. The main difference between the definitions of virtual subnetworks and virtual routers is as follows: virtual subnetwork formation sees virtual routing as a combination of several physical (LAN) interfaces with access routers to form virtual subnetworks or channels in an ATM link. The concept of virtual routers sees virtual routing as the expansion of the router architecture to the complete ATM backbone, including route servers and Layer 2/3 switches. Both concepts use the advantages of modern routing, namely safety functions and broadcast suppression. Once again, the main disadvantages are the entirely proprietary implementation, the increased broadcast load on the backbone, and the reduction of the network operation to routable protocols.

Relational Subnetworks

This approach implements a further step in the automation of VLANs. It is proposed by one manufacturer: Agile Networks (under the leadership of Wellfleet founder, William Seiffert). The hardware consists of ATM Ethernet switches and a central management console. This runs central control software, the distributed relation manager. If an end station announces itself by broadcast or multicast, the packet is forwarded to the distributed relation manager which reads the Layer 2 and Layer 3 information and is able to decide to which VLAN the end station should be allocated. A VLAN corresponds either to a logical subnetwork (IP, IPX, DECnet, AppleTalk) or to a broadcast domain (LAT, NetBIOS).

The switch ports no longer need to be assigned to specific VLANS by manual configuration they automatically learn the available Layer 2 and Layer 3 subnetworks from the connected end stations. The VLAN allocation may be changed manually later, if required.

One restriction with this concept is the fact that all devices which operate a non-routable protocol are automatically grouped in a common VLAN: a common VLAN for all LAT users, a common VLAN for all NetBIOS users. Under some circumstances, it may be necessary to perform a subsequent division into different VLANS. However, in the event of a move, this means reconfiguration at the distributed relation manager.

12.3 Conclusion

Virtual LANs are still are at the start of their development. All implementations with the exception of IEEE 802.10 SDE are proprietary. If any product could be described as mature, it is pure LAN switching, and even this has little operational experience. Virtual routing and building up topologically distributed logical subnetworks are not mature technology with the products available at present. 30 to 70% of all manufacturers' approaches consist of white papers.

However, there is no doubt that we have started on the way to the longed for decoupling of physical and logical network structures. Compatible VLAN concepts for different products from one manufacturer (slide-in hubs, LAN switches, routers, ATM switches) are often not yet available.

Building up of completely distributed VLANs means that the network is operated with less load efficiency: if, in every physical subnetwork (LAN), any stations are connected to any logical subnetworks, virtually no load separation is possible. The consequence is the enforced changeover to higher backbone capacity (i.e., ATM).

When using VLAN functions to make life a bit easier during network operation, we automatically ask whether there is any compatibility between different manufacturers products. Unfortunately the idea of simply connecting different LAN switch manufacturers products is false. So far, all manufacturers' concepts are proprietary. Even the information on which packet belongs to which Layer 2 or Layer-3-VLAN is provided in at least four different procedures:

- exchange of address tables

- time division multiplexing

- proprietary tagging (packet expansion with VLAN ID entry)

- group formation and tagging in accordance with the standard specification IEEE 802.10

Only last approach (Bay Networks, Cisco, Digital) offers any chance of compatibility.

In all cases, a network operator should be able to answer the following questions before deciding to use VLANs in a company network:

- How are broadcast domains formed?

- What sort of load distribution and control actually takes place?

- What are the consequences of replacing router concepts by VLANs for security and access protection?

- How easy are the newly installed VLANs to manage and maintain?

- Can users be consistently connected to another VLAN through a "Drag and Drop" management application?

- How do the installed VLAN functions affect the performance in the switches used?

- How do the installed VLAN functions affect the user data rate in partial networks and in the backbone?

- What migration steps to other products with higher performance or to product combinations (slide-in hubs, switches, routers) are possible with the installed VLANs?

- Does any manufacturer offer a consistent, scaleable product line?

- Do the products used or planned conform to the standard and do they leave open the option of moving to products made by other manufacturers?

As always, the following general principle applies to all networks:

If you see it, and it's there: it's REAL
If you don't see it, and it's there: it's TRANSPARENT
If you see it, and it's not there: it's VIRTUAL
If you don't see it, and it's not there: it's GONE!

Which is the same as saying: in virtual networks with ATM backbones, fault detection is not going to get any easier.

13 | LAN-WAN Connection

A key feature of router applications is the LAN-WAN interconnection. The WAN connections which can be implemented via routers are described. Some of these link-ups are also possible via various bridge products (X.21, Frame Relay). To avoid duplicate treatment of the WAN subject area, the possibilities with bridge products are mentioned in each case where they exist in addition to routers.

Within the public network domain, many countries, including Germany, allow only the procedures approved by the postal authorities (PTTs, in Germany Deutsche Post AG, TELEKOM) to be used. In data communication these are international ITU-TS recommendations which Deutsche Telekom has endorsed, in particular a long list of so-called "X standards" of the ITU-TS (formerly CCITT), where the "X" identifies the public data network area. The X recommendations set higher data transmission standards than the much simpler V recommendations (the best known probably being V.24). Against this background, two long-used ITU-TS standards, X.21 and X.25, are considered first.

Two newer standard-based procedures that are attempting to establish themselves on the strength of higher-capacity transmission are Frame Relay and ISDN. They are discussed after X.21 and X.25.

13.1 Point-to-Point Connection: X.21

The X.21 interface offers a Level 1 service in accordance with the OSI reference model. The X.21 protocol can be used as a leased line service or a dial-up
connection. This connection type is possible via both routers and bridges.
Most routers and remote bridges use dedicated connections for performance
and monitoring reasons. Because of the universal possibilities and high service
quality in comparison to other postal services, this service has the best
chances of further development in the future as a universal interface for data,
voice, and video.

X.21 defines the interface between the so-called DCE (Data Circuit
Terminating Equipment, endpoint of the network) and DTE (Data Terminal
Equipment, endpoint of the user system). Figure 13.1 shows the interface plan.

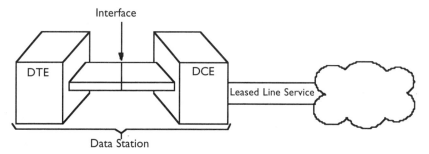

Figure 13.1 X.21 Interface

The X.21 protocol is a synchronous (symmetrical) protocol, i.e., DCE and
DTE behave identically. Coded character strings are sent, so an X.21 interface
must have a higher level of intelligence than a simple pin-to-pin transmission
functionality (V.24). Instead of allocating individual send or receive functions
to a pin-like V.24 or its American pendant RS-232C, it allocates the functions
to individual code strings. This naturally makes it much more universally
applicable than V.24.

For transmission capacities up to 9.6 kbit/sec the ITU-TS recommendation
X.27 (V.11, Balanced Interchange Circuit) is stipulated for the electrical interface on the DCE side, and X.27 or X.26 (V.10, Unbalanced Interchange Circuit)
on the DTE side. For higher transmission capacity, X.27 must be used on the
DTE side too.

X.21 includes various diagnostic functions which in case of error can record the reason why a connection was not made.

Disadvantages of using X.21 are:

- No monitoring information can be transferred during data transmission.

- Encryption must take place between DTE and DCE.

- As a rule, communication always occurs between DCE and DTE. For DTE-DTE or DCE-DCE communication, the DTE/DCE Master/Slave protocol must be changed and special crossed-wire connection cable must be used.

X.21 is not yet widespread in the USA, as the more economically implemented RS-232C is often used. Established X standards are compiled in summary form in Figures 13.2a and 4.66.

ITU-TS Recommendation	Description
X.1	International user classes of service in public data network: class 8 (2400 bps); class 9 (4800 bps); class 10 (9600 bps); or class 11 (48000 bps)
X.2	International user facilities in public data networks
X.3	Packet assembly/disassembly (PAD) facility in a public data network; lists options and defaults for interactive asynchronous terminal connection to X.25 packet networks
X.4	General structure of signals of InternationalAlphabet No. 5 (IA5) code for data transmission over public data networks (IA5 is described in CCITT V.3)
X.20	Interface between data terminal equipment (DTE) and data circuit-terminating equipment (DCE) for async transmission services on public data networks
X.20 onwards	V.21-compatible interface between DTE and DCE for async transmission services on public data network
X.21	General-purpose interface between DTE and DCE for synchronous operation on public data networks

Figure 13.2a Standards of the ITU-T X Series

ITU-TS Recommendation	Description
X.21 onwards	For use on public data networks by DTE that are designed to interface to synchronous V-Series modems
X.24	List of definitions of interchange circuits between DTE and DCE on public data networks
X.25	Interface between DTE and DCE for terminals operating in the packet mode on public data networks
X.26	Electrical characteristics for unbalanced double-current interchange circuits for data communications equipment
X.27	Electrical characteristics for balanced double-current interchange circuits for data communications equipment

Figure 13.2b Standards of the ITU-T X Series (cont.)

In-House Expansions

As a bridge or router connection to the LAN has at least MAC functionality, the simple X.21 definition is insufficient for the LAN interconnection via WAN. To satisfy the MAC layer functionality, all manufacturers implement a kind of add-on protocol (ISO OSI Level 1 and 2a) on X.21. The early solutions here were in-house protocols, frequently a "slimmed-down" HDLC. As so often, the result was incompatibility between the various manufacturers (see Figure 13.3). As it often happens that when different locations using historically different equipment are connected, the network operators are seriously affected by the incompatibility that results. This is the reason for the IETF's initiative to create implementor-compatible possibilities for LAN-WAN integrated networks. This approach is discussed in more detail in section 13.5 "Point-to-Point-Protocol."

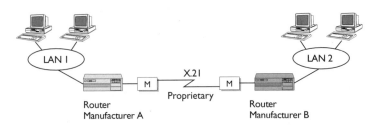

Figure 13.3: X.21 connections across different manufacturers' bridges or routers

13.2 Packet Switching: X.25

X.25 is a packet-switched network standard which has become established in many countries, though with specific national variants in each case. X.25 networks are installed in Australia, Austria, Belgium, Canada, the UK, France, Germany, Hong Kong, Republic of Ireland, Italy, Japan, Mexico, the Netherlands, Portugal, Singapore, Russia, Spain, South Africa, Switzerland, and the U.S.A. Current implementations comply with the 1984 X.25 standard or the expanded 1988 standard. Deutsche Telekom's X.25 service is known by the name Datex-P. The X.25 service is intended purely for data transmission (no voice or video transfer).

X.25 implements the bottom three layers of the ISO reference model and is supported by routers. This case involves the use of two different protocol stacks such as TCP/IP-X.25, DECnet-X.25, IPX-X.25, etc. As the conversion of two different protocol stacks (if only to Layer 3) causes a gateway association, the term "gateway router" is often used in the context of X.25 routing. The connection is made across a router pair, which is installed in each case at the LAN-WAN internetworking point between two remote LANs. In X.25 connections the LAN Layer 3 is not exchanged, but packed in the X.25 packet. Thus in the context of X.25 as a LAN-WAN connection protocol there are often representations that place X.25 at Layer 2, although the X.25 addressing is clearly recognizable as network addressing.

The interface between DTE and DCE is defined analogously to X.21, but for Layers 1 to 3 rather than Layer 1 only. Layers 1 to 3 are implemented in all DTEs and DCEs. DTEs can be hosts, individuals end stations or multiple end stations (Line concentration over multiplexer). The end-to-end connection is implemented as a virtual connection.

The X.25 connection uses the X.21 protocol at Layer 1. Within X.25 it is always used as a leased line, not a dial-up connection. Support of the speeds

- 2400 bit/sec,

- 4800 bit/sec,

- 9600 bit/sec and

- 48000 bit/sec,

is obligatory. Any speed which is possible via X.21 can be supported optionally (e.g., in Germany 64 kbit/sec is an option). The connection is full duplex (DTE and DCE can transmit from both sides simultaneously, independently of each other). The X.21 protocol works principally as HDLC (at Layer 1).

Because of the limited spread of X.21 in the USA, a variant was accepted as interim standard: the X.21bis protocol, which corresponds to the RS-232C.

Layer 2 comprises three protocols: LAP (Link Access Protocol), LAPB (Link Access Protocol Balanced), and MLP (Multilink Procedure). The first protocol was LAP; it is comparable to the HDLC Asynchronous Response Mode (ARM). As the protocol showed inconsistencies in a few procedure elements, a revised version LAPB was developed (similar to HDLC ABM, Asynchronous Balanced Mode). MLP is an enhanced protocol, which offers the option of transmitting simultaneously across several links. Analogous to the LAN technology, data at Layer 2 is framed in control information, so-called HDLC frames. HDLC defines a strict separation between data frames and control frames. Data frames are sent numbered; control frames are sent unnumbered. There are no mixed forms. With the implemented control functions, HDLC provides a high service quality in relation to freedom from errors (transmission errors, frame loss).

The maximum supported frame length can be between 128 bytes (obligatory), 1 kbyte, 2 kbytes and 4 kbytes (all three optional). A transmission size of 128 bytes between different X.25 networks is prescribed.

Layer 3 contains procedures for:

- Call set-up,

- Data transmission,

- Interruption,

- Reset,

- Restart, and

- Call clearing.

The call set-up takes place from the sending DTE via the sending DCE and receiving DCE to the receiving DTE. After successful set-up, a logical connection (logical channel) is established, which is independent of the physical line connection (it can be changed within an active connection). Errors are handled separately for individual logical channels with a "Reset, Clear, Restart" sequence. Some implementations support diagnostic packets, which display certain error situations which cannot be corrected at network level. These packets activate error correction mechanisms corresponding to higher layers. The end-to-end forwarding of the packets via the X.25 network is route-optimized according to an internal X.25 routing procedure, in which there can be one or more X.25 nodes (X.25 switches) on the route between the sending and receiving DTE, transparent to the user. The routing procedure is not specified in the standard. It is implemented differently according to the manufacturer as static routing or dynamic routing depending on the switching product.

The maximum supported data packet sequence is 8 (non-extended mode) or 128 (extended mode) frames. Several data packets can be combined in one packet (data concentration).

A single X.25 interface can theoretically support a total of e.g., 4095 logical channels, with a maximum frame length of 2 kbytes on each channel and 128 successive packets (which may have to be buffered). Most X.25 switches are not yet capable of this at present. The transmission performance actually supported varies greatly depending on the product.

For connecting multiple X.25 networks, the ITU-TS recommendation X.75 "Terminal and Transmit Call Control Procedures and Data Transfer System on International Circuits Between Packet Switched Data Networks" applies. It defines in turn the interface between the X.25 networks. The interface between two X.25 networks is a kind of bridge called STE (Signal Terminal Equipment). Electrical, functional, and procedural properties are defined. As for X.25, the communication is by exchange of data and control packets. The X.25 definition applies for the packet format.

Differences

X.25 implementations occur in various products with differing complexity. Some DTEs support only a single fixed packet size (128 bytes) and permanently preset parameter values. Others support variable packet sizes and differing parameter configurations. Some DTEs support only LAPB, others LAPB, LAP, and MLP. The user must make sure that DTE and DCE support mutually corresponding values. Possible configurations for the terminal link-up are shown in Figure 13.4.

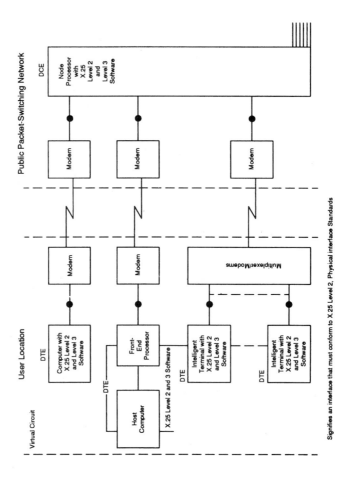

Figure 13.4 End Station Connection to X.25 networks

Bridges or Routers for X.25 Connections?

X.25 can be used considerably better with routable protocols than with bridge functions; routing complete destination networks can be mapped to X.25 dial-up numbers of the corresponding LAN access router. This does not work with bridge connections, since interconnection is based simply on the individual

MAC addresses. The few bridge products which support X.25 as protocol therefore, mostly only allow definition of point-to-point connections which use the X.25 service (lower costs).

Important Router Functions

In the context of X.25 as a LAN-WAN connection protocol, a few functional characteristics are important:

- The assignment of LAN connections to X.25 dial-up numbers should be possible per logical subnetwork.

- For multi-protocol operation, it can be desirable to assign different protocols (IP, IPX, DDP, etc.) to different X.25 channels, to achieve better capacity management.

- For multi-protocol operation with differing time-critical protocols (NetBIOS, IP, IPX), it is desirable to be able to prioritize individual protocols.

- When capacity requirements rise and selective capacity increases are required, concentration of X.25 channels should be supported for a protocol.

- With dynamic channel allocation, it is important to be able to limit the maximum number of virtual channels per protocol, so that in a peak load situation caused particularly by one protocol, the other protocols are not "starved."

- For security restrictions, the router should support the formation of Closed User Groups.

- The number of channels supported, and the X.25 options

  - incoming calls only
  - outgoing calls only
  - incoming and outgoing calls

  vary significantly with the manufacturer.

- Data compression is just as important for X.25 as for all other WAN link-up protocols. There is header compression (e.g., for IP) and data compression. In the latter case, it is important that data compression is supported for all desired routable protocols, so that the relevant routing header is preserved.

- There are two IETF specifications for compatibility in the encapsulation of LAN protocols: RFC 877 (IP) and RFC 1356 (other LAN protocols). Only if these RFCs are supported can the relevant router be connected with other manufacturers' routers via X.25. Otherwise all X.25 routers in a LAN-WAN integrated network must be from the same manufacturer.

Summary

Packet switching in accordance with the ITU-TS X.25 recommendation is presently still the most flexible method of digital long-distance transmission. Data is optimally routed via the X.25 network: both data concentration and line concentration are possible and can implement efficient resource distribution. In comparison in particular to circuit-switched services, advantages and disadvantages can be summarized as follows:

Advantages of the X.25 Service:

- Fault recognition
- error handling at network level; hence
- low error rate and
- high reliability; also
- low processing time,
- efficient transmission of a wide variety of data types, and
- overload monitoring; hence
- low overload in switching nodes,
- internationally widespread.

Disadvantages of X.25 are in the following areas:

- Complexity of the necessary equipment (DTE, DCE),
- costs for hardware and maintenance,

- necessary outlay for planning and configuration,

- necessary outlay for "reconfiguration" at intervals, corresponding to current capacity requirements,

- software support at higher level,

- Operation is only economical "at whatever the capacity limit."

Trends

In the 1988 X.25 standard, enhancements were introduced for

- Call diversion,

- Address expansion (20 bytes instead of 16 bytes).

The address recommendation was also included in the ISO standard for Connectionless Network Service (CLNS ISO 8348, Addendum 2). While X.25 traditionally works in terms of connections, there are trends in ISO standardization towards a connectionless service (ISO-OSI network levels always tend to use the datagram service). However, a connection-oriented service is still valid at present as ISO standard with X.25 (ISO 7498). Current discussions for further X.25 revisions concentrate on achieving greater compatibility between the individual X.25 standards of different nations.

In the packet-switching network environment, there is a need as in other data communications environs for more and faster transmission. Most recently Frame Relay based on the LAPD protocol is seeking acceptance as a new packet service suitable for faster transmission. This is no longer a matter "only" of data transmission: it also involves video and voice transmission, bulk data transfer and coupling of remote high-speed LANs (over 100 Mbit/sec).

13.3 ISDN

ISDN (Integrated Services Digital Network, or in user jargon: I Still Don't kNow) has become very well-established in the last two years as a LAN-WAN interconnection service. By definition, ISDN did not want to be restricted to data transmission, but rather it intended to provide integrated data, voice, and video transmission. It is not the subject of this book to discuss the objectives, advantages, and disadvantages of this integration. In this framework ISDN is only mentioned in principle as a long-range technology with the advantages and disadvantages of a LAN-WAN interconnection.

13.3.1 Standards, Function, and Areas of Application

By now ISDN is offered in most areas, even very small places, by most PTTs. In contrast to the original aim of selling broadband ISDN with 70 to 600 Mbps capacity for modern services, ISDN has gained market acceptance as a narrow band ISDN with a basic capacity of 64 kbps.

Standards, Function

The aim of ISDN is to bring together the previous different networks for data, voice, and video transmission in a common public transmission network to which every user has access through a common standardized interface. ITU-TS recommendations which relate to ISDN are set down in the I Series (I Recommendations). Figure 13.5 shows an overview plan.

Important standards for Frame Relay are [ITU-TS01], [ITU-TS02], and [ITU-TS03]:

I.121   The recommendation gives guidelines for the development of broadband standards in the ITU-TS development period 1989 to 1992.

I.122   Describes the underlying architecture and interaction mechanisms with other packet switching networks for the development of standards for ISDN-based packet switching in the ITU-TS development period 1989 to 1992.

I.441   Defines ISDN reference configurations within the framework of the user-ISDN interfaces, in particular two different concepts: functional groups and reference points (interfaces between network devices).

Instead of DTE and DCE, the following reference points are defined: TE1 (Terminal Equipment type 1) as an end system with standard ISDN interface, TE2 (Terminal Equipment type 2, requires a TA) as an end system with non-ISDN interface (V.24, X.21), TA (Terminal Adapter) as an interface adapter for linking one or more TE2 devices to the network (similar to a protocol converter). On the network side, NT2 (Network Termination) is defined as an intelligent device on the user interface to the ISDN network (multiplexer, switch), NT1 as a device with switching functionality on the network operator's interface to the user network. These clear definitions are rather more complicated when put into practice, and have led to very different ISDN devices such as ISDN end system, non-ISDN data end system, ISDN workstation, ISDN telephone, etc.

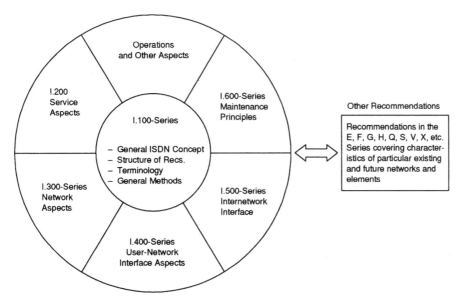

Note: Models, reference configurations, tools, methods, are contained in the appropriate I-Series Recommendations

Figure 13.5 Overview of ITU-T Recommendations in the I Series

The reference configuration specifies two channel types:

• B channel as a transparent channel with a capacity of 64 kbit/sec, which transfers the user data, whether voice or data, independently of the protocol.

• D channel as a non-transparent digital channel with 16 or 64 kbit/sec, which is used together with one or more B channels for transferring telephony and packet-switched data which requires only low bandwidth.

A basic ISDN combination is the Basic Rate Interface 2B+D (BRI), consisting of two B channels (64 kbit/sec) and one D channel (16 or 64 kbit/sec). The bit rate of this configuration amounts altogether to 192 kbit/sec, with 144 kbit/sec available to the user (64 + 64 + 16). The 16 kbps D channel is used for control information (signaling of call set-up, monitoring, call clearing). Some new applications can also use this channel for data transmission at 9.6 kbps. It is questionable however, how long the use of the D channel for data transmission will remain essentially free of charge. With intensified use of the D channel for data transmission, a tariff approximating to ISDN charges can be expected. A higher bit rate ISDN combination is the Primary Rate Interface 30B+D (PRI), consisting of 30 B channels and one D channel with 64 kbps (30 x 64 + 64). The basis for this combination is the CEPT Specification for 2,048 Mbit/sec 2B+D which is offered via the S0 interface, and 30B+D via the S2M interface. A router which does not support these interfaces must be given ISDN capability with a Terminal Adapter (as in I.441).

In the access procedure, ISDN does not differ significantly from the good old telephone service: The ISDN suppliers simply install a special ISDN telephone box at the internetworking point between WAN and LAN (usually the CC). The ISDN router is attached directly by cable to the ISDN box—if it has an S0 interface. As in the telephone system, the call is set up by dialing an ISDN number and circuit-switched through. However, call set-up is considerably faster than with an analogue telephone, taking maybe one to two seconds, so that LAN protocols which can cope with this turnaround are required. Automatic call set-up is achieved with the signaling protocol of the D channel. Call clearing is by the application, or, for inactive connections, with a time control (Inactivity Timer). Both the ISDN dial-up and the automatic termination of a call must be implemented as a router software function. If this is not done, the network operator has no choice but to fall back on a terminal adapter function.

Scenarios Application

LAN-WAN coupling with routers via B channels is now offered by many manufacturers and has gained market acceptance. The use of ISDN can essentially be divided into three areas, which in the given order helped to establish ISDN:

- Backup connection

- Bandwidth on demand

- Dial on demand

Dial Backup: For tariff or time reasons, a different service is taken for normal data transmission, and ISDN provides backup communications capacity in case of faults. This solution is attractive, as

- the basic monthly charge for an ISDN line is very low

- the protocol overhead for ISDN is very low (e.g., compared to X.25)

- an ISDN line can be operated as backup for several other interfaces/connections if it can be assumed that only one of these connections will fail at a time

Bandwidth-on-Demand: For occasional capacity excesses, a capacity increase is often not justified for the service in normal use (e.g., two parallel 64k dedicated connections would have to be converted to a 2 Mbps line). Switching in ISDN channels for the limited peak load duration can be implemented much more economically. But how does the "Bandwidth on demand" function know whether a demand situation is present? A usage threshold is defined for the normal service, and the ISDN connection is additionally activated when this threshold is exceeded. Once usage falls below the threshold again, the ISDN connection deactivates.

Dial-on-Demand: For sporadic communication with low time requirement (three to four hours per day in all), ISDN can be the most economical alternative as the basic service (for normal transmission). A call set-up occurs on transmission demand, a call clearing on inactivity. Especially in the latter case, well-devised spoofing is necessary if dynamically-routed LAN protocols are to be used. The spoofing problem will be dealt with in more detail later. ISDN is often worthwhile as the basic communication connection for firms with many small branches in which not more than four to eight devices are linked up to the network with limited needs for file transfer, download of status information or central database access.

The user must decide on one of the above options when configuring an ISDN interface. This means that if a network operator wants to safeguard a dedicated line with ISDN and at the same time wants to switch in ISDN for peak load, he or she needs two ISDN interfaces on the router! The same applies if the user wants to use an interface which is normally operated with dial-on-demand as a backup for a very important dedicated line. Only a few router manufacturers support multiple configuration of the various application options for a single ISDN interface:

- one ISDN interface as backup for several dedicated lines

- one ISDN interface configured as backup and as bandwidth-on-demand

- several ISDN interfaces combined in a pool and used according to pre-defined priorities for several dedicated lines as backup and/or as band-width-on-demand.

However, there are signs of further such development of router capabilities, at least from the high-end manufacturers in the ISDN market.

High Speed ISDN

A high speed ISDN, intended for very much higher bit rates than CEPT and T1 is B-ISDN (Broadband ISDN), which combines bandwidths of 155 Mbit/sec and 600 Mbit/sec and can therefore cope with high-speed requirements such as television, video conferencing, video telephone, video, and graphics transmission (or it could, if these options were available). Further plans are directed towards 32-44 Mbit/sec (H2), 60-70 Mbit/sec (H3) or 132-138 Mbit/sec (H4). A standard developed in parallel to B-ISDN by Bellcore is SONET (Synchronous Optical Network) with bit rates between 51 Mbit/sec and 82.5 Gbit/sec. SONET is comparable to B-ISDN in approach and in the technology applied. Both processes work asynchronously (ATM) instead of using conventional synchronous technology (X.25, LAPB), increasing throughput significantly. B-ISDN's practical implementation today is in ATM.

Fast packet transmission methods such as Frame Relay or fast packet switching require the corresponding availability of B-ISDN/ATM at present for the use of high-speed lines (or are based directly on dedicated lines).

Product Situation

Since ISDN developed first as a niche market, there are a variety of router manufacturers who offer products that are very strongly ISDN-oriented and have only a very limited number of LAN interfaces, e.g., Alicante, Ascend, Bintec, Shiva, or Telebit, in addition to the many PC packages which are mostly based in some form on the Novell MPR. The classic router manufacturers such as ACC, Bay Networks , Cisco, 3Com, or Proteon entered the ISDN market relatively late.

13.3.2 Functional Requirements of ISDN Routers

ISDN may offer an economical and flexible solution for a range of LAN applications, but in larger networks ISDN can only be used flexibly and efficiently if the routers used support some functional requirements. These are discussed below.

Protocol and LAN Support

Not every MAC process is supported by any given manufacturer for a bridge or router interconnection with ISDN. Some manufacturers only support Ethernet-ISDN or Token Ring-ISDN products. Not every manufacturer supports multi-protocol routing such that logical networks of different protocol environments could be mapped on to different ISDN dial-up numbers. Sometimes it is only possible to map all routed protocols between two locations on to the same ISDN dial-up number.

Interfaces

For standard ISDN coupling, the router must support the S0 or S2M interface. Sometimes, however, only V.35 or X.21 interfaces are offered, which must be given ISDN capability with Terminal Adapters. With increased capacity requirements, channel trunking is a desirable expansion. It then needs to be investigated whether a planned product is able to trunk at all, and if so, up to what number of channels.

Euro-ISDN

European ITU organizations have agreed on a common ISDN procedure which is operated under the name Euro-ISDN. This includes in particular the D channel signaling procedure DSS1 (Digital Signaling System Number 1). However, the assumption that a Euro-ISDN license can also be used throughout Europe is incorrect. A German Euro-ISDN license does not mean that the equipment may be operated in Great Britain, nor does a French license mean that the equipment is permitted in the Netherlands. In brief, the certification must be carried out for every European country by the national institutes. Some countries are accommodating and draw up the certificate relatively informally if another European certificate is submitted, while other countries perform a further full certification even when certification exists for several European countries. This is done at a price, of course. The operator of an international network must make sure that an ISDN router is licensed for all countries in which he or she wants to use the equipment.

PPP Support

Like X.21, ISDN simply defines a transmission method but no Data Link Layer which corresponds to the MAC function. The ISDN implementations in turn therefore need in-house expansions—or a more extensive standard protocol such as PPP—to enable multi-vendor communication. Instead of PPP, some European manufacturers use X.25 to establish compatibility: the LAN packet is packed in X.25, sent via ISDN, and unpacked again at the other end. But both PPP and X.25 mean that all in-house expansions, such as filtering and spoofing, which make significant contributions to efficiency or make ISDN at all economical, can no longer be used.

Link Control

On economic grounds, ISDN as dial-on-demand requires not only automatic call set-up, but also clearing of a connection when no more data is being sent. The call clearing should be configurable and time-controlled. The router has to keep a separate timer for this, which can be set by the network operator. A common timer value is 30 seconds, for example. The ISDN router monitors the connection for activity, i.e., it checks constantly whether there is still data on the line. If no further data packet arrives within an interval of 30 seconds for transmission over the ISDN connection, it is cleared.

Callback

By their nature, switched networks always pose a security risk: anyone can dial in. So for security reasons it is often necessary to use automatic callback to prevent unwanted intruders who try to get into the company network via ISDN dial-in with manipulated sender numbers.

Compression

Compressing data to make better use of the existing bandwidth is worthwhile up to a transmit rate of 64 kbps or 128 kbps (the cost of compression is less than the increased throughput achieved by the compression). For large data volumes, routers which also support compression for ISDN are therefore advantageous.

13.3.3 ISDN and LAN Protocols: Spoofing

While ISDN can be an economical alternative, it can also generate alarmingly high costs. A few catastrophic cases: after router installation, 50,000 DM ISDN costs in a month for a large German user; ISDN telephone bill of 40,000 SFR in a month after commissioning of ISDN routers in a large Swiss network; 70,000 FFR which a French broker paid for three days' connection to the Tokyo exchange, although he didn't transfer a single byte of data.

As ISDN service rates are based on connections and time, every call set-up and every time unit is charged. So imagine ISDN using bridge connections with Spanning Tree, source routing or router connections with dynamic routing protocols. Every 1 to 3 seconds, a Spanning Tree HELLO packet goes across the ISDN line, every route discovery is forwarded if the user doesn't set a selective filter at MAC address level, every 30 seconds RIP, SAP, DECnet routing updates go across the line. With NetWare, as well as routing updates there are also other control packets which are sent regularly from servers (see also Figure 13.6).

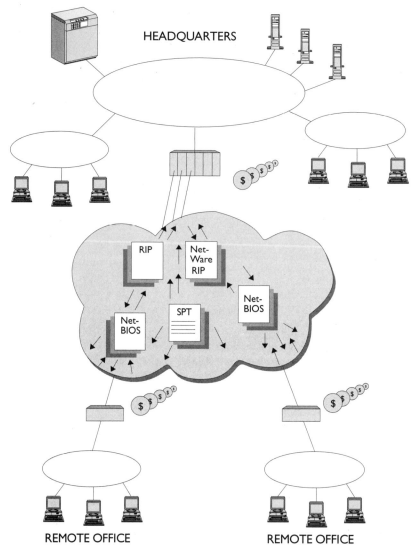

Figure 13.6: Problems with ISDN: Routing Updates and HELLOs

Spanning Tree via ISDN leads practically to a standing connection, routing updates lead at least every time to a clock pulse charge (call set-up).

If there are no changes or error situations in the network, the described update packets are actually superfluous and should therefore be kept out of the ISDN network. At the same time however, it must be ensured that faults and changes are noted as quickly as possible if they occur. Spoofing looks after both: to put it simply, spoofing is a conjurer's box which leads the LAN to believe that everything is normal, somehow suppressing really "normal" updates, but notifying actual changes.

Which packets should be spoofed? At least route discovery so far as possible, Spanning Tree HELLOs and the routing updates of all operated protocols such as IP, RIP, NetWare RIP, OSPF, NLSP, DRP, IS-IS updates; also other regular overhead packets such as NetWare SAP, NetWare Watchdog (a kind of idle polling of client sessions), NetWare Serialization (License number checking). Routing update packets, which only have to be suppressed, cause fewer problems than, for example the NetWare idle polling, since for this, like SNA polling, the spoofing must be remote and local: The server's local router must answer the watchdog packets positively, the remote router must send watchdog packets to every active client. Three manufacturer-specific methods are used in spoofing (see also Figure 13.7):

- Interval control

- Triggers

- Piggyback

Interval control: Some manufacturers (such as ACC) simply increase and standardize the time interval for update packets, to 30 minutes for instance. While this does save on ISDN line costs, it also results in errors not being noticed for 30 minutes.

Triggers: Many implementations use event triggers (e.g., Alicante, 3Com, Telebit, Shiva), meaning that all updates which don't cause a change to the routing tables or Spanning Tree are suppressed. When a routing table is changed, the next update is also forwarded via the ISDN connection. When triggers are used, the question is how often a particular ISDN router reacts to events: once per second, once in 10 seconds? The reaction speed here depends crucially on the trigger function implementation.

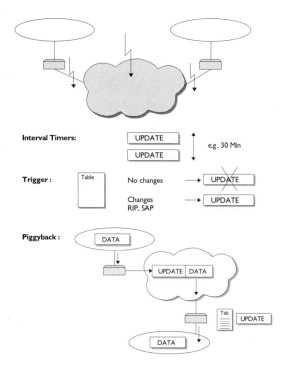

Figure 13.7: Spoofing methods in ISDN

Piggyback: Some manufacturers optimize the line costs by appending the update as a piggyback on the next data packet (e.g., Cisco). This can mean an extension of the time within which faults or network changes become known, while it saves the costs of a separate call set-up. If no packets at all are sent in the update direction, there can be no update, either.

To avoid the whole spoofing scenario as far as possible, static routing for WAN connections must be used. At least all routing update packets can then be suppressed. Not, however, other overhead packets such as NetWare Watchdog or similar.

13.3.4 ISDN with PPP

Network users who operate ISDN in WAN are apparently also interested at times in compatibility between manufacturers. Functional enhancements such as filters and spoofing have to be abandoned for this. PPP on ISDN should be used in accordance with RFC 1618 (May 1994). This document recommends a few alternatives from the rich variety of existing implementations. As the B channel is by definition a point-to-point connection, PPP can well be operated via ISDN. Theoretically, it would also work for the D channel, which, unfortunately, can often only be used until the next local ISDN switch. The reference points to which the following descriptions refer are shown in Figure 13.8.

Figure 13.8: Reference points of an ISDN configuration

Requirements on the Physical Level

PPP uses ISDN channels like bit-oriented or byte-oriented synchronous lines, which must be full duplex. The lines can be dedicated or circuit switched. Data is transferred bytewise; part-bytes are not supported. The byte-oriented data stream occurs at reference point R or T. PPP requires no control signaling. However, if it is present, the control signaling can be used by an implementation to communicate more efficiently.

The coding is not explicitly prescribed and is ultimately left to the manufacturer. As the D channel LAPD requires NRZ coding at reference point T, the use of NRZ in the B channel is suggested as default. Frames then become exchangeable between B and D channels. If the coding is configurable, NRZI is recommended for improved efficiency so that as few 1 values as possible have to be transferred via the B channel. An implementation may also wait and see which coding the distant station uses, in order to adapt automatically. This option is particularly important for devices with primary rate interface, as the 30 possible B channels could well require different codings. To find out a partner router's coding, a router can send LCP options. It must abandon this attempt after 59 seconds at the latest. However, the RFC recommends not exceeding a limit of 30 seconds.

When using Terminal Adapters, which according to V.120 are used as a terminal equipment interface, asynchronous HDLC framing is expected at the reference point R. The Terminal Adapter converts this into a synchronous data stream. Unfortunately, V.120 uses a special framing to find out the send rate, which looks like Frame Relay; it is therefore advisable from the PPP angle not to use it.

For operating several parallel channels, the "Bandwidth-On-Demand Interoperability Group" has made a suggestion called "BONDING," which uses a special initialization. This conflicts with the relatively simple PPP technique for finding out the coding. Use of the PPP Multilink Standard is therefore recommended instead of BONDING.

Framing

If there is no preconfiguration, bit-synchronous HDLC must be used at first on B channels for the initial call set-up. If a preconfiguration can be selected, RFC 1618 recommends byte-synchronous HDLC at the reference point T. Byte-synchronous HDLC must use NRZ coding.

For D channels, no data transmission is supported as default. If this is nonetheless possible by explicit configuration, an encapsulation framing such as "PPP via Frame Relay" or "PPP via X.25" can be used.

Although HDLC, LAPB, LAPD, and LAPF would be distinguishable, a single ISDN channel should use only one framing according to RFC 1618, and not several in parallel.

A PPP-compatible implementation is not obliged to support recognition of different framings, or actually switch back and forth between different framings.

Out-of-band Signaling

Experience has shown that the LLC Information Element (LLC IE) is not reliably forwarded from one end to the other, as the compatibility of the switches used on the ISDN path leaves much to be desired, and the providers' service offers differ too much. An implementation may therefore not require that the LLC IE is transferred. Furthermore, there is not yet a fixed LLC IE value for PPP.

Configuration

The LCP options for synchronous communication should be set for ISDN connections: the standard LCP sync defaults.

The frame size MRU is 1500 or more. To avoid fragmentation, the Layer 3 packet length should also not be set higher. Instead of fixed retransmission intervals, the exponential backoff method is recommended. The repetition timer should begin with 250 milliseconds and increment to 3 seconds.

Implementations which support automatic redialing (Demand Dialing, Redialing), should not go on repeating indefinitely (endless loop), but stop at some point. Examples of this are: the use of the exponential backoff method; deletion of all packets from the receive queues if the call set-up has failed; deletion of the output queue when there is an overload.

13.3.5 Conclusion

With its favorable rates, ISDN has gained market acceptance in the three areas mentioned (Backup, Bandwidth-on-Demand, Dial-on-Demand). However, its use must be very carefully planned and monitored, particularly in multi-protocol operation, dynamic routing and larger integrated networks.

As a switched procedure, ISDN should be counted among the risk services. Security measures must be activated to prevent unauthorized entry from outside.

Euro-ISDN is a good initiative (by the maxim: better an initiative than no initiative), but has still not brought about the compatibility to create a universal multinational communications capability.

13.4 Frame Relay, Cell Relay, and Fast Packet Switching

Frame Relay (FR) and Fast Packet Switching, and, in this context also Cell Relay, are newly-arising de facto standards (standard approaches from the international standardization bodies), which claim to be able to replace the traditional X.25 in future. The terms Frame Relay, Cell Relay, and Fast Packet Switching are all related in a way, are not entirely uniquely defined, and so are sometimes loosely used.

Some basic distinguishing features are therefore listed here for their further use in this book:

- Frame Relay is based on a digital frame with a format in accordance with the Frame Relay Protocol Specification which belongs at Layer 2 of the OSI reference model. Frame Relay can use Cell Relay as an underlying transmission method, and accordingly also—not quite correctly—be called Fast Packet Switching.

- Cell Relay or Cell Switching defines a transmission method in accordance with ITU-TS, with fixed length blocks, at Layer 1 of the OSI reference model. Individual blocks can be identified by set separators.

- Fast Packet Switching is a packet service at Layer 3 of the OSI reference model, and uses Cell Relay. A fast packet switching service of this kind is e.g., SMDS (Switched Multimegabit Data Service) or IEEE 802.6 DQDB. However, the pure Cell Relay transmission method at Layer 1 is also sometimes referred to as Fast Packet Switching.

Fast Packet Switching should not be lumped together with Packet Switching such as X.25, even if the name and concept seem very similar. Both services take application data, make packets out of it, and forward them over a backbone network of switching nodes until they eventually reach the desired destination station. But this is all they have in common. As SMDS has not become particularly established in the market up to now, and cannot foreseeably compete with ATM in the WAN, there will be no further consideration of SMDS at this point.

None of the specified techniques (Frame Relay, Cell Relay, Fast Packet Switching) should be confused or equated with X.25 packet switching. None of the techniques is based on the ITU-TS X.25 recommendation. Cell Relay, though used by a few Frame Relay providers, essentially belongs more with ATM than with Frame Relay: it was therefore dealt with in Chapter 11.

Frame Relay (FR) has become established on the strength of the continually improving line/transmission qualities in the WAN field and the growing inter-location LAN networking via WAN services. It is chiefly intended for the

LAN-WAN-LAN connection, rather than as a replacement for classic end stations host connections via X.25 (in which host and end station are not yet networked via LAN). Most installations are still to be found in the USA at present; the Frame Relay wave is only gradually starting up in Australia, Japan and Europe.

Some large private users begin by establishing private FR networks. Essential Frame Relay elements are

- low protocol overhead,

- packet switching,

- optional overload indicator.

Current alternatives for establishing inter-location LAN configurations are direct data links or X.25 connections, each of which belongs to one of the two possible basic categories:

- Point-to-Point connection (direct data link) or

- "Cloud" as carrier network (X.25).

For the point-to-point connection, a dedicated physical connection is explicitly created with a link between two communication endpoints (usually bridges, routers, or front-ends as location entry point, not end stations). Redundancy for intercepting failures can only be implemented by cyclic meshing of the endpoints involved (locations). In the "cloud" as carrier network, as the analogy suggests, there is a defined entry point into the wide-area network (POP, Point of Presence, i.e., next possible end stations of the carrier network), from which all destination networks can be reached by appropriate definitions. Redundancy for intercepting error situations is implemented transparently for the user within the carrier network (and with all commercial operators, private or official, unfortunately allowing the user no chance to influence it). The end user can only design the link-up to the carrier network redundantly in order to intercept error situations on this connection link. Figure 13.9 shows a comparison of point-to-point connections and "cloud" carrier networks.

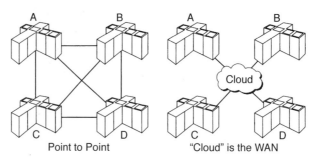

Figure 13.9 Point -to-Point Connections and Carrier Network

As a packet switching service, Frame Relay belongs to the group of "cloud" networks: location LANs are linked via a dedicated connection (direct data link) to the Frame Relay network.

The advantages of Frame Relay over point-to-point connections are that several destination networks can be reached via a single access line to the Frame Relay network, and that the necessary capacities for linking up different locations are combined in a single access line. If not all destination link-ups incessantly need the full capacity in parallel, the total capacity can be made less than the sum of the previously separated point-to-point connections.

The advantages of Frame Relay over X.25 connections can be seen in the reduced protocol overhead and the resulting increase in throughput, as well as in the support of higher transmission capacities (T1/E1).

Like X.25, Frame Relay defines an interface between DCE (WAN operator side) and DTE (private side), but in protocol intelligence X.25 also includes the OSI Layer 3, which was omitted from Frame Relay. Hand in hand with it goes support of

- Switched Virtual Circuits,

- error handling,

- (international) connection of different X.25 networks via X.75,

which Frame Relay lacks. On the other hand, the overhead is much lower than for X.25. The functions which are included in the individual X.25, and Frame

Relay protocols are listed for comparison in Figure 13.10. It becomes clear from the functional comparison that the lack of Layer 3 (OSI reference model) brings about considerable savings on the overhead but also results in functional losses.

13.4.1 Frame Relay Technology

Topics for particular attention under the technological aspects are:

- basic protocol elements

- configuration options.

Protocol

Frame Relay (FR) defines a Data Link Interface, which is at Layer 2 of the OSI reference model. FR was originally intended as a packet service for ISDN networks and HDLC frames and now can also be used in other connections (such as T1/E1). FR is defined for higher speeds (currently max. 2 MBit/sec) than are possible at present with X.25. In principle, Frame Relay acts like a "Wide Area LAN" (WALAN).

Function	X.25 in ISDN	Frame Relay
Flag Recognition/Generation	X	X
Transparency	X	X
FCS Checking/Generation	X	X
Recognize Invalid Frames	X	X
Discard Incorrect Frames	X	X
Address Transaction	X	X
Fill Interframe Time	X	X
Manage V(S) State Variable	X	
Buffer Packets Awaiting Acknowledgement	X	
Manager Timer T1/E1	X	
Acknowledge Received I-Frames	X	
Check Received N(S) against V(R)	X	
Generation of Rejection Message	X	
Respond to Poll/Final Bit	X	
Keep Track of Number of Retransmissions	X	

Figure 13.10 X.25 and Frame Relay Functions

Function	X.25 in ISDN	Frame Relay
Act Upon Reception of Rejection Message	X	
Respond to Receiver Not Ready (RNR)	X	
Respond to Receiver Ready (RR)	X	
Multiplexing of Logical Channels	X	
Management of D Bit	X	
Management of M Bit	X	
Management of W Bit	X	
Management of P(S) Packet Sent	X	
Management of P(R) Packet Received	X	
Detection of Out-of-Sequence Packets	X	
Management of Network Layer RR	X	
Management of Network Layer RNR	X	

Figure 13.10 X.25 and Frame Relay Functions (cont.)

At Layer 1 non-switched connections (PVCs) are used, e.g., with bridges or routers via X.21 or in future E1. SVCs are not supported. The PVCs are occupied with a guaranteed access capacity (CIR, Committed Information Rate). The CIR can be briefly exceeded for intercepting bursts (see section 13.4.2).

The interface between DTE and Frame Relay network is specified as shown in Figure 13.11. For the physical transfer at Layer 1, bit stuffing is used as it is for HDLC (for five successive 1 values a 0 is inserted, and removed again). The format and the data link transmission procedures are specified at Layer 2.

Frame Relay implements protocol intelligence up to Layer 2 of the OSI reference model (based on LAP-D of the ITU-TS), and, accordingly, supports the essential functions required for transporting a sequenced frame:

- Frame delimitation

- Frame structuring

- Transparency of user data (including all higher protocol information)

- Multiplexing using the address field

- Length checking (correct and complete number of bytes)

- Detection (not correction) of transmission faults

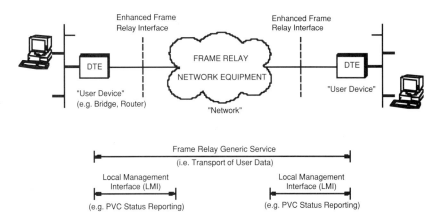

Figure 13.11 Frame Relay Interface Specifications

The format of a transmission unit, called a frame as in Local Area Networks, is subdivided just as in LANs into start flag, destination address, data field, CRC field, and end flag. An incoming packet is checked by the receiver for correctness and, if faulty, discarded. A correct (valid) frame has the following properties:

• Flag at the beginning and the end (an end flag can also be the start flag for the next frame)

• At least 5 bytes between the flags (i.e., all control information bytes and at least one data byte)

• An integer length in bytes (as coding is always of complete bytes only)

• A correct checksum (CRC) in the last two bytes before the end flag

• A maximum length of 4506 bytes (StrataCom)

• A maximum length of 1600 bytes (Digital Equipment)

• A maximum length of 8 kbytes (Cisco)

The frame format is shown in Figure 13.12. As the connection is non-switched, only a link ID need be given, the source and destination address is not required as it is in LANs. This DLCI (Data Link Connection Identifier) occupies the first six bits of the second byte (the first is the flag) and the first four bits of the third byte. The bits in between are used for control parameters:

- C/R bit for Command/Response, which is not actively used by Frame Relay (in contrast to other methods, which could interpret the packet). The C/R bit is set as wished and transferred transparently via the Frame Relay network.

- EA bit for the end of the address field (Extended Address). It is the last bit of bytes two and three; a 0 means "further address bits in the next byte", a 1 means "no further address bits." Normally there is a 0 in byte two and a 1 in byte three.

- The DE (Discard Eligibility) bit for overload control: A set DE bit indicates that the frame may be discarded in preference to other frames if an overload occurs.

- The BECN bit for Backward Explicit Congestion Notification indicates that because of an overload, if possible, control procedures should be activated in the reverse direction of the transmitted frame.

- The FECN bit for Forward Explicit Congestion Notification indicates that because of an overload, if possible, control procedures should be activated in the direction of the transmitted frame.

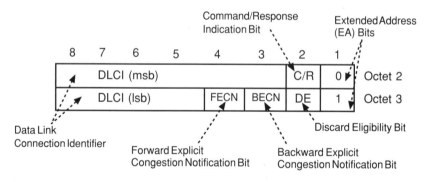

Figure 13.12 Frame Relay Frame Format

The DLCI specifies the connection number of a non-switched connection between two endpoints in the Frame Relay network. These can be different on the send and receive side: for a connection between Frankfurt and Berlin, Frankfurt can use DLCI 40 and Berlin DLCI 55. When transmitting from

Frankfurt to Berlin, Frankfurt enters 40 in the address fields, and at the output from the Frame Relay network in Berlin the ID is changed to 55 before the frame is forwarded to the end station. This addressing technique is comparable to the logical channels in X.25. Like X.25 addresses, the network addresses of the LAN protocol for source and destination network are mapped on to a source and destination DLCI. Different IDs can be used at both endpoints of the connections, e.g., for the connection between Berlin and Munich, 50 for Berlin and 33 for Munich. A plan of the addressing is shown in Figure 13.13.

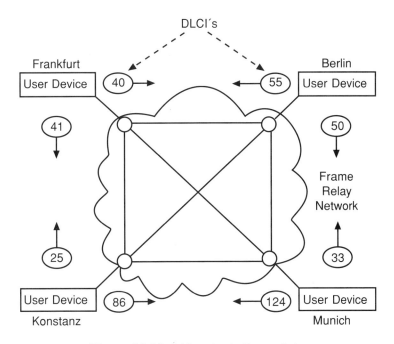

Figure 13.13 Addressing in Frame Relay

As can be seen from the description of the control fields, simple error indications and correct data transmission (with CRC) are implemented, but error correction and overload control must be performed by higher protocols. In particular this means that within the Frame Relay network there is no Store & Forward technique, which would cause retransmission on this section of the connection when a packet was lost between two switches. In this case the packet would have to be retransmitted end to end from the sending LAN to the receiving LAN.

Digression: Frame Relay for Beginners

BECN is not a call to "be evermore cool now" (although the management of the Frame Relay network has given you a few gray hairs), it refers to Backward Explicit Congestion Notification: a bit flag that is set by a switch to indicate overload in the reverse direction of the transmitted frame, in the hope that (a) all components between switch and sender do not delete the bit and (b) the sender shows understanding and reduces the traffic.

CIR specifies the guaranteed data rate (Committed Information Rate) that can be exploited via an FR access.

DLCI is not a Dual Link Communication Interface for the price of a Single Link Interface, it is the connection number (Data Link Connection Identifier) of a Frame Relay connection, remotely comparable to the X.25 channel number. It does not necessarily need to be the same at both endpoints of a connection.

DE identifies discard frames (Discard Eligibility). It is a bit flag that is set in frames which are given priority to be removed from the buffer in overload situations, and not transported any further.

FECN refers to Forward Explicit Congestion Notification, a bit flag that is set to indicate overload in the direction of the transmitted frame, in the hope that the destination station, by reducing its receive window, can cause the sender to decrease the traffic production.

LMI is the Local Management Interface, a management specification for Frame Relay communication, drafted by the Frame Relay Forum.

POP is not a musical accompaniment to data transmission; it is the next access point (Point of Presence, switch location) of the Frame Relay network operator which the user has chosen.

PVC refers to the underlying dedicated connection of an FR communication, the Permanent Virtual Circuit. The CIR for example, is set with the PVC parameters.

Access rate is the transmission capacity (bit rate) of the dedicated connection to the next POP.

Product Situation

Frame Relay? Of course we support Frame Relay, any internetworking provider/manufacturer will say with great conviction. But what really supports a Frame Relay box? It cannot always be decided at a glance whether a product is a switch, router, PAD (FRAD) or multiplexer. To add to this, the availability of interoperability tests can be described as rudimentary at best. Even when such a test verifies the functionality of connecting two devices and exchanging frames, how the same device will behave in a multivendor environment cannot be predicted.

Internetworking elements which support Frame Relay can basically be divided into two categories:

- Switches
- Access Devices

The first category (Switches) forms the Frame Relay Backbone (the inside of the cloud), receives and sends essentially only Frame Relay frames, directs packets between any transmitting and destination points, and correspondingly supports many physical connections. The second category can be seen as the endpoint of the network, from the point of view of the Frame Relay cloud: it allows access to Frame Relay networks for "Non-Frame-Relay environments" such as LANs, and for this purpose provides a limited number of physical connections. Switching functionality within the Frame Relay cloud is not included in the functionality of category 2.

Switches

Switch? If these are already in a class of their own, for different products based on the same architectural principles, much has been missed out. First there are switches (e.g., from BT North America, BBN) which have developed by re-engineering from an X.25 switch. They are based on a design which is set for the higher protocol overhead of X.25 or its processing. Among other things, this means a longer processing delay: the switch receives Frame Relay packets and encapsulates them in X.25 packets. The original intention of actually reducing the protocol overhead is thus made futile. The advantage on one hand is that the user/operator of the FR network needs no new equipment but can upgrade the existing devices. On the other hand, a "Frame-Relay-X.25 switch" can support both kinds of link-up, and thus represents an economical migration option. A disadvantage is the restricted support of higher transmission capacities: the X.25 switches are not designed to support T1/E1, and T3 is not supported in any case.

The second, forward-looking variant does handle native Frame Relay packets from corresponding access devices (routers, FRADs), but uses the Cell Relay (see Chapter 11) method for transmission (e.g., from Stratacom, Northern Telecom, Siemens/MCI); i.e., it works as a Cell Switch. All the better—should the high processing speed of Cell Relay transmission be made usable for Frame Relay too? The adaptation has the consequence that the Frame Relay header (and trailer) is removed, and the frame is partitioned into blocks for Cell Relay and is transmitted and assembled again at the other end. The use of the overload indication, deliberately provided by FR (FECN, BECN, DE), is thus made impossible. The original information is not available at the "FR" network exit point, quite apart from the fact that within the "FR" network these bits can be interpreted, set, and occupied with corresponding actions.

The overload control envisaged in the FR standard is replaced (or not) in this case by in-house functional modules. Stratacom for instance, assumes that overload is regulated in the source network (LAN). If too high a transmission rate is used, the switch's internal buffer (2 MB) first fills up, and then the surplus frames are ignored (discarded).

The higher LAN protocols must arrange a corresponding retransmission and possibly a reduction of the transmit rate.

Thirdly, there are switches which were developed purely as FR switches (and could be described as thoroughbred representatives of their category), instead of grafting the Frame Relay technology on to a quite different method. FR switches are designed from the outset to support the corresponding frame sizes and the overload functions (e.g., from Amnet, Ascom Timeplex, Cascade, Frame Relay Technologies, Netrix). The development cost for a pure FR switch is rather higher than giving an existing Cell Switch FR capability.

This approach was nevertheless chosen by the manufacturers mentioned, in order to be able to use the overload mechanisms planned for FR throughout the network.

Thus the overload bits BECN, FECN, and DE can also be set when an overload situation has arisen at a switch within the FR network, even if the CIR would not have been exceeded at any access point. The FECN/BECN and DE bits can be set into a kind of hysteresis loop if a certain upper load threshold is exceeded on a switch port, the bits being unset when the load falls below a lower threshold. If an absolute upper limit (higher than the threshold for setting the overload bits) is passed, frames are discarded (removed from the buffer).

It is worth investigating which architecture a particular switch is actually based on: conclusions can often be derived from the architecture about the management options and performance. However, if the user does not want to establish an FR network, but to use commercial providers' services, he or she has to depend on actually obtaining this information from the service provider.

Mixing with MUXes

A switch is not necessarily always a stand-alone box. Several multiplexer manufacturers (Ascom Timeplex, NET, Newbridge Networks) have developed plug-in cards into switches which support FR to some degree. Behind this is the idea of operating Frame Relay effectively as an overlay network on a TDM basis. In this case the total capacity of the multiplexer is shared between Frame Relay and X.21 applications. Frame Relay data is then received by FRADs, routers, or bridges, non-Frame-Relay data as before by front ends, cluster controllers, PBXs, and similar switches. The Frame Relay card itself sometimes already has FRAD functionality, so that no interposed FRAD is necessary.

Access Components

In a complex case, access components can be routers, which link up entire LANs with a large number of end stations; or in the simplest case, FRADs, which like PADs convert incoming packets to Frame Relay format while passing them through (for end systems which have not yet recognized the trend, such as hosts, FEPs, etc.). In between are a range of components. Altogether qualifying as access components are:

- Routers,

- Bridges,

- FRADs,

- Concentrators,

- PC cards.

As the term "LAN Transport Technology" for Frame Relay suggests, bridges, and routers are the most commonly used access devices for an FR network. In many cases routers can be judged the better suited for the FR link-up, since for routable LAN protocols, FRs seal off local overhead from the WAN area, and since no Spanning Tree overhead arises across boundaries (in contrast, the overhead of corresponding router protocols in dynamic routing can be classed as lower). However, applications which do not use routable protocols cannot profit from this advantage. A corresponding bridge interconnection is appropriate here.

Most router manufacturers now support Frame Relay as an interface (ACC, Cisco, 3Com, Digital, NSC, Proteon, Timeplex). This means that the bridge/router takes a data packet from the LAN, generates a Frame Relay header and trailer for encapsulation and sends it into the FR network, usually to the switch. Since there is still no standard valid for all LAN protocols for handling the encapsulation, compatibility problems occur here between the products of different manufacturers. A standardization initiative is RFC 1294, which specifies the encapsulation for TCP/IP. As bridges and routers use appropriate LAN protocol algorithms to decide the port to which the frame will be forwarded, they implement a higher functionality than a concentrator or FRAD.

The changeover from direct connections to Frame Relay in a bridge or router network leads to distinct configuration changes: networks with point-to-point connections are mostly configured in ring form, possibly with an additional redundancy loop (see Figure 13.14).

In Frame Relay networks, bridges/routers have a sort of corner position with a link-up to the switch, which is positioned centrally within the "cloud."

Like PADs, FRADs convert incoming packets to Frame Relay format while passing them through (for end systems which have not yet recognized the trend, such as hosts, FEPs,etc.). Concentrators basically behave like FRADs but combine several input links in one output connection to the (next) switch

(Adax, Dowty Communications, Frame Relay Technologies, Sync Research). Typically, synchronous protocols such as HDLC or SNA are given Frame Relay capability via FRADs and concentrators, poll spoofing sometimes being used to reduce the WAN load for SNA.

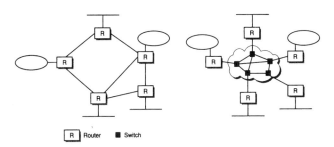

Figure 13.14 Topology change from dedicated connections to Frame Relay

For the UNIX or PC user who is determined to operate his or her equipment as a switch or FRAD, there are cards and software from Adax or Amnet. The $6,000 price tag may be tempting, but the capability of such a solution is clearly restricted.

Possible configurations for linking heterogeneous LAN and host environments to a Frame Relay network are shown in Figure 13.15.

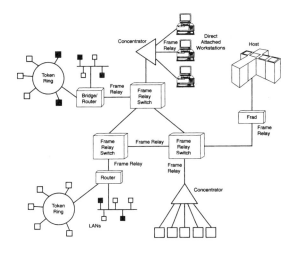

Figure 13.15 Configurations for Frame Relay Access

13.4.2 Design and Management

The advantage of Frame Relay use instead of permanent point-to-point connections lies in better exploitation of the available bandwidth.

Capacity Planning

If for example, five point-to-point connections between 10 LANs, a capacity of 64 kbit each is possible, the load between all networks might be handled by a single supply link to the Frame Relay network which only has 256 kbit/sec (instead of 320 kbit/s), since not all networks need the full 64 kbit/sec capacity at the same time.

A further example: Location A has a 64 kbit/sec link-up to location B, a 112 kbit/sec link-up to location C and a 64 kbit/sec link-up to location D (see Figure 13.16). These link-ups can be combined in a 256 kbit/sec supply link to the Frame Relay network, which could cost less than the three separate point-to-point connections (plus corresponding redundancy).

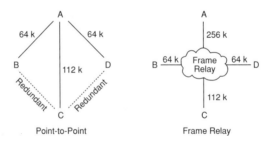

Figure 13.16 Configuration comparison

If some LANs are very lightly used at that time, considerably more than 64 kbit/sec is available for the other LANs. At maximum, if only one LAN is active at that time, the full bandwidth can be used for this traffic. As relevant measurements prove that LAN peaks only occur for about 15% to 20% of the total usage time, there is something to be said for this strategy. Figure 13.17 depicts a more complex example. The capacity of the supply link in all cases is lower than the sum of the CIR values of the individual PVCs.

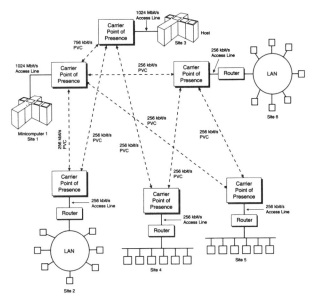

Figure 13.17 Access line capacities and CIR

In addition to this, the entire network does not need to be redesigned when new locations are linked in (as possibly with a meshed network of point-to-point connections) as capacity and access are independent of other link-ups.

In general it can be said that Frame Relay networks hardly go beyond the performance of direct data links, but with correspondingly low-error applications still enable a higher throughput than X.25 connections.

Determining the necessary capacity requires an exact knowledge of the load profile occurring on the LAN-WAN-LAN connection. Experts dispute about the choice of entry capacity: "Choose a sufficiently high capacity, experience shows you always need more than you expect," or again: "Choose a low entry capacity, you can always upgrade by small stages."

Overload Control

For indication (and possibly reaction) in overload situations, the Frame Relay protocol provides (optionally) three bit flags: BECN, FECN, and DE Bit. The function of the BECN/FECN bits is best understood by considering a transmitting station, which initiates the communication, and a receiving station (see Figure 13.18).

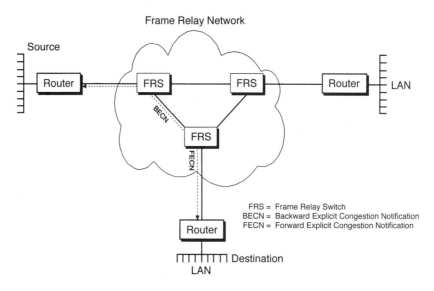

Figure 13.18 Congestion indication in the Frame Relay network

The BECN bit is set when the send flow should be reduced in the reverse direction to the transmitted frame. (Principle: the transmitting station controls the data flow, e.g., in host-end station communication.)

The FECN bit is set when the transmit flow should be reduced in the direction of the transmitted frame. (Principle: the receiver controls the data flow, e.g., by reducing the receive window size in TCP/IP.)

Unfortunately, for effective setting of the FECN/BECN bits, it is necessary for data frames to be sent into the corresponding destination and source LANs, and to arrive there correctly. If this is not the case, no transmission load reduction can be achieved. The Frame Relay standard does not provide for generating separate control frames for overload control.

The DE bit is set to indicate that the frame has priority for discarding in case of severe overload. This mechanism naturally only functions if everyone behaves fairly, otherwise the applications/frames with this bit set are at a disadvantage compared to the others. A standard has not been set for when the bit is set, for which protocols, and by which components (router, switch), and the attitude of manufacturers who do not implement the DE bit for their users' benefit (or not to disadvantage them) is understandable to a degree. On the other hand, applications which set the DE bit have better control over the potential packet loss, as they can set the DE bit in the "less important" packets. This increases the probability that the other packets (e.g., composite acknowledgments) are not destroyed in a buffer overload on a switch.

Most switches can read and set the FECN/BECN bits. Nearly all routers, FRADs, and concentrators can at least read (interpret) the bits. But very few products convert their discoveries from the bit interpretation into corrective actions. The maximum control activity for a router is simply to intercept an overload indirectly, by no longer sending with the full CIR and storing packets briefly in its buffer before sending them, e.g., if several successive frames with set BECN bit are received on a PVC. This reduces the throughput, higher protocols receive acknowledgments at longer intervals and reduce the transmit rate accordingly. However, most routers do no more than read the set bits and possibly create logfile statistics about the number of FECN/BECN bits seen, which can only be used for making trend statements and introducing preventive tuning measures if the statistics rise.

However, this lack of direct router actions cannot be blamed entirely on the manufacturers' laziness. The real problem is that no standard concept has been established for how a router can make an end system produce a lower network load. Most LAN protocols simply do not provide for it (lacking awareness that capacity bottlenecks could sometime happen here).

Source quench packets in TCP/IP are an exception (and here experiments have shown that the use of source quench packets have not led to overload reduction in the FR network, as sending source quench packets increases the LAN load, in total conflict with the original intention).

Similar difficulties arise in supporting the DE bit. Most products interpret the bit, but cannot set it or start resulting actions. Here again the argument is used that the standard only provides for optional support and gives no ruling for the application in relation to different LAN protocols. Router manufacturers point out that a router cannot judge which application (which protocol) is more important than others.

In the context of high load situations, it is repeatedly mentioned that Frame Relay networks, or the switches and routers, can cope with short bursts. But what is a "short burst"? Usually not more than a maximum size Ethernet frame, as the buffer size is mostly about 2 MB. The robustness against bursts can therefore be seen as limited.

The future success or failure of Frame Relay will depend not least on the continued development of the management situation, which is currently unsatisfactory. Functions which still have to be implemented are cost calculation, real-time error messages, and interface activation/deactivation, as well as automated allocation of DLCIs. Direct intervention possibilities in overload situations are also important.

Continuing standard initiatives for Link Management protocols that supplement the Frame Relay specification are already in progress: CLLM (Consolidated Link Layer Management ANSI T1.617 Annex D) is the ANSI approach on this matter, and LMI (Local Management Interface) is the rival paper from the Frame Relay Forum. Both procedures specify separate management control frames and use the same DLCI for management control frames, namely 1023. The packet formats differ slightly. The consequence is that even willing Frame Relay product manufacturers cannot support both management initiatives at the same time.

CLLM frames give the cause of the high load/overload in an 8-bit encryption, and also all DLCIs which should reduce their transmit rate. On receiving such management information, the endpoint should reduce the CIR accordingly. If an FR access point receives successive frames with set BECN flags, it should reduce its CIR stepwise to 0.675, 0.5, and 0.25 of the original CIR value, according to the ANSI recommendations. After normalization (no more frames arriving with set BECN bits), the transmit rate is raised stepwise by the factor 0.125.

LMI information comprises the current active DLCIs, status reports about removal or failure of DLCIs, and status information on the physical and logical link between FR network and terminal device. LMI also introduced "keep alive" packets between FR network and LAN (CPE). Global addressing is a further improvement that should be achieved with LMI. In LMI only PVCs are supported, while ANSI CLLM also provides for SVCs.

The limitation accepted with the use of CLLM or LMI is not obvious at first glance. In a single status message (about 1400 bytes), the status of all polled DLCIs must be reported. This limits the number of possible DLCIs to 364. This is still sufficient for a medium-sized router network, but not for host-end system environments.

13.4.3 Interoperability

Since Frame Relay is inherently simpler than X.25, fewer interoperability problems should arise here. This is partially true, as far as "implementation compatibility" is concerned. This simply means recognizing and forwarding Frame Relay formats. Thus a series of carrier certificates state only that the identical FR access products (e.g., routers), connected point-to-point via the specially certified network, can exchange data with one another.

Though the creation of such carrier certificates should be regarded as a positive beginning, it says little about the behavior in more complex network environments with several switches and widely varying LAN applications.

Admittedly there are not too many options for building a complex test environment, as the cost is enormous. Those who think more extensive Frame Relay tests are really a matter for the Frame Relay Forum feel disappointed in their expectations: laboratory work is not in the statutes, which according to Thomas Jones (President of the Forum Board) only involve implementation agreements (like the OSI NM Forum). His argument: "What interests the user is the behavior of Frame Relay in actual productive operation. No laboratory can test that." At least the FR forum supplies a list of manufacturers laboratories who are making efforts with tests.

The implementation agreements were also forwarded to relevant standardization bodies such as NIST and OIW for the development of corresponding conformity tests. Output in relation to this can be expected in about 1993.

In the meantime there are test environments resulting from manufacturer initiatives, e.g., from HP/Idacom, Tekelec, GN/Navratel. Many manufacturers are carrying out their own tests, and on request can name one or more other Frame Relay products (chiefly router/switch combinations) with which they are compatible.

13.4.4 Aspects and Criteria for Use

In deciding for or against Frame Relay, or in choosing the product/service, there is a range of criteria to be considered.

Costs

In deciding for or against Frame Relay, a high priority should be given to weighing up the investments to be made against the expected savings from lower transmission costs.

Tariff Comparison

How are the tariff structures of the service alternatives for comparable capacities in the required capacity area? Is the tariff fixed or load-related?

Provision

Frequently the user does not have the means to establish a private network and, accordingly, is dependent upon public networks (the postal organizations or commercial providers). Most of these in Europe do not offer Frame Relay.

Link-up

How far away is the next entry point to the desired network access? Often the costs of the direct data link for the supply to the operator's network make up a considerable proportion of the total costs.

CIR

How does the FR service provider operate guaranteed bandwidths, are there guaranteed average throughputs? What happens when the CIR is exceeded? Is the tariff then increased?

Product Choice

The compatibility between the chosen router products in an individual network and the network operator's switches should be verified by corresponding tests or certificates or written commitments from the manufacturers.

Interoperability, similarly implemented overload control, and compatible management support should be taken into account.

Service Quality

How important are throughput, reliability, and user-friendliness for a specific Frame Relay user? Are the line qualities adequate for the desired applications? Are X.25 and Frame Relay supported?

Management

Several aspects should be mentioned here:

- Who makes backup arrangements? Are these offered by the operator?

- Can the connection points and FR network be designed redundantly?

- What management options and security mechanisms are available? Which is it obligatory to install?

- Are a performance monitor and a log book for faulty frames with set FECN/BECN/DE bits available?

- Does the router as an entry point into the Frame Relay network reduce the send rate in case of high load/overload?

- How do the installed LAN applications react to a reduction in the transmit rate?

Support

What support structure is present? How is the Frame Relay network maintained, what error correction times are assured? How are the responsibilities regulated?

Within the scope of this book, the list of criteria cannot make any claims to completeness.

13.4.5 Conclusion

Like all other possible inter-location LAN-WAN-LAN connection services, Frame Relay has advantages as well as disadvantages.

Advantages of using Frame Relay include:

- high throughput because of low overhead, and therefore
- lower transmission times, and
- lower necessary band width;
- dynamic distribution of the bandwidth to several connection points,
- full transparency for all higher (LAN) protocols, and
- relatively easy installation as a simple software modification to HDLC.

The following are disadvantages:

- lack of error correction, flow control, overload control (indication only)
- no functionality at network level, i.e., in particular no routing;
- no support of SVCs;
- no global network addressing (unique address per network node instead of connection-related addresses);
- limited management possibilities;
- lack of specification for the communication between Frame Relay networks to X.75 for X.25 networks, so restriction to national networks;
- limited suitability for video and voice transfer.

Interoperability

"Implementation compatibility," i.e., recognizing and forwarding Frame Relay formats, is given in many cases. Carrier certificates give information on switch/router pairs which work together. Beyond this, available interoperability tests can at best be described as rudimentary.

The Frame Relay Forum does not conduct independent test activities. It only forwards implementation agreements to relevant standardization bodies such as NIST and OIW for the development of corresponding conformity tests. In the meantime, test environments resulting from manufacturer initiatives, (e.g., from HP/Idacom, Tekelec, GN/Navratel) have been developed.

High-Speed Transmission

Presently, it is still questionable whether Frame Relay will actually come into use on high speed lines such as T3 (45 MBit/sec). The selected dedicated connection mode (PVC) calls effective usage of the high bandwidths into question. Furthermore, Cell Relay is more suitable as a transmission method for these high speeds than the transfer of variable frame lengths. Using speeds of up to 2 MBit/sec, however, the throughput compared to X.25 (with the functional losses mentioned) can be significantly increased.

Integration of Different Data Types

Voice and video transmission (e.g., video conferencing) is problematic as a Frame Relay application. For one thing, there is no guaranteed maximum delay between two transmitted packets, which manifests itself in voice fluctuations and distorted video or delayed screen set-up. For another thing, individual frames can be lost; this can have a relatively fatal effect on many video transmission methods which need the previous frame in each case to set up the successive one. So, for voice and video transmission, the direct data link is still recommended.

Costs

Although Frame Relay equipment is usually no more expensive than X.25 equipment, existing hardware should be taken into account. Protection of previous investments in X.25 equipment should be compared with possible savings in transmission costs. The decision on Frame Relay is easier to make if a network is being newly established. If a very large X.25 network is already present, it is easier to decide on a step-by-step migration (conversion to Frame Relay) than on a complete conversion—provided the applications permit reasonable expectations about the transmission cost savings.

Trend

There are estimates which forecast a growth in investment in Frame Relay networks from $68 million in 1992 to $1.8 billion in 1996. Even DB Telekom, under the influence of the new technology wave, decided to carry out a pilot study, following which it was decided that Telekom's service would be expanded by FR. It remains to be seen whether all that will finally be left of FR are the headaches acquired by a lot of network planners and managers in dealing with the topic, or whether it will become established as the appropriate migration for X.21/X.25 networks. The current hesitant development of higher-capacity procedures based on ATM leads one to expect the latter.

13.5 Point-to-Point Protocol

The problems of linking various location LANs, in which historical developments of router products from different manufacturers are used, was already mentioned in this chapter. The encapsulation techniques, with which bridges and routers transport their packets via WAN connections, have been one of the last bastions for proprietary manufacturing solutions. The consequence for the user was the continual battle with incompatibility, as soon as different products were required to communicate between sites.

The first attempts to eliminate or at least improve this difficult situation began in 1989 with the individual definitions of the Point-to-Point Protocol (PPP) for point-to-point connections. The second step involved expansions for any desired concentration of WAN connections for any desired higher protocols with the Multilink PPP definition. The term Point-to-Point Protocol covers a range of IETF specifications, which should enable LAN protocols to be connected with manufacturer compatibility via WANs. In the meantime there may be the third revision of the basic version and the second generation for individual higher protocols. The following is a list of significant PPP RFCs.

Point-to-Point Protocol Standards

1764   Senum, S. The PPP XNS IDP Control Protocol (XNSCP). 1995 March; 5p. (Format: TXT= 9525 bytes)

1763   Senum, S. The PPP Banyan Vines Control Protocol (BVCP). 1995 March; 10p. (Format: TXT= 17817 bytes)

1762   Senum, S. The PPP DECnet Phase IV Control Protocol (DNCP). 1995 March; 7p. (Format: TXT= 12709 bytes) (Obsoletes RFC 1376)

1717   Sklower, K.; Lloyd, B.; McGregor, G.; Carr, D. The PPP Multilink Protocol (MP). 1994 November; 21 p. (Format: TXT=46264 bytes)

1663   Rand, D. PPP Reliable Transmission. 1994 July; 8 p. (Format: TXT=17281 bytes)

1662   Simpson, W., ed. PPP in HDLC-like Framing. 1994 July; 25 p. (Format: TXT=48058 bytes) (Obsoletes RFC 1549)

1661   Simpson, W., ed. The Point-to-Point Protocol (PPP). 1994 July; 52 p. (Format: TXT=103026 bytes) (Obsoletes RFC 1548)

1638   Baker, F.; Bowen, R., eds. PPP Bridging Control Protocol (BCP). 1994 June; 28 p. (Format: TXT=58477 bytes)

1634   Allen, M. Novell IPX Over Various WAN Media (IPXWAN). 1994 May; 23 p. (Format: TXT=55347 bytes) (Obsoletes RFC 1551)

1619   Simpson, W. PPP over SONET/SDH. 1994 May; 4 p. (Format: TXT=8893 bytes)

1618   Simpson, W. PPP over ISDN. 1994 May; 6 p. (Format: TXT=14896 bytes)

1598   Simpson, W. PPP in X.25. 1994 March; 7 p. (Format: TXT=13835 bytes)

1570   Simpson, W., ed. PPP LCP Extensions. 1994 January; 18 p. (Format: TXT=35719 bytes) (Updates RFC 1548)

1552   Simpson, W. The PPP Internetwork Packet Exchange Control Protocol (IPXCP). 1993 December; 14 p. (Format: TXT=29174 bytes)

1549 Simpson, W.,ed. PPP in HDLC Framing. 1993 December; 18 p. (Format: TXT=36353 bytes)

1547 Perkins, D. Requirements for an Internet Standard Point-to-Point Protocol. 1993 December; 21 p. (Format: TXT=49811 bytes)

1378 Parker, B. The PPP AppleTalk Control Protocol (ATCP). 1992 November; 16 p. (Format: TXT=28497 bytes)

1377 Katz, D. The PPP OSI Network Layer Control Protocol (OSINLCP). 1992 November; 10 p. (Format: TXT=22110 bytes)

1334 Lloyd, B.; Simpson, W. PPP Authentication Protocols. 1992 October; 16 p. (Format: TXT=33249 bytes)

1333 Simpson, W. PPP Link Quality Monitoring. 1992 May; 15 p. (Format: TXT=29965 bytes)

1332 McGregor, G. The PPP Internet Protocol Control Protocol (IPCP). 1992 May; 12 p. (Format: TXT=17613 bytes) (Obsoletes RFC 1172)

1331 Simpson, W. The Point-to-Point Protocol (PPP) for the Transmission of Multi-protocol Datagrams over Point-to-Point Links. 1992 May; 66 p. (Format: TXT=129892 bytes) (Obsoletes RFC 1171, RFC 1172; Obsoleted by RFC 1548)

1172 Perkins, D.; Hobby, R. Point-to-Point Protocol (PPP) initial configuration options. 1990 July; 38 p. (Format: TXT=76132 bytes) (Obsoleted by RFC 1332)

1171 Perkins, D. Point-to-Point Protocol for the transmission of multi-protocol datagrams over Point-to-Point links. 1990 July; 48 p. (Format: TXT=92321 bytes) (Obsoletes RFC 1134; Obsoleted by RFC 1331)

Two significant basic standards, RFC 1661 and the extension RFC 1717, are now considered in detail.

13.5.1 RFC 1661: PPP for Point-to-Point Connections

PPP was developed to enable compatibility between manufacturers for LAN-WAN connections, which could not be achieved purely on the basis of X.21 or HDLC (see also Figure 13.19).

Various higher protocols, or to be precise, all protocols selected by configuration, can be multiplexed via the same PPP connection; PPP implements multiplexing/demultiplexing at the Link Level. According to RFC 1638, protocols which are not routable can be bridged transparently or by source routing. The connection can be a dedicated connection, or it can be a dial-up connection such as ISDN if the necessary extensions (e.g., RFC 1618, RFC 1619) are implemented.

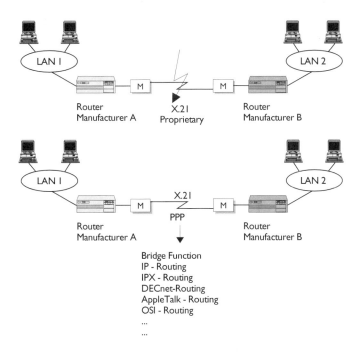

Figure 13.19: LAN-WAN connection with interconnection components from different manufacturers

PPP contains three core elements:

Encapsulation: Defines the encapsulation of datagrams of higher LAN protocols. A maximum of 8 bytes is required to pack a LAN packet; this can optionally be reduced to 2 or 4 bytes. Only one field of this must be read in order to be able to demultiplex packets of different protocols at the receiver.

LCP Protocol: A protocol for call set-up and clearing, and for configuration and testing of the connection (Link Control Protocol). The options cover the widest possible area of application for different LAN protocols and line speeds and qualities. Loopback errors can be recognized with LCP. Link quality authentication and monitoring is also supported by selecting appropriate options in the LCP phase.

NCP Protocols:Problems of higher LAN protocols are sometimes intensified by the use of point-to-point connections, e.g., allocation and management of IP addresses via a Dial-Up Modem Server. A series of individual PPP protocols, so-called Network Control Protocols (NCP), regulate the specific communication requirements for a LAN protocol at each network level, e.g., IP, IPX, DECnet, AppleTalk, OSI, VINES, XNS (see the previously listed RFCs).

RFC 1661 describes the encapsulation and configuration options which are negotiated during call set-up. For a basic communication capability, default values are set in RFC 1661 which every implementation must support. This ensures that implementations conforming to the standard can in any case communicate. At the start of a communication phase, any changes of the default values or additional functions are negotiated during call set-up with LCP, when each partner announces the parameters which he or she supports. If a partner chooses an option not supported by the other side, then both sides use the default value. However, the efficiency can be significantly increased by the selection of parameter enhancements.

RFC 1661 contains the description of a definite automatic status device for the necessary protocol actions; this cannot be dealt with in more detail within the scope of this book. Interested readers are referred to /RFC1661/.

Encapsulation

The encapsulation as in RFC 1661 is an enhancement of the HDLC encapsulation. The PPP frame overhead consists of one or two bytes protocol discriminator. This is followed by the information field, padded if necessary to a multiple of 4 bytes (see Figure 13.20). The information contains either data or the control information (overhead) for the applied PPP protocols such as LCP, BCP,

IPCP. Framing is needed for recognizing the beginning and end of a PPP packet, e.g., HDLC-like as specified in RFC 1662.

Figure 13.20: Format of the PPP encapsulation

Different LAN protocols are demultiplexed by interpretation of the protocol field. This is based on ISO 3309 (Expansion of address fields): All protocols are given an odd code, the last bit is always "1." In addition, the Least Significant Bit (LSB) of the Most Significant Byte must be set to "0." All received protocol fields which don't satisfy these restrictions are treated as unknown (and discarded).

The values of the protocol field are subdivided:

- 0x"0***" to 0x"3***" identifies network protocols of special packets (e.g. 0x"0031" for bridged packets)

- 0x"8***" to 0x"B***" identifies the NCPs of the LAN network protocols (e.g. 0x"8021" for IP, 0x"8031" for BCP)

- 0x"4***" to 0x"7***" identifies protocols for which no NCP was defined.

- 0x"C***" to 0x"F***" identifies Link Layer control protocols such as LCP, PAP, CHAP.

The PPP Connection

From the first PPP packet to a correctly set up connection, the PPP link runs through several phases, which are shown in Figure 13.21. Establish, Configuration (Options Negotiation), and Terminate are subject to LCP control; authentication is implemented by separate protocols.

After a call is successfully set up, the connection control is passed for a routed call to an NCP and for a bridge connection to the Bridge Control Protocol (BCP).

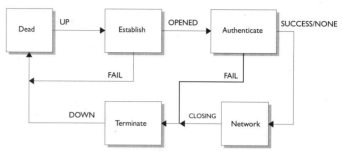

Figure 13.21 Different phases from the start to the end of a PPP connection

The LCP Protocol

In order to set up a call, the configuration parameters must first be negotiated. The switching elements involved do this via the Link Control Protocol (LCP). The default parameters which every device must support are set in such a way that so far as possible a connection is always completed.

If a parameter is set differently, this must be proposed with configuration options and acknowledged by the distant station. An example of two PPP switching elements Hugo and Otto clarifies this: Hugo sends a configure request in which the desired changes are listed. If Otto accepts the chosen parameters, he repeats them in a packet acknowledgment (ACK). If Otto wants other parameters, he can suggest these in a negative acknowledgment (configure NACK). Thus two things are achieved at the same time: Otto confirms receipt of the configure request, and the NACK packet contains the new desired values for all options which Otto wants to change.

If Hugo does not acknowledge the options changed by Otto, the default parameters are used. In a few cases the connection is closed down if the partner station doesn't support the desired parameters. For example: If a bridge wants to operate source routing, but the other side doesn't support this, there is no point in setting up a call, since the data packets could not be handled correctly. In practice this should not happen, as two devices which don't both support source routing should not even be given the chance of call set-up by the network operator.

If Hugo wants an option which is not supported at all by Otto, he refuses the configure request with a configure reject. If a Configure packet which Otto cannot interpret actually arrives, he answers with a Code Reject. Hugo must then fully relinquish the desired option.

Now take a closer look at the possible options: An option is only sent when a change of one or more default parameters are needed. All configuration options should be understood as half duplex, typically in the receive direction as seen from the send station. For example: If Hugo sends the option "Maximal Receive Unit" with extended packet length 2048 bytes, this means that the station Hugo can receive 2048 byte long packets. The options have been specified with the following design philosophy:

- The options mean additional functions or requests. An implementation that does not support a single option should nonetheless still be able to communicate with an implementation which supports all options.

- A default is therefore specified for each option. This default allows the connection to be normally operated without needing any options. A lower performance and service quality may then have to be accepted, but the basic communication capacity is given.

- Provided an RFC does not explicitly specify otherwise, the acknowledgment of the option does not necessarily mean that it is used. The partner station that acknowledges an option can still use the default values for sending.

The following options are currently specified in the RFC 1661:

0   Reserved
1   Maximum packet length
3   Authentication
4   Protocol for the connection quality
5   Magic Number
7   Protocol field compression
8   Address and control field compression

Further options were defined in an LCP extension (RFC 1570):

9   FCS alternatives (no FCS, 2 byte FCS, 4 byte FCS)
10   Recognizable padding
13   Callback (for dial-up connections)
15   Compound frames (Combining several LAN frames in a PPP packet)

The RFC 1661 options are now described in detail. The reader is referred to /RFC1570/ for details and formats of the extended options.

Maximum packet length (Default 1500 bytes): The desired packet length MRU (Maximum Receive Unit) is entered in the configure request.

Authentication (Default: No): The sending station expects the distant station to authenticate itself. It enters exactly one desired authentication protocol (e.g., CHAP, PAP) in the configure request for this. If this is rejected by the receiving station, then the next best protocol can be applied for in a further request. If the protocol request is acknowledged, the receiving station must authenticate itself to the sending station using this protocol. Authentication can be half duplex, e.g., if clients have to authenticate themselves to a server, but not conversely. Similarly, different authentication protocols can be used in the send and receive directions.

Protocol for the connection quality (Default: No): Use of a protocol for monitoring connection quality is desired (Link Quality Monitoring). This concerns values such as throughput and data loss. A station which sends a configure request with the Link Quality option expects the distant station to communicate its monitoring values in the acknowledgment. The monitoring can be half duplex if only one side wants this option.

Magic Number (Default: No): The Magic Number option allows interface errors and undesired loops (Loopback) to be recognized. Before the option is selected by both sides, the magic number is set to 0. Afterwards it is set so that it is very probably unique in the entire network (e.g., serial number of a device, hardware MAC address, system time or similar). The magic number entered in a received configure request is compared with the local magic number: if the values are identical, there is a loopback, and if the values differ, there is no loopback. This applies analogously to configure NACKs as well.

Protocol Field Compression (Default: No): The stations involved can agree on a reduction of the PPP header to a single byte (instead of 2 bytes).

Address and control field compression (Default: No): The stations involved can agree to compression of the address and control fields of the Data Link Layer. However, the compression may not be applied to LCP packets.

See /RFC1661/ for a closer study of the options and the associated formats.

Once the connection is "up and running," it remains active in normal operation until it is closed by an explicit LCP packet or NCP packet. This can be initiated by the application at any time. However, there are also disconnect situations resulting from faults: circuit outage, incorrect authentication, inadequate connection quality, time-outs, and similar situations.

If one side sends a call clearing request (Terminate Request), it has to wait a while for an acknowledgment (Terminate ACK). Only when a corresponding wait timer has expired may the connection be powered down, even without an acknowledgment. If the cleardown is from the NCP, it only applies for the corresponding protocol. However, if it is from the LCP, it applies for all activated protocols.

13.5.2 Other Important PPP Protocols

NCP Protocols

For every routable protocol, a separate Control Protocol was specified, dealing with the special parameters and boundary conditions of the particular LAN protocol (Layer 3). Each of these NCPs (IPCP for TCP/IP, DNCP for DECnet, BVCP for Banyan VINES, ATCP for AppleTalk, OSINLCP for OSI, IPXWAN for NetWare) must be separately activated and deactivated, just like the multi-protocol routing in the local area.

As a considerable space of time can be needed during call set-up for determining the link quality, and this time is also variable, implementation of a fixed time-out after which an NCP start must follow should be avoided. Otherwise it is highly probable that the NCP configuration will fail to be completed because of continual time-outs.

Protocol for Bridged Connections: BCP

The Bridge Control Protocol (BCP) was defined for connections on which bridge function is desired or necessary (when non-routable protocols are used). It is specified in RFC 1638 and handles bridge connections which use either Spanning Tree or source routing (with Spanning Tree for Single Route Broadcast). Translation bridges between Spanning Tree and source routing are not considered in RFC 1638. This means that the conversion from Ethernet/FDDI to Token Ring must always be carried out as.a LAN interface operation of the bridge.

As for routed connections, someone must decide for the implementation whether the devices at both ends of the WAN link together represent one bridge (Split Bridge model), or whether they both count as a full bridge (Independent Bridge model). In its Remote Bridge Document (IEEE 801.1G), the IEEE favors a kind of Independent Bridge model. PPP follows this approach and has set the default to "Full Bridge," also in particular for source routing bridges. This means that the WAN connection must be set with a segment number, which is unique within the entire Token Ring network and must be the same for both bridges at the end of the connection.

Some interesting network load optimization functions were drafted for BCP:

- Preserves the checksum (FCS) end-to-end

- No padding on the WAN link (if there was padding with 0 bits)

- LAN codes for further subdivision of the bridged network into network groups

BCP packets (control overhead) use the PPP protocol discriminator 0x"8031," data packets or BPDUs (packets of the bridge protocol according to IEEE 802.1D) are given the code 0x"0031." Since packets in a bridge connection are not fragmented, it is important that in the BCP phase a maximum packet size (MRU) is selected which is also sufficient for handling the occurring MAC frames. With the encapsulation in PPP, the MRU of 1500 bytes can be exceeded, as can Token Ring or FDDI packets, whose net length can be 2048 bytes or 4500 bytes.

With regard to the Magic Number option, RFC 1638 expressly recommends support. This seems entirely reasonable, as it is especially important for bridges to recognize loops.

BCP supports three different Spanning Tree protocols, which are coded in a control field in the encapsulation of BPDUs:

0x"0201" IEEE 802.1 (either IEEE 802.1D or IEEE 802.1G)

0x"0203" IBM Source Route Bridge (Single Route Broadcast)

0x"0205" DEC LANbridge 100 (DEC Spanning Tree)

The format of a BPDU packet is shown in Figure 13.22.

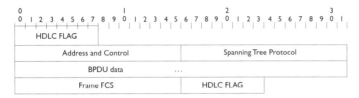

Figure 13.22: PPP Format of a Spanning Tree BPDU

A range of configuration options is defined in BCP; a correct selection guarantees that the data packets to be transported can be properly processed:

1   Bridge identification (Default: correct preconfiguration)
2   Line identification (Default: correct preconfiguration)
3   MAC support
4   Tinygram compression (Default: No)
5   LAN identification (Default: No)
6   MAC address
7   Spanning Tree protocol (Default: IEEE 802.1D or no SPT)

Bridge identification must be selected if the bridges are to work as half bridges (Single Bridge model). Both bridges must then agree on a common bridge number and notify each other which LAN interfaces they link (so that each knows its "other half"). Normally the network operator should already have configured the bridge numbers so that they are the same at both ends of the connection. If the operator doesn't do this, and the two bridges announce different numbers, the bridge with the lower number can adopt the higher number. However, it can also abort the connection. If bridge identification is selected, LAN identification may not be selected at the same time.

Line identification must be selected if the bridges are to work as full bridges (Independent Bridge model). In this case, the bridges must agree on a common virtual LAN number for the WAN connection. If the two bridges announce different values, the bridge with the lower number can adopt the higher number, but it can also abort the connection. If line identification is selected, bridge identification may not be selected at the same time.

MAC support: With this option a bridge indicates which MAC packets it can receive and process: 802.3, 802.5, FDDI. As default, a bridge is sent all packets which could be supported according to its other announced configuration parameters. If for example, a bridge selects MRU 4500 bytes, then theoretically it is able to process Token Ring and FDDI packets. Naturally, implementations work more reliably if they explicitly indicate the MAC protocols they support: if the MAC option is set, a bridge is only sent the packets of the type set in the option.

Tinygram compression: A bridge indicates with this option that it can process packets in which the padding was suppressed on the WAN link in order to save bandwidth. Before sending it to the LAN, it pads out the relevant frame again (with 0 bits) to 64 bytes.

LAN identification: The LAN frames are given an additional 4 byte field, in which a unique LAN ID is coded. This creates different network groups, between which there is no further frame transport. It is comparable to the formation of virtual LANs by tagging. If a bridge selects this option, it indicates that it can process and correctly forward frames in which the LAN ID is entered.

MAC Address: A bridge announces its MAC address with this option. It is represented in canonical form (LSB first). If the bridge sends the address 00_00_00_00_00_00, it is seen as a request for the distant station to allocate an address to the bridge.

Spanning Tree: With this option, the bridges involved agree on a common Spanning Tree protocol. There are five values (hex):

00 Zero (no SPT support)
01 IEEE 802.1D
02 IEEE 802.1G
03 IBM Source Route Spanning Tree Protocol
04 DEC LANbridge 100 Spanning Tree Protocol

Both sides agree on the lowest value. If a bridge supports several protocols, it concatenates the values, e.g., 0x"0103" for IEEE 802.1D and IBM source routing. If the distant station only supports Token Ring, it sends a Configure_NACK with the value 0x"03." Since 03 is a lower value than 0103, they agree on 0x"03." The default for this option can have two values: 0x"01" and 0x"00," i.e., IEEE 802.1D or no Spanning Tree at all.

13.5.3 RFC 1717: Multilink Enhancement for PPP

As the name PPP says, it was all devised for point-to-point connections, and thus by its nature it has a relatively restricted area of utilization. However, the construction of present-day WAN integrated networks tends to owe more to alchemy: take a liter of ISDN, add a few drops of Frame Relay, throw in a few routers, stir well, and seal the lid with a dedicated connection. So far the basic version of the network formula.

For compatible, interoperable networks though, the formula is rather more complicated, and at least the Multilink PPP (MLPPP) should also be added. MLPPP according to RFC 1717 allows parallel links to be utilized between two locations and operated with different services (see /RFC1717/). In particular, packet switching and dialed services such as ISDN, Frame Relay and ATM are permitted here, in order to switch endpoints between two connections according to capacity requirements. The ISDN access router manufacturers were the quickest to jump on this bandwagon. They use the MLPPP for concentrating 64 kbps B channels.

The use of MLPPP offers the following advantages:

- Different WAN services can be utilized for the connection between two endpoints (see Figure 13.23).

- When the active channels are heavily used, further channels can be activated automatically according to demand.

- When existing connections fail, backup connections can be activated automatically.

- All established higher protocols can be operated (increasingly) compatibly via MLPPP (IP, IPX, NetBIOS, SNA, DECnet, OSI).

- As for PPP, configuration parameters are negotiated for a particular connection during call set-up, to optimize the transfer (service quality, packet length, etc.).

- Spoofing procedures are available with MLPPP, which keep overhead packets out of the WAN connection if they are not essential (e.g., keep-alive packets, routing update packets without actual changes, etc.).

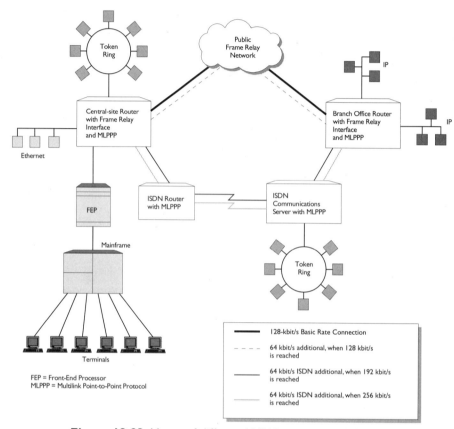

Figure 13.23: Usage of different WAN services with MLPPP

Functional Method

The MLPPP protocol functionality is based on PPP and is an intermediate module between PPP and the LAN protocol based on it, as shown in Figure 13.24. PPP sessions which are independent of one another are merged with MLPPP, and the incoming packets are forwarded correctly in a single (mixed) data stream to the higher protocol levels. The function thus belongs in the Data Link Layer and can be compared with an inverse multiplexer: several WAN connections behave towards the LAN like a single connection with the corresponding total capacity of the individual connections. In contrast to the line-based multiplexing which inverse multiplexers perform, MLPPP implements a packet-based inverse multiplexing as a software function.

It should be noted here that MLPPP does not implement a point-to-multipoint connection, it simply implements the concentration of different connections between exactly two WAN endpoints (inverse multiplexing).

As a result of the fact that MLPPP as a software function is based on PPP, it is independent in principle of the underlying physical WAN connection and can use firstly more than one connection and secondly more than one WAN service in parallel. Line-based inverse multiplexers, on the other hand, can only support one WAN service. MLPPP regulates the dynamic bandwidth allocation (activating and deactivating additional links) according to capacity requirement. Depending upon the WAN service used, both PVCs and SVCs are supported. MLPPP works in effect as though many virtual PPP modules (more formally: entities) are working away in parallel alongside one another.

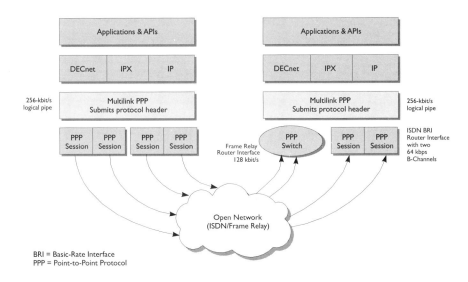

Figure 13.24: Positioning of MLPPP in the Protocol Hierarchy

In call set-up via LCP, a switching element indicates to the partner device with the multilink option that it wants to use the multilink functionality. If the distant station acknowledges the option, parallel connections can be opened. A significant problem that MLPPP confronted was the packet order in the context of fragmentation: a Layer 3 packet may have to be divided into several packets to be forwarded via WAN. These fragments can overtake one another on parallel links, so that the order of the individual fragments is not preserved. The same applies to small successive packets of a Layer 3 protocol, which are sent over parallel connections. MLPPP must therefore insert a header with corresponding packet numbering and fragment numbering, which allows the packets to be correctly put together again and sorted at the other end of the LAN-WAN connection.

MLPPP Formats and Parameters

The PPP header of multilink packets uses the address 0x"FF," control field 0x"03," and the protocol discriminator 0x"003D." For the fragmentation and reassembly described above, an additional 4 byte header field is used. The first byte contains two flags (B=begin, E=end) to signal the first and last fragment of a packet. The remaining 6 bits are always set to 0. If a packet is transported whole, both flags are set (B=1, E=1). The next 3 bytes contain the sequence number. The format is shown in Figure 13.25. A 12 bit short sequence number can also optionally be chosen; the B/E flags are then separated only by two 0 bits of the sequence number. The format can be seen in Figure 13.26.

The applied method is similar to the multilink protocol according to ISO 7776, but in addition enables packets to be pulled apart and put back together (Splitting and Recombining). The latency of a single fragment is thereby reduced, and the MRU increased if necessary. In contrast to ISO, packet acknowledgment is not explicitly required: it is only an option.

Packets which are sent with the multilink protocol are encapsulated as if the following options had been set:

- no async control character map
- no magic number
- no link quality monitoring
- Address and control field compression

- Protocol field compression

- no compound frames

- no recognizable padding

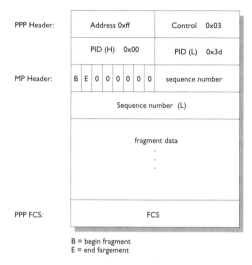

Figure 13.25: MLPPP format with long sequence number

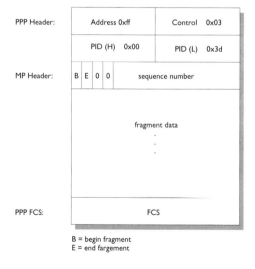

Figure 13.26: MLPPP format with short sequence number

The LCP option selection must be made per individual link, i.e. before the multilink activation and link concentration. No options are selected for complete link groups.

The additional options negotiated in multilink activation are

- multilink MRRU Maximum Received Reconstructed Unit (LCP option type 17)

- multilink Short Sequence Header (LCP option type 18)

- Endpoint discriminator (LCP option type 19)

The MRRU option indicates that a system uses the multilink protocol and all received packets will be processed according to this procedure, provided the multilink protocol is not rejected by the distant station. The default value for the MRRU is 1600 bytes.

In the LCP call set-up of a multilink, the so-called endpoint discriminator option is sent, by which the sender's address is signaled. A sender thus enables the receiver to recognize whether there are already links to this system. If so, the new link must be added to the existing multilink group. If this is not the case, a new, possibly additional, link group must be activated.

Flexibility

With MLPPP it is not only possible to concentrate various physical interfaces in a logical connection, the connection can also be partitioned into individual channels with differing access authorization. The example that follows should clarify the flexibility of MLPPP. The newly founded UBM (United Business Marketing) has achieved growth which necessitates, a change from WfW to NetWare and a move to a bigger building in another part of town. However, UBM continues to co-operate closely with UBD/Stouberg Ltd. UBM uses the existing customer database on the SNA host and accesses development and make files and pictures/video by file transfer (NFS) for preparing marketing documents.

A dedicated connection with 64k and an ISDN connection with 2 B-channels are set up for this. All three connections are concentrated in a logical channel. This has the advantage that the maximum bandwidth is at the disposal of each application if the other application is not in use at the time. As communication volumes increase however, it is found that the file transfer with NFS leads to long response times for the host application in peak situations. Analytical measurements show that NFS is occupying 70% of the available bandwidth. The staff is instructed to leave costly file transfers until the evening, but even this does not improve the situation. A further dedicated connection is therefore set up, and SNA and NFS are each allocated a dedicated connection and an ISDN channel (see also Figure 13.27).

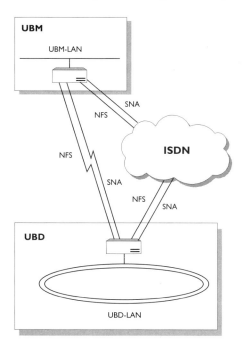

Figure 13.27: Application of MLPPP for UBM and UBD/Stouberg Ltd.

However, the last described configuration can only be implemented in accordance with RFC 1717 by activating several "Link groups" each with different endpoint identifiers, as according to RFC 1717, all Layer 3 protocols are normally defined for a complete link grouping.

Thresholds and Spoofing

As discussed in the chapters on bridge function and routing procedures, LAN traffic generates a lot of overhead packets which say only that everything is still in order and working. These packets must be suppressed as far as possible on a WAN connection, particularly as an occasionally used dial-up connection is otherwise transformed into a permanently used expense. MLPPP could counter this difficulty with threshold values and spoofing.

Threshold values cause a dial-up connection to be activated only above a certain load on the existing connections (e.g., dedicated connections), and deactivated automatically when the load on the original line has fallen back below a specific level (hysteresis process). For dynamic overhead like routing update packets, the necessary capacity cannot always be estimated very well. It also changes as the network configuration increases, and the update packets are also entirely superfluous as long as they do not communicate any actual changes. Spoofing suppresses these packets in the WAN, in that all routers only send and answer update packets to their LAN ports, so long as the routing tables don't change.

Unfortunately RFC 1717 remains silent on this. It is the task of a specific implementation to power down the connection with a Terminate Request for spoofing and when the load falls below the threshold. This function is thus again manufacturer-specific. A corresponding enhancement of RFC 1717 would be desirable.

Device Technology

The advantage for the installed routers (and bridges) is important: Increased bandwidth is achieved by adding a further channel or a further physical interface (further line connection) to the total existing connection. Without MLPPP, adding a new connection or a new channel means changing all routing tables and often setting up a new network for this connection.

13.5.4 Conclusion

PPP is beginning to emerge as the protocol suite for multi-vendor WAN connection of LAN applications. The basic RFCs have been widely accepted among manufacturers and users.

A range of problems remain unsolved, and these problems should not be concealed at this point:

- Not all NCP RFCs are equally good. The best compatibility is achieved, as before, with bridged connections (BCP with IEEE 802.1 D SPT) or for IP (IPCP).

- Some of the RFC documents show interpretation loopholes, which have led to incompatible implementations. A typical gap is, for example, the definition of whether two routers which are connected via a WAN link, act as "half routers" or as "full routers." In the first case, the connection is operated "virtually," hence without numbering, while in the second case the WAN link must be configured as a network and receive a network address.

- Further incompatibilities occur when the routing tables are exchanged.

- For IPX there are several documents. Novell presently supports IPX-WAN, other manufacturers have implemented IPXCP. Thus once again there are incompatible products.

- Functional enhancements which many manufacturers offer as add-ons, such as SDLC tunneling, DLSw, load distribution, and spoofing are naturally not supported by PPP, which was based only on the published de facto standards of the routable protocols.

- The multilink expansion is still relatively young, correspondingly unspecified, and, so far, implemented only by a few manufacturers.

For the network operator in any case: When a manufacturer puts PPP support on its spec sheet, the operator needs to know exactly how many PPP RFCs the manufacturer actually supports, and which ones they are.

14 | Examples of Hardware Architecture

T his chapter presents the architecture of a few available products which support the bridge function, LAN switching or routing.

14.1 Bridges

Now that the functions of a bridge has been described, the hardware on which it all runs is considered in more detail.

Bridges are supplied either as a "box" with corresponding firmware and software, or as a software program which can run on practically any DOS PC (especially in the Token Ring area). In the latter case the performance depends decisively on which PC is installed. The bandwidth here goes from an 80286 processor with 16 MHZ to the Pentium with 90 MHZ. Microchannel PCS as bridges can be found at IBM and Olicom (Token Ring). The "box" architectures are either PC-based or higher, e.g., with 68040 or 68060 processors from Motorola, or RISC chips, e.g., from AMD and sometimes backplanes with several hundred Mbps capacity. With growing requirements of throughput and the demand for multiport bridges, a "box" architecture with fast bus and the possibility of multiprocessor use is interesting.

The RND bridge OpenGate is taken as an example. OpenGate has a newer architecture, and with a software enhancement can also be operated as a router. State of the art is currently a chassis into which modular slot-in system cards and/or, according to the specific user requirements, LAN/WAN cards are inserted. The trend is clearly towards multiprocessor architectures, although nowadays the basic structure with a single CPU card (system board) still predominates.

OpenGate

This multiport bridge, which can also be expanded to a router with the relevant software, is a modular device with 12 slide-in modules for interface cards in the biggest configuration level. There is also a 4-slot model, which works with the same slide-in modules. A front view can be seen in Figure 14.1.

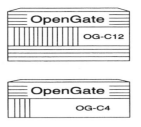

Figure 14.1 OpenGate chassis for slide-in modules

The 12-slot chassis occupies 6 rack units in the 19″ cabinet. There are basically two different slide-in modules: interface cards for LAN and WAN interfaces, and control modules. A possible configuration with 2-port Ethernet interface and 2-port WAN interface is shown in Figure 14.2.

Interface cards and control module(s) talk to one another via separate control lines. The received packet data is transported back and forth internally between modules via a proprietary passive 32-bit backplane bus with a bit rate of 640 Mbps. The bus is a FIFO-Bus, which nonetheless prioritizes FDDI modules for access.

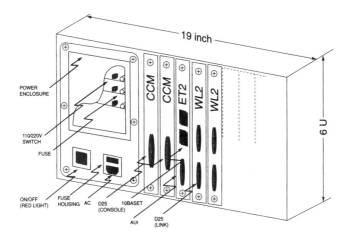

Figure 14.2 OpenGate rear

Up to 5 PSUs (Power Supply Units) provide the power: Each three interface cards need a power supply, the fifth power supply is redundant and intercepts the failure of any PSU. If not all interface slots are occupicd, not all PSUs are needed. The PSUs are built into the back of the device, which unfortunately makes the corresponding maintenance and interchange work more difficult, as the OpenGate has to be taken out of the 19″ cabinet each time, if it is not accessible from both sides. To prevent the device becoming too hot, 4 ventilators (in the 4-slot version 2 ventilators) are incorporated (FANs).

A control module is called a CCM (Central Control Module); each OpenGate is supplied as standard with one CCM. The 12-slot device can optionally be given a redundant CCM. If no redundant CCM is fitted, the slot can be used for a further interface card (No. 13). However, this is not recommended on performance and security grounds. The control module CCM is responsible for system control, control of the LED displays, software initialization (which must be done by rebooting when new software releases are read in), control of the passive backplane bus, memory management of the common memory for configuration data, and packet buffering and management of the routing tables, if routing software is installed.

The CPU on the controller card is an Intel 80186, and the RAM memory for configuration data and packets to be buffered is 4 MB. The operating software and configuration are stored in 1.5 MB Flash EPROM and non-volatile storage of 512 KB. The controller card controls all internal packet forwarding via the 640 Mbit/sec backplane bus from interface card to interface card. A packet which has to be handled is equipped with a destination interface code, transported via the bus into the main memory of the CCM, fetched from there by the interface card with the addressed output interface and forwarded to the destination network. The interplay between controller module, interface cards and system bus is sketched as an architecture plan in Figure 14.3.

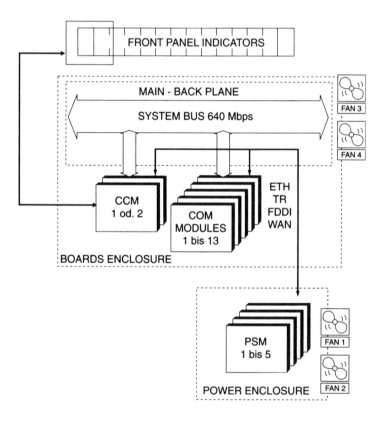

Figure 14.3 OpenGate Architecture

The Interface cards are called COM (Communication Module). They exist for Ethernet (1, 2, 4 ports), Token Ring (2 ports), FDDI (1 port, 2 slots) and WAN link-up (2 ports). A COM module consists of two parts, a main card which is mounted at the back, and an LED card which is mounted at the front. The COM card has interface logic, RISC-CPU Intel i960, LAN chip set (e.g., Intel's Ethernet 82596), 2 MB onboard memory, jumpers and other hardware, and is connected to the backplane bus and the control lines to the CCM. During operation, software is active on every COM module, implementing the bridge function (possibly router function), i.e., the packet transport. This software is stored at the same time in the CCM flash memory, and is loaded into the COM module again after a reset. The LED card is linked via an LED bus to the CCM modules and is controlled by the CCM through this bus.

The user who doesn't have a 19″ cabinet accessible from both sides has the agony of choice: if the user wants to see the LED displays he or she can no longer exchange the modules from the front, while if he or she would like the modules to be easily exchangeable from the front, it has to be done without the LED displays.

14.2 LAN Switches

LAN switches are becoming accepted in the market as standalone devices and as slide-in modules in hub systems. An example from both product groups is described.

14.2.1 3Com LinkSwitch 2700

As an example of LAN switch development, this is a LAN switch which simultaneously supports migration to the new ATM technology: the 3Com LinkSwitch 2700. The device was developed in Israel and supplies 12 Ethernet Ports (Twisted Pair, RJ-45), which are linked via an ATM Uplink to an ATM backbone. Hence the LinkSwitch 2700 can also be classified as an "ATM linking component" and a LAN-ATM converter.

If nothing else configured the LinkSwitch works as a LAN Switch, which connects the 12 Ethernet ports via ATM LE with other subnetworks in the enterprise network. Operating modes which can be set are Store & Forward (SF) and Cut Through (CT); the default setting is Cut Through. Even in the CT mode, though, the first 64 bytes of a packet are buffered and checked to suppress collisions.

As a functional enhancement, it is possible to group ports in virtual LANs (see Chapter 12), as described later.

Architecture

The heart of the architecture is an ASIC called ZipChip2, as shown in Figure 14.4. It ensures that all packets which are received at an Ethernet interface or the ATM interface are temporarily buffered in the so-called Cell RAM (1 MB or 4 MB). As the name reveals, this buffer works in ATM orientation as a cell buffer, i.e., all incoming Ethernet packets are immediately divided into 48-byte cells and forwarded via a 400 Mbps bus to the ZipChip. They are transported from there via an 800 Mbps bus into the "cell buffers," which have a fixed size of 64 bytes. Arriving ATM packets already have the correct size and need no further change. The cells are only put together again at the output port as Ethernet packets if the output port is an Ethernet port. If the output port is the ATM port, ATM LAN emulation packets are made from the cells.

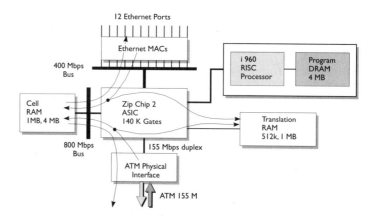

Figure 14.4: Architecture of the 3Com LinkSwitch 2700

The LinkSwitch has no input buffer per port, rather the Cell RAM acts as a shared output buffer memory. This avoids blocking situations at the input buffers (see also Chapter 7). In a 64-byte buffer, 48 data bytes and further control information are stored. This means that for a minimum Ethernet packet of 64 bytes, 2 buffers are provided, hence 128 bytes. For a longer packet, e.g., 230 bytes, 5 buffers (320 bytes) are provided. This dynamic packet buffering allows an optimized buffer utilization with peak loads in contrast to statically allocated buffers, as these must be designed for the maximum packet size. For example: With static buffers, only 500 packets can be buffered in 1 MB memory with 2K buffer size (there is control information in addition to the 1546 byte Ethernet packet length), even if they are all only 64 bytes long. With the dynamic buffering described above, a minimum of 8000 64 byte Ethernet packets can be buffered in 1 MB.

What the ZipChip2 does not do is left as a software function, and is processed by an i960 processor and LAN switch program code, for which 4 MB DRAM are available. The software functionality is, e.g., learning the MAC addresses in accordance with IEEE 802.1D, aging and managing static address entries.

For the packet processing and transformation of LAN cells into ATM LE cells, a separate address memory is used (Translation RAM, 512 KB or 1 MB), in which the MAC address tables and the VPI/VCIs and assignments are held. A 2 MB flash memory is used for storing the configuration and operating software, and the boot software is stored on a separate flash EPROM.

VLAN Function

An Ethernet port can be assigned to a VLAN, resulting in a partition of the ports into VLANs. A VLAN can correspondingly consist of 1 to maximum 12 Ethernet ports, plus the ATM port, which can belong to all VLANs. The LinkSwitch 2700 works for each VLAN like an isolated multiport bridge. This also means a separate Spanning Tree entity per VLAN, as with a common Spanning Tree VLAN internal redundancy would not be possible. The VLANs can be extended across devices by ATM LE via an ATM backbone, each VLAN having its own LES, BUS, and LECS as described in Chapter 11. External routers are necessary for coupling VLANs (see also Chapter 12).

A cascade of LinkSwitch 2700 devices via Ethernet ports is possible but not desirable because only the expansion of a single VLAN would be possible per cascaded port (an Ethernet "Uplink port" can be assigned to exactly one VLAN).

ATM Connection

The ZipChip2 is coupled to the ATM interface by a Duplex connection with 155 Mbps capacity in both directions and implements the ATM level (SAR) and AAL type 5. The architecture favors ATM packets, as the buffering of all packets is always in the ATM cell size and ATM packets therefore do not have to be recopied further. They are simply formatted into ATM LE packets and sent on the necessary VC into the ATM backbone. Between each two LE clients, a bi-directional VC is used. This is set up in the first LE ARP. Multiple–between LE clients are only possible with the Telecom Version Link Switch 2700 TLI. For linking up a LEC to the BUS, LECs, and LES, a bidirectional point-to-point VC is set up, and from the BUS and LES a unidirectional point-to-multipoint VC is set up (see also Chapter 11). ATM traffic flow control is implemented implicitly through the ATM interface.

MAC addresses from LAN subnetworks on the other side of the ATM backbone are learned not only from LE ARPs, but also from arriving ATM packets, whose MAC source addresses are associated with the remote LEC.

Packet Transport

Packet filtering, packet forwarding, flooding of broadcasts and multicasts, VLAN assignment and VC selection are implemented by the ZipChip2 ASIC. If the packet is local traffic, it is discarded in the Cell RAM and not further processed. If the packet has to be transported, the ZipChip searches in the address table for the output port and if necessary the VC (for ATM). The address table (TRAM) consists of two areas, which are hash-organized and use 15-bit indexing. This results in a manageable size of maximum 2*32K entries (see Figure 14.5). An entry consists of a 6 byte MAC address and additional information such as the associated port, the associated VLAN, the associated VC.

An incoming packet is handled by the ZipChip2 as follows:

- If source and destination address are on the same port, the packet is deleted from the Cell RAM (local traffic).

- If the destination address is on a LAN port of the switch, the cells are sent to this port and assembled there as a LAN packet, leaving the LAN port as a normal LAN packet.

- If the destination address belongs to the same VLAN and is linked via a remote LinkSwitch and the ATM backbone, the cells are formatted into ATM LE packets and sent to the corresponding VC of the ATM Uplink.

- If the destination address is the address of the LinkSwitch, it is forwarded to the bridge software (bridge protocol packets or SNMP packets).

- If the destination address is not found, the packet is forwarded to all ports belonging to the same VLAN as the port on which it was received. In addition, it goes as a broadcast on the ATM Link and thus to all other ATM components.

- Multicast packets are treated as unknown destination addresses.

- A broadcast packet is passed on to the bridge software and to all ports belonging to the same VLAN as the port on which it was received.

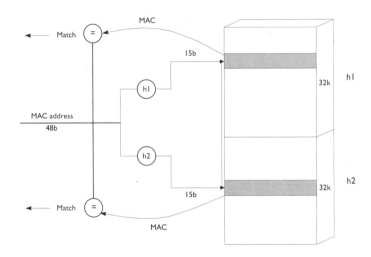

Figure 14.5: Hash table for address entries in the LinkSwitch 2700

14.2.2 3Com/Chipcom ONcore InfiNET Switch

As a supplementary example, a description follows of the core architecture of a hub slide-in module, which works as a LAN switch. The InfiNET Switch Controller for the ONcore hub system includes as a significant new development the ASIC ISC4000, which implements Ethernet LAN switching and translation bridging according to FDDI.

The LAN switch works in Store & Forward mode and as a special functional enhancement supports protocol prioritization. For each port, a protocol type filter can be defined with a high priority. Time-critical protocols can thus be given preferential treatment. Up to 200 filters can be defined, and a port can be set with any defined filter.

The ISC4000 has a link-up to the packet switching backplane (1.8 Gbps) of the ONcore system, a 200 Mbps bus connection for every two switch modules, and internal data buses to the packet buffer (3 MB) and to the DRAM for addresses and switch software (2 to 18 MB). An architecture plan is shown in Figure 14.6. The address table is hash-organized as usual and can manage up to 32K entries. The software functions are controlled by a Motorola 68040 CPU (25 MIPS).

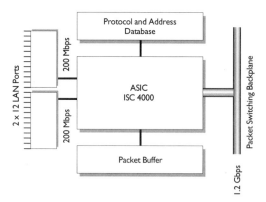

Figure 14.6: InfiNET Switch Module for the ONcore, 3Com/Chipcom

The switch modules each have up to 12 ports (10 Mbps Ethernet) and support 10BaseT, 10BaseFL/FB, 100BaseTX, 100BaseFX, and FDDI.

14.3 Routers

This chapter supplements the basic study of routers with a description of their hardware. Multi-protocol routers which are presently well-established on the market are described as examples: Bay Networks, Cisco, and 3Com (in alphabetical order). The manufacturers each have different platforms for devices with low, medium (entry-level model), and high upgradability.

14.3.1 Bay Networks

The essential elements of a Bay Networks router are:

- CPU module,

- Interface card, and

- System bus.

The architecture can roughly be described as shown in Figure 14.4. For every interface card there is a CPU board which is plugged together with the interface card and communicates via a 32-bit connection bus (processor link module Interconnect). CPU boards are called FRE (Fast Routing Engine) and interface cards are called Link Modules. Both together form an ILI (Intelligent Link Interface)—every manufacturer has its own language. With Bay Networks (to judge by the naming), speed and intelligence are obviously combined. FREs interact among themselves via the system bus. Which is made up of four parallel single buses (250 Mbit/sec), so has a total 1 Gbit/sec bit rate. Presumably after the Orient Express or some other luxury train, the bus is called Parallel Packet Express (PPX). Each FRE is connected to each of the four parallel buses (see Figure 14.7). The FRE-FRE interaction over this bus is controlled by a system controller (CPU basic module).

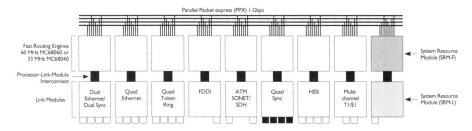

Figure 14.7: Bay Networks Multiprocessor Architecture

CPU Interface Board (ILI)

The Link Modules provide the interfaces and direct send and receive buffers. Essentially they do nothing other than forward the received packets into the temporary buffer and retrieve those for sending from the buffer and dispatch them (see Figure 14.8). The only packet processing function performed here is the bridge function (load separation of the local traffic for Ethernet and FDDI), if this is activated on an interface. In contrast to other manufacturers who implement this function in software, the address filtering is done here with a CAM (Content Addressable Memory). Otherwise a received packet is simply forwarded by the Link Module across the Link Interface to the processor card packet buffer which is shared by all interfaces which are connected via a Link Module to the processor card.

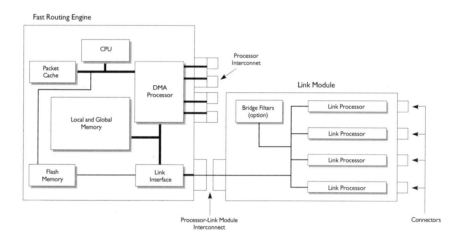

Figure 14.8: Link Interface and Processor card

Each FRE has the complete routing software and a complete routing table for all activated routed protocols. Each FRE therefore occasionally sends update information about the routing tables via the PPX to the other FREs. In order to reduce the processing effort for particularly computer-bound procedures such as OSPF, the Link State Algorithm is performed by a single processor module, the result being forwarded to all other processors.

An FRE has a Motorola 68060 (60 MHZ) or 68040 processor for handling the routing protocols for the connected Link Module, and a 680X0 DMA processor for forwarding packets via the PPX to another board (board-to-board routing). The processor module's memory amounts to 8 to 32 MB and is partitioned into local memory for operating code and global memory for packet buffering. Both processors access a further storage area for the temporary buffering, a 4 KB data cache and 4 KB instruction cache. An architecture plan of the FRE is shown in Figure 14.9. Flash memory is used for storing the operating software and the router configuration.

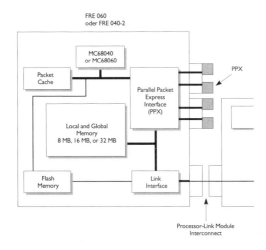

Figure 14.9: Processor card, "Fast Routing Engine"

As before, Bay Networks uses CISC rather than RISC processors, as in the manufacturer's opinion the former can cope better than the latter with I/O-intensive routing tasks.

Expansion

For the migration to ATM, a special ATM processor card was developed (ARE, ATM Routing Engine), which, instead of 680xx, uses two PowerPC processors from Motorola. It has 32 MB memory and an 8 MB Flash Card, for storing the configuration. The Flash Card can be used for booting the entire router. In a further enhancement, FREs should also support Flash Cards, which could then be used as backup. The associated Link Module has an ATM interface with 155 Mbps capacity. Unfortunately only UNI 3.0 and not UNI 3.1 is supported in the first version.

Modularity

Bay-"boxes" can appear in various sizes, depending upon how many interface cards should be possible as maximum. Different expandable (max. 4 and max. 13 slots) basic units are used for this. Cards can be exchanged between the medium- and high-end models. As in all models the same interface cards are plugged into compatible CPU boards (FRE), which access the same bus (PPX). All cards are the same size, so the available slots can be used in any way.

There are double and quadruple Ethernet boards, and double and quadruple Token Ring boards; FDDI boards at present have a maximum of one. Serial boards have two or four ports or one High Speed Port (HSSI); mixed LAN/WAN boards are also possible (see also Figure 14.7).

A second product line is a cheaper alternative, the Access Stack Nodes, with which up to four router units can be connected together. Unfortunately these devices are not module-compatible to the Link Node product line, which makes a migration from one line to the other more difficult.

14.3.2 Cisco

The Cisco 7500 products are the first routers which implement the Cisco-Fusion architecture with regard to software and hardware. They were announced in the Autumn of 1995.

Modularity

The 7500 line consists of three models with 4, 5, and 11 slots for interfaces; the last two models support redundant power supply and redundant supply lead. In this new line, Cisco seems to have learned for the first time that backward compatibility and a sensible migration concept are important to customers: the interfaces of the 7000 systems also fit in the new 7500 systems, and conversely 7500 interfaces can also be incorporated in 7000 devices (with lower performance, since they are subject to the restrictions of the 7000 architecture, e.g., 500 Mbps bus).

CPU Board and Backplane

The 7500 architecture is shown in diagram form in Figure 14.10. The computing load for routing/bridging/switching is distributed across several processors, which nevertheless do not have equal rights. There is a central processor (optionally doubled), called the Route Switch Processor (RSP), which unites the functions of the route processor and switch processor. It is based on a MIPS R4600 RISC chip and additional ASICs. The RSP takes care of the configuration memory, monitoring of the individual modules, memory management, interface statistics, and the table construction for routing and multilayer switching. In the 7-slot and 11-slot system, a double RSP can be fitted, the memory of the second CPU then also being used in normal operation by the primary CPU. In case of error the secondary CPU takes over operation (a reboot takes place). Each RSP is equipped as standard with 2 MB buffer memory for packets. The main memory has 16 MB and can be upgraded to 128 MB per RSP. The new CyBus has a capacity of 1.066 Gbps and can likewise be doubled. This makes most sense when the central CPU is also doubled. Each RSP can be linked to both system buses and thus use an internal system bit rate of 2.132 Mbps.

For microcode and configuration software the RSP has 8 MB flash memory (not configurable) and 8 MB configurable PCMCIA card.

Interface Cards

The versatility of the new interfaces is that different interfaces can be combined in one VIP, for example LAN and WAN, or 10 Mbps and 100 Mbps Ethernet: a VIP has two port adapters or child cards. Each child card can be given different interfaces. The loophole for Bay Networks was obviously closed here. However, the advantage over Bay is the higher modularity of the exchangeable child cards compared to permanently configured interface cards with LAN-WAN interface combinations. Each VIP has 512 KB own packet buffer. Second generation VIPs will handle functions such as compression, encryption and queues for priority control, which are presently still performed by the RSP.

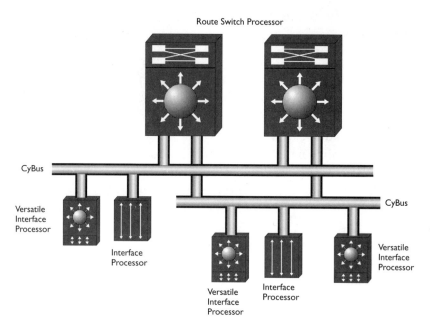

Figure 14.10: Architecture of the Cisco 7500

In the first launch there are four different VIP cards: one port 100 Mbps Ethernet; two port 100 Mbps Ethernet; 4-fold Ethernet/4-fold serial; and one port 100 Mbps Ethernet/4-fold Ethernet.

Despite the capacity increase, 7000 Series interfaces can also (by upgrade to the current Revision Level) be linked to the new CyBus. A single interface card (Interface Processor (IP), from the 7000 line and Versatile Interface Processor (VIP), from the 7500 line) can be linked to either the primary or secondary system bus (CyBus).

14.3.3 3Com

This section describes the architecture of the modular 3Com router NetBuilderII. NetBuilderII comes in two variants, a 4-slot model and an 8-slot model. Ethernet, Token Ring, and FDDI modules and a very wide range of WAN interface modules are available.

NetBuilderII has a single processor architecture; there is an architecture plan in Figure 14.10. The central CPU module CEC (Communication Engine Card) is fitted with a RISC processor AMD 29000, 25 MHZ. It controls through an 800 Mbit/sec system bus the interface cards which are connected to the bus via CMPI ASICs (Core Memory Peripheral Interface). The main memory is quite big with 3x4 MB; 4 MB for AMD commands, 4 MB for routing tables and data structures, 4 MB as shared RAM for packet buffering. Memory transfers and the bus are controlled by several ASICs: BSC (Bus Switch Controller), DMC (Dynamic Memory Controller) for the AMD control-signal storage unit and CMC (Core Memory Controller) for the shared RAM. The configuration and operating software is stored on a flash memory card with PCMCIA format. Figure 14.11 shows a block diagram with FDDI and Ethernet module.

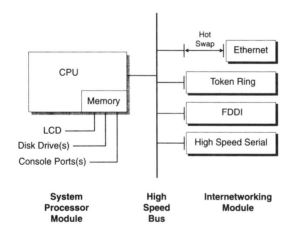

Figure 14.11 NetBuilder II Architecture

The FDDI module is fitted with a CAM (Content Addressable Memory), to allow a maximum of 8000 address entries for the bridge function. Thus the module works with hardware filtering, if it is operated as a bridge module (see Figure 14.12).

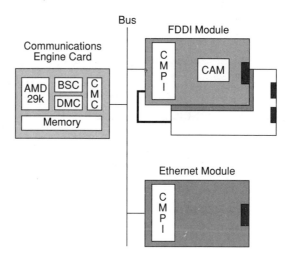

Figure 14.12 NetBuilder II with FDDI and Ethernet Module

Expansion

Further development of the NetBuilder II architecture is towards multiprocessor operation: the interface modules have a separate RISC processor (AMS 29030), which takes over the packet handling and forwarding. The central CPU (CEC) then only has to take on the routing table computation for the activated protocols. At the same time the new cards offer a higher interface concentration, e.g., six Ethernet interfaces (RJ-45 contacts).

14.4 Hub System Slide-in Modules

14.4.1 Technical Aspects

In the course of the expansion from terminal concentrator to internetworking box, the hub gained bridge, router, and LAN switch functionality in the form of slide-in modules, referred to below as B/R modules. B/R modules are often OEM adaptations from established internetworking manufacturers such as Cisco, Bay Networks, Retix, ACC etc. These modules occupy one to several slots and are integrated in different levels in the hub system:

- Chassis integration

- Half integration
- Full integration

At all integration levels, the power consumption of the B/R module of hub systems should particularly be taken into account in configuration planning. In some cases the power supply is insufficient for a concentration of more than three to four B/R modules per hub.

Chassis Integration

The B/R module uses the hub system's power supply. The available interfaces of the B/R module are linked externally, i.e., via a separate cable from a B/R module interface port to cable segments or further hub systems. The link can also be to a concentrator card in the hub in which the B/R module is installed.

Half Integration

The B/R module uses the hub system's power supply and can also be linked with an internal interface to a hub LAN bus. The second and all further interfaces are cabled to external segments or further hub systems. The link can also be to a concentrator card in the hub in which the B/R module is installed.

Full Integration

The B/R module can be linked flexibly to two (or more) hub-internal buses or external segments. If ports are used externally, the link-up can also be to a concentrator card in the hub in which the B/R module is installed. For a two-port module, which is configured as an internal-internal coupling, consequently, no external cabling is present at all.

With the integration levels described above, the following coupling options arise, as represented in Figures 14.13 to 14.15:

- external—external
- internal—external
- internal—internal

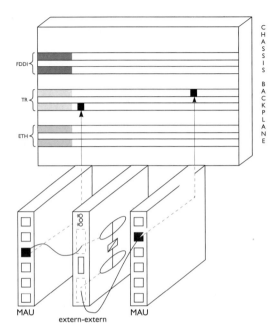

Figure 14.13: Bridge module with external–external coupling

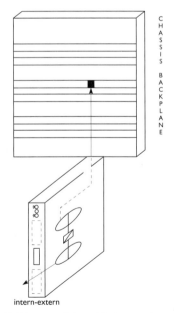

Figure 14.14: Bridge module with internal–external coupling

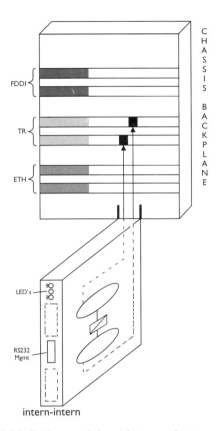

Figure 14.15: Bridge module with internal–internal coupling

The costs of B/R modules as hub slide-in modules are usually higher than separate devices with the same number of ports. The manufacturers quote the integration work done in hub management as an argument for them. However, in many cases this is restricted to very basic functions only (e.g., port on/off). For full configurability a separate application, at best on the same management platform, must be called as before.

Application Scenario

To clarify areas of application for B/R modules in hub systems, a further UBD development phase is now described:

As the doll product spectrum continues to grow and the operating margin consequently becomes narrower, UBD decides to relocate production of masculine dolls to cheap production countries, as the outfits and accessories are significantly simpler to produce than those for the female dolls. In internal company usage, the Far Eastern branch is called ATM (All Terrific Men). The manager is Pro To Col.

Location ATM needs access to the central IBM host, to the development department and occasionally to PC servers. SNA, TCP/IP, and IPX must be operated over the WAN connection to be established (at least so long as NetWare has not migrated to TCP). The link to the UBD headquarters is via a WAN link by satellite with 9.6 kbps capacity. A multi-protocol router module with bridge functionality is fitted in the backbone hubs of both locations (see Figure 14.16).

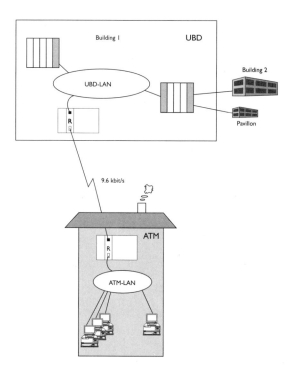

Figure 14.16: UBD headquarters and location ATM

14.4.2 Hub Modules Versus Standalone Devices

This chapter describes some significant differences, advantages and disadvantages in using B/R modules in hub systems compared to separate bridge/router devices.

Functionality

- The space used is small compared to standalone devices (an advantage for narrow distribution cabinets).

- B/R modules in hubs mostly have two ports; the number of parts is small compared to standalone devices.

- Remote ports are restricted to 1 to 2 per B/R module.

- The response time is up to twice as long compared to a pure repeater coupling.

- Each port is attached to a "segment;" there is usually no broadband common backplane.

- Special functions, such as filters, load distribution, etc., are only supported with restrictions.

- For OEM modules, a change of OEM partner can mean a change of product strategy. This means no further enhancement of the "old" B/R modules.

- In the migration of B/R modules in the concentrator to standalone devices, compatibility problems can arise.

Management

- Concentrators and bridges/routers can be managed with the same management system (operating advantage).

- In the Token Ring area, support of the IBM LAN Manager is not always given.

- B/R modules sometimes need separate configuration programs (as SW on a PC/NMS) or are initially configured by a Telnet session.

- For the status display, there are mostly only LEDs, not LCDs.

- For management with SNMP, an IP address should be assigned at least per B/R module, sometimes per B/R port (take into account in planning)

- "Hot swappable" only means exchangeability during operation, not automatic reinstallation of the configuration of the previous module. The configuration is stored in the B/R module.

- A concentrator with integrated B/R module intensifies the Single-Point-of-Failure problems.

Costs

- The costs for a hub chassis are lower than those for a B/R chassis.

- A B/R module as slide-in unit is usually dearer than the same device in the standalone version.

- The integrated operation reduces the support service complexity; hubs and bridges can be obtained from one source.

- Integration of B/R modules allows the number of hubs used to be reduced.

- The modest space requirement saves expensive space in the distribution cabinet/room.

Conclusion

Using B/R modules yields advantages from:

- Load separation

- Fault isolation

- Space savings

- Lower number of hubs

- Structured formation of subnetworks across tiers with Collapsed Backbone

- Usage of the hub management

Using B/R modules yields disadvantages from:

- Single Point of Failure (SPoF)

- Lack of independence in product selection

- More limited functionality

- Lower performance values than separate bridges or routers in the upper product level

- Compatibility problems in migration to standalone devices

15 Deployment and Operation

15.1 Management Aspects

Network management—not just in the context of bridges and routers, although increasingly in relation to them—has become an important subject in recent years. A separate chapter is therefore devoted to it. The chapter restricts itself to network management in the context of bridges and routers, as otherwise it would go beyond the scope of the book. See [KAU01] and [TERP91] for more extensive references. Two aspects are to be considered: on one hand the management of the devices themselves; their handling qualities and user-friendliness, i.e.,

- Management of bridges and routers based on:
  Ethernet
  Token Ring
  FDDI

and on the other hand the global management within an overall integrative strategy including bridges and routers, i. e.,

- Management with bridges and routers based on an overall concept which includes all network components. This poses a range of questions which should be the basis of the examination:

- Which network management functions can be implemented with bridges?

- Which network management functions can be implemented with routers?

- How can the use of management systems from bridge and router manufacturers be assessed?

- How can different coupling elements be implemented into an integrative overall management of the enterprise network?

- How can investment protection be achieved, in the sense of linking existing components and those to be installed in the future in an enterprise network management?

- Which migration paths should be aimed for, from the present situation of isolated network islands and differently-managed interconnection components to common management?

The chapters which follow deal with the concepts and questions mentioned, beginning with the victim of the whole development: the user.

15.1.1 Management by Structuring

When setting up a complex network, suitable structure planning and implementation with corresponding documentation will set the conditions for the future network management and also put into practice some fundamental management aspects. This happens chiefly by the principle "divide and rule" (the ancient Romans quoted once more): structured networks are clearer in topology, easier to handle when searching for errors, better upgradable when there are performance bottlenecks, and so on. Networks can be subdivided by geographical, topological, and logical structuring.

Topological Structuring

Geographical structuring represents the classic approach since the development of more complex networks. Included are:

- Complete networks at one site

- Backbone networks (at one site)

- Subnetworks

- Floor subnetworks

which in each case are separated from other network parts, and simultaneously linked with them, by bridges, LAN switches or routers as relay elements. For Local Area Networks, backbone formation (location sites), and building separation, geographical/topological structuring can be seen as state of the art. With regard to floor separation, star-shaped twisted pair cabling increasingly offers an organizational subnetwork structure instead of the less flexible (de)coupling of whole floors.

Logical Structuring

Logical structuring means an application- and organization-related partitioning of the network, related to different application groups (departments, work groups) and protocol groups (DECnet, NetWare, SNA, etc.). It is particularly gaining acceptance at present against topological floor coupling (see above), but should also be considered for inter-building aspects, e.g., in assigning priorities (Spanning Tree bridges), assigning path costs (router metrics), or setting filters at MAC/network level for controlling the path selection or traffic flow in redundant network structures (which are presupposed as present in all the more complex networks). Such logical networks are, for example (see Figure 15.1):

- Department networks (where a department is normally distributed over several floors, and this situation mostly continues over a long period because of frequent moves or, after a concentration on one floor is achieved, rapidly returns following expansion).

- PC networks for adequate operation of computer applications, whose users tend to spread throughout all departments of all buildings without any recognizable structure (secretaries' offices, users' workstations, etc.).

- CAD networks in the field of constructive and development-oriented activities.

- Production networks in production environments, which are usually subject to special operating conditions (the geographical and logical structuring coincide best here, as production areas are often self-contained).

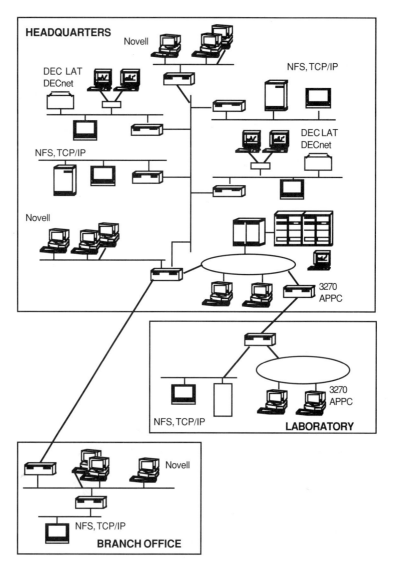

Figure 15.1: Subnetwork-structured Enterprise Network

15.1.2 User Interface

In deciding whether or not to buy a particular product, the ease of operation and the user interface supplied are not least among the considerations. A good user interface does not make up for a bad performance or lack of filter functionality; but user-friendliness (or lack of it) should not be underestimated, both for daily operation and for error situations.

User-friendliness is a sore point with most computer products, and similarly with LAN switches, bridges, and routers. The manuals should be considered first; often they are not available in the required language, have poor glossaries, and as for helping the user to find a command or study the given cross-references, their structure is more reminiscent of a paper chase than a course for user guidance. Secondly, the possibilities for device management and configuration are far removed from any OSF standard or any other usable GUI (Graphical User Interface). Some menu prompting reminds you rather of the beginnings of self-written DOS batches.

These can be controlled via various configurations, as shown in Figure 15.2:

- locally-connected console (VT100 terminal) and V.24 connection

- PC with terminal emulation and V.24 connection

- PC with network connection (e.g., Ethernet) and logging in to the bridge or the router with a standard protocol (e.g., TELNET)

- remotely via modem (RS232) with Telnet and/or in-house protocols using SLIP or PPP basis

Dialing in from any network PC is the most flexible, but in the fewest bridges and routers with full function possibility; e.g., sometimes not all commands are allowed under TELNET, or not all system messages are displayed. If this is not implemented, the option of a remote login should be made an indispensable requirement, i.e., the possibility of logging in from a network component (then installed in the management center) to all other bridges operated in the network. Even better is a remote modem connection option. The bridge/router can then be in an enclosed room and the management console in the CC linked by a modem connection. However, with several parallel login options, the integrity principle must be preserved: if a local manager is logged into the bridge at the same time, configuration consistency must be implemented (e.g., by the motto "the first one wins, the second no longer gains access" or "local login has priority over login via the network").

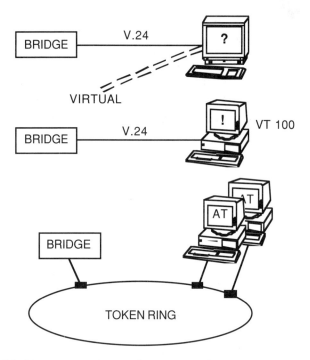

Figure 15.2: Management Access Options with Internetworking Components

As the configuration and operation of routers is clearly more difficult than for bridges, the era of the command interpreter (often called the Network Control Language (NCL)) sometimes still prevails for routers (unless the customer buys an expensive graphic proprietary network management system at the same time). As user interface for the configuration and administration of a bridge, there is normally a choice of menu prompting or a command interpreter; most bridges, fortunately, already use menu prompting instead of a command interpreter. The menu prompting differs considerably according to product in the queriable help functions, nesting depth of the menu tree, and logically associative context of the various menus (see also Figure 15.3). Menu prompting often proves to be more user-friendly than the command interpreter, provided the menus are laid out with sufficient consistency and clarity. In particular, this means:

- Menu tree depth not more than 6,

- Change of associated variables, in particular setting and deletion of the same variables in the same menu, and

- Menu texts which are unique in interpretation (under the key words "Performance statistics" for instance, the user expects performance data rather than timing markers for overflow situations).

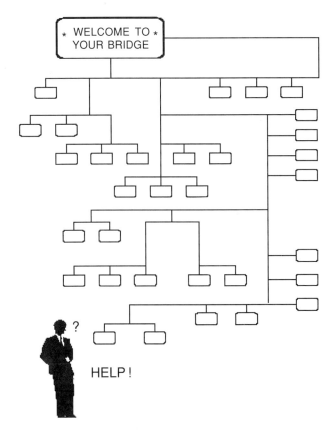

Figure 15.3: Confusing Menu Prompting for Device Configuration

A good command interpreter may be preferable to a miserable menu prompting system; but in general, menu prompting is easier to manage, and therefore worth pursuing.

A well-known bridge product, whose name is omitted here out of courtesy, has several hundred menu screens and a menu tree depth of about 8 levels in its fully-configured state. Some parameters are activated on the fifth tree level but can only be deactivated again on the first level. Such a perfect example of user-friendly menu prompting can indeed make life difficult for the long-suffering network operator. Unless an operator spends daily breaks on configuration, he or she has very little chance of getting a permanent grasp of the various functions and contexts of the management menus. Every action to be taken with the bridges will be correspondingly lengthy and tedious.

There are also counter-examples in which the efforts towards user-friendliness can be recognized, e.g., good command overviews, quick references, graphic overview plans of the menu tree, and so on. Unfortunately, user friendliness often has to take second place to the explosive development of new features (more ports, new hardware interfaces for 100BaseX and ATM, new software versions, bootPROMs, SNMP agents, etc.). These functional properties are often much better researched in a purchasing decision than the available user interface—with some justification. The problem is simply that those responsible for the network have to be plagued day by day with the practical operation of all these wonderful functions.

For the future, it is hoped that as bridges and routers are integrated in correspondingly all-embracing network management systems with full access functionality, the configuration and management of these interconnection components will, in fact, become more user friendly.

15.1.3 System-inherent Management Possibilities

When you log in via a directly-connected end system, via network or modem inband or outband into an internetworking component, there are several functions at your disposal without the use of any further management tool. As the investment of $100,000 or more for a management platform system is not justified in every network, the simpler possibilities that an interconnection component offers with its system software should be described in more detail.

15.1.3.1 Bridge functions

Like backup connections, management and analysis functions in bridges for complex networks are extremely important functions for securing the service quality. Management functions which can be executed with bridges act chiefly in the field of configuration and error management. Functions for performance, accounting management, and security management are only present on a limited scale.

The management functions are now described, according to the five functional areas specified by OSI: "Configuration," "Fault," "Performance," "Accounting," and "Security."

Configuration Management

A range of parameters and management actions should be considered for configuration management by and with bridges:

Login

All convenient bridges nowadays implement the option of remote login (logging in from one bridge into all others), if logging in from any network PC is not possible (e.g., via TELNET). The assignment of logical alias names, which naturally can be handled more conveniently than hex digits, makes operation and management easier, but is not implemented in all products.

Implementation of the full command range in remote login mode is necessary. The demand seems obvious, but is not satisfied in all cases. Depending on the product, one or more management connections are possible in parallel to different bridges. A remote integrity check should be implemented in any case, i.e., if an administrator is logged in, the device must be locked for further parallel administrative access by other persons.

Booting

If the bridge has only a diskette and no bootPROM, there can be no download in case of faulty software. A new diskette must be brought to the site (the network operator gets into his car). BootPROM with download option is the alternative worth pursuing, but unfortunately it is not always implemented.

Passwords

It goes without saying that firstly, password protection is implemented and secondly, all passwords can be set and changed with software. This will be dealt with in more detail in the functional area "Security."

Ports

It should be possible to activate and deactivate ports by management action. When a port is deactivated, the bridge should remain active (in contrast to this demand, the IBM bridge program crashes when a port is deactivated). When booting, the bridge must check all available ports for operability and activation and issue corresponding management messages. It must be possible to query and set the port speed (LAN and WAN), which in particular for remote ports must be accompanied by buffer administration corresponding to the speed. Especially luxurious devices allow the buffer size to be selected, but mostly this is internally regulated (which, in many cases, suits the ignorance of the users and likewise their unwillingness to have to deal with buffer management). In the context of load distribution, it should be noted that FIFO traffic can sometimes be assigned to a particular port, i.e., this port is not linked in to the load distribution, but only sends packets along the SPT route.

Address Tables

Address tables must be both viewable and editable, in order that the status of learned addresses and static entries can be checked and manipulated. There are products with a central table for all ports and some with a table per port. The latter can make handling more difficult with multiport bridges, as several tables cannot be viewed simultaneously. The display options here vary from simple scrolling of addresses to display by entry number, address masks, etc. In the context of address tables, it is pointed out once more that it should be possible to activate and deactivate aging and the learning mode, and to set the aging interval.

Filters

The manufacturers' imaginations could have free rein here. Filter configuration varies from simple address entry at the appropriate point in the menu to complex sequences of different statements in command language and x different filter tables. Because they actively influence the traffic flow in the network and affect logical network configuration, filters play an important part in configuration management. In particular, it should be possible to activate and deactivate them in the same menu; fortunately this is true of all but a few negative cases.

Spanning Tree

Active configuration design for the active network with redundant mechanisms includes being able to set all Spanning Tree parameters, especially the bridge and port priorities and path costs. These should be managed in a common menu. The configured HELLO interval influences the load on the network from bridge broadcasts for maintaining the SPT.

Source Routing

It must be possible to set Single Route Broadcast and All Routes Broadcast. The mode set by the manufacturer as default status for the ports should particularly be noted, to make sure that all ports do not transport as default when Single Route Broadcast is set.

An important demand in this context is amendment of all parameters during operation: if this is not implemented, configuration changes can only be made by the network manager after work, or network operation must be interrupted during work for reconfiguration—an unacceptable downtime for commercial enterprises.

Fault Management

When communication errors occur, e.g., "no connectivity" or "long response time," a few error checks can be performed with bridges. In certain fault situations, bridges generate warnings or alarm signaling within error management. In addition to this, bridges perform fault limitation by not transporting faulty packets out of the subnetwork, thereby limiting the error condition to the local subnetwork.

Self-test

Bridges perform a self-test during the boot process which checks the bridge hardware, bridge ports, and connections to the network cable. A message appears about faults.

Hardware Faults

Messages about port failures should also occur during operation. For network system collapses (overload, cable faults, etc.) a message should similarly appear in the bridge management system.

Spanning Tree

For hardware failures which lead to the loss of an active connection path, the SPT algorithm becomes active. This should lead to an alarm message apart from the subsequent reconfiguration.

Error Checks

For communication errors, a range of parameters can be checked with the bridge. The bridge mode can be a cause of error, if a new station cannot set up any communication outside the subnetwork because learning is switched off. A glance in the address table provides information on active stations which could be potential sources of error. Management statistics show occurring CRC errors, collisions, and buffer overflows, giving first assistance on long response times. Not least, the display of the bridge and port statuses is helpful: a deactivated bridge or a deactivated port transports nothing.

Performance/Accounting Management

Performance data can only be obtained at MAC level. It includes:

- sent/received packets
- sent/received bytes
- packet counters
- port utilization
- network load
- CPU utilization

Transmitted and received frames and bytes can sometimes be viewed in relation to individual active ports, in the corresponding statistics menus. Performance filters can sometimes be set, with which, for example, packets of a certain type or with certain addresses can be counted. The current network load is displayed for a range of products, as is the traffic on individual ports. The CPU and buffer utilization of the bridge is displayed only by a few products.

Security Management

Bridges can implement security functionality for connected subnetworks, but they must also be protected themselves against unauthorized access.

Password Protection

The login to a bridge must be protectable by password. Incidentally, it makes no sense not to use the implemented password protection. Laziness is no excuse for slipshod security precautions—no one would leave his or her front door unlocked (most of the time). In addition, bridges should not be placed on campus or in the corridor (this is not a joke—sad but true), but behind the locked door of a wiring closet.

Sometimes individual commands are given a separate password (e.g., the reboot command), or different access hierarchies can be set with different passwords (User, Local Manager, Super Manager). This is particularly useful with remote management if a support person on site can perform certain simple management actions while there is a higher-ranking person for special queries.

Access Protection

Admission security for the connected subnetworks can be achieved with positive or negative filter setting (see section Chapter 6.1)

Remote Subnetworks

For networks with remote segments which are linked via WAN connections, the described management options are even more important than for LAN-LAN interconnection. The considerably greater physical extension of the network often makes it impossible to correct errors rapidly "on site," so that management functions such as remote login (between bridges, not end stations), remote boot, statistical queries, and status information are necessary over the entire network in such a way that they can be executed across segments at a (central) console. For these reasons, remote bridges are usually more luxuriously equipped with management functions than their local counterpart. The functionality must be available at all management consoles so that if one bridge fails, fault correction is possible from another bridge.

As management functions in bridges are implemented still more variably than SPT protocols—effectively beyond all standards—the demand for uniform bridges if possible is even more justified. There is light on the horizon regarding management from the currently very well established SNMP management standard (even if significantly more functions would be desirable here), especially for bridges and routers. It gives hope that one day even internetworking components from different manufacturers will be jointly manageable via generic management functions and MIB variables.

Management Scenario

A few actions are now enumerated as examples of what can be performed with the management functions of a bridge in case of error. The error case assumed is that in the network shown (see Figure 15.4) once again no connection is possible between Asterix and Obelix. The individual actions are correspondingly numbered in Figure 15.4.

The following actions can be performed as error checks:

1. View the address table. If the station address is entered in the table, then the wanted station is at least active and known to the bridge, i.e., packets are correspondingly transported.

2. Check the port utilization. If a port is overloaded, no more packets come through and a new connection cannot be set up.

3. Check the collision rate. If the number of collisions is too high, the packet transport slows down for all packets, leading to time-outs and, accordingly, to failed connection attempts.

4. Check the CRC error rate. Many CRC errors suggest hardware faults in adapter cards or in the hardware of the cable, repeater, hub system, transceiver etc.

Points 2 to 4 can be checked for every subnetwork. This isolation technique can localize the source of error to a certain subnetwork (if it comes from a defined subnetwork).

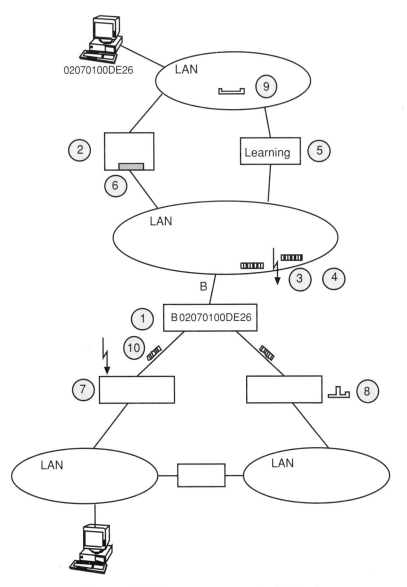

Figure 15.4 Management scenario (Bridges)

5. Check the learning mode. If the bridge is not in learning mode but in protected mode, it transports only known addresses. A newly-added station is then unable to communicate across the subnetworks.

6. Check the port status. It is advisable to do this first for the bridges on the subnetwork of the station wanting to transmit. Afterwards the check is extended successively to all bridge ports between sender and receiver. A port with status "Down" naturally cannot transport packets.

7. Check bridge status. The error "Bridge inactive" should not first be noticed when a user can no longer communicate; it should be detected by permanent monitoring immediately after a bridge has failed. Nonetheless, in case of error, all bridges between the send and receive stations should be checked for the status "active."

8. Check filter settings. Removal or reconfiguration of the network can mean that the filters set are no longer suitable for the current situation and block necessary connections (if adapting them for the new situation has been forgotten).

9. Check broadcast filters. This is analogous to point 8.

10. Check load distribution. When setting up load distribution, it can be overlooked that FIFO traffic was included in the load distribution. The corresponding protocol (e.g., LAT) does not cope with the packet reordering (see section 6.2) and crashes.

The management actions which can be taken via bridges without further management software in an error situation are basic in nature.

15.1.3.2 Router Functions

Since networks in which routers are used are generally even more complex than networks with bridges, the importance of a router's network management functionality needs no further emphasis. Management functions which can be executed with routers act chiefly in the field of configuration and error management. Functions for performance, accounting management, and security management, though more plentiful than for bridges, are still not so convenient that they cover all requirements in this functional area.

The management functions are now described, according to the five functional areas specified by OSI: "Configuration," Fault," "Performance," "Accounting," and "Security." The specified features should be understood as what is available in addition to the options for a bridge, as router management normally (except for the filter functions) covers the management options of a bridge and goes beyond them. In particular, combined multi-protocol routers, which also support bridge functionality, can do everything in management that bridge management can.

Configuration Management

To list all configuration options would go beyond the scope of this book, especially for multi-protocol routers, for which all parameters of all available routed protocols can of course be configured. Only examples of configuration options are therefore given:

Login

See Bridges. In addition: remote login (logging-in from one bridge into all others) counts as state of the art, if logging-in from any network PC is not possible (e.g., via TELNET). Unfortunately the full functionality of all commands and system messages of a TELNET session is not yet possible in all cases on a PC or other host connected to the network. The assignment of logical alias names for the individual router systems is usually implemented as management functionality.

Booting

See Bridges. In addition: it is sometimes possible to configure an automatic reboot after error situations. However, this is a two-edged sword: in an irreversible error situation, the device is not deactivated, instead, it gets hung up in an endless "reboot" loop, thereby possibly having an impact the entire network. Therefore, this option should only be used with the greatest of care.

Passwords

See Bridges.

Ports

See Bridges. In addition: the number of possible ports and different interfaces is significantly greater for routers than for bridges. Also, there is correspondingly more information data to manage. It is advisable to store it in a database.

Protocols

A single protocol router handles only a single protocol. Only the parameters of this protocol can be set. With multi-protocol routers, all protocols implemented for a system can be activated or deactivated, which is of course very useful when not all possible protocols are used (performance improvement!). Current active connections of individual protocols can be viewed.

Routing Tables

Dynamic, i.e., protocol-created routing tables can be viewed. The displayed destination routers and metric values are produced from the preconfigured parameters of the routing protocol. These can be set when the router configuration is created; the table can be seen as the result of the selected parameters. In the configuration, the value is set, e.g., for a table update. Tables for static routes can be viewed and edited. The tables are always protocol-specific, i.e., for each protocol a separate table exists for each possible route type (dynamic, static, default route, etc.).

Filters

Filters can be used in some protocols (TCP/IP, IPX, NetBIOS, etc.) at network level or higher levels. As examples, IP address filters (source, destination), TCP port filters, import routes filters, export routes filters, and SAP filters at network level and server level could be mentioned. Because filters actively influence the traffic flow in the network and effect logical network structuring, they play an important part in configuration management. In particular, it should be possible to activate and deactivate them in the same menu; this is fortunately true of all except a few negative cases.

The requirement "Amendment of all parameters during operation" is just as important for routers as for bridges.

Fault Management

When communication errors occur, e.g., "no connectivity" or "long response time," a few error checks can be performed with routers. In certain error situations, routers generate warnings or alarm messages within error management. In addition to this, they perform fault limitation by not transporting error packets (where errors are recognized up to the network level) out of the subnetwork, thereby limiting the error situation to the local subnetwork.

Self-test

See Bridges.

Hardware Faults

See Bridges.

Protocols

If a route is no longer present for a particular protocol, an error message is output; likewise for its restoration. If a particular subnetwork (i.e., the network address of a particular protocol) can no longer be reached, a message is created for the sending end station. Failed authentication attempts are likewise reported. Values for a very wide range of protocol parameters are displayed in case of error (disassembly error, wrong version numbers).

Polling

Both routers and end stations can be polled for activity. For a negative result, an error message is logged.

Log Files

There are Event and Error Logs in a very wide range of categories distinguishes e.g., "Fatal," "Service change," "Performance losses," "Warning," "Routing Events," "Link Status Events."The various categories can be displayed or suppressed. Events are, e.g., entries about negative polling attempts (see above), insufficient space for routing entries, boot attempts, de/activation of adjacent nodes, protocol de/activation, etc. Both events which concern the end station and events in router protocols (OSPF, RIP, etc.) are displayed.

MIB Database

As well as a log book, a range of products provides a MIB (Management Information Base). A wide variety of data on protocol configurations, protocol actions, hardware, storage values, and alarm messages is managed as objects and made available for viewing. The objects are organized in trees (analogous in principle to the MIB in OSI and CMIP, but in-house implementation). The number of managed objects can be several hundred. Some examples from Figure 15.5: the object "tcp" has sub-objects "Sent acknowledgments," "Number of faulty TCP segments," "Number of TCP error messages," "Number of packets received," "Number of packet repeats," etc. The object "ipx" has the sub-objects "Variables", "idp = Internet Datagram Protocol," as sub-object "Address table," "Routing table," "SAP table," etc.

Error Checks

For communication errors, a range of parameters can be checked with the router: Management menus show the loss of certain routes, overflow of routing tables, down status of adjacent routers, activated/deactivated protocols, and so on, and also as for bridges, occurring CRC errors, collisions, and buffer overflows, giving first assistance on long response times. Last but not least, the display of the bridge and port status is helpful: a deactivated router or a deactivated port transports nothing.

Performance/Accounting Management

Performance data can be obtained at MAC and network level, i.e., sent and received MAC frames and bytes can be viewed, sometimes in relation to individual active ports in the relevant statistics menus, and in addition sent/received packets and bytes are given at network level for individual protocols. A wide variety of protocol and interface-related values can be retrieved in all, e.g., about

- CPU usage,
- Buffer usage per interface,
- Free buffers per interface,
- per protocol:
  Receipt (bytes, packets), per network address,
  Sending (bytes, packets), per network address,
  Non-transport (packets), per network address,
  Broadcasts,
  Time-outs,

Hop Counts,

Disassemblies,

Reassemblies,

Number of call set-ups,

Process running time of individual protocol processes.

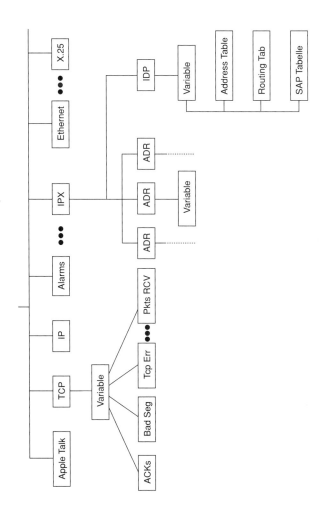

Figure 15.5 Objects of a Router MIB

Security Management

Routers must be protected on the one hand against unauthorized access, and on the other hand, should implement security functionality for connected subnetworks.

Password Protection

Often only the system admission is password-protected, not individual commands. Password protection can involve several levels (User=READ ONLY, Manager=READ/WRITE). As routers support significantly more complex configurations than bridges, it is even more advisable for routers than for bridges to activate password protection, even when it can be deactivated.

Access Protection

Admission security for the connected subnetworks can be achieved with positive or negative filter setting for individual protocols (see section 6.1). Access protection can also be achieved by setting up subnetworks within a physical segment. However, this often reduces clarity and greatly increases the complexity of the network structuring, and should therefore only be applied with great care.

Authentication

If individual protocols (and in particular router-router protocols) have implemented authentication functions (e.g., OSPF), these offer further access protection within a protocol sphere.

Routes

The data flow can be explicitly controlled by specifying static routes, so that the path of sensitive data, e.g., is precisely prescribed. Likewise "sensitive subnetworks" can be bypassed by static routing of all communication traffic which does not concern the subnetwork. When using dynamic routing, appropriate priority assignments can control which route is active in the normal case and in certain error cases. Here too, specifying the path (by appropriate setting of the cost parameters) provides an additional security factor. However, such determination should be weighed against equivalent parameter setting and thus higher usage of alternative paths (increased efficiency versus security).

Remote Subnetworks

See Bridges. As the in-house management functions in routers are implemented still more variably than standardized routing protocols—effectively beyond all standards—the demand for uniform routers if possible is even more justified. The only common platform can be provided is by SNMP at present. With the appropriate functional enhancement of SNMP, there is hope that one day even internetworking components from different manufacturers will be jointly manageable via a uniform management protocol.

Management Scenario

A few actions are now enumerated as examples of what can be performed with the management functions of a router in case of error. The error case assumed is that in the network shown (see Figure 15.6) no connection is possible between two end systems.

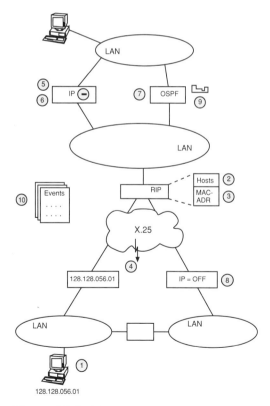

Figure 15.6: Management scenario (Routers)

The following actions can be performed as error checks:

Port usage, collision occurrence, and CRC errors can be checked for each subnetwork as for bridges. This isolation technique can localize the source of error to a particular subnetwork (if it comes from a defined subnetwork). The router and port status can be checked as for bridges. It is advisable to do this first for the routers in the subnetwork of the station wanting to transmit. Afterwards, the check is extended successively to all router ports between sender and receiver. A port with status "Down" cannot transport packets. The individual actions are correspondingly numbered in Figure 15.6.

1. View the address tables. If the network address of the station is entered in the table, then the subnetwork of the dubious station is at least known to the router, i.e., packets are correspondingly transported.

2./3. View the map tables. Is the correlation between host name and network address still correct? Is the correlation between network address and MAC address still correct?

4. Check the WAN connections. The connection can be "Down" because of error situations in the public network. The status of the WAN port and the WAN network should be checked for this.

5. View routing table. Is a route to the relevant network still present at all?

6. Check static routes. If static routes are set which are interrupted because of an error situation, then no alternative route can be used (in contrast to dynamic routing).

7. Check router-router communication. If error situations have occurred in the mutual exchange of control information between the routers, then error messages generated by the router protocol usually exist.

   Points 5 to 7 can be checked for each subnetwork. This isolation technique can localize the source of error to a particular subnetwork (if it comes from a defined subnetwork).

8. Check protocol status. Although it should always be assumed that in normal operation all protocols needed for the communication in a (multi-protocol) router are activated, this source of error cannot be ruled out entirely, especially after reconfigurations.

9. Check filter settings. Removal or reconfiguration of the network can mean that the filters set at network level or possibly higher levels are no longer suited to the current situation and prevent certain necessary connections (if adapting them for the new situation has been forgotten).

10. Finally, a glance at the Event Log can give information about error situations (time-outs, authentication errors, MAC errors, up/down of adjacent routers, router table overflow etc.)

As can be seen from the example, the management actions which can be taken via routers in an error situation are more detailed in nature than with bridges; substantially more protocol-specific data can be checked. Even so, comprehensive error management is not possible, even with routers.

15.1.4 Platform Integration

The description of the management functions which can be performed with bridges/routers makes it clear that only a few basic actions can be implemented by this method:

- Bridges cover basic management functionality at MAC level, chiefly in the area of configuration, simple faultfinding, fundamental performance data.

- LAN switches, because of the high port concentration, cover even fewer management functions than bridges.

- Routers cover basic management functionality at network level, chiefly in the area of logical and physical configuration, simple faultfinding, fundamental performance data.

- Various interconnection components are managed via various consoles. Sometimes an in-house system is necessary or strongly recommended (by the manufacturer), because only this fully supports all possible management actions of a certain product.

As network complexity grows, this starting situation makes implementation of a total concept for an enterprise network management a necessity. That means:

- Structure planning for physical and logical organization of the overall network.

- Integrated documentation of the overall network inclusive of all involved components (cable, hub systems, repeaters, highway distributors, bridges, routers, adapter cards, terminal servers, etc.).

- Integration of individual management in a standard-based management (SNMP, CMIP), usually on the basis of a platform system (see above).

- Inter-system migration planning for integration of individual management in an enterprise management.

This development is further forced by the current market situation.

Market-Associated Starting Situation

On the subject of "Integrative management," the present market situation is examined in the area of network evolution and especially interconnection components. The following aspects are significant here:

- The current market is characterized by continuing network growth, both in Europe and in the USA, which allows a forecast of further continued growth in Europe.

- The connection and integration of different networks and network islands is the objective of many companies in the 1990s.

- Three significant standards have become established in local networks and will determine the main business of network operation in the next years:

  Ethernet

  Token Ring

  FDDI

  In the future: ATM

- In the interconnection component market, a product explosion has been seen in the past eighteen months, which makes the market increasingly confusing. This lack of clarity extends to the management functionality offered by the available products.

- Manufacturers are getting into the interconnection component market "from above" from the traditional systems area and also "from below" from the traditional cabling and modem branch. According to their computer background, these manufacturers represent different network management strategies.

- As different network parts join up, interconnection components from different manufacturers are increasingly used in a company across both buildings and locations and must be integrated.

- The augmented offer of standard-based products (or those which claim to be so) is generating expectations among users, with some justification, that they can install products according to their specific suitability, independent of the manufacturer.

- The privatization of WAN services is leading increasingly to the setting up of WAN networks with industrial ownership (large end users or commercial third-party suppliers such as IBM, Info AG, Amadeus, etc.). Interfaces are created between interconnection components and management of own enterprise networks, and "private-public" WANs.

- The computer market is becoming altogether narrower, leading to a series of strategic alliances, joint ventures, and takeovers. Some users are following the "one stop shopping" trend.

- Who will survive? In the context of alliances, there is immediately a question about the survival of firms which are now active in the market. This survival issue must always be kept in mind as an underlying strategic condition for product selection, and does not make it any easier.

This section is therefore devoted to the subject: "Stepwise setting up of overall management by integration."

Network Management Platforms

Consistent enhancement of the management possibilities on the basis of network protocols created management systems which give a central overview of the entire network configuration, especially a usually graphic chart of the network topology, through which the individual interconnection components can be selected and managed/controlled (with the above functions). In the course of this development, SNMP (Simple Network Management Protocol) has become very well established as a management protocol. With this protocol routers, bridges, and hub systems, etc., which have implemented the corresponding intelligence of an SNMP agent, can be managed in a management system (though not yet with very great functionality).

The management systems mentioned have gone through three generations in their development so far: The first generation consisted predominantly of DOS-based systems whose database was organized as a simple file. They were purely intended for managing TCP/IP networks, and were produced between 1988 and 1989 (ACS 4800 V.1 from ACC, LANVIEW from Cabletron, OverView from Proteon, Wellfleet SNMP-NMS etc.). The second generation is characterized by UNIX-based workstations (e.g., Sun), with GUI and Automap of the network (Auto-topology). The database went over from files to the relational SQL database; analysis and planning were implemented to some extent. For these functional improvements, the price was approximately double that of the first generation systems (ACS 4800 V.2, NetCentral Station from Cisco, DECmcc from Digital, HP OpenView, NCRNet Manager from NCR, etc.).

The present, third generation has developed into network management platforms, which integrate more systems, support more protocols and offer more functions. Important characteristics of such platforms are:

- efforts towards integration of different manufacturers (Proxy agents),
- disclosure of interfaces,
- good documentation of APIs,
- support of SNMP,
- (future) support of CMIP,
- (future) support of CMOT,
- support of different hardware platforms.

Examples of such platform systems are SPECTRUM from Cabletron, HP OpenView, SystemView AIX from IBM (better known as NetView/6000), LANCE+ from Multinet Technology, NMCVision from Network Managers, SunNet Manager, and Solstice Enterprise Manager from Sun Microsystems.

The user should make a set of demands (and weigh them specifically), both on the use of such a system and also on bridge and router products which should be managed together with an NM platform (as in Figure 15.7). A requirements list was drafted for this in the networks user group UGNW. The requirements for configuration management, error management, and system properties, according to the UGNW, are described below.

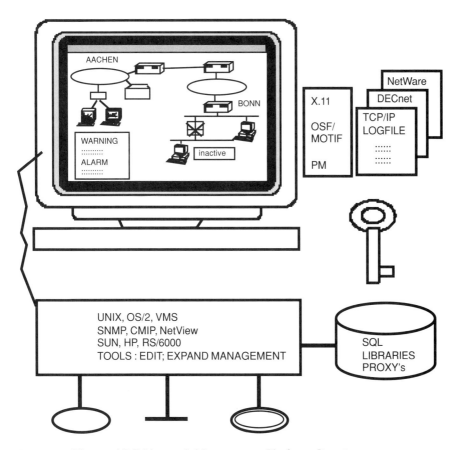

Figure 15.7 Network Management Platform: Requirements

Configuration

- At least SNMP should be supported, in future CMIP.

- All popular LANs should be supported. These include Ethernet/IEEE 802.3, Token Ring, FDDI, ATM.

- WAN support of the important interfaces is essential. These include X.21, X.25, Frame Relay.

- It must be possible to manage a very wide variety of components: hub systems, hubs, bridges, routers, terminal servers, network cards, network interfaces, highway distributors, FO converters, etc.

- The system must have sufficient capacity with regard to the number of objects to be managed. A complex network can have several thousand components which have to be captured in management.

- The system should be capable of modular expansion (when a new proxy agent or new management protocol is implemented, the complete hardware and software should not have to be exchanged).

- Amendments and updates should be possible online, as otherwise the operation runs without management monitoring for an unacceptably long time.

- Both inband and outband management should be possible (this is the true "security fanatic" speaking).

- Protocol-related subnetwork management is desirable.

- It must be possible to poll all individual components and thereby check them for activity.

- A network chart should be created for the network, with zoom functionality if possible (Location -> Building -> Floor -> Terminal).

- Inactive components should be visually identified as inactive on the graphics platform.

- An integration of the maintenance documentation is desirable (unfortunately, hardly implemented at all yet in current platform systems).

- Graphic User Interface (GUI), standards should be used (X.11, OSF/Motif, Presentation Manager/PM).

Error Management

- Alarms should be represented acoustically and by colors.

- Fault-finding procedures should lend themselves to automation or already be automated to some extent.

- The system must carry out independent plausibility checks on configuration changes.

- In error and event log files, events, and errors which have the same cause should be put together.

- The exchange of management information should be event-driven and not time-driven.

- Periodic tests should be implementable.

- Connectivity tests on any chosen stations should be possible.

System Requirements

- The system should support several standard operating systems (UNIX, VMS, OS/2).

- The system should support several hardware platforms (HP, RS/6000, Sun).

- The database must be a relational SQL database and provide import options for imports from other popular DB systems.

- Tools for editing and expanding the management functions are useful and desirable (MIB extensions, proxy agents, logbook evaluation, etc.)

- System admission must be very well protected, as the management has an extremely critical security level for the network. System admission should be graduated (several hierarchy levels), time-controlled (who can do what, and when) and action-driven (important commands). Log files should also be protected separately. Encryption options are necessary for management data.

Requirements on Bridges and Routers

*   An SNMP agent must be implemented.

*   The SNMP MIB II, bridge MIB, router MIB (as soon as adopted) etc., must be supported.

*   The supplementary in-house PRIVATE MIB must be disclosed.

*   It must be possible to read in the PRIVATE MIB into the popular NM platform systems.

*   Both READ commands (Get) and WRITE commands (Set) should be supported, so that yet another separate console is not needed for system changes.

All requirements and manufacturers' claims about fulfilling them can ultimately only be checked by testing.

Use of in-house systems from the bridge and router manufacturers is not recommended for an integrated network management solution, as these systems are generally adapted only for their own products and do not have the heterogeneous approach of systems which are designed specifically as network management platforms.

15.2 Evaluation Criteria for Bridges, Routers, and LAN Switches

The number of different manufacturers and suppliers, and the variety of products offered makes a purchasing decision difficult. Nor does it always help to rely on suppliers of complete network solutions. In product selection, the user is finally dependent upon his or her own powers of judgment. As interconnection components can less and less be described purely as a router, LAN switch or bridge, the evaluation criteria which follow are differentiated not by device classes but by functional and architectural areas. All relevant areas should be applied in each case for a component to be evaluated.

*   Bridge functions

*   Switch functions

*   Supported routing services

- Integration of SNA

- Supported WAN services

- Manageability

- Hardware/Model range

- Performance data

- Manufacturers and Support

In the following, the name "Bridge" means an interconnection component with bridge function, "Router" a switching element with router function, etc. All these functions can be implemented in a single device.

15.2.1 Bridge functions

At least the following functions should be investigated as central bridge functions. This applies also to the evaluation of LAN switches.

Address Table Management

Dynamically learned addresses and static entries can be maintained in different tables or managed in a shared table. Some address tables give the learned addresses for all ports in a single table (each marked with port number), while other address tables are set up for specific ports as "Table Port A," "Table Port B," etc. It is also useful to be able to load address tables (which have previously been edited in peace).

Loop Suppression

In principle only a bridge which has implemented loop suppression according to the IEEE 802.1D standard should be considered. If the user is faced with a larger DECnet, that user can be forced to use the Spanning Tree algorithm developed by DEC, until DEC supports the standard in its own products. An in-house implementation of loop suppression is no longer acceptable at the current state of the art, nor for LAN Switches. The user should find out which bridge products from other manufacturers an investigated product is compatible to (confirmed written test results), as the compatibility achieved can also be assessed as evidence about the quality of the standard implementation. Moreover, the demonstrable product flexibility (achieved through compatibility) is always preferable to dependence on a manufacturer.

For Token Ring environments, source routing must be available, but also source routing transparent for subnetworks with end systems which don't work with source routing. For the implementation of Single Route Broadcasting, the Spanning Tree self-configuration of bridges should in any case be selectable.

Operating Modes

Significant operating factors include "Learning," "Protected Mode," and "Aging." Switching the learning mode on and off should be possible, to allow processing time to be saved in a stable network state by deactivating learning. It must be possible to deactivate aging at the same time, otherwise the address tables are deleted after a short time, the bridge transports all packets all over the place or no longer transports anything, and the user is left "out in the cold." Which of these occurs depends on how protected mode and the learning function are linked together: some bridges freeze the learned address table when the learning function is deactivated. Some only transport the statically entered addresses and delete all learned addresses, i.e., deactivation of the learning function simultaneously means operation in protected mode.

Filter Functions

The full range of the various filter functions is involved here. Address filters on both destination and source addresses should be classed as indispensable, as are type filters. It should be noted here that some bridges can only set type filters on Ethernet frames, not on IEEE 802.3 frames. This can be balanced out with the mask filter option (which must then be given): the type filter is edited by hand as a mask filter. Broadcast filters should also be settable. It is doubtful whether a separate menu item is necessary for this, as too many filter menus lead to confusion. Logical combination of several filters can be make sense in some cases but should rather be classed as a luxury function, as it tends to make the filter programming become unclear.

15.2.2 Switch Functions

Important functions of LAN switches are described below. In addition, the functions which were described as bridge functions and which can equally be used for LAN switches should also be evaluated for a LAN switch.

Operating Modes

A very significant question is whether a LAN switch always works in Cut Through mode or in Store & Forward mode, or can be switched automatically depending on the packet loss and the error rate.

End System Attachments

Some LAN switches can only link end stations on their ports, not complete segments. However, network operators who want to link segments via 10Base2, optical fiber or even AUI, which still consist of normal users rather than power users, need this functionality. Twisted pair and optical fiber (10BaseFL, 802.5J) should be supported for the end system link-up.

Switch Connection, Uplink

If LAN switches are connected to one another by standards-based processes, there is the best chance of operating devices from different manufacturers in a network, if this becomes necessary on migration grounds (for a lot of users this is bound to become necessary, as it is foreseeable that not all switch manufacturers will stay in the market). If a network operator installs FDDI, he or she will look for a LAN switch with an FDDI Uplink; if the operator uses ATM, then he or she will want a LAN Switch with an ATM Uplink, which is compatible in as many functions as possible to his installed ATM switches.

15.2.3 Supported Routing Services

At least the following functions should be investigated as a central routing function.

Routing Table Administration

Dynamically learned addresses and static entries should be maintained in different tables. It is also useful to be able to load defined routes (which have previously been edited in peace).

Operating Modes

It should be possible to activate and deactivate dynamic routing. Static routes should be configurable parallel to dynamic routes.

Filter Functions

Filter functions generally relate to network addresses of individual routing protocols. It should be possible to set positive and negative filters. Some products also allow filter setting for subprotocol types, e.g. within the TCP/IP family (Mail, FTP, Rlogin, etc.). Broadcast filters are not a topic, as routers (if they route) suppress broadcasts in any case. For implementing firewall functionality, support of filtering in **both directions** is necessary. However, a number of the available products support only input or output filters for certain filter conditions. The number of filters is also sometimes restricted to less than 100.

Supported LAN Protocols

This includes all protocol stacks which a network operator uses, e.g., AppleTalk, DECnet, IPX, OSI, TCP/IP, XNS. If only one protocol is operated in the network, a single protocol router supporting precisely this protocol in the desired form comes into question. For multi-protocol routers, it must be checked which protocols are supported, which are only announced and which can actually be supported in parallel. For a "supported protocol" it must be checked which options going beyond the minimum consensus are implemented. It should furthermore be checked for a supported protocol whether it is included in the standard delivery range or not.

Not all routed protocols are supported for all MAC methods (Ethernet, FDDI, Token Ring etc.).

For LAN protocols without routing capability (NetBIOS, SNA, LAT, MOP) it should be checked whether, and, if so how, these protocols are bridged:

transparently or with encapsulation? Only on the same MAC levels or also from Token Ring to Ethernet?

Supported Routing Protocols

For some routable protocols (e.g., IP, IPX) there are various routing protocols, called protocol families (e.g., RIP, RIP II, OSPF, EGP, BGP, etc.). It should be checked to determine if that particular routing protocol or all the family of protocols are supported. For supported routing protocols (which are often standardized), compatibility to other router manufacturers products may also have to be checked (if in the future different locations with different devices are to be merged). This applies in particular to the standards RIP, OSPF, IS-IS.

15.2.4 Integration of SNA

We consider two essential areas for this:

- Encapsulation in TCP/IP

- APPN

Encapsulation

Support of SNA is a further topic of growing significance. Is Sync Passthrough or TCP/IP Encapsulation via LAN supported, or is SNA only supported in the form of DLC on Token Ring? Is a proprietary encapsulation operated, or is Data Link Switching supported, and if so, according to RFC 1434 or RFC 1795? To which other manufacturers is a router with DLSw compatible? Which of the options according to RFC 1795 are implemented?

APPN

APPN is the most advanced routing method, which should replace old expensive static route definitions, but router manufacturers are very hesitant about supporting it. The same applies to DLSw with APPN as routing and transport protocols.

15.2.5 Supported WAN Services

For LAN-WAN connections, the question is which WAN services can be used, and how they can be combined with LAN protocols. A number of products do not support every LAN protocol for every WAN service.

WAN Services

For this it should be checked which connections can be implemented: X.25, Frame Relay, SMDS, ISDN point-to-point or point-to-multipoint, X.21 with an "own" protocol, with HDLC or with PPP offer a wide range of possibilities here.

In particular for WAN interfaces, it is an advantage if the output queues of individual interfaces can be differently prioritized (e.g., SDLC with the highest priority, bridge traffic with the second highest, then DECnet and finally the rest of the world).

ISDN is a controversial topic, on which opinions differ about spoofing (masking out of overhead packets), dial software, automatic call-back, Euro-ISDN licensing, and configuration of point-to-multipoint connections.

Support for LAN Protocols

Especially for Frame Relay, SMDS, and ISDN, not all LAN protocols are supported. This means for example that AppleTalk functions via X.25, but not via ISDN as point-to-multipoint, or IP can be used via Frame Relay, but not DECnet, etc. When simply asked whether it supports ISDN or X.25 or Frame Relay, a manufacturer will say "Yes" in all the cases mentioned above. Thus every LAN protocol must be checked for every service with the desired functionality.

15.2.6 Manageability

Central aspects of a product's management evaluation are user interface, system admission, supported management functionality within a cross-system network management, configuration capability, security, and log file.

User Interface

The user interface should be menu-driven. Working with command interpreter and mnemonics is often not very pleasant. Nonetheless, even some leading firms continue to prize and maintain the cryptic command language.

System Admission

It is worth aiming for password-protected system admission from any PC in the network (e.g., via TCP/IP). The typical directly connected V.24 end station leads to the unpleasant situation that the person responsible for the network must set up at least one of all installed bridges under his or her own desk, as otherwise he or she cannot connect the end station. Full access from an inter-system network management system is ideal, but in many cases at present very much a vision of the future.

Most interconnection components offer the option of logging in via Telnet (they must have implemented TCP/IP themselves). However, there is often then no Graphic User Interface available, only the aforementioned command-line interpreter.

For branch offices, an outband management admission is needed, since often nobody is there with the necessary network know-how to undertake a restart or reconfiguration on site. For outband management, the supported line speeds and the basic protocol are important (in-house, SLIP, PPP). On security and compatibility grounds, the aim should be for PPP.

Management Functions

Two essential approaches should be distinguished: support of SNMP by imple-menting an SNMP agent and support of OSI management either with a few basic functions according to IEEE 802.1 or more extensively with CMIP/CMIS. Current SNMP management systems have by far the broader basis for all inter-connection components with LAN interfaces. In-house management solutions (for example on these unavoidable wretched Windows systems) may make it easier to handle special functions in configuration and in operation, but they lead to a multiplicity of management consoles on the network manager's desk, as all the different network components may have to be managed with differ-ent management systems.

Configuration

It is important to be able to configure networks in the active state. It is very unpleasant to have to reboot after setting filters, activating ports, or altering other important parameters, as it leads to a Spanning Tree reconfiguration, which in large complex networks can interrupt the communication of all end systems for several minutes. For those responsible, this means that reconfiguration is only possible at nights or weekends. For simple configuration measures, the configuration option by direct hardware access (front panel, LEDs) can also be helpful.

In the online configuration possibilities, the activation/deactivation of specific protocols, and for individual ports, should be an essential. This can be extremely helpful in fault-finding. It should likewise be possible to activate static routes online, and amend cost parameters for dynamic routes.

Creation of standard profiles for storage on servers, and configuration download via TFTP make a network operators life a lot easier for updates and error situations (non-reconstructible mis-configuration, corrupted configuration or similar situations).

Security

It is an obvious assumption that not everyone may log into a switching element and enter and exit there at will. This is prevented by sensible password protection. It makes sense to have three or four hierarchy levels in password protection so that the responsibility can be decentralized: local managers can be responsible for routine checks and less "dangerous" management actions (such as, e.g., status queries), while one central person holding the highest password level is responsible for actions which seriously affect the network operation (e.g., booting, port deactivation, etc.).

Log File

It must be required of a solid product that a log file can be kept of protocol activities (activation, deactivation, protocol errors, interface errors, dynamic route reconfiguration, etc.). If a management platform system is used, the log file must be usable via the platform. With regard to the scope, the aim should be for a middle way. If every tiny detail is logged, no network operator can evaluate the log file. The space restrictions on the log file should possibly be examined. It is also important whether a log file is overwritten when the storage space is full or whether no further messages are then recorded. In any case, a message should announce log file overflow.

15.2.7 Hardware/Model Range

Factors when considering a product's hardware are: interface range, modularity, storage, CPU, and hardware architecture.

Interfaces

Multiport devices with simple bridge function in the local area have not become established in the market; generally at least IP and IPX routing are also supported.

An interconnection component can support very variable numbers and types of interfaces; six to about 100 serial remote interfaces or local ports are possible according to the product. As regards the upper limit however, operation of this sort of concentration point should be questioned on considerations of security and availability, as a failure of such a central component would create an extreme operating crisis.

For Ethernet and Token Ring, single, double, four-fold, and six-fold interface cards are currently offered (6-fold interfaces not for Token Ring), which naturally reduces the price relation per port—if there is a corresponding demand. FDDI comes as single or double interface. The total possible number of LAN ports is also an important measure. The range here is from 3 to about 50 for bridges and routers, up to 100 for LAN switches. With regard to combination capability, it should be checked how many Ethernets can be operated with how many Token Rings and how many FDDI interfaces in one device. In particular for FDDI there are still considerable restrictions (e.g., to two or four interfaces per device).

For the remote interfaces, the supported individual capacity (9,600 bit/sec, 64 kbit/sec, 2 Mbit/sec), the supported total capacity and also the supported interfaces (X.21, V.35, G.703) for all remote ports are important. The possible combination of several LAN interfaces with several remote interfaces on an interface card should also be investigated (if the demand is there).

If newer protocols such as Frame Relay, SMDS (the poor man's ATM), or ATM are to be used to best advantage, the question should be about the switching components in the WAN area with which the routers match, i.e., can be operated.

Modularity

High modular expandability and combination of different interfaces should be positively rated. It should be investigated whether serial interfaces and LAN interfaces can be obtained on a shared board, whether dual LAN ports, dual remote ports, quad LAN ports, quad remote ports, etc. are available, and which boards can be combined in a device. The availability of different models (middle model with 3 to 5 slots, large model with 7 to 15 slots), whose modules are fully exchangeable, is important for a balanced outlay with dynamic network growth and locations of differing sizes.

Hardware/Architecture

The clear trend in hardware architecture is multi-CPU use, and use of RISC CPUs, and for LAN switches increasingly also the use of still faster, more integrated ASICs, which cast packet processing in hardware. Only a device whose architecture can offer this option will be able to cope with future performance requirements. Installed bus and installed buses between the boards, network chips, and available memory on the individual boards are also considerations for the hardware investigation.

The use of PC-based bridges/routers cannot be classed as state-of-the-art, as purpose-built "box" devices are often better for use as interconnection components than PCS. These should be reserved for use as end user devices in more complex networks with high performance and availability requirements.

Product Range

For complex networks it makes sense to look for manufacturers who offer products for the widest range of applications: the variable interconnection component with different model sizes, availability of all LAN and WAN interfaces, bridge functionality, and routing support for all desired higher protocols is wanted. This also gives a picture of a manufacturer's background experience in the internetworking field. Unfortunately many manufacturers come either from the "Ethernet world" or from the "Token Ring world," and have less mature products to offer on their "less special side."

The LAN switching and ISDN markets in particular have formed "niches" with small manufacturers, who currently offer top functionality, but whose survival is not guaranteed. This makes the installation of Ethernet, Token Ring, and FDDI, LAN-WAN interconnection components from one supplier tricky. On functional grounds therefore, the decision is sometimes for different manufacturers.

15.2.8 Performance Data

The performance data to be considered concerns primarily filter rate, throughput and processing time (delay, latency) and starting times.

Filter Capacity

The filter capacity or filter rate specifies how many packets a device, usually with bridge functionality, can analyze in order to make a transport decision; in brief: how many ordered packets a bridge can receive and store until it is able to decide on transport. The filter rate is usually specified for frames of minimum size, as this gives the largest value. The filter rate specified per port is important. With simultaneous usage of several ports the filter rate can be significantly lower than the sum of the individual filter rates as the bridge performance may be impaired by high parallel usage.

Filter capacity or filter rate should also be investigated for products which route and bridge in parallel. It is then less important to know the absolute filter rates in exclusive bridge operations (only these will be given in the spec sheets), than the actual filter rates, when e.g., three protocols are routed in parallel to the bridge operation.

Throughput

The throughput rate or forwarding rate gives the number of packets which can in fact be transported. This is less than the filter rate, as the packet processing only actually begins after the positive transport decision. Throughput rates in packets per second and in bytes per second should be distinguished. In the first case minimum packets are generally sent for the measurement; in the second case, maximum packets, as this produces the least overhead thus giving the highest data throughput. The throughput rate is also usually given with only a single port in use and can be considerably lower for parallel usage of two or more interfaces. It is very important here to find out whether a device behaves in a stable way with a peak load, i.e., remains at maximum throughput and does not show any degradation. This applies particularly to LAN switches, as compared to bridges and routers, they still have limited product maturity.

The throughput for onboard routing is typically higher than for routing between different boards. If many filters (MAC or Layer 3) are set, the performance similarly drops, as all filter conditions have to be checked before possible transport.

The performance measure PPS (Packets Per Second) relates in some cases to both interfaces; that is, all packets which the router receives and sends are computed. Correctly, a packet should count as "put through" when it has been received, processed, and sent again. The actual manufacturers' figures should be researched on this point. Switch manufacturers especially shine with fantasy numbers here.

If a product can be operated in parallel with routing and bridge functionality, the performance with an active parallel bridge function may be significantly lower than with pure routing. The same applies for parallel operation of several routing protocols in a multi-protocol router. Routing via equal LANs (Ethernet-Ethernet) therefore often gives better performance than routing between different LANs (e.g., Ethernet-Token Ring). The manufacturers' figures relating to throughput should therefore be examined very closely (preferably with an independent test external to the manufacturer; in-house tests should be appraised with care, as often the performance levels of rival products almost complement one another in different manufacturers' tests).

The total capacity of the internal bus is important: What use is expandability to 30 LAN ports, if the total capacity is "only" 80 Mbit/sec?

Processing Time

Not only total throughputs but also the processing time for a packet should be examined. It gives an impression of how fast or slowly packet queues can ever be cleared when there is an overload. It is important how the processing time was measured here: receipt of the last bit of a packet and sending of the first bit or receipt of the last bit and sending of the last bit? Make sure that rival manufacturers don't start making comparisons of different things. The battle over 10 μsec more or less is pointless anyway if Store & Forward devices are involved. The buffering of a single 1500 byte Ethernet packet takes 1.2 milliseconds.

Reconfiguration, Reboot

For the case of a Spanning Tree reconfiguration because of occurring hardware errors or a reboot (e.g., after parameter changes), the time all bridges need for a Spanning Tree recalculation should be investigated. It can sometimes produce astonishing findings in quite simple test configurations: namely that all sessions are interrupted because the recalculation takes so long.

For the case of a reconfiguration of the active routes because of occurring network errors or a reboot (e.g., after parameter changes, if they aren't possible online), the time all routers need for a recalculation of the routes according to the active routing protocols should be investigated. It can sometimes produce astonishing findings in quite simple test configurations: namely that all sessions are interrupted, because the recalculation takes so long. While the boot time is not a central performance parameter, it is nonetheless interesting especially for networks which are frequently reconfigured or expanded.

If the operating software of a device becomes so muddled that a restart is necessary, or if some parameters (precisely the ones the user keeps having to change) cannot be reconfigured online, the reboot time becomes significant. This, too can take up to several minutes.

15.2.9 Manufacturers and Support

Anyone who makes a purchase decision purely on functional and performance aspects must either have an appropriately large network support team or risk suffering afterwards with problems (which were non-existent according to the manufacturer beforehand) when the support is not forthcoming. A few factors are mentioned in this context, for inclusion in a product investigation.

Support

What support does the manufacturer/supplier offer? Is there in-house training, and if so at what cost? How is the support network structured, what response times can be agreed? Is there a Hotline? When can this be reached? How does the Hotline perform with a test query? Are difficult questions forwarded to the manufacturer?

Experience

Extensive manufacturing/supply experience, both in years and in product diversity and number of implemented networking projects, can be rated as a mark of quality for a range of products (provided the manufacturer has kept abreast of the trends). However, this criterion is very debatable: new products from young manufacturers often represent the peak of technological development, and are optimally suited to current needs. It is then very difficult to decide how the future development of the product and manufacturer will turn out. Deciding against a young, small, specialist firm may mean choosing the second best in functional terms.

Market Position

Manufacturer's market position and product's market share are further indices of a product's acceptance and good functionality. Here again, though, "young" products are at a disadvantage, even when they could be the best choice. It is important here to look at the development of the last three years and not just the current product status.

Security of Further Development

A product investigation should also include the planned enhancements in order to sound out the future prospects for the use of the product, and determine how well the product development trends will match the needs of the specific network applications.

15.2.10 Purchase Decision

The criteria mentioned should be understood as basic information about which aspects are important and worth considering when buying a product. For a specific end user and his or her specific network with a specific development in the next years, these criteria are not all (and not all equally) noteworthy. For an individual purchase decision, a specific investigation of the computer and network situation is required.

Price/Performance

The luxury product is not always the best choice for a particular network, and the budget is usually insufficient for implementing a "luxury solution" in any case. It is important to ask what particular upgrades and options cost, in order to avoid trouble later. A precise specification of the desired minimum and maximum functionality now and in the next years is necessary in order to be able to choose the right product (in relation to the price). Follow-up costs (maintenance, training, spare parts, etc.) should also be taken into account.

16 | Comparison and Future Perspectives

16.1 Comparison: Bridges versus Routers

Bridges and routers, as "simple" representatives of their type (i.e., purely as a bridge or a router), implement interconnection components for network structuring with very different functionality.

Both have their specific areas and rights of application. LAN switches are not dealt with separately here; while they have their own area of application, they can be equated functionally in many respects with multiport bridges.

16.1.1 The Most Important Differences

The implementation of a communication functionality in accordance with Layer 2 or Layer 3 of the OSI Reference Model for bridges and routers presupposes a series of basic differences in the working mode of bridges and routers, which are compared on the following page.

Bridge	Router
lower functionality	higher functionality
protocol transparency	no protocol transparency
flat structuring	hierarchical structuring
simple operation	complex operation
more limited management possibilities	greater management possibilities
alternative routes only in case of error by activation of hot standby lines	alternative routes also in normal case by use of "real" routing procedures

Functionality According to the OSI Reference Model

Bridges connect subnetworks with a functionality according to OSI Layer 2, routers connect subnetworks with a functionality according to OSI Layer 3. This means that only routers implement routing functionality (path selection) in the strict sense, as it is quite clearly in Layer 3.

Packet Transport and Load Separation

While a bridge generally does not alter the packets in transport (exception: bridges between different MAC layers), a router must always create a new MAC address and recalculate the CRC.

For the transport decision, bridges maintain port-related address tables with MAC addresses of the end stations. The table size grows with the number of connected end systems. Routers maintain tables with the addresses of networks which can be reached, and the addresses of the routers to be addressed for these. The table size grows with the number of logical subnetworks at network level. Their number is generally the same as or smaller than the number of physical subnetworks: a logical subnetwork at Layer 3 can easily comprise several subnetworks bridged at Layer 2. In exceptional cases a Layer 2 subnetwork can be structured into two or more logical network subnetworks. However, this does not require a further load separation within a Layer 2 subnetwork but rather a further access control.

As default, i.e., if there is no information on the source and destination of a packet, a bridge will transport the packet. If it is a multiport bridge, it transports it on all linked ports (with the exception of the port on which it has received it). Load separation therefore only occurs for those packets for which the bridge has learned the source and destination address. In contrast to this, the router does not transport as default. It interprets only packets which are directed specifically to its MAC address and which address destination networks known to it as accessible. If one of these cases does not apply, the packet is discarded and an error message may be generated for the sending station.

There is no flow control, or acknowledgment of received packets, between bridges, or bridges and end stations. (Exception: pairs of remote bridges which are connected together via a WAN line sometimes apply HDLC as WAN protocol, which uses packet acknowledgment.) Depending on the routable protocol in use between routers, both flow control and packet acknowledgment are applied.

Addressing

When subnetworks are coupled with bridges, packets are addressed end-to-end, i.e., from the sender to the destination station with unique MAC addresses. The bridge interprets the MAC addresses without changing them. When subnetworks are coupled with routers, addressing at network level is end-to-end, but at MAC layer from the sending station to the first router, from router to router, from the last router to the receiving station. The router interprets the network addresses and converts the MAC addresses accordingly.

Operating Mode

A bridge is always dedicated (i.e., without any other application function) in use and works in Promiscuous Mode, i.e., it receives and processes all incoming packets, until it has made a transport decision. For implementing routing functions, both hosts with routing intelligence and also dedicated routers can be used. They don't process all packets, but only those addressed directly to them.

Structuring Hierarchy

The addressing at MAC level can be termed "flat addressing," as it is related purely to the end stations. The addressing at network level can be termed "hierarchical addressing," as it is related both to the end station and to the network (network and host part). Accordingly a flat structuring is created for bridge coupling, and a hierarchical structuring of the subnetworks for router coupling; this applies in particular to newer router protocols such as OSPF and IS-IS. In addition, the last two router protocols in particular also differentiate "classes" of routers (Level 1, Level 2 or Area, Backbone), which establish a network hierarchy of at least two levels. This is not envisaged for bridges.

Filters

In the configuration of both bridges and routers, filters can be set for more extensive access control. Bridge filters always relate to MAC packets, usually MAC addresses or protocol type details in MAC frames; less commonly, any masked parts of a MAC frame. Filter setting in routers is always carried out within the scope of the configuration data for a specific protocol. Other routed protocols remain unaffected by the set filters. Router filters relate to network addresses or subprotocol type details for a protocol family (e.g., TCP/IP or DECnet) in packets.

Broadcasts

As default, bridges must forward broadcasts from end systems to all ports, if no broadcast filter is set to suppress forwarding (and hence also communication). Routers don't forward broadcasts of end systems to all ports; instead they

- forward them selectively to the addressed destination network, where the broadcast is answered by the destination station, or

- answer them if applicable with their own address in order then to forward incoming packets selectively to the addressed destination network.

Protocol Dependence

Bridges and routers behave in a complementary fashion with regard to protocol dependence: While routers are protocol-dependent towards the upper communication layers, the connections are effectively bridges in many cases for the lower layers, especially the MAC layer, because they connect similar LANs at a common MAC layer. (The connection of different MAC layers, theoretically allowed according to OSI, still creates difficulties, especially regarding differing packet sizes and the required protocol transparency "upwards.") While a bridge coupling based on a uniform configuration allows the connection of different protocol environments based on a LAN, for single routable protocols the router offers a clean interface under which various LANs are exchangeable without problems (e.g., handling of different packet sizes).

Path Selection, Routing

Bridge coupling allows only a static path allocation for the packet guidance during a communication session. In particular, when applying the Spanning Tree method, there is always only one unique path active between two end systems; only in case of errors are alternative paths used, which were previously in backup mode. When routers and corresponding router protocols are used, dynamic routes can be established which allow different paths between routers depending on the load situation, even within a session. In addition, when routers are used, static routes can be defined (e.g., on security grounds), which can be used in parallel to dynamic routes for certain networks. For different protocol families, different routing methods, i.e., router protocols, can be used (e.g., RIP, OSPF, EGP, IS-IS, DECnet, etc.).

Implementation

Bridges require no additional configuration in the end stations of the subnetworks which they connect. In the simplest case they can be inserted into an existing network without any significant interruption of operations. Even in more complex network structures with multiple redundancy and many bridges, the recalculation of active connection paths with the Spanning Tree algorithm takes only a few minutes. It is more trouble to insert an additional bridge if there is complex filter programming.

If on the other hand, a network is to be structured by installing routers, a corresponding configuration is necessary in all end stations, which is especially bad in the migration from bridge- to router-structured networks, as in many cases all end stations have to be converted to router operation and correspondingly configured at the same time. The structure and assignment of network addresses (especially for the different address Classes in the IP) should be planned with the greatest of care and designed for anticipated future expansion.

Operation

The installation of bridges can be characterized with the catch-phrase "Plug and Play," while for routers by comparison the expression "Plug & Call Hotline" or "Don't Plug, First Call Hotline" is more appropriate. While a bridge works in self-learning mode when in doubt and enables communication across subnetworks, the connection capability must be configured step by step in routers and end stations when routers are installed. Considerably more know-how is called for than for bridge installation, not only in order to configure the necessary parameters optimally in end stations and routers, but simply to get the routers and end stations in functioning communication. This know-how should already be built up in advance of router installation, in order that adequate preliminary work can be done in planning the connection structures.

16.1.2 Installation Criteria

If a network's structuring is to be refined because of its growing size and complexity, the installation of bridges or routers (or both) should be carefully planned. In current planning and also in the near future, the network operator is faced with the following situation: the market has not yet produced the interconnection component which is all things to all people. If the price advantage of bridges over routers is to be exploited, "only" a structuring at MAC layer and on the basis of MAC frames is available; if the advantage of "real" routing methods is to be exploited, the purchaser simultaneously loses the protocol transparency for the upper levels; further trade-offs can be found. To list the key points:

Bridge	Router
lower price and lower functionality	higher price and higher functionality
protocol transparency and flat, non-dynamic structuring; alternative routes only in case of error by activation of backup lines in normal operation	protocol dependence and hierarchical, dynamic structuring alternative routes by use of "real" routing methods
simple operation and more limited management possibilities	complex operation and greater management possibilities
simple configuration of a common cost metric for all protocol used	complex configuration of different metrics per protocol used

There is no "patent recipe" by which it can be decided whether bridges or routers should be used in a particular enterprise network. The specific boundary conditions of each network are too varied for that, and the forms of mixed bridge and router installation are too complex. However, a few basic criteria can be formulated for the use of bridges or routers.

The following network factors favor the use of bridges:

- The architecture is open for the heterogeneous use of all protocols and should also remain so for an expanded service offer.

- Protocols which are not routable are to be used.

- The handling of the interconnection components should be as simple as possible.

- The number of stations is low.

- The network consists of a manageable number of segments.

- The spread of the network is small.

- Simple management functions are sufficient.

- On cost grounds, no expensive interconnection components can be installed.

The following network factors favor the use of routers:

- The network architecture is clearly organized into different protocol environments.

- Few standard protocols are to be used.

- Many stations must be managed and grouped.

- The spread of the network is large, and in particular WAN connections are to be used.

- Many broadcasts occur at MAC layer.

- Various location LANs should be integrated in an enterprise "Internetwork."

- More complex management functions are necessary.

- There will be an SNA link-up via a multi-protocol backbone.

It is often unnecessary for small networks to install routers. As the complexity and number of end stations increase—and with them the complexity of the network operation—subnetworks (e.g., single locations or buildings) can be structured internally by bridges, while larger subnetworks are connected among themselves by routers. Figure 16.1 shows a typical mixed configuration, in which for example, internal location subnetworks are coupled by bridges to a location backbone, but inter-location connections are implemented with routers. An increased level of support capacity should be planned beforehand for configuration and operation in the changeover from bridges to routers. The necessary capacity and the necessary know-how must be built up in advance of the implementation.

16.1.3 Hierarchy

The functional range and also the processing complexity increase from the bridge through the router to the multi-protocol router with a high-level bridge functionality (Figure 16.1). The term filter bridge can be used for a static bridge or "simple bridge," learning bridge, routing bridge/router; all these bridges have filter functionality in the sense of a more or less refined load separation between subnetworks. The names are assigned according to the manufacturer. Remote and multiway bridges are generally self-learning and implement path selection functions (SPT).

A general tendency can be observed at present to bring bridges and routers in different product ranges into line with each other, in order to combine the advantages of both systems as far as possible (Figure 16.2). The supply of "pure" bridges and "pure" routers becomes increasingly scarce, especially in the multi-protocol-router sphere, as these devices are specially designed to be able to handle all protocols of a network in parallel so far as possible—which means that the non-routable protocols must be adapted for handling in these interconnection components by means of additional bridge functionality.

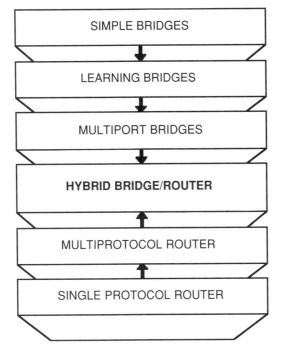

Figure 16.1 Bridge-Router Hierarchy

16.2 Future Perspectives

The necessary integration of developed protocol environments and LAN structures leads increasingly to the solution of installing a common backbone for connecting individual logical or physical subnetworks; all installed protocols can be operated in parallel on this backbone. Various solution approaches for implementing a multi-protocol backbone based on bridge or router use are now presented to illustrate the complexity of the necessary decisions, in a kind of management business game: "Enterprise with several locations and heterogeneous computer landscape seeks backbone solution."

Multi-protocol Backbone

A fictitious, but realistic, enterprise with several locations is used as a basis. It consists of eight branch offices and four regional headquarters, thus a total of twelve locations to be connected. Each branch office has four LANs and is connected to one central location by a 2 Mbit/sec line; each central location has one LAN and is connected with all other central locations by a 2 Mbit/sec line. The distance between branch offices and headquarters is less than 15 km, the individual headquarters are 50 to 100 km apart from one another. As similar applications are used at all locations throughout the enterprise, using TCP/IP, DECnet Phase IV, SNA, LAT, and IPX, all these protocols must be transferable via the common backbone. (Admittedly the protocol combination is rather maliciously chosen, as LAT is not routable; the combination is nonetheless not at all uncommon in a larger enterprise.) Various established manufacturers were asked for a solution for the required backbone structure, taking into consideration an annual increase of approximately 35% in data traffic. Bridge backbones, router backbones, and backbones with mixed bridges and routers were allowed. In order to connect all protocol environments, the choice could be:

- a single-protocol backbone with gateways and protocol converters (e.g., for SNA or DECnet) as transition to the uniform backbone protocol, or alternatively

- a multi-protocol backbone with parallel protocol handling via integrating interconnection components.

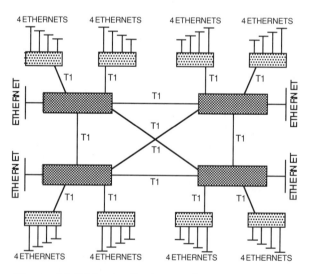

Figure 16.2 Merging Bridge and Router Functionality

The selected solution should be based on the LAN standards Ethernet or Token Ring. Cisco, Digital, IBM, HP, Proteon and were asked. Only the principal solutions can be looked at within this book. Cisco, HP (market routers), and Proteon proposed a solution with hybrid multi-protocol routers (additional bridge functionality, e.g., for LAT) (see Figure 16.2). In this solution all protocols are processed in parallel in the backbone node and, according to protocol type, routed (DECnet, IPX, TCP/IP), or bridged (LAT, SNA). Depending on the installed router product, the number of interconnection components needed differs between twelve (Cisco), and sixteen (Proteon), as the devices have different capacities with regard to the maximum number of interfaces supported.

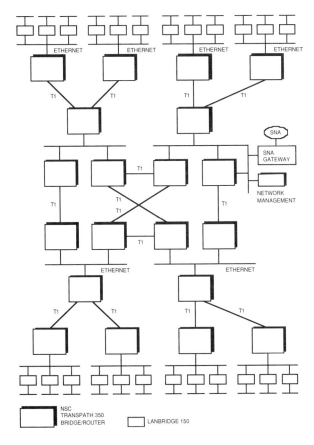

Figure 16.3 Multi-protocol backbone with DEC LAN bridges and hybrid routers TransPath

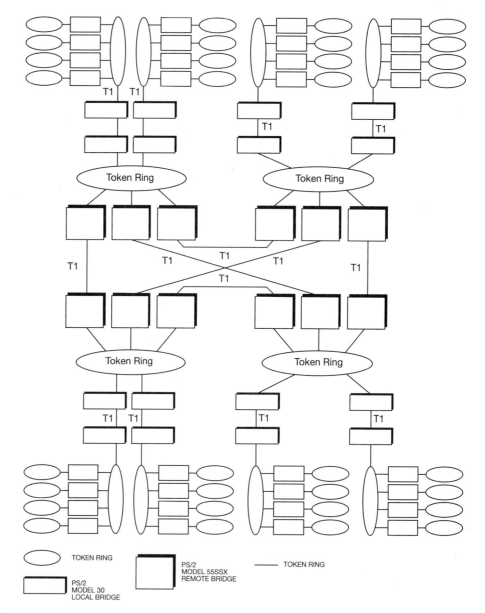

Figure 16.4 Enterprise backbone with IBM Token Ring bridges

Digital made a proposal with DEC LAN bridges and hybrid routers with bridge functionality, which led to 44 interconnection components, as the DEC LAN bridges only supported two ports each (see Figure 16.3).

IBM made no proposal; an IBM consultant was asked later instead. The solution was based exclusively on local and remote Token Ring bridges, which because of the maximum two supported ports in each case led to the planned installation of 60 interconnection components (bridges) (see Figure 16.4).

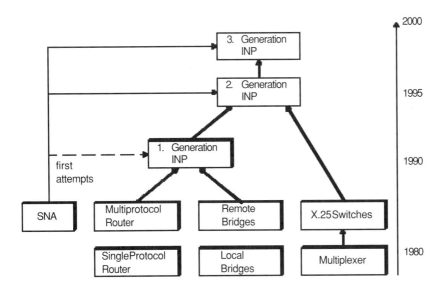

Figure 16.5 INP Evolution

Both Digital and IBM felt they were confronted in this game with the disadvantages of pure bridge backbones in order to be able to implement the solution with their own products: broadcast loads, more limited management possibilities, installation of many individual devices because of the low number of supported ports. This deficiency has led to the partnerships of large computer manufacturers with router manufacturers, which have become established in the last two years on the basis of marketing (HP/IBM/Digital/Proteon) or "Installation in large numbers in house" (IBM).

The costs (hardware, software, maintenance, transmission fees) were highest for the Digital solution, followed by IBM and Cisco, followed at some distance by HP and Proteon. For hardware, software, and maintenance there were different proportions of the total costs in each case, but it is notable that after five operating years the transmission costs averaged nearly 90%. This means that the outlay on hardware and software is hardly of significance after an operating phase of several years; attention should rather be directed to optimizing the PTT charges and the operating costs for the necessary support staff. On the basis of these criteria, a decision on a suitable solution for a real network should be made with care, and will generally involve a mixture of the solutions mentioned.

Outlook

In the last five years LANs and LAN-WAN integration have become so well established in enterprises that traditional hierarchical host structures (IBM, HP, DEC, etc.) are being increasingly weakened. LANs have become the basic components of today's enterprise networks, and LAN interconnection structures the basic architecture—very much faster than observers of computer communication development would have expected five years ago. As the need increased for interconnection components such as bridges and routers, the demands also increased on the functionality of a high-end interconnection component: from the simple bridge to the multiport bridge with DLS, from the single protocol router with a LAN, and a WAN port to the multi-protocol multiport concentrator with parallel bridge functionality.

The new generation of multifunctional interconnection components has a range of integrating features, which reflect the heterogeneous nature of the subnetworks being connected in relation to the admission methods applied and the higher communication protocols in the LAN and WAN spheres:

- Multiport capability in the LAN area with

- integration of the established standard LANs (Ethernet, Token Ring, FDDI) and

- multi-protocol capability in relation to routable protocols;

- bridge functionality for non-routable protocols;

- translation bridge functionality between different MAC layers;

- Multiport capability in the WAN area with

- support of different WAN standards (HDLC, X.25, FR, SMDS and ATM)

- future integration of WAN switches;

- CPU capacity and design of the system bus for high-grade concentration of LAN and WAN interfaces in a interconnection component.

This new generation of interconnection components will form the basis of enterprise backbone structures for multi-protocol operation. After the functional integration of the bridge and router functionality, they should not be called either bridges or routers, but rather INPs—InterNetwork Processors. With increasing possibilities for peer-to-peer communication, data will in the future be exchanged beyond department and location boundaries to a growing extent on cost and efficiency grounds, essentially making the availability of higher LAN capacities in the location backbone as well as in inter-location WAN connections. Applications that are at the beginning of their life cycle for the described networking phase are for example, video transmission, video conference, multimedia, and distributed applications (the last one more in the LAN area). Three generations of INPs are currently foreseeable:

- Integration of bridge and router functionality (1st generation),

- Integration of the switching functionality of current WAN nodes and partial SNA integration (2nd generation),

- Integration of different data streams on the basis of broadband communication and SNA integration (3rd generation).

The future generations of INPs will combine multiplexer, bridge, and router functionality after the described integration is completed (see Figure 16.5).

It is hard at present to estimate the functional complexity to which such an INP will be enhanced in the future. Above all, it is very unclear what capabilities of SNA integration an INP can and must offer in future, and what will be the future degree of maximum protocol and interface concentration. The break-even point between efficiency and support complexity for this type of multifunctional backbone concentrator cannot be forecast without wider dissemination and practical experience. For future development, a range of aspects are relevant:

- Development of the router functionality to the gateway,

- SNA integration,

- Weighing up of router use against pure X.25 switching on the basis of multiplexers and X.25 switches,

- Multi-protocol operation against migration to OSI as common backbone protocol,

- Authorization and limits of bridge backbones against router backbones for parallel multi-protocol operation.

These aspects will have to be considered in the context of INP use and when setting up integrated enterprise networks.

The integration trend is leading to an increasingly confusing product market: Hub manufacturers are integrating bridge, LAN switching, and router functionality; bridge and router manufacturers are integrating hub functionality (concentrator modules for end station link-up), WAN switch manufacturers are integrating LAN interfaces. Each manufacturer claims to cover all functions. In fact, a specific manufacturer's strength is always in the functional environment where it has traditionally operated. The assessment of a product's strengths and weaknesses can sometimes only be deduced from many years of watching the market—too bad for the newcomer. Even here, though, a word of comfort can be said: sometime in the course of the next three years a counter-trend towards "Low Price Single Function Boxes" will probably set in—as is already beginning to emerge in the ISDN router area. The single boxes will then simply be connected together in a stack (the first signs can be seen today in 3Com's Superstack, Bay Networks Access Stack or Cisco's Switch Stack 5000), and there it is.

17 Appendix

17.1 Literature

/ATMF01/   The ATM Forum, Technical Committee: LAN Emulation over ATM-Version 1.0; 1995

[BELLC]   Bellcore: Generic System Requirements in Support of Switched Multimegabit Data Service; Technical Advisory, TA-TSY-000772, Issue 3, October 1989.

[BGNW]   BGNW Benutzergruppe Netzwerke (User Group Networks [UGNW], c/o ComConsult Kommunikationstechnik GmbH, Aachen.

/BLAC94/   Black, Ulysses. Emerging Communications Technologies; Prentice Hall 1994

/BORO01/   Borowka, Petra and Mathias Hein. Hub-Systeme, Funktionen-Konzepte-Einsatzgebiete (Hub Systems, Functions—Concepts—Areas of Application); DATACOM Publishing Company Bergheim; 1994.

/BORO02/ Die 90er Jahre-Internetworking Dekade (The 90s—Internetworking Decade); DATACOM September 1993, November 1993, January 1994, April 1994.

[CCITT01] CCITT I.121. Broadband Aspects of ISDN.

[CCITT01] CCITT I.122. Framework for Providing Additional Packet Mode Bearer Services.

[CCITT03] CCITT I.441. ISDN User Network Interface Data Link Layer Specification.

[CHHE87] Chylla, Peter and Heinz-Gerd, Hegering. Ethernet LANs. Planung, Realisierung und Netz-Management. (Ethernet LANs. Planning, Implementation and Network Management.) DATACOM Publishing Company, Pulheim, 2nd edition 1988.

[COME88] Internetworking with TCP/IP. Principles, Protocols and Architecture. Prentice Hall 1988.

[COME 91] Internetworking with TCP/IP. Principles, Protocols and Architecture. Prentice Hall 1991.

[DATA95] Token Ring Switching, Speed Switch 100; DATACOM 1995.

[3COM91] 3TECH; The 3COM Technical Journal. Vol. 1, No. 4, 1991.

[DNSFR] Digital Equipment Corporation, Northern Telecom Inc., StrataCom Inc.: Frame Relay Specification with Extensions, Based on Proposed T1S1 Standards, Doc. No. 001-208966, Revision 1.0. September 1990.

[GOEKAU] Gohring, Hans-Georg and Franz-Joachim Kauffels. Token Ring. Grundlagen, Strategien, Perspektiven. (Token Ring. Basic Principles, Strategies, Perspectives.) DATACOM Publishing Company, Bergheim 1993.

[HEGL90] Hein, Mathias, Gerhard Glaser, Vogl Gerhard, and Johannes Vogl. TCP/IP. Protokolle, Projektplanung, Realisierung. (TCP/IP. Protocols, Project Planning, Implementation.) DATACOM Publishing Company, Pulheim 1990.

/IBM01/   APPN Architecture and Product Implementations Tutorial; IBM International Technical Support Centers; Form Number GG24-3669-02.

[IEEE01]   IEEE 802.1B/D18. LAN/MAN Management. May 1991.

[IEEE02]   IEEE 802.1D.MAC Bridges.

[IEEE03]   IEEE 802.1G/DZ. Remote MAC Bridging. May 1991.

[IEEE04]   IEEE 802.5M-90. Token Ring Source Routing Tutorial. September 1990.

[IEEE05]   IEEE 802.5M/D4. Token Ring Source Routing Supplement to MAC Bridges. June 1991.

[IEEE06]   IEEE 802.5M/E1. SRT Route Determination Entity. June 1991.

[ISO01]   ISO/IEC CD 10028.3. Information processing systems. Data communications. Definition of the relaying functions of a network layer intermediate system.

[ISO02]   ISO/IEC TR 9575. Information technology. Telecommunications and information exchange between systems. OSI Routing Framework. 1990/06/01.

[ISO03]   ISO 9542. Information processing systems. Telecommunications and information exchange between systems. End system to intermediate system routing exchange protocol for use in conjunction with the protocol for providing the connectionless-mode network service. (ISO 8473).

[ISO04]   ISO/IEC 10030. Information technology. Telecommunications and information exchange between systems. End system routing information exchange protocol for use in conjunction with ISO 8878.

[ISO05]   ISO/IEC 10030-2. Information technology. Telecommunications and information exchange between systems. End system routing information. Exchange protocol for use in conjunction with ISO 8878, Part 2: Protocol Implementation Conformance Statement (PICS).

[ISO06]   ISO 10589. Information processing systems. Intermediate system to intermediate system routing protocol.

[ISO07]   ISO 8648: 1988. Information processing systems. Open Systems Interconnection. Internal organization of the Network Layer.

[ISO08]   ISO 10747. Protocol for the exchange of inter-domain routing information among Intermediate Systems to support forwarding of ISO 8473 PDUs.

[ISO09]   ISO 8473: 1988. Protocol for Providing the Connectionless-Mode Network Service.

[ISO10]   ISO 8473 DAD 2: 6/1988. Protocol for Providing the Connectionless-Mode Network Service, Addendum 2: Formal Description of ISO 8473.

[ISO11]   ISO 8473 ADD 3: 1989. Protocol for Providing the Connectionless-Mode Network Service, Addendum 3: Provision of the underlying service assumed by ISO 8473 over subnetworks which provide the OSI Data Link Service.

[ISO12]   DIS 10038 DAM 2: MAC bridging—Amendment 2: MAC bridging—source routing supplement.

[ISO13]   PDTR 10734: MAC sublayer interconnection (MAC bridging)—Guidelines for bridged LAN source operation by End Systems.

[John92a]   Johnson, J.T. Frame Relay Products; Data Communications, May 1992.

[John92b]   Johnson, J.T. Coping with Public Frame Relay: A delicate balance; Data Communications, January 1992.

[KAU01]   Kauffels, Franz-Joachim. Netzwerk-Management. Probleme, Standards, Strategien. (Network Management. Problems, Standards, Strategies.) DATACOM Publishing Company, 2nd enlarged edition, Bergheim 1992.

[KAU02]	Kauffels, Franz Joachim. Lokale Netze. Systeme fur den Hochleistungsinformationstransfer. (Local Networks. Systems for High-Performance Information Transfer.) DATACOM Publishing Company, 5th edition, Bergheim 1991.
/KLES95/	Klessig, Bob. The Status of ATM Data Networking Interoperability Specifications; 3TECH, July 1995.
/KYAS93/	Kyas, Othmar. ATM-Netzwerke (ATM Networks); Datacom Publishing Company Bergheim; 1993.
[LIPP90]	Lippis, Nick. The Internetwork Decade. Data Communications International 10.91, McGraw-Hill.
[MMOS87]	Mues, Olsowsky, Suppan. Ethernet-Handbuch. (Ethernet Handbook). DATACOM Publishing Company, Pulheim 1987.
[MSKR93]	Sonu Mirchandani and Khanna Rama. FDDI. John Wiley & Sons, 1993.
/PRYK93/	DePryker, Martin. Asynchronous Transfer Mode; Solution for Broadband ISDN; 2nd edition; Ellis Horwood, 1993.
[RFC1042]	A Standard for the Transmission of IP Datagrams over IEEE 802 Networks; February 1988.
[RFC1131]	The OSPF Specification. October 1989.
[RFC1195]	RFC 1195. Use of OSI IS-IS for Routing in TCP/IP and Dual Environments. Digital Equipment Corporation, December 1990.
[RFC1247]	OSPF Version 2, July 1991.
/RFC1331/	Simpson, W. The Point-to-Point Protocol (PPP) for the Transmission of Multi-protocol Datagrams over Point-to-Point Links, May 1992.
/RFC1483/	Multi-protocol Encapsulation over ATM Adaptation Layer 5; July 1993.
/RFC1552/	Simpson, W. The PPP Internetwork Packet Exchange Control Protocol (IPXCP), December 1994.

/RFC1577/   Classical IP and ARP over ATM; January 1994.

/RFC 1634/   Allen, M. "Novell IPX Over Various WAN Media (IPX-WAN)," 05/24/1994. (Pages-23) (Format=.txt) (Obsoletes RFC1551, 1362).

/RFC1764/   Senum, S. The PPP XNS IDP Control Protocol (XNSCP). 1995 March; 5p. (Format; TXT=9525 bytes).

/RFC1763/   Senum, S. The PPP Banyan Vines Control Protocol (BVCP). 1995 March; 10p. (Format TXT=12709 bytes) (Obsoletes RFC 1376).

/RFC1717/   Sklower, K., B. Lloyd, G. McGregor, and D. Carr. The PPP Multilink Protocol (MP). 1994 November; 21p. (Format TXT=46264 bytes).

/RFC1663/   Rand, D. PPP Reliable Transmission. 1994 July; 8p. (Format: TXT=17281 bytes).

/RFC1662/   Simpson, W., ed. PPP In HDLC-like Framing. 1994 July; 25p. (Format: TXT=48058 bytes) (Obsoletes RFC 1549).

/RFC1661/   Simpson W., ed. The Point-to-Point Protocol (PPP). 1994 July; 52p. (Format: TXT=103026 bytes) (Obsoletes RFC 1548).

/RFC1638/   Baker, F. and R. Bowen, eds. PPP Bridging Control Protocol (BCP). 1994 June; 28p. (Format: TXT=58477 bytes).

/RFC1634/   Allen, M. Novell IPX Over Various WAN Media (IPX-WAN). 1994 May; 23p. (Format: TXT=55347 bytes) (Obsoletes RFC 1551).

/RFC1619/   Simpson, W. PPP over SONET/SDH. 1994 May; 4p. (Format: TXT=8893 bytes).

/RFC1618/   Simpson, W. PPP over ISDN. 1994 May; 6p. (Format: TXT=14896 bytes).

/RFC1598/   Simpson, W. PPP in X.25. 1994 March; 7p. (Format: TXT=13835 bytes).

/RFC1570/   Simpson, W., ed. PPP LCP Extensions. 1994 January; 18p. (Format: TXT=35719 bytes) (Updates RFC 1548).

/RFC1552/   Simpson, W. The PPP Internetwork Packet Exchange Control Protocol (IPXCP). 1993 December; 14p. (Format: TXT=29174 bytes).

/RFC1549/   Simpson, W., ed. PPP in HDLC Framing. 1993 December; 18p. (Format: TXT36353 bytes).

/RFC1547/   Perkins, D. Requirements for an Internet Standard Point-to-Point Protocol. 1993 December; 21p. (Format: TXT=49811 bytes).

/RFC1378/   Parker, B. The PPP AppleTalk Control Protocol (ATCP). 1992 November; 16p. (Format: TXT=28497 bytes).

/RFC1377/   Katz, D. The PPP OSI Network Layer Control Protocol (OSINLCP). 1992 November; 10p. (Format: TXT=22110 bytes).

/RFC1334/   Lloyd, B. and W. Simpson. PPP Authentication Protocols. 1992 October; 16p. (Format: TXT=33249 bytes).

/RFC1333/   Simpson, W. PPP Link Quality Monitoring. 1992 May; 15p. (Format: TXT=29965 bytes).

/RFC1332/   McGregor, G. The PPP Internet Protocol Control Protocol (IPCP). 1992 May; 12p. (Format: TXT=17613 bytes) (Obsolctes RFC 1172).

/RFC1331/   Simpson, W. The Point-to-Point Protocol (PPP) for the Transmission of Multi-protocol Datagrams over Point-to-Point Links. 1992 May; 66p. (Format: TXT=129892 bytes) (Obsoletes RFC 1171, RFC 1172, Obsoleted by RFC 1548).

/RFC1172/   Perkins, D. and R. Hobby. Point-to-Point Protocol (PPP) initial configuration options. 1990 July; 38p. (Format: TXT=76132 bytes) (Obsoleted by RFC 1332).

/RFC1171/   Perkins, D. Point-to-Point Protocol for the transmission of multi-protocol datagrams over Point-to-Point links. 1990 July; 48p. (Format: TXT=92321 bytes) (Obsoletes RFC 1134; Obsoleted by RFC 1331).

/ROUT94/ Routt, Thomas J. APPN and TCP/IP: Plotting a Backbone Strategy; Data Communications, March 1994.

[SEIF90] Seifert, William. SPF: The Only Way to Travel. Data Communications, September 1990.

[STOE91] Stottinger, Klaus. X.25 Datenpaketvermittlung (X.25 Packet Switching) DATACOM Publishing Company, Bergheim 1991, 2nd edition: 1995.

[TANE89] Tanenbaum, Andrew S. Computer Networks. Englewood Cliffs, 2nd edition, New Jersey, 1989.

[TERP91] Terplan, Kornel, and Christian H. Voigt. LAN Management. Funktionen, Instrumente, Perspecktiven (Functions, Instruments, Perspectives). DATACOM Publishing Company, Bergheim 1991.

/TOLL95/ Tolly, Kevin. TCP/IP's Rise Has APPN on the Ropes; Data Communications, February 1995.

[WEID91] Weidenhammer, D. Netzwerk-Management. Grundlagen van SNMP.BGNW-Treffen 15.07.1991. (Network Management. SNMP Basics. UGNW Meeting 15.07.1991).

17.2 Manufacturers Directory

Manufacturers of Bridges, Routers, LAN-Switches

ACC	Alantec Fore Systems
Allied Telesyn	Andrew
Ascend	Atlantis
AVM	Bay Networks
Cabletron	Centillion/Bay Networks
Cisco	Chipcom (3Com)
	CrossComm
Cray Communications	Digicomm
Digital Equipment	
3Com	Eicon
Fibronics	Fore Systems

Hewlett Packard
IBM

ITK	Kalpana Cisco
Madge/Lannet	LANart
LANtronix	Lightning
Microcom	Madge
Nashoba	NetCorp
Netronix	NetVantage
Network Peripherals	Network Systems Corp.
NetEdge	Newbridge
Olicom	Penril
Proteon	Racal Datacom
Retix	RND
Shiva/Spider	SMC/Cabletron
Telebit Cisco	Timeplex
UB Networks	Whittaker Communications
Xedia Bay Networks	Xylan NSC
Xyplex	

17.3 Abbreviations

A

AAL	ATM Adaptation Layer
ABM	Asynchronous Balanced Mode
ABR	Available Bit Rate
ACC	Advanced Computer Communications
ACE	Advanced Communication Engine
ACF	Access Control Field (ATM)
ACF	Advanced Communications Facility (IBM, SNA)
ACK	Acknowledgement
ACSE	Application Control Service Elements
AFI	Authority and Format Identifier
ANR	Automatic Network Routing
ANSI	American National Standards Institute
APE	All Paths Explorer Frame
API	Application Programming Interface

APPI	Advanced Peer to Peer Internetworking
APPN	Advanced Peer-to-Peer Networking
ARE	All Routes Explorer
ARM	Asynchronous Response Mode (HDLC)
ARP	Address Resolution Protocol
ARPA	Advanced Research Projects Agency
AS	Autonomous System (OSPF)
ASE	Application Service Element
ASIC	Application Specific Integrated Circuit
ASN	Abstract Syntax Notation
ATCP	AppleTalk Control Protocol (PPP)
ATDM	Asynchronous Time Division Multiplexing
ATM	Asynchronous Transfer Mode
AURP	AppleTalk Update Routing Protocol

B

BCP	Bridge Control Protocol (PPP)
Bellcore	Bell Communications Research
B-ICI	Broadband Intercarrier Interface
BN	Bridge Number (Source Routing)
BPDU	Bridge Protocol Data Unit
BECN	Backward Explicit Congestion Notification
bps	bit per second
BRAM	Broadcast Recognition Access Method
BRD	Bundesrepublik Deutschland
BRI	Basic Rate Interface (ISDN)
BSC	Binary Synchronous Communication
BSD	Berkeley Software Distribution
BUS	Broadcast and Unknown Server (ATM)
BVCP	Banyan VINES Control Protocol (PPP)

C

CAD	Computer Aided Design
CAM	Content Addressable Memory
CBR	Constant Bit Rate

CCITT	Comité Consultatif International Télégrafique et Téléfonique (now ITU-TS)
CCR	Commitment, Concurrency and Recovery
CEPT	Conférence Européenne des Postes et de Télécommunication
CHAP	Challenge Handshake Authentication Protocol
CISC	Complex Instruction Set Computer
CLNP	Connectionless Network Protocol
CLNS	Connectionless Network Service
CLP	Cell Loss Priority (ATM)
CMIP	Common Management Information Protocol
CMIS	Common Management Information Services
CMISE	Common Management Information Service Elements
CMOL	CMIP over Logical Link
CMOT	CMIP over TCP
CMT	Connection Management (FDDI)
CP	Circuit Priority
CPCS	Common Part Convergence Sublayer
CPE	Customer Premises Equipment
CPI-C	Common Programming Interface for Communications (MPTN)
CRC	Cyclic Redundancy Check
CS	Configuration Server (ATM)
CS	Convergence Sublayer (ATM)
CSMA	Carrier Sense Multiple Access
CSMA/CD	Carrier Sense Multiple Access with Collision Detection
CSNP	Complete Sequence Numbers PDU
CSU	Channel Switching Unit
CT	Cut Through
CTC	Channel-To-Channel
CTS	Common Transport Semantics (MPTN)
CUGID	Closed User Group ID
CUT	Cluster Unit Terminal, Control Unit Terminal

D

DAC	Dual Attachment Concentrator
DAS	Dual Attachment Station
DB	Designated Bridge
DBP	Deutsche Bundespost
DCE	Data Circuit Terminating Equipment
DCE	Distributed Computing Environment (OSF)
DDV	Datendirektverbindung (Direct Data Connection)
DEC	Digital Equipment Corporation
DECnet	Digital Equipment Corporations Proprietary Network
DED	Dynamical Established Data
DFT	Distributed Function Terminal
DFV	Datenfernverarbeitung (Teleprocessing)
DIS	Draft International Standard
DIX	Digital, Intel, Xerox
DLC	Data Link Control (IBM)
DLCI	Data Link Connection Identifier (Frame Relay)
DLM	Data Link Mapping
DLPI	Data Link Provider Interface
DLS	Distributed Load Sharing
DLS	Data Link Switch
DLSw	Data Link Switching
DLUR	Dependent LU Requester
DLUS	Dependent LU Server
DMA	Direct Memory Access
DME	Distributed Management Environment
DNA	Digital Networks Architecture
DNCP	DECnet Phase IV Control Protocol (PPP)
DPDU	Data Link Protocol Data Unit
DQDB	Distributed Queue Dual Bus
DRAM	Dynamic Random Access Memory
DRP	DECnet Routing Protocol
DS	Digital Signaling
DSAP	Destination Service Access Point
DSP	Domain Specific Part
DSU	Data Switching Unit

DTE	Data Terminal Equipment
DVA	Distance Vector Algorithm
DXI	Data eXchange Interface

E

EA	Extended Address (Frame Relay)
EAB	Extended Attributes
ECS	EtherConnect System (TM ISOLAN)
EDH	European Digital Hierarchy
EDS	ENDEC Data Separator (FNS 7090)
EEPROM	Electrical Erasable Programmable Read Only Memory
EGP	Exterior Gateway Protocol
ELAN	Emulated LAN
ENDEC	Encoder/Decoder
ENVM	Environmental Monitor Card
EP	Error Protocol
EPROM	Electrical Programmable Read Only Memory
ERIP	Extended RIP
ES	End System
ESI	End System Identifier
ES-IS	End System to Intermediate System Protocol
ETSI	European Telecommunications Standards Institute

F

FCA	Flow Control Acknowledgement
FCI	Flow Control Indication
FCO	Flow Control Operator
FCS	Frame Check Sequence
FDDI	Fiber Distributed Data Interface
FDE	Full Duplex Ethernet
FDT	Full Duplex Token Ring
FECN	Forward Explicit Congestion Notification
FEP	Front End Processor (IBM)
FIFO	First In First Out
FNS	FDDI Netzwerk-System (AEG)

FORMAC	Fiber Optic Ring Media Access Controller
FR	Frame Relay
FTAM	File Transfer Access and Manipulation
FUNI	Frame-based UNI

G

GA	Group Address
GDMI	Generic Definition of Management Information
GDS	General Data Stream
GFC	Generic Flow Control
GOSIP	Government OSI Profile
GUI	Graphical User Interface

H

HDLC	High Level Data Link Control
HP	Hewlett-Packard
HPR	High Performance Routing
HS-LAN	High Speed LAN
HSSI	High Speed Serial Interface

I

IAB	Internet Architecture Board
IBM	International Business Machines
IC	Input Controller
ICMP	Internet Control Message Protocol
ICV	Integrity Check Value (IEEE 802.10)
ID	Identifier
IDP	Initial Domain Part (OSI)
IDP	Internet Datagram Protocol (Xerox)
IDRP	Interdomain Routing Protocol
IDV	Individual Data Processing
IEC	InterExchange Carrier
IEEE	Institute of Electrical and Electronics Engineers
IETF	Internet Engineering Task Force

IF	Interface
IGP	Interior Gateway Protocol
IGRP	Inter-Gateway Routing Protocol (Cisco)
ILI	Intelligent Link Interface
ILMI	Interim Local Management Interface
IMP	Interface Message Processor
INP	Internetwork Nodal Processor
IP	Internet Protocol
IPCP	IP Control Protocol (PPP)
IPG	Inter-Packet Gap
IPNNI	Integrated Private Network-to-Network Interface (ATM)
IPX	Internetwork Packet eXchange
IS	Intermediate System
ISDN	Integrated Services Digital Network
IS-IS	Intermediate System-to-Intermediate System Protocol
ISO	International Standardization Organization
ITU-T	International Telecommunications Union – Telecommunication Standards (previously CCITT)
ITU-TS	International Telecommunications Union – Telecommunication Standards Section
IW2	IPxWAN Version 2

K

kbps	Kilobit per second

L

LAN	Local Area Network
LANE	LAN Emulation
LAP	Link Access Procedure (X.25)
LAPB	Link Access Procedure Balanced (X.25)
LAP-D	Link Access Procedure-D
LAT	Local Area Transport (Digital)
LAVC	Local Area Vax Cluster
LCP	Link Control Protocol
LE	LAN Emulation

LEC	Local Exchange Carrier
LECID	LE Client Identifier
LECS	LAN Emulation Configuration Server
LES	LAN Emulation Server (ATM)
LED	Light Emitting Diode
LEN	Low Entry Networking
LLC	Logical Link Control
LMI	Local Management Interface
LSA	Link State Algorithm
LSA	Link State Advertisement
LSAP	Logical Link Service Access Point
LSB	Least Significant Bit
LSP	Link State Protocol
LSP	Link State Protocol Data Unit
LTH	Length Field (Source Routing)
LU	Logical Unit
LUNI	LAN Emulation UNI

M

MAC	Media Access Control
MAN	Metropolitan Area Network
MAP	Manufacturing Automation Protocol
MAPDU	Management Application Protocol Data Unit
Mbps	Megabit per Second
MDF	Management-Defined Field (IEEE 802.10)
MEC	Multiport Ethernet Controller
MHS	Message Handling System
MIB	Management Information Base
MIC	Media Interface Connector
MIN	Multistage Interconnection Network
MIPS	Million Instructions Per Second
MIT	Management Information Tree
MLMA	Multi-Level Multi-Access
MLP	Multilink Procedure (X.25)
MLPPP	Multilink PPP

MNP	Microcom Networking Protocol (TM Microcom)
MOP	Maintenance Operations Protocol (Digital)
MP	Multi-Protocol
MPOA	Multi-protocol over ATM
MPR	Multi-protocol Router (Novell)
MPTN	Multi-protocol Transport Networking
MRRU	Maximum Received Reconstructed Unit (MLPPP)
MRU	Maximum Receive Unit (PPP)
MSAP	Mini Slotted Alternating Priorities
MSB	Most Significant Bit (Source Routing)
MSD	Maximal Splitting Degree (NLSP)
MTBF	Mean Time Between Failure
MTU	Maximum Transmission Unit

N

NC	Network Connection
NCL	Network Control Language
NCP	NetWare Core Protocol
NCP	Network Control Protocol (PPP)
NCP	Network Control Program (IBM)
NDIS	Network Driver Interface Specification
NetBIOS	Network Basic Input Output System
NFS	Network File System (Sun Microsystems)
NIC	Network Interface Card (Novell)
NILS	Network Internal Layer Service
NIST	National Institute for Standards and Technology
NLPID	Network Layer Protocol ID
NLRI	Network Layer Reachability Information
NM	Network Management
NML	Native Mode LAN
NMS	Network Management System
NNI	Network to Network Interface
NPDU	Network Protocol Data Unit
NRZ	No Return to Zero
NRZI	No Return to Zero Inverted

NS	Network Service
NS	Network Services (HP)
NSAP	Network Service Access Point
NSC	Network Systems Corporation
NT	New Technology (Microsoft)

O

OAM	Operation, Administration and Maintenance (ATM Switch)
OC	Output Controller
OC1	Optical Carrier Type 1
ODI	Open Data Link Interface (Novell)
OIR	Online Insertion and Removal
OLE	Object Linking and Embedding
OSF	Open Systems Foundation
OSI	Open Systems Interconnection
OSINLCP	OSI Network Layer Control Protocol (PPP)
OSPF	Open Shortest Path First
OUI	Organizational Unit Identifier

P

PARC	Palo Alto Research Center
PAP	Password Authentication Protocol
PC	Personal Computer
PCMCIA	Personal Computer Memory Card International Association
PDH	Plesiochrone Digital Hierarchy
PDU	Protocol Data Unit
PHY	Physical Layer Protocol (FDDI)
PIR	Protocol Independent Routing
PLCP	Physical Layer Convergence Procedure (SMDS, DQDB)
PM	Physical Medium (ATM)
PMD	Physical Medium Dependent (FDDI)
PNNI	Private Network-to-Network Interface (ATM)
POH	Path Overhead (SDH)
POP	Point of Presence
PPP	Point-to-Point Protocol (TCP/IP)

PPX	Parallel Packet Express
PR	Public Relations
PRI	Private Rate Interface (ISDN)
PSU	Power Supply Unit
PSNP	Partial Sequence Numbers PDU
PTI	Payload Type Identifier
PTT	Post, Telegraph and Telephone
PU	Physical Unit
PVC	Permanent Virtual Circuit

Q

QoS	Quality of Service

R

RAM	Random Access Memory
RC	Route Control-Feld
RD	Route Designator-Feld
RFC	Request For Comment; TCP/IP Standard Document
RI	Routing Information
RIB	Routing Information Base
RIF	Routing Informations Feld
RII	Routing Information Indicator
RIP	Routing Information Protocol
RISC	Reduced Instruction Set Computer
RMON	Remote MONitoring (SNMP)
RMT	Ring Management (FDDI)
RN	Ring-Nummer (Source Routing)
RND	RAD Network Devices
RNR	Receive Not Ready
ROM	Read Only Memory
ROSE	Remote Operations Service Elements
RP	Root Port
RR	Receive Ready
RT	Routing Type
RTMP	Routing Table Maintenance Protocol
RTP	Rapid Transport Protocol

S

SAA	Systems Application Architecture
SABME	Set Asynchronous Balanced Mode Extended
SAID	Secure Association Identifier (IEEE 802.10)
SAP	Service Access Point (ISO OSI)
SAP	Service Advertising Protocol (Novell NetWare)
SAR	Segmentation and Reassembly
SAS	Single Attachment Station
SDLC	Synchronous Data Link Control
SDE	Secure Data Exchange (IEEE 802.10)
SDH	Synchronous Digital Hierarchy
SEAL	Simple and Efficient Adaptation Layer
SEF	Source Explicit Forwarding
SF	Store & Forward
SGMP	Simple Gateway Monitoring Protocol
SIP	SMDS Interface Protocol
SLIP	Serial Line Interface Protocol
SMAP	Station Management Application Program (FDDI)
SMDS	Switched Multimegabit Data Service
SMFA	Specific Management Functional Area
SMI	Structure of Management Information
SMT	Station Management (FDDI)
SN	Subnetwork
SNA	Systems Network Architecture
SNAP	Subnetwork Access Protocol (RFC 1042)
SNMP	Simple Network Management Protocol
SNRM	Set Normal Response Mode
SOH	Section Overhead (SDH)
SONET	Synchronous Optical Network
SONIC	Systems Oriented Network Interface Controller (TM National Semiconductor)
SPA	Spanning Tree-Algorithmus
SPF	Shortest Path First
SPT	Spanning Tree
SQE	Signal Quality Error
SQL	Standard Query Language

SR	Source Routing
SRAM	Static Random Access Memory
SRB	Source Route Bridging
SRF	Specific Routed Frame: RII=1, RT=11x
SRT	Source Routing Transparent
SR-TB	Source Routing –Transparent Bridging
SSAP	Source Service Access Point
SSCS	Service Specific Convergence Sublayer
SSP	Switch-to-Switch Protocol (DLSw)
STE	Spanning Tree Explorer: RII 01, RT=110
STM1	Synchronous Transport Module 1
STP	Shielded Twisted Pair
SVC	Switched Virtual Circuit

T

TB	Transparent Bridging
TC	Transmission Convergence (ATM)
TCP	Transmission Control Protocol
TDM	Time Division Multiplexing
TELNET	TELetype NETwork
TFTP	Trivial File Transfer Protocol (TCP/IP)
THT	Token Holding Time
TI	Texas Instruments Inc.
TIC	Token Ring Interface Coupler
TOP	Technical Office Protocol
ToS	Type Of Service
TPDU	Transport Protocol Data Unit
TROLI	Token Ring Optimized Line Interface (TM of Pulse Engineering)
TSD	Transmission System Dependent Layer (SMDS, DQDB)
TSF	Transparent Spanning Frame

U

UA	Unnumbered Acknowledgement
UB	Ungermann Bass (now UB Networks)

UDP	User Datagram Protocol
UI	Unnumbered Information
UNI	User to Network Interface (ATM)
UTP	Unshielded Twisted Pair

V

VBR	Variable Bit Rate
VC	Virtual Circuit
VC	Virtual Channel
VCC	Virtual Channel Connection
VCI	Virtual Channel Identifier
VDRAM	Video DRAM
VLAN	Virtual LAN
VLSI	Very Large Scale Integration
VMEbus	Versa Module Europe Bus
VCI	Virtual Channel Identifier
VPI	Virtual Path Identifier
VSB	VME Subsystem-Bus
VT	Virtual Terminal
VTAM	Virtual Terminal Access Method (IBM, SNA)
VTS	Virtual Terminal Service

W

WAN	Wide Area Network
WDAD	Addendum with Status Working Draft

X

XNS	Xerox Network Systems
XRF	Extended Recovery Facility

Index